POLITICS IN POST-REVOLUTIONARY TURKEY, 1908-1913

SOCIAL, ECONOMIC AND POLITICAL STUDIES OF THE MIDDLE EAST AND ASIA
(S.E.P.S.M.E.A.)

(Founding editor: C.A.O. van Nieuwenhuijze)

Editor

REINHARD SCHULZE

Advisory Board
Dale Eickelman (Dartmouth College)
Roger Owen (Harvard University)
Judith Tucker (Georgetown University)
Yann Richard (Sorbonne Nouvelle)

VOLUME 70

POLITICS IN POST-REVOLUTIONARY TURKEY, 1908-1913

BY

AYKUT KANSU

BRILL
LEIDEN · BOSTON · KÖLN
2000

This book is printed on acid-free paper.

Library of Congress Cataloging-in-Publication Data

Kansu, Aykut, 1955-
    Politics in post-revolutionary Turkey, 1908-1913 / Aykut Kansu.
        p. cm. — (Social, economic, and political studies of the
    Middle East and Asia, ISSN 1385-3376 ; v. 70)
        Includes bibliographical references (p.   ) and index.
        ISBN 9004115870 (cloth : alk. paper)
        1.Turkey—Politics and goverment—1909-1918.   I. Title.   II. Series.
    DR576.K356   1999
    320.956.1'09'041—dc21   99-053922
                                                                     CIP

Die Deutsche Bibliothek - CIP-Einheitsaufnahme
Kansu, Aykut:
Politics in post-revolutionary Turkey, 1908 - 1913 / Aykut Kansu.-
Leiden ; Boston ; Köln : Brill, 1999
    (Social, economic, and political studies of the Middle East & Asia ; Vol 70)
    ISBN 90-04-11587-0

ISSN   1385-3376
ISBN   90 04 11587 0

PRINTED IN THE NETHERLANDS

CONTENTS

ACKNOWLEDGEMENTS

This book is a continuation of my *1908 Devrimi* (İstanbul: İletişim Yayınevi, 1995), and *The Revolution of 1908 in Turkey* (Leiden, New York and Cologne: E. J. Brill, 1997). The story of the transformation of Turkey from an absolutist 'pre-modern' state to a modern one continues in this book. As in the previous volume, I try to tell the political history of modern Turkey in a radically different fashion. I hope that readers will readily notice my standpoint on this issue, as they have done so in the previous book.

During my studies at M.I.T. and research at Harvard University I have had the good fortune of meeting academics who have helped me in more ways than one. First and foremost, I must thank—once again—Professor Philip S. Khoury, Department of History, and Professor Suzanne Berger, Department of Political Science—both at M.I.T. Feroz Ahmad of the University of Massachusetts at Boston, Department of History—and his wife, Bedia Ahmad, have always encouraged me in my pursuit—although Professor Feroz Ahmad would have been happier had my conclusions been somewhat different.

My thanks also go to Selim İlkin, a former professor and mentor, of the Statistical, Economic and Social Research and Training Centre for Islamic Countries at Ankara, Professors Sina Akşin and İlber Ortaylı—both of Ankara Üniversitesi, Siyasal Bilgiler Fakültesi—and, Professor Erik Jan Zürcher, of the Rijksuniversiteit Leiden, Instituut voor Geschiedenis, for their helpful criticisms.

I must also register my thanks to Friedrich-Ebert-Stiftung, Bonn, Germany. It was through a grant provided by this foundation that I was able to do extensive research in several archives—Bundesarchiv at Bonn, and the archives at Merseburg, and Potsdam—and libraries—Staatsbibliothek Preußischer Kulturbesitz and Amerika-Gedenkbibliothek as well as the libraries of the Humboldt-Universität and the Freie Universität Berlin, all in Berlin—during the Winter of 1991-1992. Professor Barbara Kellner-Heinkele of the Freie Universität Berlin and Professor Suraiya Faroqhi of the Ludwig-Maximilian Universtität in Munich have invited me to their respective universities to share my views with their graduate students.

Two colleagues—Professor Emeritus Fatma Mansur Coşar of the Middle East Technical University, and Professor Huricihan İslamoğlu, of Sabancı University—deserve special thanks. Their spiritual guidance have continued to contribute to this volume as well. In addition, colleagues in my new department—Middle East Technical University, Department of History—have been most helpful. I especially owe thanks to Professors Seçil Karal Akgün, İsenbike Togan, and Uygur Kocabaşoğlu for their departmental support. I am also extremely grateful to Professor Süha Sevük, President of the Middle East Technical University, and Professor Ayşen Ergin, Advisor to the President, Middle East Technical University, for making academic life at the University bearable.

Last, but not least, I must thank my students—both undergraduate and graduate—at the Middle East Technical University, Department of Political Science and Public Administration, and Department of History, who have made the retelling of a familiar story exciting. During the process of getting the manuscript ready for publication I have been helped by quite a number of enthusiastic former students and research assistants, among whom I must mention F. Hasan Arol, İlker Evrim Binbaş, Seçil Deren, Cem Karadeli, Alev Patlak, Nesim Şeker, and Tümay Timuçin Şeker.

Ankara, September 1999

CHAPTER ONE

INTRODUCTION

This book is about domestic politics following the Revolution of 1908 in Turkey. To be more precise, it is about parliamentary politics and extra-parliamentary opposition to that ideal. Parliamentary politics was something completely new to the Turkish scene. Never before in Turkish history Turkey was ruled with a government responsible and answerable to a parliament which was composed of members elected through a competitive mechanism—*i.e.*, general elections. Therefore, it is appropriate that the book starts with the opening of the Parliament in December of 1908, and ends with the restitution of constitutional rule in early 1913.

Although seemingly straightforward in its telling of events from the opening of the Parliament to the re-capture of constitutional government in early 1913, this book is built upon a premise that is fundamentally different from previous studies—which are relatively few in number.[1] Whereas previous studies—especially Feroz Ahmad's *The Young Turks: The Committee of Union and Progress in Turkish Politics, 1908-1914* and Sina Akşin's *Jön Türkler ve İttihat ve Terakki*—deal with the period as if conditions were normalised immediately after the Revolution of 1908 I take the view that the period un-

---

[1] There are only two scholarly books that exclusively deal with this period of Turkish political history. Feroz Ahmad's *The Young Turks: The Committee of Union and Progress in Turkish Politics, 1908-1914* is a ground breaking book which retains its value even thirty years after its appearance. The second book, Sina Akşin's *Jön Türkler ve İttihat ve Terakki*, traverses basically the same path although it covers both the pre-revolutionary years between 1889 and 1908, and the period between 1913 and 1918. In addition to these works, there are two recent books that deal with the same period but with a specific interest in the relationship between the Turks and the Arabs during the post-revolutionary decade (Sabine Prätor, *Der arabische Faktor in der jungtürkischen Politik: Eine Studie zum osmanischen Parlament der II. Konstitution, 1908-1918*, and Hasan Kayalı, *Arabs and Young Turks: Ottomanism, Arabism, and Islamism in the Ottoman Empire, 1908-1918*).

der scrutiny is a relentless struggle over the political future of Turkey. The Revolution of 1908 was no mere 'restoration' of the Constitution of 1876. It tried to bring about a fundamental change in the political structure of Turkey. In more senses than one, the Revolution brought about the end of the Ottoman Empire. If the Ottoman Empire stood for everything that reminded one of absolutism and the practices associated with it, 'Young Turkey' represented a radical break with that past. A modern, centralised state actively engaged in both promoting capitalist relations of production in the economy, and upholding a parliamentary form of government in politics replaced the absolutist state symbolised in the autocratic personality of Abdülhamid II. Therefore, from 1908 onwards although the official name of the empire remained unchanged and people still referred to the land as the Imperial Dominions—or, Memalik-i Mahruse-i Şahane—the label 'Ottoman Empire' was used mostly by the monarchists and their sympathisers in the conservative press, and the label 'Turkey,' or 'Young Turkey' was preferred by those who sympathised with the Revolution.[2] Rather than reflecting a restricted geographical locality, the label 'Turkey' accurately reflected the post-revolutionary political structure that still entailed the imperial possessions in the Middle East and the Balkans.[3]

First, and foremost, this book builds upon the premises of my previous book—*The Revolution of 1908 in Turkey*—where I have argued that what happened in the Summer of 1908 was a *real* revolution and not a simple and sudden change of government. As opposed to the conventional wisdom concerning this period of Turkish history, I have argued that the events cannot be interpreted as a reform project executed by a group of civilian and military bureaucrats from above—nor, can it be

---

[2] The title of a recent book by A. L. Macfie—*The End of the Ottoman Empire, 1908-1923*—testifies to the reality of the situation.

[3] I, therefore, think that a reviewer of my *The Revolution of 1908 in Turkey* has misunderstood my intention by focusing his attention exclusively on my use of the term 'Turkey,' and, thus, has completely missed the substance of my arguments (Donald Quataert's review of *The Revolution of 1908 in Turkey* in the *British Journal of Middle Eastern Studies*, 25 (1998), pp.306-307).

interpreted as a 'revolution from above.'[4]

What this Revolution entailed—or, aimed to achieve—was to constitute a liberal democratic regime in Turkey.[5] This meant doing away with old political practices and, more importantly, destroying the basis of the old political structure upon which the absolutist regime had maintained itself up until then. What distinguished the absolutist regime from the new era was its dependence upon the bureaucracy—civilian or military—to rule the country. Politics, so far as it publicly existed, was conducted in an environment where no established mechanism—*i.e.*, a parliament—functioned as a medium. This did not mean that decisions taken were not political in nature or that the system was totally strange to politics. Of course, the *ancien régime* was as politically active as the one following it. Yet, the arena where politics was conducted was immune to the public at large and was not accountable to the propertied classes in Turkey. Court politics with all of its 'intrigues' was the norm. This type of politics naturally revolved around the 'distinguished' members of the state bureaucracy, and the Court—the Yıldız Palace, where Sultan Abdülhamid maintained an extensive bureaucracy separate from the state bureaucracy, not to mention a secret service totally under his direct supervision.

High-level bureaucrats were all involved in politics. Under such a system, no high-level bureaucrat—*i.e.*, pasha—could afford remaining aloof to court politics. Survival under such a system of politics meant constant involvement in daily political affairs—'disgusting Byzantine intrigues,' as conservative historians would lament. The pashas' power bases naturally emanated not from a political system open to institutionalised competition—such as elections, political parties, parliament—and from the 'modern' society and its constituent dominant groups organised around distinct class interests, as one would imagine under a liberal democratic environment, but from a pre-modern political structure which was mainly built upon

---

[4] Aykut Kansu, *The Revolution of 1908 in Turkey*, pp.1-27.

[5] For the struggles for liberal democracy in modern Turkish political history, and the importance of the Revolution of 1908 in this respect see, Aykut Kansu, "Dünden Bugüne 1908 Devrimi," pp.4-11.

'feudal' or communal ties on the one hand, and on the state bureaucracy, on the other. Under the *ancien régime*, influential pashas had communal ties. Many an important pasha claimed Albanian, Kurdish or Arab heritage. Albania, Kurdistan and Arabia—mainly Iraq and Syria—were three of the most significant geographical areas upon which high court politics heavily depended. Feudal, or pre-modern, communal ties, as opposed to ties and relationships peculiar to modern—capitalist—societies functioned as prerequisites to this old style politics. Furthermore, so long as foreign interference was part and parcel of this system, representatives of foreign powers were also means for leverage for the politically ambitious pashas. That is why certain pashas, Kâmil and Said Pashas, for instance, were known as pro-British, while Mahmud Şevket Pasha, for instance, had a reputation for being pro-German.

Since high politics among the pashas of the *ancien régime* did not interest the society at large, their political conduct was not easily observed by the public. This was politics behind closed doors. Kept for the privileged few, the political 'market,' was not freely accessible for most of the politically ambitious members of the society. Its transactions were, of course, neither public nor accountable. To the public eye this kind of high politics was 'state politics.' It excluded the society—meaning, this kind of politics was not conducted on behalf of the society. Played among the privileged few, this high level politics among members of the state and court bureaucracy and their feudal allies had little, or nothing, to do with the desires of the public, including the interests of the bourgeoisie. Unseen by the public at large, and totally irrelevant to, if not against, the interests of the bourgeoisie, this kind of politics was condoned by conservative historians as 'state politics.' Under these circumstances one can understand, if not accept, why historians tend to refrain from calling these pashas 'politicians,' but applauding them as 'statesmen.' In an environment where politics was the exclusive domain of the pashas, the word 'politics,' so long as it implied questions concerning the society, was not to be uttered. 'Politics' under circumstances where absolutism reigned supreme could only mean one thing: 'underground subversive activity.'

With the Revolution in 1908 the old world and its absolutist system collapsed, but a totally new system could not be put in its place in such a short time. The old had died but the new had yet to be born. It is to the credit of the Unionists that they insisted upon and succeeded in holding general elections for the parliament immediately after the political chaos ended in late August of 1908. The public was ready for the idea of parliamentary rule mostly because the revolutionaries had been continually demanding the establishment of parliamentary rule for at least two years previous to the Revolution.[6] One can argue that both the concerned public—new 'citizens,' not the old 'subjects'—and the Unionists were mentally ready for the changes that were to come with the new regime. Not only the idea of a political party—the Committee of Union and Progress—but also the establishment of its local branches in most constituencies by the beginning of the electoral process was a real achievement—especially when one considers that Turkish political life had seen none of these institutions before.

Under these revolutionary circumstances, politicians of the *ancien régime* had difficulty in organising themselves in a political party of their own—not only because they were thrown into disarray by the upheaval of the established order but also because the idea of conducting politics through a political party in a competitive environment was totally alien to their mentality. Therefore, partisans of the *ancien régime* could neither organise a viable political party nor effectively compete in the general elections of 1908. The Liberal Union—a conglomeration of politicians of the *ancien régime*—which was founded to oppose the Committee of Union and Progress both during the elections and, afterwards, in the parliament, found it extremely difficult to survive under the completely new circumstances, let alone participate meaningfully in the new style politics.[7]

Although those politicians resisting the Revolution came together under one roof in this umbrella organisation—Liber-

---

[6] Aykut Kansu, *The Revolution of 1908 in Turkey*, pp.29-72; and, H. Zafer Kars, *1908 Devrimi'nin Halk Dinamiği, passim*.

[7] For the party's electoral campaign see, Fevzi Demir, İkinci Meşrutiyet Dönemi Meclis-i Mebusan Seçimleri, 1908-1914, pp.56-60.

al Union—the party lacked strong leadership. This was not because there were no competent politicians—or, pashas— who could steer the party. Rather, the reason again lay in the mentality of the *ancien régime*: no self-respecting pasha of the mentality of the absolutist regime could 'debase' himself by working in a political party. For them, political struggle outside of the state bureaucracy was unthinkable. Despite his advanced age, Kâmil Pasha, for instance, was a shrewd and able politician. He had the ambition as well as the resources at his disposal to lead such a political party. Yet, he did not for- mally lead a political party, because he judged it to be below his station in life. It was more like his style to work behind the scenes. Political observers and the public at large knew per- fectly well that the Liberal Union was advised and led by, and dependent upon—both financially and intellectually—Kâmil Pasha and Prince Sabahaddin. But both of these ambitious po- liticians found it more palatable to remain behind the facade of the party organisation.[8] It was mostly through lesser and parochial politicians, like the Albanian İsmail Kemal Bey— who would declare himself head of the provisional govern- ment of independent Albania in late 1912—that the Liberal Union and its successor formations—most importantly, En- tente Libérale—would operate in day-to-day politics in and out of the Chamber of Deputies.

The monarchist opposition, therefore, organised itself in and around a political party—the Liberal Union, first, and the Entente Libérale, from late 1911 onwards—out of necessity. Changed circumstances forced them to emulate their political opponents' strategies. Although this monarchist organisation was registered as a political party, it did not operate as a regu- lar political party one would normally observe functioning under a liberal democratic regime. Its leadership—Kâmil Pasha and Prince Sabahaddin—remained outside of the Chamber of Deputies, and the leadership tried to control and direct parliamentary debate through elected deputies of the

---

[8] Tarık Zafer Tunaya, *Türkiye'de Siyasi Partiler, 1859-1952*, pp.239-246. For Prince Sabahaddin's leading role in the Liberal Union see, for instance, Noel Buxton, "The Young Turks," p.23.

party—deputies for whom the leadership had little respect.[9] A s
they held the conviction that deputies on the Chamber floor
were beneath themselves, monarchist politics necessarily
stood at a disadvantageous position *vis-à-vis* its rival, the
Committee of Union and Progress. Whereas almost all of the
leaders of the Committee of Union and Progress were
functioning as deputies in the Chamber, and were immersed
in public debate, defending and arguing for their political
stand on each and every issue the Chamber debated,
monarchist politicians' style only reflected their contempt for
open debate. One can only recall the reluctance of Kâmil
Pasha to appear before the Chamber of Deputies to defend his
cabinet's position on certain issues, while, on the other hand,
one can observe how Unionist-backed cabinets' grand
veziers—especially, Hakkı Pasha—argued on the Chamber
floor for hours' end to convince deputies before asking for
their support. The behind-the-scene leaders of the monarchist
political parties had little respect for the rules as well as the
rituals of competitive politics. One can argue that they never
accepted the new rules. Their style of rule was fundamentally
different; and, this was totally in line with their archaic
worldview. The problem was that this archaic worldview was
almost totally incompatible with the changing times.

One can find elements of the monarchist worldview in
their party programmes. Of course, neither the Liberal Union
nor the Entente Libérale could publicly and openly state that
their fundamental aim was to return to *status quo ante* and restore the *ancien régime*. Yet, their programmes advocated
quite honestly policies not in line with the changed circumstances, but in line with old practices. Their idea of decentralisation—which Prince Sabahaddin is famous for its intellec-
tual content as well as its 'elegant' formulation, and presentation to the public through pamphlets—was nothing but an argument for the reconstitution, if not wholesale restoration, of
the political system along the lines of pre-revolutionary practices.[10]

---

[9] See Rıza Nur's complaints in his *Hürriyet ve İtilâf Fırkası Nasıl Doğdu,
Nasıl Öldü?* pp.13-14.

[10] For Prince Sabahaddin's views on 'decentralisation' see his various pam-

Under the *ancien régime*, both communities, and regions with a recognised majority of a particular ethnic composition or confessional denomination had certain privileges that kept them as separate entities from the rest of the empire. While religious communities kept their educational and religious systems almost intact they were in turn left out of the main-stream political life of the country. Legal arrangements and privileges granted to recognised communities also made it almost impossible for a unified court system to function within the boundaries of the empire. Exemptions from certain rights and obligations, such as from conscription or taxation, under the *ancien régime* had produced a political system that was highly fragmented, although it had the outward appearance of having an absolutist—and, highly centralised—state apparatus. [11]

The Revolution of 1908 tried to do away with almost all of these traditional privileges. The Unionist policy as advocated before and during the electoral campaign of 1908 was to create a unified and centralised state apparatus. They aimed at unifying the Ottoman subjects under Turkish citizenship. All parochial privileges were to be discarded. The medium of instruction in all state schools would be Turkish, although local languages would be respected and continued to be taught as a second language. Official business along with court procedures were also to be conducted in Turkish. Since the parliament had become the locus of political activity, all parochial or local bases of political power were to be suppressed. Localities were to have full representation in the Chamber of Deputies according to the strength of their respective population figures. Therefore, proportional representation of all communities were aimed at in the Chamber of Deputies. Every 'subject' was to be transformed into a 'citizen' with equal rights and obligations. This meant, for example, that every

---

phlets on this subject in Nezahet Nurettin Ege (Ed.), *Prens Sabahaddin: Hayatı ve İlmî Müdafaaları*, pp.159-201.
   [11] For the legal status of non-Muslim subjects under the absolutist regime see, Gülnihâl Bozkurt, *Alman-İngiliz Belgelerinin ve Siyasî Gelişmelerin Işığında Gayrimüslim Osmanlı Vatandaşlarının Hukukî Durumu, 1839-1914*. For the educational system in existence under the *ancien régime* see, İlhan Tekeli and Selim İlkin, *Osmanlı İmparatorluğu'nda Eğitim ve Bilgi Üretim Sisteminin Oluşumu ve Dönüşümü*.

citizen was obligated to pay taxes without exception—even if
he were an Albanian—and to serve in the military—even if
he were Greek, Armenian, or Jewish. In short, the stated aim
of the Unionists were to make everybody a 'first-class' citizen.
Full representation rights were granted in return for the elimination of traditional and communal exclusionary privileges.
Individual rights would take precedence, or completely over-
shadow, communal rights.[12]

It is not surprising that the Unionists' vision for a unified
Turkey where all citizens would enjoy the same rights as
well as have the same obligations would not be welcomed by
the traditional leaderships of the officially recognised communities. Not only the church organisations—especially the
Greek Ecumenical Patriarchate—but also the 'secular' traditional notables of various communities—Muslim or Christian—had objections to the new system.[13] In the *ancien régime* the Sultan had managed to keep himself in power
through granting special privileges to communities in return
for their support, or at least tacit acceptance, of the established
order without questioning its injustices. It is true that in the
process the absolutist state had lost effective control over many
a geographical area. In the outlying areas of the empire, almost no taxes were collected by the central authority. In these
areas, for example in Kurdistan and Albania, the state had
even been forced to officially recognise private armies of the
feudal lords. Paradoxically, the absolutist state could remain in
power so long as it did not persist on having *absolute* control of
the periphery. When the Revolution changed the existing
relations of power in the state apparatus, the whole precarious
system was bound to collapse and reaction to appear especially
in the peripheral areas of the empire.

All this meant that opposition to the Committee of Union
and Progress organised under the banner of the Liberal
Union, and later, Entente Libérale, which professed 'decen-

---

[12] For the party platform of the Committee of Union and Progress during the
general elections of 1908 see, Aykut Kansu, *The Revolution of 1908 in Turkey*,
pp.157-176.

[13] Kudret Emiroğlu, *Anadolu'da Devrim Günleri: İkinci Meşrutiyet'in İlânı,
Temmuz-Ağustos 1908*, pp.307-308; and, Aykut Kansu, *The Revolution of 1908 in
Turkey*, pp.163-192.

tralisation,' was composed of two distinct but related sets of discontented groups: pashas—*i.e.*, the politicians of the absolutist
regime—representing the political interests of the absolutist
state, and local notables and officially recognised communal
organisations—such as the local ulema, muftis, and *naqib al-
ashraf*, representing the Muslim population, and the numerous patriarchates of the various Christian sects and their local
school and church organisations—representing disenchanted
communities. Therefore, opposition to the Committee of
Union and Progress manifested itself not in a modern and
contemporary set of conservative political beliefs and attitudes,
but in a totally reactionary garb—in the name re-establishing
or restoring communal practices and privileges.[14] When the

---

[14] Written in the aftermath of the counter-revolutionary *coup* attempt of April
1909, a contemporaneous analysis made by Halid Halid, a Unionist sympathiser
living in England, on the composition and purpose of the Liberal Union is quite
clear on these points:

"With the indirect support of this Prince [Sabahaddin] a new party was
then created. This party, which calls itself the 'Ahrar,' and which is styled by its
European sympathisers the 'Liberal Union,' has amongst its members Said Pasha,
the son of the late Vizir Kiamil Pasha, who was notorious for his tyrannical deeds
under the old *régime*; Ismail Kemal Bey, the Albanian separatist deputy; and
many other persons who could not find a seat in the Council of the Committee of
Union and Progress. Several high officials, who betrayed an amazing degree of
reactionary tendency on the success of the dastardly deeds of revolt perpetrated by
the fanatical mob, had favoured the 'broader' principles of the Constitution pro-
pounded by the 'Liberal Union party.' The political propaganda of the party had
also appealed forcibly to the pan-Hellenic imagination of the Greeks, most of
whose deputies and journalists have given the party a helping hand. The party
leaders knew how to win the sympathies of certain foreign concession-hunters
who have been making a mad rush to Turkey to exploit her resources, by giving
them to understand that if their party came into power they would have a much
better chance of getting what they sought. Curiously enough, the adherents of the
'Liberal Union party,' by displaying an excessive degree of Anglophil tendencies,
have won the support of some English newspaper correspondents in Constantinople. It must be within the recollection of those who follow the trend of events in
the Near East, that those English papers which have been carrying on a campaign
against what is called the 'illegal' authority of the Committee of Union and
Progress have praised the political ideals of the leaders of the Liberal Union. They
were true Liberals, these English correspondents told us, who promised equal
chances to all nationalities in Turkey to develop on their own nationalist lines;
while, on the other hand, the Young Turks, who adhered to the Committee, were
Chauvinists running their politics on the narrow Turkish lines. It seems strange
to have started an agitation of this sort against the position of the Committee, and
to advise it to dissolve, at the very moment when a White Book relating to the recent constitutional movement in Turkey was being published by his Brittanic
Majesty's Government, in which the patriotic work done by the Committee is
highly praised" (Halil Halid, "The Origin of the Revolt in Turkey," pp.757-758).

My analysis, therefore, is in complete disagreement with Feroz Ahmad's
allegation that both the Committee of Union and Progress and the Entente Libérale were against absolutism. Likewise, I can not accept his allegation that the
differences between these two political worldviews pertained almost exclusively to
economic policy choices (Feroz Ahmad, *The Making of Modern Turkey*, pp.33-35).

opposition talked of 'rights' they had in mind not the 'liberal' rights which an individual should rightfully enjoy in a liberal democratic state but the rights communities would collectively enjoy against the modern and centralised state apparatus. Monarchists had in mind not personal liberties but communal privileges—privileges which were, more often than not, used to keep the individual members of these communities under the strict control and oppression of their traditional leaders, disallowing any personal freedom to individual members of an ethnic or religious community. Liberation of the individual, and promotion and extension of liberal rights to individuals was not the motive of the political struggle conducted by the Ententists.

The political history of the period from late 1908—when the parliament opened—to early 1913—when the Unionists recaptured power from an illegitimate government through a non-constitutional method—reflects the constant struggle between the proponents of the new regime working through, and depending upon, the newly created parliament, and the monarchist forces who aimed at restoring the *ancien régime* at all costs. One cannot but observe that this is no ordinary parliamentary struggle of two opposing political groups to capture political power through mutually agreed upon principles of liberal democratic politics. Although a superficial look at parliamentary debates and press reports might give that impression, a closer scrutiny of the content of those debates and the reason for, as well as the nature of, the arguments and disagreements show it with absolute clarity that here was a case of a continuous struggle between the old, absolutist mentality and the new, liberal worldview.[15]

The development of events from late 1908 onwards shows that although the general elections produced a Chamber of Deputies where there were many sympathisers of the Com-

---

[15] For all his sensitivity to the issue, Erik J. Zürcher, for instance, fails to give a satisfactory analysis for the period between 1908 and 1913 precisely because he thinks political struggle after the Revolution of 1908 was being conducted under 'normalised' conditions—as if the constitutional future of Turkey was not discussed, debated and contested at all (Erik J. Zürcher, *Turkey: A Modern History*, Revised Edition, pp.100-113).

mittee of Union and Progress, the Unionists were by no
means the strongest group in the Chamber. As I have argued
in *The Revolution of 1908 in Turkey* that the general elections
of 1908 did not return a overwhelmingly Unionist Chamber, I
do not go into the details of the numerical strength of the
Unionists here.[16] Well-informed observers of the Turkish political scene often assessed the situation as really precarious—
and their observations and predictions proved to be absolutely
correct in most of the cases. Unionist leadership, on their part,
also knew very well that they could only count on a slim and
shaky majority on really divisive issues—sometimes, even
that majority could not be taken for granted. Unionists were
well aware of their highly precarious situation in the Chamber. I think an historian should interpret the events from late
1908 to early 1913 keeping this most important factor in
mind.[17]

My understanding of the real parliamentary strength of
the Unionists, therefore, is fundamentally different from the
dominant view perpetuated by mis-informed debates and by
the lack of thorough analyses of concrete situations—inside
and outside the Chamber of Deputies. Unionists, at certain
junctures—or, opportune moments—were strong enough to
resist opposition in the Chamber. There are abundant cases,
the most important of which are mentioned, as well as the results shown, in the following chapters of the present book. Part
of the misapprehension among historians about a realistic assessment of the parliamentary strength of the Committee of
Union and Progress lay in the fact that the Unionists themselves preferred to mislead the public as to their real strength.
From their point of view, it was quite natural, for tactical purposes, to give a false impression to the public at large. They
had every reason to disguise, so far as possible, their parlia-

---

[16] Aykut Kansu, *The Revolution of 1908 in Turkey*, pp.237-241.

[17] I can not therefore accept Ahmad and Kayalı's arguments that "the Young
Turks ... did not see in themselves the capacity to rule. Therefore they never
considered taking up high governmental posts" (Feroz Ahmad, *The Young Turks:
The Committee of Union and Progress in Turkish Politics, 1908-1914*, p.17), or,
that "[the Committee of Union and Progress] lacked self-confidence and organization. ... Therefore, it was not prepared to make a bid for exclusive political
power ..." (Hasan Kayalı, *Arabs and Young Turks: Ottomanism, Arabism, and
Islamism in the Ottoman Empire, 1908-1918*, p.53).

mentary—and, extra-parliamentary—weaknesses. This false sense of a comfortable majority could be achieved, and the myth perpetuated, partly because practically all of the deputies in the Chamber had participated in the elections of 1908 under the Unionist banner. Political legitimacy in the Fall of 1908, when the general elections took place, could most easily be achieved by associating oneself with the most popular force in the country. Therefore, political expediency helped shape future historiography: Both the Unionists and their opponents had every reason, in the early months of the Revolution, to convince themselves as well as the public that the new parliament was Unionist-dominated. Almost every deputy, in the early months of the Revolution, publicly took pride in boasting to have been a member of the Committee of Union and Progress.[18]

On another front, one can also argue that the Unionists were even successful in neutralising opposition within the bureaucracy—both civilian and military—in most cases. Yet, there were also times when they were totally overawed by extra-parliamentary forces. They were especially vulnerable to attacks or hostilities emanating from the military bureaucracy. Contrary to conventional wisdom, Unionists did not enjoy universal support even from among the low ranking officers, from the ranks of whom some Unionists like Enver Bey—later, Pasha—had managed to survive. An accurate and more realistic assessment of the relationship between the military bureaucracy and the Committee of Union and Progress would suggest, for at least during the period under discussion, that the Unionists could not unequivocally depend on the support of even the majority of the junior officers. Support for the Unionist cause among the upper echelons of the military bureaucracy, especially among the military pashas, were minimal and almost always shaky; and that 'support' was dependent upon circumstances. It was mostly the patriotism of these high ranking pashas that allied them with the policies of the Committee of Union and Progress—so long as Unionist poli-

---

[18] Sina Akşin also seems to accept these arguments at face value and assumes that the Chamber of Deputies consisted overwhelmingly of Unionists (*Jön Türkler ve İttihat ve Terakki*, p.160).

cies corresponded to the patriotic ideal these pashas held.[19]
Patriotic duty—for instance, the resistance against unconditional surrender of the Kâmil Pasha Cabinet immediately after the First Balkan War in 1912—brought honest members of
the military and civilian bureaucracy and the Unionist politicians together.

It is against this background that events from late 1908 onwards should be judged. One can observe how the Unionists
tried to capture political power through parliamentary means.
Although they were not successful in their first attempt of
interpellation to bring down the Kâmil Pasha Cabinet in early
1909, Kâmil Pasha's attempt for the restoration of monarchist
practices in cabinet formation in early February of that year
presented itself as a good opportunity to rally the majority in
the parliament against absolutism. Although this move was
successful in bringing down Kâmil Pasha, Unionist were not
strong enough to form a cabinet of their own. However, as the
events showed shortly afterwards, even a moderate 'coalition'
cabinet was not to the liking of the monarchists; and, the
counter-revolutionary *coup* attempt of 'March 31' took place.
Kâmil Pasha and other monarchist politicians—some of
whom were deputies themselves—acted in close collaboration
with the Hamidian entourage to bring down a constitutionally
formed government through illegitimate means. In this counter-revolutionary *coup* attempt one can see clearly how determined the Unionists were to defend the new regime and how
opportunistically the monarchists acted in trying to bring
down the newly established order. This event showed how in-
tolerant the monarchists were towards the principles of liberal
democratic politics and parliamentary rule.

This event presented an opportunity to demonstrate the
strength of the Unionists as well as their determination to
defend constitutional rule at all costs. Therefore, it is totally ab-

---

[19] For a similar viewpoint see, Feroz Ahmad, "Great Britain's Relations with
the Young Turks, 1908-1914," p.305: "If the senior officers co-operated with the
Unionists, it was because they too wanted to save the Empire. The Unionists 'co-operated' with them because they had the power. The officers were always suspect;
ideologically both were poles apart."

surd to interpret the coup attempt of March 31 as the result of
the mistakes of the Unionists, and blame them for it—as some
historians tend to think. Just as it is to be rejected that this *coup*
came about as a result of the dissatisfaction with the Unionists
and because of the 'blunders' they are alleged to have committed, the allegations of some monarchists that this was part of a
conspiracy on the part of the Unionists to get rid of their opponents are equally baseless and absurd.[20] Nor is it justified to
interpret the 'Event of March 31' as a simple uprising on the
part of disaffected troops stationed at the Yıldız Palace.[21] One
cannot also interpret this *coup* attempt as a religious reaction
on the part of some Muslim fanatics against the secular practices of the new regime.[22] Searching the cause of the 'Event of
March 31' in the religious fanaticism of an angry mob is
tantamount to missing the whole issue of counter-revolutionary agenda of the monarchists.[23]

'The Event of March 31' was, pure and simple, a counter-
revolutionary attempt at restoring the absolutist regime. The
historian should have no doubt as to the motive of this *coup* attempt. One can only investigate the causes of its failure within
two weeks. The monarchists failed partly because they did not
expect the Unionists to gather so much support in such a short
time from around the country in favour of the constitutional
regime. They also did not expect to have the military bureaucracy so divided within itself to afford the needed support for a
successful absolutist takeover. Once the Unionists managed to
galvanise support from among the troops of the Third Army

---

[20] For arguments along these lines see, İsmail Hami Danişmend, *Sadr-ı-a'zam Tevfik Paşa'nın Dosyasındaki Resmi ve Hususi Vesikalara Göre: 31 Mart Vak'ası.*

[21] Victor R. Swenson, "The Military Rising in Istanbul, 1909," pp.171-184. William Hale seems to have accepted this simplistic view (William Hale, Turkish Politics and the Military, pp.40-41).

[22] Bernard Lewis, *The Emergence of Modern Turkey*, 2nd Edition p.215. See also, David Farhi, "The Şeriat as a Political Slogan—or the 'Incident of the 31st Mart'," pp.275-299. Similar interpretations can be found in Ecvet Güresin, *31 Mart İsyanı*; and, Cemal Kutay, *Bir 'Geri Dönüş'ün Mirası: 31 Mart'ın 90. Yılında Laik Cumhuriyet Karşısında Derviş Vahdetiler Cephesi*, 2nd printing.

[23] For an excellent analysis of the historiographical controversy over the counter-revolutionary *coup* attempt of April 13, 1909 and the dethronement of Ab-dülhamid see, Claudia Kleinert, *Die Revision der Historiographie des Osmanischen Reiches am Beispiel von Abdülhamid II: Das späte Osmanische Reich im Urteil türkischer Autoren der Gegenwart, 1930-1990*, pp.106-141.

Corps stationed at Salonica along with gathering large numbers of volunteers at their power base in Salonica to rush to the
defence of constitutional rights, there was little hope of afford-
ing meaningful resistance by solely deploying the troops stationed at Istanbul and the Yıldız Palace.

After the suppression of the *coup* attempt, the Unionists insisted on the restoration of the constitutional government that
functioned before the events took place—even though they
knew that at least part of the blame lay with the Hüseyin Hilmi Pasha Cabinet. His Cabinet was restored not because the
Unionists had trust in Hüseyin Hilmi Pasha but that his restoration would signify return to normalcy—a psychological factor as well as a constitutional necessity deemed indispensable
by the leadership of the Committee of Union and Progress.
Judging by the results of the court martial proceedings during
the Summer of 1909 one can see that political forces within the
country were such that the leadership cadres of the monarchist opposition could not be punished for their roles in the
counter-revolutionary *coup* attempt to the full extent of the law.
Leading figures of the monarchist opposition were practically
left free to resume their clandestine operations. This also
shows how delicate the balance of power was between the
forces of revolution and the forces of reaction. Unionists had to
be very tactful and careful not to upset the delicate balance that
was now in their favour. It was in their political interest not to
pursue the issue through legal means.

One can say that the Hakkı Pasha Cabinet was the first
government which can be interpreted as Unionist-dominated.
Hakkı Pasha thus became the first grand vezier that the
Unionists felt comfortable with. He was trustworthy enough
for the Unionists to have him registered on the ballot as a
Committee of Union and Progress candidate in the elections
of 1908. He had lost the contest due to Kâmil Pasha's successful
counter-propaganda.[24] It was no accident that it was during his
term of office—during the Summer of 1910—that another plot
to overthrow the constitutional regime was uncovered. Again,
the same set of monarchists were involved in the plot.

---

[24] Hüseyin Kâzım Kadri, *Meşrutiyet'ten Cumhuriyet'e Hatıralarım*, pp.67-68.

Although evidence for monarchist agitation was conclusive, no severe punishments could be given to the conspirators. Besides, since some of the leaders of the conspiracy—Prince Sabahaddin and Şerif Pasha—had already escaped and were living in exile, it was impossible to bring each and every one of them before justice.

It is after these failed attempts to bring about the downfall of constitutional order that the monarchists turned their attention to the Committee of Union and Progress. Thus, from late 1910 and early 1911 onwards, monarchists concentrated their efforts to put a wedge within the party itself. Calling itself the New Faction—or, Hizb-i Cedid—monarchists almost managed to bring about a division in the party in April of 1911. Demands of the New Faction, if they were to be accepted, would definitely mean a return to the absolutist regime. It was only through the skillful manipulation of the deputies in the Chamber that the Unionist leadership managed to stave off the danger posed against the very survival of the party, let alone the parliamentary regime. When the monarchists could not succeed in conquering the Committee of Union and Progress from within, there was one last resort—before attempting another *coup*. That was the establishment of an opposition party within the Chamber of Deputies that was to bring together monarchist and separatist deputies under one roof and oppose the government as well as the regime *via* an organised political party.

This party, Entente Libérale, was formed in October of 1911 in order to challenge the new regime as well as to afford an organised opposition to the Unionist-backed Hakkı Pasha Cabinet in the Chamber. As the results of the by-election, conducted in Istanbul shortly after the formation of the party, showed, Unionists were by no means justified to assume that they had the overwhelming majority of the public, so far as the İstanbul constituency was concerned, behind their policies. Yet, although successful in challenging and winning the vacant seat for Istanbul in the Chamber of Deputies, the monarchist opposition organised under the banner of Entente Libérale had a structural weakness. This weakness showed itself in the composition of its members and its formal leadership. Just as it as the case in the previous experiences of establishing monarchist opposition parties, this party too lacked a strong leadership. Again, politicians of the *ancien régime* preferred not to 'debase' themselves by taking formal responsibility of the party leadership. Although it was known that Kâmil Pasha and Prince Sabahaddin were behind the party, both formally kept their 'distance.' Furthermore, totally confined to the Chamber of Deputies, this party lacked a strong organisation in the provinces.

A second weakness lay in the composition of the party's membership. Once again, the party brought the disaffected communities'—the Albanians', the Greeks', part of the Armenians', and the Arabs'—separatist leaders and their monarchist allies together. This was a conglomeration of various communities that had no common interest except for the overthrow of the new regime which they detested because of the havoc it had caused by destroying the rights and privileges with which the traditional leaders of these communities wielded power in their own communities. Thus it remained a political organisation defending the communal rights of the minorities rather than aggregating various interests. It is mainly for this reason that this party lacked strong support from among the Turkish community. Those Turkish deputies—like Dr. Rıza Nur, who professed to uphold nationalistic sentiments—were so deeply involved in counter-revolutionary plots that they saw no contradiction, for instance, in helping separatist Albanians secede from Turkey during the Spring insurrection of 1912. To the extent that the party appealed to citizens of Turkish origin, its main line of propaganda consisted of religious arguments. Accusing the Unionists for being irreligious, monarchists made political use of Muslim religious dogma and fanaticism conveniently forgetting that they were cooperating with conservative Christians belonging to the Orthodox and Catholic sects on the issue of restoring the *ancien régime.*

It is against this background that one has to judge the fate of the general elections of 1912. For the most part, historians accept, without critically examining the facts or the circumstances, the allegation of the monarchists that the general elections of 1912 were wrought with gross irregularities and were rigged. We have only very few research findings on how the general elections of 1912 were actually held in various localities.[25] However, recent investigations show the extent of religious provocation on the part of the Entente Libérale, and the separatist arguments upon which the party platform was built.[26] While monarchist forces of the Entente Libérale were actively engaged in supporting Albanian insurrection which would result in independence before the end of 1912, some of those Albanian separatists were running as candidates under the Entente Libérale banner in the general elections for a parliament which they had no intention of being a member. Alongside these separatist candidates, there were the monarchist allies who were contesting seats in the Chamber while they were simultaneously bent on destroying, or robbing the parliament of its fundamental function. It was under these circumstances that the elections were concluded. Outright monarchists and outspoken Albanian separatists were, in most cases, successfully prevented from being elected to the Chamber. Exclusion of staunch supporters of the *ancien régime* and outspoken Albanian separatists has been interpreted by some historians as proof that these elections were not fair and square.

One only has to remember that arguments over the fairness of these elections were used as a pretext for a *coup d'état* and provided a much needed official excuse to close down the parliament and 'call for new elections' in the Summer of 1912. The history of the coming of the *coup d'état* has not yet been written. However, there are quite a number of memoirs mostly written by junior members of the *coup*—who were used as instruments or accessories to the *coup*, rather than being the organisers themselves—that tell the story of this *coup* in al-

---

[25] Rashid Khalidi, "The 1912 Election Campaign in the Cities of *bilad-al-Sham*," pp.461-474; İhsan Güneş, "1912 Seçimleri ve Eskişehir'de Meydana Gelen Olaylar," pp.459-482; Stojan Makedonski, "Le Regime Jeune-Turc et les Deuxiemes Elections Parlamentaires de 1912 en Macedoine et Thrace Orientale," pp.58-71; and, Kudret Emiroğlu, "Trabzon'da Sopalı Seçimler, 1912," , pp.41-46.

[26] İhsan Güneş, "1912 Seçimleri ve Eskişehir'de Meydana Gelen Olaylar," pp.459-482; and, Fevzi Demir, İkinci Meşrutiyet Dönemi Meclis-i Mebusan Seçimleri, 1908-1914, pp.90-121.

most minute detail.[27] When one knows that the *coup* was being organised and action was taken before and during the general elections, the allegations that the elections were rigged—and, therefore, the argument that it had to be declared null and void—gains a totally new meaning and importance. It is no coincidence that the monarchist *İkdam* printed news of voting irregularities and alleged election frauds at exactly the time when monarchists were pushing for a new, 'independently-led' cabinet and the dissolution of the parliament— that is to say, long after the elections had been concluded. The impatience with parliamentary practice was so blatantly obvious that the new cabinet formed by the *ancien régime* pashas after the *coup* immediately began searching for a 'legal' way to dissolve the parliament for good.

Preliminary measures taken, the Chamber of Deputies was declared 'temporarily' dissolved on August 5, 1912. New elections would be called for and the parliament would re-open with freshly elected deputies. This was a mid-way solution for the restoration of the absolutist regime where pashas of the *ancien régime* would rule without a parliament. It was at this juncture that the Entente Libérale declared the closure of its local branches. The official communiqué from the party leadership stated that since a trustworthy cabinet had taken over the reigns of government, there was no need for political activity now.[28] Had there been a genuine intention of holding general elections, nothing would be more absurd than closing down a party desperately in need of being represented in the parliament. The raid on the offices of the Committee of Union and Progress a few days later further cleared up the situation. The absolutist intention became much more clearer when the conspirator behind the *coup*, Kâmil Pasha, took over the leadership of the cabinet—thus, ending the fiction that this was a cabinet of 'disinterested pashas.' Kâmil Pasha's one of

---

[27] Ahmed Bedevi Kuran, *İnkılâp Tarihimiz ve İttihad ve Terakki*, idem, *İnkılâp Tarihimiz ve 'Jön Türkler*, and, *idem*, *Osmanlı İmparatorluğunda İnkılâp Hareketleri ve Milli Mücadele*; Rıza Nur, *Cemiyet-i Hafiye*, and *idem*, *Hürriyet ve İtilâf Fırkası Nasıl Doğdu, Nasıl Öldü?*; and, Hasan Amca, *Doğmayan Hürriyet: Bir Devrin İçyüzü, 1909-1918.*

[28] Şehbenderzade Filibeli Ahmed Hilmi, *Muhalefetin İflâsı: İtilâf ve Hürriyet Fırkası*, pp.62-63.

the first executive orders was to indefinitely postpone the holding of the general elections in view of the war with the Balkan powers. Thus, Kâmil Pasha dispersed all doubt, if there had been such doubt, about the real intentions of the monarchists, and cleared up any misunderstanding that might have been left concerning the monarchist project for the future of Turkey.

Under the circumstances, Unionists had been left with very few options. Half of its leadership exiled and some of the remaining leaders being sought after and imprisoned by the monarchist martial law authorities, the Committee of Union and Progress' days were thought to be numbered. The monarchist press had been celebrating the 'air of freedom after four years of oppression under the despotism of the Committee of Union and Progress' since July of 1912.[29] According to monarchist propagandists a new era had just dawned. It was no exaggeration that many felt the hope of a liberal democratic future for Turkey had been utterly shattered. In the words of a foreign observer intimately involved with the domestic politics of Turkey, Count Ostrorog, the situation from July 1912 onwards reminded him of the events of 'March 31'—the only difference was that this one had succeeded.[30]

It was under these circumstances that the war against the Balkan powers was fought. Declaring war on October 8, 1912, Montenegro was the first to attack Turkey. A week later full fledged war had started when Bulgaria, Serbia and Greece joined in. Coupled with the swiftness with which the Balkan countries simultaneously made their attacks on several fronts, decimation of the troops by the cholera epidemic, and demoralisation and political division among the staff officers left the Turkish Army in total disarray. This situation brought about retreat sooner than the Cabinet feared. Bulgarian armies reached the Çatalca lines—the last lines of defence before the gates of İstanbul—by early November. Armistice was sought

---

[29] Şefik Esad, "Her Millet Lâyık Olduğu Hükûmete Nail Olur," *İktiham*, July 12, 1328/July 25, 1912, p.1; and, Ferhan, "Abdülhamid Gelecekmiş!" *İktiham*, July 21, 1328/August 3, 1912, p.1.

[30] Mehmed Cavid, "Meşrutiyet Devrine Ait Cavid Bey'in Hatıraları: 166," *Tanin*, February 16, 1944, p.2.

after and negotiated on very unfavourable terms. The Kâmil Pasha Cabinet furthermore immediately asked for the diplomatic help of Great Britain and her allies in reaching a negotiated settlement. Backing the Balkan countries, Great Britain and her allies put forward demands that practically meant unconditional surrender for Turkey. Kâmil Pasha insistently rejected the German and the Austrian advice to hold out.

Thus, it was on the very day Kâmil Pasha Cabinet convened to formally accept the harsh terms of the great powers that the Unionists along with the patriotic pashas in the military—Mahmud Şevket Pasha figuring prominently among them—decided to take the matter into their own hands. They put the plan to 'raid the Sublime Porte' into execution—forcing the Cabinet to resign at gunpoint, and shooting Nâzım Pasha in the process. Kâmil Pasha was exiled to Egypt shortly afterwards.[31] Thus came the end of an epoch in Turkish history.

---

[31] In Egypt he would lose no time in organising another *coup* that would totally eliminate the Committee of Union and Progres and restore the monarchists to power. According to Feroz Ahmad, he seemed to have secured British support in return for promises to surrender the key administrative and financial positions in the government to foreign experts (*The Young Turks: The Committee of Union and Progress in Turkish Politics, 1908-1914*, pp.126-129).

CHAPTER TWO

UNIONIST BID FOR POLITICAL POWER
IN EARLY 1909

Conventional recounting of events in late 1908 and early 1909
often give a wrong impression of what the real political situation was. As the standard accounts of the Revolution dismiss the genuinely revolutionary character of the movement
and portray it as a mere governmental change, or takeover, by
a modernising elite, composed of enlightened military and
civilian bureaucrats, they take it for granted that these bureaucrats who called themselves Unionists—or 'revolutionaries
from above,' as the proponents of dependency theory would
like to label them—ruled without encountering serious opposition. Given the conventional belief that the general elections
turned out a Chamber which was overwhelmingly, if not totally, Unionist, there remains no reason, from a conventional
viewpoint, to question the validity of these assumptions.

However, as I have argued elsewhere, the Revolution was
genuine—meaning that it was not a simple takeover of state
apparatus by a 'modernising elite' represented by enlightened
bureaucrats.[1] The upheaval in the upper echelons of the civilian and military bureaucracy which took place immediately
after the Revolution partly illustrates the true nature of the
events. Furthermore, the Kâmil Pasha Cabinet which was
formed during the initial days of the Revolution also illustrates the transitional, or provisional, character of political rule.
Although nominally supported by the Unionist leadership,
the government was neither constituted by the Unionists nor
represented the real aspirations of the Revolution. Kâmil Pasha
was far from being a revolutionary figure, and everybody

---

[1] Aykut Kansu, *The Revolution of 1908 in Turkey*, pp.1-29. See also, Aykut
Kansu, "Dünden Bugüne 1908 Devrimi," pp.4-11.

knew that a change in government was inevitable after the opening of the parliament.

The results of the general elections, contrary to common belief among historians, did not turn out to be a total success for the Unionists. The elections did not give the Unionists the overwhelming majority in the Chamber they had hoped for.[2] Nevertheless, being the only organised body in the Chamber, they stood a good chance of challenging the Kâmil Pasha Cabinet. Therefore, it was only natural to expect that a government having the confidence of the Unionists take over the reigns of power as soon as the Chamber started to function.

Though not more than about two hundred deputies had reached the capital, Parliament was scheduled to open on December 17.[3] Whereas representatives of the *ancien régime*, statesmen who survived the thirty shameful years of the absolutist regime, would dominate the Senate, the Chamber of Deputies would largely consist of men of the younger generation, less experienced than their colleagues in the Senate, though inspired with a more confident temper and a much more patriotic fervour. Kurds, Arabs, Albanians, Slavs, Armenians, Greeks, and Jews would be proportionally represented in the Chamber.[4]

On the morning of the scheduled opening, all of İstanbul was in movement—troops preparing for the ceremony, artisans feverishly putting finishing touches to the decorations which had been commissioned for the event, festive crowds surging across the bridges over the Golden Horn into İstanbul. The Sultan, whom Kâmil Pasha had persuaded to preside over the ceremony, would drive from the Yıldız Palace by way of Pera, the Mahmud Bridge, and Eski Saray to the Hagia Sophia, in the shadow of which stood the Parliament Building. Long before the procession began, crowds of men took up

---

[2] Aykut Kansu, *The Revolution of 1908 in Turkey*, pp.237-241.
[3] Hüseyin Cahid [Yalçın], "Meclis-i Mebusan İnikadı," *Tanin*, December 4, 1324/December 17, 1908, p.1.
[4] "The Turkish Chamber of Deputies," *The Times*, December 17, 1908, p.12. For the complete list of deputies in the Chamber see, Aykut Kansu, *The Revolution of 1908 in Turkey*, Appendix One, pp.243-301. For the list of senators see, Appendix Two, pp.303-310.

every vantage point along the route, patiently awaiting the Sultan's passage, while women, dispensing with the veil, gathered in windows and along the rooftops. The route was profusely decorated with the Crescent and Star on red and green fields. Newly-clad troops lined the streets and causeways, and all crossroads were picketed with cavalry, and staff officers in brilliant uniforms. Despite extensive planning, however, the square which faced the Hagia Sophia and the Parliament Building became so crowded that cavalry had to be called in to help the Albanian infantry stationed there to keep the pressure under control. The lower roofs of the Hagia Sophia and even the lower rim of the main dome were reportedly 'black' with sightseers. In front of the Parliament gate was a guard of honour, and there were also detachments of students from the classical, technical, military, naval, and civil schools.[5]

By eleven fifteen, everyone was in his place as the first deputies arrived, preceded by red and green silk banners. A trumpet called the troops to attention, and military bands clashed out the Constitutional Hymn. At half past twelve, the Royal carriage arrived, with Abdülhamid, his son, Prince Burhaneddin, and the Grand Vezier. As the carriage swung past to the sound of the Hamidian Anthem, the crowd burst into singing, and cheering for the Constitution. Exactly at ten minutes to one, the Turkish flag over the Parliament Building gave way to the Royal ensign and for a second time, Abdülhamid stood before the assembled representatives of his people.[6]

In the Chamber, facing the tribune sat some two hundred deputies, the monotony of the black stambulines and red fezzes relieved by the white and green turbans of the ulema and hodjas and the blue uniforms of a dozen military deputies. Between the tribune and the deputies were ranged the dignitaries of the Muslim, Christian, and Jewish faiths.

---

[5] Edwin Pears, *Forty Years in Constantinople: The Recollections of Sir Edwin Pears, 1873-1915*, p.253; *idem, Life of Abdul Hamid*, pp.301-302; Hasan Amca, *Doğmayan Hürriyet: Bir Devrin İçyüzü, 1908-1918*, pp.68-71; Yusuf Hikmet Bayur, *Türk İnkılâbı Tarihi, 1/2*, p.137; "Opening of Parliament by the Sultan: Scenes in Stambul," *The Times*, December 18, 1908, p.5.

[6] "Opening of Parliament by the Sultan: Scenes in Stambul," *The Times*, December 18, 1908, p.5.

Beyond the Christian prelates, on the extreme right of the tribune, were the senators—Marshals and Generals in full uniform, and ex-Ministers covered with gold lace. Of all, perhaps the most interesting figure among the senators was that of Said Pasha, who thirty years ago, ambitious of power, and sceptical of constitutionalism, had aided Abdülhamid to overthrow the Parliament of 1876 and laid the foundations of the system of Palace government.[7]

Written with Kâmil Pasha's knowledge, the speech from the throne began with a justification for the Constitution's abrogation. The Sultan stated that "the first Parliament was temporarily dissolved until the education of the people had been brought to a sufficiently high level by the extension of instruction throughout the Empire."[8] The deputies listened without even smiling at what was surely the strangest defence an autocrat had ever offered for the suppression of liberty. But when the Sultan spoke of foreign interference and of the cabinet's need for complete parliamentary support, and when he reiterated his pledge to stand by and preserve the Constitution, the deputies positively erupted into applause. When Abdülhamid left, all were in high spirits. The deputies then chose Naki Bey, deputy for Trabzon and the senior member present, as temporary President of the Chamber.[9] The session ended with all present swearing allegiance to the Constitution and the Sultan, as long as the latter should maintain the Constitution.[10]

Outside, huge crowds had waited patiently until half past one, when an officer on the summit of Hagia Sophia waved a white flag. Another immediately answered from the Ministry of War, and a moment later the first of one hundred and

---

[7] "Opening of Parliament by the Sultan: Scenes in Stambul," *The Times*, December 18, 1908, p.5.

[8] "Nutk-u İftitahi-i Hazret-i Padişahi," I/I/1, December 4, 1324/December 17, 1908, *Meclis-i Mebusan Zabıt Ceridesi*, *1*, pp.2-3.

[9] I/I/1, December 4, 1324/December 17, 1908, *Meclis-i Mebusan Zabıt Ceridesi*, *1*, p.3; "Opening of Parliament by the Sultan: Scenes in Stambul," *The Times*, December 18, 1908, p.5; and, "Opening of Parliament: Speech from the Throne," *The Levant Herald and Eastern Express*, December 18, 1908, p.1. See also, Edwin Pears, *Life of Abdul Hamid*, pp.302-303; and, Yusuf Hikmet Bayur, *Türk İnkılâbı Tarihi*, *1/2*, pp.137-138.

[10] I/I/1, December 4, 1324/December 17, 1908, *Meclis-i Mebusan Zabıt Ceridesi*, *1*, pp.3-6; "Opening of Parliament by the Sultan: Scenes in Stambul," *The Times*, December 18, 1908, p.5; and, "Opening of Parliament: Speech from the Throne," *The Levant Herald and Eastern Express*, December 18, 1908, p.1.

one guns told the capital that the Sultan had fulfilled his promise to the people. A great shout went up and the amassed bands
again played the Constitutional Hymn. The crowd took up the
Hymn, and for nearly an hour after, snatches of the Hymn
came up to the Chamber of Deputies, mingled with loud
cheering as the Sultan, the Ministers, Ambassadors, and the
deputies successively left the Parliament Building.[11]

On the whole, the press greeted the opening of Parliament
with satisfaction, gave expression to the joy of the nation, and
counselled the people to support the labours of the deputies in
whom the nation had placed its confidence.[12]

The Speech from the Throne was also generally greeted
with enthusiasm, though *Tanin* criticised its brevity and
vagueness, and its editor, Hüseyin Cahid [Yalçın], condemned Kâmil Pasha for his involvement in its conception.
Tanin also expressed the hope that the Austrian and Bulgarian
difficulties would be settled as soon as possible in order to
allow Parliament to devote itself to domestic questions.[13]

With the inauguration of the Parliament, the Committee of
Union and Progress headquarters at Salonica sent a telegram
to the Sultan, reiterating its claim that a system of government
based on deliberation was a national right in accordance with
the teachings of history and the prescriptions of the Muslim
faith. The telegram went on to express the joy of the nation,
and wished the Sultan a peaceful and happy reign.[14]

The opening of the Parliament was greeted with celebrations in the provincial centres. At Salonica, the stronghold of
the Committee of Union and Progress, and the surrounding
towns of Kavalla and Drama, similar rejoicings took place on
the day of the opening of the Parliament.[15] There were cele-

---

[11] "Opening of Parliament by the Sultan: Scenes in Stambul," *The Times*, December 18, 1908, p.5.
[12] "The Turkish Parliament," *The Times*, December 19, 1908, p.5.
[13] Hüseyin Cahid [Yalçın], "Nutuk İftahı," *Tanin*, December 5, 1324/Decem-
ber 18, 1908, p.1; see also, "The Turkish Parliament," *The Times*, December 19,
1908, p.5. For an additional description of and comment on the events of the day
from a Unionist point of view see, Babanzade İsmail Hakkı, "Tarihi bir Gün,"
Tanin, December 5, 1324/December 18, 1908, p.1. See also, Hüseyin Cahid [Yal-
çın], "Mebusan-ı Osmani ve Avrupa," *Tanin*, December 6, 1324/December 19,
1908, p.1; and, Hüseyin Cahid [Yalçın], "Nutuk İftahı ve Tesiratı," *Tanin*, December 9, 1324/December 22, 1908, p.1.
[14] "The Turkish Parliament," *The Times*, December 22, 1908, p.5.
[15] "Lettre de Salonique," and "Lettre de Drama," *The Levant Herald and East-*

brations in the Anatolian towns as well. At Erzurum, a crowd
of about thirty thousand people gathered in front of the government building where speeches were made and loyalty to constitutional regime expressed.[16] In towns all over Anatolia—for
instance, in Trabzon, Adana, Bursa, İzmit and Bandırma—the
population greeted the opening of the Parliament with extreme joy.[17]

The great majority of the deputies were genuinely anxious to
help in the task of reorganising the nation's internal administration and were united in their advocacy of reforms such as
the introduction of the principle of ministerial responsibility to
the Constitution, the alteration of laws concerning the powers
of provincial authorities, and the extension of conscription to
non-Muslims. Matters of parliamentary procedure would have
to be discussed: a President and two Vice-Presidents would
have to be elected, a budget, which would inevitably excite debate, would have to be passed; a variety of schemes prepared
by the different Ministries would have to be sanctioned.[18] *Le
Temps*, in reference to an interview which one of its correspondents had with Dr. Nâzım Bey, remarked that the proposal to amend the Constitution of 1876 so as to determine once
and for all the nature of ministerial responsibility, and to establish a constitutional basis for national sovereignty, was the
rock on which the first Russian Duma had split, and that it
would constitute the real test of the aims and strength of the
Unionists.[19]

The President and the two Vice-Presidents of the Chamber
had not yet been appointed. By Article 74 of the Constitution of
1876, the Sultan would choose these from a list prepared by the
Chamber, but it was doubtful whether Abdülhamid would

---

ern Express, December 24, 1908, p.3; and, "Lettre de Cavalla," *The Levant Herald
and Eastern Express*, December 23, 1908, p.3.
    [16] "Rejoicings at Erzerum," *The Levant Herald and Eastern Express*, De-
cember 18, 1908, p.1.
    [17] "Lettre de Brousse," "Lettre d'Ismidt," and "Lettre de Panderma," *The Lev-
ant Herald and Eastern Express*, December 24, 1908, p.3; and, "Lettre d'Adana,"
and "Lettre de Trebizonde," *The Levant Herald and Eastern Express*, December 30,
1908, p.3.
    [18] "The Turkish Chamber of Deputies," *The Times*, December 17, 1908, p.12.
    [19] "The Turkish Parliament: French Views," *The Times*, December 19, 1908,
p.5.

have much freedom in the matter. Ahmed Rıza Bey, formerly editor of *Meşveret*, and one of the chief organisers of the
Unionist movement outside the Empire, was believed to have
an excellent chance of gaining the presidency, in spite of his
unpopularity among religious circles. Of the other candidates,
İsmail Kemal Bey, the monarchist Albanian deputy for Berat,
was also a serious contender: an administrator of proven ability, he was experienced, ambitious, and witty, though detested
by the Unionists who accused him of having duped them on
the issue of Albanian autonomy.[20]

The election of the President of the Chamber took place on
December 23, and the names of Ahmed Rıza Bey, Azmi Bey,
and Emrullah Efendi were subsequently submitted to the Sultan. As Ahmed Rıza had received a commanding two hundred and five votes, he was expected to be the Sultan's choice.
İsmail Kemal Bey came in fourth, receiving sixty-eight
votes.[21]

The following day, the first round of elections of three candidates for the First Vice-Presidency of the Chamber began.
Talât Bey, deputy for Edirne and one of the leaders of the
Committee of Union and Progress, came first with two hundred and sixteen votes. Şefik Bey, deputy for Balıkesir, received one hundred votes, Hagop Babiguian, Armenian deputy for Rodosto, sixty-one votes, Mustafa Asım Efendi, deputy
for İstanbul, thirty-seven votes, Abd al-Nafi Pasha, deputy for
Aleppo, thirty-seven votes, İsmail Kemal Bey, Albanian deputy for Berat, thirty-six votes, Ebuzziya Tevfik Bey, deputy for
Antalya, thirty votes, Aristidi Pasha Yorgandjioglu, Greek
deputy for İzmir, eighteen votes, Cavid Bey, deputy for Salonica, eighteen votes, Necib Draga, Albanian deputy for Üsküb,
fourteen votes, and Krikor Zohrab, Armenian deputy for İstan-
bul, ten votes.[22] On the second round—for the third position—

---

[20] "The Turkish Chamber of Deputies," *The Times*, December 17, 1908, p.12.

[21] I/I/4, December 10, 1324/December 23, 1908, *Meclis-i Mebusan Zabıt Ceridesi, 1*, pp.40-42; "The Turkish Parliament," *The Times*, December 24, 1908, p.3;
and, "The Turkish Parliament," *The Times*, December 25, 1908, p.5. See also, Hüseyin Cahid [Yalçın], "Meclisimiz," *Tanin*, December 11, 1324/December 24,
1908, p.1.

[22] I/I/4, December 11, 1324/December 24, 1908, *Meclis-i Mebusan Zabıt Ceridesi, 1*, pp.46-47; "The Turkish Parliament," *The Times*, December 25, 1908, p.5;
and, "A la Chambre Ottomane," *The Levant Herald and Eastern Express*, December 26, 1908, p.2.

İsmail Kemal Bey received one hundred and fifteen votes and Hagop Babiguian, sixty votes. As a result, the three deputies whose names were to be submitted to the Sultan—Talât Bey, deputy for Edirne, Şefik Bey, deputy for Balıkesir, both of the Committee of Union and Progress, and İsmail Kemal Bey, monarchist deputy for Berat—had been decided upon.[23]

The December 26 sitting of the Chamber opened with the announcement that the Sultan had named Ahmed Rıza Bey President of the Chamber. The announcement was received with the utmost enthusiasm, and Ahmed Rıza Bey took the floor and addressed the Chamber. He described how, twenty years before, he had left Bursa and made his way to Paris, where he worked, with the help of devoted patriotic friends, for constitutional liberties. He urged the Chamber to put aside old quarrels and unite for the general good, for the eyes of the nation, and of all of Europe as well, were upon it. He declared that the Committee of Union and Progress would carry out its task with the calm and dignity which had thus far marked its policy, and expressed the hope that his comrades would not allow themselves to be influenced by personal interests in the performance of their duties.[24] He then announced that Talât Bey had been selected First Vice-President.[25] Three candidates were then chosen for the post of Second Vice-President— Aristidi Pasha Yorgandjioglu, Greek deputy for İzmir, with one hundred and twenty-two votes, Necib Draga, Albanian deputy for Drama and member of the Üsküb branch of the Committee of Union and Progress, with one hundred and twenty-nine votes, and Ruhi al-Khalidi, Arab deputy for Jerusalem, with one hundred and nine votes. The Sultan was expected to select Aristidi Pasha Yorgandjioglu for the post.[26]

[23] I/I/4, December 11, 1324/December 24, 1908, *Meclis-i Mebusan Zabıt Ceridesi, I*, p.48; "The Turkish Parliament," *The Times*, December 26, 1908, p.4.
[24] I/I/5, December 13, 1324/December 26, 1908, *Meclis-i Mebusan Zabıt Ceridesi, I*, pp.50-52. For a highly favourable comment on his speech see, Hüseyin Cahid [Yalçın], "Ahmed Rıza Bey'in Nutku," *Tanin*, December 15, 1324/December 28, 1908, p.1.
[25] I/I/5, December 13, 1324/December 26, 1908, *Meclis-i Mebusan Zabıt Ceridesi, I*, p.52.
[26] I/I/5, December 13, 1324/December 26, 1908, *Meclis-i Mebusan Zabıt Ceridesi, I*, pp.52-54; "The Turkish Parliament: Election of Officers," *The Times*, December 28, 1908, p.3; and, "A la Chambre Ottomane," *The Levant Herald and Eastern Express*, December 28, 1908, p.1.

That same day, draft copies of the Chamber's reply to the Speech from the Throne were circulated in the lobbies. The reply began by blaming the calamities and oppression of the previous thirty years on the Sultan's former advisors. With regard to foreign affairs, it declared that Turkey was animated by the most pacific intentions and that the Chamber would give its fullest support to "a Cabinet which, according to the spirit of the Constitution, should be responsible to the Chamber and possess its confidence."[27] Though this somewhat vaguel y worded passage was expected to arouse considerable discussion, the draft was passed by a large majority on December 28.[28]

It was generally expected—since August of 1908—that, once Parliament was convened and the Chamber's executives elected, the Committee of Union and Progress would begin a concerted attack on the Kâmil Pasha Cabinet: the Committee would clearly require men of bolder and more modern ideas.[29] Whether or not this attack would be prompted by honest motives remained to be seen. Whatever the case, the early days of 1909 promised to test the nation's commitment to a truly constitutional regime, and whether or not that commitment would extent to Kâmil Pasha's removal.[30]

The question of a vote of confidence for the Kâmil Pasha Cabinet was therefore of continued interest in the Chamber. Though the position of independent Turkish deputies was uncertain, the Greek deputies, and a majority of the Albanian

---

[27] I/I/5, December 13, 1324/December 26, 1908, *Meclis-i Mebusan Zabıt Ceridesi, 1*, pp.55-60; and, "The Turkish Parliament," *The Times*, December 28, 1908, p.3. See also, Yusuf Hikmet Bayur, *Türk İnkılâbı Tarihi, 1/2*, pp.138-139.

[28] I/I/6, December 15, 1324/December 28, 1908, *Meclis-i Mebusan Zabıt Ceridesi, 1*, pp.64-68; and, "The Turkish Parliament: The Sultan and the Deputies," *The Times*, December 29, 1908, p.4.

[29] "The Young Turkish Revolution," in G. P. Gooch and H. Temperley (Eds.), *British Documents on the Origins of the War, 1898-1914, 5: The Near East*, p.259; Sir Gerard Lowther to Sir Edward Grey, Constantinople, August 25, 1908, printed in "The Young Turkish Revolution," in G. P. Gooch and H. Temperley (Eds.), *British Documents on the Origins of the War, 1898-1914, 5: The Near East*, p.267. Hüseyin Cahid Yalçın, "Meşrutiyet Hatıraları, 1908-1918," *Fikir Hareketleri, 4* (April 25-October 19, 1935), p.214.

[30] "The Young Turkish Revolution," in G. P. Gooch and H. Temperley (Eds.), *British Documents on the Origins of the War, 1898-1914, 5: The Near East*, pp.259-260. See also, "Die Parteibildung im türkischen Parlament," *Berliner Tageblatt und Handels-Zeitung*, January 4, 1909, p.1.

and Armenian deputies, were believed to support the Cabinet.[31] Syrian deputies, along with other deputies from Arabia, had already made it public that they had decided to support Kâmil Pasha's maintenance as Grand Vezier.[32]

With the elections in the Chamber complete, the leadership of the Committee of Union and Progress then took steps to provoke an immediate vote of confidence with the intention of bringing down the Kâmil Pasha Cabinet, and replacing it with a cabinet headed by Hüseyin Hilmi Pasha.[33] Hoping to embarrass the Government on the Cretan Question, Hüseyin Cahid [Yalçın], on December 30, proposed that a day be scheduled for a discussion of the Cabinet's foreign and domestic policy.[34] The date of Kâmil Pasha's statement of policy had not yet been scheduled, but it was expected that the Grand Vezier would defend his conduct of affairs on January 2, 1909, after which the Chamber would adjourn for the Kurban Bayram holidays.[35] Hüseyin Cahid [Yalçın]'s proposal, however, only weakened the Committee's already tenuous majority, galvanised opposition against the Committee of Union and

---

[31] "The Turkish Parliament," *The Times*, December 24, 1908, p.3.
[32] "The Turkish Parliament," *The Times*, December 19, 1908, p.5.
[33] A. A. Türkei 159, No.2/482, Telegram from Marschall, Pera, December 3, 1908; A. A. Türkei 159, No.2/437, Telegram from Tschirschky, Vienna, December 4, 1908; A. A. Türkei 159, No.2/490, Telegram from Marschall, Pera, December 8, 1908. *Şura-yı Ümmet*, the official organ of the Committee of Union and Progress, wanted a new cabinet instead of the Kâmil Pasha Cabinet (A. A. Türkei 159, No.2/516, Telegram from Marschall, Pera, December 26, 1908). See also, Gerald H. Fitzmaurice to Mr. Tyrrell, Constantinople, January 11, 1909, printed in "The Young Turkish Revolution," in G. P. Gooch and H. Temperley (Eds.), *British Documents on the Origins of the War, 1898-1914, 5: The Near East*, p.271.
[34] I/I/7, December 17, 1324/December 30, 1908, *Meclis-i Mebusan Zabıt Ceridesi, 1*, pp.80-84; Hüseyin Cahid Yalçın, "Meşrutiyet Hatıraları, 1908-1918," *Fikir Hareketleri*, 4 (April 25-October 19, 1935), p.245; "A la Chambre Ottomane," *The Levant Herald and Eastern Express*, December 31, 1908, p.2; "Deputiertenkammer," *Osmanischer Lloyd*, January 1, 1909, p.1; "A la Chambre Ottomane," *The Levant Herald and Eastern Express*, January 2, 1909, p.2; and, Ali Fuad Türkgeldi, *Görüp İşittiklerim*, p.16. Hüseyin Cahid [Yalçın] also published a criticism of the Kâmil Pasha Cabinet's domestic and foreign policy in his editorial the same day ("Buhranın En Son Safhası," *Tanin*, December 17, 1324/December 30, 1908, p.1). He continued to criticise Kâmil Pasha's policy of the past four months the next day (Hüseyin Cahid [Yalçın], "Kâmil Paşa Politikası," *Tanin*, December 18, 1324/December 31, 1908, p.1). Writing in the *Yeni Gazete*, Cenab Şahabeddin questioned the motives of Hüseyin Cahid [Yalçın] in calling for the interpellation and suspected that he was doing it for personal gain ("Die türkische Presse," *Osmanischer Lloyd*, January 9, 1909, p.2).
The population of the island of Crete had made a declaration on October 12, 1908 by which the island cededed from Turkey and became part of Greece (Cemal Kutay, *Üç Paşalar Kavgası*, p.43).
[35] "Turkish Internal Affairs," *The Times*, December 31, 1908, p.4.

Progress, and prevented further immediate action against Kâmil Pasha at this juncture. The Greek and Christian deputies
in the Chamber supported the Government; yet, amid much
confusion and debate, the request for interpellation was accepted.[36] Though supporting a review of Kâmil Pasha's policy,
however, the Chamber voted to postpone the debate for a fortnight.[37] The debate was expected to be held on January 11.[38]

The opposition papers, *İkdam*, and *Yeni Gazete* were openly in support of Kâmil Pasha.[39] In addition, a Greek language
newspaper reported that the Albanian deputies intended to
support the Liberal Union's policy of decentralisation and, implicitly, Kâmil Pasha.[40] Though *Tanin* and *Şura-yı Ümmet*
continued to criticise the Grand Vezier's domestic and foreign
policy, it was believed that, pending settlement with Austria
and Bulgaria, the Salonica Committee had decided to support
Kâmil Pasha's maintenance, ostensibly in an effort to pacify
its own dissenters.[41] It was also rumoured that a majority of the
one hundred members of the Deputies' Club had resolved to
support the Cabinet in the January 11 debate.[42]

Preparing for his appearance before the Chamber, Kâmil
Pasha ordered the Ministries to prepare summaries of reforms
and budgets over the past five months, all of which the Cabinet
would review in an extraordinary meeting on January 9. Os-

---

[36] I/I/8, December 18, 1324/December 31, 1908, *Meclis-i Mebusan Zabıt Ceridesi*, *1*, pp.91-99; and, Hüseyin Cahid Yalçın, "Meşrutiyet Hatıraları, 1908-1918,"
Fikir Hareketleri, *4* (April 25-October 19, 1935), p.245.

[37] "The Turkish Parliament," *The Times*, January 1, 1909, p.6.

[38] "The Near East: The Boycott of Austrian Goods," *The Times*, January 2,
1909, p.5.

[39] Hüseyin Cahid Yalçın, "Meşrutiyet Hatıraları, 1908-1918," *Fikir Hareket-
leri*, *4* (April 25-October 19, 1935), p.245; A. A. Türkei 159, No.2/7, Telegram from
Marschall, Pera, January 7, 1909; A. A. Türkei 159, No.2/10, Telegram from
Marschall, Pera, January 9, 1909; and, "Die türkische Presse," *Osmanischer Lloyd*,
January 9, 1909, p.2. See also, Mehmet Tevfik Biren, *II. Abdülhamid, Meşrutiyet ve
Mütareke Devri Hatıraları*, *2*, p.9.

[40] "The Turkish Parliament," *The Times*, January 5, 1909, p.6.

[41] "The Turkish Parliament," *The Times*, January 5, 1909, p.6. For the criticism of the Kâmil Pasha Cabinet and its supporters in the columns of *Tanin* see,
Hüseyin Cahid [Yalçın], "Kâmil Paşa Politikası," *Tanin*, December 18, 1324/De-
cember 31, 1908, p.1; "The Near East: The Boycott of Austrian Goods," *The Times*,
January 2, 1909, p.5; Hüseyin Cahid [Yalçın], "Vükelâdan İstizah," *Tanin*, December 21, 1324/January 3, 1909, p.1; Hüseyin Cahid [Yalçın], "Girit Meselesi ve Boy-
kotaj," *Tanin*, December 25, 1324/January 7, 1909, p.1; Hüseyin Cahid [Yalçın],
"Kâmil Paşa ve Tarafdarları," *Tanin*, December 26, 1324/January 8, 1909, p.1; and,
Hüseyin Cahid [Yalçın], "Kâmil Paşa ve İngiliz Dostluğu," *Tanin*, December 27,
1324/January 9, 1909, p.1.

[42] "The Turkish Parliament," *The Times*, January 5, 1909, p.6.

tensibly, Kâmil Pasha's speech would emphasise the progress made since the Revolution, highlighting the various schemes for administrative reform which would be submitted to the Chamber. [43]

The day of the Cabinet's extraordinary session, the Unionists held a demonstration at the Sultan Ahmed Square to protest the Greek Government's intention to annex Crete. Twenty thousand people attended, among them Arabs, Bosnians, Albanians and Kurds, all of whom displayed great enthusiasm, especially when one of the meeting's numerous orators reminded them that, in the economic boycott, Turkey possessed a weapon of proven efficacy, and that, in case of need, it could also be employed against Greece. After a number of speeches had been delivered, the majority of the demonstrators marched to Sublime Porte whereupon they sent delegates to present their resolution to the Grand Vezier: that the Government do everything in its power to oppose Greek annexation of Crete. [44]

Kâmil Pasha appeared before the crowd, stating that the Greek Government had formally declared that the solution to the Cretan question would be left in the hands of the four Powers; there was no foundation to the rumours, which Unionist newspapers had spread, that the Cretan question was about to be raised. He ended by saying that Crete remained an Ottoman province and that, should necessity demand it, he would not fail in his duty to the nation and the Empire. The speech, which was received with loud cheers, was followed by a demonstration in support of the Grand Vezier—an unforeseen and unpleasant turn of events to those who had organised the meeting in the specific hope of discrediting the Government. [45]

On January 10, *Şura-yı Ümmet*, the Unionist organ, published a severe criticism of certain deputies who were accused

---

[43] "Turkey: The Progress of Reform," *The Times*, January 9, 1909, p.6.

[44] "Girit Havadisi," *İkdam*, December 30, 1324/January 12, 1909, p.3; "The Cretan Question: Speech by Kiamil Pasha," *The Times*, January 11, 1909, p.7. See also the editorial in *Tanin* (Hüseyin Cahid [Yalçın], "Büyük bir Gün—Büyük bir Millet," *Tanin*, December 28, 1324/January 10, 1909, p.1).

[45] "The Cretan Question: Speech by Kiamil Pasha," *The Times*, January 11, 1909, p.7.

of forming nationalist—*i.e.*, separatist—'parties' in the Chamber. The paper declared that the safety of the country was jeopardised by such conduct, called the deputies in question fools or knaves, and urged Ahmed Rıza Bey to bring about unity within the Chamber.[46] The attack was not well received; Hasan Bey, the Albanian deputy for Prishtnë, denounced the *Şura-yı Ümmet* article in the January 11 session of the Chamber.[47] In its January 11 issue, *Şura-yı Ümmet* published a letter from Ahmed Rıza Bey in which he defended the deputies, affirming that they were indeed working for the general interests of the nation.[48] There was, however, considerable lobbying effort on the part of the deputies opposing the Committee of Union and Progress against Ahmed Rıza's presidency of the Chamber.[49] In response to opposition, *Şura-yı Ümmet* not only publicly disavowed responsibility for the editorial, but bowing to criticism from the opposition deputies as well as from the moderate Unionists, also removed the editor and manager of the newspaper. They were replaced by members of the staff of *İttihad ve Terakki*, the Salonica organ of the Committee of Union and Progress.[50] The paper also ceased to mention underneath its title that it was the official organ of the Committee of Union and Progress. Instead, it began writing that it was the organ of all interests.[51]

Throughout January, monarchist opposition strengthened. A British newspaper, the *Daily Mail*, even printed rumours of an insurrection against the constitutional regime involving some twenty thousand conspirators. After imprisoning the Grand Vezier and the President of the Chamber, these reportedly planned to close the Parliament, abrogate the Constitution, and appoint a new Caliph. The conspiracy was said to

---

[46] *Şura-yı Ümmet*, December 28, 1324/January 10, 1909, quoted in "The Turkish Parliament," *The Times*, January 12, 1909, p.6; and, "The Nationalists," *The Levant Herald and Eastern Express*, January 11, 1909, p.1.

[47] "A la Chambre Ottomane," *The Levant Herald and Eastern Express*, January 12, 1909, p.2. See also, Hüseyin Cahid [Yalçın], "Meclis-i Mebusan'da," *Tanin*, December 30, 1324/January 12, 1909, p.1; and "Das türkische Kabinett," *Berliner Tageblatt und Handels-Zeitung*, January 12, 1909, pp.1-2.

[48] *Şura-yı Ümmet*, December 29, 1324/January 11, 1909, quoted in "The Turkish Parliament," *The Times*, January 12, 1909, p.6.

[49] "Deputientenkammer," *Osmanischer Lloyd*, January 12, 1909, p.1.

[50] "The Turkish Parliament," *The Times*, January 12, 1909, p.6.

[51] "Die Fedakjaran-i-milet," *Osmanischer Lloyd*, January 17, 1909, p.1.

have spread throughout Turkey.[52]

On January 12, the police raided the offices of the reactionary newspaper *Hukuk-u Umumiye*, seized a quantity of arms, and arrested several people, all members of the Devotees of the Nation, accused of plotting to overthrow the constitutional regime.[53] The police investigation proved that the offices of *Hukuk-u Umumiye* had served as headquarters for a gang of political adventurers and blackmailers known as the Devotees of the Nation who appeared to have obtained and distributed arms for the purpose of intimidating both the Government and the Committee of Union and Progress.[54] Some forty members of the organisation, including İsmail Hakkı Efendi, the editor of *Hukuk-u Umumiye*, were subsequently arrested, a majority of whom were released by the end of the month.[55] *Hukuk-u Umumiye* resumed publication on January 22.[56] In light of the releases, the police action came under heavy attack.[57]

On January 13, Kâmil Pasha appeared before the Chamber and defended his Cabinet's programme.[58] After referring to the enthusiasm with which the new regime had been re-

---

[52]   *Tanin*, January 13, 1324/January 26, 1909, quoted in Hüseyin Cahid Yalçın, "Meşrutiyet Hatıraları, 1908-1918," *Fikir Hareketleri*, 4 (April 25-October 19, 1935), p.277.

[53]   "A Suspected Turkish Plot," *The Times*, January 13, 1909, p.5; and, "Les 'Fédakiarans'," *The Levant Herald and Eastern Express*, January 15, 1909, p.2. See also, Mustafa Şahin, "Cemiyet mi, Eşkıya Çetesi mi?" pp.57-59.

[54]   "Turkish Internal Affairs: The Suspected Plot," *The Times*, January 15, 1909, p.5; "Die Gesellschaft der Fedakiaran-i Millet," *Osmanischer Lloyd*, January 16, 1909, p.1; and, "Les 'Fédakiarans'," *The Levant Herald and Eastern Express*, January 16, 1909, p.2.

[55]   "Turkish Internal Affairs: The Suspected Plot," *The Times*, January 15, 1909, p.5; "Die Fedakjaran-i-milet," *Osmanischer Lloyd*, January 17, 1909, p.1; "Les Fédakiarans," *The Levant Herald and Eastern Express*, January 18, 1909, p.1; "News Items," *The Levant Herald and Eastern Express*, January 20, 1909, p.1; "Turkey: Disorderly Military Students," *The Times*, January 28, 1909, p.5; and, "Politische Nachrichten: Die Fedakjaran-i-milet," *Osmanischer Lloyd*, February 3, 1909, p.2.

[56]   "Les Fédakiarans," *The Levant Herald and Eastern Express*, January 23, 1909, p.2.

[57]   "Turkey: Disorderly Military Students," *The Times*, January 28, 1909, p.5.

[58]   I/I/11, December 31, 1324/January 12, 1909, *Meclis-i Mebusan Zabıt Ceridesi*, *1*, pp.164-170; Hüseyin Cahid Yalçın, "Meşrutiyet Hatıraları, 1908-1918," *Fikir Hareketleri*, 4 (April 25-October 19, 1935), p.246; "Turkish Policy: Speech by Kiamil Pasha," *The Times*, January 14, 1909, p.5; "A la Chambre Ottomane: L'exposé Grand Véziriel," *The Levant Herald and Eastern Express*, January 15, 1909, p.1; Yusuf Hikmet Bayur, *Türk İnkılâbı Tarihi*, *1/2*, pp.139-140; and, Ali Fuad Türkgeldi, *Görüp İşittiklerim*, p.17. See also, Hüseyin Cahid [Yalçın], "Sadrâzam Paşanın İzahatı," *Tanin*, January 1, 1324/January 14, 1909, p.1; and, Ali Kemal, "Kâmil Paşa'nın Beyanatı," *İkdam*, January 1, 1324/January 14, 1909, p.1.

ceived as well as to the extraordinary discipline and moderation displayed by the people, he declared that it was, first and foremost, due to the Sultan that disturbance and bloodshed had been avoided. The Sultan, he argued, had put himself at the head of the Revolution, dissociated himself from the group of evil advisors, and had thus earned the nation's gratitude. Having defended Abdülhamid and exonerated him from any personal wrong doing, Kâmil Pasha went on to pay lip service to the various groups which had brought about the Revolution: warm thanks were due to the army, which had identified itself with the nation's aspirations, and to the men, who, undaunted by exile and oppression, had worked perseveringly to overthrow despotism.[59]

He then summarised the administrative reforms which his cabinet had initiated. The military, he said, had made great strides since the Revolution, and though the Navy's fleet had been allowed to fall into an absolutely disorganised condition under the old regime, the expenditure of 300,000 TLs in the preceding five months had made it possible to commission all vessels. Extensive programme of public works would be submitted to the Chamber, with a number of demands for concessions on the part of foreign capitalists. Though the Ministries of Public Works, and Mines and Forests, in particular, had the benefit of foreign assistance, he warned that the influx of foreign capital would depend on the practice of sound finance, and a wary, unadventurous foreign policy. British capitalists, who had shunned Turkish investments under the old regime, had lately co-operated with French and German financiers and would, he hoped, continue to aid in the development of the Empire.[60]

---

[59] I/I/11, December 31, 1324/January 12, 1909, *Meclis-i Mebusan Zabıt Ceridesi, I,* pp.164-166; "Turkish Policy: Speech by Kiamil Pasha," *The Times,* January 14, 1909, p.5; "Deputiertenkammer," *Osmanischer Lloyd,* January 14, 1909, p.1; "Das Exposé Kiamil Paschas," *Berliner Tageblatt und Handels-Zeitung,* January 14, 1909, p.15; and, "A la Chambre Ottomane: L'exposé Grand Véziriel," *The Levant Herald and Eastern Express,* January 15, 1909, p.1.

[60] I/I/11, December 31, 1324/January 12, 1909, *Meclis-i Mebusan Zabıt Ceridesi, I,* pp.166-168; "Turkish Policy: Speech by Kiamil Pasha," *The Times,* January 14, 1909, p.5; "Deputiertenkammer," *Osmanischer Lloyd,* January 14, 1909, p.1; "Das Exposé Kiamil Paschas," *Berliner Tageblatt und Handels-Zeitung,* January 14, 1909, p.15; and, "A la Chambre Ottomane: L'exposé Grand Véziriel," *The Levant Herald and Eastern Express,* January 15, 1909, p.1.

Turning to foreign affairs, the Grand Vezier pointed out that the Government had devoted its attention to the strengthening of its relations with the Powers. Certain political schemes, however, had of late hampered its efforts. The Bulgarian declaration of independence was followed by Austria-Hungary's annexation of the occupied provinces and the evacuation of the sandjak of Novi Bazar. The Government had vigorously protested these acts of lawlessness, and had formally requested the Great Powers to convene a European Conference. In the meantime, the populations of Bosnia and Herzegovina had shown signs of considerable excitement, as was the case in Serbia and Montenegro. The Government decided to accept the recommendation of the Powers—amounting to a financial arrangement with the concerned parties—and the immediate danger of war had been averted. As to the Cretan Question, the Grand Vezier stated that the four Protecting Powers had promised to achieve a settlement in accordance with Turkish interests.[61]

In conclusion, Kâmil Pasha stressed that the Government had faced great external and internal difficulties during the last five and a half months. He hoped that, with Divine aid and the patriotic support of the Chamber, the state would emerge from its troubles, taking its place among the proud nations of the world.[62]

The speech over, deputies sprang to their feet and cheered the Grand Vezier for several minutes. Rıza Nur, deputy for Sinob, proposed an informal vote of confidence which was unanimously carried, amid frantic cheers.[63] The move had

---

[61] I/I/11, December 31, 1324/January 12, 1909, *Meclis-i Mebusan Zabıt Ceridesi*, *1*, pp.168-170; "Turkish Policy: Speech by Kiamil Pasha," *The Times*, January 14, 1909, p.5; "Deputiertenkammer," *Osmanischer Lloyd*, January 14, 1909, p.1; "Das Exposé Kiamil Paschas," *Berliner Tageblatt und Handels-Zeitung*, January 14, 1909, p.15; and, "A la Chambre Ottomane: L'exposé Grand Véziriel," *The Levant Herald and Eastern Express*, January 15, 1909, p.1.

[62] I/I/11, December 31, 1324/January 12, 1909, *Meclis-i Mebusan Zabıt Ceridesi*, *1*, p.170; "Turkish Policy: Speech by Kiamil Pasha," *The Times*, January 14, 1909, p.5; "Deputiertenkammer," *Osmanischer Lloyd*, January 14, 1909, p.1; "Das Exposé Kiamil Paschas," *Berliner Tageblatt und Handels-Zeitung*, January 14, 1909, p.15; and, "A la Chambre Ottomane: L'exposé Grand Véziriel," *The Levant Herald and Eastern Express*, January 15, 1909, p.1.

[63] I/I/11, December 31, 1324/January 12, 1909, *Meclis-i Mebusan Zabıt Ceridesi*, *1*, p.170; "Vertrauensvotum der türkischen Kammer für den Grosswesir," *Berliner Tageblatt und Handels-Zeitung*, January 14, 1909, p.1; and, "Turkish Policy: Speech by Kiamil Pasha," *The Times*, January 14, 1909, p.5.

mobilised the monarchists who succeeded in rallying to the side of Kâmil Pasha all those who could be won over from the Unionist cause. As a result, the parliamentary majority of the Committee of Union and Progress became shaky, and this prevented the Unionists from taking open action against Kâmil Pasha at this juncture.[64] When the President asked Hüseyin Cahid [Yalçın] if he had anything to add, the latter declined to speak, and with the session over, deputies poured into the lobbies still cheering the Grand Vezier.[65] This was a political victory for the anti-Unionists.[66]

Characteristically, the monarchist anti-Unionist press made the most of Kâmil Pasha's latest success.[67] The *İkdam* of January 15 ridiculed the Committee of Union and Progress for its failure to bring about the fall of Kâmil Pasha.[68] Admitting defeat, Hüseyin Cahid [Yalçın] wrote that whatever his opinion of Kâmil Pasha's policy, he could not but refrain from joining his colleagues in their applause of the former's masterly defence.[69] The speech was generally well-received. Non-Muslim elements were gratified by the Grand Vezier's reaffirmation that military service and state-sponsored education would be open to them, a promise originally made by the Unionists. On their part, members of the Committee of Union and Progress appreciated his complimentary references to their efforts on behalf of national liberties. Criticism was suspended for the moment, and deputies, senators, and the gen-

---

[64]   G. H. Fitzmaurice to Mr. Tyrrell, Constantinople, January 11, 1909, printed in "The Young Turkish Revolution," in G. P. Gooch and H. Temperley (Eds.), *British Documents on the Origins of the War, 1898-1914, 5: The Near East*, p.271; and, Yusuf Hikmet Bayur, *Türk İnkılâbı Tarihi, 1/2*, p.140.

[65]   I/I/11, December 31, 1324/January 12, 1909, *Meclis-i Mebusan Zabıt Ceridesi, 1*, pp.171-180; "Turkish Policy: Speech by Kiamil Pasha," *The Times*, January 14, 1909, p.5; Hüseyin Cahid Yalçın, "Meşrutiyet Hatıraları, 1908-1918," *Fikir Hareketleri, 4* (April 25-October 19, 1935), p.246; and, Ali Fuad Türkgeldi, *Görüp İşittiklerim*, p.18.

[66]   "Der Sieg Kiamil Paschas," *Berliner Tageblatt und Handels-Zeitung*, January 14, 1909, Evening Edition, p.2; and, "Kiamil und die Jungtürken," *Berliner Tageblatt und Handels-Zeitung*, January 15, 1909, Evening Edition, p.2.

[67]   "Der Eindruck des Exposees Kiamil Paschas," *Osmanisher Lloyd*, January 16, 1909, p.1.

[68]   Ali Kemal, "Noksanımız, Yine Noksanımız," *İkdam*, January 2, 1324/January 15, 1909, p.1. See also, Hüseyin Cahid Yalçın, "Meşrutiyet Hatıraları, 1908-1918," *Fikir Hareketleri, 4* (April 25-October 19, 1935), p.246.

[69]   Hüseyin Cahid [Yalçın], "Sadrâzam Paşanın İzahatı, *Tanin*, January 1, 1324/January 14, 1909. See also, "Kiamil Pasha's Speech: General Turkish Approval," *The Times*, January 15, 1909, p.5.

eral public, almost without exception, expressed satisfaction with the result of Hüseyin Cahid [Yalçın]'s interpellation.[70]

The reception of the Grand Vezier's speech was thoroughly unexpected. Only three weeks before, even the majority of Kâ-mil Pasha's own supporters believed a vote of non-confidence was inevitable. At that time, a segment of the Committee of Union and Progress—composed partly of young and zealous politicians who disapproved of the Grand Vezier's appoint-ments, of senators who resented his independence and were inclined to mistake his caution for timidity, and of those who were personally hostile towards the old statesman—had ob-tained the control of *Şura-yı Ümmet*, the organ of the Commit-tee of Union and Progress, and had gained *Tanin*'s support, whose editor Hüseyin Cahid [Yalçın] was carrying on a vig-orous campaign against the Grand Vezier.[71]

The older and more conservative members of the Committee of Union and Progress not only appreciated Kâmil Pasha's political abilities, but realised that 'swapping horses while crossing the stream' was both impractical and inadvis-able with respect to the long-term plans of the party, and given the apparent extent of his popularity, downright dangerous for the Committee. Under the leadership of İsmail Kemal Bey, the monarchist Albanian deputy for Berat, non-Turkish depu-ties—among them Greeks, Arabs, and Albanians—as well as some Turks came out in open support of the Government. De-spite such support from the conservative deputies, *Şura-yı Üm-met* continued its campaign against the Grand Vezier until the Unionist leadership forced a personnel and policy change in the paper. Nonetheless, its efforts had served a purpose, namely, to provide cover for the Committee's general retreat.[72]

The attack, however, was not over. During the January 16 sitting of the Chamber, Abdülaziz Mecdi [Tolon] called on Ziya Pasha, the Minister of Finance, to account for the delay

[70] "Kiamil Pasha's Speech: General Turkish Approval," *The Times*, January 15, 1909, p.5.
[71] "Kiamil Pasha's Speech: General Turkish Approval," *The Times*, January 15, 1909, p.5. See also, "Kâmil Paşa'ya Beyan-ı İtimad," *Ikdam*, January 4, 1324/January 17, 1909, p.3.
[72] "Kiamil Pasha's Speech: General Turkish Approval," *The Times*, January 15, 1909, p.5.

in the publication of the Budget. Speaking in defence of his Ministry, Ziya Pasha stated that other ministries had not yet sent in their respective estimates, and that, though he had succeeded in drawing up revenue estimates for the upcoming financial year, he was unable to give any estimate of expenditures. At the moment, he could not, regretfully, fix a date for the communication of the Budget to the Chamber. Ziya Pasha's defence did nothing to promote his reputation among the deputies. A short debate followed, and the Chamber finally voted the order of the day.[73]

Likewise, on January 18, Babanzade İsmail Hakkı Bey, the Unionist deputy for Baghdad, demanded that the ministries of Public Works and Foreign Affairs provide the Chamber with information on the Baghdad Railway. He pointed out that the agreements concluded by the Government with foreign promoters had been kept from the Turkish people and that it was only through the European press that any information on the subject was known. The Turkish people, he said, had the right to a full explanation on this and other points. The Chamber decided that the responsible Ministers should report to the Chamber on January 30.[74]

The January 23 session was devoted to a series of similar interpellations. Şemseddin Bey, the Minister of Pious Foundations, who had appeared to answer questions on the state of his ministry, caused considerable unrest when he declared that while he was ready to answer certain questions, he was unwilling to recognise the Chamber's competency in matters of

---

[73] I/I/13, January 3, 1324/January 16, 1909, *Meclis-i Mebusan Zabıt Ceridesi*, *1*, pp.205-210; "The Turkish Parliament," *The Times*, January 18, 1909, p.7. For Hüseyin Cahid [Yalçın]'s interpretation of the sitting, see his editorial, "Tasfiye-i Hesabat," *Tanin*, January 4, 1324/January 17, 1909, p.1.

[74] I/I/14, January 5, 1324/January 18, 1909, *Meclis-i Mebusan Zabıt Ceridesi*, *1*, p.241; I/I/16, January 8, 1324/January 21, 1909, *Meclis-i Mebusan Zabıt Ceridesi*, *1*, pp.275-284; "Turkish Internal Affairs: The Baghdad Railway Scheme," *The Times*, January 20, 1909, p.5; and, "Politische Nachrichten," *Osmanischer Lloyd*, January 30, 1909, p.1. See also, Hüseyin Cahid [Yalçın], "Ecnebi Mütahassıslar ve Posta İslahatı," *Tanin*, January 7, 1324/January 20, 1909, p.1.; and, Hüseyin Cahid [Yalçın], "Mühim bir İstizah," *Tanin*, January 8, 1324/January 21, 1909, p.1. His editorial was commented upon in the *Osmanischer Lloyd*: "Eine wichtige Interpellation," *Osmanischer Lloyd*, January 22, 1909, p.1. Hüseyin Cahid [Yalçın] wrote two more editorials, one on the Hedjaz Railway and the other on the commerical activities of foreigners in the Empire (Hüseyin Cahid [Yalçın], "Nazik bir Nokta," *Tanin*, January 9, 1324/January 22, 1909, p.1; and, Hüseyin Cahid [Yalçın], "Memalik-i Osmaniye'de Ecnebi Teşebbüsat-ı Ticariyesi," *Tanin*, January 10, 1324/January 23, 1909, p.1).

a purely religious nature. He further stated that thus far he had been unable to introduce any reforms in his ministry, and concluded his speech with an Arabic prayer. The Chamber protested the use of an unofficial language in Parliament, though Ahmed Rıza Bey, succeeded in easing tensions by explaining that the Arabic phrases in question were not a part of the Minister's speech, but were a private prayer. After a long debate, in which a number of deputies deplored the inefficiency of Şemseddin Bey's leadership, the Chamber voted the Minister's explanations adequate, and proceeded to discuss an interpellation concerning the choice of the members of the Council of State. Lütfi Bey argued that twenty-nine of the Council's thirty members owed their positions to nepotism or other undue influences. Hasan Fehmi Pasha's replies were found somewhat unconvincing. The Chamber in his case contended itself with voting the order of the day.[75]

Signed by fifty deputies, on February 9, another interpellation demanded that the Minister of the Interior, Hüseyin Hilmi Pasha, account for the absence of order throughout the Empire. The issue caused heated debate, and was finally rejected by a large majority.[76]

Kâmil Pasha was by no means a great patriot nor even a constitutionalist. He had quarrelled with Sultan Abdülhamid in the past not because he wanted the latter to summon a parliament but because he wanted the Sultan to give him more power. The principal trait in his character was personal ambition, not liberalism.[77] With political pressure from the Committee of Union and Progress for the resignation of the cabinet, however, Kâmil Pasha and other monarchist politi-

---

[75] I/I/17, January 10, 1324/January 23, 1909, *Meclis-i Mebusan Zabıt Ceridesi*, *I*, pp.297-307; Hüseyin Cahid [Yalçın], "İstizahların Neticesi," *Tanin*, January 12, 1324/January 25, 1909, p.1; and, "The Turkish Parliament," *The Times*, January 26, 1909, p.5.

[76] I/I/25, January 27, 1324/February 9, 1909, *Meclis-i Mebusan Zabıt Ceridesi*, *I*, pp.540-551; "The Turkish Parliament," *The Times*, February 10, 1909, p.10. About a week ago, Hüseyin Cahid [Yalçın] had began writing on the deteriorating situation in Macedonia (Hüseyin Cahid [Yalçın], "Makedonya Düğümü," *Tanin*, January 18, 1324/January 31, 1909, p.1; and, Hüseyin Cahid [Yalçın], "Makedonya Meselesi," *Tanin*, January 20, 1324/February 2, 1909, p.1). See also, "Die Makedonische Frage," *Osmanischer Lloyd*, February 2, 1909, p.1; and, "Die türkische Presse," *Osmanischer Lloyd*, February 4, 1909, p.2.

[77] Francis McCullagh, *The Fall of Abd-ul-Hamid*, pp.32-33.

cians forgot about their quarrels with Sultan Abdülhamid. By this time, Abdülhamid, too, had come to perceive that monarchist politicians like Kâmil Pasha were his allies, rather than enemies, in the fight against the Unionists.

The public display of an alliance between Sultan Abdülhamid and monarchist politicians had come about on January 15, when the Sultan had conferred the Grand Cordon of the Mecidiye Order upon Kâmil Pasha in recognition of the services rendered by him and his success in obtaining the confidence of the Chamber of Deputies.[78]

By late January, the public began to fully see Kâmil Pasha's true colours. On January 26, as part of celebrations for the 610th anniversary of the Ottoman Dynasty, the Liberal Union gave a dinner party.[79] The Grand Vezier's presence at this function, which had been privately organised by the Liberal Union, was generally regarded as a political move signalling his preference for monarchy and the opposition party over the Constitutional regime and the Committee of Union and Progress thanks to whom he had initially come to power.[80] The joining of forces between the monarchists and the Liberal Union, on the one hand, and the Liberal Union and Kâmil Pasha on the other heralded the beginning of hostilities between Kâmil Pasha and the Committee of Union and Progress.[81] Ahmed Rıza Bey did not attend the dinner; he also told Kâmil Pasha that he had done wrong in attending the function him-

---

[78] "Honour for Kiamil Pasha," *The Times*, January 16, 1909, p.7; and, "Kâmil Paşa'ya Beyan-ı İtimad," *Ikdam*, January 4, 1324/January 17, 1909, p.3. Kutay mistakenly gives the date as January 17, 1909 (Cemal Kutay, *Üç Paşalar Kavgası*, p.51).

[79] "News Items," *The Levant Herald and Eastern Express*, January 26, 1909, p.1; "Anniversary of the Foundation of the Ottoman Empire," *The Levant Herald and Eastern Express*, January 27, 1909, p.1; "Osmanlı Ahrar Fırkası ve Dün Geceki Ziyafet," *Ikdam*, January 14, 1324/January 27, 1909, p.2; "La banquet de l'Union Libérale," *The Levant Herald and Eastern Express*, January 27, 1909, p.2; Ali Kemal, "İstiklâl-i Osmaniye," *Ikdam*, January 15, 1324/January 28, 1909, p.1; "Osmanlı Ahrar Fırkası ve Büyük bir Ziyafet," *Ikdam*, January 15, 1324/January 28, 1909, pp.2-3; and, Cemal Kutay, *Üç Paşalar Kavgası*, p.52. See also, Şerif, *Bir Muhalifin Hatıraları: İttihat ve Terakki'ye Muhalefet*, p.31.

[80] Ziya Şakir [Soko], "Hürriyet ve İtilâf Nasıl Doğdu? Nasıl Yaşadı? Nasıl Battı? 4: Yeni Fırka da Programını Hazırlayarak İşe Girişti," *Tan*, November 2, 1937, p.9; Tarık Zafer Tunaya, *Türkiye'de Siyasi Partiler, 1859-1952*, p.242; and, "The Turkish Cabinet: Critical Situation," *The Times*, February 13, 1909, p.7.

[81] "Das jungtürkische Comité und seine Gegner," *Berliner Tageblatt und Handels-Zeitung*, February 10, 1909, Evening Edition, p.2. See also, Şerif, *Bir Muhalifin Hatıraları: İttihat ve Terakki'ye Muhalefet*, p.31.

self.[82] The monarchist *Serbesti*, attaching great importance to the dinner party, wrote that it heralded the commencement of a strong opposition party in the Chamber.[83]

In a concerted effort to publicise the issues monarchist readers would be most interested in, *Serbesti* started publishing interviews with the politicians of the old regime who were being held under house arrest in the Prince Islands. The first of these interviews, which was published on February 2, was with Abu-l Huda who claimed that he was innocent and that his captivity was totally unjustified.[84] In the February 3 issue, *Serbesti* interviewed Memduh Pasha, the ex-Minister of the Interior under the old regime. Complaining about his forced stay in the island, Memduh Pasha said that he was still kept under house arrest because he had not agreed to pay for his freedom, giving the example of Rıza Pasha, who had returned his ill-gotten wealth to the Treasury, and consequently been released.[85] The publication of these interviews at this juncture served no purpose other than prepare the ground for an organised attack on the constitutional regime and the Committee of Union and Progress.

The news that Kâmil Pasha and his cabinet were preparing a bill which would restrict press freedom aroused further discontent with those sympathetic to the Revolution.[86] On February 7, a protest meeting was organised during which speeches against such restrictions were warmly received. Later, a delegation met with Ahmed Rıza Bey, the President of the Chamber of Deputies.[87] Additionally, students of the Military School of Medicine expressed their dissatisfaction with the

[82] "Explanatory Memorandum by the Late Grand Vizier, Kiamil Pasha," in Demetrius Georgiades, *Is the Regeneration of Turkey Possible?* pp.157-158; and, "The Turkish Cabinet: Critical Situation," *The Times*, February 13, 1909, p.7.

[83] *Serbesti*, January 15, 1324/January 28, 1909, cited in "Le parti libérale ottoman," *The Levant Herald and Eastern Express*, January 29, 1909, p.2.

[84] "Les 'relégués' à Prinkipo," *The Levant Herald and Eastern Express*, February 3, 1909, p.2.

[85] "Interview with Memduh Pasha," *The Levant Herald and Eastern Express*, February 4, 1909, p.1.

[86] For an editorial in support of Kâmil Pasha's proposals see, "Matbuat Kanunu," *İkdam*, January 28, 1324/February 10, 1909, p.1.

[87] Hüseyin Cahid Yalçın, "Meşrutiyet Hatıraları, 1908-1918," *Fikir Hareketleri*, 4 (April 25-October 19, 1935), p.277. See also, "Yeni Matbuat Kanunu," *İkdam*, January 26, 1324/February 8, 1909, p.3; and, Cemal Kutay, *Üç Paşalar Kavgası*, p.54.

Government's intentions, declaring in a memorandum that they were ready to protect the freedom of the press with every available means. Telegrams poured in from the provinces defending the accomplishments of the Revolution. Public anxiety, however, only increased with the news that Kâmil Pasha intended to dismiss certain Ministers from his Cabinet.[88]

On February 10, Kâmil Pasha dismissed the Ministers of War and of the Navy.[89] Because he did so in the manner of one who was discharging a banal, everyday duty, his subordinates were under the impression that the pashas in question had asked to be relieved of office, that they had forced the Grand Vezier to accept their resignations, and that, at all events, the matter was one which could have no possible interest for anybody except for the dismissed Ministers themselves. Though Kâmil Pasha acted with consummate skill, inducing Arif Hikmet Pasha, the Minister of the Navy, to resign quietly, the Unionists afterwards encouraged Arif Hikmet Pasha to complain of the wrong that had been done to him, and even to deny that he had resigned at all. On the other hand, Ali Rıza Pasha, the Minister of War, resigned only under duress and after a vigorous fight, as he later told the Chamber of Deputies.[90] Kâmil Pasha immediately appointed Nâzım Pasha, the Commander of the Second Army Corps, as Minister of War, and Hüsnü Pasha as acting Minister of the Navy.[91]

What had prompted Kâmil Pasha to force Ali Rıza Pasha's resignation was the latter's reluctance to send certain troops

---

[88] Hüseyin Cahid Yalçın, "Meşrutiyet Hatıraları, 1908-1918," *Fikir Hareketleri*, 4 (April 25-October 19, 1935), p.277.

[89] "Ministerial Changes," *The Levant Herald and Eastern Express*, February 11, 1909, p.1; "Der Ministerwechsel," *Osmanischer Lloyd*, February 12, 1909, p.1; A. A. Türkei 159, No.2/50, Telegram from Marschall, Pera, February 11, 1909; Ali Cevad, *İkinci Meşrutiyetin İlânı ve Otuzbir Mart Hadisesi*, p.35; Ali Fuad Türkgeldi, *Görüp İşittiklerim*, p.19; and, Hilmi Kâmil Bayur, *Sadrazam Kâmil Paşa: Siyasi Hayatı*, p.293. The events are totally distorted in the official history concerning this period (Yusuf Hikmet Bayur, *Türk İnkılâbı Tarihi*, 1/2, p.164). See also, Şerif, *Bir Muhalifin Hatıraları: İttihat ve Terakki'ye Muhalefet*, p.28.

[90] Francis McCullagh, *The Fall of Abd-ul-Hamid*, p.33. For a completely misleading interpretation of the whole affair see, for instance, Ahmet Turan Alkan, *İkinci Meşrutiyet Devrinde Ordu ve Siyaset*, pp.88-91.

[91] "Nâzım Paşa," *İkdam*, December 30, 1324/January 12, 1909, p.1; Edwin Pears, *Life of Abdul Hamid*, p.306; and, Cemal Kutay, *Üç Paşalar Kavgası*, p.55. For a distorted version of the appointment see, Yusuf Hikmet Bayur, *Türk İnkılâbı Tarihi*, 1/2, p.165.

loyal to the constitutional regime away from İstanbul, replacing them with troops loyal to the Sultan. The troops in question
were primarily responsible for protecting the Sultan and the
Palace.[92] Kâmil Pasha had summarily ordered that these
troops be dispatched to Janina. The Ministry of War along
with Ali Rıza Pasha opposed the move, and stood firm. The
Cabinet had not been informed of Kâmil Pasha's decision.[93]

Of course, the posts in question were exactly those which
Abdülhamid had, in July 1908, struggled to reserve for his
own nominees. Even after he had signed the imperial order
reviving the Constitution, on July 31, the Sultan refused to
yield his right to fill these two vital posts, as well as that of
Minister of Justice, and would not give way until the Unionists made it clear that he had little choice. The Sultan did finally give in, but because of his stubbornness and reluctance
in the matter, the Committee of Union and Progress had kept
careful watch over these posts, and when its nominees were
suddenly dismissed, protest was immediate and vocal.[94]

It was Admiral Said Pasha, Kâmil Pasha's son and a corrupt
monarchist, who was intimately involved with the scheme to
restore control of the Army and Navy to Abdülhamid.[95] The
attempt was by no means isolated; it was part and parcel of the
monarchists' general agenda since the advent of the constitutional regime. The Unionists had driven Kâmil Pasha's predecessor Mehmed Said Pasha, out of office in August of 1908
precisely because he had insisted that the Sultan retain the
right to fill the very same posts.[96]

After dismissing Ali Rıza Pasha from the Ministry of War

---

[92]   On October 19, battalions from Salonica had been brought to İstanbul to
replace the Sultan's troops in the capital in a move to further disarm the Sultan
who was suspected of using these troops in a reactionary insurrection. The sus-
picion was not without foundation. On October 31 some of the members of the battalions replaced by the ones who came from Salonica opened fire to the newly arrived troops, but they were suppressed by the Salonica troops (Cemal Kutay, *Üç Paşalar Kavgası*, p.45).

[93]   Hüseyin Cahid Yalçın, "Meşrutiyet Hatıraları, 1908-1918," *Fikir Hareketleri*, 4 (April 25-October 19, 1935), pp.277-278.

In an attempt to legitimise his action, Kamil Pasha alleged that Ali Rıza
Pasha was an ineffective Minister who was incapable of making his orders re-
spected ("Explanatory Memorandum by the Late Grand Vizier, Kiamil Pasha," in
Demetrius Georgiades, *Is the Regeneration of Turkey Possible?* p.154).

[94]   Francis McCullagh, *The Fall of Abd-ul-Hamid*, p.34.
[95]   Francis McCullagh, *The Fall of Abd-ul-Hamid*, p.39.
[96]   Francis McCullagh, *The Fall of Abd-ul-Hamid*, pp.39-40.

Kâmil Pasha named Nâzım Pasha as his replacement on the same day.[97] Because Nâzım Pasha had suffered for his political views under the old regime, no one could openly accuse him of being a tool of reaction. Nevertheless, he was a soldier, with all the soldier's hatred for politics, and while in command of the Second Army Corps at Edirne, he had distinguished himself by his stern repression of the Committee of Union and Progress among his officers. As a result, the troops at Edirne could now be counted on the monarchist side.[98]

Clearly, Nâzım Pasha's appointment as Minister of War was an indication of Kâmil Pasha's hitherto veiled antagonism towards the Committee of Union and Progress, and many felt that the repressive tactics which had been confined to Edirne might soon be applied to the whole of the army.[99] On the day of Nâzım Pasha's appointment, Dr. Nâzım Bey, one of the leaders of the Committee of Union and Progress, visited Kâmil Pasha, expressing the Committee's surprise at such a sudden change in the cabinet. He then asked Kâmil Pasha how he dared to act without the consent of the Committee of Union and Progress in such an important matter.[100]

In the Chamber of Deputies, the issue of the dismissals came to a head on February 11 when deputies discussed giving the Cabinet a vote of no confidence.[101] The Unionists were

---

[97] "The Turkish Cabinet: New Minister of War," *The Times*, February 11, 1909, p.5; Ali Fuad Türkgeldi, *Görüp İşittiklerim*, p.19; and, Ali Cevad, *İkinci Meşrutiyetin İlânı ve Otuzbir Mart Hadisesi*, p.36.

[98] Francis McCullagh, *The Fall of Abd-ul-Hamid*, pp.33-34.; and, Ahmet Turan Alkan, *İkinci Meşrutiyet Devrinde Ordu ve Siyaset*, p.90. For Nâzım Pasha's allegiance to Abdülhamid and his distaste for liberal ideas see his letter of intent when he accepted the position of Minister of War (Yusuf Hikmet Bayur, *Türk İnkılâbı Tarihi*, 1/2, p.165).

[99] Francis McCullagh, *The Fall of Abd-ul-Hamid*, p.34; and, "Explanatory Memorandum by the Late Grand Vizier, Kiamil Pasha," in Demetrius Georgiades, *Is the Regeneration of Turkey Possible?* p.151.

[100] "Explanatory Memorandum by the Late Grand Vizier, Kiamil Pasha," in Demetrius Georgiades, *Is the Regeneration of Turkey Possible?* p.152. See also, Yusuf Hikmet Bayur, *Türk İnkılâbı Tarihi*, 1/2, p.168.

[101] I/I/26, January 29, 1324/February 11, 1909, *Meclis-i Mebusan Zabıt Ceridesi*, *1*, pp.570-573; Hüseyin Cahid Yalçın, "Meşrutiyet Hatıraları, 1908-1918," *Fikir Hareketleri*, *4* (April 25-October 19, 1935), p.278; "Meclis-i Mebusan'da Dünkü İstizah," *İkdam*, January 30, 1324/February 12, 1909, p.1; "Deputiertenkammer," *Osmanischer Lloyd*, February 12, 1909, p.1; "A la Chambre Ottomane," *The Levant Herald and Eastern Express*, February 12, 1909, p.2; Hilmi Kâmil Bayur, *Sadrazam Kâmil Paşa: Siyasi Hayatı*, p.294; Yusuf Hikmet Bayur, *Türk İnkılâbı Tarihi*, 1/2, p.167; and, Fahri Çoker, II. Meşrutiyet Meclisi'nde Sadrazamın Çekilmesine Neden Olan Bahriyeliler," p.11.

now determined to overthrow Kâmil Pasha and his cabinet, and the Grand Vezier was called to appear before the Chamber on February 13, exactly one month after he had been called upon to defend the conduct of his cabinet. The session was likely to be momentous. A majority of the Turkish deputies, most of whom were Unionist, were hostile to the Grand Vezier, who nonetheless could rely on the support of most non-Turkish deputies.[102] In an editorial which appeared in *Tanin* on February 12, Hüseyin Cahid [Yalçın] wrote that Kâmil Pasha's tactics were reminiscent of those of the absolutist regime, and that the future of the Constitution was indeed precarious with someone as irresponsible as Kâmil Pasha at the helm of the government.[103]

By February 12, however, it was uncertain whether the Grand Vezier would answer the Chamber's interpellation: it was generally felt that he would postpone his answer in order to let the excitement exhaust itself.[104] Fearing for the worst, the Committee of Union and Progress immediately dispatched special envoys to Edirne and Salonica. The envoys delivered the message to the Unionist officers in the Second and Third Army Corps that there was a serious possibility of an attempt for the restoration of the absolutist regime. The Unionists leadership ordered these officers to hold themselves in

---

[102] By this time, it was estimated by independent observers that the Committee of Union and Progress could safely count on the support of one hundred and fifty deputies in the Chamber ("Die jungtürkische Aktion gegen Kiamil Pascha," *Berliner Tageblatt und Handels-Zeitung*, February 13, 1909, Morning Edition, p.15). In a dispatch of February 13 just before the voting began, the correspondent of the *Berliner Tageblatt und Handels-Zeitung* estimated that the Committe of Union and Progress could muster one hundred and fifty votes while Kiamil Pasha could get as high as one hundred votes in support of his cabinet ("Die türkische Konstitutionskrisis," *Berliner Tageblatt und Handels-Zeitung*, February 13, 1909, Evening Edition, pp.1-2). See also, Francis McCullagh, *The Fall of Abd-ul-Hamid*, p.34; and, "The Turkish Cabinet: Critical Situation," *The Times*, February 13, 1909, p.7.

[103] Hüseyin Cahid [Yalçın], "Tebdil-i Vükelâ," *Tanin*, January 30, 1324/February 12, 1909, p.1. His editorial was commented upon in "Der Ministerwechsel," *Osmanischer Lloyd*, February 13, 1909, p.1. See also, A. A. Türkei 159, No.2/52, Telegram from Marschall, Pera, February 12, 1909; Hüseyin Cahid Yalçın, "Meşrutiyet Hatıraları, 1908-1918," *Fikir Hareketleri*, 4 (April 25-October 19, 1935), p.278; Hasan Amca, *Doğmayan Hürriyet: Bir Devrin İçyüzü, 1908-1918*, pp.84-85; Yusuf Hikmet Bayur, *Türk İnkılâbı Tarihi, 1/2*, p.167; and, Hilmi Kâmil Bayur, *Sadrazam Kâmil Paşa: Siyasi Hayatı*, p.294. Even non-Unionists, such as Mahmud Muhtar Pasha, were of the opinion that what Kamil Pasha had done was against principles of parliamentary rule (Mahmud Muhtar, *Maziye bir Nazar*, p.104).

[104] "The Grand Vizier," *The Levant Herald and Eastern Express*, February 13, 1909, p.1; and, "Turkey," *The Times*, February 13, 1909, p.7.

readiness for action, and telegrams were sent to other towns and cities, informing that the Second and Third Army Corps were ready to defend the Constitution.[105]

According to an article published in its February 12 issue, *Şura-yı Ümmet* announced that Ali Rıza Pasha intended to protest his removal from office before the Chamber. The editorial in *Şura-yı Ümmet* went on to say that the Grand Vezier's actions constituted a despotic *coup*, not a mere reconstruction of the Cabinet as the latter had claimed. Such conduct being otherwise inexplicable, the editorial concluded, the Grand Vezier's plan could only be to annihilate the Constitution.[106] *Tanin* also continued in its attacks on Kâmil Pasha, stating that a minister, unlike a governor, could not be changed at will—particularly if that minister enjoyed the confidence of the Chamber. The Grand Vezier's behaviour, *Tanin* said, encroached the Chamber's rights and violated constitutional principles.[107] Even *Hukuk-u Umumiye*, a conservative, and *Tercüman-ı Hakikat*, an independent newspaper, though they supported the new appointments, were doubtful of the legitimacy of Kâmil Pasha's action. *Yeni Gazete* and *İkdam*, two staunchly anti-Unionist newspapers supporting Kâmil Pasha, were silent.[108] Yet, *Yeni Gazete* implicitly expressed its support for the new appointment to the Ministry of War by stating that Nâzım Pasha had received a large number of congratulatory telegrams.[109]

The monarchist press, however, did not remain silent when it came to the Committee of Union and Progress. As if it

---

[105] "Explanatory Memorandum by the Late Grand Vizier, Kiamil Pasha," in Demetrius Georgiades, *Is the Regeneration of Turkey Possible?* pp.147-148.

[106] "Meşruti İdareye Mühim bir Darbe," *Şura-yı Ümmet*, January 30, 1324/ February 12, 1909, quoted in "The Turkish Cabinet: Critical Situation," *The Times*, February 13, 1909, p.7, "Der Ministerwechsel," *Osmanischer Lloyd*, February 13, 1909, p.1, and in Feroz Ahmad, *The Young Turks: The Committee of Union and Progress in Turkish Politics, 1908-1914*, p.34. See also, "Explanatory Memorandum by the Late Grand Vizier, Kiamil Pasha," in Demetrius Georgiades, *Is the Regeneration of Turkey Possible?* p.160.

[107] Hüseyin Cahid [Yalçın], "Tebdil-i Vükelâ," *Tanin*, January 30, 1324/February 12, 1909, p.1; "Der Ministerwechsel," *Osmanischer Lloyd*, February 13, 1909, p.1; "The Turkish Cabinet: Critical Situation," *The Times*, February 13, 1909, p.7; and, Hilmi Kâmil Bayur, *Sadrazam Kâmil Paşa: Siyasi Hayatı*, p.294.

[108] "The Turkish Cabinet: Critical Situation," *The Times*, February 13, 1909, p.7.

[109] *Yeni Gazete*, January 30, 1324/February 12, 1909, cited in "The Minister of War," *The Levant Herald and Eastern Express*, February 13, 1909, p.1. See also, "Nâzım Paşa," *İkdam*, January 30, 1324/February 12, 1909, p.1.

were thoroughly abnormal for a political party to question the actions of a cabinet it doubted and to aspire to take over the reigns of government by garnering votes in the Chamber, *İkdam* accused the Committee of Union and Progress of political ambition and interference in the affairs of the government.[110]

As the dismissals were clearly unconstitutional, Hüseyin Hilmi Pasha, the Minister of the Interior, and Manyasizade Refik Bey, the Unionist Minister of Justice, resigned in protest on February 12.[111] The February 13 issue of *Şura-yı Ümmet* contained an interview with Hüseyin Hilmi Pasha in which the ex-minister stated that his resignation had been prompted by the fact that the Grand Vezier had not informed him of those matters which had supposedly made the dismissals necessary, matters which would normally have been of the utmost importance to his ministry.[112] This statement, added to those already made by the dismissed ministers themselves, inflamed public opinion, and further assertions that the Minister of War had been dismissed because of his resistance to remove the four chasseur battalions—which had been sent some months ago from Salonica by the Committee of Union and Progress to prevent any attempt at the overthrow of the Constitution by a *coup de main*—only added fuel to the fire.[113] On February 13, Cemaleddin Efendi, the Sheikh-ul-Islam, Ziya Pasha, the Minister of Finance, and Hasan Fehmi Pasha, the President of the Council of State, also tendered their resignations.[114]

---

[110] "Cemiyetler, Fırkalar," *İkdam*, January 31, 1324/February 13, 1909, p.1. See also, "Yeni Türkiye ve Ordusu," *İkdam*, January 31, 1324/February 13, 1909, p.1.

[111] The resignations were announced on the same day's issue of *Tanin* ("Tebdil-i Vükelâ," *Tanin*, January 30, 1324/February 12, 1909, p.3); and "Differenzen im türkischen Kabinett," *Berliner Tageblatt und Handels-Zeitung*, February 12, 1909, Morning Edition, p.3. "Explanatory Memorandum by the Late Grand Vizier, Kiamil Pasha," in Demetrius Georgiades, *Is the Regeneration of Turkey Possible?* p.152; Cemal Kutay, *Üç Paşalar Kavgası*, p.55; Ali Fuad Türkgeldi, *Görüp İşittiklerim*, p.19; "Ministerial Changes," *The Levant Herald and Eastern Express*, February 13, 1909, p.1; and, "The Turkish Cabinet: Critical Situation," *The Times*, February 13, 1909, p.7. See also, Yusuf Hikmet Bayur, *Türk İnkılâbı Tarihi*, 1/2, p.167.

[112] *Şura-yı Ümmet*, January 31, 1324/February 13, 1909, quoted in "The Turkish Cabinet: Fall of Kiamil Pasha," *The Times*, February 15, 1909, p.7.

[113] "The Turkish Cabinet: Fall of Kiamil Pasha," *The Times*, February 15, 1909, p.7.

[114] "Explanatory Memorandum by the Late Grand Vizier, Kiamil Pasha," in Demetrius Georgiades, *Is the Regeneration of Turkey Possible?* p.152; "Ministerial

February 13 came and by half past twelve o'clock Kâmil
Pasha had still not appeared before the Chamber, much less
communicated his intentions to its president. The atmosphere
was charged as deputies paced the lobbies discussing the situation, among them several well known Unionist deputies
who had not often been seen in Parliament of late. Representatives of foreign embassies were also seen mingling, apparently in an attempt to assess the future of the Cabinet. At
two o'clock, the President's bell announced that he had taken
the chair, and although the Grand Vezier's reply had not yet
arrived, the session began with the announcement that the
Ministers of the Interior, of Justice, and of Finance, along with
the Sheikh-ul-Islam had resigned. The Chamber resolved to
call the Sublime Porte, where the Grand Vezier had arrived,
in order to urge his presence.[115]

It was then that his long-expected answer arrived. The
Grand Vezier stated that though he had intended to reply personally, vital questions of foreign policy left him constrained,
in the interests of the nation, to postpone a detailed answer until February 17.[116] He added that reports regarding the intended removal of chasseur battalions from İstanbul to Salonica and Ali Rıza Pasha's reluctance to carry out such instructions had been falsely disseminated to excite public opinion
and embarrass the Grand Vezier. The appointment of Nâzım
Pasha, he argued, whose capabilities were unquestionable, offered the strongest proof of his desire to uphold the constitu-

Changes," *The Levant Herald and Eastern Express*, February 13, 1909, p.1; "Die
jungtürkische Aktion gegen Kiamil Pascha," *Berliner Tageblatt und Handels-
Zeitung*, February 13, 1909, Morning Edition, p.15; "Vükelânın İstifası," *Ikdam*,
February 1, 1324/February 14, 1909, p.3; "Kiamil Pasha's Downfall," *The Levant
Herald and Eastern Express*, February 15, 1909, p.1; Mehmed Cemaleddin, *Siyasi
Hatıralar, 1908-1913*, p.48; Cemal Kutay, *Üç Paşalar Kavgası*, p.55; and, Ali Fuad
Türkgeldi, *Görüp İşittiklerim*, pp.19-20.

[115] "The Turkish Cabinet: Fall of Kiamil Pasha," *The Times*, February 15,
1909, p.7; and, Hüseyin Cahid Yalçın, "Meşrutiyet Hatıraları, 1908-1918," *Fikir
Hareketleri*, 4 (April 25-October 19, 1935), p.278. See also, Yusuf Hikmet Bayur,
Türk İnkılâbı Tarihi, 1/2, p.169.

[116] I/I/27, January 31, 1324/February 13, 1909, *Meclis-i Mebusan Zabıt Ceridesi*, 1, p.591; "Explanatory Memorandum by the Late Grand Vizier, Kiamil
Pasha," in Demetrius Georgiades, *Is the Regeneration of Turkey Possible?* p.149;
and, "The Turkish Cabinet: Fall of Kiamil Pasha," *The Times*, February 15, 1909,
p.7; and, "A la Chambre ottomane," *The Levant Herald and Eastern Express*, February 15, 1909, p.2. See also, Yusuf Hikmet Bayur, *Türk İnkılâbı Tarihi*, 1/2,
pp.169-170.

tional regime.[117]

Violent protests frequently interrupted the reading of Kâmil Pasha's reply. The President then read protests by the Ministers of War and the Navy. The Minister of War declared that he had been removed from office without reason and against the dictates of the Constitution, and had been appointed to another post which he had not asked for. He protested this unconstitutional procedure and entrusted the Chamber with his defence. Arif Hikmet Pasha, the Minister of the Navy, said that although he had tendered his resignation only a fortnight ago, it had not been accepted: his dismissal, he argued, was clearly arbitrary.[118]

The President then read a telegram sent by a group of navy officers. These protested the Grand Vezier's actions, urging the Chamber to take measures against the danger which they felt threatened the nation's safety and welfare. They further declared that until Hüsnü Pasha was replaced, they would recognise no other authority than the Chamber.[119] A similar ultimatum had also been sent by officers of the Second Army Corps to Nâzım Pasha, telling him that they would not be party to giving strength to an unconstitutionally formed Government.[120] This was more or less tantamount to mutiny which, because some officers of the First and Second Army Corps stationed at İstanbul and Edirne respectively had sent

---

[117] "The Turkish Cabinet: Fall of Kiamil Pasha," *The Times*, February 15, 1909, p.7; "A la Chambre ottomane," *The Levant Herald and Eastern Express*, February 15, 1909, p.2; and, Yusuf Hikmet Bayur, *Türk İnkılâbı Tarihi, 1/2*, p.170..

[118] 1/I/27, January 31, 1324/February 13, 1909, *Meclis-i Mebusan Zabıt Ceridesi, 1*, pp.591-592; "The Turkish Cabinet: Fall of Kiamil Pasha," *The Times*, February 15, 1909, p.7; Hüseyin Cahid Yalçın, "Meşrutiyet Hatıraları, 1908-1918," *Fikir Hareketleri*, 4 (April 25-October 19, 1935), p.278; "A la Chambre ottomane," *The Levant Herald and Eastern Express*, February 15, 1909, p.2; and, Fahri Çoker, II. Meşrutiyet Meclisi'nde Sadrazamın Çekilmesine Neden Olan Bahriyeliler," p.11.

[119] 1/I/27, January 31, 1324/February 13, 1909, *Meclis-i Mebusan Zabıt Ceridesi, 1*, pp.598-599; "The Turkish Cabinet: Fall of Kiamil Pasha," *The Times*, February 15, 1909, p.7; Hilmi Kâmil Bayur, *Sadrazam Kâmil Paşa: Siyasi Hayatı*, p.294; Hüseyin Cahid Yalçın, "Meşrutiyet Hatıraları, 1908-1918," *Fikir Hareketleri*, 4 (April 25-October 19, 1935), p.293; "Explanatory Memorandum by the Late Grand Vizier, Kiamil Pasha," in Demetrius Georgiades, *Is the Regeneration of Turkey Possible?* p.148; Edwin Pears, *Forty Years in Constantinople: The Recollections of Sir Edwin Pears, 1873-1915*, p.272; *idem, Life of Abdul Hamid*, p.309; and, Fahri Çoker, II. Meşrutiyet Meclisi'nde Sadrazamın Çekilmesine Neden Olan Bahriyeliler," p.12.

[120] "Tebdil-i Vükelâ," *Tanin*, February 2, 1324/February 15, 1909, pp.2-3. See also, Hüseyin Cahid Yalçın, "Meşrutiyet Hatıraları, 1908-1918," *Fikir Hareketleri*, 4 (April 25-October 19, 1935), p.294.

telegrams in support of the new Minister of War, raised the spectre of civil war.[121]

Members of the Liberal Union then tried to take control of the Chamber, but despite the intervention of one of its leaders, İsmail Kemal Bey, the Chamber decided to send Kâmil Pasha a note informing him that the Chamber had declared itself in permanent session and requested that he appear before it to answer its queries. The message dispatched, debate resumed.[122]

At half past three, the session was recessed for two hours, pending the arrival of the Grand Vezier's answer, and vehement lobbying took place. Members of the Liberal Union were visibly discouraged, while the Unionists displayed growing elation: it had already been resolved to withdraw the vote of confidence which had been given a month earlier.[123]

The Grand Vezier's answer arrived some time after five o'clock. As had largely been expected, the message briefly reiterated that Kâmil Pasha would appear before the Chamber on February 17.[124] After an hour's desultory debate, during which Talât Bey, Vice-President of the Chamber, defended the Committee of Union and Progress, the order of the day, which bore one hundred and two signatures, was read. It stated that the Grand Vezier, in spite of the Chamber's repeated requests for information regarding the ministerial changes, had not complied, and that by doing so he had left the country's situation in doubt, jeopardising its liberties and its Constitution. For these reasons, the Chamber declared that the Grand Vezier no longer possessed its confidence.[125]

---

[121] Cemal Kutay, *Üç Paşalar Kavgası*, pp.58-59.

[122] I/I/27, January 31, 1324/February 13, 1909, *Meclis-i Mebusan Zabıt Ceridesi, 1*, pp.593-603; Hüseyin Cahid Yalçın, "Meşrutiyet Hatıraları, 1908-1918," *Fikir Hareketleri*, 4 (April 25-October 19, 1935), p.294; "The Turkish Cabinet: Fall of Kiamil Pasha," *The Times*, February 15, 1909, p.7; and, "Explanatory Memorandum by the Late Grand Vizier, Kiamil Pasha," in Demetrius Georgiades, *Is the Regeneration of Turkey Possible?* p.149.

[123] "Die türkische Kammer gegen den Grosswesir," *Berliner Tageblatt und Handels-Zeitung*, February 14, 1909, pp.1-2; and, "The Turkish Cabinet: Fall of Kiamil Pasha," *The Times*, February 15, 1909, p.7.

[124] I/I/27, January 31, 1324/February 13, 1909, *Meclis-i Mebusan Zabıt Ceridesi, 1*, p.603; "Explanatory Memorandum by the Late Grand Vizier, Kiamil Pasha," in Demetrius Georgiades, *Is the Regeneration of Turkey Possible?* p.149; "The Turkish Cabinet: Fall of Kiamil Pasha," *The Times*, February 15, 1909, p.7; and, Hilmi Kâmil Bayur, *Sadrazam Kâmil Paşa: Siyasi Hayatı*, p.298.

[125] I/I/27, January 31, 1324/February 13, 1909, *Meclis-i Mebusan Zabıt Ceridesi, 1*, pp.603-610; "The Turkish Cabinet: Fall of Kiamil Pasha," *The Times*, February 15, 1909, p.7; Hilmi Kâmil Bayur, *Sadrazam Kâmil Paşa: Siyasi Hayatı*,

Just as the Chamber was about to vote on this resolution, a third message arrived from the Grand Vezier, stating that he had heard the Chamber was not satisfied with his previous message. Accordingly, as the Chamber seemed unwilling to respect Article 38 of the Constitution—which declared that though any minister summoned by a majority of the Chamber was bound to reply, that minister was allowed to either send a representative in his place or, with sufficient justification and taking full responsibility, to postpone his reply—the Grand Vezier was prepared to return the seals of office and to publish an exposé in the press, leaving the Chamber with the responsibility for the consequences of his disclosures.[126] Despite the opinion of some of the deputies that this amounted to a resignation and made further steps unnecessary, the Chamber proceeded to vote.[127] Kâmil Pasha received a vote of no-confidence by a vote of one hundred and ninety-six to eight.[128]

The crisis, as the official Viennese newspaper *Fremden-blatt* observed, highlighted the absurdity of a situation where the Committee of Union and Progress, though responsible for the Revolution and still very powerful, had been forced to leave the political stage to a government which was fundamentally opposed in its ideology, and more than that, a minority.[129] Kâmil Pasha had, for one reason or another, 'trans-

---

p.298; and, Fahri Çoker, II. Meşrutiyet Meclisi'nde Sadrazamın Çekilmesine Neden Olan Bahriyeliler," p.12.

[126] I/I/27, January 31, 1324/February 13, 1909, *Meclis-i Mebusan Zabıt Ceridesi, 1*, p.610; "Explanatory Memorandum by the Late Grand Vizier, Kiamil Pasha," in Demetrius Georgiades, *Is the Regeneration of Turkey Possible?* p.150; Hilmi Kâmil Bayur, *Sadrazam Kâmil Paşa: Siyasi Hayatı*, pp.298-299; and, "The Turkish Cabinet: Fall of Kiamil Pasha," *The Times*, February 15, 1909, p.7.

[127] I/I/27, January 31, 1324/February 13, 1909, *Meclis-i Mebusan Zabıt Ceridesi, 1*, pp.610-612; "The Turkish Cabinet: Fall of Kiamil Pasha," *The Times*, February 15, 1909, p.7; and, Hüseyin Cahid Yalçın, "Meşrutiyet Hatıraları, 1908-1918," *Fikir Hareketleri*, 4 (April 25-October 19, 1935), p.294.

[128] I/I/27, January 31, 1324/February 13, 1909, *Meclis-i Mebusan Zabıt Ceridesi, 1*, pp.613-614; Hüseyin Cahid Yalçın, "Meşrutiyet Hatıraları, 1908-1918," *Fikir Hareketleri*, 4 (April 25-October 19, 1935), p.294; "Der Sturz Kiamil Paschas: Die Vorgänge in der Deputientenkammer," *Osmanischer Lloyd*, February 14, p.1; "Die türkische Kammer gegen den Grosswesir," *Berliner Tageblatt und Handels-Zeitung*, February 14, 1909, pp.1-2; "The Turkish Cabinet: Fall of Kiamil Pasha," *The Times*, February 15, 1909, p.7; "Kiamil Pasha's Downfall," *The Levant Herald and Eastern Express*, February 15, 1909, p.1; A. A. Türkei 159, No.2/55, Telegram from Marschall, Pera, February 13, 1909; Hilmi Kâmil Bayur, *Sadrazam Kâmil Paşa: Siyasi Hayatı*, p.299; and, Ali Cevad, *İkinci Meşrutiyetin İlânı ve Otuzbir Mart Hadisesi*, pp.36-37. See also, Edwin Pears, *Life of Abdul Hamid*, p.306; Yusuf Hikmet Bayur, *Türk İnkılâbı Tarihi, 1/2*, p.170.

[129] *Fremdenblatt*, February 16, 1909, quoted in "The Turkish Crisis: The New

ferred' his ostensible 'allegiance' from the Committee of Union and Progress to the substantially weaker Liberal Union. The crisis, therefore, only vindicated the principle of representative government. As one of the British sympathisers of the Revolution defended the action the Unionists took, "in a country which lived, only seven months ago, under a crushing despotism, it was natural and proper that the Chamber should be sensitive about the control of the army and the navy; if they were to come under the management of a Minister disposed in any way to compromise with Yıldız Palace, the result would be either reaction triumphant or civil war."[130] In the editorial column of the *Tanin* of February 14, Hüseyin Cahid [Yalçın] expressed similar views. He stated that the Chamber had been faced with a formidable challenge; had the Chamber succumbed to forces of absolutism, Hüseyin Cahid [Yalçın] wrote, a fatal blow would have been struck at the parliamentary regime. Fortunately, he went on, the prompt and decisive action of the deputies saved both the nation and the Constitution.[131] In a long editorial in the Evening Edition of the *Berliner Tageblatt und Handels-Zeitung* of February 15 the event was also interpreted as an important moral victory for the Committee of Union and Progress and what it stood for in politics.[132]

Hüseyin Hilmi Pasha was given the task of forming a new cabinet, and on February 14, he announced the Cabinet members.[133] Not surprisingly, Ali Rıza Pasha was re-appointed

---

Grand Vezier," *The Times*, February 17, 1909, p.5.

[130]   Noel Buxton, "The Turkish Internal Crisis: To the Editor of *The Times*," *The Times*, February 19, 1909, p.10.

[131]   Hüseyin Cahid [Yalçın], "Heyet-i Vükelâ'nın Sükutu," *Tanin*, February 1, 1324/February 14, 1909, p.1. See also, Feroz Ahmad, *The Young Turks: The Committee of Union and Progress in Turkish Politics, 1908-1914*, p.36. For similar views expressed in a French language İstanbul daily see, *Stamboul* of February 15 and 16, 1909, quoted in Korkmaz Alemdar, *İstanbul, 1875-1964: Türkiye'de Yayınlanan Fransızca bir Gazetenin Tarihi*, pp.115-116.

[132]   "Der Sieg der Jungtürken," *Berliner Tageblatt und Handels-Zeitung*, February 15, 1909, Evening Edition, p.1.

[133]   *Tanin* had published the names of ministers who were to be included in the new cabinet in its February 14, 1909 issue ("Yeni Heyet-i Vükelâ," *Tanin*, February 1, 1324/February 14, 1909, p.4). "Kiamil Pasha's Downfall," *The Levant Herald and Eastern Express*, February 15, 1909, p.1; "Der Sturz Kiamil Paschas," and, "Das Neue Ministerium," *Osmanischer Lloyd*, February 15, 1909, p.1; "Hilmi Pasha's Ministry," *The Times*, February 15, 1909, p.7; "Yeni Sadrâzam," and, "Yeni Heyet-i Vükelâ," *Tanin*, February 2, 1324/February 15, 1909, p.3; "Heyet-i Vükelâ,"

Minister of War.[134] Manyasizade Refik Bey was also re-appointed Minister of Justice.[135] Rıfat Pasha was named Minister for Foreign Affairs.[136] As Rıfat Pasha was Ambassador in London, the ex-Minister for Foreign Affairs, the monarchist Tevfik Pasha, was asked to fill in until the former's return; he refused, and Gabriel Nouradunghian, another monarchist, was appointed as acting Minister for Foreign Affairs.[137] Ziya-eddin Efendi was appointed to the Sheikh-ul-Islamate.[138]

Hüseyin Hilmi Pasha presented his cabinet's programme to the Chamber on the evening of February 17.[139] He declared that internal policy would be guided by the desire to meet all the social needs of a nation governed by liberal principles. In order to achieve this, the laws and institutions of foreign liberal regimes would be studied, and, where suitable, borrowed. But, of all the questions awaiting solution, the most important was the establishment of peace and security. Every citizen, he said, must feel that he lived under a regime of equality and justice. By means of schools and the press, the government hoped to eradicate superstition, the root of conflict between different nationalities and religions, and to enlighten the populace. In the realm of finance, he pledged to do away with the superfluous spending which was the hallmark of the

Ikdam, February 2, 1324/February 15, 1909, p.2; "Grosswesir Hussein Hilmi," *Berliner Tageblatt und Handels-Zeitung*, February 15, 1909, p.1; A. A. Türkei 159, No.2/58, Telegram from Marschall, Pera, February 15, 1909; and, Ali Cevad, *Ikinci Meşrutiyetin İlânı ve Otuzbir Mart Hadisesi*, p.38. See also, Yusuf Hikmet Bayur, *Türk İnkılâbı Tarihi, 1/2*, p.172.

[134] Hüseyin Cahid Yalçın, "Meşrutiyet Hatıraları, 1908-1918," *Fikir Hareketleri*, 4 (April 25-October 19, 1935), p.294; Cemal Kutay, *Üç Paşalar Kavgası*, p.59; and, "Hilmi Pasha's Ministry," *The Times*, February 15, 1909, p.7.

[135] He died after a few weeks of his appointment, on March 4 (Cemal Kutay, *Üç Paşalar Kavgası*, p.63). The post of the Minister of Justice was filled by Nazim Pasha, ex-Governor-General of Janina Province, on March 14 (Cemal Kutay, *Üç Paşalar Kavgası*, p.63).

[136] "The New Grand Vezier: The Foreign Ministry," *The Times*, February 18, 1909, p.7; and, Yusuf Hikmet Bayur, *Türk İnkılâbı Tarihi, 1/2*, p.172.

[137] Cemal Kutay, *Üç Paşalar Kavgası*, p.60; "The Turkish Crisis: The Foreign Office," *The Times*, February 17, 1909, p.5; and, "The Turkish Ministry: Foreign Affairs and Finance," *The Times*, February 20, 1909, p.5.

[138] Mehmed Cemaleddin, *Siyasi Hatıralar, 1908-1913*, p.49.

[139] I/I/30, February 4, 1324/February 17, 1909, *Meclis-i Mebusan Zabıt Ceridesi, 1*, pp.677-679; "Yeni Heyet-i Vükelânın Programı," *Tanin*, February 5, 1324/February 18, 1909, p.1; Ali Kemal, "Heyet-i Vükelânın Hatt-ı Hareketi," *Ikdam*, February 5, 1324/February 18, 1909, p.1; "Hilmi Paschas Programm," *Osmanischer Lloyd*, February 18, 1909, p.1; and, "A la Chambre ottomane," *The Levant Herald and Eastern Express*, February 18, 1909, p.2. For Hüseyin Cahid [Yalçın]'s views on the new cabinet, see, Hüseyin Cahid [Yalçın], "Yeni Heyet-i Vükelâ ve Programı," *Tanin*, February 5, 1324/February 18, 1909, p.1.

old regime. Implicitly, he also spoke against the monarchist scheme of decentralisation: the programme stated that loyalty to the interests of the country would be the Cabinet's only guide, counteracting those interested schemes which aimed at sowing discord throughout the country, the integrity and indivisibility of which were indispensable. He went on to say that union ensured not only the strength and greatness of a nation, but also its security, material prosperity, and prestige among other nations.[140]

A short debate followed during which İsmail Kemal Bey, the Albanian deputy for Berat and one of the leaders of the monarchist opposition in the Chamber, said that he was unable to express confidence in the new cabinet: in the first place, he did not consider it constitutional, in the second, he did not think it prudent to entrust the Ministry of War to someone who seemed unwilling to undertake improvements in the military which, by his own admission, was in an unsatisfactory state. As was the case on February 13, İsmail Kemal Bey's resistance proved ineffective, though the vote of confidence was not unanimous.[141]

In the February 18 issue of its organ *Şura-yı Ümmet*, the Committee of Union and Progress announced the formation of a parliamentary party of the same name which constituted a majority of the Chamber and would support the new Cabinet. The announcement contained a formal apology for Unionist policy since July, and, while admitting the Liberal Union's charge of having influenced the elections, defended itself on the grounds that it had acted for the national good, not out of selfish interests. The result had been the return to the Chamber of its most capable members.[142]

---

[140] I/I/30, February 4, 1324/February 17, 1909, *Meclis-i Mebusan Zabıt Ceridesi, 1*, pp.677-678; "Yeni Heyet-i Vükelânın Programı," *Tanin*, February 5, 1324/ February 18, 1909, p.1; and, "The New Grand Vezier: Statement in Parliament," *The Times*, February 18, 1909, p.7.

[141] I/I/30, February 4, 1324/February 17, 1909, *Meclis-i Mebusan Zabıt Ceridesi, 1*, pp.678-679; "The New Grand Vezier: Statement in Parliament," *The Times*, February 18, 1909, p.7; "Das Vertrauensvotum für Hilmi Pascha," *Berliner Tageblatt und Handels-Zeitung*, February 18, 1909, Evening Edition, pp.1-2; and, Cemal Kutay, *Üç Paşalar Kavgası*, p.60.

[142] *Şura-yı Ümmet*, February 5, 1324/February 18, 1909, quoted in "Die Partei der Einheit und des Fortschrittes," *Osmanischer Lloyd*, February 19, 1909, p.1, and "The Turkish Ministry: Foreign Affairs and Finance," *The Times*, February 20, 1909, p.5.

With the fall of Kâmil Pasha, those Turkish and Greek newspapers which had supported him attacked the new cabinet and the Committee of Union and Progress with great violence.[143] These were *İkdam, Sabah, Yeni Gazete, Sada-yı Millet, Hukuk-u Umumiye, Serbesti* and *Osmanlı*—the last of these was owned by Prince Sabahaddin, and began publication on March 17 as the organ of the Liberal Union.[144] A Levantine newspaper published in İstanbul, *The Levant Herald and Eastern Express*, also took the side of the Liberal Union, criticising the Committee of Union and Progress and demanding its dissolution.[145] *Serbesti*, in particular, was fully and explicitly supporting *The Levant Herald and Eastern Express* in its campaign against the Unionists.[146] There were also some conservative foreign papers, such as *L'Indépendance Belge*, which were highly critical of Hüseyin Hilmi Pasha's appointment as Grand Vezier, and the influence the Committee of Union and Progress exerted in politics.[147]

One of the issues the monarchist press tried to exploit for its own benefit was the decision of the new cabinet to introduce a draft law on the press. When Hilmi Pasha Cabinet announced its intention of introducing a moderate and most necessary press law, the Liberal Union, the Mohammedan Union and the Sultan's spies raised such a deafening outcry that people began to suspect that some terrible injustice was about to be inflicted on them. It was not the liberal minded people who ob-

---

[143] "Die türkische Presse," *Osmanischer Lloyd*, February 15, 2909, p.1; "Das neue Kabinet," *Osmanischer Lloyd*, February 17, 1909, p.1; "Die türkische Presse," *Osmanischer Lloyd*, February 19, 1909, p.1; and, Francis McCullagh, *The Fall of Abd-ul-Hamid*, p.71.

[144] "Die türkische Presse," *Osmanischer Lloyd*, February 15, 2909, p.1; Tarık Zafer Tunaya, *Türkiye'de Siyasi Partiler, 1859-1952*, p.243; Sina Akşin, "31 Mart Olayına Değin Sabahattin Bey ve Ahrar Fırkası," pp.555-557; and, Cemal Kutay, *Üç Paşalar Kavgası*, p.64. See also, Ahmed Bedevi Kuran, *İnkılâp Tarihimiz ve 'Jön Türkler,'* p.270.

[145] Hüseyin Cahid Yalçın, "Meşrutiyet Hatıraları, 1908-1918," *Fikir Hareketleri*, 4 (April 25-October 19, 1935), p.295. Beginning with its February 27 issue, the Levantine newspaper attacked *Tanin* ("Le Tanine devant l'opinion publique," *The Levant Herald and Eastern Express*, February 27, 1909, p.1; and, "Le Tanine devant l'opinion publique," *The Levant Herald and Eastern Express*, March 2, 1909, p.1). For *Tanin*'s reply see, Hüseyin Cahid [Yalçın], "Tufeylât," *Tanin*, February 15, 1324/February 28, 1909, p.1.

[146] *Serbesti*, February 22, 1324/March 7, 1909, excerpted in "Le Comité Union et Progrès et la Nation," *The Levant Herald and Eastern Express*, March 8, 1909, p.1.

[147] *L'Indépendance Belge*, February 16, 1909, quoted in Demetrius Georgiades, *Is the Regeneration of Turkey Possible?* pp.97-98.

jected to the proposed press law; it was the old regime papers, *Yeni Gazete*, which was the property of Kâmil Pasha and was really under the direction of his son, Admiral Said Pasha, *İkdam*, whose editor Ali Kemal Bey was a Palace informer, *Volkan*, organ of the Mohammedan Union, *Mizan*, whose editor Murad Bey was another Palace informer, and *Serbesti*. It was certain that these papers were being subsidised by the Yıldız Palace.[148]

In view of their weak position in the Chamber, the monarchist opposition set out to strengthen it by winning over the British Embassy. Many monarchists who had concealed their real views began to gain courage and expressed their disgust with the Unionists who had brought about the fall of Kâmil Pasha. Some monarchist deputies approached Sir Gerard Lowther, the British Ambassador, to express their alarm at the turn of events, and appealed to Great Britain for help in overthrowing the Committee of Union and Progress from political power. Abdülhamid, too, confidentially expressed to the British Ambassador his deep anxiety at the strength of the Unionists.[149]

On the night of February 25, an official communiqué was issued, stating that the Government received reports that, at the instigation of certain individuals, public meetings designed to compromise the harmony that had reigned since the Revolution would be taking place. Accordingly, pending the publication of a special law on the subject of public meetings now under consideration for submission to the Parliament, the Government had ordered surveillance of such assemblies, and was taking measures to prevent any action calculated to

---

[148] Francis McCullagh, *The Fall of Abd-ul-Hamid*, pp.57-58; Ali Cevad, *İkinci Meşrutiyetin İlânı ve Otuzbir Mart Hadisesi*, pp.39-40; and, Abdurrahman Şeref, *Son Vak'anüvis Abdurrahman Şeref Efendi Tarihi: II. Meşrutiyet Olayları, 1908-1909*, p.18.

[149] F.O. 371/761/8914, Sir Gerard Lowther to Sir Edward Grey, Pera, March 3, 1909, excerpted in Feroz Ahmad, *The Young Turks: The Committee of Union and Progress in Turkish Politics, 1908-1914*, p.37; and, Feroz Ahmad, "Great Britain's Relations with the Young Turks, 1908-1914," p.312. No doubt they had been encouraged by the favourable British public opinion on behalf of Kâmil Pasha (See, "Der Sturz Kiamils," *Berliner Tageblatt und Handels-Zeitung*, February 16, 1909, pp.1-2, for a brief account of the conservative public opinion prevalent in British politics at this time and the sympathy shown to Kâmil Pasha; and, "England und der neue Grosswesir," *Berliner Tageblatt und Handels-Zeitung*, February 19, 1909, Evening Edition, pp.1-2, for the British position *vis-à-vis* the new cabinet).

endanger public security. Henceforth, the police would have to be notified of such meetings twenty-four hours in advance; meetings without proper authorisation would be forbidden.[150] Police regulations concerning public meetings, the communiqué said, had been issued after careful consideration of similar regulations in force in Western Europe. Though the necessary authorisation would not be refused without good reason, the object of the meeting had to be clearly stated, and that during the transition from the old to the new regime, while reactionary tendencies were still observable, open attacks on the Constitution or the army would not be tolerated. Finally, the communiqué added that the introduction of such measures had been already too long delayed, citing several meetings which the Government felt had assumed an inflammatory and disruptive character.[151]

The communiqué was issued in response to an article in the monarchist newspaper *Serbesti* which had proposed a demonstration to demand the restoration of Kâmil and Nâzım Pashas to power. The proposed demonstration was to take place on February 26 in front of the respective pashas' houses.[152] The demonstration had actually been organised by Admiral Said Pasha, son of the ex-Grand Vezier Kâmil Pasha, who had distributed five thousand liras in order to gather a large crowd to protest the Government as well as the Committee of Union and Progress.[153]

The monarchist opposition created a furore over the issue of the new regulations.[154] In an interview with *Tanin*, Hüseyin Hilmi Pasha then tried to pacify opposition by claiming that the regulations concerning meetings had been misrepresented: the required official authorisation was merely a for-

---

[150] "Turkey: The Government and Public Meetings," *The Times*, February 27, 1909, p.7; and, Cemal Kutay, *Üç Paşalar Kavgası*, p.61.

[151] "Turkey: The Restriction on Public Meetings," *The Times*, March 2, 1909, p.5.

[152] "Turkey: The Government and Public Meetings," *The Times*, February 27, 1909, p.7; and, Cemal Kutay, *Üç Paşalar Kavgası*, p.61. See also, *Servet-i Fünun*, February 17, 1324/March 2, 1909, quoted in "News Items," *The Levant Herald and Eastern Express*, March 3, 1909, p.1.

[153] Hüseyin Cahid Yalçın, "Meşrutiyet Hatıraları, 1908-1918," *Fikir Hareketleri*, 4 (April 25-October 19, 1935), p.294.

[154] Hüseyin Cahid Yalçın, "Meşrutiyet Hatıraları, 1908-1918," *Fikir Hareketleri*, 4 (April 25-October 19, 1935), p.295.

mal acknowledgement of notification. Authorisation could not be refused, he said, as that would deny the right of assembly.[155]

İsmail Kemal Bey, however, took the issue to the Chamber, arguing that the regulations were unconstitutional, and demanded a hearing on March 3.[156] On March 3, the Grand Vezier appeared before the Chamber to defend the Government. Though the opposition rejected the Government's defence, after several hours of debate, the Chamber, by a vote of one hundred and fifty to forty-nine, finally declined to discuss the issue further.[157]

The monarchist campaign against the Committee of Union and Progress, nevertheless, continued unabated. On March 6, Serbesti published a 'document' implicating the Committee in blackmail to extract money from corrupt officials of the old regime.[158] A few days later, in a move calculated to discredit the Unionists, Serbesti and Serbest İzmir, another monarchist newspaper, wrote that Major Niyazi, one of the heroes of the Revolution, had resigned from the Committee of Union and Progress, on account of dissatisfaction with it.[159] This imaginary news was of course denied by Major Niyazi himself.[160]

[155] "Sadrâzam Paşa ile Mülâkat," Tanin, February 17, 1324/March 2, 1909; "Turkish Internal Affairs: The Right of Public Meeting," The Times, March 4, 1909, p.5; and, Cemal Kutay, Üç Paşalar Kavgası, p.63.
[156] I/I/37, February 18, 1324/March 3, 1909, Meclis-i Mebusan Zabıt Ceridesi, 2, p.134; Cemal Kutay, Üç Paşalar Kavgası, p.63.
[157] I/I/37, February 18, 1324/March 3, 1909, Meclis-i Mebusan Zabıt Ceridesi, 2, pp.134-154, and, 162-164; "Turkish Internal Affairs: The Right of Public Meeting," The Times, March 4, 1909, p.5. For the Unionist views on this issue see, Hüseyin Cahid [Yalçın], " Hakk-ı İctima Meselesi," Tanin, February 19, 1324/March 4, 1909, p.1; and, Babanzade İsmail Hakkı, "Ahali ve Meclis-i Mebusan," Tanin, February 19, 1324/March 4, 1909, pp.1-2.
[158] Serbesti, February 21, 1324/March 6, 1909, cited in F.O. 371/769/10792, Sir Gerard Lowther to Sir Edward Grey, Pera, March 12, 1909, quoted in Feroz Ahmad, The Young Turks: The Committee of Union and Progress in Turkish Politics, 1908-1914, p.39.
[159] "Le major Niazi bey," The Levant Herald and Eastern Express, March 18, 1909, p.1; and, Feroz Ahmad, The Young Turks: The Committee of Union and Progress in Turkish Politics, 1908-1914, p.39.
[160] Yeni Asır, March 4, 1325/March 17, 1909, cited in F.O. 195/2328, Consul-General Lamb to Sir Gerard Lowther, Salonica, March 18, 1909, in Feroz Ahmad, The Young Turks: The Committee of Union and Progress in Turkish Politics, 1908-1914, p.39; and, "Le major Niazi bey," The Levant Herald and Eastern Express, March 18, 1909, p.1.

In early March, an action of the Minister of War had precipitated unrest within the troops stationed at the Yıldız Palace. He
had proposed that all officers known to have acted as informers and spies under the old regime be dismissed from the
army, and, upon his proposal, the Government had demanded a list of officers deemed unworthy to hold a commission.[161]
On March 6, there was a disturbance involving troops
stationed in the Yıldız Palace. The official version of events
stated that a soldier who had been reprimanded for
insubordinate conduct induced some of his comrades to demonstrate in front of the Palace, cheering the Sultan. Officers
appeared and ordered the demonstrators to return to their quarters, which they did without further disorder. Reportedly,
these troops, who were responsible for the November 1908 mutiny, had been disgruntled with the Government's gradual
relocation of officers and troops identified with the old regime,
substituting with those who were considered loyal to the
Constitution. After the November mutiny had been suppressed, many were of the opinion that these troops should
have been removed from the capital altogether, and indeed,
the new Minister of War had recently proposed the summary
dismissal of officers who were known to have acted on behalf
of the old regime. But the Committee of Union and Progress
had preferred to adopt from the start a more gradual approach.
That these measures had not yet proved wholly effective was
clear, but the Committee's determination to deal resolutely
with reactionary and mutinous tendencies within the army
remained unshaken.[162]

Despite the gradual approach the Unionists took in cleaning the armed forces from reactionary elements, the move
nevertheless upset some of the high-ranking officers generally sympathetic to the old regime. Esad Pasha, replacing Abdullah Pasha who had resigned as Commander of the Fourth
Army Corps at Erzurum, also resigned.[163] İbrahim Pasha, ex-
Commander of the Second Army Corps at Edirne, was ap-

[161] "Turkey," *The Times*, March 2, 1909, p.5.
[162] "Turkey: Military Incident at Yildiz," *The Times*, March 9, 1909, p.5.
[163] "Turkey: The State of the Army," *The Times*, March 11, 1909, p.5.

pointed his successor.[164] Several senior officers of the Second
Army Corps who had served under Nâzım Pasha before his
ill-fated appointment to the Ministry of War were also said to
have tendered their resignations. These resignations were
attributed to dissatisfaction in the army with the Committee of
Union and Progress.[165]

In the days following the formation of the Hilmi Pasha Cabinet, the opposition found solace in the fact that several deputies had defected from the Committee of Union and Progress.
The concerted effort of the monarchist opposition began with
press attacks against the Committee of Union and Progress.
Dr. Rıza Nur, deputy for Sinob, whose opposition to the Unionists had long been established since his election tour in his
district, started the opposition campaign by writing a provocative article ridiculing the Unionists in the March 12 issue of
the monarchist daily İkdam.[166] At the moment when the
Constitution was proclaimed, the Committee, wrote Rıza Nur,
was inspired by lofty ideals and patriotic aims, but since then
a number persons had joined its ranks and forced their way
into its midst who were animated by considerations of personal interest. These elements, Rıza Nur continued, who
found themselves invested with immense material and moral
influence, had produced a radical change in its policy. He
then proceeded to put several questions, such as whether the
Committee constituted an irresponsible Cabinet, whether it
interfered in the acts of the responsible Government, and
whether the necessity for its continued existence was justified,
and to answer them in detail. The Committee, he alleged, was
a regular *imperium in imperio*, maintaining a whole hier-
archy in the various branches of the administration alongside

[164] "Turkey: New Army Appointments," *The Times*, March 13, 1909, p.5.
[165] "Turkey: The State of the Army," *The Times*, March 11, 1909, p.5.
[166] Dr. Rıza Nur, "Görüyorum ki İşler Fena Gidiyor," *İkdam*, February 27,
1324/March 12, 1909, p.1. This article is cited in "Le Comité Union et Progrès,"
The Levant Herald and Eastern Express, March 13, 1909, p.1. This was rebuked by
Hüseyin Cahid [Yalçın] in the *Tanin* of March 4, 1325/March 17, 1909 ("İş Fena
mı Gidiyor?" p.1). See also, Hüseyin Cahid Yalçın, "Meşrutiyet Hatıraları, 1908-
1918," *Fikir Hareketleri, 4* (April 25-October 19, 1935), p.326. Rıza Nur's attacks on
the Unionist leadership continued in the columns of *İkdam* ("Le Comité Union et
Progrès: Les révélations du Dr. Riza Nour bey," *The Levant Herald and Eastern
Express*, March 17, 1909, p.1).

the bureaucratic apparatus. Rıza Nur concluded his article by writing that the Committee of Union and Progress ought to dissolve not only its local organisations in Anatolia but also the central committee in İstanbul and the clubs affiliated to it, and confine its activities to Monastir and Salonica.[167]

A banquet was given on the evening of March 12 in Pera Palace by Damad Ferid Pasha, son-in-law of the Sultan and a senator, Prince Said Halim Pasha, and other gentlemen in honour of the Committee of Union and Progress and the army and the navy.[168] Among those present were Hilmi Pasha, the Grand Vezier, Said Pasha, the President of the Senate, Ahmed Rıza Bey, the President of the Chamber, the Ministers of War and of the Navy, Gazi Ahmed Muhtar Pasha, an influential senator, Mahmud Muhtar Pasha, the Commander of the First Army Corps, and many senators, deputies, and officers of high rank.[169]

Damad Ferid Pasha expressed his pleasure in welcoming so distinguished a gathering, and eulogised the services of the Committee of Union and Progress, the army, and the navy. Afterwards, Hilmi Pasha made a speech in which he said that having accomplished the great task of securing the country's freedom, the Unionists had then performed an equally admirable and meritorious act in handing over authority to the Parliament, in whom was vested the power of the nation, and whose decisions the Unionists did not aspire to control.[170]

However, it was the speech of Ahmed Rıza Bey, the President of the Chamber, which was the most important and most provocative. He said that the wretches, who under the old regime endeavoured, from motives of personal interest, to sow discord between the various elements of the nation were

---

[167] Dr. Rıza Nur, "Görüyorum ki İşler Fena Gidiyor," *İkdam*, February 27, 1324/March 12, 1909, p.1. This article is excerpted in "The New Regime in Turkey: The Government and the Committee," *The Times*, March 20, 1909, p.6; and Hüseyin Cahid Yalçın, "Meşrutiyet Hatıraları, 1908-1918," *Fikir Hareketleri*, 4 (April 25-October 19, 1935), p.326. See also, "Die türkische Presse," *Osmanischer Lloyd*, March 17, p.2.

[168] "Le comité Union et Progrès devant l'opinion publique: Le dîner de vendredi au Pera Palace," *The Levant Herald and Eastern Express*, March 15, 1909, p.1.

[169] "The Committee of Union and Progress," *The Times*, March 13, 1909, p.5.

[170] "The Committee of Union and Progress," *The Times*, March 13, 1909, p.5; and, "The New Regime in Turkey: The Government and the Committee," *The Times*, March 20, 1909, p.6.

naturally discontented with the formation of a new Cabinet capable of understanding and appreciating the parliamentary regime. He added that there were politicians who desired to see the past revived, and, in order to reach this end by another path, were anxious that liberty should be loosed from all control. According to him, it was they who complained of the power of the Unionists; it was they who were working to discredit it in the eyes of the ulema on the one hand and of the non-Muslim elements on the other. It was they, in short, who clamoured loudly for its extinction.[171] Accusing all those, including by implicit reference, members of the Liberal Union, who worked for the restoration of absolutist monarchy as being traitors, he added that these reactionary tendencies had to be firmly repressed.[172]

The speech delivered on the evening of March 12 by Hilmi Pasha was sharply criticised in the opposition newspapers.[173] *Yeni Gazete* noted a contradiction between the Grand Vezier's statement that the Committee of Union and Progress had transformed itself into a simple parliamentary party and had ceased to interfere in the affairs of the Government and the speech of Ahmed Rıza Bey, who had declared that the Committee's duties in relation to the change of regime had not yet terminated.[174]

Liberal Union organs and other conservative newspapers also severely criticised Ahmed Rıza Bey, accusing him of being incapable of that impartiality which should distinguish the President of the Chamber. Most signs were indicative that matters were approaching a crisis.[175]

In response to Rıza Nur's and other monarchists' attacks on

---

[171]   "The New Regime in Turkey: The Government and the Committee," *The Times*, March 20, 1909, p.6.
[172]   "The Committee of Union and Progress," *The Times*, March 13, 1909, p.5; and, Hüseyin Cahid [Yalçın], "Pera Palas Ziyafeti," *Tanin*, March 1, 1325/March 14, 1909, p.1. See also, Tarık Zafer Tunaya, *Türkiye'de Siyasi Partiler, 1859-1952*, p.242.
[173]   "Die türkische Presse," *Osmanischer Lloyd*, March 17, 1909, p.2.
[174]   *Yeni Gazete*, March 1, 1325/March 14, 1909, quoted in "Turkey: The Chamber and the Ministry," *The Times*, March 15, 1909, p.8.
[175]   "Turkey: Position of the Ministry," *The Times*, March 16, 1909, p.5; and, *Serbesti*, March 2, 1325/March 15, 1909, and Ali Kemal, "İhtilâf—İtilâf," *İkdam*, March 2, 1325/March 15, 1909, p.1, excerpted in "Le dîner du Pera Palace: Commentaires de la presse turque," *The Levant Herald and Eastern Express*, March 16, 1909, p.1.

the Committee of Union and Progress, the Committee did its best to neutralise the opposition campaign.[176] Lecturing in Monastir on the political situation, Dr. Nâzım Bey, one of the leaders of the Committee of Union and Progress, urged his audience to boycott *İkdam* and *Yeni Gazete*, who attacked the Unionists and spread baseless rumours.[177] In the March 27 session of the Chamber a vehement debate took place regarding the attitude of three monarchist foreign language İstanbul papers—*The Levant Herald and Eastern Express, Proodos,* and *Neologos*—which had recently been engaged in a fierce controversy with the leading organs of the Committee of Union and Progress concerning the political situation. A resolution demanding the expulsion of the editors of these newspapers had been forwarded by the Grand Vezier to the President of the Chamber. After the reading of this resolution, several Unionist deputies strongly urged the suspension of the newspapers and the expulsion of their editors, declaring that their attacks on the police, the army, and the nation were intolerable. The Chamber finally adopted a motion inviting the Government to apply the Press Law to all newspapers publishing inflammatory articles prejudicial to the interests of Turkey and wounding to the honour of the army and the nation.[178]

The monarchist press campaign against the interference of the Committee of Union and Progress in Government affairs appeared to be producing an effect. It was stated that the Unionists was deliberating on the advisability of abandoning inter meddling in the government of European Turkey, though maintaining a control over the Anatolian provinces.[179]

Meanwhile, the monarchists kept up the pressure on the Unionists. On March 30, Şerif Pasha, the monarchist ex-Ambassador to Stockholm who had created a furore among

---

[176] Hüseyin Cahid [Yalçın], "Pera Palas Ziyafeti," *Tanin*, March 1, 1325/March 14, 1909, p.1; and, Hüseyin Cahid [Yalçın], "Ziyafet Münasebetiyle," *Tanin*, March 2, 1325/March 15, 1909, p.1.

[177] "Doktor Nâzım Bey'in Konferansları," *İkdam*, February 27, 1324/March 12, 1909, p.3; and, "Turkey," *The Times*, March 13, 1909, p.5.

[178] I/I/47, March 14, 1325/March 27, 1909, *Meclis-i Mebusan Zabıt Ceridesi*, 2, pp.479-487; and, "Turkish Politics: The 'Foreign' Press," *The Times*, March 29, 1909, p.8.

[179] "The Committee of Union and Progress," *The Times*, March 17, 1909, p.5.

the Unionists immediately after the Revolution when he had claimed that he was the leader of the Unionist organisation in İstanbul, published an open letter in *Osmanlı* announcing his resignation from the Committee of Union and Progress as a mark of disapproval of the methods of the Unionists, which, he alleged, involved serious danger to the interests of the country.[180]

Kâmil Pasha was also active in writing in *İkdam* criticising the Unionists.[181] In the *İkdam* and *L'Indépendant Belge* of April 3, he published, in a long statement, the reasons why he had 'left' the office of the Grand Vezierate.[182] His statement drew instant attention in Government circles. In the April 4 issue of *La Turquie*, Hüseyin Hilmi Pasha replied to Kâmil Pasha's statement. The Grand Vezier declared that Kâmil Pasha's memoir explained nothing but set forth a theory of government which amounted to a negation of constitutional regime. Under the constitutional regime, Hüseyin Hilmi Pasha went on, the Grand Vezier was simply the President of the Council of Ministers, who had to explain its policy to the Chamber, not at its own pleasure, but when the Chamber desired. Returning to the events that precipitated Kâmil Pasha's downfall, Hüseyin Hilmi Pasha said that he had handed in his resignation in consequence of the dismissal of the Minister of War, but was dissuaded by Kâmil Pasha because he had understood from him that the Minister of War had accepted the post of High Commissioner in Egypt of his own accord. Furthermore, Kâmil Pasha had announced the Cabinet that the Ministers of War and of the Navy had been in-

[180] "Chérif pacha," and "Le Comité Union et Progrès et le général Chérif pacha," *The Levant Herald and Eastern Express*, March 31, 1909, p.2; and, "The Committee of Union and Progress," *The Times*, April 2, 1909, p.5. For the text of his resignation letter see, Şerif, *Bir Muhalifin Hatıraları: İttihat ve Terakki'ye Muhalefet*, pp.32-34.
[181] Hüseyin Cahid Yalçın, "Meşrutiyet Hatıraları, 1908-1918," *Fikir Hareketleri*, 4 (April 25-October 19, 1935), p.342.
[182] "Sadr-ı Sabık Kâmil Paşa Hazretleri'nin İzahnamesi," *İkdam*, March 21, 1325/April 3, 1909, pp.1-2; "Mémoire Explicatif de Kiamil Pacha," *L'Indépendant, Belge*, April 3, 1909, pp.1-2, reproduced in full in, A. A. Türkei 159, No.2; "Turkey: Kiamil Pasha and the Committee," *The Times*, April 5, 1909, p.5; and, Cemal Kutay, *Üç Paşalar Kavgası*, p.65. The French translation of his statement was published the same day in "Le mémoire explicatif de Kiamil pacha," *The Levant Herald and Eastern Express*, April 3, 1909, pp.1-2. The German translation appeared on April 4 ("Rechtfertigung Kiamil Paschas," *Osmanischer Lloyd*, April 4, 1909, p.1).

volved in a conspiracy against the Sultan. Hüseyin Hilmi Pasha said that in reality no plot existed; two ministers had been
dismissed purely from arbitrary motives. Realising this, Hüseyin Hilmi Pasha and several of his colleagues had decided
that they had no longer any choice but to resign. There was
therefore no external pressure, as Kâmil Pasha alleged.[183]

The press discussed Kâmil Pasha's accusations against the
Committee of Union and Progress with much animation. The
monarchist *Mizan, İkdam, Yeni Gazete, Serbesti,* and *Osmanlı*—organ of the Liberal Union—regarded it as a crushing indictment of the Committee of Union and Progress and the existing Cabinet.[184] Furthermore, *Serbesti* alleged that the situation of the Committee of Union and Progress was fragile,
while *Yeni Gazete* deliberately fabricated the rumour that the
Committee was about to be dissolved.[185] The leaders of the
Committee, of course, denied any such rumours.[186] *Tanin,
Şura-yı Ümmet,* and *Sabah* condemned it as misrepresenting
facts and demonstrating the weakness of the ex-Grand Vezier's case.[187]

On April 3, the official opening of the Mohammedan Union
was celebrated with a large demonstration in İstanbul consisting of religious ceremonies and public speeches by Said-i
Kürdi and Derviş Vahdeti.[188] The news of the establishment of

---

[183] *La Turquie,* April 4, 1909, cited in "Turkey: Kiamil Pasha and the Committee," *The Times,* April 6, 1909, p.5.

[184] "Le mémoire de Kiamil pacha: Les commentaires de la Presse turque,"
The Levant Herald and Eastern Express, April 5, 1909, p.1; "Turkey: Kiamil Pasha
and the Committee," *The Times,* April 6, 1909, p.5; "Die türkische Presse," *Osmanischer Lloyd,* April 7, 1909, p.2; and, Ali Cevad, *İkinci Meşrutiyetin İlânı ve
Otuzbirt Mart Hadisesi,* p.46.

[185] "La situation du Comité Union et Progrès," *The Levant Herald and Eastern
Express,* April 3, 1909, p.2.

[186] "The Committee of Union and Progress," *The Levant Herald and Eastern
Express,* April 5, 1909, p.1.

[187] Hüseyin Cahid [Yalçın], "Kâmil Paşa'nın İzahnamesi," *Tanin,* March 22,
1325/April 4, 1909, pp.1-3; Hüseyin Cahid [Yalçın], "Kâmil Paşa ve Gazeteler,"
Tanin, March 23, 1325/April 5, 1909, p.1; and, "Turkey: Kiamil Pasha and the
Committee," *The Times,* April 6, 1909, p.5. Rahmi [Aslan]'s rebuttal in the *Şura-yı
Ümmet* is also reprinted in *Tanin* ("*Şura-yı Ümmet'*ten: Kâmil Paşa Hazret-
leri'ne," *Tanin,* March 24, 1325/April 6, 1909, pp.2-3).

[188] "Abdul Hamids Besorgnisse," *Berliner Tageblatt und Handels-Zeitung,*
April 3, 1909, Evening Edition, p.1; "L'Union Mahométane," *The Levant Herald
and Eastern Express,* April 5, 1909, p.1; Edwin Pears, *Forty Years in
Constantinople: The Recollections of Sir Edwin Pears, 1873-1915,* p.273; and, Cemal
Kutay, *Üç Paşalar Kavgası,* p.65.

the Union and its by-laws as well as the list of the executive members had already been announced in the March 16 of *Volkan*, the association's organ.[189] Despite outward appearance that this was a Muslim religious organisation, it did not represent the Muslim religious establishment; in fact it had nothing to do with religion at all.[190] The association was Abdülhamid's creation, and was to be used as an instrument for the counterrevolutionary attempt. Its founders were the chief eunuch at the Yıldız Palace, Nadir Agha, the second eunuch at the Yıldız Palace, one of the Sultan's sons, one of the Sultan's nephews, Derviş Vahdeti, and several others of the same type. All of these individuals lived in the Palace.[191] Derviş Vahdeti was the only one amongst the founders of the Union who could pretend to any kind of religious character. He was, however, a *bektaşi*, therefore an unorthodox and heretical Muslim, and thus it was difficult to see how he could become fanatical on the subject of the *shari'a*. Derviş Vahdeti acted as the editor of *Volkan*.[192] Another journalist who belonged to the Mohammedan Union was Mizancı Murad Bey, who, like other tools of Abdülhamid, had begun his public life as a conspirator and exile in Paris. Then he had entered the Sultan's service as an informer, and, when the Revolution succeeded, he had tried, unsuccessfully, to infiltrate into the Committee of Union and Progress.[193] Of the five hundred and forty-three principal agitators belonging to this Union, eleven were employees in the Yıldız Palace, seventeen were journalists, and the remainder were military men and hodjas.[194]

The counter-revolutionary agitation of the Mohammedan Union had started immediately after its coming into exis-

---

[189] Cemal Kutay, *Üç Paşalar Kavgası*, p.64. Derviş Vahdeti had applied to the Palace for money to publish *Volkan* (Ali Cevad, *İkinci Meşrutiyetin İlânı ve Otuzbirt Mart Hadisesi*, pp.45-46).

[190] Francis McCullagh, *The Fall of Abd-ul-Hamid*, p.52.

[191] Francis McCullagh, *The Fall of Abd-ul-Hamid*, p.53. The most brilliant of them all was Nadir Agha, the second eunuch, who, in the tenth year of his age, was bought for the Sultan from a slave-merchant in Egypt for a hundred and fifty francs, and had developed during the last few years into Abdülhamid's most trusted advisor (Francis McCullagh, *The Fall of Abd-ul-Hamid*, p.55). See also, Edwin Pears, *Life of Abdul Hamid*, p.301.

[192] Francis McCullagh, *The Fall of Abd-ul-Hamid*, p.54.

[193] Francis McCullagh, *The Fall of Abd-ul-Hamid*, pp.54-55.

[194] Francis McCullagh, *The Fall of Abd-ul-Hamid*, p.55.

tence.[195] On March 28, their organ, *Volkan*, had published an article attributed to the leaders of the troops of Albanians who had been sent from İstanbul to Macedonia in which the soldiers allegedly complained about their situation. The paper printed the rumour that all of the regiment dissatisfied with this removal from İstanbul were to join wholesale the Mohammedan Union.[196]

It was in this climate that, on April 5, the by-election in İstanbul took place. On March 9, it had been announced that the seat in İstanbul left vacant by the death of Manyasizade Refik Bey, the late Minister of Justice, would be contested by Ali Kemal Bey, editor of *İkdam*, as candidate of the Liberal Union.[197] Despite all the efforts of the monarchist Liberal Union, the public was not very enthusiastic about the party and its members. The Unionist candidate was Rıfat Pasha, the Minister for Foreign Affairs; the candidate of the opposition Liberal Union was Ali Kemal Bey, the editor of *İkdam*.[198] Rıfat Pasha won the election by a total vote of two hundred and eighty-one as against one hundred and twenty-nine votes received by Ali Kemal Bey. Murad Bey received fifty, Prince Sabahaddin three, and Kâmil Pasha one vote. The by-election in İstanbul was an indication of the weakness of the Liberal Union against the Committee of Union and Progress.[199]

On March 29, the Palace troops composed of Albanian and Arab regiments had been removed from the Palace grounds and stationed at Taşkışla barracks.[200] On April 5, the Government obtained the Sultan's consent to the removal from İstan-

---

[195] Cemal Kutay, *Üç Paşalar Kavgası*, p.65; and, Ali Haydar Midhat, *Hatıralarım, 1872-1946*, p.207.
[196] Cemal Kutay, *Üç Paşalar Kavgası*, p.65.
[197] "Turkey: Refik Bey's Constitutency," *The Times*, March 9, 1909, p.5; "The Turkish Parliament," *The Times*, March 10, 1909, p.5; and, "Politische Nachrichten: Der liberale Kandidat für die Ersatzwahl in der Hauptstadt," *Osmanischer Lloyd*, March 23, 1909, p.2.
[198] For Ali Kemal's appeal to the electorate see, Ali Kemal, "Dersaadet Müntehib-i Sanilerine," *İkdam*, March 22, 1325/April 4, 1909, p.1.
[199] Cemal Kutay, *Üç Paşalar Kavgası*, p.65; "L'élection législative de Constantinople," *The Levant Herald and Eastern Express*, April 6, 1909, p.1; "Politische Nachrichten: Die Wahl Rifaat Paschas zum Abgeordneten von Konstantinopel," *Osmanischer Lloyd*, April 6, 1909, p.1; and, "Turkey: Kiamil Pasha and the Committee," *The Times*, April 6, 1909, p.5. For a commentary on the importance of this by-election for the Committee of Union and Progress see, "Die Bedeutung des jungtürkischen Wahlsieges," *Osmanischer Lloyd*, April 7, 1909, p.1.
[200] Ali Cevad, *İkinci Meşrutiyetin İlânı ve Otuzbir Mart Hadisesi*, p.44.

bul of the troops kept in the Taşkışla barracks. The Albanians would shortly be transferred to Kossovo, the Arab troops would be incorporated in the Fifth Army Corps, and the Kurds and the Lazes would return to their respective countries.[201] Abdülhamid, who had had long conversations with the Grand Vezier, the Minister of War, and the President of the Chamber on the subject, was stated to have been much disturbed by the departure of the troops, and to have recognised with considerable reluctance the desirability of a measure which the repeated cases of insubordination since the proclamation of the Constitution had shown to be a necessity.[202] With a view to provoke the troops and the officers against the Government and the Unionists, *Serbesti* alleged that these measures would have terrible consequences.[203]

On the night of April 6, Hasan Fehmi Efendi, editor of *Serbesti*, was assassinated in İstanbul under most mysterious circumstances.[204] The owner of *Serbesti*, Mevlânzade Rıfat Bey, was one of the founders of the anti-Unionist society called the Devotees of the Nation—or, Fedakâran-ı Millet—which had flourished in İstanbul in late 1908 and been involved with underground activities to eliminate the Committee of Union and Progress from the political scene. Abdülhamid was reported to be highly interested in this society, for which he had already made monetary contributions.[205] However, Mevlân-

---

[201] Ali Cevad, *İkinci Meşrutiyetin İlânı ve Otuzbir Mart Hadisesi*, p.45; and, "Turkey: The Troops at Yıldız," *The Times*, April 7, 1909, p.5.

[202] "Turkey: The Troops at Yıldız," *The Times*, April 7, 1909, p.5.

[203] *Serbesti*, March 24, 1325/April 6, 1909, excerpted in "L'armée et la politique," *The Levant Herald and Eastern Express*, April 7, 1909, p.1.

[204] "Assasinat," *The Levant Herald and Eastern Express*, April 7, 1909, p.1; Ali Kemal, "İlk Kurban," *İkdam*, March 26, 1325/April 8, 1909, p.1; "Cinayet Tahkikatı," *İkdam*, March 26, 1325/April 8, 1909, pp.1-2; "Die Ermordung des Redakteurs der 'Serbesti'," *Osmanischer Lloyd*, April 8, 1909, p.1; "Turkey: Murder of an Editor in Constantinople," *The Times*, April 8, 1909, p.5; "Ein politischer Mord in Konstantinopel," *Berliner Tageblatt und Handels-Zeitung*, April 8, 1909, Morning Edition, p.1; "Der Mord in Konstantinopel," *Berliner Tageblatt und Handels-Zeitung*, April 8, 1909, Evening Edition, p.4; Hüseyin Cahid Yalçın, "Meşrutiyet Hatıraları, 1908-1918," *Fikir Hareketleri*, 4 (April 25-October 19, 1935), p.357; Edwin Pears, *Life of Abdul Hamid*, p.312; and, Ali Cevad, *İkinci Meşrutiyetin İlânı ve Otuzbir Mart Hadisesi*, p.46.

[205] For a highly sympathetic view on this counter-revolutionary society see, Sina Akşin, "Fedâkâran-ı Millet Cemiyeti," pp.125-136. For the true nature and previous activities of this society see, Aykut Kansu, *The Revolution of 1908 in Turkey*, pp.202-204.

zade Rıfat Bey's resignation from that society, and his publication of *Serbesti* in which he took an ultra-nationalist stand,
attacking at the same time the Sultan and the Unionists, had
greatly annoyed Abdülhamid. Abdülhamid was so angry at
this defection that he had decided to have Mevlânzade Rıfat
Bey assassinated, and offered an assassin a large sum of
money to do the work. The assassin, however, wanted more,
whereupon Abdülhamid thought that it would be better to buy
Mevlânzade Rıfat Bey body and soul with the money than to
give it to his murderers.[206]

When Hasan Fehmi Efendi was assassinated, the crime
was put down, by the monarchists, to the Committee of Union
and Progress for obvious political motives.[207] The fact, however, was that one of the Palace police had been seen near the
scene of the murder at the time the crime was committed. It
was not impossible that the Palace had planned this murder
which would certainly provoke an outburst of public feeling
against the Unionists. This, in turn, would help the monarchists and Abdülhamid stage the *coup d'état* they had been
planning for some time.[208]

As expected, the news of the crime provoked an outburst of
indignation from the students of the Faculty of Political Science and the School of Medicine. Provoked by Ali Kemal
Bey, the editor of *İkdam* who also taught at the Faculty of
Political Science, midday on April 7, about one thousand students demonstrated before the Sublime Porte, where Hüseyin
Hilmi Pasha, who met with a mixed reception, was obliged to
appear on the steps and calm the crowd by promises that every
effort would be made to arrest the murderer. The students,
after cheering outside the offices of *Serbesti*, marched to the
Chamber of Deputies and called upon the President of the

[206] Francis McCullagh, *The Fall of Abd-ul-Hamid*, p.23; and, Ali Cevad, *İkinci Meşrutiyetin İlânı ve Otuzbir Mart Hadisesi*, p.40.
[207] Ali Cevad, *İkinci Meşrutiyetin İlânı ve Otuzbir Mart Hadisesi*, p.46; "Gov-
ernment by Secret Committee," *The Contemporary Review*, 95 (January-June 1909),
pp.747-748; Victor R. Swenson, "The Military Rising in Istanbul, 1909," p.176; Ahmed Bedevi Kuran, *İnkılâp Tarihimiz ve 'Jön Türkler,'* p276; Ahmed Bedevi
Kuran, *Osmanlı İmparatorluğunda İnkılâp Hareketleri ve Milli Mücadele*, p.510;
Edwin Pears, *Forty Years in Constantinople: The Recollections of Sir Edwin Pears,
1873-1915*, pp.274-275; idem, *Life of Abdul Hamid*, p.312; and, Yusuf Hikmet Bayur,
Türk İnkılâbı Tarihi, 1/2, p.183.
[208] Francis McCullagh, *The Fall of Abd-ul-Hamid*, pp.23-24.

Chamber to ensure that justice should be done.[209] Meanwhile, in the Chamber, Müfid Bey, the monarchist Albanian deputy for Argyrocastro, demanded that a day be fixed for the interpellation of the Minister of the Interior in regard to the murder. The great majority of the Chamber voted in favour of the motion, which was not opposed by the members of the Unionist bloc.[210]

The funeral of Hasan Fehmi Efendi took place on April 8. It was attended by at least five thousand people, among whom were a number of deputies of the Liberal Union, many theo-logical students, and Albanians. The funeral procession was used as an opportunity to demonstrate against the Hilmi Pasha Cabinet and the Unionists.[211] The opposition press hinted that the murder was an act of political vengeance. While *Osmanlı* commented on the alleged passivity of the police, *Mizan* declared that the patience of the people was about to be ex-hausted, and that the Government should either do its duty or resign.[212] *İkdam* even published a petition from its editor to the Minister of Justice in which Ali Kemal Bey declared that he warned İsmail Kemal Bey and Rıfat Bey, the assistant editor of *Serbesti*, that they had been condemned by a group of extremists in Salonica.[213] The monarchist military students

[209] Mehmed Cavid, "Meşrutiyet Devrine Dair Cavit Bey'in Hatıraları: 3," *Ta-nin*, September 1, 1943, p.2; Hüseyin Cahid Yalçın, "Meşrutiyet Hatıraları, 1908-1918," *Fikir Hareketleri*, 4 (April 25-October 19, 1935), p.357; Hasan Amca, *Doğmayan Hürriyet: Bir Devrin İçyüzü, 1908-1918*, pp.73-78; "Turkey: Murder of an Editor in Constantinople," *The Times*, April 8, 1909, p.5; and, "La mort du pre-mier martyr de la liberté," *The Levant Herald and Eastern Express*, April 8, 1909, p.1. See also, "Mekteb-i Mülkiye'deki Vak'a," *Tanin*, March 31, 1325/April 13, 1909, p.3; and, Yusuf Hikmet Bayur, *Türk İnkılâbı Tarihi*, 1/2, p.183.

[210] I/I/53, March 25, 1325/April 7, 1909, *Meclis-i Mebusan Zabıt Ceridesi*, 2, pp.651-655; "Turkey: Murder of an Editor in Constantinople," *The Times*, April 8, 1909, p.5; "Deputiertenkammer," *Osmanischer Lloyd*, April 8, 1909, p.1; and, Hü-seyin Cahid Yalçın, "Meşrutiyet Hatıraları, 1908-1918," *Fikir Hareketleri*, 4 (April 25-October 19, 1935), pp.357-358.

[211] Hüseyin Cahid Yalçın, "Meşrutiyet Hatıraları, 1908-1918," *Fikir Hareket-leri*, 4 (April 25-October 19, 1935), p.358; Hasan Amca, *Doğmayan Hürriyet: Bir Devrin İçyüzü, 1908-1918*, pp.78-81; Ahmed Bedevi Kuran, *Osmanlı İmparatorlu-ğunda İnkılâp Hareketleri ve Milli Mücadele*, p.511, who claims a crowd of one hundred thousand!; "Şehid-i Hürriyetin Cenaze Merasiminde," *İkdam*, March 27, 1325/April 9, 1909, pp.1-2; "Cenaze Alayı," *İkdam*, March 27, 1325/April 9, 1909, p.2; "Zur Ermordung Hassan Fehmis: Die Bestattung," *Osmanischer Lloyd*, April 9, 1909, p.1; and "The Murder of a Turkish Editor: Feeling in Constantinople," *The Times*, April 9, 1909, p.3.

[212] *Osmanlı* and *Mizan*, March 27, 1325/April 9, 1909, quoted in "The Kara-keui Murder," *The Levant Herald and Eastern Express*, April 10, 1909, p.1.

[213] "The Murder of a Turkish Editor: Feeling in Constantinople," *The Times*, April 9, 1909, p.3.

and officers took this opportunity to protest the Minister of War, and their protest telegrams were published in opposition newspapers in a move to create unrest and rebellion within the military.[214]

In spite of efforts of the police to discover the identity of the murderer of Hasan Fehmi Efendi, he had not been discovered. The affair was discussed at length in the press.[215] *Şura-yı Ümmet*, the Unionist organ, published a manifesto of the Committee of Union and Progress denying all complicity in the crime, which it unreservedly condemned. *Tanin*, too, defended the Committee of Union and Progress. The Armenian Revolutionary Federation also issued a manifesto condemning the crime, and appealing to the.different political parties to subordinate personal quarrels to national interests, and to combine to meet the dangers which threatened the country.[216]

The monarchist newspapers attacked the Unionists, while, at the same time, trying to capitalise on this event for political gain: disguising its real aim for increased political influence on behalf of the Liberal Union, *İkdam* of April 11 proposed a 'truce' between the two opposing parties, suggesting that İsmail Kemal Bey be made Vice-President of the Chamber, and that two monarchist politicians replace the ministers of Finance and of War.[217] While paying lip service to the necessity of rapprochement between the Committee and the Liberal Union, *İkdam*, nevertheless, continued its attack by accusing Ahmed Rıza Bey, President of the Chamber, of having declared himself in favour of an enlightened absolutism.[218]

---

[214] Hüseyin Cahid Yalçın, "Meşrutiyet Hatıraları, 1908-1918," *Fikir Hareketleri*, 4 (April 25-October 19, 1935), p.358.

[215] See, for instance, "Cinayet Tahkikatından," *İkdam*, March 27, 1325/April 9, 1909, p.2; "Cinayet Tahkikatından," *İkdam*, March 28, 1325/April 10, 1909, p.2; and, "Cinayet Tahkikatından," *İkdam*, March 29, 1325/April 11, 1909, p.2.

[216] The denial was also published in the *Tanin* ("Osmanlı İttihad ve Terakki Cemiyeti Merkez-i Umumiyesi'nden," *Tanin*, March 27, 1325/April 9, 1909, p.1). "Hüseyin Cahid [Yalçın], "Fırsattan İstifade," *Tanin*, March 27, 1325/April 9, 1909, p.1; and, "Turkish Affairs: The Internal Dissensions," *The Times*, April 10, 1909, p.3. See also, "Katil Kimdir?" *Tanin*, March 29, 1325/April 11, 1909, p.3.

[217] *İkdam*, March 29, 1325/April 11, 1909, quoted in *Tanin*, March 30, 1325/April 12, 1909 (Hüseyin Cahid Yalçın, "Meşrutiyet Hatıraları, 1908-1918," *Fikir Hareketleri*, 4 (April 25-October 19, 1935), p.358). For the Unionist replies in the *Tanin* see, Hüseyin Cahid [Yalçın], "Birleşme," *Tanin*, March 30, 1325/April 12, 1909, p.1; and, Babanzade İsmail Hakkı, "Şerait-i İtilâf," *Tanin*, March 30, 1325/April 12, 1909, p.1.

[218] "Turkish Internal Affairs: Parties and Politics," *The Times*, April 13, 1909, p.3.

Tanin, which defended the constitutional regime and the Unionists, wrote that the Liberal Union was a subversive body trying to bring back the monarchical order. The Liberal Union repudiated the designs attributed to it. Rahmi [Aslan] and Dr. Nâzım Bey, two prominent members of the Committee of Union and Progress, who were accused by Ali Kemal Bey, the editor of *İkdam*, of proposing his murder, were having recourse to the courts.[219]

With the assassination of an opposition journalist under suspicious circumstances, and the furore it helped to create in public opinion, the stage was finally set for an attempt by the monarchist opposition to capture political power from the Unionist-backed constitutional government by a *coup d'état*. Ever since the establishment of the liberal regime in July, 1908, the monarchist forces and disgruntled elements within the military had used every opportunity to return to the old regime. Reactionary attempts during the general elections and disobedience of the troops stationed at the Yıldız Palace had already given a glimpse of what might be expected from the monarchists. Therefore, the Unionist leadership was not unaware of the danger posed against the constitutional regime, and had taken measures, such as the decision of removing the Palace troops from İstanbul, in order to preserve the newly established order.

Unionist precautions, however, were not sufficient to prevent the monarchists from executing their plans for taking power through unconstitutional means. Preparations for the *coup d'état* had already been made and put into execution. It came at the small hours of April 13, and caught the Unionist leadership by surprise but not unprepared. Political power was captured by monarchists who kept it for the following ten days, while Unionist leadership was forced to go underground. These ten days tested the strength of the forces both for and against the constitutional order, and ended with the victory of the forces supporting the Constitution.

---

[219] "Turkish Internal Affairs: Parties and Politics," *The Times*, April 13, 1909, p.3.

CHAPTER THREE

THE MONARCHIST *COUP D'ÉTAT* OF APRIL 13, 1909

The *coup* attempt of April 13, 1909, the intention of which was to restore absolutist monarchy, has a peculiar place in Turkish historiography. It can not be factually ignored, since the constitutional regime established by the Committee of Union and Progress was visibly overthrown, and public order shattered for about two weeks. Moreover, this was a well-organised monarchist attempt to restore the old regime, which, as it turned out, utterly failed due to the determination of the Unionists to protect the liberal regime, and the swift intervention of a section of the military—the Third Army Corps stationed at Salonica—which remained loyal to the Revolution.[1] The counter-revolutionary *coup* attempt meant the restoration of the Sultan's powers. The mutinied soldiers at the service of the counter-revolutionaries at İstanbul openly proclaimed that, and championed Islam and the Sultan against the Unionists and the Christians. Every prominent champion of constitutional regime and liberty, except for the monarchist Liberal Union politicians, had to flee in order to escape death after the first day of the *coup*. Abdülhamid regained in large degree his former influence. The members of the Chamber of Deputies were mostly afraid to assemble.[2]

The peculiarity in Turkish historiography in general, and Kemalist historiography in particular, arises not from a suppression of facts but a gross misinterpretation of events in the days that followed the April 13, 1909 *coup*. Bent on denying the genuine character of the Revolution of 1908, Kemalist

---

[1] Officers supporting the Committee of Union and Progress acted *immediately* after the counter-revolutionary *coup* attempt (See, for instance, "Hilfsaktion der Jungtürken in Saloniki," *Berliner Tageblatt und Handels-Zeitung*, April 15, 1909, Morning Edition, pp.1-2).

[2] William M. Ramsay, *The Revolution in Constantinople and Turkey*, p.17.

historiography can not interpret the *coup* as a counter-revolutionary attempt to restore the *ancien régime*. According to established scholarship, there has not been a revolution to start with; consequently, it would be absurd to talk of a counter-revolutionary movement. Therefore, Kemalist historiography describes the *coup* as neutrally as possible, dubbing it as the 'Event of March 31'—March 31 corresponding to April 13 in the 'old' calendar.

Conveniently, this 'event' is explained away as a spontaneous religious reaction on the part of a supposedly ignorant and unenlightened population which revolted against the modernising elite, or the military and civilian bureaucrats, who had been trying to reform Turkey. This helps portray the civilian and military bureaucracy in the most favourable terms by giving undue, and, to a large extent, undeserved prominence to the role it played in the *coup's* suppression. Obsessed by the ideology of 'saving the State,' Kemalist historiography congratulates the military *and*, of course, Atatürk, who really had no part in it except for his chance presence as a junior officer in the Third Army, for preserving and protecting the state against its domestic enemies.[3]

Although this fiction currently reigns supreme thanks to the efforts of the past and present Kemalist ideologues, it is interesting to note that the *coup* of April 13, 1909 has been correctly interpreted for what it really was immediately after its failure. The true nature of the 'event' was laid bare before the eyes of the public not only in the pages of the foreign but also the Turkish press.[4] Foreign scholarship in its pre-Kemalist phase, that is to say, before it was misinformed and confused by the myths created for purposes of legitimising the Kemalist regime, described it as a *coup d'état* aiming to restore Hamidian absolutism.[5]

---

[3] See for instance, "31 Mart (13 Nisan) Ayaklanması," in Yusuf Hikmet Bayur, *Türk İnkılâbı Tarihi*, 1/2, pp.184-217. Bayur alleges that Mustafa Kemal Atatürk was the first and only officer at Salonica who formulated the idea of the 'March on İstanbul' (Yusuf Hikmet Bayur, *Türk İnkılâbı Tarihi*, 1/2, pp.197-198).

[4] Even during the events, some foreign newspapers correctly identified this 'event' as counter-revolutionary. See for instance, the leading article in a Berlin daily: "Die Gegenrevolution in Konstantinopel," *Vossische Zeitung*, April 16, 1909, Morning Edition, p.1.

[5] There are two books which stand out as examples of excellent journalism, describing and analysing the *coup d'état*. They are Francis McCullagh's *The Fall*

The *coup* began with soldiers belonging to the Rifle Division which had recently been brought from Salonica to İstanbul mutinying towards the morning of April 13.[6] The Government appeared to have been informed of the *coup* which was on foot, but its measures were purely defensive. Officers informed their men during the preceding week that they should have been prepared to disperse meetings by force. On the night of April 12, Mahmud Muhtar Pasha issued an decree couched in terms of more than Prussian rigour, ordering the troops, if necessary, to fire upon the *softas*, the religious *agents provocateurs* of the Mohammedan Union, and civilians.[7] This decided the majority of the men to mutiny. After binding some of their officers and imprisoning others, messages were sent from barrack to barrack and, at dawn, soldiers, led in the first instance by an Albanian corporal and by a Kurdish hodja, member of the Mohammedan Union marched out of their barracks to the Hagia Sophia Square, in front of the Parliament Building, shouting slogans in favour of the Sultan and the *shari'a*.[8] In addition to a large number of persons in religious garb, there were also many ex-officers, who had been laid off with the reforms in the army following the Revolution, in soldiers' uniforms among the mutinied soldiers. All indicated that the march was planned well in advance; there was nothing spontaneous. By late morning, the Parlia-

of Abd-ul-Hamid, and Paul Farkas' *Staatsstreich und Gegenrevolution in der Türkei*.

[6] "Militärrevolte in Konstantinople," *Berliner Tageblatt und Handels-Zeitung*, April 13, 1909, Evening Edition, p.1; and, "Bericht unseres Korrespondenten," *Berliner Tageblatt und Handels-Zeitung*, April 14, 1909, Evening Edition, p.2.

[7] "Military Revolt in Turkey," *The Times*, April 14, 1909, p.5; and, "Die Vorgänge vom 13. April: Weitere Einzelheiten der Meuterei, *Berliner Tageblatt und Handels-Zeitung*, April 15, 1909, Morning Edition, p.2. See also, Edwin Pears, *Life of Abdul Hamid*, p.314. For information on the Mohammedan Union see, "Das Komitee 'Ittiad Muhammedi,'" *Vossische Zeitung*, April 17, 1909, Morning Edition, p.2.

[8] "Die Urheber der Agitation," *Berliner Tageblatt und Handels-Zeitung*, April 13, 1909, Evening Edition, p.2; and, "Military Revolt in Turkey," *The Times*, April 14, 1909, p.5; "Die Militärrevolution in Konstantinopel, *Berliner Tageblatt und Handels-Zeitung*, April 14, 1909, Morning Edition, pp.1-2. See also, "Neue Proklamationen der Ulemas," *Vossische Zeitung*, April 18, 1909, Morning Edition, pp.2-3; Hüseyin Işık, "İkinci Meşrutiyet'in İlânında ve Korunmasında Silahlı Kuvvetlerimizin Rolü," pp.54-55; and, Mevlânzade Rıfat, *31 Mart: Bir İhtilâlin Hikâyesi*, pp.51-53.

ment Building was surrounded by about five to six thousand fully armed mutinied soldiers.[9] The organisers of the *coup d'état* also disguised many men as hodjas, and induced some *softas* to raise the cry of 'Religion in danger!' Many soldiers were provoked by being told that the Committee of Union and Progress and the Cabinet had decided to force all Muslims to become Christians.[10]

The mutineers assassinated Emir Muhamed Arslan Bey, deputy for Latakia, whom they mistook for Hüseyin Cahid [Yalçın], the prominent Unionist deputy for İstanbul and editor-in-chief of *Tanin*. They also killed Nâzım Pasha, the Minister of Justice, whom they mistook for Ahmed Rıza Bey, and wounded Ali Rıza Pasha, Minister of War.[11]

The Captain of the destroyer *Asar-ı Tevfik*, Ali Kabuli Bey, tried to prevent his crew from joining the mutinied soldiers. Though partly successful in keeping order at first, Ali Kabuli Bey subsequently lost control of his crew and was captured by the mutineers, who carried him through the streets of İstanbul in front of the Palace. There, the mutineers cheered for the Sultan and the *shari'a* until Abdülhamid appeared before the Palace. Under the seemingly approving eyes of Abdülhamid, the mutineers lynched Ali Kabuli Bey, after which they hanged him on a tree on the Palace grounds.[12]

---

[9] Celal Bayar, *Ben de Yazdım, 1*, p.141; "Die Militärrevolution in Konstantinopel," *Berliner Tageblatt und Handels-Zeitung*, April 14, 1909, Morning Edition, pp.1-2; "Bericht unseres Korrespondenten," *Berliner Tageblatt und Handels-Zeitung*, April 14, 1909, Evening Edition, p.2; Edwin Pears, *Forty Years in Constantinople: The Recollections of Sir Edwin Pears, 1873-1915*, p.266; and, Edwin Pears, *The Crisis in Turkey*," p.511.

[10] Edwin Pears, "Turkey: Developments and Forecasts," p.713; and, Hüseyin Işık, "İkinci Meşrutiyet'in İlânında ve Korunmasında Silahlı Kuvvetlerimizin Rolü," p.54.

[11] Celal Bayar, *Ben de Yazdım, 1*, p.142, and, p.145; "Die Straßenkämpfe in Stambul," *Berliner Tageblatt und Handels-Zeitung*, April 14, 1909, Evening Edition, p.2; "Die Militärrevolution in Konstantinopel: Niederlage des jungtürkischen Comités—Ermordung des Justizministers," *Berliner Tageblatt und Handels-Zeitung*, April 14, 1909, Evening Edition, p.1; "Zur Ermordung Nâzım Paschas," *Berliner Tageblatt und Handels-Zeitung*, April 14, 1909, Evening Edition, p.2; "Das türkische Revolution," *Vossische Zeitung*, April 14, 1909, Evening Edition, p.1; Ahmed Bedevi Kuran, *Osmanlı İmparatorluğunda İnkılâp Hareketleri ve Milli Mücadele*, p.514; Ahmed Bedevi Kuran, *İnkılâp Tarihimiz ve 'Jön Türkler,'* p278; Mevlânzade Rıfat, *31 Mart: Bir İhtilâlin Hikâyesi*, p.43; Edwin Pears, *Forty Years in Constantinople: The Recollections of Sir Edwin Pears, 1873-1915*, p.261; Abdurrahman Şeref, *Son Vak'anüvis Abdurrahman Şeref Efendi Tarihi: II. Meşrutiyet Olayları, 1908-1909*, p.155, and p.165; and, Yusuf Hikmet Bayur, *Türk İnkılâbı Tarihi, 1/2*, p.185.

[12] "Unter den Fenstern des Sultans," *Berliner Tageblatt und Handels-Zeit-*

Throughout the city, the mutineers sought and killed military students wherever they found them. This was more an act of revenge of the ex-officers, who, under Abdülhamid's absolutist regime, had been promoted despite their lack of proper education and experience, and were dismissed from the army following the Revolution.[13]

Apparently, all the mutinied soldiers had received money. Many observers had seen gold in the hands of privates on both April 13 and 14. Most of them were seen in the bazaars, spending large amounts of money which they could have neither earned nor saved. Many rode about in street carriages, and when the cabbies hesitated to take them, they pulled out money to show they could pay.[14]

The April 13 issues of the opposition papers *Serbesti* and *Mizan* contained articles which indicated that their authors had advance knowledge of the events that were to take place on April 13. While *Serbesti* argued for the formation of a new Cabinet along the lines of that of Kâmil Pasha's, *Mizan*'s editorial tried to discredit the Committee of Union and Progress and its management of the country by way of criticising the parliamentary form of government.[15]

That day, the offices of *Tanin* and *Şura-yı Ümmet*, as well as those of the Committee of Union and Progress were stormed and looted while the Women's Club, an affiliate of the Committee of Union and Progress, was closed.[16] The offices of the Committee of Union and Progress had been com-

---

ung, April 16, 1909, Morning Edition, pp.1-2; and, Celal Bayar, *Ben de Yazdım, 1,* pp.142-143. See also, Hasan Amca, *Doğmayan Hürriyet: Bir Devrin İçyüzü, 1908-1918,* p.87; Ahmed Bedevi Kuran, *Osmanlı İmparatorlugunda İnkılâp Hareketleri ve Millî Mücadele,* p.516; Ahmed Bedevi Kuran, *İnkılâp Tarihimiz ve 'Jön Türkler,'* p280; Mevlânzade Rıfat, *31 Mart: Bir İhtilâlin Hikâyesi,* pp.159-160; and, Yusuf Hikmet Bayur, *Türk İnkılâbı Tarihi, 1/2,* pp.191-192.

[13] Celal Bayar, *Ben de Yazdım, 1,* p.144.

[14] "Die Jungtürken vor Konstantinopel: Die Stimmung in der belagerten Stadt," *Berliner Tageblatt und Handels-Zeitung,* April 19, 1909, Morning Edition, pp.1-2; and, Edwin Pears, "The Crisis in Turkey," p.519.

[15] Sina Akşin, *31 Mart Olayı,* pp.28-30.

[16] "The Counter-Revolution and the Fall of Abdul-Hamid," in G. P. Gooch and H. Temperley (Eds.), *British Documents on the Origins of the War, 1898-1914, 5: The Near East,* p.314. These were the only buildings that were destroyed during the reign of terror (Francis McCullagh, *The Fall of Abd-ul-Hamid,* p.137). See also, Edwin Pears, "The Crisis in Turkey," p.511; *idem, Life of Abdul Hamid,* p.313; and, Mevlânzade Rıfat, *31 Mart: Bir İhtilâlin Hikâyesi,* pp.165-166.

pletely wrecked, even the wooden frames having been torn out of the windows. The printing machines of the two Unionist papers, *Tanin* and *Şura-yı Ümmet*, had been destroyed and the type scattered in the streets.[17]

Bent on killing Hüseyin Cahid [Yalçın], counter-revolutionaries instead killed Emir Muhammed Arslan Bey, another deputy in the Chamber, who apparently resembled Yalçın.[18] The latter took refuge in the Russian Embassy, while Cavid Bey hid in the house of a stock broker friend.[19]

The military's lack of response in İstanbul was both noticeable and revealing, indicating that its sympathies lay with the monarchist *coup*. The Grand Vezier, Hüseyin Hilmi Pasha, and the Commander-in-Chief of the First Army Corps, Mahmud Muhtar Pasha, were both to blame for allowing the *coup* to unfold without much resistance.[20] Because of Hüseyin Hilmi Pasha's reputation for having played the Hamidian regime and the European Powers off one another in pre-revo-

---

[17] "*Şura-yı Ümmet ve Tanin,*" *İkdam,* April 2, 1325/April 15, 1909, p.2; Mary A. Poynter, *When Turkey Was Turkey,* p.61; "Die Lage am gestrigen Mittwoch," *Berliner Tageblatt und Handels-Zeitung,* April 15, 1909, Morning Edition, p.1; and, "The Revolution in Turkey: Newspaper Offices Wrecked," *The Times,* April 15, 1909, p.3. See also, Abdurrahman Şeref, *Son Vak'anüvis Abdurrahman Şeref Efendi Tarihi: II. Meşrutiyet Olayları, 1908-1909,* p.156, and pp.163-164; and, Mevlânzade Rıfat, *31 Mart: Bir İhtilâlin Hikâyesi,* pp.165-166.

[18] I/I/56, April 3, 1325/April 16, 1909, *Meclis-i Mebusan Zabıt Ceridesi, 3,* p.22; Babanzade İsmail Hakkı, "Cehennemi Bir Gün," *Tanin,* April 13, 1325/April 26, 1909, reproduced in Hüseyin Cahid Yalçın, "Meşrutiyet Hatıraları, 1908-1918," *Fikir Hareketleri,* 5 (October 26, 1935-April 18, 1936), p.6; Mevlânzade Rıfat, *31 Mart: Bir İhtilâlin Hikâyesi,* p.43; and, Yusuf Hikmet Bayur, *Türk İnkılâbı Tarihi, 1/2,* p.185.

[19] Hüseyin Cahid Yalçın, "Meşrutiyet Hatıraları, 1908-1918," *Fikir Hareketleri,* 5 (October 26, 1935-April 18, 1936), p.7; "Die Militärrevolution in Konstantinopel: Niederlage des jungtürkischen Comités—Ermordung des Justizministers," *Berliner Tageblatt und Handels-Zeitung,* April 14, 1909, Evening Edition, p.1; "Die türkische Revolution," *Vossische Zeitung,* April 14, 1909, Evening Edition, p.1; "The Revolution in Turkey: Fate of Committee Members," *The Times,* April 15, 1909, p.3; and, "Die Lage am gestrigen Mittwoch," *Berliner Tageblatt und Handels-Zeitung,* April 15, 1909, Morning Edition, p.1. See also, Edwin Pears, *Forty Years in Constantinople: The Recollections of Sir Edwin Pears, 1873-1915,* p.266; Mevlânzade Rıfat, *31 Mart: Bir İhtilâlin Hikâyesi,* p.58; and, Yusuf Hikmet Bayur, *Türk İnkılâbı Tarihi, 1/2,* p.186.

[20] The Committee of Union and Progress was of the same opinion. In a proclamation addressed to the nation on the first anniversary of the July 24, 1908 Revolution, the Committee of Union and Progress accused Hüseyin Hilmi Pasha, among others, by saying that "it was the cowardice, indecision and incapacity of these men, who had been believed to be able men and who had been in office for a year, that had opened in the bosom of the Fatherland those two almost mortal wounds—the İstanbul insurrection of April 13, and the tragic calamities of Adana" (Francis McCullagh, *The Fall of Abd-ul-Hamid,* p.79). See also, Mevlânzade Rıfat, *31 Mart: Bir İhtilâlin Hikâyesi,* p.59.

lutionary Macedonia, some conceded that he was probably the worst Grand Vezier Turkey could have had at such a moment.[21]

Murad Bey, editor of *Mizan*, appeared at the Sublime Porte, demanding the resignation of the cabinet as well as that of Ahmed Rıza Bey, the President of the Chamber of Deputies.[22] Ahmed Rıza Bey was forced to resign his Presidency of the Chamber of Deputies.[23] Though still in İstanbul, Ahmed Rıza Bey had been forced into hiding with Talât Bey, Dr. Nâzım Bey, and other leaders of the Committee of Union and Progress.[24] Nonetheless, the Chamber of Deputies met under the presidency of the deputy for Aleppo, Mustafa al-'Ayntabi Efendi.[25] Only twenty-five deputies—almost all of them monarchist—were in attendance.[26]

A monarchist, Mustafa al-'Ayntabi Efendi, the deputy for Aleppo, had published an article in the April 7 issue of *al Islam*, in fact, only its second issue, praising the *shari'a*. The newspaper had printed other reactionary editorials in which the Constitution and the constitutional regime was strongly criticised.[27]

---

[21] Francis McCullagh, *The Fall of Abd-ul-Hamid*, pp.92-93.

[22] Ahmed Rıza, *Meclis-i Mebusan ve Ayan Reisi Ahmed Rıza Bey'in Anıları*, p.36. See also, Sina Akşin, *31 Mart Olayı*, p.42.

[23] "Die Militärrevolution in Konstantinopel," *Berliner Tageblatt und Handels-Zeitung*, April 14, 1909, Morning Edition, pp.1-2; Ahmed Rıza, *Meclis-i Mebusan ve Ayan Reisi Ahmed Rıza Bey'in Anıları*, pp.36-37. His letter of resignation was printed in the *Takvim-i Vekayi* of April 7, 1325/April 20, 1909 (Celal Bayar, *Ben de Yazdım*, *1*, p.156n). See also, Mevlânzade Rıfat, *31 Mart: Bir İhtilâlin Hikâyesi*, pp.89-90; and, Hüseyin Cahid Yalçın, "Meşrutiyet Hatıraları, 1908-1918," *Fikir Hareketleri*, *5* (October 26, 1935-April 18, 1936), p.37.

[24] Ahmed Rıza, *Meclis-i Mebusan ve Ayan Reisi Ahmed Rıza Bey'in Anıları*, p.37; and, A. A. Türkei 159, No.2/114, Telegram from Marschall, Pera, April 13, 1909. See also, "Die Militärrevolution in Konstantinopel: Niederlage des jungtürkischen Comités—Ermordung des Justizministers," *Berliner Tageblatt und Handels-Zeitung*, April 14, 1909, Evening Edition, p.1; "Das türkische Revolution," *Vossische Zeitung*, April 14, 1909, Evening Edition, p.1; "Die Lage am gestrigen Mittwoch," *Berliner Tageblatt und Handels-Zeitung*, April 15, 1909, Morning Edition, p.1; Sina Akşin, *31 Mart Olayı*, p.44n; Edwin Pears, *Forty Years in Constantinople: The Recollections of Sir Edwin Pears, 1873-1915*, p.266; and, Mevlânzade Rıfat, *31 Mart: Bir İhtilâlin Hikâyesi*, p.58. See also, Yusuf Hikmet Bayur, *Türk İnkılâbı Tarihi*, *1/2*, pp.185-186.

[25] Sina Akşin, *31 Mart Olayı*, p.44.

[26] "Die Lage am gestrigen Mittwoch," *Berliner Tageblatt und Handels-Zeitung*, April 15, 1909, No.2/114, Morning Edition, p.1. Bayur alleges that about forty deputies had assembled in the Chamber (Yusuf Hikmet Bayur, *Türk İnkılâbı Tarihi*, *1/2*, p.186).

[27] *al Islam* was the organ of the newly established religious association, al Islam Cemiyeti, whose structure of organization was based on Prince Sabahaddin's principles (Sina Akşin, *31 Mart Olayı*, p.45n).

The deputies were convened to 'discuss' the demands of the monarchist Liberal Union which had been forwarded to the mutinied soldiers for submission to the Chamber. The monarchist opposition demanded strict adherence to the rules of *shari'a*; the dismissals of the Grand Vezier, the Minister of War, the Commander of the First Army Corps, the Commander of Taşkışla barracks, and the resignation of the President of the Chamber of Deputies.[28] The monarchists also called for the dismissal of Ahmed Rıza Bey, Hüseyin Cahid [Yalçın], Rahmi [Aslan], Talât Bey, and Cavid Bey—in effect, the leadership of the Committee of Union and Progress—from the Chamber of Deputies as well as the dissolution of their party. Finally, Kâmil Pasha was to be appointed Grand Vezier, Nâzım Pasha, Minister of War, and İsmail Kemal Bey, President of the Chamber of Deputies.[29]

İsmail Kemal Bey urged the deputies to give the Hüseyin Hilmi Pasha Cabinet a vote of no confidence, and sending the result immediately to Abdülhamid. Those few Unionist deputies in attendance—Babanzade İsmail Hakkı, Bedros Haladjian, and Vartkes Serengülyan—tried to dissuade their colleagues.[30] Later in the day, eighty monarchist deputies would succeed in passing a resolution demanding the Cabinet to step down.[31] İsmail Kemal Bey also urged the Chamber to elect a temporary Minister of War. He nominated İsmail Hakkı [Mumcu] Pasha, the monarchist deputy for Amasya, as the candidate for the post of Acting Minister of War, and the deputies of the monarchist Liberal Union—the only deputies sitting in the Chamber—immediately accepted.[32] İsmail Kemal

---

[28]   Sina Akşin, *31 Mart Olayı*, p.45.
[29]   "Die Militärrevolution in Konstantinopel: Niederlage des jungtürkischen Comités—Ermordung des Justizministers," *Berliner Tageblatt und Handels-Zeitung*, April 14, 1909, Evening Edition, p.1; "Bericht unseres Korrespondenten," *Berliner Tageblatt und Handels-Zeitung*, April 14, 1909, Evening Edition, p.2. See also, Mevlânzade Rıfat, *31 Mart: Bir İhtilâlin Hikâyesi*, pp.61-62.
[30]   Sina Akşin, *31 Mart Olayı*, p.47. Babanzade İsmail Hakkı, "Cehennemi Bir Gün," *Tanin*, April 13, 1325/April 26, 1909, reproduced in Hüseyin Cahid Yalçın, "Meşrutiyet Hatıraları, 1908-1918," *Fikir Hareketleri*, 4 (April 25-October 19, 1935), p.405.
[31]   "Die Militärrevolution in Konstantinopel: Niederlage des jungtürkischen Comités—Ermordung des Justizministers," *Berliner Tageblatt und Handels-Zeitung*, April 14, 1909, Evening Edition, p.1; "Vom türkischen Parlament," *Vossische Zeitung*, April 16, 1909, Evening Edition, p.2; and, Sina Akşin, *31 Mart Olayı*, p.48.
[32]   Ismail Kemal, *The Memoirs of Ismail Kemal Bey*, pp.334-335; and, Mev

was then elected to the presidency of the Chamber by the votes of the sixty Liberal Union deputies.[33]

At two o'clock that afternoon, Hüseyin Hilmi Pasha tendered his resignation.[34] Abdülhamid immediately accepted his resignation along with those of his Cabinet. The Ministers were then summoned to the Palace to sign their resignation letters later in the afternoon, after which, Tevfik Pasha was appointed the new Grand Vezier.[35]

Chief of Staff İzzet Pasha felt that a permanent Minister of War had to be appointed as quickly as possible. He was offered the job and accepted. Having secured the nomination of İsmail Hakkı [Mumcu] Pasha as Acting Minister of War, İsmail Kemal Bey now ardently supported İzzet Pasha's nomination.[36]

At about the same time, it was announced that Abdülhamid had pardoned those soldiers who had mutinied, thus legitimating the *coup* and absolving those involved of all charges.[37] Though by no means a supporter of the Unionists, Mahmud Muhtar Pasha, the Commander of the First Army Corps, had proposed resisting the mutiny with armed force, which would have, in effect, crushed the *coup*. This was the last thing that the monarchists, who were bent on accomplishing the fall of the constitutionally formed government, wanted. Therefore, he was ordered not to use force, and that evening he was dismissed from command.[38] Later, İsmail

---

lânzade Rıfat, *31 Mart: Bir İhtilâlin Hikâyesi*, pp.69-71.

[33] Ismail Kemal, *The Memoirs of Ismail Kemal Bey*, p.335; and, Mevlânzade Rıfat, *31 Mart: Bir İhtilâlin Hikâyesi*, pp.79-80.

[34] "Military Revolt in Turkey: Resignation of Hilmi," *The Times*, April 14, 1909, p.5; and, Sina Akşin, *31 Mart Olayı*, pp.42-43.

[35] "Suret-i İrade-i Seniye," *İkdam*, April 1, 1325/April 14, 1909, p.1; "Die Militärrevolution in Konstantinopel: Niederlage des jungtürkischen Comités—Ermordung des Justizministers," *Berliner Tageblatt und Handels-Zeitung*, April 14, 1909, Evening Edition, p.1. "Die Lage am gestrigen Mittwoch," *Berliner Tageblatt und Handels-Zeitung*, April 15, 1909, Morning Edition, p.1. See also, Sina Akşin, *31 Mart Olayı*, p.43, Mevlânzade Rıfat, *31 Mart: Bir İhtilâlin Hikâyesi*, p.87 and p.95; Edwin Pears, *Forty Years in Constantinople: The Recollections of Sir Edwin Pears, 1873-1915*, p.266; and, Hüseyin Cahid Yalçın, "Meşrutiyet Hatıraları, 1908-1918," *Fikir Hareketleri*, 5 (October 26, 1935-April 18, 1936), p.37. With the same imperial decree Edhem Pasha was appointed Minister of War (Hüseyin Cahid Yalçın, "Meşrutiyet Hatıraları, 1908-1918," *Fikir Hareketleri*, 5 (October 26, 1935-April 18, 1936), p.37).

[36] Sina Akşin, *31 Mart Olayı*, pp.36-38.

[37] Yusuf Hikmet Bayur, *Türk İnkılâbı Tarihi*, 1/2, p.187; and, "The Revolution in Turkey: Behaviour of the Troops," *The Times*, April 15, 1909, p.3.

[38] Sina Akşin, *31 Mart Olayı*, pp.36-38; and, "The Revolution in Turkey: Be-

Kemal Bey publicly announced that Edhem Pasha would be the new Minister of War.[39]

At half past ten at night, Edhem Pasha arrived in the Hagia Sophia Square and was greeted with loud cheers by the mutineers, whom he addressed, urging that they should return calmly to barracks and announcing his appointment as Minister of War. Some fifteen thousand rifles were discharged during the next half hour in token of joy by the soldiers.[40]

The Liberal Union wanted to have Kâmil Pasha as Grand Vezier and Nâzım Pasha as the Minister of War.[41] Although the mutineers had no clear idea who they supported, the *İkdam* of April 14 wrote that the troops wanted to see these pashas in the new cabinet.[42] *Osmanlı*, another monarchist organ, also wrote that the mutineers wanted İsmail Kemal Bey to replace Ahmed Rıza Bey as the President of the Chamber. At the same time, the paper also announced—prematurely—that Kâmil Pasha had been appointed Grand Vezier and Nâzım Pasha, Minister of War.[43] Meanwhile, *Mizan* warmly welcomed the *coup d'état*, congratulating the military for its restraint and orderliness, while other monarchist papers, among them *Volkan*, printed editorials also praising the *coup*, and condemning the Committee of Union and Progress.[44]

By the afternoon of April 14, Tevfik Pasha had formed his Cabinet.[45] Of the new appointees, Zihni Pasha, President of the

---

haviour of the Troops," *The Times*, April 15, 1909, p.3. See also, Edwin Pears, *Forty Years in Constantinople: The Recollections of Sir Edwin Pears, 1873-1915*, pp.261-264.

[39] "Die Militärrevolution in Konstantinopel: Niederlage des jungtürkischen Comités—Ermordung des Justizministers," *Berliner Tageblatt und Handels-Zeitung*, April 14, 1909, Evening Edition, p.1; and, Sina Akşin, *31 Mart Olayı*, p.53.

[40] "Das türkische Revolution," *Vossische Zeitung*, April 14, 1909, Evening Edition, p.1; "The Revolution in Turkey: Behaviour of the Troops," *The Times*, April 15, 1909, p.3; Mevlânzade Rıfat, *31 Mart: Bir İhtilâlin Hikâyesi*, p.64; and, Yusuf Hikmet Bayur, *Türk İnkılâbı Tarihi*, 1/2, p.188.

[41] "Die Militärrevolution in Konstantinopel: Niederlage des jungtürkischen Comités—Ermordung des Justizministers," *Berliner Tageblatt und Handels-Zeitung*, April 14, 1909, Evening Edition, p.1. See also, Mevlânzade Rıfat, *31 Mart: Bir İhtilâlin Hikâyesi*.

[42] Sina Akşin, *31 Mart Olayı*, p.46; and, Hüseyin Cahid Yalçın, "Meşrutiyet Hatıraları, 1908-1918," *Fikirt Hareketleri*, 5 (October 26, 1935-April 18, 1936), p.22.

[43] Sina Akşin, *31 Mart Olayı*, p.46.

[44] Sina Akşin, *31 Mart Olayı*, pp.67-68.

[45] A. A. Türkei 159, No.2/125, Telegram, Pera, April 14, 1909; "Suret-i Hatt-ı

Council, would resign within twenty-four hours, as would Emin Pasha, Minister of the Navy, who was refused admittance to the Admiralty by the sailors.[46]

Once again, Abdülhamid insisted on retaining the exclusive right to appoint the Ministers of War and of the Navy. Despite this, Tevfik Pasha allegedly opposed the Sultan on the ground of constitutionality.[47] Nonetheless, Abdülhamid clearly controlled the military appointments made after the *coup*.

Tevfik Pasha offered the Ministry of Justice to İsmail Kemal Bey. İsmail Kemal Bey, however, rejected the offer, believing that the presidency of the Chamber of Deputies would be his after Ahmed Rıza Bey's dismissal from that office.[48] Additionally, Ömer Rüşdü Pasha, who had been offered the post of Commander of the First Army Corps, declined the offer. Upon hearing this, İsmail Kemal Bey used his influence in Nâzım Pasha's favour, and Nâzım Pasha was duly appointed Commander of the First Army Corps. As its attempts to get him appointed Minister of War had failed, this was a partial victory for the Liberal Union.[49]

The remainder of the Tevfik Pasha Cabinet consisted of the following: Sheikh-ul-Islam, Ziyaeddin Efendi; Minister of the Interior, Rauf Pasha (appointed April 16); Minister for Foreign Affairs, Rıfat Pasha; Minister of War, Edhem Pasha; Minister of the Navy, Emin Pasha; Minister of Justice, Hasan Fehmi Pasha (resigned April 21); President of the Council of State, Zihni Pasha (resigned April 15), Raif Pasha (resigned April 16); Minister of Commerce and Public Works, Gabriel Nou-

Hümayun," *Ikdam*, April 2, 1325/April 15, 1909, p.1; "Das neue türkische Kabinett," *Berliner Tageblatt und Handels-Zeitung*, April 15, 1909, Morning Edition, p.1; "Das neue Kabinett," *Osmanischer Lloyd*, April 15, 1909, p.1; and, "Vom türkischen Parlament," *Vossische Zeitung*, April 16, 1909, Evening Edition, p.2. See also, Mevlânzade Rıfat, *31 Mart: Bir İhtilâlin Hikâyesi*, pp.97-98; and, Yusuf Hikmet Bayur, *Türk İnkılâbı Tarihi*, 1/2, p.188.

[46] "Die Gärung in der Türkei: Ernste Stimmung in Konstantinopel," *Berliner Tageblatt und Handels-Zeitung*, April 16, 1909, Evening Edition, p.4; and, "The Counter-Revolution and the Fall of Abdul-Hamid," in G. P. Gooch and H. Temperley (Eds.), *British Documents on the Origins of the War, 1898-1914, 5: The Near East*, p.314.

[47] Sina Akşin, *31 Mart Olayı*, p.57; and, Yusuf Hikmet Bayur, *Türk İnkılâbı Taihi*, 1/2, pp.188-189.

[48] Sina Akşin, *31 Mart Olayı*, pp.57-58.

[49] Sina Akşin, *31 Mart Olayı*, pp.59-60; and, "The Revolution in Turkey," *The Times*, April 16, 1909, p.3.

radunghian; Minister of Finance, Nuri Bey; Minister of Education, Abdurrahman Şeref Bey; Minister of Forests, Mines, and Agriculture, Dimitraki Mavrocordato; Minister of Pious Foundations, Khalil Hammada Pasha.[50]

Although a Cabinet had at length been formed, the real power in the capital was the Sultan. Within a few days, stories to this effect began to circulate. Pointing out the fact that Palace spies had again been at work and that each soldier of the Fourth Rifle Battalion had received five liras, many believed that the mutiny in İstanbul had been engineered from the Palace itself. And the fact that the Sultan had issued a complete pardon to the mutineers was considered proof of Abdülhamid's complicity.[51]

The Committee of Union and Progress was quick in trying to enlighten public opinion as to the true nature of recent events. While the monarchists maintained the fiction that the *coup* was just a party movement against the Committee of Union and Progress, the Unionists insisted that the new constitutional regime was under attack, and that the new Cabinet represented the first reactionary step towards the abolishing of the Constitution and the re-establishment of absolute monarchy.[52] Unionist representatives were immediately dispatched to the provinces in an effort to explain the true nature of the events and gather support for the constitutional regime.[53] In response, the Government issued a series of manifestos which

---

[50] "Suret-i Hatt-ı Hümayun," *İkdam*, April 2, 1325/April 15, 1909, p.1; "Das neue türkische Kabinett," *Berliner Tageblatt und Handels-Zeitung*, April 15, 1909, Morning Edition, p.1; "The Revolution in Turkey: Composition of the New Cabinet," *The Times*, April 15, 1909, p.3; "Das neue Kabinett," *Osmanischer Lloyd*, April 15, 1909, p.1; and, Ali Cevad, *İkinci Meşrutiyetin İlânı ve Otuzbir Mart Hadisesi*, p.191. Dimitraki Mavrocordato and Gabriel Noradunghian had the same posts in the previous cabinet.

[51] "The Counter-Revolution and the Fall of Abdul-Hamid," in G. P. Gooch and H. Temperley (Eds.), *British Documents on the Origins of the War, 1898-1914*, 5: *The Near East*, p.315; and, Edwin Pears, *Forty Years in Constantinople: The Recollections of Sir Edwin Pears, 1873-1915*, p.284.

[52] "Der Vormarsch der Jungtürken: Ein jungtürkisches Ultimatum," *Berliner Tageblatt und Handels-Zeitung*, April 17, 1909, Morning Edition, p.1; and, "The Counter-Revolution and the Fall of Abdul-Hamid," in G. P. Gooch and H. Temperley (Eds.), *British Documents on the Origins of the War, 1898-1914*, 5: *The Near East*, p.315. See also, Abdurrahman Şeref, *Son Vak'anüvis Abdurrahman Şeref Efendi Tarihi: II. Meşrutiyet Olayları, 1908-1909*, p.36.

[53] "The Counter-Revolution and the Fall of Abdul-Hamid," in G. P. Gooch and H. Temperley (Eds.), *British Documents on the Origins of the War, 1898-1914*, 5: *The Near East*, p.315.

stated that the Constitution was in no way threatened, pointing to the fact that the Chamber was sitting as usual.[54] Monarchist propaganda, however, had little effect. The manifestos of the Committee of Union and Progress had not only been the first to arrive, but representatives had also seen to it that Government propaganda and pro-government newspapers would not reach the provinces. The proclamations of the Government and the Chamber, telegraphed to all the provincial authorities, were equally ineffectual.[55] Reports from the European provinces indicated that the recent events in İstanbul were considered to be a *coup d'etat* and a reaction to the Constitution. Loyalist troops of the Third Army Corps at Salonica were apparently preparing to start for the capital.[56] In the Anatolian provinces, support for the Unionists and the Constitution was said to be equally unanimous.[57]

In Salonica, the Central Committee of the Committee of Union and Progress and the Third Army Corps had taken action the moment news of the *coup* arrived.[58] Midhat Şükrü [Bleda], Secretary General of the Committee of Union and Progress, had been kept informed of all developments. He, in turn, communicated with the Unionist Governor of Edirne, Reşid Pasha, and with Mahmud Şevket Pasha.[59] At a meeting

---

[54] "The Counter-Revolution and the Fall of Abdul-Hamid," in G. P. Gooch and H. Temperley (Eds.), *British Documents on the Origins of the War, 1898-1914, 5: The Near East*, p.315; and, Yusuf Hikmet Bayur, *Türk İnkılâbı Tarihi, 1/2*, pp.192-193.

[55] "The Counter-Revolution and the Fall of Abdul-Hamid," in G. P. Gooch and H. Temperley (Eds.), *British Documents on the Origins of the War, 1898-1914, 5: The Near East*, p.316; Abdurrahman Şeref, *Son Vak'anüvis Abdurrahman Şeref Efendi Tarihi: II. Meşrutiyet Olayları, 1908-1909*, pp.36-37; and, Yusuf Hikmet Bayur, *Türk İnkılâbı Tarihi, 1/2*, p.193.

[56] "Hilfsaktion der Jungtürken in Saloniki," *Berliner Tageblatt und Handels-Zeitung*, April 15, 1909, Morning Edition, pp.1-2; and, "The Counter-Revolution and the Fall of Abdul-Hamid," in G. P. Gooch and H. Temperley (Eds.), *British Documents on the Origins of the War, 1898-1914, 5: The Near East*, p.316.

[57] "Der Vormarsch der Jungtürken: Ein jungtürkisches Ultimatum," *Berliner Tageblatt und Handels-Zeitung*, April 17, 1909, Morning Edition, p.1; and, "The Counter-Revolution and the Fall of Abdul-Hamid," in G. P. Gooch and H. Temperley (Eds.), *British Documents on the Origins of the War, 1898-1914, 5: The Near East*, p.316.

[58] "Hilfsaktion der Jungtürken in Saloniki," *Berliner Tageblatt und Handels-Zeitung*, April 15, 1909, Morning Edition, pp.1-2; "Die Anarchie im ottomanischen Reiche: Die Gegenaktion in Saloniki und Adrianopel," *Berliner Tageblatt und Handels-Zeitung*, April 15, 1909, Evening Edition, p.4; "Der Vormarsch der Jungtürken: Ein jungtürkisches Ultimatum," *Berliner Tageblatt und Handels-Zeitung*, April 17, 1909, Morning Edition, p.1; and, Sina Akşin, *31 Mart Olayı*, p.55.

[59] Midhat Şükrü Bleda and Salahattin Güngör, "İttihat ve Terakki'nin Kâtib-i Umumisi Midhat Şükrü Hatıralarını Anlatıyor," *İstanbul Ekspres*, November 24,

with Mahmud Şevket Pasha, it was decided that troops dispatched from Rumelia would be mobilised to crush the *coup*.[60] Mahmud Şevket Pasha then sent a telegram informing the Ministry of War that preparations were being made to march on İstanbul. Edhem Pasha, the newly appointed Minister of War, replied that because the events in the capital was under control, there was no need for such an action.[61]

On April 14, a demonstration was held in Salonica, the stronghold of the Committee of Union and Progress. Thirty thousand people attended, publicly swearing to protect the Constitution. Many volunteered to enlist in the fight against the monarchist *coup*.[62]

Praising the *coup*, the *İkdam* of April 15 also quoted several monarchist Greek papers which supported the recent developments in the capital.[63] The *Volkan* of April 15 also praised the *coup* and congratulated the military for its restrained behaviour.[64] *Volkan* also prematurely announced that İsmail Kemal Bey had been 'appointed' the new President of the Chamber of Deputies, while Ali Kemal and Murad Beys would be elected deputies, replacing Hüseyin Cahid [Yalçın] and Cavid Bey who had fled. Finally, the paper hinted that Murad Bey might enter the Cabinet.[65]

The Sultan, the Grand Vezierate, and the Chamber of Deputies, however, all received an increasing number of telegrams denouncing the counter-revolutionary *coup* attempt. These poured in from most of the towns and cities of Turkey, though particularly from Rumelia. Some were sent by local branches of the Committee of Union and Progress, some by the local population, and others by members of provincial military clubs. Some were even sent by the provincial civilian bureaucracy. Clearly, the Committee of Union and Progress had

1952, quoted in Sina Akşin, *31 Mart Olayı*, p.56n.
    [60] Sina Akşin, *31 Mart Olayı*, p.56.
    [61] Sina Akşin, *31 Mart Olayı*, p.64.
    [62] Sina Akşin, *31 Mart Olayı*, p.65; "The Revolution in Turkey: Resistance Threatened at Salonica," *The Times*, April 16, 1909, p.3; and, "Selânik'te Neler Cereyan Etti?" *İkdam*, April 7, 1325/April 20, 1909, p.2.
    [63] Sina Akşin, *31 Mart Olayı*, p.69.
    [64] Sina Akşin, *31 Mart Olayı*, p.70.
    [65] *Volkan*, April 15, 1909, quoted in Sina Akşin, *31 Mart Olayı*, p.63n.

orchestrated this latest campaign against the Government.[66] In one of its telegrams sent to the Sultan, the Central Committee of the Committee of Union and Progress informed Abdül-hamid that if he wanted to avoid bloodshed, he would have to restore the Hüseyin Hilmi Pasha Cabinet to power and re-institute Ahmed Rıza Bey to the presidency of the Chamber of Deputies.[67] Another telegram of the Central Committee, addressed to the Sultan, threatened all those who were responsible for the *coup*. In its third telegram, the Central Committee of the Committee of Union and Progress the Unionists blamed Ahmed Cevdet Bey, the owner of *İkdam*, Ali Kemal Bey, its editor, Murad Bey, editor of *Mizan*, Abdullah Zühdü, owner of *Yeni Gazete*, Said Pasha, son of Kâmil Pasha, Mevlânzade Rıfat, and Derviş Vahdeti for the *coup*, adding that Abdülhamid would be held accountable if these were to escape from justice.[68]

The army of constitutional forces which had assembled at Salonica, left on the night of April 15. Tevfik Pasha, the Grand Vezier, Nâzım Pasha, the Minister of War, and İzzet Pasha, Chief of Staff, were immediately informed.[69]

While leading members of the monarchist Government along with Nâzım Pasha, the newly appointed Commander of the First Army Corps stationed at İstanbul, publicly expressed optimism for their success, many were cognisant of the shakiness of their position, and, therefore, were uneasy.

The monarchists were, nevertheless, powerful enough to threaten even the moderate supporters of the constitutional regime. On April 16, four naval officers—including the late Minister of the Navy, Arif Hikmet Pasha—were forced to take asylum on board a British ship and leave the country.[70] Mah-

---

[66] Yusuf Hikmet Bayur, *Türk İnkılâbı Tarihi, 1/2*, p.193; and, Sina Akşin, *31 Mart Olayı*, p.92.

[67] "Der Vormarsch der Jungtürken: Ein jungtürkisches Ultimatum," *Berliner Tageblatt und Handels-Zeitung*, April 17, 1909, Morning Edition, p.1; and, Sina Akşin, *31 Mart Olayı*, p.93.

[68] Sina Akşin, *31 Mart Olayı*, p.93.

[69] "Der Vormarsch der Jungtürken: Die jungtürkische Expedition gegen Konstantinopel," *Berliner Tageblatt und Handels-Zeitung*, April 17, 1909, Morning Edition, p.1; and, Sina Akşin, *31 Mart Olayı*, p.85.

[70] "The Counter-Revolution and the Fall of Abdul-Hamid," in G. P. Gooch and H. Temperley (Eds.), *British Documents on the Origins of the War, 1898-1914, 5*:

mud Muhtar Pasha, who as Commander of the First Army
Corps had recommended the use of force against the mutineers, took refuge with Sir William Whittall, an English
friend in İstanbul, and narrowly escaped with his life, the
house having been surrounded by monarchist troops.[71]

That day, Rauf Pasha, Governor of the Aydın province and
ex-Commissioner General of Egypt, was appointed the new
Minister of the Interior.[72] Later, he, along with the other
members of the new Cabinet, was received in the Yıldız
Palace and was graciously recognised by the Sultan as the
duly appointed Minister of the Interior.[73] With the exception of
the Sultan and the monarchist members of the Chamber of
Deputies, however, no one seemed to acknowledge his appointment as legitimate. Provincial governors largely disre-
garded his circulars, and in some cases, his telegrams were
returned to İstanbul unopened. Many governors simply
replied that they did not recognise him as the Minister of the
Interior.[74] Others accused the Tevfik Pasha Cabinet of uncon-
stitutionality, urged its resignation, and demanded the restoration of the constitutionally established Cabinet of Hüseyin Hilmi Pasha. Some telegrams indicated that the Liberal Union
and the Mohammedan Union were to be held responsible for
the *coup*.[75]

The most important of these telegrams was sent by İbrahim
Pasha, Commander of the Fourth Army Corps stationed at
Erzincan, who attacked both the *coup* and the Cabinet, and de-
clared that the Fourth Army Corps also was ready to march

The Near East, pp.315-316.

[71] Edwin Pears, *Forty Years in Constantinople: The Recollections of Sir Edwin Pears, 1873-1915*, pp.261-264; and, "The Counter-Revolution and the Fall of Abdul-Hamid," in G. P. Gooch and H. Temperley (Eds.), *British Documents on the
Origins of the War, 1898-1914, 5: The Near East*, p.316; Mary A. Poynter, *When
Turkey Was Turkey*, pp.61-62; and, Abdurrahman Şeref, *Son Vak'anüvis Abdurrahman Şeref Efendi Tarihi: II. Meşrutiyet Olayları, 1908-1909*, p.167.
[72] "Der Sultan und die Meuterer," *Berliner Tageblatt und Handels-Zeitung*,
April 17, 1909, Morning Edition, p.2; and, Cemal Kutay, *Üç Paşalar Kavgası*, p.69.
Sina Akşin, *31 Mart Olayı*, p.109.
[73] Francis McCullagh, *The Fall of Abd-ul-Hamid*, p.180; Cemal Kutay, *Üç Paşalar Kavgası*, p.69; and, Sina Akşin, *31 Mart Olayı*, p.107.
[74] Francis McCullagh, *The Fall of Abd-ul-Hamid*, pp.180-181.
[75] İsmail Hami Danişmend, *Sadr-ı-a'zam Tevfik Paşa'nın Dosyasındaki Resmi ve Hususi Vesikalara Göre: 31 Mart Vak'ası*, pp.34-83. See also, Sina Akşin, *31
Mart Olayı*, pp.107-108. Swenson, who has a totally misleading interpretation of
the counter-revolutionary coup attempt of March 31, alleges that the Tevfik Pasha
Cabinet was a legitimate government.

on İstanbul to restore the Constitution.[76] The Tevfik Pasha Cabinet tried in vain to restore confidence in itself by issuing telegrams to the provinces which claimed that all was well, that the Constitution was still in force, that the new Cabinet contained seven Ministers from the previous Cabinet, and that its policies would be the same.[77]

With one hundred and eighty-eight members in attendance, the Chamber of Deputies met and 'accepted' the resignation of Ahmed Rıza Bey.[78] The Chamber, however, could not elect a new President in his place as none of the five candidates—Mustafa al-'Ayntabi Efendi, deputy for Aleppo, Nail Bey, deputy for Canik, İsmail Kemal Bey, deputy for Berat, Ahmed Mahir Efendi, deputy for Kastamonu, and Şefik Bey, deputy for Karesi—could muster enough votes to gain the necessary half of the deputies in attendance.[79] At an impasse, the Chamber elected its oldest member Ali Naki Efendi, deputy for Trabzon, as acting President. The Chamber then proclaimed that it was 'upholding the principles of the Constitution,' at the same time, forgiving the mutiny as the product of public dissatisfaction with Unionist policy.[80]

Later, during the same proceedings, Krikor Zohrab, the monarchist deputy for İstanbul, read a petition which supported the *coup* and bore the signatures of thousands of soldiers from the First, Second, Third, Fourth, Fifth, Sixth, and Seventh Army Corps. On the one hand, the petition indicated that support for the *coup* was widespread among the military; on

---

[76] *Takvim-i Vekayi*, April 8, 1325/April 21, 1909, cited in Sina Akşin, *31 Mart Olayı*, p.109.

[77] Sina Akşin, *31 Mart Olayı*, p.109.

[78] I/I/56, April 3, 1325/April 16, 1909, *Meclis-i Mebusan Zabıt Ceridesi*, 3, p.23; "Die Gärung in der Türkei: Eine Proklamation des türkischen Parlaments," *Berliner Tageblatt und Handels-Zeitung*, April 16, 1909, Evening Edition, p.4; and, Sina Akşin, *31 Mart Olayı*, p.75.

[79] Cemal Kutay, *Üç Paşalar Kavgası*, p.69. Mustafa Efendi received 93 votes, Nail Bey, 82, Ismail Kemal Bey, 68, Ahmed Mahir Efendi, 54, and Şefik Bey 54. 95 votes were required to get elected (I/I/56, April 3, 1325/April 16, 1909, *Meclis-i Mebusan Zabıt Ceridesi*, 3, p.23; "Die Gärung in der Türkei: Eine Proklamation des türkischen Parlaments," *Berliner Tageblatt und Handels-Zeitung*, April 16, 1909, Evening Edition, p.4; and, Sina Akşin, *31 Mart Olayı*, pp.75-76).

[80] Cemal Kutay, *Üç Paşalar Kavgası*, p.69. Ali Cevad, *İkinci Meşrutiyetin İlânı ve Otuzbir Mart Hadisesi*, pp.132-133. Sina Akşin, *31 Mart Olayı*, p.76. For the complete text of the proclamation see "Mebusan Beyannamesi," *İkdam*, April 3, 1325/April 16, 1909, p.1—which is also reproduced in Hüseyin Cahid Yalçın, "Meşrutiyet Hatıraları, 1908-1918," *Fikir Hareketleri*, 5 (October 26, 1935-April 18, 1936), p.101.

the other hand, it suggested that the *coup* had been prepared well in advance and that conspiracy had reached to every army corps spread in the country.[81]

The Chamber, however, also received a telegram from Janina in support of the constitutional regime and the Committee of Union and Progress, and called for the immediate resignation of the Tevfik Pasha Cabinet and the reinstatement of the old Cabinet. Despite monarchist efforts to have it read in closed session, the telegram was read in the Chamber. It ended with the threat of military action against the capital.[82]

By now, under Mahmud Şevket Pasha's command, the two battalions loyal to the constitutional regime which had left Salonica on the night of April 15 had taken possession of the Salonica-Demotika railway.[83] At the outset, it seemed almost certain that the Macedonians could only enter İstanbul over the dead bodies of the Edirne troops. In the first place, the Unionists had never been strong in the Second Army Corps, whose former Commander, Nâzım Pasha, was no friend of the Committee of Union and Progress, and had sternly refused to allow his officers to join any political association, or to mix themselves up in any way with politics. Secondly, antagonism between the two army corps was high due to the fact that it was the Salonica officers who had induced the Chamber to oust Kâmil Pasha in February over the issue of Nâzım Pasha's appointment to the Ministry of War. Finally, the Second Army Corps was numerically superior to the Third Army Corps.[84] Midhat Şükrü [Bleda] went to Edirne to assess the situation and reported that the Edirne troops would support

[81] I/I/56, April 3, 1325/April 16, 1909, *Meclis-i Mebusan Zabıt Ceridesi*, 3, pp.24-26.

[82] I/I/56, April 3, 1325/April 16, 1909, *Meclis-i Mebusan Zabıt Ceridesi*, 3, pp.26-27; "Die Aussichten der jungtürkischen Gegenaktion," *Berliner Tageblatt und Handels-Zeitung*, April 16, 1909, Morning Edition, p.1; "Vom türkischen Parlament," *Vossische Zeitung*, April 16, 1909, Evening Edition, p.2; and, Sina Akşin, *31 Mart Olayı*, p.82. For the text of the telegramme sent from Janina, see Hüseyin Cahid Yalçın, "Meşrutiyet Hatıraları, 1908-1918," *Fikir Hareketleri*, 5 (October 26, 1935-April 18, 1936), pp.101-102. See also, Yusuf Hikmet Bayur, *Türk Inkılâbı Tarihi*, 1/2, p.194, where the date given is wrong.

[83] "The Counter-Revolution and the Fall of Abdul-Hamid," in G. P. Gooch and H. Temperley (Eds.), *British Documents on the Origins of the War, 1898-1914*, 5: *The Near East*, p.316.

[84] Francis McCullagh, *The Fall of Abd-ul-Hamid*, p.158.

the Third Army Corps.[85]

On the afternoon of April 16, two military trains, consisting of forty-seven carriages carrying troops numbering fifteen thousand soldiers loyal to the Constitution, had arrived at Çatalca, only seventy-two kilometres from İstanbul.[86] One of these had gone on to Isparta Kule, and more were reportedly on their way both from Edirne and Salonica. A great Constitutionalist army was assembling in the environs of İstanbul.[87]

Members of the Liberal Union met with representatives of the Mohammedan Union, the Albanian Union, the Kurdish Club, and the Albanian dominated Üsküb and Scutari branches as well as the Edirne branch of the Committee of Union and Progress to discuss the elimination of the Committee of Union and Progress from the political arena. The last three groups had broken away from the central Committee of the Union and Progress during the preceding two weeks apparently in consequence of the dissatisfaction felt with the policy of its leaders, especially Ahmed Rıza Bey and Hüseyin Cahid [Yalçın]. They decided to send a deputation to Salonica to inform the Unionists of their intention.[88] This deputation never left İstanbul.

About forty deputies with monarchist leanings held a meeting and decided to send deputations into the various provincial centres to allay concern for the Constitution's safety. The following morning, however, it was clear that such action was already too late. Only one group of deputies actually left—to meet with the loyalist troops who were expected at Çatalca.[89]

---

[85] Midhat Şükrü Bleda and Salahattin Güngör, "İttihat ve Terakki'nin Kâtib-i Umumisi Midhat Şükrü Hatıralarını Anlatıyor," *İstanbul Ekspres*, November 25, 1952, quoted in Sina Akşin, *31 Mart Olayı*, p.85.

[86] "Der Vormarsch der Jungtürken: Die jungtürkische Expedition gegen Konstantinopel," *Berliner Tageblatt und Handels-Zeitung*, April 17, 1909, Morning Edition, p.1; "Der jungtürkische Versuch eines Gegenschlages," *Vossische Zeitung*, April 17, 1909, Evening Edition, p.1; Edwin Pears, "The Crisis in Turkey," p.525; and, Francis McCullagh, *The Fall of Abd-ul-Hamid*, p.170.

[87] Francis McCullagh, *The Fall of Abd-ul-Hamid*, p.170; and, "Die jungtürkische Aktion gegen Konstantinopel: Einnahme von Tschataldscha durch die Comitétruppen," *Berliner Tageblatt und Handels-Zeitung*, April 17, 1909, Evening Edition, p.1.

[88] "The Revolution in Turkey: A Delegation to Salonika," *The Times*, April 17, 1909, p.7; and, Sina Akşin, *31 Mart Olayı*, pp.103-104.

[89] "The Counter-Revolution and the Fall of Abdul-Hamid," in G. P. Gooch and H. Temperley (Eds.), *British Documents on the Origins of the War, 1898-1914, 5: The Near East*, p.316.

Apparently, their aim was to pacify the advancing army.[90]

Nâzım Pasha was confident that a compromise would be reached in Çatalca. The deputation, composed of eight persons, among whom were Halis Efendi, a military instructor to whom the general supervision of the *softas* was entrusted, and the deputies from Üsküb and Bursa, however, failed, and was not even allowed to return to İstanbul. One of the members of the deputation, a hodja on whom a pistol and papers proving his complicity in the revolt were found was beaten and imprisoned.[91] A second deputation headed by İzzet Halil Pasha, the Grand Master of the Artillery, was equally unsuccessful, but was permitted to return.[92]

The only real assurance the Government could obtain was the guarantee that loyalist troops would not enter the capital as long as it was clear that no preparations for resistance were being made. The representatives of the loyalist troops, assured of the safety of the Constitution, insisted, among other things, on the reinstatement of the late Cabinet and the punishment of those responsible for political violence. Meanwhile, troops continued to arrive at Çatalca, without resistance. The monarchist artillery garrison had long since retreated to the capital where it was graciously received at the Palace.[93]

By this time, the monarchist Government was convinced that the loyalist forces meant to occupy İstanbul. The Cabinet was so alarmed at the prospect of a conflagration that it sent Rıfat Pasha, Minister for Foreign Affairs, to the British Embassy for mediation. The Minister for Foreign Affairs told

[90] "Die jungtürkische Aktion gegen Konstantinopel: Einnahme von Tscha-taldscha durch die Comitétruppen," *Berliner Tageblatt und Handels-Zeitung,* April 17, 1909, Evening Edition, p.1.

[91] "The Situation in Turkey: Ineffective Deputations," *The Times,* April 19, 1909, p.5; and, "The Counter-Revolution and the Fall of Abdul-Hamid," in G. P. Gooch and H. Temperley (Eds.), *British Documents on the Origins of the War, 1898-1914,* 5: *The Near East,* p.316.

[92] "The Counter-Revolution and the Fall of Abdul-Hamid," in G. P. Gooch and H. Temperley (Eds.), *British Documents on the Origins of the War, 1898-1914,* 5: *The Near East,* p.316.

[93] "Die Jungtürken vor Konstantinopel: Die jungtürkische Vorhut," *Berliner Tageblatt und Handels-Zeitung,* April 17, 1909, Evening Edition, p.4; "Vor den Mauern Konstantinopels," *Berliner Tageblatt und Handels-Zeitung,* April 18, 1909, p.1; "Der Vormarsch der Jungtürken," *Berliner Tageblatt und Handels-Zeitung,* April 18, 1909, p.2; and, "The Counter-Revolution and the Fall of Abdul-Hamid," in G. P. Gooch and H. Temperley (Eds.), *British Documents on the Origins of the War, 1898-1914,* 5: *The Near East,* p.316.

British officials that the Cabinet contemplated of sending another deputation to Çatalca for negotiations with the loyalist
troops, and asked the British to accompany them, since the
Unionist forces would more readily credit the statement that
there was no attack on the Constitution if it were made by a
representative of the British Embassy.[94] Although the British
initially accepted to mediate the dispute, later other counsels
prevailed and the British Embassy decided that the monarchist deputies should go to Çatalca alone. This latest deputation
fared no better than its predecessors, and indeed failed even to
obtain a hearing.[95]

On April 17, Abdülhamid summoned Tevfik Pasha, the
Grand Vezier, to the Palace and met with him at length. He
then received members of the Cabinet and discussed the state
of the nation. Finally, the Sultan declared that the Government would remain faithful to the Constitution, adding that
those who tried to overthrow the Constitution would be severely punished. He also announced that a special commission
would be sent to Çatalca 'to re-establish calm among the
troops.'[96]

Still largely unaware of the military situation, the capital
was already labouring under a deluge of proclamations.
Prince Sabahaddin, the eloquent leader of the Liberal Union,
began issuing a series of long and wordy appeals to the clergy, the soldiers, and the nation in general in the vain hope of
addressing the crisis. His proclamation to the monarchist soldiers congratulated them for their attachment to religion.[97]

Elsewhere in İstanbul, a group of fifth-rate politicians came
together and formed a new 'party' under the name of the
Ottoman Union—or, Heyet-i Müttefika-i Osmaniye. They
then proceeded to draw up an almost interminable 'proclama-

---

[94] "The Counter-Revolution and the Fall of Abdul-Hamid," in G. P. Gooch and
H. Temperley (Eds.), *British Documents on the Origins of the War, 1898-1914, 5:
The Near East*, p.316.

[95] "The Counter-Revolution and the Fall of Abdul-Hamid," in G. P. Gooch and
H. Temperley (Eds.), *British Documents on the Origins of the War, 1898-1914, 5:
The Near East*, p.317.

[96] Francis McCullagh, *The Fall of Abd-ul-Hamid*, p.182.

[97] Francis McCullagh, *The Fall of Abd-ul-Hamid*, p.183; Ahmed Bedevi Kuran, *Osmanlı İmparatorluğunda İnkılâp Hareketleri ve Milli Mücadele*, p.515;
and, Ahmed Bedevi Kuran, *İnkılâp Tarihimiz ve 'Jön Türkler,'* p.280.

tion,' in which they undertook "to put aside all differences and to defend with one accord the country, engaging themselves at the same time to maintain the constitutional laws."[98] According to the proclamation, the founders of this union included the Committee of Union and Progress, the Liberal Union, various Armenian, Greek, Albanian, Kurdish, Circassian, and Bulgarian political clubs, as well as the alumni association of the Faculty of Political Science, and the Association of Medical Doctors.[99] This document was reportedly signed by representatives from eleven associations, as well as by the editors of the monarchist press. The Central Committee of the Committee of Union and Progress at Salonica promptly repudiated the signature of the İstanbul branch of the Committee appended to this document.[100]

The Chamber of Deputies met and, at the insistence of İsmail Kemal Bey and Tevfik Pasha 'discussed' the temporary Budget Bill. The Bill was passed by one hundred and twenty-six votes to twelve.[101] In the same sitting, deputies held elections for the seat left vacant by the forced resignation of Ahmed Rıza Bey, the President of the Chamber. Three candidates were selected, and their names, according to the Constitution, were promptly presented to the Sultan for the final choice. Mustafa Nail Bey, deputy for Canik, and Mustafa al-'Ayntabi Efendi, deputy for Aleppo, both received one hundred and eleven votes. Hacı Ahmed Mahir Efendi, deputy for Kastamonu, received ninety-six, Şefik Bey, sixty, and İsmail Kemal Bey, forty-seven.[102]

---

[98] "Heyet-i Müttefika-i Osmaniye'nin Beyannamesi," *Ikdam*, April 5, 1325/April 18, 1909, p.1; "Die Situation in Konstantinopel," *Berliner Tageblatt und Handels-Zeitung*, April 18, 1909, pp.1-2; Francis McCullagh, *The Fall of Abd-ul-Hamid*, p.183. See also, Sina Akşin, *31 Mart Olayı*, pp.122-123; and, Yusuf Hikmet Bayur, *Türk İnkılâbı Tarihi, 1/2*, p.195.

[99] "Heyet-i Müttefika-i Osmaniye'nin Beyannamesi," *Ikdam*, April 5, 1325/April 18, 1909, p.1; Sina Akşin, *31 Mart Olayı*, p.122; and, "Die Situation in Konstantinopel," *Berliner Tageblatt und Handels-Zeitung*, April 18, 1909, pp.1-2. Bayur wrongly alleges that members of the 'Ottoman Union' were supporters of the constitutional, *i. e.*, liberal democratic, regime (Yusuf Hikmet Bayur, *Türk İnkılâbı Tarihi, 1/2*, p.195).

[100] Francis McCullagh, *The Fall of Abd-ul-Hamid*, p.183.

[101] I/I/57, April 4, 1325/April 17, 1909, *Meclis-i Mebusan Zabıt Ceridesi, 3*, pp.33-36.

[102] I/I/57, April 4, 1325/April 17, 1909, *Meclis-i Mebusan Zabıt Ceridesi, 3*, pp.37-38, and 55-56; "Meclisi-i Mebusan Riyaseti," *Ikdam*, April 5, 1325/April 18, 1909, pp.2-3.

The Chamber then chose thirty deputies for the latest deputation to Çatalca, after which telegrams which arrived from the provinces were read. These were sent by various popular representatives, army commanders, and local branches of the Committee of Union and Progress. All assailed the military *coup*, made it clear that the new developments were considered a return to absolutism, and refused to recognise the Tevfik Pasha Cabinet.[103]

İsmail Kemal Bey tried to sway the increasingly anxious members of the Chamber in the *coup*'s favour, claiming that everything that had been done, had been done constitutionally. Many deputies, among them, Nazareth Daghavarian, Mehmed Ali Bey, Mustafa Arif [Kocabaş], and Pantoleon Cosmidis, argued that the *coup* was a blow to the supremacy of constitutional rule and the prestige of the Chamber. As long as deputies were afraid for their lives, they insisted, one could not speak of normalcy.[104]

Realising that the capital was surrounded, monarchist newspapers quickly changed the tone of their editorials.[105] *İkdam*, so enthusiastic about the *coup* in its early days, stated that the maintenance of Hamidian absolutism could only ruin the country. It went on to criticise the destruction of pro-Unionist newspaper offices, and stressed that deputies be allowed to live in safety.[106] Yet, *İkdam* did not fail to print telegrams sent from the provinces in support of the *coup*. The editorial praised this support, admonishing the population not be taken in by the lie that the Constitution was in danger.[107] *Osmanlı*, controlled by Prince Sabahaddin, asked for the Sultan's immediate abdication in the interest of peace.[108] Derviş Vah-

---

[103] I/I/57, April 4, 1325/April 17, 1909, *Meclis-i Mebusan Zabıt Ceridesi, 3*, pp.43-49; and, Sina Akşin, *31 Mart Olayı*, p.116. See also, "Elliyedinci İctima-ı Umumi," *İkdam*, April 5, 1325/April 18, 1909, pp.3-4.

[104] I/I/57, April 4, 1325/April 17, 1909, *Meclis-i Mebusan Zabıt Ceridesi, 3*, pp.49-54; "Elliyedinci İctima-ı Umumi," *İkdam*, April 5, 1325/April 18, 1909, pp.3-4; and, Sina Akşin, *31 Mart Olayı*, pp.117-118.

[105] Sina Akşin, *31 Mart Olayı*, p.110.

[106] Ali Kemal, "En Büyük Tehlike Nedir?" *İkdam*, April 4, 1325/April 17, 1909, p.1. Repentance came too late, for *İkdam* was suppressed indefinetely as soon as the troops from Salonica entered the city (Francis McCullagh, *The Fall of Abd-ul-Hamid*, p.184).

[107] Ali Kemal, "En Büyük Tehlike Nedir?" *İkdam*, April 4, 1325/April 17, 1909, p.1. See also, Sina Akşin, *31 Mart Olayı*, pp.110-111.

[108] Francis McCullagh, *The Fall of Abd-ul-Hamid*, p.184.

deti's editorial in *Volkan*, however, claimed that the 'events' of April 13 were, in fact, only a continuation of the Revolution of 1908; in a desperate attempt to legitimate the *coup*, he asked that readers join the 'movement,' the roots of which, after all, began with Niyazi and Enver Beys.[109]

Messages from every part of Turkey poured in to the Ministry of War. Marshal İbrahim Pasha, Commander of the Fourth Army Corps at Erzincan, and General Salih Pasha, Commander of the Second Army Corps at Edirne, stated that "having learned that armed men had dared to come to the walls of the Chamber," they were both "ready to march on the capital." Similar messages came from Prizren, Yenice, Vardar, Prishtnë, Geilan, Burhaniye, İzmir, Janina, Van, Kastamonu, Ankara, Bursa, Kossovo, Beirut, Nablus, Tripoli, Bartın, Durazzo, Mitrovitza, Sivas, Erzincan, Üsküb and a score of other places, all demanding the dissolution of the Tevfik Pasha Cabinet, all declaring that the signatories had decided to take up arms against İstanbul.[110]

In fact, it seemed the Sultan had lost all of European Turkey, with the exception of a few barracks in the capital, as well as all the Anatolian provinces which were advanced enough to take an interest in politics. Four battalions had embarked at Trabzon; a battalion of sharpshooters had left Erzurum, and other battalions were on their way to İstanbul via Konya. All the best generals and officers were either in Salonica or on their way to join the forces surrounding İstanbul. Ali Rıza Pasha, ex-Minister of War, and Mahmud Muhtar Pasha, ex-Commander of the First Army Corps, had reached Salonica and were now among those on their way to join the besieging army.[111] İstanbul's general population was still unaware of these developments.

The news that the Edirne troops, in particular, had rallied to the Unionist cause considerably strengthened its position, and dealt the Government a severe blow. Although there had been

---

[109] Derviş Vahdeti, "Öteberi," *Volkan*, April 4, 1325/April 17, 1909, quoted in Sina Akşin, *31 Mart Olayı*, p.111.

[110] Francis McCullagh, *The Fall of Abd-ul-Hamid*, pp.178-179.

[111] "Die Vorgänge im Orient: Die jungtürkische Gegenbewegung," *Vossische Zeitung*, April 18, 1909, Morning Edition, p.2; and, Francis McCullagh, *The Fall of Abd-ul-Hamid*, p.180.

some hesitation for the previous two days, on April 17, the garrison's officers met and decided to throw their lot in with the Committee of Union and Progress. The very force on which the monarchist Government had been relying on as a check on the action of the Unionists was now its declared enemy.[112]

However, thinking that it might be needed to defend the Bulgarian frontier in the not unlikely event of foreign intervention, Mahmud Şevket Pasha did not ask the Second Army Corps for much material support. Accordingly, the Second Army Corps only sent an infantry and a cavalry brigade to İstanbul. What was infinitely more important, the Second Army sent assurance that it was with Mahmud Şevket Pasha heart and soul, and that it could be relied upon to guard his flank.[113]

The deputation chosen from among the members of the Chamber met with the representatives of the Salonica Army, and in a telegram sent to the Ministry for Foreign Affairs, the president of the delegation—Esad Pasha Toptan, the independent deputy for Durazzo—informed the Cabinet that the loyalist forces intended to enter the capital peacefully in order to restore law and order.[114] The deputation learned that ten other trains were following. In a telegram sent to the Chamber in the afternoon, the deputation informed the deputies that fifteen thousand soldiers would advance to the city if any preparations were made to resist.[115]

On the morning of April 18, most in İstanbul believed that the Second Army Corps had routed the Salonica troops, and towards evening, everyone was convinced that there would be no trouble. The peaceful manifesto of the Ottoman Union had been published; the monarchist newspapers were extremely hopeful; the Grand Vezier, in a public appearance, ridiculed

[112] "The Counter-Revolution and the Fall of Abdul-Hamid," in G. P. Gooch and H. Temperley (Eds.), *British Documents on the Origins of the War, 1898-1914, 5: The Near East*, p.317. See also Francis McCullagh, *The Fall of Abd-ul-Hamid*, pp.158-159.

[113] Francis McCullagh, *The Fall of Abd-ul-Hamid*, p.159.

[114] "Die Vermittelungsaktion der Parlamentarier," *Berliner Tageblatt und Handels-Zeitung*, April 19, 1909, p.2; Yusuf Hikmet Bayur, *Türk İnkılâbı Tarihi, 1/2*, p.199; and, Sina Akşin, *31 Mart Olayı*, pp.120-121.

[115] Edwin Pears, "The Crisis in Turkey," p.525.

the idea of civil strife, and the representatives of several European banks sent reassuring messages to their head offices.[116]

In an editorial for *Ikdam*, Ali Kemal Bey reiterated the Government's claim that the *coup* in no way threatened the constitutional regime, though he then went on to praise it for having put an end to the political reign of the Committee of Union and Progress. In this connection, he lauded the formation of the Ottoman Union as its successor. The *coup*, he said, would allow the nation's political life to proceed on firmer ground.[117] In *Osmanlı*, Prince Sabahaddin published an open letter to the nation's religious leaders, in which he thanked them for their co-operation with those troops involved in the *coup*, and urged them to support the newly established Ottoman Union.[118] *Mizan* also welcomed the establishment of the Ottoman Union. Its editorial disparaged party politics in general, and praised the political unity which Ottoman Union represented.[119]

Volkan, meanwhile, printed a list of demands addressed to the members of the Committee of Union and Progress. Though the paper tolerated the party's existence, it did accuse Unionists of having misappropriated funds during their rule, and demanded that these be returned to the nation forthwith. The accusation was completely unsupported.[120]

At the opening of its session, the Chamber was informed that Abdülhamid had chosen Mustafa al-'Ayntabi Efendi, deputy for Aleppo, as its President.[121] Throughout, the remnant of the Chamber tried hard to persuade itself that the events of the

---

[116] Francis McCullagh, *The Fall of Abd-ul-Hamid*, p.170.

[117] Ali Kemal, "Yine Meyus Olmamalıyız," *Ikdam*, April 5, 1325/April 18, 1909, p.1.

[118] Prince Sabahaddin, "Sultanzade Sabahaddin Beyefendi'nin Ulema-ı Kirama Hitaben Açık Mektupları," *Osmanlı*, April 5, 1325/April 18, 1909, quoted in Sina Akşin, *31 Mart Olayı*, pp.128-129. See also, Ahmed Bedevi Kuran, *Inkılâp Tarihimiz ve 'Jön Türkler,'* p.280.

[119] "Cemiyetlere İhtar-ı Mühim," *Mizan*, April 5, 1325/April 18, 1909, quoted in Sina Akşin, *31 Mart Olayı*, p.129.

[120] "Meclis-i Mebusan İttihad ve Terakki Azalarına Selâmet-i Vatan Namına Ricamız," *Volkan*, April 5, 1325/April 18, 1909, quoted in Sina Akşin, *31 Mart Olayı*, p.127.

[121] I/I/58, April 5, 1325/April 18, 1909, *Meclis-i Mebusan Zabıt Ceridesi, 3*, pp.59-60; "Ellisekizinci İctima-ı Umumi," *Ikdam*, April 6, 1325/April 19, 1909, pp.3-4; Sina Akşin, *31 Mart Olayı*, p.132; Abdurrahman Şeref, *Son Vak'anüvis Abdurrahman Şeref Efendi Tarihi: II. Meşrutiyet Olayları, 1908-1909*, p.42; and, "Report in the Chamber," *The Times*, April 19, 1909, p.5.

last few days had been perfectly regular, and the Chamber's monarchist deputies issued a declaration to that effect. "The Chamber," it said, "had called on the Cabinet of Hüseyin Hilmi Pasha to resign. Then an imperial decree, issued in conformity with a vote of the Chamber, had accorded a general amnesty to those who had taken part in the demonstration, and all the soldiers had returned to their barracks with joy and confidence, thus giving a proof of their order and discipline."[122]

In this extra-ordinary session of the Chamber, the deputation which had been to Çatalca reported its findings. Members of the deputation spoke of the firm determination of the loyalist troops not to return, or even to cease advancing, until they had secured guarantees for the Constitution. All were in accord as to the admirable discipline of the regiments which they saw. One of the members of the deputation, himself deputy for Üsküb, stated that the officers were under the impression that the lives of the deputies in İstanbul were in danger. Another stated that if the Chamber itself did not put the First Army Corps in order, the loyalist Third Army Corps would do so. On the proposal to send a further deputation to give advice, Süleyman Bey, another member of the deputation, said plainly that the leaders at Çatalca had told them they had no need for it.[123]

During the proceedings, telegrams supporting the Constitution and condemning the *coup* were also read. Most of these reiterated the claim that the Tevfik Pasha Cabinet was illegitimate.[124] Encouraged by the abundance and vehemence of such telegrams, Unionist deputies—who had been noticeably reticent throughout—decided to give their version of the current situation, brushing aside the monarchists' claim

---

[122] I/I/58, April 5, 1325/April 18, 1909, *Meclis-i Mebusan Zabıt Ceridesi, 3,* pp.61-69; Francis McCullagh, *The Fall of Abd-ul-Hamid,* p.171; and, Mevlânzade Rıfat, *31 Mart: Bir İhtilâlin Hikâyesi,* pp.83-84.

[123] I/I/58, April 5, 1325/April 18, 1909, *Meclis-i Mebusan Zabıt Ceridesi, 3,* p.60; Edwin Pears, "The Crisis in Turkey," p.525; "Report in the Chamber," *The Times,* April 19, 1909, p.5; and, "Das türkische Parlament und die Freiheitstruppen," *Berliner Tageblatt und Handels-Zeitung,* April 19, 1909, Evening Edition, p.4.

[124] I/I/58, April 5, 1325/April 18, 1909, *Meclis-i Mebusan Zabıt Ceridesi, 3,* pp.72-80; "Der türkische Ministerrat," *Berliner Tageblatt und Handels-Zeitung,* April 19, 1909, Morning Edition, p.2; and, Sina Akşin, *31 Mart Olayı,* p.135.

that everything was in perfect order. Nesim Masliah, the Unionist deputy for İzmir, made a speech in which he said that the telegrams clearly proved the people's loyalty to the Constitution, adding that they had seen through the lies propagated by the *coup*'s supporters. Using violent language, he denounced the wrecking of *Şura-yı Ümmet*'s offices, "which had for twenty years defended, in exile, the cause of freedom." "The Chamber," he continued, "had deceived the nation by issuing lying proclamations." He ridiculed the Government's assertion that the Constitution was safe in light of the fact that the leadership of the Committee of Union and Progress and most deputies were in flight or in momentary danger of assassination.[125]

That day, the combined forces from Edirne—commanded by Salih Pasha—and Salonica—commanded by Hüseyin Hüsnü Pasha, father-in-law of the prominent Unionist Rahmi [Aslan]—advanced to Isparta Kule, some thirty kilometres from the walls of İstanbul. An advance post of six hundred and fifty men had already been established at Küçük Çekmece, fifteen kilometres closer to the capital.[126] The main body was nearly eight thousand strong, included cavalry and artillery, and its discipline was described as perfect. That evening, the monarchist Government made a last attempt at reconciliation, sending Chief of the Staff İzzet Pasha, who was supposed to be favourably regarded by the Unionists. The attempt, however, was fruitless, and İzzet Pasha returned to İstanbul the following morning, without achieving any result.[127]

On April 19, the monarchist press continued to downplay the

---

[125] I/I/58, April 5, 1325/April 18, 1909, *Meclis-i Mebusan Zabıt Ceridesi*, 3, pp.80-82; and, Francis McCullagh, *The Fall of Abd-ul-Hamid*, p.171. See also the defence of the Constitution by other members of the Chamber, including Boso Efendi, Vasif Bey, Dağavaryan Efendi and Mustafa Arif Bey, in Sina Akşin, *31 Mart Olayı*, pp.132-136.

[126] Edwin Pears, "The Crisis in Turkey," p.525; Midhat Şükrü Bleda, *İmparatorluğun Çöküşü*, p.67; "20 Kilometer von Konstantinopel," *Berliner Tageblatt und Handels-Zeitung*, April 19, 1909, Morning Edition, p.2; and, Sina Akşin, *31 Mart Olayı*, p.143.

[127] "Die Vermittelungsaktion der Parlamentarier," *Berliner Tageblatt und Handels-Zeitung*, April 19, 1909, Morning Edition, p.2; Sina Akşin, *31 Mart Olayı*, p.143, and "The Counter-Revolution and the Fall of Abdul-Hamid," in G. P. Gooch and H. Temperley (Eds.), *British Documents on the Origins of the War, 1898-1914, 5: The Near East*, p.317.

significance of the *coup*. In *İkdam*, Ali Kemal Bey tried his best to persuade the public that the existing regime was in no danger.[128] The same paper also published another open letter from Prince Sabahaddin to the monarchist soldiers, celebrating the *shari'a*.[129]

Troops in İstanbul, however, had already started defecting to the loyalists. Whole squadrons of cavalry went over at a time. On April 19, the troops of the Rami barracks welcomed the Salonica troops, joined them, and kindly presented them with six machine gun batteries.[130]

By now, the population could not but be aware of the situation, and students poured out of İstanbul in a steady stream. Law School students marched through the streets with a flag, on their way to join the Salonica troops at Bakırköy. They were followed by students and professors of the Pangaltı Military School, the Engineering School, the Commercial School, and many others.[131]

Hüseyin Cahid [Yalçın] and Cavid Bey, who had escaped from İstanbul to Odessa several days earlier, returned by train via Budapest, and were now on their way to Salonica. At the border, Turkish soldiers welcomed them, shouting "Down with Abdülhamid!" and for the rest of the trip, Hüseyin Cahid [Yalçın] and Cavid Bey were cheered on at every station. That night they reached Salonica where a large crowd had assembled despite the fact that the army had banned all demonstrations. They were immediately taken to a hall to address the population.[132]

When İzzet Pasha returned to İstanbul with the news that the loyalists were prepared to march on İstanbul, the monarchists panicked. İsmail Kemal Bey suggested resisting the

---

[128] Ali Kemal, "Neye Muhtacız?" *İkdam*, April 6, 1325/April 19, 1909, p.1. See also, Sina Akşin, *31 Mart Olayı*, p.138.

[129] "Sultanzade Sabahaddin Beyefendi'nin Osmanlı Askerine Hitaben Açık Mektubu: Asker Kardeşler!" *İkdam*, April 6, 1325/April 19, 1909, p.2.

[130] Francis McCullagh, *The Fall of Abd-ul-Hamid*, p.181. See also, "Die Vorgänge im Orient: Der jungtürkische Gegenstoß," *Vossische Zeitung*, April 20, 1909, Evening Edition, p.1.

[131] Francis McCullagh, *The Fall of Abd-ul-Hamid*, p.181.

[132] "Cahid ve Cavid Beyler," *İkdam*, April 8, 1325/April 21, 1909, p.2; Hüseyin Cahid Yalçın, "Meşrutiyet Hatıraları, 1908-1918," *Fikir Hareketleri*, 5 (October 26, 1935-April 18, 1936), pp.133-134, and pp.148-149. They were at Bakırköy on April 20 ("Die Vorgänge im Orient: Der jungtürkische Gegenstoß," *Vossische Zeitung*, April 20, 1909, Evening Edition, p.1).

Salonica army by the monarchist troops still loyal to them, and enlisting the help of foreign powers to bolster the Government's weakened defences. The German and Russian Embassies had already refused their co-operation, and that afternoon, he met with Sir Gerard Lowther, the British Ambassador. Although the latter did not rule out the possibility of intervention on behalf of the monarchists, he let it be known that Abdülhamid could not be defended.[133]

Meanwhile, Nâzım Pasha went to the Taksim barracks and gave orders to resist the approaching Salonica army with every available means. He was in no mood to simply give up and surrender.[134]

That day, Tevfik Pasha presented his Cabinet's programme to the Chamber. Assessing the current situation, he blamed the *coup* on the struggle between the political parties, though he repeated that the Constitution was in no way under attack, and that his Cabinet would protect the Constitution. Not surprisingly, he welcomed the appearance of the Ottoman Union, as a stabilising presence. While admitting that the citizens had expressed their dissatisfaction with the existing state of affairs, he expressed the hope that it would soon dissipate.[135] Finally, with the news of loyalist advances, the Chamber had been pushing for the opportunity to give the Tevfik Pasha Cabinet a vote of no confidence. In order to avoid the likely possibility that his Cabinet might get a vote of no confidence from the Chamber which had become reassured of victory for the constitutional regime, Tevfik Pasha met with monarchist deputies and secured a postponement of the vote.[136]

In the afternoon of April 19, rumours began to circulate that the Committee of Union and Progress had demanded the abdication of the Sultan and was prepared to back its demand

---

[133] Sina Akşin, *31 Mart Olayı*, p.143.
[134] Ziya Şakir Soko, *Sultan Hamid'in Son Günleri*, p.153; and, Sina Akşin, *31 Mart Olayı*, p.152.
[135] I/I/59, April 6, 1325/April 19, 1909, *Meclis-i Mebusan Zabıt Ceridesi*, 3, pp.98-99; and, "Ellidokuzuncu İctima-ı Umumi," *İkdam*, April 7, 1325/April 20, 1909, pp.1-2. For the text of the cabinet programme see also, Abdurrahman Şeref, *Son Vak'anüvis Abdurrahman Şeref Efendi Tarihi: II. Meşrutiyet Olayları, 1908-1909*, p.43.
[136] Ali Fuad Türkgeldi, *Görüp İşittiklerim*, p.30.

with force if necessary.[137] The conviction that the Palace would be attacked was so strong that inhabitants of the surrounding neighbourhoods, Beşiktaş and Ortaköy, quickly deserted their homes.[138] Such a message had in fact been sent to the Palace, and Tevfik Pasha relayed this information to the British Embassy through an envoy, indicating that the Committee of Union and Progress had also sent a second telegram demanding that several people whom it considered responsible for recent events be handed over into its custody. İsmail Kemal Bey was among them.[139]

Later that night, Hüseyin Hüsnü Pasha, Commander of the Salonica troops, drafted a proclamation intended to explain the loyalists' position and motives to the people of İstanbul. Describing the events of the past week as a counter-revolutionary *coup* designed to bring back the absolutist regime, he called all those involved with the events as reactionaries and informed the public that the loyalists were marching on İstanbul in order to restore the Constitution, and punish those who sought to destroy.[140] The proclamation was distributed throughout the capital the following day.[141]

In a second telegram, which would be sent to the Headquarters of the Chief of Staff to be relayed to the General Staff of the First Army Corps, Hüseyin Hüsnü Pasha expressed regret that the First Army Corps had sided with the forces of reaction, but asked the Headquarters to advise the troops of the

---

[137] "Gerüchte über die Abdankung des Sultans," *Berliner Tageblatt und Handels-Zeitung*, April 20, 1909, Morning Edition, p.1; and, "Zur Abdankung des Sultans," *Berliner Tageblatt und Handels-Zeitung*, April 20, 1909, Evening Edition, p.4.

[138] "The Counter-Revolution and the Fall of Abdul-Hamid," in G. P. Gooch and H. Temperley (Eds.), *British Documents on the Origins of the War, 1898-1914, 5: The Near East*, p.317.

[139] "The Counter-Revolution and the Fall of Abdul-Hamid," in G. P. Gooch and H. Temperley (Eds.), *British Documents on the Origins of the War, 1898-1914, 5: The Near East*, p.317.

[140] "Hareket Ordusu Kumandanı Tarafından İstanbul Ahalisine Beyanname," *İkdam*, April 8, 1325/April 21, 1909, p.1; "Der Anmarsch der Truppen: Zwei Proklamationen des Höchstkommandierenden der Einschließungsarmee," *Osmanischer Lloyd*, April 21, 1909, p.1; "Die Proklamationen des jungtürkischen Feldherrn," *Berliner Tageblatt und Handels-Zeitung*, April 21, 1909, Morning Edition, p.3; and, Sina Akşin, *31 Mart Olayı*, pp.149-150. See also, Yusuf Hikmet Bayur, *Türk İnkılâbı Tarihi, 1/2*, pp.200-201, where he alleges that this proclamation was written by Mustafa Kemal Atatürk.

[141] Sina Akşin, *31 Mart Olayı*, p.149n.

First Army Corps not to resist the loyalist advance.[142] The leaders of the Committee of Union and Progress, Talât Bey and Dr. Nâzım Bey, had previously discussed the contents of the telegram with İzzet Pasha.[143]

The Salonica army continued its march towards İstanbul and during the night reached San Stefano and Bakırköy.[144] Tevfik Pasha and Edhem Pasha, Minister of War, tendered their resignations; the Sultan refused to accept them, as he would of Nâzım Pasha and Memduh Pasha.[145]

On the morning of April 20, İsmail Kemal Bey, whose arrest was requested by the Unionists, sought and was granted asylum in the British Embassy. He was then escorted to an outbound Egyptian ship.[146] That same day, Nâzım Pasha fled to the Prince Islands.[147] The flight of the counter-revolutionaries had started. Trains for Anatolia were curiously full of passengers in religious garb; deserting soldiers fled to the interior of the country on foot.[148]

Mahmud Şevket Pasha, Commander of the Third Army Corps in Salonica, sent an ultimatum to the Cabinet which gave it twenty-four hours to resign. It also stated that martial law would be declared throughout the capital but that order would be established and maintained by police force and

---

[142] "Hareket Ordusu Kumandanı Tarafından Erkân-ı Harbiye-i Umumiye Riyaseti'ne Telgrafname," *İkdam*, April 8, 1325/April 21, 1909, p.1; "Der Anmarsch der Truppen: Zwei Proklamationen des Höchstkommandierenden der Einschließungsarmee," *Osmanischer Lloyd*, April 21, 1909, p.1; "Die Proklamationen des jungtürkischen Feldherrn," *Berliner Tageblatt und Handels-Zeitung*, April 21, 1909, Morning Edition, p.3; and, Sina Akşin, *31 Mart Olayı*, pp.150-151. See also, Yusuf Hikmet Bayur, *Türk İnkılâbı Tarihi, I/2*, pp.201-203, where he alleges, again, that this proclamation too was written by Mustafa Kemal Atatürk.
[143] Celal Bayar, *Ben de Yazdım, 2*, pp.624-629. See also, Sina Akşin, *31 Mart Olayı*, p.153.
[144] "Das Vorrücken der Comitétruppen," *Berliner Tageblatt und Handels-Zeitung*, April 20, 1909, Morning Edition, p.2; and, Sina Akşin, *31 Mart Olayı*, p.145.
[145] "The Counter-Revolution and the Fall of Abdul-Hamid," in G. P. Gooch and H. Temperley (Eds.), *British Documents on the Origins of the War, 1898-1914, 5: The Near East*, p.317; and, "Gnadenfrist für das Kabinett Tewfik," *Berliner Tageblatt und Handels-Zeitung*, April 20, 1909, Evening Edition, p.4.
[146] Ismail Kemal, *The Memoirs of Ismail Kemal Bey*, p.345; and, "The Counter-Revolution and the Fall of Abdul-Hamid," in G. P. Gooch and H. Temperley (Eds.), *British Documents on the Origins of the War, 1898-1914, 5: The Near East*, p.317.
[147] Ismail Kemal, *The Memoirs of Ismail Kemal Bey*, p.345.
[148] *İkdam*, April 8, 1325/April 21, 1909, quoted in Sina Akşin, *31 Mart Olayı*, p.161n.

gendarmes brought in from Macedonia. The Chamber of Deputies would then be convened according to the rules of the Constitution, to elect a new President. Naturally, a new Cabinet would be also formed.[149]

Out of desperation and in the hope of provoking foreign intervention on his behalf, the Sultan made arrangements to have one of the warships moored off Beşiktaş open fire on the German, Russian, Austrian, and French Embassies the moment loyalist troops entered İstanbul.[150]

That afternoon, Hüseyin Hüsnü Pasha's proclamations, addressed to the people of İstanbul and the General Staff of the Army respectively, were made public. The second proclamation was the more interesting as it was clearly intended to reassure to the mutinous troops whom it considered the victims of monarchist designs. The proclamation began with the assertion that the *coup* was the result of reaction, that those responsible meant to subvert the Constitution all along, and that by appealing to the religious feelings of the troops, the latter had been misled to mutiny, bringing dishonour to the immaculate Turkish Army. To wipe out this stain, detachments of the Second and Third Army Corps had come to San Stefano and Küçük Çekmece to see the Constitution, by the grace of the Almighty, restored. Hüseyin Hüsnü Pasha made two demands: first, that the troops in İstanbul take a solemn oath to follow their superiors' orders, and to henceforth abstain from all interference in politics; second, that the troops in no way interfere with measures taken to punish the guilty, nor could they even look askance at the men of the Second and Third Army Corps whom they were asked to consider their brothers. Accordingly, they were asked to denounce those officers and spies who had incited them to mutiny.[151]

---

[149] Sina Akşin, *31 Mart Olayı*, pp.162-163.

[150] "Das Ultimatum an den Sultan," *Berliner Tageblatt und Handels-Zeitung*, April 20, 1909, Evening Edition, p.4. This plan was reported to Rıfat Pasha, Minister for Foreign Affairs, who, in turn, informed the British Embassy of this provocation ("The Counter-Revolution and the Fall of Abdul-Hamid," in G. P. Gooch and H. Temperley (Eds.), *British Documents on the Origins of the War, 1898-1914, 5: The Near East*, p.318).

[151] "Hareket Ordusu Kumandanı Tarafından Erkân-ı Harbiye-i Umumiye Riyaseti'ne Telgrafname," *İkdam*, April 8, 1325/April 21, 1909, p.1; "Der Anmarsch der Truppen: Zwei Proklamationen des Höchstkommandierenden der Einschließungsarmee," *Osmanischer Lloyd*, April 21, 1909, p.1; and, "The Counter-Revo-

For those who had participated in the *coup*, the first proclamation to the population of İstanbul was not very reassuring.
Hüseyin Hüsnü Pasha stated that the task of dealing with the
traitors and malcontents would be left to the military. These
would be severely punished so as to protect the constitutional
regime and prove that there could never be a force superior to
the Constitution, founded as it was on *shari'a*. Those *agents
provocateurs* who, in the guise of religious leaders, had fos-
tered the *coup* would, in particular, be dealt with harshly.[152]

It was now several days after the ex-President of the
Chamber, Ahmed Rıza Bey, had escaped to San Stefano, and
most of the Unionist deputies, upon the call of the parliamentary deputation that had gone to San Stefano on April 19, chose
this moment to join him, indicating that they were prepared
to recognise him as the Chamber's legitimate President.[153]

By April 21, the monarchists had lost all hope of retaining
political power in their hands; they were in total disarray.
Most tried to save their skins by disclaiming any responsibility with the whole affair. In his editorial of April 21 in the
İkdam, Ali Kemal Bey denied that he had ever supported the
coup.[154] Ahmed Cevdet Bey, the owner of *İkdam*, also defended his actions, though he quickly escaped to Vienna.[155]
Murad Bey's editorial in the *Mizan* was very conciliatory; he
described the role of the monarchist press in the *coup* as moderate, and stated that although the existence of political parties
in the Chamber was desirable, the Ottoman Union should

lution and the Fall of Abdul-Hamid," in G. P. Gooch and H. Temperley (Eds.),
British Documents on the Origins of the War, 1898-1914, 5: The Near East, p.318.
    [152] "Hareket Ordusu Kumandanı Tarafından İstanbul Ahalisine Beyanname,"
İkdam, April 8, 1325/April 21, 1909, p.1; and, "The Counter-Revolution and the
Fall of Abdul-Hamid," in G. P. Gooch and H. Temperley (Eds.), *British Documents
on the Origins of the War, 1898-1914, 5: The Near East,* p.318. See also, "Die Vor-
gänge im Orient: Friede und Freundschaft!" *Vossische Zeitung,* April 22, 1909,
Morning Edition, p.2.
    [153] "Die Zernierung Konstantinopels," *Berliner Tageblatt und Handels-Zeit-
ung,* April 21, 1909, Morning Edition, p.1; and, Sina Akşin, *31 Mart Olayı,* pp.165-
166.
    [154] Ali Kemal, "Bir Haftadan Beri," *İkdam,* April 8, 1325/April 21, 1909, p.1.
See also, Sina Akşin, *31 Mart Olayı,* pp.169-170.
    [155] *İkdam,* April 9, 1325/April 22, 1909, quoted in Sina Akşin, *31 Mart Olayı,*
p.170; "Vor der Verständigung," *Berliner Tageblatt und Handels-Zeitung,* April
22, 1909, Morning Edition, p.1; and, Celal Bayar, *Ben de Yazdım, 1,* pp.188-192.

provide the guiding spirit.[156]

The Tevfik Pasha Cabinet met and prepared a response to Mahmud Şevket Pasha's ultimatum. In essence, they accepted all demands; thus, accepting an unconditional surrender.[157] Nonetheless, Mahmud Şevket Pasha left Salonica to head the army in besieging İstanbul.[158]

The number of deputies gathered at San Stefano now amounted to one hundred. They met and decided to schedule a joint session with the Senate the following day.[159]

In his *İkdam* editorial of April 22, Ali Kemal Bey wrote that true patriots had nothing to fear from the Salonica army.[160]

As planned, the Chamber of Deputies held a joint session with the Senate at San Stefano. Said Pasha, the ex-Grand Vezier and President of the Senate, jointly presided over the proceedings with Ahmed Rıza Bey, who was reinstituted as President of the Chamber.[161] Calling itself the National Assembly, this parliament-in-exile quickly got down to business and in closed session, began discussing the issue of Abdülhamid's dethronement. Later in the afternoon, the Assembly issued a declaration supporting Hüseyin Hüsnü Pasha's two proclamations.[162] Said Pasha then met with

---

[156] Murad, "Artık Çocukluğumuza Nihayet Verelim," *Mizan*, April 8, 1325/ April 21, 1909, quoted in Sina Akşin, *31 Mart Olayı*, p.171.

[157] "Die Jungtürken und der Sultan: Verhandlungen mit der Anmarscharmee," *Berliner Tageblatt und Handels-Zeitung*, April 21, 1909, Evening Edition, p.1; "Die Bedingungen der Anmarscharmee," *Vossische Zeitung*, April 23, 1909, Morning Edition, p.2; and, Sina Akşin, *31 Mart Olayı*, p.172.

[158] "Abfahrt der Oberbefehlshaber zur Operationsarmee," *Berliner Tageblatt und Handels-Zeitung*, April 22, 1909, Evening Edition, p.1; and, Cemal Kutay, *Üç Paşalar Kavgası*, p.76.

[159] "Die Jungtürken und der Sultan: In Erwartung der Entscheidung," *Berliner Tageblatt und Handels-Zeitung*, April 21, 1909, Evening Edition, p.1; "Im Hauptquartier von San Stefano," *Berliner Tageblatt und Handels-Zeitung*, April 22, 1909, Morning Edition, p.1; "Das unentschiedene Los des Sultans," *Berliner Tageblatt und Handels-Zeitung*, April 22, 1909, Evening Edition, p.1; "Vom türkischen Parlament," *Vossische Zeitung*, April 22, 1909, Morning Edition, p.2; "Vom türkischen Parlament," *Vossische Zeitung*, April 22, 1909, Evening Edition, p.2; and, Sina Akşin, *31 Mart Olayı*, p.175.

[160] Ali Kemal, "Telâş Fenadır," *İkdam*, April 9, 1325/April 22, 1909, p.1.

[161] "Die Nationalversammlung in San Stefano," *Osmanischer Lloyd*, April 23, 1909, p.1; "Die konstituierende Nationalversammlung," *Berliner Tageblatt und Handels-Zeitung*, April 23, 1909, p.3; "Der Beginn der Nationalversammlung," *Berliner Tageblatt und Handels-Zeitung*, April 23, 1909, Evening Edition, pp.1-2; and, Sina Akşin, *31 Mart Olayı*, pp.181-182.

[162] "Das Rumpfparlament der Jungtürken," *Berliner Tageblatt und Handels-Zeitung*, April 23, 1909, Morning Edition, p.1; "Die Nationalversammlung für die

Mahmud Şevket Pasha.[163]

It had become quite clear that the Sultan was willing to come to terms with the Committee of Union and Progress, and that he would forsake his own agents and supporters to do it. The evening papers carried a list of thirty-five persons de- scribed as fomenters of the April 13 *coup*. Among them was the eminent editor of *İkdam*, Ali Kemal Bey, who barely had not enough time to escape. Though only thirty-five were named, the complete list was said to name some five hundred and forty-three—some of whom belonged to the Liberal Union, others who were friends and associates of the Sultan.· It was announced that the Sultan himself had provided the list, and had denounced them to the Unionists.[164]

News soon arrived that loyalist troops sent from İzmir were now holding positions at Eskişehir. Ostensibly, the defence of İstanbul would have to be conducted on two fronts.[165]

The exodus of the wealthier population, among whom were monarchist pashas, their households, as well as those wealthy Greeks and Armenians who had supported the *coup*, gained momentum throughout April 23, and every outgoing ship was filled beyond capacity.[166]

Meanwhile, the Ottoman Union held a meeting during which all the opposition forces against the Committee of Union and Progress tried to devise a strategy to survive the *coup*'s failure. These elected a commission of seven members to meet with the National Assembly in the hopes of gaining a measure of legitimacy.[167]

Finally, the Salonica troops began their march on İstan- bul.[168] They captured the barracks of Davud Paşa and Rami

Abdankung des Sultans," *Berliner Tageblatt und Handels-Zeitung*, April 23, 1909, Evening Edition, p.1; "Die Vorgänge im Orient: Absetzung des Sultans?" *Vossi- sche Zeitung*, April 23, 1909, Evening Edition, p.1; Sina Akşin, *31 Mart Olayı*, p.182 and p.185; and, Cemal Kutay, *Üç Paşalar Kavgası*, p.76.

[163] Cemal Kutay, *Üç Paşalar Kavgası*, p.76; and, Edwin Pears, *Forty Years in Constantinople: The Recollections of Sir Edwin Pears, 1873-1915*, pp.284-285.

[164] Sina Akşin, *31 Mart Olayı*, p.179; and, William M. Ramsay, *The Revolu- tion in Constantinople and Turkey*, p.74.

[165] Sina Akşin, *31 Mart Olayı*, p.177.

[166] Mary A. Poynter, *When Turkey Was Turkey*, p.62; and, William M. Ramsay, *The Revolution in Constantinople and Turkey*, p.78, and p.87.

[167] Sina Akşin, *31 Mart Olayı*, pp.189-192.

[168] "Der Kampf un Konstantinopel," *Berliner Tageblatt und Handels-Zeitung*,

Çiftlik, and though monarchist troops put up some resistance at Edirnekapı, these were quickly forced to surrender.[169]

On April 24, the Salonica troops entered İstanbul from Topkapı and Edirnekapı, taking control of police stations on the way and capturing the Ministry of War.[170] They, however, encountered resistance at the Fatih Mosque barracks, at the Sublime Porte, and at the officers' club adjoining the Sublime Porte.[171] Lasting over three hours, the battle for control of the government buildings at the Sublime Porte was the fiercest. When it was over, the loyalists had forty-four dead and ninety-five wounded, the monarchists, fifty-seven dead and one hundred and ten wounded.[172] The Sublime Porte had great gashes made by shells in front and on one side, and some of the buildings in its immediate vicinity were "pitted like a smallpox patient."[173]

Resistance at the Taksim and Taşkışla barracks was also considerable, though by the afternoon both would be in the hands of the loyalists.[174] The battle at these barracks left fifty-three dead and sixty-five wounded among the loyalists, two hundred forty dead and four hundred and seventy-five wounded among the monarchists.[175] By late afternoon, the

---

April 24, 1909, Morning Edition, p.1; and, Cemal Kutay, *Üç Paşalar Kavgası*, p.76.

[169] "Der Kampf un Konstantinopel," *Berliner Tageblatt und Handels-Zeitung*, April 24, 1909, Morning Edition, p.1; "Der Einmarsch der Comitétruppen in Konstantinopel," *Berliner Tageblatt und Handels-Zeitung*, April 24, 1909, Morning Edition, p.3; Edwin Pears, *Forty Years in Constantinople: The Recollections of Sir Edwin Pears, 1873-1915*, pp.278-279; and, Cemal Kutay, *Üç Paşalar Kavgası*, pp.76-77. See also, "Der Strassenkampf am Sonnabend," *Berliner Tageblatt und Handels-Zeitung*, April 26, 1909, Morning Edition, p.1.

[170] Yusuf Hikmet Bayur, *Türk İnkılâbı Tarihi*, 1/2, p.205; Mevlânzade Rıfat, *31 Mart: Bir İhtilâlin Hikâyesi*, pp.173-175; and, Cemal Kutay, *Üç Paşalar Kavgası*, p.77.

[171] Francis McCullagh, *The Fall of Abd-ul-Hamid*, p.217.

[172] *İkdam*, April 18, 1325/May 1, 1909, quoted in Sina Akşin, *31 Mart Olayı*, p.196n.

[173] Mary A. Poynter, *When Turkey Was Turkey*, p.70.

[174] "Die Einnahme Konstantinopels: Kapitulation des Jildis," *Berliner Tageblatt und Handels-Zeitung*, April 24, 1909, Evening Edition, p.1; "Die Vorgänge im Orient: Die Einnahme Konstantinopels," *Vossische Zeitung*, April 24, 1909, Evening Edition, p.1; Sina Akşin, *31 Mart Olayı*, p.196; Hüseyin Işık, "İkinci Meşrutiyet'in İlânında ve Korunmasında Silahlı Kuvvetlerimizin Rolü," p.55; Edwin Pears, *Forty Years in Constantinople: The Recollections of Sir Edwin Pears, 1873-1915*, p.279; Mevlânzade Rıfat, *31 Mart: Bir İhtilâlin Hikâyesi*, pp.173-174; and, Cemal Kutay, *Üç Paşalar Kavgası*, p.77.

[175] "Die Operationstruppen in Konstantinopel: Der Kampf um Taschkischla—Der Kampf um die Taximkaserne—Bei den Taximkasernen nach dem Kampfe—

Yıldız Palace was completely surrounded.[176] Mahmud Şevket Pasha issued a proclamation, giving a summary of the events that had taken place in the capital that day.[177]

All through the night, the Bosphorus was black with little boats carrying fleeing soldiers and reactionaries across from the Yıldız Palace to the Asian shore.[178]

On April 25, the Yıldız Palace and some barracks were still holding out. The Palace defences were said to include some four thousand troops.[179] Reports further indicated that the Palace guns were prepared to fire on Pera, destroying the European quarter where the Embassies were situated, if any attack were initiated. The Selimiye barracks on the Asiatic side were also still held by the Sultan's troops, and these reportedly declared that they too would fire on Pera in the event of an attack on the Yıldız Palace.[180] However, when surrounded, there was no resistance at the Selimiye barracks. When the Salonica troops arrived, half of the garrison had already fled, and those who remained surrendered at once.[181]

Der zweite Angriff auf die Taschkischla," *Osmanischer Lloyd*, April 25, 1909, p.1; *İkdam*, April 18, 1325/May 1, 1909, quoted in Sina Akşin, *31 Mart Olayı*, p.196n; Edwin Pears, *Forty Years in Constantinople: The Recollections of Sir Edwin Pears, 1873-1915*, p.279; *idem, Life of Abdul Hamid*, p.316; H. G. Dwight, *Constantinople: Old and New*, pp.439-444; and, Mary A. Poynter, *When Turkey Was Turkey*, p.70. In the Court Martial that followed the re-institution of the constitutional regime the commander of the Taşkışla barracks was found guilty and given capital punish- ment (*Tanin*, July 7, 1325/July 20, 1909, quoted in Sina Akşin, *31 Mart Olayı*, p.197n).

[176] "Die Einnahme Konstantinopels: Kapitulation des Jildis," *Berliner Tage- blatt und Handels-Zeitung*, April 24, 1909, Evening Edition, p.1; "Die Vorgänge im Orient: Die Einnahme Konstantinopels," *Vossische Zeitung*, April 24, 1909, Evening Edition, p.1; "Die Belagerung des Jildis Kiosk," *Berliner Tageblatt und Handels-Zeitung*, April 25, 1909, p.1; "Drohungen der Comitésoldaten," *Berliner Tageblatt und Handels-Zeitung*, April 25, 1909, pp.1-2; and, William M. Ramsay, *The Revolution in Constantinople and Turkey*, p.97. See also, Yusuf Hikmet Bayur, *Türk İnkılâbı Tarihi, 1/2*, p.205-206.

[177] Die Proklamation vor dem Einmarsch," *Berliner Tageblatt und Handels- Zeitung*, April 24, 1909, Evening Edition, p.4; "Einmarsch der Truppen—Prokla- mation des Generalissimus," *Osmanischer Lloyd*, April 24, 1909, p.1; and, Cemal Kutay, *Üç Paşalar Kavgası*, p.77.

[178] Mary A. Poynter, *When Turkey Was Turkey*, p.69; and, Hasan Amca, *Doğ- mayan Hürriyet: Bir Devrin İçyüzü, 1908-1918*, p.88.

[179] William M. Ramsay, *The Revolution in Constantinople and Turkey*, p.99.

[180] William M. Ramsay, *The Revolution in Constantinople and Turkey*, pp.99- 100.

[181] "Die Aktion an der asiatischen Küste," *Berliner Tageblatt und Handels- Zeitung*, April 26, 1909, Morning Edition, p.1; "Der einsame Sultan," *Berliner Tageblatt und Handels-Zeitung*, April 26, 1909, Evening Edition, p.1; "Der Fall der Selimie-Kaserne," *Berliner Tageblatt und Handels-Zeitung*, April 26, 1909, Even-

By late afternoon, all the barracks had been taken; the Sultan surrendered without a fight. He was now in the hands of the military pending the arrival of the National Assembly from San Stefano.[182] In the meantime, Mahmud Şevket Pasha declared martial law throughout the city and informed the National Assembly which, in turn, approved the measure.[183] Mahmud Şevket Pasha also told the National Assembly that it was safe to return to İstanbul to the Parliament building, and the Assembly decided to meet there the following day.[184]

Those counter-revolutionary leaders who were to stand trial were detained at the Unionist club of Bakırköy.[185] Derviş Vahdeti was caught at İzmir while transferring from the ship he had left İstanbul with to another ship.[186] Nâzım Pasha, who had replaced Mahmud Muhtar Pasha as Commander of the First Army Corps after the *coup*, was dismissed; Mahmud Muhtar Pasha was reinstituted.[187]

On April 26, the military began making arrests, and a special Tribunal was immediately created.[188] Most of the staff at the

---

ing Edition, p.4; and, William M. Ramsay, *The Revolution in Constantinople and Turkey*, p.104.

[182] "Der Belagerungszustand über Konstantinopel—Die Kapitulation der Jildistruppen," *Osmanischer Lloyd*, April 26, 1909, p.1; "Der gefangene Sultan: Die Umzingelung des Jildis—Der Widerstand auf dem asiatischen Ufer," *Berliner Tageblatt und Handels-Zeitung*, April 26, 1909, Morning Edition, p.1; "Abdülhamid Nasıl Teslim Oldu?" *İkdam*, April 16, 1325/April 29, 1909, p.1; and, William M. Ramsay, *The Revolution in Constantinople and Turkey*, p.105. See also, Hüseyin Işık, "İkinci Meşrutiyet'in İlânında ve Korunmasında Silahlı Kuvvetlerimizin Rolü," p.55; and, Hasan Amca, *Doğmayan Hürriyet: Bir Devrin İçyüzü, 1908-1918*, pp.87-88.

[183] "İdare-i Örfiye Beyannamesi," *İkdam*, April 13, 1325/April 26, 1909, p.1; "Militärdiktatur," *Berliner Tageblatt und Handels-Zeitung*, April 26, 1909, Evening Edition, p.1; "Dersaadet Umum İnzibat Dairesi'nin İlân-ı Resmisi," *İkdam*, April 13, 1325/April 26, 1909, p.1; Cemal Kutay, *Üç Paşalar Kavgası*, p.77; and, Sina Akşin, *31 Mart Olayı*, pp.201-208. See also, Mevlânzade Rıfat, *31 Mart: Bir İhtilâlin Hikâyesi*, p.187; and, Yusuf Hikmet Bayur, *Türk İnkılâbı Tarihi, 1/2*, p.206.

[184] "Beratung der Nationalversammlung," *Berliner Tageblatt und Handels-Zeitung*, April 26, 1909, Evening Edition, p.1; Cemal Kutay, *Üç Paşalar Kavgası*, p.77; and, Sina Akşin, *31 Mart Olayı*, p.208.

[185] "Die Kämpfe des Sonntags," *Berliner Tageblatt und Handels-Zeitung*, April 26, 1909, Evening Edition, p.1; Sina Akşin, *31 Mart Olayı*, p.202.

[186] *İkdam*, April 13, 1325/April 26, 1909, quoted in Sina Akşin, *31 Mart Olayı*, p.203.

[187] *İkdam*, April 13, 1325/April 26, 1909, quoted in Sina Akşin, *31 Mart Olayı*, p.203. Nâzım Pasha's letter of resignation reached the Grand Vezirate on April 26 (Sina Akşin, *31 Mart Olayı*, p.215).

[188] "Die Hinrichtung der Schuldigen," *Berliner Tageblatt und Handels-Zeitung*, April 27, 1909, Morning Edition, p.2; and, Sina Akşin, *31 Mart Olayı*, p.209.

Yıldız Palace was taken into custody, put aboard outbound ships, and summarily exiled.[189] More than five thousand prisoners were taken to the camps set up along the Golden Horn. Among the soldiers taken to the camps for confinement, there were also persons dressed as hodjas as well as some high officials of the Palace.[190]

Printed in Salonica and appearing for the first time since the *coup*, *Tanin* published editorials by Hüseyin Cahid [Yalçın] and Cavid Bey which advocated the necessity of harsh measures against the counter-revolutionaries in order to guarantee the success of the Revolution of 1908.[191]

Leaving Salonica by train the previous night, Hüseyin Cahid [Yalçın] and Cavid Bey entered İstanbul on the morning of April 27.[192] They immediately went to the Chamber of Deputies where they were given a warm welcome.[193]

The Chamber decided to remove Abdülhamid from the throne, replacing him with Mehmed Reşad.[194] With the exception of the Ministers of Justice, War, and the Navy, the Tevfik Pasha Cabinet was allowed to remain in office until it was replaced by the Hüseyin Hilmi Pasha Cabinet on May

---

[189] Sina Akşin, *31 Mart Olayı*, p.216.

[190] "Die Hinrichtung der Schuldigen," *Berliner Tageblatt und Handels-Zeitung*, April 27, 1909, Morning Edition, p.2; "Massenverhaftungen in Konstantinopel," *Berliner Tageblatt und Handels-Zeitung*, April 27, 1909, Evening Edition, p.1; and, Mary A. Poynter, *When Turkey Was Turkey*, pp.69-70.

[191] *Tanin*, April 14, 1325/April 27, 1909, quoted in Sina Akşin, *31 Mart Olayı*, pp.212-213.

[192] Hüseyin Cahid Yalçın, "Meşrutiyet Hatıraları, 1908-1918," *Fikir Hareketleri*, 5 (October 26, 1935-April 18, 1936), p.165.

[193] Cemal Kutay, *Üç Paşalar Kavgası*, p.77.

[194] "Absetzung des Sultans!" *Berliner Tageblatt und Handels-Zeitung*, April 27, 1909, Evening Edition, p.1; "Die Enthronung Abdul Hamids," *Osmanischer Lloyd*, April 27, 1909, p.1; "VAE VICTIS! Abdul Hamids Abschied—Neue Verhaftungen—Mohammeds V. Eidesleistung," *Berliner Tageblatt und Handels-Zeitung*, April 28, 1909, Morning Edition, p.1; "Zur Absetzung Abdul Hamids: Das Fetwa des Scheikh-ûl-Islam," *Berliner Tageblatt und Handels-Zeitung*, April 28, 1909, Morning Edition, p.3; "Der Thronwechsel in der Türkei," *Vossische Zeitung*, April 28, 1909, Morning Edition, p.1; "Der Thronwechsel," *Osmanischer Lloyd*, April 28, 1909, p.1; "Der Thronwechsel in der Türkei: Der historische Tag in Konstantinopel," *Berliner Tageblatt und Handels-Zeitung*, April 28, 1909, Evening Edition, p.4; Cemal Kutay, *Üç Paşalar Kavgası*, p.77; Sina Akşin, *31 Mart Olayı*, pp.216-218; and, Hüseyin Cahid Yalçın, "Meşrutiyet Hatıraları, 1908-1918," *Fikir Hareketleri*, 5 (October 26, 1935-April 18, 1936), p.165. See also, Mevlânzade Rıfat, *31 Mart: Bir İhtilâlin Hikâyesi*, pp.177-180; Edwin Pears, *Forty Years in Constantinople: The Recollections of Sir Edwin Pears, 1873-1915*, pp.284-285; and, Yusuf Hikmet Bayur, *Türk İnkılâbı Tarihi*, 1/2, p.209.

5.[195]

The leadership of the Liberal Union had either fled or been arrested. Prince Sabahaddin, the leader of the party, had been arrested on April 26 at his estate in Pendik.[196] Kâmil Pasha, another leader, was under house arrest; Kâmil Pasha's son, Said Pasha, had been deeply compromised in the counter-revolutionary *coup* attempt.[197] However, Said Pasha had escaped to Egypt along with Mevlânzade Rıfat, editor-in-chief of *Serbesti*, Rıza Nur, deputy for Sinob, and Nureddin Ferruh [Alkend], Secretary-General of the Liberal Union.[198] The British and French Embassies, however, came to Prince Sabahaddin's defence, managing to secure his release on April 29. He was subsequently exiled.[199] It was felt that because Prince Sabahaddin had for years lived in exile in Paris, his imprisonment would unduly prejudice French public opinion against the newly re-established regime.[200]

On the night of April 27, Abdülhamid and his household were escorted from the Yıldız Palace to a special train destined for Salonica.[201] With the successful suppression of the *coup*

---

[195] "Der Rücktritt des Kabinetts Tewfik," *Berliner Tageblatt und Handels-Zeitung*, April 29, 1909, Morning Edition, p.2; "Das neue Kabinett Tewfik Pascha," *Osmanischer Lloyd*, May 2, 1909, p.1; and, Sina Akşin, *31 Mart Olayı*, p.219.

[196] "Das Strafgericht," *Berliner Tageblatt und Handels-Zeitung*, April 28, 1909, Morning Edition, p.2; William M. Ramsay, *The Revolution in Constantinople and Turkey*, p.114, and p.116; Sina Akşin, *31 Mart Olayı*, p.209; Ahmed Bedevi Kuran, *Osmanlı İmparatorluğunda İnkılâp Hareketleri ve Milli Mücadele*, p.521; and, Ahmed Bedevi Kuran, *İnkılâp Tarihimiz ve 'Jön Türkler,'* p.282.

[197] "Das Geständnis der gefangenen Meuterer," *Berliner Tageblatt und Handels-Zeitung*, April 29, 1909, Morning Edition, p.2; and, William M. Ramsay, *The Revolution in Constantinople and Turkey*, p.114. Kâmil Pasha was kept under house arrest until May 29, 1909 (A. A. Türkei 159, No.2/252, Telegram from Marschall, Therapia, May 31, 1909). Yusuf Hikmet Bayur, the official historian of the period and a relative of Kâmil Pasha, denies his involvement in the *coup* attempt (Yusuf Hikmet Bayur, *Türk İnkılâbı Tarihi*, 1/2, p.185). However, Kâmil Pasha was pointed out as one of the conspirators (A. A. Türkei 159, No.2/197, Telegram from Marschall, Pera, April 29, 1909. For Mahmud Şevket Pasha's declaration to that effect to the German Ambassador Marschall see, A. A. Türkei 159, No.2/243, Telegram from Marschall, Therapia, May 24, 1909).

[198] A. A. Türkei 159, No.2/52, Copy of Oppenheim's report, "Türkische Flüchtlinge in Egypten," Cairo, April 28, 1909.

[199] "Verhaftungen und Freilassungen," *Vossische Zeitung*, April 29, 1909, p.1; and, William M. Ramsay, *The Revolution in Constantinople and Turkey*, pp.116-117, and p.134. See also, Ahmed Bedevi Kuran, *İnkılâp Tarihimiz ve 'Jön Türkler,'* p.282; Ahmed Bedevi Kuran, *Osmanlı İmparatorluğunda İnkilâp Hareketleri ve Milli Mücadele*, p.521; and, Yusuf Hikmet Bayur, *Türk İnkılâbı Tarihi*, 1/2, p.185—all of which ignore the fact that Prince Sabahaddin was let free because of foreign pressure.

[200] William M. Ramsay, *The Revolution in Constantinople and Turkey*, p.135.

[201] "Abdul Hamid in Saloniki," *Berliner Tageblatt und Handels-Zeitung*,

and the removal of Sultan Abdülhamid from the throne, the Unionists in alliance with the Third Army Corps reestablished constitutional rule.[202]

The *coup* was a well-organised monarchist scheme to restore the absolutist regime.[203] It is not, as most historians still continue to argue, a spontaneous outburst of religious reaction on the part of the İstanbul mob which, nevertheless, served the purpose of those who wanted a return to the Hamidian regime. As events at İstanbul amply demonstrated, the *coup* was well-planned ahead, and the Palace as well as monarchist pashas and politicians were intimately involved with its execution. The fact that it was conceived by top-level monarchists well in advance has further been born out by events that occurred simultaneously in the provinces.

The Albanian troops which had been sent away from İstanbul reached Salonica on April 11. They were in such a dangerous frame of mind that two Constitutionalist battalions had to be sent to overawe them before they got on the train which was to take them into the interior.[204]

On the night of April 12, the same night that the counter-revolutionary *coup* began, anti-Unionist feeling erupted in the barracks of the Salonica battalions, where ex-officers and hodjas had worked up the troops to such a point that they demanded "the land be freed of those atheists, traitors, enemies

April 28, 1909, Evening Edition, pp.1-2; "Die Abfahrt Abdul Hamids nach Saloniki," *Berliner Tageblatt und Handels-Zeitung*, April 29, 1909, Morning Edition, p.1: "Das 'Gefängnis' des entthronten Sultans," *Berliner Tageblatt und Handels-Zeitung*, April 29, 1909, Morning Edition, p.2; "Abdul Hamid in Saloniki: Die Ankunft," *Berliner Tageblatt und Handels-Zeitung*, April 29, 1909, Evening Edition, p.4; "Abdul Hamid," *Vossische Zeitung*, April 29, 1909, Evening Edition, p.1; "Abdülhamid Selânik'e Nasıl Gitti?" *İkdam*, April 18, 1325/May 1, 1909, pp.1-2; "Selânik'te Abdülhamid," *İkdam*, April 18, 1325/May 1, 1909, p.2; Cemal Kutay, *Üç Paşalar Kavgası*, p.77; Edwin Pears, *Forty Years in Constantinople: The Recollections of Sir Edwin Pears, 1873-1915*, p.287; idem, *Life of Abdul Hamid*, pp.322-323; Abdurrahman Şeref, *Son Vak'anüvis Abdurrahman Şeref Efendi Tarihi: II. Meşrutiyet Olayları, 1908-1909*, pp.61-63; and, William M. Ramsay, *The Revolution in Constantinople and Turkey*, p.133. See also, Yusuf Hikmet Bayur, *Türk İnkılâbı Tarihi, 1/2*, p.213.
[202] "Die Jungtürken an der Regierung," *Vossische Zeitung*, April 29, 1909, Evening Edition, p.1.
[203] For a political commentary along these lines which is published *immediately* after the march on İstanbul see, Paul Michaelis, "Politische Wochenschau," *Berliner Tageblatt und Handels-Zeitung*, April 25, 1909 p.1.
[204] Francis McCullagh, *The Fall of Abd-ul-Hamid*, p.149.

of Islam, who called themselves Unionists." Early the following morning, soldiers rushed on their unsuspecting officers
and detained them. Thus insurrection at the Salonica barracks
started at about the same time as it started in İstanbul.[205]

Disguised as ulemas, many reactionary agents travelled
throughout Anatolia preaching against the Unionists and the
constitutional regime. The clergy in İstanbul, however,
exposed them as fakes by wiring to the provincial centres.[206]

Immediately before the *coup* of April 13, *agents provocateurs* had spread the word in Erzincan to the effect that there
would soon be a revolt to establish *shari'a* during which not
only military students and officers but also the Armenians
would be massacred. The rumours proved to be correct in Erzincan; on April 13, the same day of the *coup* in İstanbul,
soldiers mutinied, making a pro-monarchist march through
the town carrying Korans. The mutinied soldiers gathered at
the main square of the town where they put their demands to
İbrahim Pasha, Commander of the Fourth Army Corps, and to
Sheikh Hacı Fevzi Efendi, a prominent religious leader of Erzincan. One of the mutinied soldiers threatened İbrahim Pasha with a sword but the pasha acted quick enough to stave off
the danger to his life. Both İbrahim Pasha and the Sheikh
managed to control the mutinied soldiers with promises to
listen to their demands the following day. As the mob dispersed it destroyed the local office of the Committee of Union
and Progress.[207]

The next day, the mutineers along with their leaders appeared before the Army Headquarters to see İbrahim Pasha.
As soon as İbrahim Pasha came out of the building, loyalist
soldiers in the garrison trapped the mutineers upon İbrahim
Pasha's signal. All mutineers were subsequently rounded off
and disarmed. Having controlled the situation at Erzincan, İb-
rahim Pasha left the town for Erzurum, from where news of
reactionary activity had reached the Fourth Army Headquar-

[205] Francis McCullagh, *The Fall of Abd-ul-Hamid*, p.70.
[206] Francis McCullagh, *The Fall of Abd-ul-Hamid*, p.52.
[207] Alpaslan Orhon, "Erzurum ve Erzincan'da '31 Mart Olayı' ile İlgili Ayaklanmalar ve Bastırılışları," pp.98-106; and, Celal Bayar, *Ben de Yazdım*, *I*, pp.159-
160.

ters.[208]

Another pro-monarchist outbreak in Erzurum was prepared to coincide with the *coup* in İstanbul. Emissaries from İstanbul made promises to the soldiers and gave them money, aided and abetted by reactionary *ulemas* and the Commander Yusuf Pasha himself.[209] Although no direct evidence linked Yusuf Pasha to this plot, many believed that Yusuf Pasha had been conspiring with discontented elements in the Fourth Army Corps.[210] He had been named Military Commander of Erzurum in February of 1909. Evidence showed that he had scarcely reached his new post when he began instigating reactionary intrigues, for, as one of the Sultan's most capable adherents, he immediately saw that the Sultan's interests were threatened by the new constitutional regime.[211]

Having foreknowledge of the monarchist plot, the local members of the Committee of Union and Progress, who were in considerably stronger position than their colleagues at Erzincan, foiled the monarchists' plans by arranging a demonstration to denounce the *coup* before the monarchists could even act.[212] In addition to the arrival into town of a contingent of cavalry, including well-known Unionist revolutionaries, their task in organising a demonstration was made easier since public feeling against the *coup* to bring back the old regime was very strong in Erzurum.[213] The demonstration took place on Friday, April 16. A crowd of ten to fifteen thousand, consisting of Muslims, Christians, and soldiers, assembled in front of the Government building, along with a group of high officials, including Tahir Pasha, the Governor of Erzurum, İbrahim Pasha, the Commander of the Fourth Army Corps, and Yusuf Pasha, the Military Commander of Erzurum. Speeches were delivered by the members of

---

[208] Celal Bayar, *Ben de Yazdım, I*, pp.160-161.
[209] F.O. 424/219, Consul Shipley to Sir Gerard Lowther, Erzerum, April 29, 1909, p.133.
[210] Alpaslan Orhon, "Erzurum ve Erzincan'da '31 Mart Olayı' ile İlgili Ayaklanmalar ve Bastırılışları," pp.95-97; and, F.O. 424/219, Consul Shipley to Sir Gerard Lowther, Erzerum, April 29, 1909, p.133.
[211] Francis McCullagh, *The Fall of Abd-ul-Hamid*, p.142.
[212] Celal Bayar, *Ben de Yazdım, I*, p.161.
[213] Celal Bayar, *Ben de Yazdım, I*, p.161; and, F.O. 424/219, Consul Shipley to Sir Gerard Lowther, Erzerum, April 23, 1909, p.131.

the local Committee of Union and Progress, by representatives of the Muslim and Christian communities, and by several of the *ulema*. Amid much enthusiastic cheering, resolutions were passed affirming the determination of all present to adhere to the principles of the Constitution, and to defend these to the last. İbrahim Pasha sent telegrams to this effect to İstanbul and Salonica, adding that the Fourth Army Corps was with the population and that it was ready to furnish a contingent if required.[214]

Yusuf Pasha, however, gained influence over the troops, non-commissioned officers, and some of the subaltern officers of the garrison, and on April 20, sent the 2nd Battalion of the 26th Regiment to the Governor's office in order to repeat the İstanbul drama of a week earlier. The mutineers encountered no resistance, and Yusuf Pasha took advantage of the situation in order to exile fifty-three Unionist officers under the pretext that the soldiers had insisted on this being done.[215] He also closed the local Unionist headquarters and there was direct evidence that he had personally been involved in the removal of the two leading civilian members of the Committee of Union and Progress.[216] Yusuf Pasha's plans for full scale re-action, however, were cut short when several functionaries of the local telegraph office, members of the Committee of Union and Progress, informed Mahmud Şevket Pasha of these developments. Mahmud Şevket Pasha ordered Marshall İbrahim Pasha, Commander of the Fourth Army Corps, to arrest the traitor. As Abdülhamid had fallen in the interval, throwing the monarchist elements in Erzurum into panic, this was fairly easy. Yusuf Pasha was subsequently sent to İstanbul under guard to face the Government's special Tribunal.[217]

At El-Shukurd, Veil Baba and Kara Kilise, similar monar-

---

[214] F.O. 424/219, Consul Shipley to Sir Gerard Lowther, Erzerum, April 23, 1909, p.131; Celal Bayar, *Ben de Yazdım, 1*, p.163; and, "Die Jungtürken vor Konstantinopel: Der Rachezug," *Berliner Tageblatt und Handels-Zeitung*, April 19, 1909, Morning Edition, p.1. See also, "Die Vermittelungsaktion der Parlamentarier," *Berliner Tageblatt und Handels-Zeitung*, April 19, 1909, Morning Edition, p.2.

[215] Francis McCullagh, *The Fall of Abd-ul-Hamid*, p.142.

[216] F.O. 424/219, Consul Shipley to Sir Gerard Lowther, Erzerum, April 29, 1909, p.133.

[217] F.O. 424/219, Consul Shipley to Sir Gerard Lowther, Erzerum, April 29, 1909, p.133; and, Francis McCullagh, *The Fall of Abd-ul-Hamid*, p.142.

chists conspiracies were carried out, ending in violence. That a dozen massacres did not occur in Anatolia instead of one or two was due to the efforts of the Unionist officers, who were able to preempt further bloodshed by forging official tele-grams and announcing the Sultan's dethronement before the event had actually taken place.[218]

Although a massacre had been planned in Aleppo, it did not materialise owing to the fact that, on the eve of the out-break, the military commander went to the Governor, told him he was aware of the monarchist plan for a massacre and his complicity in this plot, and threatened the Governor's life if massacres were to take place. The Governor apparently collapsed and remained incapacitated until all danger of an outbreak had passed. Meanwhile, the military patrolled the streets, with orders to arrest anyone who showed the slightest signs of provocation.[219]

Between April 14 and 16, the bloody massacre of the Arme-nians at Adana took place—several days after the arrival of a member of the Sultan's personal guard.[220] Based on certain absolutely reliable evidence, the Committee of Union and Progress later learned that the Sultan himself had given the orders, that not only the Armenians, but all members of the local Committee of Union and Progress had been targeted, and that the violence had originally been planned for April 23.[221] As had happened elsewhere, Cevad Bey, the Governor of Adana, remained aloof, thus letting the massacre plans of the monarchists take its course. He did not even interfere to stop

---

[218] Francis McCullagh, *The Fall of Abd-ul-Hamid*, p.142.
[219] Abdurrahman Şeref, *Son Vak'anüvis Abdurrahman Şeref Efendi Tarihi: II. Meşrutiyet Olayları, 1908-1909*, p.129; and, Francis McCullagh, *The Fall of Abd-ul-Hamid*, p.143.
[220] William M. Ramsay, *The Revolution in Constantinople and Turkey*, p.130, p.136, and p.205. See also, Feroz Ahmad, "Unionist Relations with the Greek, Armenian, and Jewish Communities of the Ottoman Empire, 1908-1914," p.420. Quotations from various sources and official reports on the massacre of the Armeni-ans at Adana see, Abdurrahman Şeref, *Son Vak'anüvis Abdurrahman Şeref Efendi Tarihi: II. Meşrutiyet Olayları, 1908-1909*, pp.66-129. For a completely different ac-count, which blames the victims—*i.e.*, Armenians—for the massacres, see, Salâhi R, Sonyel, "The Turco-Armenian 'Adana Incidents' in the Light of Secret British Documents, July 1908-December 1909," pp.1291-1338. For similar allegations see, Yusuf Hikmet Bayur, *Türk İnkılâbı Tarihi, 1/2*, p.196.
[221] The testimony of Hüseyin Cahid [Yalçın]'s wife, in William M. Ramsay, *The Revolution in Constantinople and Turkey*, pp.182-183.

the tins of petroleum stored in the Government depots from being taken out to set on fire the Armenian quarter of the city.[222] During the attack on the Armenians, some seventeen thousand were massacred, while about nineteen hundred of the attackers were killed by Armenians who tried to repel the attack.[223] Large sections of Adana had been completely burned down by the mob.[224] The only satisfactory fact was that the Muslim religious leaders of Adana immediately denounced the outrages and joined with the Armenian Church leaders to show their sympathy with the victims, thus preventing further massacres.[225] Similar events also took place in closeby towns, Mersin and Tarsus, where Armenians were attacked and their neighbourhoods burned down by mobs provoked by *agents provocateurs*.[226] At Kozan and Maraş, too, reactionary mobs had attacked the Armenians.[227] If the monarchists were thinking of Adana, it was highly likely that they had also had their minds directed to parts of Anatolia closer to the capital.[228]

· Whether Abdülhamid was involved in the massacres or not, in many cases it was more than likely that local governors knew what was coming and that, if they did not wholeheartedly approve, they were at least willing to look the other way.[229] Others were reportedly paralysed with fear.

Immediately after the *coup* attempt on April 13, three *agents provocateurs* disguised as hodjas arrived at Konya, and preaching in the mosques, urged people to make a holy war

---

[222]   Edwin Pears, "Turkey: Developments and Forecasts," p.708.

[223]   İsmail Hami Danişmend, *Sadr-ı-a'zam Tevfik Paşa'nın Dosyasındaki Resmi ve Hususi Vesikalara Göre: 31 Mart Vak'ası*, p.123.

[224]   Sina Akşin, *31 Mart Olayı*, p.145.

[225]   Edwin Pears, "Turkey: Developments and Forecasts," p.708.

[226]   "Die Metzeleien in Mersina und Adana," *Berliner Tageblatt und Handels-Zeitung*, April 18, 1909, p.2; "Die Massacres von Mersina," *Berliner Tageblatt und Handels-Zeitung*, April 19, 1909, Morning Edition, p.2; "Der Scheich ul Islam gegen die Absetzung: Der gestrige Ministerrat," *Berliner Tageblatt und Handels-Zeitung*, April 21, 1909, Morning Edition, p.3; "Die Unruhen in Kleinasien," *Berliner Tageblatt und Handels-Zeitung*, April 21, 1909, Evening Edition, p.4; "Die Metzeleien in Kleinasien," *Berliner Tageblatt und Handels-Zeitung*, April 30, 1909, Morning Edition, p.2; and, Sina Akşin, *31 Mart Olayı*, p.145.

[227]   "Der Scheich ul Islam gegen die Absetzung: Der gestrige Ministerrat," *Berliner Tageblatt und Handels-Zeitung*, April 21, 1909, Morning Edition, p.3; Abdurrahman Şeref, *Son Vak'anüvis Abdurrahman Şeref Efendi Tarihi: II. Meşrutiyet Olayları, 1908-1909*, p.129; and, Sina Akşin, *31 Mart Olayı*, p.168.

[228]   William M. Ramsay, *The Revolution in Constantinople and Turkey*, p.130.

[229]   Francis McCullagh, *The Fall of Abd-ul-Hamid*, p.141.

against the Christians. Though panic seized the town for several days, the population of Konya refused to rise, and actually arrested one of the hodjas, as he was preaching massacre in front of one of the mosques.[230] The Governor of Konya, in the meantime, remained secluded in his house for six days, reportedly ill, allowing events to take their course. Hundreds of Armenian refugees gathered in the grounds of the British Consulate at Konya. With the help of the Çelebi Efendi, an officer, who had been an exile of Abdülhamid's time, calmed the excited crowd and averted catasthrophe.[231] The Çelebi Efendi, head of the Mevlevi dervishes, delivered a speech in which he declared that all men were the children of God; he urged the Turks not to rise against their brethren.[232]

In Kayseri, the attempt to start riot and massacre was prevented by the decided and energetic action of Cemal Bey, the Governor, who foiled the plans of the monarchists.[233]

In various other towns order was maintained with more or less difficulty. That violence and massacre had been planned, and systematically preached by *agents provocateurs*, who either had or pretended to have a religious character as hodjas and dressed accordingly, was beyond dispute. The almost simultaneous appearance of *agents provocateurs* throughout the provinces and the similarity of the circumstances indicated that everywhere a single plan was in execution, and most felt that the Palace was at the centre of it all.[234]

The intention was obvious. The Unionists relied on Christian as much as they relied on Muslim political support. They had preached fraternity and equality, and denounced violence; their ideal was to bring about a unity of races and religions in a well-governed state. The violence organised by monarchists and the Yıldız Palace was designed to make this

---

[230] William M. Ramsay, *The Revolution in Constantinople and Turkey*, pp.201-202.

[231] William M. Ramsay, *The Revolution in Constantinople and Turkey*, pp.201-202.

[232] Francis McCullagh, *The Fall of Abd-ul-Hamid*, pp.141-142; and, William M. Ramsay, *The Revolution in Constantinople and Turkey*, p.202.

[233] William M. Ramsay, *The Revolution in Constantinople and Turkey*, p.202; Abdurrahman Şeref, *Son Vak'anüvis Abdurrahman Şeref Efendi Tarihi: II. Meşrutiyet Olayları, 1908-1909*, p.129; and, Sina Akşin, *31 Mart Olayı*, pp.168-169.

[234] William M. Ramsay, *The Revolution in Constantinople and Turkey*, pp.202-203.

impossible. Had the plan come to fruition, the monarchists could have denounced the Unionist ideal as an empty dream, shown that the Committee of Union and Progress did not have the strength to establish its authority over Turkey, and righteously declared that the old regime was the only form of government which could preserve peace.[235]

---

[235] William M. Ramsay, *The Revolution in Constantinople and Turkey*, pp.203-204.

CHAPTER FOUR

RE-ESTABLISHMENT OF CONSTITUTIONAL RULE AND THE CONTINUING STRUGGLE BETWEEN THE UNIONISTS AND THE MONARCHIST FORCES

After the restoration of the constitutional regime, all power was virtually in the hands of Mahmud Şevket Pasha, though, at first, he did not exercise this power directly.[1] Although he had ostensibly come from Salonica to protect the Constitution, Mahmud Şevket Pasha soon made it abundantly clear that he himself intended to be free of all constitutional checks. He also dissociated himself from the Committee of Union and Progress. In a communiqué he issued on May 3, Mahmud Şevket Pasha insisted on the army's entire independence of any political party, and stated that any officers who continued to be members of any political organisation would be dismissed from the army.[2] On May 18, without precedent, he became the Inspector-General of the first three Army Corps.[3] The position had clearly been created to meet the prevailing political situation; it placed Mahmud Şevket Pasha outside the Cabinet's authority, and this included that of the Minister of War.[4]

Because all decisions were made under his personal supervision, the Committee of Union and Progress was almost powerless.[5] Besides, the *coup* had left the Unionists' entire İstanbul

---

[1] Edwin Pears, "Turkey: Developments and Forecasts," p.718; and, Halid Ziya Uşaklıgil, *Saray ve Ötesi*, *1*, pp.44-45.

[2] "The Turkish Outlook: The Army and Politics," *The Times*, May 4, 1909, p.5.

[3] "Turkey: Army Appointments," *The Times*, May 19, 1909, p.5.

[4] Feroz Ahmad, *The Young Turks: The Committee of Union and Progress in Turkish Politics, 1908-1914*, pp.48-49; and, "Eski Bir Nazırın Siyaset Hatıraları," *Tan*, January 21, 1937, quoted in İbnülemin Mahmud Kemal İnal, *Osmanlı Devrinde Son Sadrıazamlar*, p.1884.

[5] E. J. Dillon, "A Clue to the Turkish Tangle," pp.750-753; Mahmud Muhtar Pasha, *Maziye Bir Nazar*, quoted in İbnülemin Mahmud Kemal İnal, *Osmanlı*

organisation in disarray. Faced with the task of reconstruction, the Unionists were unable to really compete for direct power.[6] Moreover, there was still opposition to the policies of the Committee of Union and Progress within the military. Even the Third Army Corps which had restored the constitutional regime at the cost of some lives contained elements which were not particularly pro-Unionist. This included some high level officers—notably, Mahmud Şevket Pasha himself. Thus, the position of the Unionists were quite shaky, although appearance suggested otherwise.[7] This was publicly confirmed by a report published in the May 11 issue of *Neues Wiener Tageblatt*. According to the article, a prominent Unionist leader at Salonica had admitted during the course of an interview with an Austrian diplomat that most of the Unionist leadership considered the situation very dark and confused. The difficulty of the situation, as the prominent Unionist leader stated, lay in the fact that there was still secret agitation carried on by the supporters of the old regime.[8] The leadership of the Committee of Union and Progress, however, skilfully kept up the appearance of strength, if not dominance, and succeeded in convincing the public that both it and the constitutional regime enjoyed the full support of the military.[9]

After the suppression of the *coup* the monarchists attempted once more to stay in power.[10] Tevfik Pasha made some changes in his cabinet on April 29: he named Salih Pasha, the Commander of the Second Army Corps, Minister of War, Ali Rıza Pasha Minister of the Navy, Ürgüplü Hayri Bey, deputy for Niğde, Minister of Justice, and Cavid Bey, deputy for Salonica, Minister of Finance.[11] Tevfik Pasha had named Ür-

Devrinde Son Sadrıazamlar, p.1884; and, Feroz Ahmad, *The Young Turks: The Committee of Union and Progress in Turkish Politics, 1908-1914*, p.48.

[6] Halid Ziya Uşaklıgil, *Saray ve Ötesi*, *1*, p.44; and, Edwin Pears, "Turkey: Developments and Forecasts," p.718.

[7] Hüseyin Cahid Yalçın, "Meşrutiyet Hatıraları, 1908-1918," *Fikir Hareketleri*, *5* (October 26, 1935-April 18, 1936), p.373.

[8] *Neues Wiener Tagblatt*, May 11, 1909, excerpted in "Task of the Young Turks," *The Times*, May 13, 1909, p.5.

[9] Hüseyin Cahid Yalçın, "Meşrutiyet Hatıraları, 1908-1918," *Fikir Hareketleri*, *5* (October 26, 1935-April 18, 1936), p.373.

[10] Mehmed Cavid, "Mesrutiyet Devrine Ait Cavit Bey'in Hatıraları: 8," *Tanin*, September 6, 1943, p.2.

[11] "New Cabinet," *The Levant Herald and Eastern Express*, April 30, 1909, p.1; and, Mehmed Cavid, "Meşrutiyet Devrine Ait Cavit Bey'in Hatıraları: 8," *Tanin*,

güplü Hayri and Cavid Beys, two Unionist deputies, ministers in his reconstituted cabinet without informing either of them. As the Committee of Union and Progress was against the retention of Tevfik Pasha, Ürgüplü Hayri and Cavid Beys immediately handed in their resignations, rejecting the positions offered in an attempt to force Tevfik Pasha leave office.[12] Still trying to cling to power, Tevfik Pasha appointed Sabri Bey, a member of the Chamber, Minister of Justice. The Ministry of the Interior was offered to Hüseyin Hilmi Pasha, who declined it, while the Minister for Foreign Affairs and the Ministers of Public Works and of Pious Foundations were unchanged.[13] On April 30, he appointed Avlonyalı Ferid Pasha, the ex-Grand Vezier under the old regime, Minister of the Interior.[14]

Meanwhile, the Unionist leadership at İstanbul met and discussed the political situation on April 30. As the political climate, especially the opposition against the Committee of Union and Progress within the military, was not favourable for the formation of a Unionist cabinet at this juncture, the leadership decided to press for the appointment of either Hüseyin Hilmi Pasha or Hakkı Bey as Grand Vezier, and the creation of under-secretaryships in the ministries to be filled with Unionist deputies.[15] That same day, the Unionists prepared a cabinet list with Hüseyin Hilmi Pasha as Grand Vezier, Salih Pasha as Minister of War, Arif Hikmet Pasha as Minister of the Navy, Talât Bey as Minister of the Interior, Hakkı Bey as Minister for Foreign Affairs, Bedros Haladjian as Minister of Public Works, Cavid Bey as Minister of Finance, Hüseyin Cahid [Yalçın] as Minister of Education, Ürgüplü Hayri Bey as Minister of Justice, Mısırlı Khalil Hammada Pasha as Minister of the Pious Foundations, and Aristidi

September 6, 1943, p.2.

[12] Mehmed Cavid, "Meşrutiyet Devrine Ait Cavit Bey'in Hatıraları: 8," *Tanin*, September 6, 1943, p.2; and, "The Fall of Abdul Hamid: The Formation of a New Ministry," *The Times*, April 30, 1909, p.5.

[13] "The Fall of Abdul Hamid: The Formation of a New Ministry," *The Times*, April 30, 1909, p.5.

[14] "The Situation in Turkey," *The Times*, May 1, 1909, p.7.

[15] Mehmed Cavid, "Meşrutiyet Devrine Ait Cavit Bey'in Hatıraları: 8," *Tanin*, September 6, 1943, p.2, and "Meşrutiyet Devrine Ait Cavit Bey'in Hatıraları: 9," *Tanin*, September 7, 1943, p.2.

Pasha Yorgandjioglu as Minister of Agriculture, Mines, and Forests. Though under a neutral Grand Vezier, this cabinet list was dominated by prominent Unionist deputies.[16]

However, the monarchists had little intention of leaving the Grand Veziership to even a neutral person, such as Hüseyin Hilmi Pasha. Upon monarchist pressure, Tevfik Pasha was, once again, given the task to form a cabinet with an imperial decree dated May 1.[17] He appointed Galib Bey, a senator, as the new Minister of Justice, and Rıfat Bey as the new Minister of Finance.[18] The list of ministers included monarchists and old regime pashas such as Avlonyalı Ferid Pasha as the new Minister of the Interior, Gabriel Nouradunghian as the new Minister of Commerce and Public Works, and Dimitraki Mavrocordato as the new Minister of Agriculture, Mines, and Forests. Salih Pasha and Ali Rıza Pasha were retained as Minister of War and Minister of the Navy, respectively.[19]

The cabinet had a decidedly monarchist bent. Among the members of the new cabinet, Raif Pasha, the President of the Council of State, Ali Rıza Pasha, the Minister of the Navy, and Dimitraki Mavrocordato, the Minister of Agriculture, Mines, and Forests, were fierce opponents of the Committee of Union and Progress, who demanded the imprisonment of Unionists as soon as they took office.[20] Avlonyalı Ferid Pasha's appointment caused considerable discussion. Unionists held that his record, especially as Grand Vezier during the last year of the absolutist regime, was not of a character to inspire confidence in the nation.[21]

Naturally, the cabinet was opposed by the Committee of

---

[16] "The Situation in Turkey: Proposed Young Turk Cabinet," *The Times*, May 1, 1909, p.7.

[17] I/I/64, April 19, 1325/May 2, 1909, *Meclis-i Mebusan Zabıt Ceridesi, 3*, pp.158-159; and, "Das neue Kabinett Tewfik Pascha," *Osmanischer Lloyd*, May 2, 1909, p.1. The translation of the imperial decree can be found in "The Situation in Turkey: Rescript by Mahomed V," *The Times*, May 3, 1909, p.7.

[18] "The Situation in Turkey: Rescript by Mahomed V," *The Times*, May 3, 1909, p.7; and, "Le Cabinet Tevfik pacha," *The Levant Herald and Eastern Express*, May 3, 1909, p.1.

[19] "Le Cabinet Tevfik pacha," *The Levant Herald and Eastern Express*, May 3, 1909, p.1; and, "The Situation in Turkey: The New Ministry," *The Times*, May 3, 1909, p.7.

[20] Mehmed Cavid, "Meşrutiyet Devrine Ait Cavit Bey'in Hatıraları: 9," *Tanin*, September 7, 1943, p.2.

[21] "The Situation in Turkey: The New Ministry," *The Times*, May 3, 1909, p.7.

Union and Progress. Many deputies expressed their dissatisfaction with the reconstituted Tevfik Pasha Cabinet, and it was
obvious that it lacked the confidence of the majority of the
Chamber.[22] Even *Yeni Gazete*, a monarchist daily, predicted
that the new cabinet would fail to obtain a vote of confidence
in the Chamber.[23]

Despite Unionist opposition and the prevailing uncertainty,
the Tevfik Pasha Cabinet proceeded to draw up a programme.[24] On May 3, Tevfik Pasha tried to get help from the
deputies in the Chamber for the drawing up of the programme
but the Unionist deputies flatly refused to get involved with a
monarchist cabinet.[25] In fact, Ahmed Rıza Bey, the President
of the Chamber, echoing the sentiment in the Chamber, was
insistent on the immediate resignation of the Tevfik Pasha
Cabinet. Talât Bey, the Vice-President of the Chamber, con-
veyed the sentiment of the deputies to Tevfik Pasha through
the intermediary of Ali Fuad [Türkgeldi], making it clear
that neither the Chamber nor the Committee of Union and
Progress wanted to see Tevfik Pasha remain in power. After a
joint meeting of the representatives of the Chamber on May
5—Talât Bey, and Aristidi Pasha Yorgandjioglu, the Second
Vice-President of the Chamber—and the cabinet, Tevfik Pasha
handed in his resignation.[26]

Besides the names of Hüseyin Hilmi Pasha and Hakkı
Bey, the Unionist leadership had also circulated the name of
Mahmud Şevket Pasha as a possible Grand Vezier. Actually,
Talât Bey, one of the leaders of the Committee of Union and
Progress, had already formally asked Mahmud Şevket Pasha
to accept the grand veziership. Fearing that he might lose his

---

[22] "The Situation in Turkey: The New Ministry," *The Times*, May 3, 1909, p.7.

[23] "The Fall of Abdul Hamid: The Formation of a New Ministry," *The Times*,
April 30, 1909, p.5; and, "The Cabinet," *The Levant Herald and Eastern Express*,
May 3, 1909, p.1.

[24] "The Turkish Outlook: Position of the Government," *The Times*, May 4,
1909, p.5; and, Mehmed Cavid, "Meşrutiyet Devrine Ait Cavit Bey'in Hatıraları:
9," *Tanin*, September 7, 1943, p.2.

[25] Mehmed Cavid, "Meşrutiyet Devrine Ait Cavit Bey'in Hatıraları: 9," *Tanin*, September 7, 1943, p.2.

[26] Ali Fuad Türkgeldi, *Görüp İşittiklerim*, pp.40-41; "Das neue Kabinett," *Osmanischer Lloyd*, May 6, 1909, p.1; "New Turkish Ministry: Composition of the
Cabinet," *The Times*, May 6, 1909, p.5; and, İbnülemin Mahmud Kemal İnal, *Osmanlı Devrinde Son Sadrıazamlar*, p.1712.

prestige and influence within the army if he accepted a political position, Mahmud Şevket Pasha declined the offer, suggesting, instead, the name of Gazi Ahmed Muhtar Pasha as a
possible candidate for the grand veziership.[27] When Gazi Ahmed Muhtar Pasha, too, declined the offer for similar reasons,
the Unionists' choice fell on Hüseyin Hilmi Pasha, who was
re-appointed as Grand Vezier, as the Committee of Union and
Progress had originally demanded.[28]

Hüseyin Hilmi Pasha was appointed to the Grand Vezierate
on May 5.[29] Public sentiment was by now largely behind his
re-appointment—indicating as it would that the *coup* had
failed, but that the Constitution was back in force.[30] However,
the Cabinet members remained mostly unchanged: Hüseyin
Hilmi Pasha retained Raif Pasha, President of the Council of
State, Rıfat Bey, Minister of Finance, Rıfat Pasha, Minister for
Foreign Affairs, Salih Pasha, Minister of War, Gabriel Nouradunghian, Minister of Commerce and Public Works, Khalil
Hammada Pasha, Minister of Pious Foundations, and Avlonyalı Ferid Pasha, Minister of the Interior, who was intimately
connected with the old regime.[31] Aristidi Pasha Yorgandjioglu replaced monarchist Dimitraki Mavrocordato as the new
Minister of Agriculture, Mines, and Forests; Nail Bey re-

[27] Colmar Von der Goltz, "Erinnerungen an Mahmud Schewket Pascha,"
Deutsche Rundshau, October-December 1913, p.198, quoted in Glen Wilfred Swanson, Mahmud Sevket Pasha and the Defense of the Ottoman Empire, pp.75-76.
[28] Glen Wilfred Swanson, Mahmud Sevket Pasha and the Defense of the Ottoman Empire, p.75; "Le nouveau Cabinet," *The Levant Herald and Eastern Express*, May 6, 1909, p.1; and Tevfik Pasha's statement, in İbnülemin Mahmud Kemal İnal, *Osmanlı Devrinde Son Sadrazamlar*, pp.1712-1713.
   The imperial decree announcing Hüseyin Hilmi Pasha's appointment as
Grand Vezier is dated Rebiulahir 15, 1327/April 22, 1325/May 5, 1909. The text of
the decree can be found in İbnülemin Mahmud Kemal İnal, *Osmanlı Devrinde
Son Sadrazamlar*, p.1671.
[29] "New Turkish Ministry," *The Times*, May 6, 1909, p.5; "Das neue Kabinett," *Osmanischer Lloyd*, May 6, 1909, p.1; and, Cemal Kutay, *Türkiye İstiklâl ve
Hürriyet Mücadeleleri Tarihi, 17*, pp.9543-9544.
[30] Halid Ziya Uşaklıgil, *Saray ve Ötesi, 1*, pp.80-81; and Ali Fuad Türkgeldi,
Görüp İşittiklerim, p.40. See also, Celal Bayar, *Ben de Yazdım, 2*, p.399.
[31] "Le nouveau Cabinet," *The Levant Herald and Eastern Express*, May 6, 1909,
p.1; "New Turkish Ministry: Composition of the Cabinet," *The Times*, May 6, 1909,
p.5; Mehmed Cavid, "Meşrutiyet Devrine Ait Cavit Bey'in Hatıraları: 9," *Tanin*,
September 7, 1943, p.2; Hüseyin Cahid Yalçın, "Meşrutiyet Hatıraları, 1908-1918,"
Fikir Hareketleri, 5 (October 26, 1935-April 18, 1936), p.389; and, Feroz Ahmad,
*The Young Turks: The Committee of Union and Progress in Turkish Politics,
1908-1914*, p.53.

placed Abdurrahman Bey as the new Minister of Education; and, Arif Hikmet Pasha replaced Ali Rıza Pasha as the new Minister of the Navy.[32] Sahib Molla was appointed Sheikh-ul-Islam.[33] His appointment was widely approved. He commanded very general respect and liking, and the disfavour with which he had been regarded by the Palace during the last years of Abdülhamid's reign bore testimony to the liberalism of his opinions.[34] When Hakkı Bey, Ambassador at Rome, refused the post of the Ministry of Justice, it was offered to Ürgüplü Hayri Bey, Unionist deputy for Niğde and Chairman of the Judicial Committee of the Chamber of Deputies.[35] However, monarchist opposition effectively blocked his appointment. Thereupon, Necmeddin [Kocataş], the Governor of Baghdad who was a capable official, was appointed to the post on May 17, and thus replaced Galib Bey as the new Minister of Justice.[36] Despite these changes, and the appointment of Cavid Bey as Under-Secretary of the Ministry of Finance, the reconstituted Cabinet of Hüseyin Hilmi Pasha was not totally devoid of monarchist Ministers who had come into power by the *coup* of April 13.[37]

Though previously supreme and unchallenged, the *coup* had also left the Committee of Union and Progress weakened in the Chamber. Supported by the military, those deputies who opposed the Unionists had begun a campaign to discredit them by blaming the *coup* on their 'irresponsible' behaviour. The tactic of blaming the *coup* on its victims proved largely successful, so much so that there would have been consid-

---

[32] "Le nouveau Cabinet," *The Levant Herald and Eastern Express*, May 6, 1909, p.1; and, "New Turkish Ministry: Composition of the Cabinet," *The Times*, May 6, 1909, p.5. See also, Celal Bayar, *Ben de Yazdım*, 2, p.399, and Ali Fuad Türkgeldi, *Görüp İşittiklerim*, p.41.

[33] "New Turkish Ministry: Composition of the Cabinet," *The Times*, May 6, 1909, p.5.

[34] "The New Turkish Ministry: Favourable Public Opinion," *The Times*, May 7, 1909, p.5.

[35] "The Turkish Outlook: Reported Change in the Ministry," *The Times*, May 8, 1909, p.7.

[36] "Turkey," *The Times*, May 18, 1909, p.5. See also, "Necmeddin Molla Kocataş," in İbrahim Alaettin Gövsa, *Türk Meşhurları Ansiklopedisi*, p.219.

[37] Mehmed Cavid, "Meşrutiyet Devrine Ait Cavit Bey'in Hatıraları: 9," *Tanin*, September 7, 1943, p.2. Tevfik Çavdar, citing the monarchist criticism of Hüseyin Hilmi Pasha Cabinet, mistakenly assumes that this Cabinet was really dominated by the Committee of Union and Progress (Tevfik Çavdar, *Talât Paşa: Bir Örgüt Ustasının Yaşam Öyküsü*, p.160).

erable opposition both within the military as well as monarchist circles had the Committee of Union and Progress openly
asked for positions in the new Hüseyin Hilmi Pasha Cabinet.[38]

Nonetheless, the Committee of Union and Progress was
displeased with the new Cabinet, principally with the fact that
all of its members had been chosen from among the 'experienced' and decorated pashas. Although these had supposedly
been selected for their personal integrity and ministerial competence, their high positions in the old regime made their
commitment to the Revolution's political and economic reform programme somewhat dubious. After all, deep down,
these pashas were monarchists.[39] By May 16, it had become
clear that only about one hundred and fifty deputies had
promised their votes for Hüseyin Hilmi Pasha. Although this
number was quite sufficient for the vote of confidence, it was
significant that the Grand Vezier was opposed by part of the
Committee of the Union and Progress, who accused him of
having shown culpable weakness on April 13—an accusation
to which Hüseyin Hilmi Pasha had already replied at length
in the Turkish press.[40]

On May 24, Hüseyin Hilmi Pasha appeared before the
Chamber to present his programme and ask for a vote of
confidence. The programme was similar in essentials to that
which he had laid before the Chamber when he was first
appointed Grand Vezier. With regard to the state of the interior, after declaring that strict application of the law in the
case of the reactionary agitators who caused the outbreak in
the capital would be indispensable, he pointed out that the disturbances at Adana were brought about by the same reactionary forces. The state of siege proclaimed at Adana was extended by order of the government to Maraş and Antakya. He
added that the Governor of Adana and the Sub-Governor of
Cebel-i Bereket had been relieved of their posts on account of
failure to do their duties. Hüseyin Hilmi Pasha also informed
the Chamber that a scheme for the thorough reorganisation of

---

[38] Hüseyin Cahid Yalçın, "Meşrutiyet Hatıraları, 1908-1918," *Fikir Hareketleri,* 5 (October 26, 1935-April 18, 1936), p.374.
[39] Hüseyin Cahid Yalçın, "Meşrutiyet Hatıraları, 1908-1918," *Fikir Hareketleri,* 5 (October 26, 1935-April 18, 1936), p.374.
[40] "Turkey: Hilmi Pasha's Ministry," *The Times,* May 17, 1909, p.6.

the police and gendarmerie had been adopted, and was beginning to be applied. He concluded his statement with a review of the legislative enactments under consideration, among which he specially mentioned the laws concerning the press and public meetings, which he hoped the Chamber would pass without loss of time.[41]

Following his statement, the Committee of Union and Progress deputies made their displeasure clear.[42] Though he came under heavy attack, the Chamber finally approved his cabinet by a vote of one hundred and ninety to five. There were several abstentions. The result was not unexpected. The necessity for supporting the only possible cabinet left when once the idea of appointing ministers from the ranks of the Committee of Union and Progress was excluded, was so obvious as to diminish its importance as a sign of the real feeling of the Chamber.[43] Some suggested that Mahmud Şevket Pasha and the threat of a complete military takeover had forced the Chamber to support the new cabinet.[44]

The press in general accepted the programme of the government with satisfaction, if without great enthusiasm, and expressed the hope that it would be rapidly carried out. The disappointments of the preceding month had undoubtedly caused its reception to be less enthusiastic than would otherwise have been the case.[45] *Tanin*, however, lost no time in criticising the new Hüseyin Hilmi Pasha Cabinet.[46] Hüseyin Cahid [Yalçın] began the attack in early June, describing the current situation as a war between the old and the new, between the forces of conservatism and those of progress. After

---

[41] I/I/78, May 11, 1325/May 24, 1909, *Meclis-i Mebusan Zabıt Ceridesi, 3,* pp.635-636; "Heyet-i Vükelâ'nın Programı," *Tanin*, May 12, 1325/May 25, 1909, p.2; and, "Turkey: Ministerial Statement of Policy," *The Times*, May 25, 1909, p.5.

[42] Hüseyin Cahid [Yalçın], "Kabinenin Programı," *Tanin*, May 12, 1325/ May 25, 1909, p.1; and, "Heyet-i Vükelâ'nın Programı," *Tanin*, May 12, 1325/May 25, 1909, p.2. See also, Feroz Ahmad, *The Young Turks: The Committee of Union and Progress in Turkish Politics, 1908-1914,* p.50.

[43] "Ministerial Programme Voted by Chamber," *The Levant Herald and Eastern Express*, May 25, 1909, p.1; and, "Turkey: A Vote of Confidence," *The Times*, May 25, 1909, p.5.

[44] Feroz Ahmad, *The Young Turks: The Committee of Union and Progress in Turkish Politics, 1908-1914,* p.50.

[45] "Turkey: The Press and the Government," *The Times*, May 26, 1909, p.5.

[46] Hüseyin Cahid [Yalçın], "Kabinenin Programı," *Tanin*, May 12, 1325/ May 25, 1909, p.1.

the Revolution of 1908, he said, the old regime's bureaucrats
had been allowed to retain their hold on nation's management, a mistake that had almost lost the nation its Constitution.[47] In another editorial, he argued that it was foolish to expect a political cadre which had opposed the Constitution from
the very start to overcome the barriers to a fully liberal democratic regime. This task, he stated, could only be entrusted to
those young partisans of the Revolution who had risked their
lives for the Constitution. He added that the existing cabinet
was not one which would carry out the policies of the Committee of Union and Progress.[48]

Gabriel Nouradunghian, Minister of Commerce and Public
Works in the Hüseyin Hilmi Pasha Cabinet, defended the
monarchist position. In an interview with the editor of *La
Turquie*, he began by criticising the procedure by which the
cabinet was formed. In his view, the selection of Ministers
from among members of the Chamber, subject to Chamber's
approval, had the drawback of making the cabinet 'dependent'
on the Parliament.[49] Clearly, this position was tantamount to
advocating the restoration of the absolutist regime whereby
the Sultan alone appointed and dismissed the Ministers. Hüseyin Cahid [Yalçın] countered the monarchists' arguments,
vehemently defending the principle of representative government, responsible to the Chamber of Deputies and not to the
whims of an absolute monarch.[50]

Immediately following the suppression of the *coup* attempt,
the government, prevailed upon by the Third Army Corps
and the Committee of Union and Progress, started arresting
those suspected of instigating the events. The pursuit of Ha-

---

[47] Hüseyin Cahid [Yalçın], "Çevirme Hareketi,"*Tanin*, May 19, 1325/June 1,
1909, p.1. See also, Hüseyin Cahid Yalçın, "Meşrutiyet Hatıraları, 1908-1918," *Fikir Hareketleri, 5* (October 26, 1935-April 18, 1936), p.374.
[48] Hüseyin Cahid [Yalçın], "Tenviri Lâzım bir Nokta," *Tanin*, May 23, 1325/
June 5, 1909, p.1. See also, Hüseyin Cahid Yalçın, "Meşrutiyet Hatıraları, 1908-
1918," *Fikir Hareketleri, 5* (October 26, 1935-April 18, 1936), p.374.
[49] The Interview was excerpted in *Tanin*, May 19, 1325/June 1, 1909 (Hüseyin
Cahid Yalçın, "Meşrutiyet Hatıraları, 1908-1918," *Fikir Hareketleri, 5* (October 26,
1935-April 18, 1936), p.375).
[50] Hüseyin Cahid [Yalçın], "Şekl-i Hükûmet," *Tanin*, May 16, 1325/May 29,
1909, p.1. See also, Hüseyin Cahid Yalçın, "Meşrutiyet Hatıraları, 1908-1918," *Fikir Hareketleri, 5* (October 26, 1935-April 18, 1936), p.389.

midian spies and reactionaries continued with unabated vigour.[51] A Court Martial was established in İstanbul, which began trying the counter-revolutionaries who had been arrested after the Third Army Corps had captured the capital.[52]

One of the first acts of the Court Martial was the trial of thirteen leaders of the mutiny, one a major on the retired list and thirteen belonging to the Fourth Battalion of Chasseurs. Found guilty as charged, they were sentenced to death, and were hanged in public on the morning of May 3.[53] Two military officers, Major Mehmed Ferid, of the Selimiye Barracks at İstanbul, and Adjutant Major Mehmed Namık were sentenced by the Court Martial to expulsion from the army and five years' hard labour.[54] Another trial that took place on May 3 was of the murderers of Ali Kabuli Bey, the Commander of the ironclad *Asar-ı Tevfik*, who had been killed while trying to stop the mob at Beşiktaş. The condemned men, who were all sentenced to death, included sailors, marines, a military *imam*, and a sub-lieutenant attached to the torpedo factory.[55] Their executions also took place in public on May 12.[56] On May 17, two rankers and three policemen who were found guilty of mutiny on April 13 were hanged in public.[57]

The Court Martial, at its May 3 sitting, did not give judge-

---

[51] "The Fall of Abdul Hamid: Press Opinions on the Revolution," *The Times*, April 30, 1909, p.5; and, Edwin Pears, *Forty Years in Constantinople: The Recollections of Sir Edwin Pears, 1873-1915*, pp.301-302.

[52] Ahmed Bedevi Kuran, *İnkılap Tarihimiz ve İttihad ve Terakki*, p.255; and, Edwin Pears, *Forty Years in Constantinople: The Recollections of Sir Edwin Pears, 1873-1915*, p.302.

[53] "The Turkish Outlook: Executions in the Capital," *The Times*, May 4, 1909, p.5; and, Zekeriya Türkmen, *Osmanlı Meşrutiyetinde Ordu-Siyaset Çatışması*, p.103. For the list of those hanged see, Abdurrahman Şeref, *Son Vak'anüvis Abdurrahman Şeref Efendi Tarihi: II. Meşrutiyet Olayları, 1908-1909*, pp.210-212.

[54] "Army Appointments and Punishments," *The Times*, May 8, 1909, p.7.

[55] "News Items," *The Levant Herald and Eastern Express*, May 4, 1909, p.1. See also, "The New Turkish Ministry," *The Times*, May 7, 1909, p.5; Hüseyin Işık, "İkinci Meşrutiyet'in İlânında ve Korunmasında Silahlı Kuvvetlerimizin Rolü," p.56; and, Abdurrahman Şeref, *Son Vak'anüvis Abdurrahman Şeref Efendi Tarihi: II. Meşrutiyet Olayları, 1908-1909*, pp.212-214.

[56] "Execution of the Murderers of Ali Kabuli Bey," *The Levant Herald and Eastern Express*, May 12, 1909, p.1; "Turkey: Further Executions," *The Times*, May 13, 1909, p.5; and, Zekeriya Türkmen, *Osmanlı Meşrutiyetinde Ordu-Siyaset Çatışması*, p.103. See also, *Resimli Kitab*, 2 (April-September 1909), p.762; "More Executions Fixed," *The Times*, May 12, 1909, p.5; and, Hüseyin Işık, "İkinci Meşrutiyet'in İlânında ve Korunmasında Silahlı Kuvvetlerimizin Rolü," p.56.

[57] "Turkey: Executions in Constantinople," *The Times*, May 18, 1909, p.5; and, Hüseyin Işık, "İkinci Meşrutiyet'in İlânında ve Korunmasında Silahlı Kuvvetlerimizin Rolü," p.56.

ment in the case of Murad Bey, editor of *Mizan*.[58] Described
by the foreign press as a monarchist infiltrator in the Committee of Union and Progress and a secret agent working for Sultan Abdülhamid, Murad Bey was accused of trying to incite
people against the constitutional regime and thus preparing
the ground for a civil war.[59] He was one of the few leaders of
the *coup* who could not escape from İstanbul when the attempt
had failed, and, consequently, he had been arrested on April
24.[60]

He defended himself in court on May 31.[61] In his defence,
despite evidence to the contrary, he denied any foreknowledge of or involvement with the *coup* attempt. He even
denied the role his newspaper *Mizan* played, despite the fact
that his editorials clearly supported the *coup* and the restoration of the absolutist regime of Abdülhamid.[62] A day later, totally unconvinced by Murad Bey's defence, the Court Martial
found him guilty as charged, and sentenced him to exile for
life in Rhodes.[63] On June 19, along with sixty-three other
monarchists found guilty on charges of attempting to overthrow the constitutional regime, he was put on board a ship
bound for Rhodes.[64]

Sabah of May 7 printed the contents of a *jurnal* written by
Ali Kemal Bey, editor-in-chief of *İkdam*, in which he assured

[58] "News Items," *The Levant Herald and Eastern Express*, May 4, 1909, p.1.
[59] "Les Evénements de Turquie," *La Paix*, May 2, 1909, p.1, quoted in Birol
Emil, *Mizancı Murad Bey: Hayatı ve Eserleri*, p.214n.
[60] Birol Emil, *Mizancı Murad Bey: Hayatı ve Eserleri*, pp.212-213. See also,
L'Eclaire, April 30, 1909, p.3, and *L'Independence Belge*, April 30, 1909, p.1, cited
in Birol Emil, *Mizancı Murad Bey: Hayatı ve Eserleri*, p.214n.
[61] Fevziye Abdullah Tansel, "Mizancı Mehmed Murad Bey," p.87.
[62] The text of his defence can be found in Mehmed Murad, *Tatlı Emeller, Acı
Hakikatler* (İstanbul, 1330 [1914]), pp.359-369, reproduced in full in Birol Emil,
Mizancı Murad Bey: Hayatı ve Eserleri, pp.213-219.
[63] "News Items," *The Levant Herald and Eastern Express*, June 8, 1909, p.1;
"Birinci Divan-ı Harb-i Örfi," *Tanin*, May 26, 1325/June 8, 1909, p.2; "News
Items," *The Levant Herald and Eastern Express*, June 14, 1909, p.1; Zekeriya Türkmen, *Osmanlı Meşrutiyetinde Ordu-Siyaset Çatışması*, p.105; Hüseyin Işık, "İkinci
Meşrutiyet'in İlânında ve Korunmasında Silahlı Kuvvetlerimizin Rolü," p.56;
and, Fevziye Abdullah Tansel, "Mizancı Mehmed Murad Bey," p.88. See also, Birol Emil, *Mizancı Murad Bey: Hayatı ve Eserleri*, p.213; and, Abdurrahman Şeref,
*Son Vak'anüvis Abdurrahman Şeref Efendi Tarihi: II. Meşrutiyet Olayları, 1908-
1909*, pp.133-134.
[64] "Situation politique," *La Paix*, June 23, 1909, p.2, and, Mehmed Murad, *En-
kaz-ı İstibdad İçinde Zügürdün Tesellisi* (İstanbul, 1329 [1913]), p.46, all quoted in
Birol Emil, *Mizancı Murad Bey: Hayatı ve Eserleri*, p.220. See also, Zekeriya Türkmen, *Osmanlı Meşrutiyetinde Ordu-Siyaset Çatışması*, p.104.

the Sultan that he was always a faithful servant, and that in western Europe and Egypt he had informed him of the Unionist activities.[65] Additional *jurnals* of Ali Kemal Bey were published in the *Sabah* of May 17.[66]

On May 6, Ahmed Fazlı [Tung], editor of *Osmanlı* and one of the most prominent figures of the monarchist opposition headed by Prince Sabahaddin, was arrested.[67] On June 3, he was brought before the Court Martial. He was acquitted the same day, and was permitted to resume publication of *Osmanlı*.[68] Leaving Turkey for the summer months, he returned to İstanbul on September 28.[69]

The Court Martial authorities issued a proclamation concerning the monarchist newspaper proprietors and editors who had fled the country when the *coup* attempt failed.[70] Ahmed Cevdet Bey, proprietor of *İkdam*, Ali Kemal Bey, editor of *İkdam*, Derviş Vahdeti, proprietor of *Volkan*, and Mevlânzade Rıfat Bey, proprietor of *Serbesti*, who were all accused of being the principal organisers as well as inciters of the *coup* attempt, were granted a delay of ten days to appear before the Court Martial. If they failed to appear within the specified time period, they would automatically be considered outlaws, tried by default, and their properties would be confiscated.[71] Meanwhile, the Court Martial, at its May 26 sitting, sentenced Ömer Lütfi Bey, one of the editors of *Volkan*, to death.[72]

The Court Martial proceeded to hand down judgements on the monarchist newspaper proprietors and editors on July 18, after it became apparent that they had no intention of coming back to Turkey to face the Court. At the July 18 sitting of the Court Martial, Ahmed Cevdet Bey, the proprietor of *İkdam*,

---

[65] "News Items," *The Levant Herald and Eastern Express*, May 7, 1909, p.1.

[66] "Les Djournals," *The Levant Herald and Eastern Express*, May 17, 1909, p.1.

[67] "Une arrestation," *The Levant Herald and Eastern Express*, May 7, 1909, p.2.

[68] "Birinci Divan-ı Harb-i Örfi," *Tanin*, May 22, 1325/June 4, 1909, p.3; and, "News Items," *The Levant Herald and Eastern Express*, June 4, 1909, p.1.

[69] "News Items," *The Levant Herald and Eastern Express*, September 29, 1909, p.1.

[70] "The Court Martial," *The Levant Herald and Eastern Express*, May 18, 1909, p.1; and, Ahmed Bedevi Kuran, *İnkılap Tarihimiz ve İttihad ve Terakki*, p.255.

[71] "The Court Martial," *The Levant Herald and Eastern Express*, May 18, 1909, p.1.

[72] "Turkey: Death Sentences," *The Times*, May 27, 1909, p.5.

was acquitted of all charges.[73] Cleared of all charges, Ahmed
Cevdet Bey and his wife arrived at İstanbul from Vienna on
August 5. He announced his intention of resuming *İkdam*'s
publication.[74]

However, Ali Kemal Bey, the editor of *İkdam*, was sentenced, *in absentia*, to banishment from İstanbul for having
worked in the interests of Abdülhamid, the deposed Sultan.[75]
Having already escaped from the country, Ali Kemal Bey began publication of a newspaper in exile. This paper, *Yeni Yol*,
was prohibited to be circulated in Turkey by a decision of the
cabinet taken on November 15.[76]

On July 21, the Court Martial sentenced Mevlânzade Rıfat
Bey, editor of *Serbesti, in absentia*, to ten years' banishment
from İstanbul.[77] During the trials of other defendants, documents had been produced, establishing the fact that Mevlânzade Rıfat Bey had, on one occasion, taken the considerable
sum of seventy liras from Abdülhamid as compensation for
his monarchist agitation in the columns of *Serbesti*.[78] On August 10, the government forbade the circulation in Turkey of
Serbesti which was being published first in Cairo and after
July 27 in Paris by Mevlânzade Rıfat Bey with the financial
support of Şerif Pasha.[79] The Court Martial further announced
that persons caught selling or buying *Serbesti* would be liable
to pay a fine of two to fifteen liras. The Court Martial decision

---

[73] "Birinci Divan-ı Harb-i Örfi," *Tanin*, July 6, 1325/July 19, 1909, p.3; "News
Items," *The Levant Herald and Eastern Express*, July 19, 1909, p.1; and, "Executions
in Constantinople," *The Times*, July 20, 1909, p.5.

[74] "News Items," *The Levant Herald and Eastern Express*, August 6, 1909, p.1.

[75] "Birinci Divan-ı Harb-i Örfi," *Tanin*, July 6, 1325/July 19, 1909, p.3; "News
Items," *The Levant Herald and Eastern Express*, July 19, 1909, p.1; and, "Executions
in Constantinople," *The Times*, July 20, 1909, p.5. See also, Charles Donald
Sullivan, Stamboul Crossings: German Diplomacy in Turkey, 1908 to 1914, p.142.

[76] "News Items," *The Levant Herald and Eastern Express*, November 16, 1909,
p.1.

[77] "Birinci Divan-ı Harb-i Örfi," *Tanin*, July 9, 1325/July 22, 1909, p.3; "News
Items," *The Levant Herald and Eastern Express*, July 22, 1909, p.1; and, "News
Items," *The Levant Herald and Eastern Express*, August 20, 1909, p.1.

[78] The *jurnal* of Hüseyin Tayyar, quoted in full in Celal Bayar, *Ben de Yazdım*, 2, p.394.

[79] "News Items," *The Levant Herald and Eastern Express*, August 11, 1909, p.1;
and, "News Items," *The Levant Herald and Eastern Express*, August 20, 1909, p.1.
For the legal arrangement between Mevlânzade Rıfat Bey and Şerif Pasha concerning the publication of *Serbesti*, see Şerif, *Bir Muhalifin Hatıraları: İttihat ve
Terakki'ye Muhalefet*, pp.53-55; and, Ahmed Bedevi Kuran, *İnkılap Tarihimiz ve
İttihad ve Terakki*, pp.256-257. See also, Ahmed Bedevi Kuran, *İnkılâp Tarihimiz
ve 'Jön Türkler*,' p.285.

had been taken on account of the persistence of *Serbesti* in its monarchist propaganda against the constitutional rule. *Serbesti* had printed that the government was an organ of oppression operating under the influence of the Committee of Union and Progress, and that the sentences handed down by the Court Martial were in contradiction to constitutional law.[80]

Meanwhile, the Court Martial also took action against the old regime pashas who had already been found guilty and been exiled immediately after the Revolution. On the morning of May 17, Memduh Pasha, the ex-Minister of the Interior under the old regime, was arrested at the Prince Islands, where he had been exiled, and was taken to the Ministry of War.[81] On May 23, the Court Martial decided to degrade him as well as the other pashas of the old regime, send them to exile for five years, and confiscate their properties. The Court Martial had discovered proofs of their complicity in reactionary intrigues since their exile to the Prince Islands off the coast of İstanbul. These sentences applied, among others, to ex-Ministers who had, immediately after the Revolution, been accused of misappropriating public funds. It was expected that similar judgement would be passed on İzzet Pasha, the ex-Chamberlain, Selim Melhame, and Necib Melhame.[82] The government also banned the distribution of *Moayyad*, the organ of the monarchist Egyptians, within Turkey, as its editor and proprietor, Sheikh Ali Yusuf, was believed to be in close communication with İzzet Pasha, whose agents were reported to be active in the Arab world.[83]

The pashas in question, Tahsin, Mehmed Rıza, Ragıb, Ahmed Ratib, Saadeddin, Reşid, and İsmail, in addition to Mem-

---

[80] "News Items," *The Levant Herald and Eastern Express*, August 24, 1909, p.1. See also, Erol Şadi Erdinç and Faruk Ilıkan, "Osmanlı İttihad ve Terakki Cem'iyyeti Merkez-i Umûmî'si Yazışmalarından Örnekler," pp.40-41.

[81] "News Items," *The Levant Herald and Eastern Express*, May 17, 1909, p.1. See also, Zekeriya Türkmen, *Osmanlı Meşrutiyetinde Ordu-Siyaset Çatışması*, p.104; and, Abdurrahman Şeref, *Son Vak'anüvis Abdurrahman Şeref Efendi Tarihi: II. Meşrutiyet Olayları, 1908-1909*, p.136.

[82] "The Magnates of the Old Regime," *The Levant Herald and Eastern Express*, May 24, 1909, p.1; Hüseyin Işık, "İkinci Meşrutiyet'in İlânında ve Korunmasında Silahlı Kuvvetlerimizin Rolü," p.56; and, Zekeriya Türkmen, *Osmanlı Meşrutiyetinde Ordu-Siyaset Çatışması*, p.104. See also, Abdurrahman Şeref, *Son Vak'anüvis Abdurrahman Şeref Efendi Tarihi: II. Meşrutiyet Olayları, 1908-1909*, p.139.

[83] "Turkey: The Egyptian Nationalist Press," *The Times*, May 26, 1909, p.5.

duh, were taken from the Prince Islands on the night of May 24 and imprisoned at the Ministry of War. All lost their right to a pension.[84] On May 26, Mahmud Şevket Pasha announced that the old regime pashas at the Prince Islands would be exiled to Lymnos, Bodrum, Mytilene, and Chios.[85] Their departure from İstanbul was affected without delay; on the night of May 27, they were put on a ship to take them to their places of exile. Tahsin Pasha, the ex-First Secretary to the Sultan, Memduh Pasha, the ex-Minister of the Interior, and Reşid Pasha, the ex-Prefect of İstanbul, would reside at Chios; Mehmed Rıza Pasha, the ex-Minister of War at Mytilene; Rami Pasha, the ex-Minister of the Navy, Zeki Pasha, the ex-Grand Master of Ordnance, Ahmed Ratib Pasha, the ex-Governor-General of the Hedjaz, and Saadeddin Pasha, the ex-Commander of the First Division of the Guard, at Rhodes; İsmail Pasha, the ex-Inspector-General of Military Schools at Bodrum; and, Ragıb Pasha, ex-Chamberlain to the Sultan, at Cos.[86]

At his interrogation by the Court Martial on May 8, Nadir Agha, a palace official who was also a defendant, had told the Court Martial authorities that Derviş Vahdeti's editorials in *Volkan* had pleased Abdülhamid. Nadir Agha went on to say that the Sultan had given Derviş Vahdeti a considerable sum of money for his services, as well as a monthly stipend for the publication of *Volkan*.[87]

Derviş Vahdeti who was a fugitive was finally arrested at İzmir in late May.[88] During the last days of the *coup*, when it

---

[84] "News Items," *The Levant Herald and Eastern Express*, May 26, 1909, p.1; "Turkey: Proceedings Against Reactionaries," *The Times*, May 26, 1909, p.5; and, "Turkey: Punishment of Reactionaries," *The Times*, May 27, 1909, p.5. See also, Hüseyin Işık, "İkinci Meşrutiyet'in İlânında ve Korunmasında Silahlı Kuvvetlerimizin Rolü," p.56; and, Abdurrahman Şeref, *Son Vak'anüvis Abdurrahman Şeref Efendi Tarihi: II. Meşrutiyet Olayları, 1908-1909*, pp.136-141.

[85] "News Items," *The Levant Herald and Eastern Express*, May 27, 1909, p.1.

[86] "The Magnates of the Old Regime," *The Levant Herald and Eastern Express*, May 28, 1909, p.1; and, Zekeriya Türkmen, *Osmanlı Meşrutiyetinde Ordu-Siyaset Çatışması*, p.104.

[87] Celal Bayar, *Ben de Yazdım*, 2, p.389. Nadir Agha was acquitted by the Court Martial on May 26 ("Turkey: Punishment of Reactionaries," *The Times*, May 27, 1909, p.5). See also, "Nadir Ağa ile Mülâkat, 1: Nadir Ağa'nın Başına Gelenler," *Tanin*, May 14, 1325/May 27, 1909, pp.1-2; "Nadir Ağa ile Mülâkat, 2: Yıldız Ahvaline Dair Bazı İfşaat," *Tanin*, May 15, 1325/May 28, 1909, p.1.

[88] "News Items," *The Levant Herald and Eastern Express*, May 26, 1909, p.1; "Derviş Vahdeti Melununun Tutulması," *Tanin*, May 13, 1325/May 26, 1909, p.1; and, "Vahdeti Nasıl Tutuldu?" *Tanin*, May 14, 1325/May 27, 1909, p.2. See also, Hüseyin Işık, "İkinci Meşrutiyet'in İlânında ve Korunmasında Silahlı Kuvvetlerimi-

had become apparent that it would fail, he had first gone to Admiral Said Pasha, Kâmil Pasha's son and one of the organisers of the *coup*, for help. When he could not find refuge in the Palace of Prince Vahideddin, he took the train to Gebze. From there he proceeded over land to Bergama, and then to İzmir.[89] In İzmir, he was informed to the authorities, and was arrested.[90] On May 30, he was brought back to İstanbul under police escort, and was imprisoned at the Ministry of War.[91] In his interrogation, Derviş Vahdeti confessed, and admitted that he had been to the palace where he had taken money from Abdülhamid for the services he rendered in his *Volkan* for the monarchist cause.[92] His trial continued until early July. Finally, the Court Martial sentenced him to death on July 6.[93]

At its July 19 sitting, the Court Martial also notified Said Pasha, Kâmil Pasha's son, who was accused of having been one of the principal instigators of the *coup* attempt of April 13, that he must surrender himself within ten days for trial. If not, he would be condemned by default and suffer the loss of civil rights and the confiscation of his property. A similar warning was also sent to Niyazi Bey, ex-deputy for Argani-Maden. However, neither Said Pasha nor Niyazi Bey was expected to put in an appearance.[94]

By May 4, Yusuf Pasha, the Military Commander of Erzurum, was ordered to resign his command and proceed to the headquarters of the Fourth Army Corps at Erzincan.[95] Later, he was brought to İstanbul to face charges. The May 19 issue of *Tanin* published a letter from Erzurum which declared that the responsibility for the military outbreak there in connection with the *coup* attempt of April 13 must be assigned to Yu-

---

zin Rolü," p.56.

[89] Celal Bayar, *Ben de Yazdım*, 2, pp.380-381. See also, "Derviş Vahdeti Nasıl ve Nerede İhtifa Eylemiş?" *Tanin*, May 14, 1325/May 27, 1909, p.2.

[90] Hüseyin Işık, "İkinci Meşrutiyet'in İlânında ve Korunmasında Silahlı Kuvvetlerimizin Rolü," p.56; and, Celal Bayar, *Ben de Yazdım*, 2, p.382.

[91] "News Items," *The Levant Herald and Eastern Express*, May 31, 1909, p.1.

[92] Celal Bayar, *Ben de Yazdım*, 2, p.392.

[93] "News Items," *The Levant Herald and Eastern Express*, July 7, 1909, p.1; and, "News Items," *The Levant Herald and Eastern Express*, July 14, 1909, p.1. For the full text of the decision of the Court Martial, see Celal Bayar, *Ben de Yazdım*, 2, pp.383-384. See also, Hüseyin Işık, "İkinci Meşrutiyet'in İlânında ve Korunmasında Silahlı Kuvvetlerimizin Rolü," p.56.

[94] "Executions in Constantinople," *The Times*, July 20, 1909, p.5.

[95] "The Turkish Outlook: Affairs in Anatolia," *The Times*, May 5, 1909, p.5.

suf Pasha.[96] The Court Martial sentenced Yusuf Pasha to death on account of his support for the monarchist *coup*.[97]

On the morning of July 19, thirteen persons sentenced to death were executed at Bayezid, Sultan Ahmed Square, and Fatih. Among them were Yusuf Ziya Pasha, the Military Commander of Erzurum, Çerkes Şevket Mehmed Pasha, Derviş Vahdeti, Colonel Nuri Bey, Hakkı Bey, a notorious spy, and Colonel İsmail Bey. Çerkes Şevket Mehmed Pasha, popularly known as 'Kabasakal,' *i.e.*, 'twisted beard,' was a torturer and former aide-de-camp of Abdülhamid.[98]

At the May 1 sitting of the Chamber of Deputies a lively debate had taken place on the Armenian massacres at Adana. Mehmed Cevad Bey, Governor of Adana during the disturbances, and the Assistant Minister of the Interior had been violently attacked and stigmatised as creatures of the Hamidian regime. Finally, after an agitated sitting, a resolution had been passed almost unanimously in favour of the formation of a Court Martial at Adana to try the guilty parties and of dispatching a parliamentary commission of inquiry and sending immediately a sum of twenty thousand liras to relieve the distress at Adana.[99] The Court Martial which proceeded to Adana on May 6 to try those guilty of the massacres had been formed of officers of the Third Army Corps.[100] In an interview published in the May 14 issue of *La Turquie*, Mahmud Şevket Pasha declared that ten battalions of trustworthy troops of the Second and Third Army Corps had been sent to Adana, where the Court Martial had been ordered to inflict the death

[96] "The Situation in Asiatic Turkey," *The Times*, May 25, 1909, p.5.

[97] Hüseyin Işık, "İkinci Meşrutiyet'in İlânında ve Korunmasında Silahlı Kuvvetlerimizin Rolü," p.55; Abdurrahman Şeref, *Son Vak'anüvis Abdurrahman Şeref Efendi Tarihi: II. Meşrutiyet Olayları, 1908-1909*, p.209; and, "News Items," *The Levant Herald and Eastern Express*, July 14, 1909, p.1.

[98] "News Items," *The Levant Herald and Eastern Express*, July 19, 1909, p.1; "Executions in Constantinople," *The Times*, July 20, 1909, p.5; Hüseyin Işık, "İkinci Meşrutiyet'in İlânında ve Korunmasında Silahlı Kuvvetlerimizin Rolü," p.55; Edwin Pears, *Forty Years in Constantinople: The Recollections of Sir Edwin Pears, 1873-1915*, pp.302-303; Abdurrahman Şeref, *Son Vak'anüvis Abdurrahman Şeref Efendi Tarihi: II. Meşrutiyet Olayları, 1908-1909*, pp.131-132; and, Zekeriya Türkmen, *Osmanlı Meşrutiyetinde Ordu-Siyaset Çatışması*, pp.104-105. See also, *Resimli Kitab*, 2 (April-September 1909), p.843.

[99] I/I/63, April 18, 1325/May 1, 1909, *Meclis-i Mebusan Zabıt Ceridesi*, 3, pp.119-136; and, "The Massacres in Asia Minor: Relief Voted by the Chamber," *The Times*, May 3, 1909, p.7.

[100] "The New Turkish Ministry," *The Times*, May 7, 1909, p.5.

sentence on persons found guilty of murder and incitement to riot.[101]

The May 24 issue of *Tanin* printed an interview with Avlonyalı Ferid Pasha, Minister of the Interior, who informed the public that several soldiers who had taken part in the Armenian massacres in Cilicia had been arrested. Nine persons had already been condemned to death by the Adana Court Martial. With regard to the responsibility for the outbreak, the Minister said that, while he could not definitely ascribe it to official prompting, certain officials had failed to do their duties, among them the Sub-Governor of Cebel-i Bereket, who had been imprisoned pending an inquiry into his conduct. Avlonyalı Ferid Pasha declared that the government had made up its mind to discover the criminals and to inflict on them the most severe punishment.[102] His statement, however, was not entirely satisfactory. His desire to satisfy the public would be more likely to be crowned with success were steps taken to inquire into the conduct of Mehmed Cevad Bey, the ex-Governor of Adana, whose conduct throughout the massacres could only be ascribed to complicity. The mere dismissal of this official was hardly a sufficient punishment for having left Adana for more than a week the prey of monarchist agitators and mutinied soldiers.[103]

On July 15, the government decided to try the ex-Governor of Adana, and the ex-Sub-Governor of Cebel-i Bereket. They were sent to Adana under a strong escort to face the Court Martial there. In addition, some twenty leading Muslim notables of Adana who had already been arrested would be immediately brought before the Court Martial.[104]

In its report, the Court Martial appointed to inquire into the massacres at Adana found that various causes led to excessive

---

[101] *La Turquie*, May 14, 1909, excerpted in "Turkey: The Massacres at Adana," *The Times*, May 15, 1909, p.7.

[102] *Tanin*, May 11, 1325/May 24, 1909, quoted in "Turkey: The Adana Massacres," *The Times*, May 31, 1909, p.5.

[103] "Turkey: The Adana Massacres," *The Times*, May 31, 1909, p.5.

[104] "The Adana Massacres: Manifesto to be Addressed to Moslems," *The Times*, July 16, 1909, p.5. The Unionists continually pressed for their trials. See, for example, Hüseyin Cahid [Yalçın], "Hakikat İsteriz!" *Tanin*, June 27, 1325/July 10, 1909, p.1; and, "Adana'da İğtişaş Nasıl Hızırlandı?: Eski Hükûmet Uyuyordu," *Tanin*, June 27, 1325/July 10, 1909, p.1.

animosity between Christians and Muslims. It dwelt on the incapacity and lack of energy displayed by the Governor, while other local authorities were also censured. The report concluded that, in addition to fifteen people who had been already hanged, eight hundred deserved death, fifteen thousand deserved hard labour for life, and eighty thousand deserved minor sentences.[105]

The Court Martial at Adana sentenced Mehmed Cevad Bey, the ex-Governor of Adana, to suspension from public service for six years on account of his complicity with the monarchists who had organised and carried out the Armenian massacres.[106] His connections with the Palace went as far back as 1889, when he had entered the Yıldız Palace as imperial secretary and worked there for eleven years before being appointed Sub-Governor of Jerusalem in 1901, and, later, Governor of Ankara, Konya, and Adana.[107] Remzi Pasha, the ex-Military Commander of Adana, was also sentenced to three years' imprisonment.[108] The trial by Court Martial at Antakya of the persons implicated in the massacres resulted in about fifteen of those accused being sentenced to death. In addition, a number of notables were exiled.[109]

Meanwhile, İsmail Kemal Bey, the monarchist deputy for Berat who had been deeply involved in the *coup* attempt and had escaped after its failure, remained in Athens during May. Due to constant representations to the Greek Government by the Turkish Government concerning İsmail Kemal Bey's stay in Greece, he was forced to leave Athens for Corfu in early June. Some forty fugitives belonging to his party were disarmed and interned by the authorities upon landing at

---

[105] "The Adana Massacres," *The Times*, July 19, 1909, p.5. See also, "Adana Faciası Hakkında iki Vesika," *Tanin*, July 17, 1325/July 30, 1909, pp.1-2; "Adana Faciası Hakkında iki Vesika," *Tanin*, July 18, 1325/July 31, 1909, pp.1-2; "Adana Faciası Hakkında iki Vesika," *Tanin*, July 19, 1325/August 1, 1909, pp.1-2; "Adana Faciası Hakkında iki Vesika," *Tanin*, July 20, 1325/August 2, 1909, pp.1-2; "Adana Faciası Hakkında iki Vesika," *Tanin*, July 21, 1325/August 3, 1909, pp.1-2; "Adana Faciası Hakkında iki Vesika," *Tanin*, July 22, 1325/August 4, 1909, pp.1-2; and, "Adana Faciası Hakkında iki Vesika," *Tanin*, July 23, 1325/August 5, 1909, p.1.

[106] "News Items," *The Levant Herald and Eastern Express*, September 6, 1909, p.1.

[107] Ali Çankaya, *Yeni Mülkiye Tarihi ve Mülkiyeliler*, *3*, pp.189-190.

[108] "News Items," *The Levant Herald and Eastern Express*, September 6, 1909, p.1.

[109] "The Massacres in Asia Minor," *The Times*, September 23, 1909, p.3.

Corfu. He was not expected to stay at Corfu for long. However, his return to his native town of Vlorë had been rendered impossible owing to measures taken against him there.[110] Therefore, he left for Rome.

At the Chamber of Deputies' July 8 sitting, Mahmud Şevket Pasha made a formal demand for the surrender of İsmail Kemal Bey on account of the discovery of papers bearing his signature in the house of a person who had been condemned and of the seizure of letters, in which the Albanian deputy for Berat made an uncomplimentary reference to several of the Unionist leaders and described the Court Martial as 'executioners.' İsmail Hakkı Bey, deputy for Gümülcine, read the report of the parliamentary commission of inquiry into the conduct of the deputy in question. In an eloquent speech, he declared that the commission found no proof of the allegation that İsmail Kemal Bey provoked or attempted to profit by the *coup* attempt of April 13. All that could be said was that he appeared to have felt personal satisfaction at the overthrow of his political opponents. Even this statement was challenged by one of the Arab deputies, who said that he had seen İsmail Kemal Bey moved to tears by the events which accompanied the outbreak. After a long discussion, a large majority voted that İsmail Kemal Bey should not be given up to the military tribunals in the absence of all proof of guilt. Thus the Chamber acquitted him as well as Müfid Bey, another monarchist Albanian deputy for Argyrocastro, who had escaped from İstanbul at about the same time. The result was joyfully received by the Albanian deputies.[111]

Ali Haydar Bey, another prominent anti-Unionist working with Prince Sabahaddin, arrived at İstanbul on July 13.[112] He had escaped to Paris after the *coup* attempt had failed.

Excluded from cabinet-level office, the Committee of Union and Progress devised a reform plan which would rely less on

[110] "Ismail Kemal Bey," *The Times*, June 2, 1909, p.7.

[111] I/I/108, June 25, 1325/July 8, 1909, *Meclis-i Mebusan Zabıt Ceridesi*, 5, pp.267-277; "Turkey: The Chamber and Ismail Kemal Bey," *The Times*, July 9, 1909, p.5; and, "Ismail Kemal Bey Innocent," *The Levant Herald and Eastern Express*, July 9, 1909, p.1.

[112] "News Items," *The Levant Herald and Eastern Express*, July 14, 1909, p.1.

the cabinet and more on those responsible for the nation's day to day management; the Unionists hoped to gain those key management positions in the Ministries not just for its own adherents, but specifically for its deputies, which was unheard of. By placing Unionist deputies in the various Ministries as Under-Secretaries, the Unionists hoped to influence the cabinet indirectly.[113] Already the Unionists had secured their position in the Palace with the appointment of Halid Ziya [Uşaklıgil] as First Secretary and Tevfik Bey as Second Chamberlain.[114] The Under-Secretaries were expected to serve a similar though more important function with respect to the cabinet.

The Unionist leadership discussed its plan, and on May 6, Cavid and Talât Beys met with Mahmud Şevket Pasha in the hopes of gaining his support. He summarily dismissed the idea.[115] They then went to see Hüseyin Hilmi Pasha whose response was no less discouraging.[116] He particularly objected to the idea of effectively giving under-secretaries cabinet-level influence, unprecedented as it was in any nation. The Unionist leadership interpreted this resistance as the resistance of the old regime, dedicated as it was to monopolising political power.[117] The monarchist members of the cabinet, especially Gabriel Nouradunghian, Raif Pasha, and the Sheikh-ul-Islam were also vehemently opposed to the idea.[118] Monarchist resistance in general gained momentum with Mahmud Şevket Pasha's resistance. Publicly, he still supported the Committee of Union and Progress; privately, he did

---

[113] Hüseyin Cahid Yalçın, *Talât Paşa*, p.37. The issue was brought before the public eye in mid-May (Hüseyin Cahid [Yalçın], "Müsteşarlık Meselesi," *Tanin*, May 6, 1325/May 19, 1909, p.1). For a discussion of this issue see, Ahmet Mehmet-efendioğlu, "İttihat ve Terakki ve Siyasi Müsteşarlıklar," pp.32-37.

[114] Feroz Ahmad, *The Young Turks: The Committee of Union and Progress in Turkish Politics, 1908-1914*, p.50.

[115] Mehmed Cavid, "Meşrutiyet Devrine Ait Cavit Bey'in Hatıraları: 10," *Tanin*, September 8, 1943, p.2.

[116] Mehmed Cavid, "Meşrutiyet Devrine Ait Cavit Bey'in Hatıraları: 10," *Tanin*, September 8, 1943, p.2.

[117] Hüseyin Cahid Yalçın, *Talât Paşa*, p.37. Also see, Hüseyin Cahid [Yalçın], "Müsteşarlık Meselesi," *Tanin*, May 6, 1325/May 19, 1909, p.1; and, Feroz Ahmad, *The Young Turks: The Committee of Union and Progress in Turkish Politics, 1908-1914*, p.51.

[118] Mehmed Cavid, "Meşrutiyet Devrine Ait Cavit Bey'in Hatıraları: 10," *Tanin*, September 8, 1943, p.2.

everything he could to stop them—particularly on this issue.[119]

Discouraged but undaunted, the Committee of Union and Progress decided to take the matter before the Chamber. If deputies were to be allowed to hold the office of Under-Secretary, Article 67 of the Constitution would have to be modified. This article stated that a deputy could not hold any other government appointment.[120] Amendments to the Constitution required a two-thirds majority in the Chamber, a majority which the Unionist theoretically had. But the Committee of Union and Progress itself was divided. Some opposed the idea of having Unionist deputies hold two positions on the grounds that it would risk offending public opinion; the Committee of Union and Progress would be viewed not as patriotic, but as power-hungry.[121] The leadership tried to consolidate control over its deputies by officially forming, on June 12, the Parliamentary Party of Union and Progress. Some within the Committee of Union and Progress, however, felt that this was largely a concession to those critics who claimed that the party was still some sort of a secret organisation.[122]

The proposal for the Amendment of Article 67 was presented to the Chamber of Deputies on June 1. Hüseyin Hilmi Pasha read the modified version of the Article and then submitted the text to the Committee for the Revision of the Constitution.[123] On June 14, the issue came up for discussion. Though debate was long and heated, the proposal was finally put to the vote by open ballot. It passed. When Ahmed Rıza Bey, President of the Chamber, announced that the motion had been accepted by a majority, however, there was an uproar. Several deputies demanded a second vote by ballot, and the President acquiesced. Because the result of the vote was one hundred and four for and seventy-two against, and not a

---

[119] Hüseyin Cahid Yalçın, *Talât Paşa*, p.37.
[120] Tarhan Erdem (Compilor), *Anayasalar ve Seçim Kanunları, 1876-1982*, p.9.
[121] Hüseyin Cahid Yalçın, *Talât Paşa*, p.37.
[122] "Meclis-i Mebusan-ı Osmani'de Müteşekkil İttihad ve Terakki Fırkası'nın Nizamname-i Dahilisi," *Tanin*, May 30, 1325/June 12, 1909, quoted in Tarık Zafer Tunaya, *Türkiye'de Siyasi Partiler*, pp.210-211. See also, Feroz Ahmad, *The Young Turks: The Committee of Union and Progress in Turkish Politics, 1908-1914*, p.54.
[123] I/I/84, May 19, 1325/June 1, 1909, *Meclis-i Mebusan Zabıt Ceridesi, 4*, pp.97-98; and, *Takvim-i Vekayi*, May 21, 1325/June 3, 1909, p.8, quoted in Feroz Ahmad, *The Young Turks: The Committee of Union and Progress in Turkish Politics, 1908-1914*, p.51.

two-thirds majority, the question was left undecided.[124] On June 17, discussion was again re-opened, but opposition was still too strong, and Talât Bey withdrew the motion on behalf of the Committee of Union and Progress.[125]

Having failed to amend the Constitution, the Unionists decided to simplify their strategy: They decided to push directly for Cabinet positions. The policy of moderation and coexistence with the Hüseyin Hilmi Pasha Cabinet was thus brought to an end. At the same time, measures were taken to enforce unity and discipline within its parliamentary party group as its defeat in the Chamber was largely the result of internal dissension.[126]

Cavid Bey, one of the most prominent leaders of the Committee of Union and Progress and deputy for Salonica, was the first real Unionist in a cabinet office, joining the Hüseyin Hilmi Pasha Cabinet in late June as Minister of Finance.[127] Rıfat Bey, Minister of Finance had, in fact, resigned, stating that Cavid Bey was infinitely more qualified for the job.[128] Indeed, reporter to the Budget Commission, Cavid Bey's activi-

---

[124] I/I/92, June 1, 1325/June 14, 1909, *Meclis-i Mebusan Zabıt Ceridesi, 4,* pp.357-367, and, 370-371. For Hüseyin Cahid Yalçın's criticism of the opposition press on this issue see, Hüseyin Cahid [Yalçın], "Bir Halet-i Ruhiye," *Tanin,* June 3, 1325/June 16, 1909, p.1. See also, Feroz Ahmad, *The Young Turks: The Committee of Union and Progress in Turkish Politics, 1908-1914,* p.51-52, where he mistakenly gives the date as June 12.

[125] I/I/95, June 4, 1325/June 17, 1909, *Meclis-i Mebusan Zabıt Ceridesi, 4,* p.445; "Turkey: The Chamber and Under-Secretaries," *The Times,* June 18, 1909, p.5; and, "The Young Turk Committee and the Chamber," *The Times,* June 26, 1909, p.5.

[126] Feroz Ahmad, *The Young Turks: The Committee of Union and Progress in Turkish Politics, 1908-1914,* p.52.

[127] "New Turkish Minister of Finance," *The Times,* June 28, 1909, p.5; "Der neue Finanzminister," *Osmanischer Lloyd,* June 29, 1909; p.1; and, F.O. 317/777, Sir Gerard Lowther to Sir Edward Grey, Therapia, June 28, 1909, quoted in Feroz Ahmad, *The Young Turks: The Committee of Union and Progress in Turkish Politics, 1908-1914,* p.52. See also, Yusuf Hikmet Bayur, *Türk İnkılâbı Tarihi, 1/2,* p.214.

Manyasizade Refik Bey had been the first Unionist to be named Minister; he had been appointed Minister of Police on August 10, 1908 ("The New Era in Turkey: Ministers and Reform," *The Times,* August 11, 1908, p.5; and, Aykut Kansu, *The Revolution of 1908 in Turkey,* p.129). On November 30, 1908, he was appointed Minister of Justice (Feroz Ahmad, *The Young Turks: The Committee of Union and Progress in Turkish Politics, 1908-1914,* p.31). He was not, however, to be in the Cabinet for long, as he died shortly after taking office, in early March of 1909.

[128] Hüseyin Cahid Yalçın, "Meşrutiyet Hatıraları, 1908-1918," *Fikir Hareketleri,* 5 (October 26, 1935-April 18, 1936), p.389; and, Ali Fuad Türkgeldi, *Görüp İşittiklerim,* p.45.

ty in the Chamber and in parliamentary committee was one of the most encouraging features of the first session of the Chamber of Deputies. He was certainly one of the ablest of the younger men who had come to the front since the Revolution of 1908. He had been rapidly joining the necessary practical training to a sound theoretical education in economics and finance, and it was expected that his honesty, energy, and oratorical gifts would carry him far. His appointment to the Ministry was received with general satisfaction, and was of special significance in that he was the first leading member of the Committee of Union and Progress who had accepted cabinet rank.[129]

By July 1909, the Unionists began to consider the possibility of ousting the government out of office by a vote of non-confidence, and setting up a new one with a more pronounced Unionist presence. They secretly approached Kâmil Pasha and offered him the Grand Vezierate on just this condition—Talât Bey, in particular, was to be named Minister of the Interior. Though he did not reject the proposal, Kâmil Pasha let it be known that he did not consider the Unionist candidates worthy of ministerial consideration. The matter was dropped.[130]

The Unionists had also begun to attack the Cabinet in the press. The *Tanin* of July 20 accused it of containing members attached to the old regime, and demanded that the Government be handed over to the active, honourable, and trustworthy men of the new regime.[131] Three days later, on the first anniversary of the Revolution, the Central Committee in Salonica issued a proclamation, stating that as Ottomans, all factions should put away their differences in the interests of the nation as a whole. Declaring that the administration of the

---

[129] "New Turkish Minister of Finance," *The Times*, June 28, 1909, p.5. See an interview with the newly appointed Cavid Bey in "Eine Unterredung mit dem Finanzminister: Die Lage des Staatsschätzes," *Osmanischer Lloyd*, July 10, 1909, p.1. For Yalçın's comments on Cavid Bey's appointment to this post see, Hüseyin Cahid [Yalçın], "'Tecrübesiz'ler," *Tanin*, June 17, 1325/June 30, 1909, p.1.

[130] F.O. 800/78, Sir Gerard Lowther to Sir Edward Grey, Constantinople, July 20, 1909, quoted in Feroz Ahmad, *The Young Turks: The Committee of Union and Progress in Turkish Politics, 1908-1914*, p.53.

[131] Hüseyin Cahid [Yalçın], "Girit ve Efkâr-ı Umumiye, *Tanin*, July 7, 1325/ July 20, 1909, p.1; and, "Turkish Politics: The Press and the Cretan Question," *The Times*, July 21, 1909, p.5.

country was in hands which showed themselves weak on April 13, citizens were urged to push for a new and younger cabinet, as only youthful vitality and enterprise could save the country from the tradition of the old regime.[132] Yet, at a meeting held on July 26 to discuss cabinet change, it turned out that the Unionist deputies were divided on the issue. Ultimately, it was decided to have a secret vote. The vote showed that the majority of the Committee of Union and Progress was in favour of the maintenance of the Hilmi Pasha Cabinet for the time being.[133] Nevertheless, party leadership continued working to get rid of some of the cabinet members.

By the end of July, there remained little doubt that there would be major changes in the cabinet.[134] It was expected that Hüseyin Hilmi Pasha would resign and would be requested to form a new cabinet which would be still more strongly Unionist than the existing one. Avlonyalı Ferid Pasha would certainly be replaced by Talât Bey. Rıfat Pasha, who had accepted the portfolio of Foreign Affairs with reluctance, was expected to retire. In the opinion of many competent observers Gabriel Nouradunghian would probably not be included in the next cabinet.[135]

The August 3 issue of *Tanin* published what purported to be a secret report transmitted by Avlonyalı Ferid Pasha to Yıldız Palace.[136] As a result of Unionist pressure, Avlonyalı Ferid Pasha, whose name was intimately connected with the old regime, was forced to resign his post on August 5 as Minister of the Interior.[137] His resignation was precipitated by the

---

[132] "Osmanlı İttihad ve Terakki Cemiyeti'nin İstanbul Heyet-i Merkeziyesi Beyannamesidir," *Tanin*, July 10, 1325/July 23, 1909, p.1; "İttihad ve Terakki Cemiyeti'nin—İd-i Milli Münasebetiyle—Osmanlılara Beyannamesi," *Tanin*, July 12, 1325/July 25, 1909, p.1; "Proklamation an das türkische Volk anläßlich des Nationalfestes," *Osmanischer Lloyd*, July 25, 1909, p.1; and, "Turkey: The Political Situation," *The Times*, July 27, 1909, p.5.
[133] "The Cabinet," *The Levant Herald and Eastern Express*, July 27, 1909, p.1.
[134] "Tebdil-i Vükelâ Şayiaları," *Tanin*, July 16, 1325/July 29, 1909, p.1.
[135] "Turkish Affairs: Coming Ministerial Changes," *The Times*, August 4, 1909, p.7.
[136] "Abdülhamid-i Sani Devrinin Tarz-ı İdaresi ve Rical-i Hükûmet," *Tanin*, July 21, 1325/August 3, 1909, p.1; "Turkey: The Attacks on Ferid Pasha," *The Times*, August 5, 1909, p.3; and, "Ferid Paschas Rücktritt," *Osmanischer Lloyd*, August 7, 1909, p.1.
[137] "The Ministry of the Interior," *The Levant Herald and Eastern Express*, August 6, 1909, p.1; "Ferid Paschas Rücktritt," *Osmanischer Lloyd*, August 7, 1909, p.1; F.O. 371/761, Sir Gerard Lowther to Sir Edward Grey, Constantinople, August

attacks in the press, and the unconcealed mistrust of Hüseyin Hilmi Pasha and his colleagues in the cabinet. His tenure of office was only remarkable for certain appointments, which were not believed to be entirely due to his initiative, of Unionists to provincial governorships, and his determined but unsuccessful attempt to stifle the inquiry into the Adana massacres.[138]

Talât Bey, who was on a state visit to London, was immediately named his successor.[139] He had won golden opinions as Vice-President of the Chamber of deputies, and was among the recognised leaders of the Committee of Union and Progress.[140] This was a crucial step for the Committee of Union and Progress, and most felt the appointment boded for the eventual establishment of a fully liberal democratic regime.[141]

The successful campaign against Avlonyalı Ferid Pasha encouraged the Unionists to put pressure, this time, on Gabriel Nouradunghian, another monarchist cabinet member. *Tanin* published highly critical editorials against both his decidedly monarchist political philosophy and his conduct in the Ministry of Commerce and Public Works.[142] Thereupon, Gabriel Nouradunghian brought a law suit against Hüseyin Cahid [Yalçın].[143] Nouradunghian's lawyer was Krikor Zohrab, the anti-Unionist deputy for İstanbul, while Hüseyin Cahid [Yalçın] was defended by Yusuf Kemal [Tengirşenk], Union-

---

7, 1909, quoted in Feroz Ahmad, *The Young Turks: The Committee of Union and Progress in Turkish Politics, 1908-1914*, p.53.

[138] "The Turkish Cabinet: Resignation of Ferid Pasha," *The Times*, August 7, 1909, p.5.

[139] "News Items," *The Levant Herald and Eastern Express*, August 9, 1909, p.1; and, Tevfik Çavdar, *Talât Paşa: Bir Örgüt Ustasının Yaşam Öyküsü*, p.160. See also Ali Fuad Türkgeldi, *Görüp İşittiklerim*, pp.43-44.

[140] "The Turkish Deputation," *The Times*, July 7, 1909, p.5. For Hüseyin Cahid Yalçın's comments on the appointment see, Hüseyin Cahid [Yalçın], "Yeni Dahiliye Nazırı," *Tanin*, July 29, 1325/August 11, 1909, p.1.

[141] Hüseyin Cahid Yalçın, "Meşrutiyet Hatıraları, 1908-1918," *Fikir Hareketleri*, 5 (October 26, 1935-April 18, 1936), p.406. See also, Hüseyin Kâzım, "Genç Türkiye'nin Genç Nazırlarına," *Tanin*, August 10, 1325/August 23, 1909, pp.1-2.

[142] Hüseyin Cahid [Yalçın], "Nafia Nezareti'nde: Yeni Usuller Tatbik Ediliyor!" *Tanin*, July 30, 1325/August 12, 1909, p.1; "Nafia Nazırı," and "Nafia Nezareti'ndeki Yolsuzluklar," *Tanin*, August 5, 1325/August 18, 1909, p.1; Hüseyin Cahid [Yalçın], "Nafia Nazırı'nın İtirafatı," and "Nafia Nezareti'ndeki Yolsuzluklardan: Binde bir Numune," *Tanin*, August 6, 1325/August 19, 1909, p.1; and, "Nouradunghian Efendi Hazretlerine," *Tanin*, August 7, 1325/August 20, 1909, p.1.

[143] "News Items," *The Levant Herald and Eastern Express*, August 24, 1909, p.1; and, Ali Fuad Türkgeldi, *Görüp İşittiklerim*, p.44.

ist deputy for Kastamonu.[144] On September 2, three ministers threatened to resign unless Gabriel Nouradunghian resigned the portfolio of Commerce and Public Works.[145] It was an open secret that Nouradunghian had for some time past failed to gain the confidence of some of his colleagues in the cabinet.[146] The efforts made to bring about an understanding between the Minister of Commerce and Public Works and his colleagues having failed, Nouradunghian's resignation was regarded in Unionist circles as certain to take place shortly.[147] While the law suit was still being tried at the court, Nouradunghian was forced to resign on the evening of September 7, thus averting a cabinet crisis.[148] He was immediately succeeded by Bedros Haladjian, a pro-Unionist Armenian deputy for İstanbul.[149] Haladjian was a young man, a lawyer, and had been educated in Europe. He was legal advisor to the Public Debt Administration, and he had succeeded Cavid Bey as reporter of the Budget Committee.[150] In his part, Hüseyin Cahid [Yalçın] was acquitted on the charge of libel, but was fined five liras for having used insulting language against Nouradunghian.[151]

---

[144] "News Items," *The Levant Herald and Eastern Express*, August 26, 1909, p.1; and, "Le procés du 'Tanine'," *The Levant Herald and Eastern Express*, September 2, 1909, p.2.

[145] "Dissensions in the Turkish Cabinet," *The Times*, September 3, 1909, p.3.

[146] "Turkish Cabinet Dissensions," *The Times*, September 4, 1909, p.3.

[147] "Turkey: The Cabinet Dissensions," *The Times*, September 6, 1909, p.4. See, "Nafia Nazırı Meselesi," and, [Karekin] Pasturmadjian, "Nafia Nazırı Gabriel Nouradunghian Efendi'ye Açık Mektup," *Tanin*, August 25, 1325/September 7, 1909, p.1.

[148] "Nouradunghian Efendi," *Tanin*, August 26, 1325/September 8, 1909, p.1; "Turkey: Change in the Cabinet," *The Times*, September 9, 1909, p.3; "Der Rücktritt Gabriel Effendis," *Osmanischer Lloyd*, September 9, 1909, p.1; and, "Gabriel Effendi Noradunghian," *The Levant Herald and Eastern Express*, September 9, 1909, p.1.

[149] "Nafia Nezareti," *Tanin*, August 27, 1325/September 9, 1909, p.1.

[150] "Gabriel Effendi Noradunghian," *The Levant Herald and Eastern Express*, September 9, 1909, p.1; "Turkey: Change in the Cabinet," *The Times*, September 9, 1909, p.3; "Der neue Minister der öffentlichen Arbeiten," *Osmanischer Lloyd*, September 10, 1909, p.1; and, Ali Fuad Türkgeldi, *Görüp İşittiklerim*, p.44. Haladjian's appointment was heavily criticised by members of the anti-Unionist opposition (Rıza Nur, *Hayat ve Hatıratım*, 2, p.327). For various press reviews on Haladjian's appointment see, "Die türkische Presse," *Osmanischer Lloyd*, September 10, 1909, p.2; and, "Der Empgfang der Presse im Ministerium der öffentlichen Arbeiten," *Osmanischer Lloyd*, September 14, 1909, p.1. For Hüseyin Cahid Yalçın's comments on the appointment see, Hüseyin Cahid [Yalçın], "Yeni Nafia Nazırı," *Tanin*, August 29, 1325/September 11, 1909, p.1.

[151] "News Items," *The Levant Herald and Eastern Express*, September 20, 1909, p.1; and, "Der Prozeß Nuradunghian contra 'Tanin'," *Osmanischer Lloyd*, Septem-

Summer recess over, the Parliament convened on November 14.[152] There was considerable opposition to Ahmed Rıza Bey's re-election as President of the Chamber. On November 12, one hundred and ten deputies of the Committee of Union and Progress had unanimously decided to support the re-election of Ahmed Rıza Bey. As some twenty-five other deputies who were still absent from the capital had pledged their support, his re-election could be regarded as certain.[153] Indeed, the Unionist leadership managed to rally its deputies, and he was re-elected with a comfortable majority.[154]

The leadership of the Committee of Union and Progress had already made party cohesion and unity a priority. Now, with a battle possibly in the offing, unity only seemed that much more important. Following the establishment of the Parliamentary Party in the Chamber of Deputies, the Unionist leadership urged its members to act in unison on matters of importance before the Chamber. Before the Second Congress of the Committee of Union and Progress took place in October, Hüseyin Cahid [Yalçın] presented the positions of the Committee of Union and Progress and the Parliamentary Party Group in the columns of *Tanin*, reiterating the need for unity and discipline, and pointing out that those deputies who had been elected under the Unionist ticket were bound to support its programme. To those who could not, he suggested they

---

ber 21, 1909, p.1.

[152] I/II/1, November 1, 1325/November 14, 1909, *Meclis-i Mebusan Zabıt Ceridesi, 1*, pp.2-4; Hüseyin Cahid [Yalçın], "Meclis-i Mebusan'ın Açılması," *Tanin*, November 2, 1325/November 15, 1909, p.1; "Meclis-i Mebusan: İkinci Devre-i İctimaiyesinin Resm-i İftitahı," *Ikdam*, November 2, 1325/November 15, 1909, p.1; "İkinci Devre-i İctima," *Ikdam*, November 2, 1325/November 15, 1909, p.2; "The Opening of the Second Parliamentary Session," *The Levant Herald and Eastern Express*, November 15, 1909, p.1; and, "Zur Eröffnung der zweiten Parlaments-session," *Osmanischer Lloyd*, November 15, 1909, p.1.

[153] "İttihad ve Terakki Fırkası'nın Dünkü Müzakeresi," *Ikdam*, October 31, 1325/November 13, 1909, p.3; "The Turkish Chamber," *The Times*, November 13, 1909, p.5; and, "Parlament und Parteien: Die Versammlung der Komiteepartei," *Osmanischer Lloyd*, November 14, 1909, p.1.

[154] I/II/1, November 1, 1325/November 14, 1909, *Meclis-i Mebusan Zabıt Ceridesi, 1*, p.4; "Ahmed Riza Elected President," *The Times*, November 15, 1909, p.6; Hüseyin Cahid Yalçın, "Meşrutiyet Hatıraları, 1908-1918," *Fikir Hareketleri, 6* (April 25-October 17, 1936), p.55. Ahmed Rıza Bey received one hundred and sixty-four votes (I/II/1, November 1, 1325/November 14, 1909, *Meclis-i Mebusan Zabıt Ceridesi, 1*, p.4; "The Opening of the Second Parliamentary Session," *The Levant Herald and Eastern Express*, November 15, 1909, p.1; and, "Die Präsidentenwahl in der Kammer," *Osmanischer Lloyd*, November 16, 1909, p.1).

make up their own programme and form a separate party.[155]

Prompted by rumours of the establishment of an opposition party, *i.e.*, the Moderate Liberals, the Committee of Union and Progress announced that it would welcome at least one other party in the Chamber, adding that the existence of a visible opposition functioning within the principles of a constitutional liberal regime could only strengthen the existing regime.[156]

The announcement had partly to do with the fact that Unionists felt increasingly uncomfortable with the presence of the military in political life. Ever since the restoration of constitutional order in late April, the military had been intricately involved in politics, criticising the Unionists for having participated in the political affairs of the country. With the object of allaying the concerns of the military with respect to Unionist intentions in the editorial columns of *Tanin* first by announcing on September 26 that the Committee of Union and Progress had transformed itself into a parliamentary group in the Chamber of Deputies, and, a day later, on September 27, by informing the public that the Committee of Union and Progress had no desire to work as a political party, Hüseyin Cahid [Yalçın] had tried to pacify the opposition against the Unionists with the information that the Committee and its provincial branches would work as a cultural club dedicated to social work and promotion of education.[157]

Having made these declarations, the leadership decided to tackle the problem head on during the annual congress of the Committee of Union and Progress in October of 1909. Hüseyin Cahid [Yalçın] wrote that although the army had valiantly defended the Constitution, further intervention was unnecessary now that the constitutional regime was firmly reestablished. He warned that continued interference could be harm-

---

[155] Hüseyin Cahid [Yalçın], "Cemiyet ve Fırka," *Tanin*, August 25, 1325/September 7, 1909, p.1. For the debate in the 1909 Congress of the Committee of Union and Progress on this and other issues see, Ahmet Mehmetefendioğlu, "İttihat ve Terakki'nin 1909 Kongresi," pp.20-29.

[156] Hüseyin Cahid [Yalçın], "Meclis-i Mebusan'da Fırkalar," *Tanin*, October 23, 1325/November 5, 1909, p.1; Hüseyin Cahid [Yalçın], "Meclis-i Mebusan'da," *Tanin*, November 3, 1325/November 16, 1909, p.1.

[157] Hüseyin Cahid [Yalçın], "Selânik Kongresi Münasebetiyle," *Tanin*, September 13, 1325/September 26, 1909, p.1; "Cemiyet'in Klübleri," *Tanin*, September 14, 1325/September 27, 1909, p.1; and, Hüseyin Cahid [Yalçın], "Memnun Olacak bir Hal," *Tanin*, September 15, 1325/September 28, 1909, p.1.

ful both for the state as well as for military discipline, adding that in the future soldiers would not be accepted as members of the Committee of Union and Progress and its clubs, nor would they be allowed any other connection. Finally, the article expressed the conviction that officers, although they would not be allowed to become members, would continue supporting the policies of the Committee of Union and Progress.[158] Thus, while the Committee of Union and Progress desired to keep the senior officers out of politics, it expected junior officers continue supporting the party.

In addition, the Committee of Union and Progress hoped to minimise the role of the Sultan in political affairs by emphasising the restricted role of a monarch in a constitutional monarchy. During a state reception given by the Sultan, the Unionist deputies refused to kiss the hem of his robe, making it clear that they would not take a subservient role to the monarch.[159]

The first formal counter-revolutionary opposition party to appear after the *coup* was the Moderate Liberals—or, the Mutedil Hürriyetperveran Fırkası.[160] By August, the anti-Unionist opposition had already begun organising—for the first time since the counter-revolutionary *coup* attempt was suppressed. There were press reports that Lütfi Fikri Bey and Gümülcineli İsmail Bey were preparing to head this opposition in the Chamber.[161] Dr. Rıza Nur was also actively working to organise the opposition party in the Chamber. Around September, monarchist Damad Ferid Pasha had invited Rıza Tevfik [Bölükbaşı], Dr. Rıza Nur and Lütfi Fikri Bey to discuss the possibility of establishing a formal monarchist opposition in the parliament.[162] The decision to establish a monarchist party

---

[158] Hüseyin Cahid [Yalçın], "Selânik Kongresi Münasebetiyle," *Tanin*, September 13, 1325/September 26, 1909, p.1; and, Hüseyin Cahid [Yalçın], "Askerler ve Cemiyet," *Tanin*, October 13, 1325/October 26, 1909, p.1.

[159] Hüseyin Cahid Yalçın, "Meşrutiyet Hatıraları, 1908-1918," *Fikir Hareketleri, 6* (April 25-October 17, 1936), p.54.

[160] "Mutedil Hürriyetperveran Fırkası (Mutedil Liberaller)," in Tarık Zafer Tunaya, *Türkiye'de Siyasi Partiler, 1859-1952*, pp.277-285. See also, Şehbenderzade Filibeli Ahmed Hilmi, *Muhalefetin İflâsı: İtilâf ve Hürriyet Fırkası*, p.32.

[161] Hüseyin Cahid Yalçın, "Meşrutiyet Hatıraları, 1908-1918," *Fikir Hareketleri, 6* (April 25-October 17, 1936), p.23.

[162] Rıza Nur, *Hayat ve Hatıratım*, 2, pp.336-337.

having been taken during this and the following meetings, Dr. Rıza Nur first contacted the Arab deputies. Their leader, Abd al-Hamid az-Zahrawi, deputy for Hama, first, declared that they preferred to remain as an Arab bloc opposed to the Unionists, without joining with other monarchists in the Chamber. Later, however, they decided to join in with Rıza Nur group.[163]

The monarchists also held talks with Colonel Sadık Bey, a military figure within the ranks of the Committee of Union and Progress who was believed to have considerable following in the army.[164] Despite the clandestine nature of the talks with Colonel Sadık Bey, the Unionist leadership learned of these meetings. The situation could have been very critical if there were to be defections from the party at this juncture, especially when Hüseyin Hilmi Pasha, in whom the Unionist leadership did not fully trust, was in power. The Unionists were worried about Hüseyin Hilmi Pasha's influence over the Sultan; they tried to take counter-measures with a view to neutralise any attempt on the part of either Hüseyin Hilmi Pasha or other anti-Unionist and monarchist figures whose regular meetings with the Sultan might turn him decidedly against the Committee of Union and Progress.[165]

Meanwhile, organisers of the Moderate Liberals met with Ahmed Reşid [Rey], and worked on the programme of the party.[166] Ahmed Reşid [Rey]'s relation with the Unionists were far from being on the best of terms. The Unionists were aware of his anti-Unionist and monarchist sentiments. His activities on behalf of the monarchists during the general elections at Aleppo were still in memory. After Talât Bey's appointment as Minister of the Interior, Ahmed Reşid [Rey], who had been the Governor of Aleppo since June of 1908, was relieved of his post in September of 1909 and was summoned

---

[163] Rıza Nur, *Hayat ve Hatıratım*, 2, p.334. See also, Rashid Khalidi, "Ottomanism and Arabism in Syria Before 1914: A Reassessment," p.59; and, Hasan Kayalı, *Arabs and Young Turks: Ottomanism, Arabism, and Islamism in the Ottoman Empire, 1908-1918*, pp.97-99. For the political career of Abd al-Hamid az-Zahrawi see, Ahmed Tarabein, "Abd al-Hamid al-Zahrawi: The Career and Thought of an Arab Nationalist," pp.97-119.
[164] Rıza Nur, *Hayat ve Hatıratım*, 2, pp.335-336.
[165] Halid Ziya Uşaklıgil, *Saray ve Ötesi*, 2, pp.10-20.
[166] Rıza Nur, *Hayat ve Hatıratım*, 2, p.336.

to the capital where he was confronted at the Ministry with complaints and accusations of bribery lodged against him. Talât Bey additionally confronted him on the issue of his *jurnals*, or secret reports, presented to Abdülhamid.[167]

Soon after his dismissal from government service, Ahmed Reşid [Rey] began publishing *Şahrah*, a paper vehemently opposed to the Committee of Union and Progress and the principles it upheld. The paper was being financed by Tahir Hayreddin Bey, Mehmed Hayreddin Bey, and Salih Pasha—all of whom were sons of Tunuslu Hayreddin Pasha. The paper encouraged many monarchists, including Colonel Sadık Bey, who were up until then hesitant to openly speak up against the Committee of Union and Progress. Colonel Sadık Bey readily joined in the monarchist opposition by working with Ahmed Reşid [Rey] and others.[168]

During the second half of October 1909, rumours began to circulate that a formal opposition party along the lines of the Liberal Union was in the offing, and by November 9, news of this appeared in the press.[169] The party, Moderate Liberals—or, Mutedil Hürriyetperveran Fırkası—was formally established and presented to the public on November 22.[170] Among the founders of the party were İsmail Kemal Bey, deputy for Berat, Abd al-Nafi Pasha, deputy for Aleppo, Abd al-Mahdi Efendi, deputy for Kerbela, Volçetrinli Hasan Bey, deputy for Prishtnë, Hızır Lütfi Efendi, deputy for Zor, Shafiq al-Mu'ayyid al-'Azm, deputy for Damascus, Shukri al-Asali, deputy for Damascus, and Rushdi al-Sham'a, deputy for

[167] Ahmed Reşid Rey, *Gördüklerim, Yaptıklarım, 1890-1922*, pp.115-121.

[168] Ahmed Reşid Rey, *Gördüklerim, Yaptıklarım, 1890-1922*, pp.126-127.

[169] "Meclis-i Mebusan'da Fırkalar ve Vakıf-ı Ahval bir Zatın Mütalaatı," *İkdam*, October 27, 1325/November 9, 1909, p.1; "Neue Parteien," *Osmanischer Lloyd*, November 10, 1909, p.1; "Les partis nouveaux," *Osmanischer Lloyd*, November 10, 1909, p.4; and, "The Turkish Parliament," *The Times*, November 17, 1909, p.5. *İkdam* of November 13 printed that the name of the party was still undecided ("Ahrar Fırkası," *İkdam*, October 31, 1325/November 13, 1909, p.3).

[170] Rıza Nur, *Hayat ve Hatıratım*, 2, p.337; and, *Sabah*, November 9, 1325/November 22, 1909, quoted in Tarık Zafer Tunaya, *Türkiye'de Siyasi Partiler, 1859-1952*, p.278n. Kutay gives the date as November 21, 1909 (Cemal Kutay, *Türkiye İstiklâl ve Hürriyet Mücadeleleri Tarihi, 17*, p.9733). See also, "Zur Bildung der gemäßigt liberalen Partei," *Osmanischer Lloyd*, November 24, 1909, p.1; *Sada-yı Millet*, November 12, 1325/November 25, 1909, and "Yeni Fırkalar," *Yeni Gazete*, November 22, 1325/December 5, 1909, both quoted in Tarık Zafer Tunaya, *Türkiye'de Siyasi Partiler, 1859-1952*, p.278n.

Damascus, as well as Colonel İsmail Hakkı Bey.[171] The new party was clearly under Albanian, Arab, and Greek control.[172] İsmail Kemal Bey, deputy for Berat and one of the most ardent supporters of the monarchist *coup*, was named its leader; he would remain in that position until 1911.[173]

The monarchist and counter-revolutionary press openly supported the new party. *Sada-yı Millet* was the most enthusiastic.[174] Diran Kelekyan, editor of *Sabah*, another monarchist paper, praised it for espousing both liberal and conservative principles.[175] Nonetheless, as the Moderate Liberals were only able to open branches in Rize and Basra, the party's activity was restricted to the Chamber.[176]

On December 2, a number of deputies belonging to the Moderate Liberals held a meeting in order to lay down the basis of their programme. Addressing the deputies, Lütfi Fikri Bey, one of the moderate members of the opposition, suggested that the new party should adopt, in principle, the views of the Committee of Union and Progress with respect to the particulars of the constitutional system. His proposal, however, was rejected. Qasim Zainal Efendi, deputy for Jiddah, pro-

---

[171] Tarık Zafer Tunaya, *Türkiye'de Siyasi Partiler, 1859-1952*, p.277. He mistakenly identifies Shafiq al-Mu'ayyid al-'Azm as deputy for Zor. The names of Lütfi Fikri Bey and of Colonel İsmail Hakkı Bey are mentioned by Kutay (Cemal Kutay, *Türkiye İstiklâl ve Hürriyet Mücadeleleri Tarihi*, 17, p.9733). Lütfi Fikri Bey, deputy for Dersim, joined the party later—in 1911—when his demands were met (Tarık Zafer Tunaya, *Türkiye'de Siyasi Partiler, 1859-1952*, p.281). See also, "Zur Bildung der gemäßigt liberalen Partei," *Osmanischer Lloyd*, November 24, 1909, p.1.

[172] "Türkiye'de İki Yeni Fırka," *İkdam*, November 20, 1325/December 3, 1909, p.1, excerpting *Le Temps* editorial of October 30, 1909. See also "Meclis'te Üç Fırka: İttihad ve Terakki Fırkası—Mutedil Hürriyetperveran—Meşrutiyet Fırkası—Acaba Hakikat-ı Hal İtibariyle Fırka Var mı?—Efkâr ve Eşhas," *İkdam*, November 21, 1325/December 4, 1909, p.1. For similar information see *Sabah* issues of December 7, 1325/December 20, 1909 and December 21, 1325/January 3, 1910, and *Sada-yı Millet* issues of November 12, 1325/November 25, 1909, January 5, 1325/January 18, 1910, January 10, 1325/January 23, 1910, and February 2, 1325/February 15, 1910 (Tarık Zafer Tunaya, *Türkiye'de Siyasi Partiler, 1859-1952*, p.278n). On the role of Arab deputies see, Rashid Khalidi, "Ottomanism and Arabism in Syria Before 1914: A Reassessment," p.59.

[173] Tarık Zafer Tunaya, *Türkiye'de Siyasi Partiler, 1859-1952*, p.281.

[174] "Fırkalar Nâzım-ı Meşrutiyettir: Şan-ı Ahrar," *Sada-yı Millet*, November 3, 1325/November 16, 1909, "*Sada-yı Millet* Gazetesine," *Sada-yı Millet*, November 6, 1325/November 19, 1909, "Fırkalar ve Islahat," *Sada-yı Millet*, November 7, 1325/November 20, 1909, and "Tekâmül-ü Meşrutiyet," *Sada-yı Millet*, November 8, 1325/November 21, 1909 (Tarık Zafer Tunaya, *Türkiye'de Siyasi Partiler, 1859-1952*, p.280n).

[175] Diran Kelekyan, "Hem Hürriyetperver Hem Muhafazakâr," *Sabah*, November 12, 1325/November 25, 1909 (Tarık Zafer Tunaya, *Türkiye'de Siyasi Partiler, 1859-1952*, p.280n).

[176] Cemal Kutay, *Türkiye İstiklâl ve Hürriyet Mücadeleleri Tarihi*, 17, p.9733.

posed the principle of decentralisation as the main philosophical pillar of the new party.[177] The meeting ended with the election a commission consisted of Traianos Nallis, deputy for Monastir, Murad Boyadjian, a prominent member of the Armenian Social Democrat Hnchakian Party, Dr. Rıza Nur, deputy for Sinob, Volçetrinli Hasan Bey, deputy for Prishtnë, Qasim Zainal Efendi, deputy for Jiddah, and Lütfi Fikri Bey, deputy for Dersim, to work on the programme of the party.[178]

The İstanbul press reported that members of the Liberal Union, which had ceased to exist as an active party since its repression after the April *coup*, had joined the newly-founded Moderate Liberals.[179] Dr. Rıza Nur not only denied the story, he also denied that the Liberal Union had ever ceased to exist.[180] Nonetheless, members of the Liberal Union were active participants in the new party.

The differences between the Hüseyin Hilmi Pasha Cabinet, the opposition, and the Unionists came to a head in December of 1909 during what came to be known as the 'Lynch Affair.'[181] It began with a plan to force the amalgamation of Hamidiye, a state-owned steamer company on the Euphrates River, and the Euphrates and Tigris Steam Navigation Company Limited, popularly known as the Lynch Company, a Brit-

---

[177] "New Liberal Party," *The Levant Herald and Eastern Express*, December 3, 1909, p.1.

[178] "Un nouveau Parti," *The Levant Herald and Eastern Express*, December 3, 1909, p.2.

[179] These news were published in *Osmanischer Lloyd* ("Zur Bildung der gemäßigt liberalen Partei," *Osmanischer Lloyd*, December 2, 1909, p.1; "Die neue liberale Partei," *Osmanischer Lloyd*, December 4, 1909, p.1) and *Neologos*, and were quoted in the December 3 to 5, 1909 issues of the Turkish language dailies. See, for instance, "Yeni Ahrar Fırkası," *Tanin*, November 22, 1325/December 5, 1909, pp.2-3; and, "Ahrar Fırkası," *Tanin*, November 23, 1325/December 6, 1909, p.3.

[180] *Sada-yı Millet*, November 22, 1325/December 5, 1909, and *Sada-yı Millet*, November 27, 1325/December 10, 1909 (Tarık Zafer Tunaya, *Türkiye'de Siyasi Partiler, 1859-1952*, p.246n). See also, "Fırkalara Dair," *Tanin*, November 23, 1325/December 6, 1909, p.3. The declaration that the Liberal Union had decided to cease to exist was made by Nureddin Ferruh Alkend, one of the leaders of the Liberal Union, upon his return to Turkey from exile in France on January 30, 1910 (*Sada-yı Millet*, January 17, 1325/January 30, 1910. The text of the declaration is printed in Tarık Zafer Tunaya, *Türkiye'de Siyasi Partiler, 1859-1952*, pp.253-254).

[181] For a short article on this issue see, Ahmet Mehmetefendioğlu, "Hüseyin Hilmi Paşa Hükümetinin İstifası ve Lynch Şirketi," pp.13-19.

ish steamer concern.[182] By imperial decrees of 1834 and 1841, British vessels had been granted the right to navigate the Euphrates and Tigris Rivers, and, since 1862, the Lynch Company had had the right to operate steamers on both.[183] The concession was for an indefinite period.[184] The Committee of Union and Progress favoured a new arrangement which would put the British company on equal footing with the Turkish one, ending the Lynch Company's concessionary right. Half of the new company would be owned by the Turkish Government, the other half by the Lynch Company. Although directorship of the company would be left to a British citizen, the company would be registered as a Turkish company.[185] This, in effect, would signal the transformation of what had been so long an entirely British concession into a Turkish company of which Lynch would own a share.[186] The duration of the new concession was to be seventy-five years, though the Government reserved the right to nationalise the company thirty-seven years after the signing of the new concession.[187] Importantly, Lynch did not acquire any new rights. On the contrary, by amalgamating its interests with those of a Turkish company, Lynch surrendered those he had enjoyed for so many years.[188] Clearly, the new arrangement

---

[182] "Steamship Navigation in Turkey: The Proposed Amalgamation," *The Times*, December 2, 1909, p.5.

[183] Memorandum of the British Ambassador in Berlin, Sir Edward Goschen, presented to the German Foreign Ministery, January 14, 1910, in Johannes Lepsius, Albrecht Mendelssohn Bartholdy and Friedrich Thimme (Eds.), *Die Grosse Politik der Europäischen Kabinette, 1871-1914*, 27/2, p.618. See also, Marian Kent, "Great Britain and the End of the Ottoman Empire, 1900-23," pp.180-183.

[184] The text of the Concession, dated Shaban 1250, can be found in Hüseyin Cahid Yalçın, "Meşrutiyet Hatıraları, 1908-1918," *Fikir Hareketleri*, 6 (April 25-October 17, 1936), p.70.

[185] No.9978, Der Botschafter in Konstantinopel Freiherr von Marschall an den Reichkanzler von Bethmann Hollweg, Pera, November 22, 1909, in Johannes Lepsius, Albrecht Mendelssohn Bartholdy and Friedrich Thimme (Eds.), *Die Grosse Politik der Europäischen Kabinette, 1871-1914*, 27/2, p.592. See also, Hüseyin Cahid [Yalçın], "Lynch İşine Dair," *Tanin*, November 14, 1325/November 27, 1909, p.1; and, "Lynch Meselesi," *Tanin*, November 14, 1325/November 27, 1909, p.2.

[186] Memorandum of the British Ambassador in Berlin, Sir Edward Goschen, presented to the German Foreign Ministry, January 14, 1910, in Johannes Lepsius, Albrecht Mendelssohn Bartholdy and Friedrich Thimme (Eds.), *Die Grosse Politik der Europäischen Kabinette, 1871-1914*, 27/2, p.618.

[187] Hüseyin Cahid Yalçın, "Meşrutiyet Hatıraları, 1908-1918," *Fikir Hareketleri*, 6 (April 25-October 17, 1936), p.70.

[188] Memorandum of the British Ambassador in Berlin, Sir Edward Goschen, presented to the German Foreign Ministery, January 14, 1910, in Johannes Lep-

was more favourable to the Government, although Lynch's position was, in a weakened form, secured for the next thirty-seven years.

The presence of a British navigation concern had posed something of a problem for the German Government which was interested in Mesopotamia and was, at the time, negotiating for the Baghdad Railway concession that would connect Baghdad to İstanbul. German interests wanted the Lynch negotiations postponed until after their own negotiations for the Baghdad Railway were successfully completed.[189] When this did not happen, *Osmanischer Lloyd*, the newspaper defending German interests in İstanbul, accused Hüseyin Hilmi Pasha, in its November 25 issue, of succumbing to British interests.[190]

Some senators, mainly pashas of the old regime with strong monarchist and counter-revolutionary leanings, saw this as their opportunity to put pressure on what they considered to be heavily Unionist Hüseyin Hilmi Pasha Cabinet. They hastily prepared a draft law which stipulated that the government submit for the Chamber's approval every concessionary agreement involving a foreign company. The Unionists countered by arguing that concessions which did not involve a financial burden on the part of the government should be exempt from such scrutiny.[191] The monarchists then tried to capitalise on the lack of cohesion within the Unionist ranks by driving a wedge between the leadership and the party's rank and file. The monarchist daily *Yeni Gazete* took up the Lynch concession and, defining the cab-

---

sius, Albrecht Mendelssohn Bartholdy and Friedrich Thimme (Eds.), *Die Grosse Politik der Europäischen Kabinette, 1871-1914,* 27/2, p.618.

[189] Hüseyin Cahid Yalçın, "Meşrutiyet Hatıraları, 1908-1918," *Fikir Hareketleri,* 6 (April 25-October 17, 1936), p.84. See also, E. T. S. Dugdale (Ed.), *German Diplomatic Documents, 1871-1914, 3: The Growing Antagonism, 1898-1910,* pp.363-392.

[190] "Die Lynchangelegenheit," *Osmanischer Lloyd,* November 25, 1909, p.1. This is quoted in Hüseyin Cahid Yalçın, "Meşrutiyet Hatıraları, 1908-1918," *Fikir Hareketleri,* 6 (April 25-October 17, 1936), p.70. See also, "Lynch Meselesi," *Ikdam,* November 9, 1325/November 22, 1909, p.2; "Lynch Meselesi," *Ikdam,* November 14, 1325/November 27, 1909, p.2; "Lynch Meselesi," *Ikdam,* November 15, 1325/November 28, 1909, p.4; "Lynch Meselesi Hakkında," *Ikdam,* November 16, 1325/November 29, 1909, p.2; and, "Lynch Meselesi," *Ikdam,* November 18, 1325/December 1, 1909, p.2.

[191] Hüseyin Cahid Yalçın, "Meşrutiyet Hatıraları, 1908-1918," *Fikir Hareketleri,* 6 (April 25-October 17, 1936), p.85.

inet as Unionist, attacked its supposedly collaborationist policy. Other opposition papers also attempted to drum up disaffection.[192] Among these, *Sada-yı Millet*, was one of the fiercest in its criticism of the proposed amalgamation of the Turkish and English navigation companies. Its November 16 editorial was deemed to be too provocative, and, consequently, the Court Martial suspended *Sada-yı Millet* on November 30.[193] Most of the authors writing in the opposition papers were anti-Unionist Arab deputies, including Muhammad Shawkat ibn Rif'at Pasha, deputy for Divaniye, Hızır Lütfi Efendi, deputy for Zor, Emir Amin Arslan Bey, deputy for Latakia, and Shafiq al-Mu'ayyad al-'Azm, deputy for Damascus.[194] The monarchist campaign to divide the Committee of Union and Progress proved largely successful.

Opposition was not confined to monarchist deputies alone; some Unionist deputies were also bitterly opposed to the fusion. Even before debate opened in the Chamber of Deputies, Babanzade İsmail Hakkı Bey, deputy for Baghdad and a prominent Unionist, as well as other deputies from the Arab provinces issued statements saying they believed that the proposed amalgamation masked an ingenious design on the part of Great Britain to effect the economic conquest of Iraq.[195] On November 9, deputies of the parliamentary party of the Committee of Union and Progress met to discuss parliamentary strategy. Due to stubborn opposition, however, no decision was taken on the question whether the party should give or refuse its support to the government on the proposed fusion of the two companies.[196]

In the face of this opposition from among the ranks of the

---

[192] No.9978, Der Botschafter in Konstantinopel Freiherr von Marschall an den Reichkanzler von Bethmann Hollweg, Pera, November 22, 1909, in Johannes Lepsius, Albrecht Mendelssohn Bartholdy and Friedrich Thimme (Eds.), *Die Grosse Politik der Europäischen Kabinette, 1871-1914*, 27/2, p.593.
[193] "News Items," *The Levant Herald and Eastern Express*, December 1, 1909, p.1.
[194] Cemal Kutay, *Türkiye İstiklâl ve Hürriyet Mücadeleleri Tarihi*, 17, p.9621.
[195] "Steamship Navigation in Turkey: The Proposed Amalgamation," *The Times*, December 2, 1909, p.5; and, "Turkey: The Committee and the Ministry," *The Times*, December 11, 1909, p.5. See also, Ferdinand L. Leipnik, "The Future of the Ottoman Empire," p.298.
[196] "Turkey: The Committee and the Ministry," *The Times*, December 11, 1909, p.5.

Committee of Union and Progress, the Unionist leadership decided not to open discussion in the Chamber. Hüseyin Cahid [Yalçın], in an eloquent editorial in the December 10 issue of *Tanin*, declared that the cabinet had decided not to submit the 'Lynch Affair' to the Chamber of Deputies. After defending this decision and accusing the deputies of allowing themselves to be influenced by German intrigues, Hüseyin Cahid [Yalçın] called upon the Unionist deputies to support the cabinet. He pointed out that, owing to the paucity of outstanding political personalities in the Empire, the task of finding worthy successors to the existing cabinet would prove well-nigh impossible.[197]

Despite Unionist reluctance to bring the issue before the Chamber, the 'Lynch Affair' was discussed on the December 11 sitting. Both sides were prepared to defend their positions to the bitter end.[198] Hüseyin Hilmi Pasha rose to reply to the interpellation on the navigation of the Euphrates and the Tigris. He explained and defended the policy of the government. He maintained that by virtue of Article 118 of the Constitution the Cabinet considered itself entitled to act independently, the more so since it was not granting a new concession, but was modifying, in accordance with the national interests, the terms of one which already existed. After describing the terms of the new arrangement he remarked that the government was not willing to agree to grant an indemnity to the new company for losses which might eventually be caused by irrigation. If such guarantees of indemnification had been granted, and if the state had been thus committed to future financial disbursements, the cabinet would agree to submit the

---

[197] Hüseyin Cahid [Yalçın], "Buhran," *Tanin*, November 27, 1325/December 10, 1909, p.1—which is also excerpted in, "Turkey: The Committee and the Ministry," *The Times*, December 11, 1909, p.5. See also, Hüseyin Cahid [Yalçın], "Lynch Meselesinde Müesserat," *Tanin*, November 28, 1325/December 11, 1909, p.1. See also, F.O. 424/221, Mr. Marling to Sir Edward Grey, Constantinople, December 13, 1909, *Further Correspondence Respecting the Affairs of Asiatic Turkey and Arabia*, No.9618, pp.148-149.

[198] I/II/13, November 28, 1325/December 11, 1909, *Meclis-i Mebusan Zabıt Ceridesi*, *1*, pp.245-265; "Mebusan-ı Kiramımıza Açık Mektup," *İkdam*, November 28, 1325/December 11, 1909, p.1; Hüseyin Cahid [Yalçın], "Dünkü Meclis," *Tanin*, November 29, 1325/December 12, 1909, p.1; and, "Kabine Şimdilik Yerinde: Lynch Meselesi," *İkdam*, November 29, 1325/December 12, 1909, p.1. See also, Hüseyin Cahid Yalçın, "Meşrutiyet Hatıraları, 1908-1918," *Fikir Hareketleri*, *6* (April 25-October 17, 1936), p.85.

convention to the approval of the Chamber; otherwise not. As for the question of monopoly, there was nothing in the terms of the convention to prevent private owners from using their own steamers to carry their own cargoes, and sailing boats and rafts would continue to ply their trade undisturbed. Hüseyin Hilmi Pasha concluded by announcing that, if his explanations were not accepted, he and his colleagues would resign.[199]

On the Chamber floor, the 'Lynch Affair' provoked spirited debate.[200] It was immediately apparent that the ranks of the Committee of Union and Progress were not in total agreement. Deliberations of the parliamentary group of the party on November 22 on this issue had already shown that there were many Unionist deputies opposed to the new plan.[201] Nonetheless, the leadership expected a majority of Unionist deputies support its position—though a large number of the Chamber's deputies were expected to oppose it.[202] During the debate which followed, Ahmed Ferid [Tek], editor-in-chief of the Unionist organ *Şura-yı Ümmet* and one of the Secretaries of the Chamber, defected from the official Unionist position and argued against the concession.[203] İsmail Kemal Bey, deputy for Berat and one of the leaders of the counter-revolutionary *coup*, also spoke against the scheme.[204] Other deputies who

---

[199] I/II/13, November 28, 1325/December 11, 1909, *Meclis-i Mebusan Zabıt Ceridesi*, *1*, pp.245-262; "Critical Debate in the Turkish Chamber," *The Times*, December 13, 1909, p.5; Hüseyin Cahid Yalçın, "Meşrutiyet Hatıraları, 1908-1918," *Fikir Hareketleri*, 6 (April 25-October 17, 1936), p.85; and, Cemal Kutay, *Türkiye İstiklâl ve Hürriyet Mücadeleleri Tarihi*, *17*, p.9621. See also, "Yine Lynch Meselesine Dair İzahat," *İkdam*, November 29, 1325/December 12, 1909, pp.3-4.

[200] I/II/13, November 28, 1325/December 11, 1909, *Meclis-i Mebusan Zabıt Ceridesi*, *1*, pp.248-265; "Die Lynchaffaire in der Kammer," *Osmanischer Lloyd*, December 12, 1909, p.1; Feroz Ahmad, *The Young Turks: The Committee of Union and Progress in Turkish Politics, 1908-1914*, p.57; and, Rıza Nur, *Hayat ve Hatıratım*, 2, pp.337-338.

[201] No.9978, Der Botschafter in Konstantinopel Freiherr von Marschall an den Reichkanzler von Bethmann Hollweg, Pera, November 22, 1909, in Johannes Lepsius, Albrecht Mendelssohn Bartholdy and Friedrich Thimme (Eds.), *Die Grosse Politik der Europäischen Kabinette, 1871-1914*, 27/2, p.593.

[202] *Le Jeune Turc*, December 12, 1909, enclosed in F.O. 371/781, Marling to Sir Edward Grey, Constantinople, December 14, 1909, quoted in Feroz Ahmad, *The Young Turks: The Committee of Union and Progress in Turkish Politics, 1908-1914*, p.56n; and, Hüseyin Cahid Yalçın, "Meşrutiyet Hatıraları, 1908-1918," *Fikir Hareketleri*, 6 (April 25-October 17, 1936), p.85.

[203] I/II/13, November 28, 1325/December 11, 1909, *Meclis-i Mebusan Zabıt Ceridesi*, *1*, pp.262-263; and, Hüseyin Cahid Yalçın, "Meşrutiyet Hatıraları, 1908-1918," *Fikir Hareketleri*, 6 (April 25-October 17, 1936), p.85.

[204] I/II/13, November 28, 1325/December 11, 1909, *Meclis-i Mebusan Zabıt Ce-

openly opposed the Lynch concession were Lütfi Fikri Bey, deputy for Dersim, and Talib Bey, monarchist deputy for Basra.[205] Both the Arab deputies and the Iraqis themselves feared British expansion.[206] Muhammad Shawkat·ibn Rif'at Pasha, independent deputy for Divaniye, declared that the concession would bring ruin to Iraq.[207] After Shawkat Pasha, deputy for Divaniye, had replied to the Grand Vezier, Halil [Menteşe], leader of the parliamentary party of the Committee of Union and Progress, rose and declared that the Chamber ought to come to a satisfactory arrangement with the cabinet. To the stupefaction of a great part of the deputies, Halil [Menteşe] enlarged upon the fact that machinery destined for the company would be admitted duty free, and laid a resolution before the Chamber. This was an attempt on the part of Halil [Menteşe] to placate opposition. Admitting that the concession was equivalent to a monopoly of river navigation, in that it contained financial exemptions and restricted liberty of commerce, his resolution stated that the Chamber found the explanations of the cabinet sufficient, on condition that the Act of the Concession be submitted to it for ratification. The motion was immediately put to vote and carried by a great majority. The protests of the Grand Vezier were drowned in the general clamour, and the President of the Chamber suspended the sitting.[208]

During the interval Halil [Menteşe] conferred with the

---

ridesi, 1, p.256; Cemal Kutay, Türkiye İstiklâl ve Hürriyet Mücadeleleri Tarihi, 17, p.9624.

[205] Cemal Kutay, Türkiye İstiklâl ve Hürriyet Mücadeleleri Tarihi, 17, p.9625.

[206] While the question was being discussed in the Chamber, there had been protest meetings in Bagdad against the concession being granted to an English concern (Stamboul, December 22, 1909, and von Marschall, Constantinople, October 26, 1909 and November 6, 1909, German Diplomatic Documents, 3, p.368, and p.385, quoted in Feroz Ahmad, The Young Turks: The Committee of Union and Progress in Turkish Politics, 1908-1914, p.67). After the debate in the Chamber and the vote of confidence for the Hüseyin Hilmi Pasha Cabinet, the situation in Bagdad and Basra became so serious that the Government had considered proclaiming Martial Law (The Levant Herald and Eastern Express, December 29, 1909, quoted in Feroz Ahmad, The Young Turks: The Committee of Union and Progress in Turkish Politics, 1908-1914, p.67).

[207] I/II/13, November 28, 1325/December 11, 1909, Meclis-i Mebusan Zabıt Ceridesi, 1, pp.248-250; and, Cemal Kutay, Türkiye İstiklâl ve Hürriyet Mücadeleleri Tarihi, 17, p.9621.

[208] I/II/13, November 28, 1325/December 11, 1909, Meclis-i Mebusan Zabıt Ceridesi, 1, p.250-251; Cemal Kutay, Türkiye İstiklâl ve Hürriyet Mücadeleleri Tarihi, 17, p.9621; and, "Critical Debate in the Turkish Chamber," The Times, December 13, 1909, p.5.

Ministers, whom his motion had placed in such a difficult position. But on the resumption of the debate, the Grand Vezier announced that the cabinet persisted in its demand for a free hand as regards the concessions; otherwise it would resign. Cavid Bey, Minister of Finance, then spoke with bitter eloquence, declaring that the financial exemptions of which deputies complained were granted in every state to concessionnaires. He argued that if every concession were submitted article by article to the Chamber, that body would scarcely succeed in passing four in a year. He claimed that the policy of the Chamber was, apparently, to tie the hands of Ministers—a course which could only endanger the Constitution. He went on to say that the cabinet was resolved to submit no concessions to the approval of the Chamber unless they involved expenditure on the part of the state. He concluded his speech by the warning that if the attitude of the cabinet displeased the opposition deputies, they were free to form a cabinet to their own liking. These words were followed by loud cheers and uproar, ending in a general tumult and the suspension of the sitting.[209]

On the resumption of the debate, Halil [Menteşe], basing himself on an article of the Constitution which permitted the rediscussion of a question on which differences of opinion existed between the Chamber and the cabinet, obtained a vote for the continuation of the debate. This was proof that the government was not yet beaten. During the debate that followed, Babanzade İsmail Hakkı Bey, Emrullah Efendi, and Ahmed Ferid [Tek] criticised the government. Ahmed Ferid [Tek] raised the spectre of British absorption of the Middle East.[210] Babanzade İsmail Hakkı Bey opposed the concession on the grounds that Britain was already powerful in Iraq—control of the river system would only make her even more powerful.[211]

---

[209] I/II/13, November 28, 1325/December 11, 1909, *Meclis-i Mebusan Zabıt Ceridesi*, *1*, pp.252-257; "Critical Debate in the Turkish Chamber," *The Times*, December 13, 1909, p.5; and, Cemal Kutay, *Türkiye İstiklâl ve Hürriyet Mücadeleleri Tarihi*, *17*, pp.9621-9624.
[210] I/II/13, November 28, 1325/December 11, 1909, *Meclis-i Mebusan Zabıt Ceridesi*, *1*, pp.257-265; and, "Critical Debate in the Turkish Chamber," *The Times*, December 13, 1909, p.5.
[211] I/II/13, November 28, 1325/December 11, 1909, *Meclis-i Mebusan Zabıt Ceridesi*, *1*, pp.258-260; *Le Jeune Turc*, December 12, 1909, enclosed in F.O. 371/781,

He went as far as to say that any Minister of the Interior who approved such a scheme could only be a traitor to his country. It was only through the skilful intervention of Talât Bey, Minister of the Interior and one of the leaders of the Committee of Union and Progress, that tempers were temporarily calmed.[212] Nevertheless, deputies from Iraq demanded the interpellation of the cabinet. The general excitement reached to such a pitch that the sitting was adjourned.[213]

The parliamentary group of the Committee of Union and Progress convened on December 12 and forced Ahmed Ferid [Tek] to resign as he had violated party unity on this important matter.[214] Party discipline having been strengthened, debate was resumed on December 13. After four and a half hours' debate, Halil [Menteşe] proposed a motion. The motion stated that if the government's last proposals regarding compensation were accepted by the Lynch Company, this and all other concessions which did not involve the government in financial liability should be left to the decision of the cabinet and not submitted to the Chamber for ratification. The Chamber expressed confidence in the cabinet, and the motion was carried by one hundred and sixty-three votes to eight, with forty deputies abstaining.[215]

Believing that the military had largely been responsible

Marling to Sir Edward Grey, Constantinople, December 14, 1909, quoted in Feroz Ahmad, *The Young Turks: The Committee of Union and Progress in Turkish Politics, 1908-1914*, p.56n; and, Hüseyin Cahid Yalçın, "Meşrutiyet Hatıraları, 1908-1918," *Fikir Hareketleri*, 6 (April 25-October 17, 1936), p.85.

[212] No.9978, Der Botschafter in Konstantinopel Freiherr von Marschall an den Reichkanzler von Bethmann Hollweg, Pera, November 22, 1909, in Johannes Lepsius, Albrecht Mendelssohn Bartholdy and Friedrich Thimme (Eds.), *Die Grosse Politik der Europäischen Kabinette, 1871-1914*, 27/2, p.593.

[213] "Critical Debate in the Turkish Chamber," *The Times*, December 13, 1909, p.5.

[214] "İttihad Fırkası İctimaı," *İkdam*, November 30, 1325/December 13, 1909, p.1; Ahmed Ferid [Tek], "*İkdam* Gazetesi Müdüriyetine," *İkdam*, December 1, 1325/December 14, 1909, p.1; Hüseyin Cahid Yalçın, "Meşrutiyet Hatıraları, 1908-1918," *Fikir Hareketleri*, 6 (April 25-October 17, 1936), p.100; and, "The Turkish Chamber: Vote of Confidence in the Cabinet," *The Times*, December 14, 1909, p.5.

[215] I/II/14, November 30, 1325/December 13, 1909, *Meclis-i Mebusan Zabıt Ceridesi, 1*, pp.268-293; Hüseyin Cahid [Yalçın], "Dünkü Meclis," *Tanin*, December 1, 1325/December 14, 1909, p.1; Hüseyin Cahid Yalçın, "Meşrutiyet Hatıraları, 1908-1918," *Fikir Hareketleri*, 6 (April 25-October 17, 1936), p.85 and p.100; "Schluß der Kammerdebatte über die Lynchangelegenheit," *Osmanischer Lloyd*, December 14, 1909, p.1; and, *Stamboul*, December 14, 1909 and *The Levant Herald and Eastern Express*, December 14, 1909, quoted in Feroz Ahmad, *The Young Turks: The Committee of Union and Progress in Turkish Politics, 1908-1914*, p.67.

for the opposition, Unionists accused Mahmud Şevket Pasha of concerted action with the Germans. In particular, Mahmud Şevket Pasha was said to have conspired with General von der Goltz to overthrow the Committee of Union and Progress in order to set up a military regime devoted to German interests. *Tanin* was particularly vitriolic in its attacks, so much so that some believed Hüseyin Cahid [Yalçın] would be summoned before the military's special Tribunal.[216] Though this did not take place, the Court Martial did suspend *Tanin*'s publication on December 22.[217] In spite of the Chamber's apparent mandate, Hüseyin Hilmi Pasha tendered his resignation on December 28.[218] He had understood that it would be dangerous to grant the concession to the Lynch Company.[219]

The monarchist press, which had earlier denounced the Hüseyin Hilmi Pasha Cabinet as thoroughly Unionist, now intimated that the Committee of Union and Progress had forced his resignation.[220] Halil [Menteşe], leader of the Parliamentary party of the Committee of Union and Progress in the Chamber, categorically denied that the Unionists had exerted any pressure on Hüseyin Hilmi Pasha, along with Ömer Naci Bey, another prominent Unionist, who denied the charges made by the opposition and invited Hüseyin Hilmi Pasha to publicly give the details of his resignation.[221]

---

[216] Hüseyin Cahid [Yalçın], "Almanlar ve Osmanlılar," *Tanin*, December 4, 1325/December 17, 1909, p.1. See, F.O. 371/992, Mr. Marling to Sir Edward Grey, Constantinople, December 26, 1909, quoted in Feroz Ahmad, *The Young Turks: The Committee of Union and Progress in Turkish Politics, 1908-1914*, p.57.

[217] "La liberté de la Presse," *The Levant Herald and Eastern Express*, December 23, 1909, p.1; "Turkey: Leading Newspaper Suppressed," *The Times*, December 23, 1909, p.3; and, Feroz Ahmad, *The Young Turks: The Committee of Union and Progress in Turkish Politics, 1908-1914*, p.57.

[218] I/II/19, December 16, 1325/December 29, 1909, *Meclis-i Mebusan Zabıt Ceridesi, 1*, p.393; "Turkey: Resignation of the Grand Vizier," *The Times*, December 29, 1909, p.3; "The Resignation of Hilmi Pasha," *The Times*, December 30, 1909, p.3; "The Ministerial Crisis," *The Levant Herald and Eastern Express*, December 30, 1909, p.1; "Die Ministerkrise," *Osmanischer Lloyd*, December 30, 1909, p.1; "Sadrâzamın İstifası," *İkdam*, December 16, 1325/December 29, 1909, p.1; and, Feroz Ahmad, *The Young Turks: The Committee of Union and Progress in Turkish Politics, 1908-1914*, p.57. See also, Halid Ziya Uşaklıgil, *Saray ve Ötesi, 2*, pp.21-30.

[219] Feroz Ahmad, *The Young Turks: The Committee of Union and Progress in Turkish Politics, 1908-1914*, p.67.

[220] "Hüseyin Hilmi Paşa'nın Beyanatı," *İkdam*, December 18, 1325/December 31, 1909, p.2.

[221] "Beyanname," *Yeni Tanin*, December 25, 1325/January 7, 1909, p.1; Hüseyin Cahid Yalçın, "Meşrutiyet Hatıraları, 1908-1918," *Fikir Hareketleri, 6* (April 25-October 17, 1936), p.101; "The Committee and the Government," *The Levant Herald and Eastern Express*, January 6, 1910, p.1; and, "Déclaration," *The Levant*

In response, Hüseyin Hilmi Pasha announced that his resignation, contrary to rumours spread by the foreign press, had not been the result of Unionist pressure, that there was no disagreement between the Unionists and himself, and that, as he had made his decision based on personal reasons, the Unionists had not even had advance knowledge of his resignation.[222]

In a *Tanin* editorial, Babanzade İsmail Hakkı Bey disparaged the claim that Hüseyin Hilmi Pasha's resignation was the result of a power struggle between Great Britain and Germany over Mesopotamia and the Lynch Concession as had been suggested in the domestic and foreign press.[223] However, as Hüseyin Cahid [Yalçın] had suggested, it was more than likely that the military—which had enjoyed German support since the 1890s and was firmly anti-Unionist— had engineered the resignation following its apparent defeat on the Lynch issue.[224]

Herald and Eastern Express, January 8, 1910, p.1.

[222] "The Resignation of Hussein Hilmi Pasha," *The Levant Herald and Eastern Express*, January 8, 1910, p.1. The text of the open letter by Hüseyin Hilmi Pasha is dated Zilhicce 25, 1327/January 7, 1910 and printed in full in İbnülemin Mahmud Kemal İnal, *Osmanlı Devrinde Son Sadrıazamlar*, p.1673. See also Cemal Kutay, *Türkiye İstiklâl ve Hürriyet Mücadeleleri Tarihi, 17*, p.9626.

[223] Babanzade İsmail Hakkı, "Buhran ve Vükelâmız," *Yeni Tanin*, December 16, 1325/December 29, 1909, quoted in Hüseyin Cahid Yalçın, "Meşrutiyet Hatıraları, 1908-1918," *Fikir Hareketleri, 6* (April 25-October 17, 1936), p.101; and, Ahmet Mehmetefendioğlu, "Hüseyin Hilmi Paşa Hükümetinin İstifası ve Lynch Şirketi," p.18.

[224] Hüseyin Cahid Yalçın, "Meşrutiyet Hatıraları, 1908-1918," *Fikir Hareketleri, 6* (April 25-October 17, 1936), p.101; and, Ahmet Mehmetefendioğlu, "Hüseyin Hilmi Paşa Hükümetinin İstifası ve Lynch Şirketi," p.18. For the German point of view of the 'Lynch Affair' see, A. A. Türkei 159, No.2, Copy No.4, "Lynchfrage und Demission Hilmi Paschas,", Pera, January 4, 1910.

CHAPTER FIVE

THE HAKKI PASHA CABINET

There was considerable speculation as to who would succeed Hüseyin Hilmi Pasha. Although Hakkı Bey, Kâmil, Said and Avlonyalı Ferid Pashas were all said to have been considered, İbrahim Hakkı Bey was finally chosen.[1] Publicly, Halil [Menteşe] declared that Hakkı Bey and Said Pasha had been considered as possible Grand Veziers by the Committee of Union and Progress, and their names had been presented to the Sultan.[2] Depite the public announcement that the Sultan had chosen Hakkı Bey over Said Pasha as the new Grand Vezier, it was clear that the Unionists had pressed for Hakkı Bey's appointment. The appointment of Said Pasha, for example, was successfully opposed by Cavid and Talât Beys.[3] Kâmil, Said, and Avlonyalı Ferid Pashas had all served the monarchist regime for all their lives, and were thoroughly anti-Unionist; furthermore, Kâmil and Avlonyalı Ferid Pashas, in particular, had been involved with the counter-revolutionary *coup*.

---

[1] "Sadrâzam Kim Olacak?" *İkdam*, December 16, 1325/December 29, 1909, pp.1-2; "Yeni Kabineyi Kim Teşkil Edecek?" *İkdam*, December 30, 1909, p.1; "Le nouveau Grand-Vézir," *The Levant Herald and Eastern Express*, December 31, 1909, p.1; "Hakki Bej Großwesir," *Osmanischer Lloyd*, December 31, 1909, p.1; "New Turkish Grand Vizier," *The Times*, December 31, 1909, p.3; and, "Yeni Kabine," *Yeni Tanin*, December 19, 1325/January 1, 1910, p.1.

[2] "La Presse Ottomane," *The Levant Herald and Eastern Express*, January 3, 1910, p.2.

[3] "The Resignation of Hilmi Pasha," *The Times*, December 30, 1909, p.3. See the interview Talât Bey gave to the correspondent of *Osmanischer Lloyd* ("Der Minister des Jnnern über die Kabinettskrise," *Osmanischer Lloyd*, January 5, 1910, p.1). Count Aehrenthal, the Austrian Minister for Foreign Affairs, told the British Ambassador at Vienna that "in his opinion, the new regime at Constantinople had taken a step backward in the appointment of Hakki Bey as Grand Vizier, and not a step forward." The reason was that "instead of asserting himself, [he] would merely be an instrument of the Committee" (F.O. 424/222, Sir F. Cartwright to Sir Edward Grey, Vienna, January 5, 1910, *Further Correspondence Respecting the Affairs of Asiatic Turkey and Arabia*, No.9707, p.41).

Being the least tainted with involvement in the absolutist regime, Hakkı Bey was the most acceptable candidate from the point of view of the Committee of Union and Progress. And the fact that he had been legal advisor to the Government as well as Ambassador to Rome gave him roots in the traditional bureaucracy which would render him acceptable to the monarchists. After graduating from Mekteb-i Mülkiye where he had been a highly successful student, he was appointed lecturer at the Law School. This experience made him more open to youth and new ideas than previous Grand Veziers, and he was highly regarded for his teaching abilities and his liberal views by both students and intellectuals alike.[4] In Abdülhamid's days he had never hesitated in private conversation to let his opinion on public events be known, and many had often been struck by his power of seeing both sides of a question and by his judicial habit of mind.[5]

After some hesitation and negotiation, Hakkı Bey, who was at Rome as Turkish Ambassador, accepted the post and arrived in İstanbul on January 9, 1910.[6] An imperial decree announcing his appointment was issued on January 12.[7] As the Grand Vezier was customarily required to have the title of pasha, he had been elevated to the rank of pasha immediately before his appointment was made official.[8] Hakkı Pasha had only accepted on the guarantee that he be allowed to form a cabinet

---

[4] Hüseyin Cahid Yalçın, *Talât Paşa*, p.36; Halid Ziya Uşaklıgil, *Saray ve Ötesi*, 2, pp.44-46; and, İbnülemin Mahmud Kemal İnal, *Osmanlı Devrinde Son Sadrıazamlar*, pp.1783-1790. See also, "Hakkı Bey'in Tercüme-i Hali," *İkdam*, December 21, 1325/January 3, 1910, p.2.

[5] Edwin Pears, "Developments in Turkey," p.699.

[6] "Hakkı Bey'in Kayd-ı İhtiyatiyesi: İttihad Fırkası'yla Hasbıhal," *İkdam*, December 18, 1325/December 31, 1909, p.1; "Hakkı Bey'in Şeraiti," *İkdam*, December 19, 1325/January 1, 1910, p.1; "Hakkı Bey'in Şeraiti," *İkdam*, December 20, 1325/January 2, 1910, p.1; "The Turkish Grand Vizier," *The Times*, January 3, 1910, p.5; "Sadr-ı Cedid Hakkı Beyefendi Hazretleri'nin İstikbali," *İkdam*, December 28, 1325/January 10, 1910, p.2; and, "The Turkish Grand Vizier," *The Times*, January 10, 1910, p.3.

[7] *Yeni Tanin*, December 31, 1325/January 13, 1910, quoted in Feroz Ahmad, *The Young Turks: The Committee of Union and Progress in Turkish Politics, 1908-1914*, p.57. The text of the imperial decree for his appointment, dated Zilhicce 30, 1327/January 12, 1910, can be found in İbnülemin Mahmud Kemal İnal, *Osmanlı Devrinde Son Sadrıazamlar*, p.1766.

[8] Hüseyin Cahid Yalçın, "Meşrutiyet Hatıraları, 1908-1918," *Fikir Hareketleri*, 6 (April 25-October 17, 1936), p.101; and, İbnülemin Mahmud Kemal İnal, *Osmanlı Devrinde Son Sadrıazamlar*, p.1766.

without any monarchist intervention.[9] While he was unable to obtain the acceptance of certain conditions which he attempted to impose before deciding to accept the grand vezierate, he had formulated certain desiderata which he would discuss with his colleagues and the leadership of the Committee of Union and Progress before taking up office. The most important of these desiderata was that the Unionists should pledge themselves to abstain from interpellations of a nature to embarrass the Grand Vezier and the cabinet for a time.[10]

He then appointed Mahmud Şevket Pasha as Minister of War in the hopes of curtailing the latter's influence.[11] In his dual capacity as Chief Administrator of Martial Law and Inspector-General of the first three Army Corps, Mahmud Şevket Pasha had been intricately involved in political affairs, but largely independent of ministerial authority.[12] By bringing Mahmud Şevket Pasha into the Cabinet Hakkı Pasha hoped, in particular, to put an end to Martial Law which, because it persisted long after the situation had normalised, now made a mockery of liberal principles.[13] Not only did he fail to lift the state of emergency, but he soon found that Mahmud Şevket Pasha's inclusion in the Cabinet did nothing to control the military, and in fact, only weakened the Unionist position,

[9] Feroz Ahmad, *The Young Turks: The Committee of Union and Progress in Turkish Politics, 1908-1914*, p.68. Hakkı Bey was strongly disliked by the monarchists. His appointment to the Grand Veziership drew heavy criticism from the ranks of the monarchists and the reactionaries. See, for instance, Mehmed Salahaddin, *Bildiklerim: İttihad ve Terakki Cemiyeti'nin Maksad-ı Tesis ve Suret-i Teşkili ve Devlet-i Âliye-i Osmaniye'nin Sebeb-i Felâket ve İnkısamı*, p.29; and İbnülemin Mahmud Kemal İnal, *Osmanlı Devrinde Son Sadrıazamlar*, p.1766n.

[10] "The Turkish Grand Vizier," *The Times*, January 3, 1910, p.5; and, "Mahmud Schefket Pascha Kriegsminister," *Osmanischer Lloyd*, January 12, 1910, p.1.

[11] Hüseyin Cahid Yalçın, "Meşrutiyet Hatıraları, 1908-1918," *Fikir Hareketleri*, 6 (April 25-October 17, 1936), pp.116-117. See also Feroz Ahmad, *The Young Turks: The Committee of Union and Progress in Turkish Politics, 1908-1914*, p.68. For a different interpretation of the circumstances surrounding Mahmud Şevket Pasha's appointment as the Minister of War, see Glen Wilfred Swanson, *Mahmud Şevket Paşa and the Defense of the Ottoman Empire*, p.80.

[12] "The Turkish Cabinet," *The Times*, January 13, 1910, p.5; and, Hüseyin Cahid Yalçın, "Meşrutiyet Hatıraları, 1908-1918," *Fikir Hareketleri*, 6 (April 25-October 17, 1936), pp.116-117. See also Feroz Ahmad, *The Young Turks: The Committee of Union and Progress in Turkish Politics, 1908-1914*, p.68.

[13] Feroz Ahmad, *The Young Turks: The Committee of Union and Progress in Turkish Politics, 1908-1914*, p.69. For İbrahim Hakkı Pasha's programme see, "Kabinenin Programı," *Yeni Tanin*, January 13, 1325/January 26, 1910, p.1.

especially with regard to economic matters and financial reform.[14]

The new cabinet contained prominent members of the Committee of Union and Progress: Talât Bey and Cavid Bey retained their respective portfolios as Minister of the Interior and Minister of Finance.[15] Although Hüseyin Cahid [Yalçın], deputy for İstanbul, and Babanzade İsmail Hakkı Bey, deputy for Baghdad, were considered for the post of Minister of Education, finally Emrullah Efendi, deputy for Kırk Kilise, was appointed.[16] Although Sahib Molla was first named the Sheikh-ul-Islam in the list provided to the press, a few days later Hüseyin Hüsnü Efendi was appointed in his place.[17] Later, on July 12, he resigned and was replaced by Musa Kâzım Efendi, a Unionist senator.[18] Sharif Ali Haydar Bey, who was an Arab and a respected member of the Senate, was appointed Minister of Pious Foundations.[19] Finally, Bedros

[14] Feroz Ahmad, *The Young Turks: The Committee of Union and Progress in Turkish Politics, 1908-1914*, p.69.

[15] "The New Cabinet," *The Levant Herald and Eastern Express*, January 11, 1910, p.1; "Yeni Kabine," *İkdam*, December 29, 1325/January 11, 1910, p.1; "Heyet-i Vükelâ ve Teşekkül-ü Katiyesi," *İkdam*, December 30, 1325/January 30, 1910, p.1; "Die Ernennung Hakki Paschas und die Verfassung," *Osmanischer Lloyd*, January 13, 1910, p.1; and, "The Turkish Cabinet," *The Times*, January 13, 1910, p.5. For Cavid Bey's views on the policy of the new cabinet see, "Dschavid Bej über die Politik des Kabinetts," *Osmanischer Lloyd*, January 16, 1910, p.1.

[16] "The New Cabinet," *The Levant Herald and Eastern Express*, January 11, 1910, p.1; "Turkey: The Cabinet," *The Times*, January 12, 1910, p.5; "Heyet-i Vükelâ ve Teşekkül-ü Katiyesi," *İkdam*, December 30, 1325/January 12, 1910, p.1; and, Cemal Kutay, *Türkiye İstiklâl ve Hürriyet Mücadeleleri Tarihi*, 17, p.9628. Tevfik Çavdar, *Talât Paşa: Bir Örgüt Ustasının Yaşam Öyküsü*, p.165; *Tanin*, December 30, 1325/January 12, 1910, quoted in Hüseyin Cahid Yalçın, "Meşrutiyet Hatıraları, 1908-1918," *Fikir Hareketleri*, 6 (April 25-October 17, 1936), p.116.

[17] "The New Cabinet," *The Levant Herald and Eastern Express*, January 11, 1910, p.1; and, "Heyet-i Vükelâ ve Teşekkül-ü Katiyesi," *İkdam*, December 30, 1325/January 12, 1910, p.1. Çavdar mistakenly writes that Musa Kâzım Efendi, a trusted Unionist member of the Senate, was appointed Sheikh-ul-Islam (Tevfik Çavdar, *Talât Paşa: Bir Örgüt Ustasının Yaşam Öyküsü*, p.165). "The Turkish Cabinet," *The Times*, January 13, 1910, p.5; and, "Le nouveau Cabinet," *The Levant Herald and Eastern Express*, January 13, 1910, p.1.

[18] "The Sheikh-ul-Islam," *The Times*, July 13, 1910, p.5; and, "Empire News: The Capital," *The Orient*, 1/14 (July 18, 1910), p.4. See also, Ambassador Oscar S. Strauss to Secretary of State, Constantinople, July 20, 1910, in *Records of the Department of State Relating to Internal Affairs of Turkey, 1910-1929*, Roll 4.

[19] "The Turkish Cabinet," *The Times*, January 13, 1910, p.5; "Le nouveau Cabinet," *The Levant Herald and Eastern Express*, January 13, 1910, p.1; "Die Ernennung Hakki Paschas und die Verfassung," *Osmanischer Lloyd*, January 13, 1910, p.1; and, Cemal Kutay, *Türkiye İstiklâl ve Hürriyet Mücadeleleri Tarihi*, 17, p.9628. Ürgüplü Hayri Bey, the Unionist deputy for Niğde, was made Minister of Pious Foundations in early January, 1911 ("The Ottoman Parliament," *The Orient*, 1/42 (February 1, 1911, p.2).

Haladjian, another prominent Unionist, was named Minister of Commerce and Public Works.[20] Minister of Justice and President of the Council of State was Necmeddin [Kocataş], another prominent Unionist.[21] Rıfat Pasha, who had been Minister for Foreign Affairs in the Hüseyin Hilmi Pasha Cabinet, retained his position.[22] The only outright monarchist in the cabinet was Dimitraki Mavrocordato, who was appointed Minister of Agriculture, Forests and Mines.[23]

Hakkı Pasha presented his cabinet's programme to the Chamber on January 24.[24] The basic points of the programme were the establishment of internal peace, judicial reform with a view to change pre-revolutionary absolutist laws, amending the Constitution so as to fully bring it into conformity with the principles of a constitutional monarchy, and preparation of a balanced budget—in fact, most of the points advocated by the Unionist leadership. One of the most important feature of his programme was the reference to martial law. After pointing out the necessity of exceptional measures for the prevention of disorder, Hakkı Pasha stated that it would be the policy of his

[20] "The New Cabinet," *The Levant Herald and Eastern Express*, January 11, 1910, p.1; "Heyet-i Vükelâ ve Teşekkül-ü Katiyesi," *Ikdam*, December 30, 1325/ January 12, 1910, p.1; and, Cemal Kutay, *Türkiye İstiklâl ve Hürriyet Mücadeleleri Tarihi, 17*, p.9628. İnal mistakenly writes that "for four months from the date of the formation of his Cabinet İbrahim Hakkı Pasha himself took upon the duties of Acting Minister of Commerce and Public Works" (İbnülemin Mahmud Kemal İnal, *Osmanlı Devrinde Son Sadrıazamlar*, p.1767).

[21] "The New Cabinet," *The Levant Herald and Eastern Express*, January 11, 1910, p.1; "Heyet-i Vükelâ ve Teşekkül-ü Katiyesi," *Ikdam*, December 30, 1325/January 12, 1910, p.1; "Die Ernennung Hakki Paschas und die Verfassung," *Osmanischer Lloyd*, January 13, 1910, p.1; and, Cemal Kutay, *Türkiye İstiklâl ve Hürriyet Mücadeleleri Tarihi, 17*, p.9628.

[22] "The New Cabinet," *The Levant Herald and Eastern Express*, January 11, 1910, p.1; "Heyet-i Vükelâ ve Teşekkül-ü Katiyesi," *Ikdam*, December 30, 1325/January 12, 1910, p.1; and, "Die Ernennung Hakki Paschas und die Verfassung," *Osmanischer Lloyd*, January 13, 1910, p.1. When Rıfat Pasha resigned and left İstanbul for Paris in late 1911, Hakkı Pasha took up the portfolio as Acting Minister for Foreign Affairs (İbnülemin Mahmud Kemal İnal, *Osmanlı Devrinde Son Sadrıazamlar*, p.1767).

[23] "The New Cabinet," *The Levant Herald and Eastern Express*, 1910, p.1; "Heyet-i Vükelâ ve Teşekkül-ü Katiyesi," *Ikdam*, December 30, 1325/January 12, 1910, p.1; and, Cemal Kutay, *Türkiye İstiklâl ve Hürriyet Mücadeleleri Tarihi, 17*, p.9618 and p.9628.

[24] I/II/29, January 11, 1325/January 24, 1910, *Meclis-i Mebusan Zabıt Ceridesi, 1*, pp.617-620; "The Cabinet's Programme," *The Levant Herald and Eastern Express*, January 24, 1910, p.1; "Hakkı Paşa Kabinesi'nin Programı," *Ikdam*, January 12, 1325/January 25, 1910, p.1; "The Cabinet's Programme," *The Levant Herald and Eastern Express*, January 25, 1910, p.1; "Turkey: Statement by the Grand Vizier," *The Times*, January 25, 1910, p.5; and, "Kabinenin Programı," *Yeni Tanin*, January 13, 1325/January 26, 1910, p.1; .

cabinet to bring about the disappearance of this unpleasant state of affairs, and, by the gradual adoption of wise measures, to restore normal conditions.[25]

Both the cabinet and its programme came under opposition fire, led by Hızır Lütfi Efendi, deputy for Zor, Lütfi Fikri Bey, deputy for Dersim, İsmail Kemal Bey, deputy for Berat, Ahmed Ferid [Tek], deputy for Kütahya, and Dr. Rıza Nur, deputy for Sinob.[26] The monarchists' opposition to the Unionist-dominated cabinet had started as soon as it was announced. President of the Moderate Liberals, Abd al-Nafi Pasha, the Arab deputy for Aleppo, as well as İsmail Kemal Bey, the Albanian deputy for Berat, and other members of the party met with Hakkı Pasha on January 18, and had a long interview.[27] In its January 25 editorial, the monarchist *Yeni Gazete* expressed its scepticism of the new cabinet and its programme.[28] Despite monarchist opposition to the formation of the cabinet, Hakkı Pasha received a vote of confidence of one hundred and eighty-seven to thirty-four.[29]

It had become clear from the very start that though Grand Vezier, Hakkı Pasha's power was limited. Truly dedicated to the liberal ideals of a constitutional regime, his greatest problem was the smoldering power struggle between the Committee of Union and Progress on the one hand and the military and monarchist factions on the other. Clearly, to keep these

---

[25] I/II/29, January 11, 1325/January 24, 1910, *Meclis-i Mebusan Zabıt Ceridesi, 1*, pp.617-620; "Turkey: Statement by the Grand Vizier," *The Times*, January 25, 1910, p.5; Hüseyin Cahid [Yalçın], "Mukayese," *Yeni Tanin*, January 14, 1325/January 27, 1910, p.1; and, Cemal Kutay, *Türkiye İstiklâl ve Hürriyet Mücadeleleri Tarihi, 17*, pp.9632-9633.

[26] I/II/29, January 11, 1325/January 24, 1910, *Meclis-i Mebusan Zabıt Ceridesi, 1*, pp.621-630; and, Cemal Kutay, *Türkiye İstiklâl ve Hürriyet Mücadeleleri Tarihi, 17*, pp.9633-9634.

[27] "Informations Parlementaires," *The Levant Herald and Eastern Express*, January 19, 1910, p.2; and, "Die neue liberale Partei," *Osmanischer Lloyd*, January 10, 1910, p.1.

[28] "La Presse ottomane: Le programme de Hakky pacha," *The Levant Herald and Eastern Express*, January 26, 1910, p.2. For *Ikdam*'s viewpoint on the cabinet programme see, "Hakkı Paşa Kabinesi'nin Programı ve Bundan İstinbat Ettiğimiz Mana," *Ikdam*, January 12, 1325/January 25, 1910, pp.1-2.

[29] I/II/29, January 11, 1325/January 24, 1910, *Meclis-i Mebusan Zabıt Ceridesi, 1*, pp.641-643; "The Cabinet's Programme," *The Levant Herald and Eastern Express*, January 25, 1910, p.1; "Chambre des Députés," *The Levant Herald and Eastern Express*, January 25, 1910, pp.1-2; "Der Programm Hakki Paschas," *Osmanischer Lloyd*, January 25, 1910, p.1; "Turkey: Statement by the Grand Vizier," *The Times*, January 25, 1910, p.5; and, Cemal Kutay, *Türkiye İstiklâl ve Hürriyet Mücadeleleri Tarihi, 17*, p.9636.

forces in check without himself losing power would require great skill.[30]

On February 20, eight Unionist deputies resigned from the party and declared that they intended to form a second monarchist party called the People's Party—or, Ahali Fırkası.[31] The reason these conservative deputies decided to leave the Committee of Union and Progress centred around Hakkı Pasha's appointment of Hüseyin Hüsnü Efendi as Sheikh-ul-Islam. The first choice for the position of Sheikh-ul-Islam was Sahib Molla, a prominent liberal and a Unionist. A second choice was Musa Kâzım Efendi, another Unionist. When both had been successfully opposed by the conservative faction within the Committee of Union and Progress, Hüseyin Hüsnü Efendi had been appointed instead. However, even this appointment did not satisfy the conservatives, who had themselves proposed three names of their own choice for the position. These deputies believed such a post should have been reserved for someone with conservative views.[32]

The first to resign from the Committee of Union and Progress were Şeyhzade Zeynelabidin Efendi, deputy for Konya, İsmail Hakkı Bey, deputy for Gümülcine, İbrahim Vasfi Efendi, deputy for Karesi, Farhad Efendi, deputy for Tripoli, Şevket Bey, deputy for Erzurum, and, Ömer Lütfi Efendi, deputy for Burdur.[33] İsmail Hakkı Bey, deputy for Gümülcine and a

---

[30] Feroz Ahmad, *The Young Turks: The Committee of Union and Progress in Turkish Politics, 1908-1914*, p.68.

[31] *Yeni Gazete*, February 8, 1325/February 21, 1910, cited in Tarık Zafer Tunaya, *Türkiye'de Siyasi Partiler, 1859-1952*, p.294n; "Yeni Fırka," *İkdam*, February 9, 1325/February 22, 1910, p.1; "The Turkish Chamber," *The Times*, March 5, 1910, p.5; and, *Yeni Gazete*, February 14, 1325/February 27, 1910, quoted in Hüseyin Cahid Yalçın, "Meşrutiyet Hatıraları, 1908-1918," *Fikir Hareketleri*, 6 (April 25-October 17, 1936), p.117. See also, Ziya Şakir [Soko], "Hürriyet ve İtilâf Nasıl Doğdu? Nasıl Yaşadı? Nasıl Battı? 11: Bazı Mebuslar Demokratlar İçin İnsaf İstiyorlardı," *Tan*, November 11, 1937, p.9; and, Ahmed Bedevi Kuran, *Osmanlı İmparatorluğunda İnkılâp Hareketleri ve Milli Mücadele*, p.522.

[32] Hüseyin Cahid Yalçın, "Meşrutiyet Hatıraları, 1908-1918," *Fikir Hareketleri*, 6 (April 25-October 17, 1936), pp.117-118.

[33] *Yeni Gazete*, February 8, 1325/February 21, 1909, quoted in Tarık Zafer Tunaya, *Türkiye'de Siyasi Partiler, 1859-1952*, p.294n; "Yeni Fırka," *İkdam*, February 9, 1325/February 22, 1910, p.1; "Fırkadan Ayrılanlar," *Tanin*, February 14, 1325/February 27, 1910, p.3; and, Hüseyin Cahid Yalçın, "Meşrutiyet Hatıraları, 1908-1918," *Fikir Hareketleri*, 6 (April 25-October 17, 1936), p.117. The contents of the resignation letter of the six deputies were published in the *Sabah* of February 9, 1325/February 22, 1910 (Tarık Zafer Tunaya, *Türkiye'de Siyasi Partiler, 1859-1952*, p.301n).

former Vice-President of the Committee of Union and Progress, was the leader of the new party, which was generally considered to be decidedly reactionary in its tendencies.[34] According to rumours, Gümülcineli İsmail Hakkı Bey had approached the Unionist leadership for the post of the Ministry of the Interior in the new cabinet, and, when refused, had joined in the opposition.[35] On his part, Gümülcineli İsmail Hakkı Bey published letters in *Sabah*, *İkdam*, and *Yeni Gazete*, refuting the statements of *Tanin* and other papers concerning the motives which impelled his resignation from the Committee of Union and Progress. He alleged that the object of the pro-Unionist papers was to discredit the newly formed People's Party and prevent its development.[36]

In its February 21 issue, *Yeni Gazete* printed the news of the formation of the People's Party by these deputies, and published its programme.[37] With the announcement of the new party, Hoca Mustafa Sabri Efendi, deputy for Tokad, Hacı Şevket Efendi, deputy for Erzurum, İbrahim Vasfi Efendi, deputy for Karesi, Ömer Fevzi Efendi, deputy for Karahisar-ı Şarki, Ahmed Şükrü Efendi, deputy for Sivas, Ömer Lütfi Efendi, deputy for Burdur, Süleyman Sudi [Acarbay], deputy for Bayezid, Mehmed Hamdi [Yazır], deputy for Antalya, and Farhad Efendi, deputy for Tripoli, also resigned from the Committee of Union and Progress.[38] Opposition newspapers wel-

[34] "The Turkish Chamber," *The Times*, March 5, 1910, p.5; Ziya Şakir [Soko], "Hürriyet ve İtilâf Nasıl Doğdu? Nasıl Yaşadı? Nasıl Battı? 12: Ahali Fırkası bir Gün İçinde Kurulmuştu," *Tan*, November 13, 1937, p.9; and, Ziya Şakir [Soko], "Hürriyet ve İtilâf Nasıl Doğdu? Nasıl Yaşadı? Nasıl Battı? 13: Bu Yeni Teşekküle Neden Ahali Fırkası Denmişti?" *Tan*, November 14, 1937, p.9.
[35] Rıza Nur, *Hayat ve Hatıratım*, 2, p.330.
[36] "News Items," *The Levant Herald and Eastern Express*, February 25, 1910, p.1.
[37] *Yeni Gazete*, February 8, 1325/February 21, 1909, quoted in Tarık Zafer Tunaya, *Türkiye'de Siyasi Partiler, 1859-1952*, p.294n. The other opposition newspaper, *İkdam*, printed the programme of the new party on its February 9, 1325/February 22, 1910 issue. See also, "Eine türkische Volkspartei," *Osmanischer Lloyd*, February 22, 1910, p.1.
[38] "Yeni Fırka," *İkdam*, February 9, 1325/February 22, 1910, p.1; "Die neue Volkspartei," *Osmanischer Lloyd*, February 23, 1910, p.1. Mustafa Sabri Efendi's resignation was printed in *Yeni Gazete* of February 10, 1325/February 23, 1910 (Tarık Zafer Tunaya, *Türkiye'de Siyasi Partiler, 1859-1952*, p.295n). See also Rıza Nur, *Hayat ve Hatıratım*, 2, p.330, and Cemal Kutay, *Türkiye İstiklâl ve Hürriyet Mücadeleleri Tarihi*, 17, p.9733. The names of Süleyman Sudi [Acarbay] and Mehmed Hamdi [Yazır] were mentioned in the telegram sent by the Edirne branch of the Committee of Union and Progress criticising the resignations (*Yeni Tasvir-i Efkâr*, February 14, 1325/February 27, 1910 and *Yeni İkdam*, November 11, 1326/No-

comed this new party, among them *Yeni Gazete*, which had published the party's announcement and programme, *Sabah*, *Sada-yı Millet* and *İkdam*.[39] Abdullah Zühdü Bey, editor-in-chief of *Yeni Gazete*, wrote that both the nation and the Chamber of Deputies had long been in need of such a party.[40]

On their part, local branches of the Committee of Union and Progress at Edirne, Konya, Gelibolu, Erzurum and other cities strongly criticised the resignations.[41] Many of their telegrams were printed in the daily papers; and leaders of the People's Party defended their actions in the monarchist press.[42]

Pro-Unionist newspapers, however, welcomed the appearance of a distinct opposition party. *Tanin* and *Yeni Tasvir-i*

---

vember 24, 1910, published in Tarık Zafer Tunaya, *Türkiye'de Siyasi Partiler, 1859-1952*, p.301). See also, Ziya Şakir [Soko], "Hürriyet ve İtilâf Nasıl Doğdu? Nasıl Yaşadı? Nasıl Battı? 13: Bu Yeni Teşekküle Neden Ahali Fırkası Denmişti?" *Tan*, November 14, 1937, p.9

[39] *Yeni Gazete*, February 8, 1325/February 21, 1910, quoted in Tarık Zafer Tunaya, *Türkiye'de Siyasi Partiler, 1859-1952*, p.294n; "Yeni Fırka," *İkdam*, February 9, 1325/February 22, 1910, p.1; Dikran Kelekyan, "İntihabçılar ve Mebuslar," *Sabah*, February 11, 1325/February 24, 1910; and Rıza Tevfik [Bölükbaşı], "Meclis'te Fırkalar Teşkili Hakkında," *Sabah*, February 10, 1325/February 23, 1910, both cited in Tarık Zafer Tunaya, *Türkiye'de Siyasi Partiler, 1859-1952*, p.295n; "Fırka-i Ahali ve [Le] Jeune Turc, [La] Turquie, Osmanischer Lloyd Gazetelerinin Beyanatı," *İkdam*, February 12, 1325/February 25, 1910, pp.3-4; and, "Meclis-i Mebusan'da Fırkalar," *İkdam*, February 15, 1326/February 28, 1910, p.1. See also Cemal Kutay, *Türkiye İstiklâl ve Hürriyet Mücadeleleri Tarihi, 17*, p.9733; and, Ahmed Bedevi Kuran, *Osmanlı İmparatorluğunda İnkılâp Hareketleri ve Milli Mücadele*, p.522.

[40] Abdullah Zühdü, "Ahali Fırkası," *Yeni Gazete*, February 10, 1325/February 23, 1910, quoted in Tarık Zafer Tunaya, *Türkiye'de Siyasi Partiler, 1859-1952*, p.298n.

[41] "İttihad ve Terakki Fırkası'ndan Çıkan Mebuslar İçin Aldığımız Telgrafnameler," *Tanin*, February 15, 1325/February 28, 1910, p.2; "İttihad ve Terakki Fırkası'ndan Çıkan Mebuslar Hakkında Telgraflar," *Tanin*, February 16, 1325/March 1, 1910, p.2; and, "Fırka'dan Çıkan Mebuslar İçin Aldığımız Telgraflar, *Tanin*, February 17, 1325/March 2, 1910, pp.2-3.

[42] *Yeni Tasvir-i Efkâr*, February, 27, 1325/March 12, 1910; February 28, 1325/March 13, 1910; March 6, 1326/March 19, 1910; and March 30, 1326/April 12, 1910, cited in Tarık Zafer Tunaya, *Türkiye'de Siyasi Partiler, 1859-1952*, p.296n.

İsmail Hakkı Bey's reply to articles published in the *Le Jeune Turc, La Turquie*, and *Osmanischer Lloyd* appeared in the February 11, 1325/February 24, 1910 issues of the newspapers (Tarık Zafer Tunaya, *Türkiye'de Siyasi Partiler, 1859-1952*, p.297n). His reply to the local Edirne branch of the Committee of Union and Progress was published in the *İkdam* and *Yeni Gazete* of February 15, 1325/February 28, 1910 (Tarık Zafer Tunaya, *Türkiye'de Siyasi Partiler, 1859-1952*, p.302). Mustafa Sabri defended his position in letters entitled "Fırka Meselesi," *Yeni Gazete*, February 16, 1325/March 1, 1910 and "Devr-i Sabıktan Müdevver Devr-i Hazır Müraileri," *Yeni Gazete*, February 18, 1325/March 3, 1910. Haci Şevket's letter appeared in *Yeni Gazete*, February 16, 1325/March 1, 1910, and Süleyman Sudi [Acarbay]'s article on the party, "Fırkalar Dolayısıyla," appeared in *Yeni Gazete*, February 23, 1325/March 8, 1910 (Tarık Zafer Tunaya, *Türkiye'de Siyasi Partiler, 1859-1952*, p.297n).

Efkâr reminded those who were critical of the new party that the Committee of Union and Progress still had one hundred and sixty deputies in the Chamber.[43] In an interview, Halil [Menteşe], leader of the parliamentary party of the Committee of Union and Progress, added that the resignations made his party's political outlook more coherent.[44]

Overall, the People's Party remained relatively weak. Despite *The Levant Herald's*, *İkdam's* and *Sada-yı Millet's* claimed that it was some thirty deputies strong, other opposition dailies such as *Sabah*, *Le Moniteur Oriental* and *Osmanischer Lloyd* wrote that no more than twenty, or twenty-five, deputies belonged to the new party.[45] The total strength of the party, according to Dr. Rıza Nur, was seventeen.[46] Conversely, according to their own account, Unionists had the firm support of one hundred and fifty-four deputies in the Chamber.[47]

Although the formation of the People's Party was a slight blow to Unionist strength in the Chamber of Deputies, it was not the main threat to the full establishment of the liberal democratic regime in Turkey. The main threat still continued to be the monarchist opposition which was organised both inside and outside of the country. The Moderate Liberals represented the legal monarchist organisation in Turkey. Organised in exile, Parti Radical Ottoman—or, Islahat-ı Esasiye-i Osmaniye Fır-

---

[43] "İttihad ve Terakki Fırkası," *Tanin*, February 15, 1325/February 28, 1910, p.2, which gave the figure as one hundred and fifty-four. *Yeni Tasvir-i Efkâr*, March 7, 1910, which corrected this figure and published the list of all the deputies belonging to the Committee of Union and Progress (Tarık Zafer Tunaya, *Türkiye'de Siyasi Partiler, 1859-1952*, p.297n).

[44] "Halil Bey'in Beyanatı," *İkdam*, February 14, 1325/February 27, 1910, p.2. Similar views were expressed by Şehbenderzade Ahmed Hilmi, "Ahali Fırkası Münasebetiyle: Nazariyat ve Bizdeki Tatbikatı," *Yeni Tasvir-i Efkâr*, February 10, 1325/February 23, 1910 and Velid Ebuzziya, "İttihad ve Terakki Fırkası'nın Hal-i Hazırı," *Yeni Tasvir-i Efkâr*, February 22, 1325/March 7, 1910, (Tarık Zafer Tunaya, *Türkiye'de Siyasi Partiler, 1859-1952*, p.297n).

[45] "Yeni Fırka," *İkdam*, February 9, 1325/February 22, 1910, p.1; "Les partis à la Chambre," *The Levant Herald and Eastern Express*, February 24, 1910, p.2; "Der Austritt von Mitgliedern aus der Komiteepartei," *Osmanischer Lloyd*, February 24, 1910, p.1; *İkdam*, February 9, 1325/February 22, 1910, *Sada-yı Millet*, February 9, 1325/February 22, 1910, *Sabah*, February 24, 1325/March 8, 1910, and *La Moniteur Oriental*, March 10, 1910, quoted in Tarık Zafer Tunaya, *Türkiye'de Siyasi Partiler, 1859-1952*, p.299n.

[46] Rıza Nur, *Hürriyet ve İtilâf Fırkası Nasıl Doğdu, Nasıl Öldü?* p.22.

47 "İttihad ve Terakki Fırkası," *Tanin*, February 15, 1325/February 28, 1910, p.2, where the names of all these deputies are listed.

kası, a strong monarchist opposition group led and financed by Şerif Pasha and Prince Sabahaddin—supplemented the Moderate Liberals.[48]

So, by November 1909, Şerif Pasha, ex-Ambassador to Stockholm and an ardent monarchist, had established in Paris the Parti Radical Ottoman—a counter-revolutionary organisation.[49] After the Revolution of 1908, Şerif Pasha had demanded a position in the new administration. Reportedly, the London Embassy was said to have been the place he most coveted. Nominally, he was a member of the Pangaltı branch of the Committee of Union and Progress—he had joined it with the hope of receiving some high position under the new government. In actuality, however, he was an ardent opponent of the Unionists, and had been openly critical on several occasions. As such, the leadership had rejected him for consideration, and he had consequently resigned his membership in the Committee of Union and Progress. His resignation letter was published in the *İkdam* of March 23, 1909. Şerif Pasha had then left for France before the counter-revolutionary *coup* attempt in April 1909 though he was reportedly involved in counter-revolutionary activities.[50] After the *coup*, the Court Martial had tried him *in absentia*, found him guilty of conspiracy, stripped him of his rank, and sentenced him to hard labour.[51]

Immediately after the suppression of the counter-revolutionary *coup* attempt of April 1909, some of the most prominent monarchist editors had escaped to Europe. Among them were Ali Kemal Bey, editor-in-chief of *İkdam*, and Mevlânzade Rıfat Bey, editor of *Serbesti*, who had joined Şerif Pasha in

---

[48] Ahmed Bedevi Kuran, *Osmanlı İmparatorluğunda İnkılâp Hareketleri ve Milli Mücadele*, pp.531-533.

[49] "The Anti-Government Plot in Turkey: The History of the Plot," *The Times*, July 29, 1910, p.5; and, *Tesisat*, November 10, 1327/November 23, 1911, quoted in Tarık Zafer Tunaya, *Türkiye'de Siyasi Partiler, 1859-1952*, p.285.

[50] "The Anti-Government Plot in Turkey: The History of the Plot," *The Times*, July 29, 1910, p.5; and, Tarık Zafer Tunaya, *Türkiye'de Siyasi Partiler, 1859-1952*, p.286n, and p.287. See also, Şerif, *Bir Muhalifin Hatıraları: İttihat ve Terakki'ye Muhalefet*, pp.32-44.

[51] Şerif, *Bir Muhalifin Hatıraları: İttihat ve Terakki'ye Muhalefet*, pp.70-73.

Paris to continue their counter-revolutionary activities.[52] Financed by Şerif Pasha, Ali Kemal Bey started publishing *Yeni Yol*, whose first issue appeared in October 19, 1909, and, Mevlânzade Rıfat Bey continued publishing his reactionary *Serbesti* in exile at Paris.[53] Later, however, Şerif Pasha withdrew his financial support from Mevlânzade Rıfat Bey's *Serbesti*, which then continued publication with the financial backing of Hidiv Abbas Hilmi Pasha of Egypt.[54] Şerif Pasha and Prince Sabahaddin instituted a larger counter-revolutionary journal in French, *Mechroutiette*, which began publication on October 15, 1909. Claiming to be a monthly journal defending the political and economic interests as well as the rights of all Ottomans without any distinction of race or religion, *Mechroutiette* was, in essence, the French edition of *Serbesti*.[55] As E. J. Dillon, a British journalist who was by no means a Unionist sympathiser, stated, the case of *Mechroutiette* as well as the monarchist opposition in France was very illustrative. Observing that the opposition had been liberal before the Revolution of 1908, and that it had to edit its press organ in France, the opposition now was conservative or reactionary, and had to seek refuge for its newspaper in Paris; the irony of fate was in truth caustic. Here was a party—Parti Radical Ottoman— which condemned liberty of the press, yet was forced to avail itself of the hospitality of Republican France in order to publish a Turkish reactionary journal, which, to make things still more incongruous, it called *Mechroutiette, i.e.,* 'The Consti-

[52] Tarık Zafer Tunaya, *Türkiye'de Siyasi Partiler, 1859-1921*, p.290; and, Şerif, *Bir Muhalifin Hatıraları: İttihat ve Terakki'ye Muhalefet*, pp.53-61. See also, Ali Kemal, *Ömrüm*, pp.170-180.
[53] Ahmed Bedevi Kuran, *Osmanlı İmparatorluğunda İnkılâp Hareketleri ve Milli Mücadele*, p.527; A. L. C., "Journaux ottomans à Paris," p.507; and, Ali Kemal, *Ömrüm*, pp.171-174.
[54] Şerif, *Bir Muhalifin Hatıraları: İttihat ve Terakki'ye Muhalefet*, pp.55-61; Ahmed Bedevi Kuran, *Osmanlı İmparatorluğunda İnkılâp Hareketleri ve Milli Mücadele*, p.527; and, Ahmed Bedevi Kuran, *İnkılâp Tarihimiz ve 'Jön Türkler,'* p.285.
[55] A. L. C., "Journaux ottomans à Paris," pp.506-507; Ahmed Bedevi Kuran, *Osmanlı İmparatorluğunda İnkılâp Hareketleri ve Milli Mücadele*, p.527; and, Hüseyin Cahid Yalçın, "Meşrutiyet Hatıraları, 1908-1918," *Fikir Hareketleri*, 6 (April 25-October 17, 1936), p.149. The programme of the Parti Radical Ottoman was published in *Mechroutiette* (Tarık Zafer Tunaya, *Türkiye'de Siyasi Partiler, 1859-1952*, p.287n).

tution.'[56] Its editor was first İbrahim Baha Bey, then Ali Kemal Bey, and later Pertev Tevfik Bey.[57]

Both *Yeni Yol,* and *Mechroutiette* were official organs of the Parti Radical Ottoman.[58] Although the Hakkı Pasha Government had prohibited the paper's distribution within Turkey, it was, nevertheless, circulated in Turkey.[59] In order to discredit its editor, the Committee of Union and Progress released the *jurnals* of Şerif Pasha addressed to Abdülhamid before the Revolution of 1908, informing on the activities of the revolutionaries. In late February, these letters appeared in *Servet-i Fünun* and *Tanin.*[60] He would, however, continue publishing his vehemently anti-constitutional views in various politically conservative Paris newspapers and journals.[61]

Clearly, monarchist opposition outside the country was becoming organised, and Paris was its centre.[62] Counter-revolutionaries and monarchists gathered around Şerif Pasha.[63] In addition to Ali Kemal Bey and Mevlânzade Rıfat Bey, two reactionary newspaper editors, there were a number of ex-Military Academy students such as Ahmed Bedevi [Kuran],

---

[56] E. J. Dillon, "Fate's Little Ironies in Turkey," p.376.

[57] Ahmed Bedevi Kuran, *Osmanlı İmparatorluğunda İnkılâp Hareketleri ve Milli Mücadele,* p.531; and, Ahmed Bedevi Kuran, *İnkilâp Tarihimiz ve 'Jön Türkler,'* p.292.

[58] "*Tanin* Başmuharririne," *Tanin,* December 16, 1326/December 29, 1910, quoted in Tarık Zafer Tunaya, *Türkiye'de Siyasi Partiler, 1859-1952,* p.289n; and, Ahmed Bedevi Kuran, *Osmanlı İmparatorluğunda İnkılâp Hareketleri ve Milli Mücadele,* p.531.

[59] *Sada-yı Millet,* February 19, 1325/March 4, 1910, quoted in Tarık Zafer Tunaya, *Türkiye'de Siyasi Partiler, 1859-1952,* p.289n; and, "The Anti-Government Plot in Turkey," *The Times,* July 29, 1910, p.5.

[60] Hüseyin Cahid Yalçın, "Meşrutiyet Hatıraları, 1908-1918," *Fikir Hareketleri,* 6 (April 25-October 17, 1936), p.149; and, *Tanin,* February 12, 1325/February 25, 1910, and February 16, 1325/February 29, 1910, quoted in Tarık Zafer Tunaya, *Türkiye'de Siyasi Partiler,* p.286n. For his reply to *Tanin* see, "Şerif (Paşa)'nın Cevabı," *Tanin* February 27, 1325/March 12, 1910, p.2. See also, "Şerif (Paşa)'nın Jurnalleri," *Tanin,* April 3, 1326/April 16, 1910, p.2. For Şerif Pasha's own views on this issue see, Şerif, *Bir Muhalifin Hatıraları: İttihat ve Terakki'ye Muhalefet,* pp.64-66.

[61] Şerif, "Les Continuateurs d'Abdul-Hamid, I," pp.305-315; *idem,* "Les Continuateurs d'Abdul-Hamid, II: Leurs Finance—Leur Administration," pp.13-30; *idem,* "Les Continuateurs d'Abdul-Hamid, III: Le Comité 'Union et Progrès' et notre Politique Extérieure," pp.569-580; and, *idem,* "La Faillite des Continuateurs d'Abdul-Hamid," pp.35-48.

[62] Ahmed Bedevi Kuran, *Osmanlı İmparatorluğunda İnkılâp Hareketleri ve Milli Mücadele,* pp.529-533.

[63] Hüseyin Cahid Yalçın, "Meşrutiyet Hatıraları, 1908-1918," *Fikir Hareketleri,* 6 (April 25-October 17, 1936), p.133; and, Ahmed Bedevi Kuran, *Osmanlı İmparatorluğunda İnkılâp Hareketleri ve Milli Mücadele,* pp.529-533.

Veli Bosna, Pertev Tevfik Beys, who had all escaped to Europe
following the crush of the *coup* attempt of April 1909. Other
leading members of the organisation in Paris were İbrahim
Baha Bey, editor of *Mechroutiette*, Kemal Bey, Şerif Pasha's
trusted man who would be instrumental in organising the
monarchist opposition within Turkey, Hoca Kadri Efendi,
Yahya Kemal [Beyatlı], Halid Bey, brother of Fuad Bey who
worked as a diplomat in the Ministry for Foreign Affairs, Albert Fua, İzmirli Kemal Avni Bey, Köprülüzade Ressam Galib
Bey, Dr. Nihad Reşad [Belger], and Dr. Refik Nevzad Bey.
There were also a small number of ex-civilian bureaucrats
such as ex-Governor of Basra, Mardini Arif Bey, and ex-Sub-
Governor Halil Bey, who were all opposed to the new regime
and had joined the monarchist opposition in Paris.[64] Gelen-
bevizade Muhtar Bey, son of the monarchist Sheikh-ul-Islam
Cemaleddin Efendi, as well as Rüşdü Pasha, son of the monarchist ex-Minister of the Navy Hasan Pasha, and Fazıl Pasha
Toptan, a cousin of Esad Pasha Toptan, were other prominent
and wealthy monarchists who supported and actively participated in the counter-revolutionary organisation in Paris.[65]

In January of 1910, Kemal Bey, *alias* Ahmed Fehmi Bey,
came to İstanbul and took a prominent part in organising the
Parti Radical Ottoman here, being assisted by Princess Emine,
Şerif Pasha's wife, and by his own wife. Branches of this organisation were established in Bursa and some other Anatolian towns. Soon after the extension of their activities within
Turkey, the government had become fully aware of the move-
ments of the plotters, and started gathering intelligence as to
their contacts in Turkey.[66]

Gümülcineli İsmail Hakkı Bey and Colonel Sadık Bey
were not only in close contact with Şerif Pasha, they were also

---

[64] Tarık Zafer Tunaya, *Türkiye'de Siyasi Partiler, 1859-1921*, p.290; Ahmed Be-
devi Kuran, *İnkılâp Tarihimiz ve 'Jön Türkler,'* p.288; and, Ahmed Bedevi Kuran,
Osmanlı İmparatorluğunda İnkılâp Hareketleri ve Milli Mücadele, p.529-531.
[65] Ahmed Bedevi Kuran, *Osmanlı İmparatorluğunda İnkılâp Hareketleri ve
Milli Mücadele*, p.530; and, Ahmed Bedevi Kuran, *İnkılâp Tarihimiz ve 'Jön
Türkler,'* pp.288-289.
[66] "The Anti-Government Plot in Turkey: The History of the Plot," *The
Times*, July 29, 1910, p.5.

receiving his financial assistance.[67] As reported in the Greek language *Anatolikos Tahidromos*, among those who were intimately involved with Şerif Pasha's counter-revolutionary organisation within Turkey were Avlonyalı Ferid and Kâmil Pashas.[68] During the early summer of 1910, with Parliament in recess between June 28 and November 1, communication with the monarchist opposition only increased. In addition, many with foreign passports arrived in Turkey and visited members of the opposition on Şerif Pasha's behalf.[69]

What had given the counter-revolutionary organisation an opportunity to increase its efforts within Turkey was the start of the Albanian revolt in the spring of 1910.[70] An *octroi* had been imposed at İpek for the embellishment of the town. General dissatisfaction owing to the neglect of the government to do anything substantial for bettering the conditions in Albania was the principal cause of the uprising. Other causes which contributed were the proposal to take a census of the population for the purpose of taxation, universal conscription, and the determination to impose the Turkish script instead of the Latin. The Albanians resisted the *octroi*, and, after angry disputes, murdered Rüşdü Bey, the Commander, and wounded İsmail Hakkı Bey, the Sub-Governor of İpek.[71]

The Albanian revolt in Macedonia generated heated discussion in the Chamber of Deputies. Following the assassination attempt on İsmail Hakkı Bey, the Sub-Governor of İpek, on April 1 by Albanian rebels, the government had declared a state of emergency. Two days later, there were rebellions in

---

[67] Hüseyin Cahid Yalçın, "Meşrutiyet Hatıraları, 1908-1918," *Fikir Hareketleri, 6* (April 25-October 17, 1936), p.133.

[68] *Sabah*, July 9, 1910, quoted in Tarık Zafer Tunaya, *Türkiye'de Siyasi Partiler, 1859-1952*, p.290n.

[69] Cemal Kutay, *Türkiye İstiklâl ve Hürriyet Mücadeleleri Tarihi, 17*, p.9715.

[70] "The Albanian Outbreak: Turkish Losses," *The Times*, April 9, 1910, p.5.

[71] "Gayr-ı Müslimlerin Askerliği," *Tanin*, March 13, 1326/March 26, 1910, p.2; "Mesail-i Mühimme-yi Milliyeden: Efrad-ı Gayr-ı Müslimenin Müddet-i Hizmeti," *İkdam*, March 14, 1326/March 27, 1910, p.2; "Arnavutluk Ahvali ve Priştine ve İpek Vekâyi," *Yeni İkdam*, March 24, 1326/April 6, 1910, p.4; "News Items," *The Levant Herald and Eastern Express*, April 6, 1910, p.1; "İpek Hadisesi," *Yeni İkdam*, March 25, 1326/April 7, 1910, p.3; "İpek Vakası ve Millet-i Osmaniye'nin Mukadderatı," *Yeni İkdam*, March 26, 1326/April 8, 1910, pp.1-2; Edwin Pears, "Developments in Turkey," p.701; and, Cemal Kutay, *Türkiye İstiklâl ve Hürriyet Mücadeleleri Tarihi, 17*, p.9642.

Prishtnë, Vucitrn, Gjakovë and Ferizovich.[72] On April 9, Albanian deputies requested the interpellation of the Grand Vezier as well as the Minister of the Interior.[73] The Albanian rebellion was discussed in the Chamber of Deputies on April 11. Hakkı Pasha, the Grand Vezier, explained that the opposition deputies had nothing to fear from the dispatch of the fifty battalions, who, instead of drilling at the capital, "were about to perform military exercises in the plain of Kossovo Polje."[74]

Mehmed Necib Draga and other Albanian deputies who had remained within the Committee of Union and Progress had resigned from the party on April 10. On the April 11 sitting, they took to the Chamber floor and criticised the government's policy as well as some of its officials.[75] Among those who spoke against the government were İsmail Hakkı Bey, deputy for Gümülcine, Volçetrinli Hasan Bey, deputy for Prishtnë, Mehmed Necib Draga, deputy for Üsküb, İsmail Kemal Bey, deputy for Berat, Hasan Fuad Pasha, deputy for Prishtnë, Aziz Pasha Vrione, deputy for Berat, Şaban Pasha, deputy for Prishtnë, Müfid Bey, deputy for Argyrocastro, and Lütfi Fikri Bey, deputy for Dersim.[76] It was felt that at least part of this latest round of opposition had little to do with the events

---

[72] "News Items," *The Levant Herald and Eastern Express*, April 6, 1910, p.1; "Arnavutluk Vekayi ve Meclis-i Vükelâ Muharreratı," *Yeni İkdam*, March 26, 1326/April 8, 1910, p.1; "En Albanie," *The Levant Herald and Eastern Express*, April 8, 1910, p.1; "Arnavutluk Ahvali," *Yeni İkdam*, March 27, 1326/April 9, 1910, p.1; "En Albanie," *The Levant Herald and Eastern Express*, April 9, 1910, p.1; "Priştine Vekayi," *Yeni İkdam*, March 28, 1326/April 10, 1910, p.1; "Arnavutluk Ahvali," *Yeni İkdam*, March 28, 1326/April 10, 1910, p.1; and, Cemal Kutay, *Türkiye İstiklâl ve Hürriyet Mücadeleleri Tarihi*, 17, p.9642.

[73] I/II/69, March 27, 1326/April 9, 1910, *Meclis-i Mebusan Zabıt Ceridesi*, 3, pp.654-658; "Eine Interpellation Talaat Bejs," *Osmanischer Lloyd*, April 9, 1910, p.1; and, "Chambre des Députés," *The Levant Herald and Eastern Express*, April 11, 1910, p.1.

[74] I/II/70, March 29, 1326/April 11, 1910, *Meclis-i Mebusan Zabıt Ceridesi*, 4, pp.5-18; Hüseyin Cahid [Yalçın], "Dünkü İstizah," *Tanin*, March 30, 1326/April 12, 1910,p.1; "Dünkü Sualler," *Yeni İkdam*, March 30, 1326/April 12, 1910, p.1; and, "The Albanian Outbreak: Negotiations Opened," *The Times*, April 12, 1910, p.5.

[75] "Dünkü Sualler," *Yeni İkdam*, March 30, 1326/April 12, 1910, p.1; "The Albanian Outbreak: Negotiations Opened," *The Times*, April 11, 1910, p.5; and, "Albania," *The Levant Herald and Eastern Express*, April 12, 1910, p.1.

[76] I/II/70, March 29, 1326/April 11, 1910, *Meclis-i Mebusan Zabıt Ceridesi*, 4, pp.5-13; "Albania," *The Levant Herald and Eastern Express*, April 12, 1910, p.1; and, Cemal Kutay, *Türkiye İstiklâl ve Hürriyet Mücadeleleri Tarihi*, 17, pp.9644-9653.

on İpek and were to do with a distinctly monarchist agenda.[77]
At the end of deliberations, however, the government received
a vote of confidence with one hundred eighty votes to four.[78]

Albanian and other opposition deputies tried to make the
rebellion an issue once again in the May 4 sitting of the
Chamber.[79] They proposed to appoint a parliamentary commission to inquire into the causes of outbreak in northern
Albania. Their proposal, however, was defeated by one hundred and twenty-five votes to forty-four. Hakkı Pasha maintained that the revolt, which was local and diminishing in
intensity, was likely to be encouraged by the dispatch of a parliamentary commission, but he promised that the government would send a commission for the reorganisation and
reform of the Kossovo province after the suppression of the
outbreak.[80]

When the opposition's tactics to use the Albanian outbreak
as a rallying point to discredit the Hakkı Pasha Cabinet failed,
an altogether different strategy was tried out in mid-May—
this time on the question of the privacy of correspondence.
The discussion on the Budget of the Ministry of Posts and
Telegraphs on May 18 gave a number of opposition deputies
an opportunity of complaining that letters and telegrams addressed to them were not delivered or were opened. In spite of
the efforts of the leadership of the Committee of Union and
Progress, many Unionist deputies joined the opposition in
bitter protests against the action of the government, which,
they averred, had given orders to the Governors and the Post

[77] Cemal Kutay, *Türkiye İstiklâl ve Hürriyet Mücadeleleri Tarihi*, 17, pp.9644-
9653; "Hüseyin Cahid [Yalçın], "Dünkü İstizah," *Tanin*, March 30, 1326/April 12,
1910, p.1; and, Hüseyin Cahid Yalçın, "Meşrutiyet Hatıraları, 1908-1918," *Fikir
Hareketleri*, 6 (April 25-October 17, 1936), p.166.
[78] I/II/70, March 29, 1326/April 11, 1910, *Meclis-i Mebusan Zabıt Ceridesi*, 4,
pp.45-46; "Chambre des Députés," *The Levant Herald and Eastern Express*, April
12, 1910, p.1; "The Turkish Chamber," *The Times*, April 12, 1910, p.5; and, "The
Ottoman Parliament," *The Orient*, 1/2 (April 27, 1910), p.1.
[79] For the meeting of Albanian senators and deputies held on April 30 to review the situation as well as discuss the line of action in the parliament see, "Ar-
navut Âyan ve Mebusan Azalarının Dünkü İctimaı ve Arnavutluk Meselesi," *Yeni
İkdam*, April 18, 1326/May 1, 1910, p.1.
[80] I/II/82, April 21, 1326/May 4, 1910, *Meclis-i Mebusan Zabıt Ceridesi*, 4,
pp.551-580, and 583-584; Hüseyin Cahid [Yalçın], "Kabine ve Meclis," *Tanin*,
April 22, 1326/May 5, 1910, p.1; "Government Commission Promised," *The Times*,
May 5, 1910, p.5.

Office authorities to institute a system of espionage. The sitting was finally suspended amid general disorder.[81]

On the May 26 sitting of the Chamber, Talât Bey, one of the leaders of the Committee of Union and Progress and Minister of the Interior, replying to an interpellation respecting the alleged interception by the Governor of Erzurum of letters addressed to Süleyman Sudi [Acarbay], the Kurdish opposition deputy for Bayezid, denied that there had been any illegal practices, and made the matter a question of confidence. After hearing explanations from Acarbay, the Chamber, by one hundred and forty-one votes to thirty-two, declared itself satisfied.[82]

The discussion concerning the interception of correspondence was partly the result of a previous debate in the Chamber. On May 9, an exciting debate had taken place with reference to the publication of the *jurnals*, or secret reports, discovered at the Yıldız Palace, after its occupation by the army suppressing the *coup* attempt of April 1909.[83] The debate was opened by Shafiq al-Mu'ayyad al-'Azm, monarchist deputy for Damascus, who complained that *Tanin* and a Monastir newspaper had accused him of espionage. He said that as long as the *jurnals* discovered at the ex-Sultan's Palace remained unpublished, deputies and senators would be exposed to similar accusations. He therefore begged the government to take the necessary steps for their publication. He protested against the attitude of newspapers, which, he added, were generally believed to be inspired by the government.[84]

---

[81] I/II/92, May 5, 1326/May 18, 1910, *Meclis-i Mebusan Zabıt Ceridesi*, 5, pp.305-313; "Espionage in Turkey: Deputies and the Post Office," *The Times*, May 19, 1910, p.5; and, Hüseyin Cahid [Yalçın], "Bütçe Müzakeresi," *Tanin*, May 6, 1326/May 19, 1910, p.1; and, "Mektupların Açılması Meselesi," *Yeni İkdam*, May 8, 1326/May 21, 1910, p.1.

[82] I/II/98, May 13, 1326/May 26, 1910, *Meclis-i Mebusan Zabıt Ceridesi*, 5, pp.494-516, and 524-525; and, "Turkish Deputies and the Post Office," *The Times*, May 27, 1910, p.5.

[83] I/II/85, April 26, 1326/May 9, 1910, *Meclis-i Mebusan Zabıt Ceridesi*, 5, pp.8-41.

[84] I/II/85, April 26, 1326/May 9, 1910, *Meclis-i Mebusan Zabıt Ceridesi*, 5, pp.8-10; "Espionage in Turkey: The Yıldiz Secret Reports," *The Times*, May 19, 1910, p.5. For *Tanin*'s accusations against Shafiq al-Moayyad see, "Meclis-i Mebusan-ı Osmani Müzakeresi ve İzhar-ı Fikr-i İstibdadiyeden bir Mebus," *Tanin*, April 23, 1326/May 6, 1910, p.1. *Tanin* of the same day also published *jurnals* of Şerif Pasha ("Şerif (Paşa)'nın Jurnalleri," *Tanin*, April 23, 1326/May 6, 1910, p.1).

At this point, Cavid Bey, one of the most prominent leaders of the Committee of Union and Progress and Minister of Finance, protested against the insinuation, and his protest aroused a storm among the Arab deputies, who averred that the Arabs were incapable of deceit. When the tumult had been calmed, Shafiq al-Mu'ayyad al-'Azm demanded an official inquiry. Hüseyin Cahid Yalçın, Unionist deputy for İstanbul and editor-in-chief of *Tanin*, then mounted the tribune and declared that the fact that Shafiq al-Mu'ayyad al-'Azm had compared the old regime and the new, to the advantage of the former, was in itself sufficient to arouse suspicions of his political probity. Then, amidst increasing excitement, he accused Shafiq al-Mu'ayyad al-'Azm and another Arab deputy of espionage, declaring that the Court Martial was in possession of the proofs, and was proceeding to give other names of delators. He then called on the Chamber to annul the election of any deputy who should be proved to have sent *jurnals* to Yıldız.[85]

Vartkes Serengülyan, a leading Armenian deputy with Unionist sympathies, then rose to propose the publication by the government of all *jurnals* and similar documents that had been prepared by ministers, senators, deputies, provincial governors, and other high-ranking officials. He said that if the Grand Vezier feared the consequences for ministers and senators he should consent at all events to the publication of the reports composed by deputies. The debate grew most acrimonious, and a proposal to demand only the *jurnals* of Arab deputies aroused such fury among the Syrian and Yemen contingent that the President of the Chamber suspended the sitting and sent for the Grand Vezier. During the interval, Unionist deputies held a hurried meeting and decided to limit their demands to the publication of the *jurnals* of deputies.[86]

---

[85] I/II/85, April 26, 1326/May 9, 1910, *Meclis-i Mebusan Zabıt Ceridesi*, 5, pp.10-11; "Espionage in Turkey: The Yıldız Secret Reports," *The Times*, May 19, 1910, p.5. See also, Hüseyin Cahid Yalçın, "Meşrutiyet Hatıraları, 1908-1918," *Fikir Hareketleri*, 6 (April 25-October 17, 1936), pp.149-150.

[86] I/II/85, April 26, 1326/May 9, 1910, *Meclis-i Mebusan Zabıt Ceridesi*, 5, pp.11-15; and, "Espionage in Turkey: The Yıldız Secret Reports," *The Times*, May 19, 1910, p.5.

On the resumption of debate, questions were asked concerning the activity of the Commission which had been appointed by Parliament to examine the *jurnals* discovered at Yıldız. The President of the Chamber declared that the Commission had not been able to complete its task owing to the enormous amount of material before it, which filled more than three hundred and fifty chests. Hakkı Pasha deprecated the publication of any of the *jurnals* discovered at Yıldız on grounds of public interest. Ultimately, Hakkı Pasha succeeded in obtaining the support of the Committee of Union and Progress, and, although the debate was revived on May 9, the Chamber took no definite decision.[87]

Meanwhile, an opposition newspaper, *Sada-yı Millet*, had appeared in İstanbul, itself owned by Pantoleon Cosmidis, the monarchist Greek deputy for İstanbul.[88] Its editor-in-chief, Ahmed Samim Bey, was murdered on the night of June 9 while walking in company with a member of the staff of *Tanin*.[89] *Sada-yı Millet* supported not only the monarchist cause but also foreign interests. Some time before his murder, Ahmed Samim Bey had published an article in *Sada-yı Millet*, criticising the Unionist policy by pointing out that its methods of procedure in the matter of concessions and political affairs had been of a nature to forfeit foreign, especially British, sympathy.[90]

[87] I/II/85, April 26, 1326/May 9, 1910, *Meclis-i Mebusan Zabıt Ceridesi*, 5, pp.15-41; "Hüseyin Cahid [Yalçın], "Meclis-i Mebusan'da Dünkü Hadise," *Tanin*, April 27, 1326/May 10, 1910, p.1; and, "Espionage in Turkey: The Yıldız Secret Reports," *The Times*, May 19, 1910, p.5.
[88] "İstanbul Mebusu ve *Sada-yı Millet* Müdürü Cosmidis Efendi'ye," *Tanin*, March 1, 1326/March 14, 1910, p.2; and, Hüseyin Cahid Yalçın, "Meşrutiyet Hatıraları, 1908-1918," *Fikir Hareketleri*, 6 (April 25-October 17, 1936), p.180.
[89] "Bir Cinayet-i Feci," *Tanin*, May 28, 1326/June 10, 1910, p.3; Hüseyin Cahid [Yalçın], "Evvelki Geceki Vaka," *Tanin*, May 29, 1326/June 11, 1910, p.1; "Cinayet Tahkikatı," *Tanin*, May 29, 1326/June 11, 1910, p.3; "The Late Ahmed Samim Bey," *The Levant Herald and Eastern Express*, June 11, 1910, p.1; "Murder of a Turkish Editor," *The Times*, June 11, 1910, p.8; "Ermordung eines Journalisten," *Osmanischer Lloyd*, June 11, 1910, p.1; "Zur Ermordung Samim Bejs," *Osmanischer Lloyd*, June 12, 1910, p.1; "Zur Ermordung Samim Bejs," *Osmanischer Lloyd*, June 14, 1910, p.1; "Empire News: The Capital," *The Orient*, 1/9 (June 15, 1910), p.3; and, *Tanin*, May 29, 1326/June 11,1910, quoted in Hüseyin Cahid Yalçın, "Meşrutiyet Hatıraları, 1908-1918," *Fikir Hareketleri*, 6 (April 25-October 17, 1936), p.197. See also, Rıza Nur, *Hayat ve Hatıratım*, 2, pp.311-312.
[90] "Murder of a Turkish Editor," *The Times*, June 11, 1910, p.8.

On June 21, several opposition deputies brought the matter before the Chamber. Rida al-Sulh, the Arab deputy for Beirut, demanded that the allegations of the Committee of Union and Progress' involvement be clarified.[91] The opposition referred to a letter written by Ahmed Samim Bey to Kıbrıslı Şevket Bey shortly before his murder alleging that he had been 'condemned to death' by the Unionists.[92] Lütfi Fikri Bey, deputy for Dersim, made a deliberately vague statement, blaming the Unionists for the fact that the criminals had not yet been identified and arrested. Cosmidis, deputy for İstanbul and owner of *Sada-yı Millet*, blatantly accused the Unionists of complicity.[93] Rahmi [Aslan], deputy for Salonica, and Vartkes Serengülyan Efendi, deputy for Erzurum, both leading Unionists in the Chamber, defended the Committee of Union and Progress, arguing that they had nothing to gain from such an act of terror.[94] Nonetheless, İsmail Hakkı [Mumcu] Pasha, deputy for Amasya and a prominent member of the opposition, renewed the attack. Coming to the Committee's defence, Halil [Menteşe], leader of parliamentary group of the Committee of Union and Progress, suggested that the recent murder resembled the assassination of Hasan Fehmi Efendi, another opposition journalist, who had been killed a few days before the counter-revolutionary *coup* attempt in April 1909. Though the Committee of Union and Progress had initially been blamed for the murder, it later turned out that the counter-revolutionaries had themselves killed Hasan Fehmi

---

[91] I/II/119, June 8, 1326/June 21, 1910, *Meclis-i Mebusan Zabıt Ceridesi, 6,* p.460; and, Cemal Kutay, *Türkiye İstiklâl ve Hürriyet Mücadeleleri Tarihi, 17,* p.9685.

[92] "Turkey: The Murder of an Editor," *The Times*, June 15, 1910, p.5. On June 15, the entire press published a letter from Dr. Nâzım Bey, one of the leaders of the Committee of Union and Progress, who absolutely denied that his party had any part in the death of Ahmed Samim Bey ("The Murder of a Turkish Editor," *The Times*, June 16, 1910, p.5).

[93] I/II/119, June 8, 1326/June 21, 1910, *Meclis-i Mebusan Zabıt Ceridesi, 6,* pp.460-461; Cemal Kutay, *Türkiye İstiklâl ve Hürriyet Mücadeleleri Tarihi, 17,* pp.9685-9687; and, "The Murder of a Turkish Editor," *The Times*, June 22, 1910, p.7.

[94] I/II/119, June 8, 1326/June 21, 1910, *Meclis-i Mebusan Zabıt Ceridesi, 6,* pp.465467; Cemal Kutay, *Türkiye İstiklâl ve Hürriyet Mücadeleleri Tarihi, 17,* pp.9688-9689. See also, the letter dated July 28 of Talât Bey, one of the leaders of the Committee of Union and Progress and Minister of the Interior, sent to *The Times* in defence of the innocence of the Unionists in the murder ("The Murder of Ahmed Samim Bey: Letter from the Turkish Minister of the Interior," *The Times*, August 9, 1910, p.6).

Efendi as part of their efforts to provoke the *coup*. Halil [Menteşe] argued that a similar conspiracy might, once again, have been re-enacted.[95]

In July, the government discovered a conspiratorial group which came to be known as the Secret Organisation—or, Cemiyet-i Hafiye.[96] It was a sharp reminder of the fact that the new regime in Turkey, although much more firmly established than it was fifteen months ago, had not reached the stage at which attempts to overthrow it were regarded as too hopeless to be made.[97]

For some time, rumours had it that in retaliation for Ahmed Samim Bey's murder, a secret organisation had been established to assassinate prominent Unionist leaders.[98] However, the conspirators were said to have hesitated between direct attempts to assassinate the principal ministers—a plan which was abandoned owing to the impossibility of finding hit-men for the task—and an elaborate attempt to stir up popular feeling during the *Ramazan*. The scheme adopted appeared to be as follows: a number of women of the city were to be paid to disguise themselves as Muslims and in this guise behave in the streets during the holy month in an unseemly fashion calculated to rouse Muslim feeling, and to evoke the comment, 'This is what freedom has led us to.' When feeling had been sufficiently excited, an attempt was to be made to stir up a tumult simultaneously in all towns where the Unionists had branches and to overthrow the government.[99]

---

[95] I/II/119, June 8, 1326/June 21, 1910, *Meclis-i Mebusan Zabıt Ceridesi*, 6, pp.468-473; and, Cemal Kutay, *Türkiye İstiklâl ve Hürriyet Mücadeleleri Tarihi*, 17, pp.9688-9689.

[96] "Cemiyet-i Hafiye," *Tanin*, July 7, 1326/July 20, 1910, pp.1-2; "Cemiyet-i Hafiye," *Yeni İkdam*, July 7, 1326/July 20, 1910, p.2; "Cemiyet-i Hafiye," *Tanin*, July 8, 1326/July 21, 1910, p.1; "Cemiyet-i Hafiye," *Yeni İkdam*, July 8, 1326/July 21, 1910, p.3; "Cemiyet-i Hafiye," *Tanin*, July 9, 1326/July 22, 1910, p.1; "Die geheime Gesellschaft," *Osmanischer Lloyd*, July 26, 1910, p.1; and, "Die geheime Gesellschaft," *Osmanischer Lloyd*, July 27, 1910, p.1.

[97] "The Anti-Government Plot In Turkey," *The Times*, July 29, 1910, p.5.

[98] "Informations: Société secrète," *The Levant Herald and Eastern Express*, July 8, 1910, p.2, quoting "Gizli bir Cemiyet," *Sabah*, June 25, 1326/July 8, 1910—which, in turn, borrowed the news from *Neue Freie Presse*. See also, Rıza Nur, *Cemiyet-i Hafiye*, pp.31-32 for the news in *Sabah*.

[99] "The Anti-Government Plot in Turkey: The Committee for Fundamental Reforms," *The Times*, July 29, 1910, p.5. See also, Hüseyin Cahid Yalçın, "Meşrutiyet Hatıraları, 1908-1918," *Fikir Hareketleri*, 6 (April 25-October 17, 1936), p.214.

According to *Berliner Tageblatt und Handels-Zeitung* this counter-revolutionary organisation had established several branches in İstanbul—at Beşiktaş, Kadıköy, Üsküdar, Fatih, and Sultan Ahmed—and that they had about eighty members registered in these branches.[100] This secret organisation was the arm of the Parti Radical Ottoman—itself established in September 1909—operating in Turkey.[101] The leaders of the Parti Radical Ottoman, were Şerif Pasha, Mevlânzade Rıfat Bey, Ali Kemal Bey, Pertev Bey, İzmirli Kemal Avni Bey, Albert Fua, Refik Nevzad Bey and Nihad Reşad [Belger], all of whom lived in exile in France.[102] İsmail Kemal Bey, deputy for Berat and one of the monarchists who had been deeply involved in April *coup*, was also reportedly a member.[103] According to various press accounts, members within Turkey included such opposition figures as former monarchist Grand Veziers Avlonyalı Ferid and Kâmil Pashas, Mustafa Asım Efendi, Colonel Sadık Bey, Princess Emine, Şerif Pasha's wife, who was the co-ordinator in İstanbul, and Dr. Rıza Nur, who was the chief of the İstanbul branch.[104]

Colonel Sadık Bey had been a member of the Committee of Union and Progress before the Revolution of 1908; as such, he had enjoyed some political support within its ranks.[105] And it was for this reason that, after the *coup* attempt of April 1909

---

[100] "Cemiyet-i Hafiye Hakkında," *Yeni Gazete*, July 15, 1326/July 28, 1910, quoting *Berliner Tageblatt und Handels-Zeitung*. Rıza Nur cites this source and does neither dispute the existence of these branches nor the number of members (Rıza Nur, *Cemiyet-i Hafiye*, pp.139-141). See also, "The Secret Committee," *The Levant Herald and Eastern Express*, July 29, 1910, p.1.

[101] "Die geheime Gesellschaft," *Osmanischer Lloyd*, July 29, 1910, p.1. Although Şerif Pasha mentions the Secret Organisation, he conspicuously omits his involvement with it in his memoirs (Şerif, *Bir Muhalifin Hatıraları: İttihat ve Terakki'ye Muhalefet*, pp.66-70).

[102] Tarık Zafer Tunaya, *Türkiye'de Siyasi Partiler, 1859-1952*, p.290. Interestingly enough, Ali Kemal does not cite his involvement in this 'party' when he writes about his exile in Paris between 1909 and 1912 (Ali Kemal, *Ömrüm*, pp.170-180).

[103] "Arrest of a Turkish Deputy," *The Times*, July 20, 1910, p.5; and, *Progrès de Salonique*, August 6, 1910, quoted in Tarık Zafer Tunaya, *Türkiye'de Siyasi Partiler, 1859-1952*, p.290n.

[104] "Cemiyet-i Hafiye," *Sabah*, July 9, 1326/July 22, 1910, quoting *Anatolikos Tahidromos*, in Tarık Zafer Tunaya, *Türkiye'de Siyasi Partiler, 1859-1952*, p.290n; "Arrest of a Turkish Deputy," *The Times*, July 21, 1910, p.5; and, Rıza Nur, *Cemiyet-i Hafiye*, pp.87-112.

[105] Hüseyin Cahid Yalçın, "Meşrutiyet Hatıraları, 1908-1918," *Fikir Hareketleri*, 6 (April 25-October 17, 1936), p.134. There is allegation that he joined the Committee of Union and Progress after the Revolution succeeded (Ali Canip Yöntem, "Hizb-i Cedid," p.353).

was crushed, the Committee of Union and Progress tried hard
to keep him within the party. Sadık Bey was not interested.
Playing on feelings of religious bigotry and portraying the
Unionist leadership as irreligious, he only tried to increase
his support within. His own 'religiosity,' however, was sheer
propaganda. It was one of the religious figures of the Committee of Union and Progress, Hacı Mustafa [Beyman], deputy
for Ankara, who exposed Colonel Sadık Bey after the latter
had tried to win him over to his side.[106]

As a first step, the government forbade the distribution of
Mechroutiette, the monarchist paper published in Paris by Şerif Pasha.[107] It was ascertained that Mechroutiette had not only
been distributed in İstanbul but also in the provinces.[108] Arrests
followed. By July 12, twenty-six people in connection with the
secret organisation, including two employees of the French
Post Office in Galata, Hafız Sami and Saim Efendis, had been
detained.[109] Many members of the organisation were also
arrested in Bursa, İzmir, Trabzon, Damascus, and Köprülü,
and sent under escort to İstanbul.[110] According to press reports,
the government would issue a communiqué, giving the full
particulars in regard to the secret organisation after the arrest
of all the members of that body.[111] On July 20, the government
communiqué confirmed the existence of a secret organisation,
announcing that forty-eight people had been arrested and

---

[106] Hüseyin Cahid Yalçın, "Meşrutiyet Hatıraları, 1908-1918," Fikir Hareketleri, 6 (April 25-October 17, 1936), p.134.
[107] "The Anti-Government Plot in Turkey: The Committee for Fundamental
Reforms," The Times, July 29, 1910, p.5; and, "Une Association secrète?," The Levant Herald and Eastern Express, July 9, 1910, p.2. See also, Rıza Nur, Cemiyet-i Hafiye, p.36.
[108] "News Items," The Levant Herald and Eastern Express, July 12, 1910, p.1.
[109] "Informations: L'association secrète," The Levant Herald and Eastern Express, July 11, 1910, p.2; and, "News Items," The Levant Herald and Eastern Express, July 12, 1910, p.1. See also, Rıza Nur, Cemiyet-i Hafiye, pp.36-37.
[110] "News Items," The Levant Herald and Eastern Express, July 15, 1910, p.1;
"The Secret Committee," The Levant Herald and Eastern Express, July 23, 1910, p.1;
"The Secret Committee," The Levant Herald and Eastern Express, July 26, 1910, p.1;
"Cemiyet-i Hafiye Tahkikatı," Tanin, July 15, 1326/July 28, 1910, pp.1-2; "La société
secrète," The Levant Herald and Eastern Express, July 29, 1910, p.1; "Cemiyet-i Hafiye: Tahkikat Ne Merkezde?" Tanin, July 16, 1326/July 29, 1910, pp.1-2; "Informations: Association réactionnaire," The Levant Herald and Eastern Express, September 3, 1910, p.2
[111] "News Items," The Levant Herald and Eastern Express, July 19, 1910, p.1.

were to appear before the Military Tribunal.[112] Şerif Pasha was named as the organisation's leader, and in addition to plotting the murders of various Unionist and cabinet members, the organisation was accused of having tried to create dissension among those troops who were being sent to crush the Albanian rebellion.[113] Apart from specific charges, the public prosecutor accused those arrested of membership in an organisation which sought to restore those civilian and military bureaucrats who had been fired after the Revolution of 1908 to their pre-Revolutionary posts, dissolve the Chamber of Deputies, form a new government, and re-establish absolutism.[114]

Dr. Rıza Nur, deputy for Sinob, was among those detained on July 18.[115] According to *Yeni Gazete*, Dr. Rıza Nur had for the preceding two months been suspected of belonging to the secret organisation, but there had not been enough evidence against him to justify his arrest—until very serious evidence against him had been given by the other members of the organisation who had lately been arrested.[116] Dr. Münir Bey had reportedly visited Dr. Rıza Nur from abroad, bringing a letter from Şerif Pasha. Dr. Rıza Nur was charged with

---

[112] Hüseyin Cahid Yalçın, "Meşrutiyet Hatıraları, 1908-1918," *Fikir Hareketleri*, 6 (April 25-October 17, 1936), p.214. *Yeni Gazete* of July 9 printed the news that sixty-three members of the secret organisation had been arrested ("News Items," *The Levant Herald and Eastern Express*, July 9, 1910, p.1). See also, "Die geheime Gesellschaft," *Osmanischer Lloyd*, July 27, 1910, p.1.
According to Dr. Rıza Nur, Nedre Matran had informed on the organisation which resulted in the following arrests (Rıza Nur, *Cemiyet-i Hafiye, passim*).
[113] "Beyanname," *Tanin*, July 7, 1326/July 20, 1910, p.2; Hüseyin Cahid Yalçın, "Meşrutiyet Hatıraları, 1908-1918," *Fikir Hareketleri*, 6 (April 25-October 17, 1936), p.214; "La Société secrète," *The Levant Herald and Eastern Express*, July 20, 1910, p.1; and, Rıza Nur, *Cemiyet-i Hafiye*, pp.97-98.
[114] "Beyanname," *Tanin*, July 7, 1326/July 20, 1910, p.2; and, "La Société secrète," *The Levant Herald and Eastern Express*, July 20, 1910, p.1; and, Rıza Nur, *Cemiyet-i Hafiye*, pp.97-98.
[115] "Cemiyet-i Hafiye ve Rıza Nur Bey'in Tevkifi," *Tanin*, July 6, 1326/July 19, 1910, quoted in Tarık Zafer Tunaya, *Türkiye'de Siyasi Partiler, 1859-1952*, p.288n; Babanzade İsmail Hakkı, "Bir Mebusun Tevkifi," *Tanin*, July 7, 1326/July 20, 1910, p.1; "Arrest of a Turkish Deputy," *The Times*, July 20, 1910, p.5; "The Secret Committee: Arrest of a Deputy," *The Levant Herald and Eastern Express*, July 20, 1910, p.1; and, "Die geheime Gesellschaft," *Osmanischer Lloyd*, July 27, 1910, p.1. See also, Rıza Nur, *Hayat ve Hatıratım*, 2, p.338; Rıza Nur, *Cemiyet-i Hafiye*, pp.90-110; and, Hüseyin Cahid Yalçın, "Meşrutiyet Hatıraları, 1908-1918," *Fikir Hareketleri*, 6 (April 25-October 17, 1936), p.214.
[116] "The Secret Committee: Arrest of a Deputy," *The Levant Herald and Eastern Express*, July 20, 1910, p.1; and, "The Anti-Government Plot in Turkey: The Committee for Fundamental Reforms," *The Times*, July 29, 1910, p.5.

conspiracy, and kept under custody for three and a half months.[117]

In late August, the committee appointed by the İstanbul Military Tribunal to report upon the Secret Organisation concluded its report. It contained names of fifty persons, who, except those who had evaded arrest, would be brought before the Military Tribunal.[118] In early October, the Military Tribunal acquitted twenty-two of the persons accused of belonging to the Secret Organisation; the rest would stand trial.[119] The conspiracy trials began on October 17.[120] On October 22, the court set Dr. Rıza Nur free, not that there was not any hard evidence against him but that Gerald H. Fitzmaurice, the First Dragoman of the British Embassy, along with Rahmi [Aslan], the prominent Unionist deputy for Salonica, and Necmeddin [Kocataş], Unionist deputy for Kastamonu and Minister of Justice, intervened on his behalf.[121] In addition to Dr. Rıza Nur, the Military Tribunal also released Topal Osman, and some other members of the Secret Organisation.[122] However, at its October 26 sitting, the Military Tribunal sentenced Şerif Pasha and Kemal Bey, his contact within the country, to life imprisonment in a fortress; both had been tried *in absentia*. The sentences entailed the loss of their civil rights and

---

[117] Rıza Nur, *Cemiyet-i Hafiye*, pp.79-85; "Empire News: The Capital," *The Orient*, 1/27 (October 19, 1910), p.5; Hüseyin Cahid Yalçın, "Meşrutiyet Hatıraları, 1908-1918," *Fikir Hareketleri*, 6 (April 25-October 17, 1936), p.214; and, Cemal Kutay, *Türkiye İstiklâl ve Hürriyet Mücadeleleri Tarihi, 17*, p.9717.

[118] "Cemiyet-i Hafiye," *Tanin*, August 11, 1326/August 24, 1910, pp.1-2; "Turkey: Charges of Conspiracy," *The Times*, August 24, 1910, p.3; and, "Turkey: The Anti-Government Plot," *The Times*, August 25, 1910, p.3. See also, Rıza Nur, *Cemiyet-i Hafiye*, pp.178-180.

[119] "News Items," *The Levant Herald and Eastern Express*, October 5, 1910, p.1; and, "Turkey: Political Suspects Released," *The Times*, October 6, 1910, p.6.

[120] "News Items," *The Levant Herald and Eastern Express*, October 12, 1910, p.1.

[121] "Release of Dr. Riza Nour," *The Levant Herald and Eastern Express*, October 24, 1910, p.1; "Turkey: The 'Secret Committee'," *The Times*, October 24, 1910, p.7; "Empire News: The Capital," *The Orient*, 1/28 (October 26, 1910), p.5; "Die geheime Gesellschaft," *Osmanischer Lloyd*, October 29, 1910, p.1; Rıza Nur, *Hayat ve Hatıratım, 2*, pp.338-339; Hüseyin Cahid Yalçın, "Meşrutiyet Hatıraları, 1908-1918," *Fikir Hareketleri*, 6 (April 25-October 17, 1936), p.214; and, Cemal Kutay, *Türkiye İstiklâl ve Hürriyet Mücadeleleri Tarihi, 17*, p.9717. For the decision of the Military Tribunal see, Rıza Nur, *Cemiyet-i Hafiye*, pp.221-224.

[122] "Turkey: The 'Secret Committee'," *The Times*, October 24, 1910, p.7; and, "Die geheime Gesellschaft," *Osmanischer Lloyd*, October 29, 1910, p.1. See also, Rıza Nur, *Cemiyet-i Hafiye*, pp.221-224.

confiscation of their properties.[123] By November 14, fourteen of the forty-eight persons accused of belonging to the Secret Organisation were acquitted. Şerif Pasha's wife and Dr. Münir Bey, who were tried *in absentia*, were sentenced to five years' exile and fifteen years' imprisonment respectively.[124] The case of the Secret Organisation, which had been under investigation since July, was finally closed at the end of November by the condemnation of nineteen persons, who had been found guilty by the Military Tribunal.[125]

The summer recess of the Parliament ended on November 14.[126] The Committee of Union and Progress had already chosen its candidates for the Presidency and Vice-Presidencies of the Chamber at an extra-ordinary meeting of the party held on November 10; the Unionist candidates were Ahmed Rıza Bey, deputy for İstanbul, for the Presidency, Ürgüplü Hayri Bey, deputy for Niğde, and Suleiman al-Bostani, deputy for Beirut, for the Vice-Presidencies.[127] On November 14, despite opposition, these Unionist candidates were elected. Out of a total of one hundred and sixty-one deputies present at the elections, one hundred and twenty-four voted for Ahmed Rıza Bey, while twelve Greek deputies supported Rıza Tevfik [Bölükbaşı], deputy for Edirne; there were fourteen abstentions.[128]

---

[123] "The Secret Committee," *The Levant Herald and Eastern Express*, October 26, 1910, p.1; "The 'Secret Association' in Turkey," *The Times*, October 27, 1910, p.5; and, "Die geheime Gesellschaft," *Osmanischer Lloyd*, October 29, 1910, p.1. See also, Şerif, *Bir Muhalifin Hatıraları: İttihat ve Terakki'ye Muhalefet*, pp.70-73.

[124] "The Secret Committee," *The Levant Herald and Eastern Express*, November 14, 1910, p.1; and, "Die geheime Gesellschaft," Osmanischer Lloyd, November 16, 1910, p.1.

[125] "Empire News: The Capital," *The Orient*, 1/33 (November 30, 1910), p.4.

[126] I/III/1, November 1, 1326/November 14, 1910, *Meclis-i Mebusan Zabıt Ceridesi*, *1*, pp.2-4; "Hüseyin Cahid [Yalçın], "Meclis-i Mebusan'ın Açılması," *Tanin*, November 2, 1326/November 15, 1910, p.1; "Meclis-i Mebusan'ın Küşadı," *Tanin*, November 2, 1326/November 15, 1910, p.2; "Meclis-i Mebusan-ı Osmani: İlk Müzakere," *Yeni İkdam*, November 2, 1326/November 15, 1910, p.1; "Dünkü Resm-i Küşad," *Yeni İkdam*, November 2, 1326/November 15, 1910, p.1; "Opening of the Turkish Parliament: The Sultan's Speech," *The Times*, November 15, 1910, p.7; "Eröffnung der dritten Parlamentssession," *Osmanischer Lloyd*, November 15, 1910, p.1; and, Cemal Kutay, *Türkiye İstiklâl ve Hürriyet Mücadeleleri Tarihi*, *17*, p.9706.

[127] "News Items," *The Levant Herald and Eastern Express*, November 11, 1910, p.1; "Turkey: The Presidency of the Chamber," *The Times*, November 11, 1910, p.5; and, Cemal Kutay, *Türkiye İstiklâl ve Hürriyet Mücadeleleri Tarihi*, 17, pp.9706-9707.

[128] I/III/1, November 1, 1326/November 14, 1910, *Meclis-i Mebusan Zabıt Ceridesi*, *1*, p.3; "Üçüncü Devre-i İctimaiye: Birinci İctima-i Umumi," *Yeni İkdam*,

Ürgüplü Hayri Bey and Suleiman al-Bostani were elected Vice-Presidents with one hundred ten and ninety-nine votes respectively.[129]

Shortly after the opening of the Parliament, the opposition began its attack on the Hakkı Pasha Cabinet. By the end of November, *Yeni İkdam* and *Yeni Gazete* wrote that opposition parties in the Chamber, the Moderate Liberals and the People's Party, were prepared to jointly interpellate the Hakkı Pasha Cabinet after Hakkı Pasha presented his programme in the Chamber on December 5.[130] Their spokesmen were to be Lütfi Fikri Bey, deputy for Dersim, Ahmed Ferid [Tek], deputy for Kütahya, Rıza Tevfik [Bölükbaşı], deputy for Edirne, and Shafiq al-Mu'ayyad al-'Azm, deputy for Damascus.[131]

At a meeting of the parliamentary party of the Committee of Union and Progress held on November 20, at which the question whether a vote of confidence should be given to the cabinet had been discussed, several Ministers were severely criticised by the conservative faction. The party finally agreed to abstain from any decision as to its policy until it heard both Hakkı Pasha's statement of the policy of the government and the criticisms of the opposition parties.[132] According to *Yeni İkdam*, the parliamentary party of the Committee of Union

---

November 2, 1326/November 15, 1910, pp.1-2; "Chambre des Députés," *The Levant Herald and Eastern Express*, November 15, 1910, p.2; "Opening of the Turkish Parliament: The Sultan's Speech," *The Times*, November 15, 1910, p.7; and, "The Opening of Parliament," *The Orient, 1/31* (November 16, 1910), p.1.

[129] I/III/1, November 1, 1326/November 14, 1910, *Meclis-i Mebusan Zabıt Ceridesi, 1*, pp.3-4; "Üçüncü Devre-i İctimaiye: Birinci İctima-i Umumi," *Yeni İkdam*, November 2, 1326/November 15, 1910, pp.1-2; and, "Chambre des Députés," *The Levant Herald and Eastern Express*, November 15, 1910, p.2.

[130] "The Position of the Cabinet," *The Levant Herald and Eastern Express*, November 28, 1910; and, "Empire News: The Capital," *The Orient, 1/33* (November 30, 1910), p.5. For *İkdam* articles see, Lütfi Fikri, "Meşrutiyetin Bize Mahsus Şekillerinden," *Yeni İkdam*, November 8, 1326/November 21, 1910, pp.1-2; "Kabine ve Ekseriyet Fırkası," *Yeni İkdam*, November 10, 1326/November 23, 1910, p.1; Tahir Hayreddin, "Acaba Mevki-i Siyasimiz Nedir?" *Yeni İkdam*, November 10, 1326/November 23, 1910, pp.1-2; Lütfi Fikri, "Heyet-i Vükelâyı Nasıl Teşekkül Etmeli?" *Yeni İkdam*, November 14, 1326/November 27, 1910, p.1; Lütfi Fikri, "Heyet-i Vükelâyı Nasıl Teşekkül Etmeli?" *Yeni İkdam*, November 17, 1326/November 30, 1910, p.1; Tahir Hayreddin, "Bi Taraf-ı Haric," *Yeni İkdam*, November 18, 1326/December 1, 1910, p.1; and, Tahir Hayreddin, "Kuvve-i Teşriiye Nazarından Kabine," *Yeni İkdam*, November 20, 1326/December 3, 1910, p.1.

[131] "The Position of the Cabinet," *The Levant Herald and Eastern Express*, November 28, 1910; "Hüseyin Cahid [Yalçın], "Dahili Tahrikat," *Tanin*, November 16, 1326/November 29, 1910, p.1; and, "Empire News: The Capital," *The Orient, 1/33* (November 30, 1910), p.5.

[132] "The Committee of Union and Progress," *The Times*, November 21, 1910, p.5.

and Progress met again on November 25 and finally decided to support the cabinet in general while admitting the possibility that individual Ministers might be obliged in the near future to resign in consequence of the criticisms of their policy in the Chamber.[133]

Upon persistent demands of the opposition deputies within the Committee of Union and Progress, Hakkı Pasha was forced to submit his statement of the policy of the government to the party.[134] The procedure was at variance with all known parliamentary practice. His surrender, however, in no way calmed the excitement within the party, which appeared to be due to the fact that after it had been agreed that conservative Unionist deputies who were dissatisfied with the internal and external policy of the cabinet should be allowed freedom of criticism, the leaders of the party had suddenly reversed their policy. On November 28, when a copy of the Grand Vezier's speech was read to the parliamentary party, Halil [Menteşe], leader of the Committee of Union and Progress, laid a motion before his colleagues calling upon them to give pledges to abstain from comment or criticism during the debate on the Grand Vezier's speech, and at its close to record their votes in favour of the government. The motion met with vigorous disapproval from a strong minority of conservative deputies, which was unsparing of its criticisms of both Halil [Menteşe] and the Unionist Ministers who were present, and declared that gagging methods were a travesty of representative institutions. The majority finally voted in favour of [Menteşe]'s motion, but it was believed that the strength of the minority might yet force the Unionist leadership to reconsider its decision.[135]

---

[133] *Yeni İkdam*, November 13, 1326/November 26, 1910, quoted in "Turkey: The Committee and the Cabinet," *The Times*, November 28, 1910, p.5. This news was denied in "İttihad ve Terakki Fırkası," *Tanin*, November 16, 1326/November 29, 1910, pp.3-4.

[134] "İttihad ve Terakki Fırkası," *Tanin*, November 16, 1326/November 29, 1910, pp.3-4; "Sadrâzam Paşa ve Kabinenin İzahnamesi," *Yeni İkdam*, November 16, 1326/November 29, 1910, p.1; "The Committee of the Union and Progress," *The Times*, November 29, 1910, p.5; and, "Turkey: Hakki Pasha and the Committee," *The Times*, December 1, 1910, p.5.

[135] "Ministerium und Majoritätspartei," *Osmanischer Lloyd*, November 29, 1910, p.1; and, "Turkey: Hakki Pasha and the Committee," *The Times*, December 1, 1910, p.5.

On November 29, the Committee of Union and Progress held yet another meeting during which there were stormy debates. Reportedly, there was a serious divergence of opinion among the conservative section of the party. It was rumoured that the position of certain Unionist ministers was not particularly secure. The November 30 issue of *Sabah* wrote that the conservative faction of the Committee of Union and Progress demanded the overthrow of the cabinet and formation of a new cabinet by Said Pasha.[136] In the editorial of the December 3 issue of *Puzantion*, Puzant Ketchian reviewed the political situation, exaggerating the differences of opinion between Hakkı Pasha and the Committee of Union and Progress. Along with *Sabah*, the monarchist *Yeni İkdam* had already started talking about the necessity for a cabinet change, urging that a person who was not a member of the Committee of Union and Progress be the Grand Vezier.[137]

Şerif Pasha, the leader of the monarchist opposition in exile, was also active publishing in his *Mechroutiette* articles geared towards getting a hold on the army and bringing forward a counter-revolution, addressing the military officers, painting the condition of the country in dark colours. He had been declaring in the columns of *Mechroutiette* that the Unionists were ruining the country for selfish ends, that they were robbing the Ministry of Finance and the Ministry of Commerce and Public Works, that Cavid Bey had embezzled out of the loan he had negotiated with the French bankers hundreds and thousands of liras and had purchased immense farms in Dobruca. He had been openly making appeals in the name of his Parti Radical Ottoman to the military to turn against what

---

[136] "The Cabinet and the Committee," *The Levant Herald and Eastern Express,* November 30, 1910, p.1. See also, "Turkey: Ministers and Parliament," *The Times,* December 2, 1910, p.5. For the Unionist view on the results of this meeting see, "İttihad ve Terakki Fırkası," *Tanin,* November 17, 1326/November 30, 1910, p.2. The demand for the formation of a new cabinet under the leadership of an 'independent' grand vezier was rebutted by the Unionist leadership in the columns of *Tanin* ("Hüseyin Cahid [Yalçın], "Heyet-i Vükelâ Nasıl Teşekkül Etmeli?" *Tanin,* November 18, 1326/December 1, 1910, p.1).

[137] Tahir Hayreddin, "Bi Taraf-ı Haric," *Yeni İkdam,* November 18, 1326/December 1, 1910, p.1; and, "The Cabinet and the Committee," *The Orient,* 1/34 (December 7, 1910), p.1.

he called the 'evil regime' and overthrow it as it had overthrown the Hamidian regime.[138]

Meanwhile, after Hakkı Pasha's statement of the government policy at the December 3 sitting of the Chamber, Rıza
Tevfik [Bölükbaşı], deputy for Edirne, Pantoleon Cosmidis,
the Greek deputy for İstanbul, and Théodore Pavloff, the Serbian deputy for Üsküb, severely criticised the policy of the
government and condemned particularly the course pursued
in Albania and the violation of rights of individuals.[139] Rıza
Tevfik [Bölükbaşı]'s criticisms were vigorous but diffuse. He
protested against the government's tyrannical usage of its political opponents, adding that Dr. Rıza Nur's treatment reminded him of the old regime. Talât Bey here interrupted
[Bölükbaşı], but was called to order by the Speaker and covered with invectives by the opposition. Rıza Tevfik [Bölükba-
şı], continuing his speech, declared that the tyranny of the
government had provoked widespread discontent. On his part,
Pantoleon Cosmidis protested against the general unfairness
of the government's policy towards the Christians. Deploring
the conduct of the police, he mentioned the case of a Greek
who had been beaten to death in the police barracks at İs-
tanbul. After Cosmidis criticised the policy followed in Albania, Théodore Pavloff caused some sensation by giving statis-
tics of the number of persons who had been flogged during
the disarmament of the rebellious Albanian peasants. He said
that eleven had died of their injuries and sixty-four had been
crippled.[140]

---

[138] "The Cabinet and the Committee," The Orient, 1/34 (December 7, 1910),
pp.1-2.

[139] I/III/10, November 20, 1326/December 3, 1910, Meclis-i Mebusan Zabıt Ceridesi, I, pp.272-299; Hüseyin Cahid [Yalçın], "Dünkü Meclis," Tanin, November
21, 1326/December 4, 1910, p.1; "Dünkü İctima ve Kabinenin İzahatı," Yeni İk-
dam, November 21, 1326/December 4, 1910, p.1; "Das Kabinett vor der Kammer,"
Osmanischer Lloyd, December 4, 1910, p.1; "Kabinenin Siyaset-i Umumiyesi,"
Yeni İkdam, November 22, 1326/December 5, 1910, p.1; "Die Kritik des Regierungsprogramms," Osmanischer Lloyd, December 6, 1910, p.1; "The Position of the
Cabinet," and "Chambre des Députés," The Levant Herald and Eastern Express,
December 6, 1910, pp.1-2; and, "The Ottoman Parliament," The Orient, 1/34 (De-
cember 7, 1910), p.1.

[140] I/III/10, November 20, 1326/December 3, 1910, Meclis-i Mebusan Zabıt Ceridesi, I, pp.285-299; "Turkish Policy: Statement by Hakki Pasha," The Times, December 5, 1910, p.5. For a rebuttal of Cosmidis' arguments see, Hüseyin Cahid
[Yalçın], "Dünkü Meclis," Tanin, November 21, 1326/December 4, 1910, p.1.

At the following sitting on December 5, İsmail Hakkı [Mumcu] Pasha, deputy for Amasya, Hoca Vehbi Efendi, deputy for Konya, Ahmed Ferid [Tek], deputy for Kütahya, Abd al-Mahdi Efendi, deputy for Kerbela, Krikor Zohrab, deputy for İstanbul, and Shafiq al-Mu'ayyad al-'Azm, deputy for Damascus, all members of the opposition, spoke against the government.[141] Ahmed Ferid [Tek] reproached the government with having made enemies and failed to gain friends by an uncertain and purposeless foreign policy. He particularly criticised the anti-Greek policy which, he claimed, had thrown them to the arms of the Bulgarians. He also deprecated the policy pursued in Albania. He alleged that the recent campaign to repress the outbreak had broken the strength of the best bulwark of the Empire on its European side, and the Albanian chiefs who had been flogged in the presence of their wives were hardly likely to be grateful to the new regime. Krikor Zohrab also protested against the Albanian campaign. According to Zohrab, the government's foreign policy was a dead failure; the friendly Powers—i.e., Great Britain and France—which supported the monarchist cause in Turkey, were growing cold due to the government's renegotiation of the capitulations and its insistence on the four percent increase in customs duties.[142] It was quite interesting to note that both Ahmed Ferid [Tek] and Krikor Zohrab defended the line foreign powers regularly took in criticising Turkey whenever the Hakkı Pasha Cabinet upheld Turkish interests which, in turn, hurt the Europeans.[143]

At the December 7 sitting of the Chamber, the speeches criticising the policy of the government were resumed.[144] The

---

[141] I/III/11, November 22, 1326/December 5, 1910, *Meclis-i Mebusan Zabıt Ceridesi*, 1, pp.304-347; ."Die Kritik des Regierungsprogramms," *Osmanischer Lloyd*, December 6, 1910, p.1; "The Position of the Cabinet," and "Chambre des Députés," *The Levant Herald and Eastern Express*, December 6, 1910, pp.1-2; and, "The Ottoman Parliament," *The Orient*, 1/34 (December 7, 1910), p.1.

[142] I/III/11, November 22, 1326/December 5, 1910, *Meclis-i Mebusan Zabıt Ceridesi*, 1, pp.311-333; and, "The Turkish Chamber: Criticisms of the Government," *The Times*, December 6, 1910, p.5.

[143] See the editorials in *Tanin* (Hüseyin Cahid [Yalçın], "Dünkü Celse," *Tanin*, November 23, 1326/December 6, 1910, p.1; and, Hüseyin Cahid [Yalçın], "Meclis-i Mebusan'da Siyaset-i Hariciye," *Tanin*, November 24, 1326/December 7, 1910, p.1).

[144] I/III/12, November 24, 1326/December 7, 1910, *Meclis-i Mebusan Zabıt Ceridesi*, 1, pp.353-424.

speakers were Yorgos Boussios, Greek deputy for Serfidje, Dimitri Vlachoff, Serbian deputy for Salonica, Haristo Daltcheff, Bulgarian deputy for Serres, Volçetrinli Hasan Bey, Albanian deputy for Prishtnë, Vartkes Serengülyan, Armenian deputy for Erzurum, Hasan Fuad Pasha, Albanian deputy for Prishtnë, and Lütfi Fikri Bey, deputy for Dersim.[145] Vartkes Serengülyan and Dimitri Vlachoff, both of whom entertained socialist viewpoints, criticised the internal policy of the government, Vlachoff laying special stress on the suppression of trade unions and on the government's failure to initiate agrarian legislation.[146]

Lütfi Fikri Bey, one of the leaders of the opposition, then spoke for nearly three hours. With respect to internal affairs, he accused the government of having failed to apply even the unconstitutional measures which it had adopted with any pretence of equality. He emphasised the fact that the Democratic Party's organs were suspended almost daily, while the newspapers of the Committee of Union and Progress were allowed to write as they pleased. The Head of the Department of Public Security had committed the grave impropriety of officially informing the press that the government possessed proofs of Dr. Rıza Nur's guilt.[147] He then asked for the interpellation of the government on the issue of Dr. Rıza Nur's arrest.[148] He strongly criticised the Government's conduct and

---

[145] I/III/12, November 24, 1326/December 7, 1910, *Meclis-i Mebusan Zabıt Ceridesi*, *1*, pp.353-409; Hüseyin Cahid [Yalçın], "Dünkü Celse," *Tanin*, November 25, 1326/December 8, 1910, p.1; "Die letzte Phase der Debatte: Opposition und Regierung haben gesprochen—Das Komitee wird antworten," *Osmanischer Lloyd*, December 9, 1910, p.1; and, "The Ottoman Parliament," and "Speeches in Parliament by the Opposition," *The Orient*, *1/35* (December 14, 1910), pp.1-3.

[146] I/III/12, November 24, 1326/December 7, 1910, *Meclis-i Mebusan Zabıt Ceridesi*, *1*, pp.362-373; "Turkish Policy: Critics in the Chamber," *The Times*, December 8, 1910, p.5; Hüseyin Cahid [Yalçın], "Dünkü Celse," *Tanin*, November 25, 1326/December 8, 1910, p.1; and, "Die letzte Phase der Debatte: Opposition und Regierung haben gesprochen—Das Komitee wird antworten," *Osmanischer Lloyd*, December 9, 1910, p.1.

[147] I/III/12, November 24, 1326/December 7, 1910, *Meclis-i Mebusan Zabıt Ceridesi*, *1*, pp.378-401; Hüseyin Cahid [Yalçın], "Dünkü Celse," *Tanin*, November 25, 1326/December 8, 1910, p.1; "Turkish Policy: Critics in the Chamber," *The Times*, December 8, 1910, p.5; and, "Die letzte Phase der Debatte: Opposition und Regierung haben gesprochen—Das Komitee wird antworten," *Osmanischer Lloyd*, December 9, 1910, p.1. For information on the Democratic Party organs see, Ziya Şakir [Soko], "Hürriyet ve İtilâf Nasıl Doğdu? Nasıl Yaşadı? Nasıl Battı? 8: Demokratların Çıkardığı Gazeteler Kapatılıyordu," *Tan*, November 7, 1937, p.9

[148] I/III/12, November 24, 1326/December 7, 1910, *Meclis-i Mebusan Zabıt Ceridesi*, *1*, p.401; Rıza Nur, *Cemiyet-i Hafiye*, pp.259-278; Hüseyin Cahid Yalçın,

asked for a vote. After lengthy deliberations, his request for interpellation was rejected by a vote of ninety-six to seventy-three.[149]

The criticism of the Hakkı Pasha Cabinet was resumed at the December 8 sitting.[150] The speakers were İsmail Hakkı Bey, deputy for Gümülcine, Muhammad Ali Fazıl Efendi, the Arab deputy for Mosul, Sava Stoyanovich, the Serbian deputy for Prishtnë, Hacı Abdülvehab Efendi, deputy for Bolu, Pavlis Carolidis, the Greek deputy for İzmir, Hamparsoum Boyadjian, the Armenian deputy for Kozan, Jannakis Mammapoulos, the Greek deputy for Argyrocastro, Nazareth Daghavarian, the Armenian deputy for Sivas, and Esad Pasha Toptan, the Albanian deputy for Durazzo.[151]

After these criticisms, Hakkı Pasha made a four-hour long speech defending his cabinet. He declared that the government had ordered the arrest of Dr. Rıza Nur after due consideration. A postcard addressed to him by Şerif Pasha from Paris had come under the notice of the authorities. Rıza Nur had denied that he had received it, but it had certainly been addressed to him. Further, Rıza Nur was known to have burnt documents which were believed to be of a compromising nature. With respect to the disarmament in Albania and Macedonia, Hakkı Pasha said that it was necessary, adding that of-

---

"Meşrutiyet Hatıraları, 1908-1918," *Fikir Hareketleri, 6* (April 25-October 17, 1936), p.214; and, Cemal Kutay, *Türkiye İstiklâl ve Hürriyet Mücadeleleri Tarihi, 17*, pp.9720-9728. The motion was signed by fifteen deputies. Names of the thirteen of them were İsmail Hakkı Bey, deputy for Gümülcine, Lütfi Fikri Bey, deputy for Dersim, Haristo Dalcheff, deputy for Serres, Dimitri Vlahoff, deputy for Salonica, Hamparsoum Boyadjian, deputy for Kozan, Shafiq al-Moayyid, deputy for Zor, Davud Yusfani and Muhammed Ali Fazil, deputies for Mosul, Abd al-Hamid az-Zahrawi, deputy for Hama, Ömer Fevzi Efendi, deputy for Karahisar-ı Şarki, Rush-di al-Shama, deputy for Damascus, Said al-Husseini, deputy for Jerusalem, and İbrahim Vasfi Efendi, deputy for Karesi (Tarık Zafer Tunaya, *Türkiye'de Siyasi Partiler, 1859-1952*, pp.295-296n).

[149] Cemal Kutay, *Türkiye İstiklâl ve Hürriyet Mücadeleleri Tarihi, 17*, pp.9720-9728.

[150] I/III/13, November 25, 1326/December 8, 1910, *Meclis-i Mebusan Zabıt Ceridesi, 1*, pp.427-489.

[151] I/III/13, November 25, 1326/December 8, 1910, *Meclis-i Mebusan Zabıt Ceridesi, 1*, pp.427-448; "Chambre des Députés," *The Levant Herald and Eastern Express*, December 9, 1910, pp.1-2; "Die letzte Phase der Debatte: Opposition und Regierung haben gesprochen—Das Komitee wird antworten," *Osmanischer Lloyd*, December 9, 1910, p.1; and, "The Ottoman Parliament," *The Orient, 1/35* (December 14, 1910), p.1. See also, "Turkish Ministerial Policy," *The Times*, December 9, 1910, p.5; and, Hüseyin Cahid [Yalçın], "Muhalefetin İflâsı," *Tanin*, November 26, 1326/December 9, 1910, p.1.

ficials who had committed acts of cruelty would be punished. He added that the condition of the provinces was improving as rapidly as could be expected considering the confusion into which every department of the administration had fallen under the Hamidian regime.[152]

Halil [Menteşe] made a speech at the following sitting, on December 10. He deprecated the exaggerations in the criticisms contained in the speeches of the opposition deputies. He emphasised the real services rendered by the Committee of Union and Progress, praised the course of the Hakkı Pasha Cabinet, and proposed that the discussion be closed.[153] Finally, [Menteşe]'s resolution that the explanations of the government deserved a vote of confidence was passed by a vote of one hundred and twenty-one against sixty-one.[154] This was hardly a real success for the Unionists, given the fact that the Committee of Union and Progress alone numbered one hundred and sixty-two members of whom at least one hundred and fifty were present in the Chamber at the time the vote was taken.[155] While [Menteşe]'s unexpectedly conciliatory speech and promises for the relaxation of official severity had won several Greek and Bulgarian votes, some twenty-five members of the Committee of Union and Progress had abstained from voting. Secondly, many conservative Unionist deputies had been considerably impressed by hearing the arguments of the monarchist opposition which sup-

---

[152] I/III/13, November 25, 1326/December 8, 1910, *Meclis-i Mebusan Zabıt Ceridesi, 1*, pp.448-489; "Sadrâzam Paşa'nın Beyanatı," *Tanin*, November 26, 1326/December 9, 1910, pp.2-3; "Kabine Reisinin Dünkü Beyanatı ve Muhalifin," *Yeni Ikdam*, November 26, 1326/December 9, 1910, pp.1-2; "Hakkı Paşa'nın Beyanatından," *Tanin*, November 27, 1326/December 10, 1910, pp.2-3; "The Ottoman Parliament," *The Orient, 1/35* (December 14, 1910), p.1; and, "Turkish Ministerial Policy: Reply by the Grand Vizier," *The Times*, December 9, 1910, p.5.

[153] I/III/14, November 27, 1326/December 10, 1910, *Meclis-i Mebusan Zabıt Ceridesi, 1*, pp.493-503; Hüseyin Cahid [Yalçın], "Halil Bey'in Nutku," *Tanin*, November 28, 1326/December 11, 1910, p.1; "Chambre des Députés," *The Levant Herald and Eastern Express*, December 12, 1910, p.1; and, "The Ottoman Parliament," *The Orient, 1/35* (December 14, 1910), p.1.

[154] I/III/14, November 27, 1326/December 10, 1910, *Meclis-i Mebusan Zabıt Ceridesi, 1*, pp.505-507; "Der Vertrauensvotum der Kammer," *Osmanischer Lloyd*, December 11, 1910, p.1; "Vote of Confidence Adopted," *The Times*, December 12, 1910, p.5; "The Ottoman Parliament," *The Orient, 1/35* (December 14, 1910), p.1; and, Tarık Zafer Tunaya, *Türkiye'de Siyasi Partiler, 1859-1952*, p.289n.

[155] "The Position of the Government," *The Levant Herald and Eastern Express*, December 12, 1910, p.1. See also, Hüseyin Cahid [Yalçın], "Son Müzakereden Çıkan Dersler," *Tanin*, November 29, 1326/December 12, 1910, p.1.

ported the criticisms of some of the methods of the new regime made by foreign correspondents or by short-lived organs of the monarchist opposition.[156]

Despite the rejection of Lütfi Fikri Bey's interpellation by ninety-six votes to seventy-three on December 7, the closeness of the vote had already showed the extremely weakened position of the Committee of Union and Progress in the Chamber. Encouraged by the weakness of the Unionist leadership, opposition deputies as well as dissident members of the Committee of Union and Progress asked for a cabinet change. It was expected that in the next meeting of the parliamentary party of the Committee of Union and Progress the question of changes in the cabinet would be discussed.[157] The Unionist position in the cabinet somewhat strengthened on December 21, when Ürgüplü Hayri Bey, a prominent Unionist, replaced Sharif Ali Haydar as Minister of Pious Foundations.[158] On December 25, the Committee of Union and Progress held a meeting which lasted for five hours. The subject under discussion was the cabinet. Talât Bey, Minister of the Interior, was present, and his explanations resulted in a vote favourable to the cabinet. The Greek papers, however, wrote that the thirty-eight dissenting deputies had announced that if they were unsuccessful in securing the resignation of some members in the cabinet they would withdraw from the Committee of Union and Progress.[159]

The political crisis was important enough to summon Dr. Nâzım Bey, the President, and Hacı Âdil [Arda], the Secretary-General of the Committee of Union and Progress, to İstanbul to attend another meeting on December 27 to discuss the demands of the party dissidents.[160] The meeting, attended

---

[156] "Turkey: The Parliamentary Situation," *The Times*, December 12, 1910, p.5; and, "Turkey: The Parliamentary Situation," *The Times*, December 17, 1910, p.5.

[157] "The Political Situation in Turkey," *The Times*, December 21, 1910, p.5.

[158] "Kabinenin Mevkii," *Yeni İkdam*, December 8, 1326/December 21, 1910, p.2; "Kabinenin Mevkii," *Yeni İkdam*, December 9, 1326/December 22, 1910, p.1; "Turkey: Minister of Pious Foundations," *The Times*, December 22, 1910, p.5; and, "Empire News: The Capital, *The Orient*, 1/37 (December 28, 1910), p.6.

[159] "Empire News: The Capital," *The Orient*, 1/37 (December 28, 1910), p.5. See also, Ahmed Bedevi Kuran, *İnkılâp Tarihimiz ve 'Jön Türkler,'* p.301.

[160] "Incident in Parliament," *The Levant Herald and Eastern Express*, December 27, 1910, p.1; and, "Sitzung des Komitees," *Osmanischer Lloyd*, December 28, 1910, p.1.

by one hundred and twenty deputies, was stormy; dissident members were adamant in their demands, and decided to interpellate some of the ministers.[161] Unionist deputies were unable to arrive at a definite decision with regard to the cabinet, some members suggesting that cabinet changes should be brought about by the refusal of a vote of confidence in certain ministers after they had been individually interpellated by members of the party; others urged that the cabinet should be forced to collectively resign. Hakkı Pasha was believed to have expressed the intention of opposing any attempt to effect cabinet changes by the first of these methods, arguing that the latest vote of confidence was given to the cabinet as a whole.[162]

Lütfi Fikri Bey's motion demanding a parliamentary inquiry into the arrest of Dr. Rıza Nur and the ill-treatment of political prisoners was discussed in the Chamber on December 31.[163] Lütfi Fikri Bey declared that the proceedings taken against the Secret Organisation were originally inspired by private denunciations. The inquiry was carried out, not by the Department of Public Security, but by an extraordinary commission appointed *ad hoc*. Another commission, presided over by a military officer, conducted an independent inquiry, but the representative of the Military Court refused to append his signature to its report. He claimed that Dr. Münir Bey, the principal informer against Dr. Rıza Nur, had been tortured with the object of extracting a confession from him. According to Lütfi Fikri Bey, evidence thus produced was worthless. He then gave a minute and circumstantial description of the

---

[161] "Kabinenin Mevkii ve Ekseriyet Fırkasının Dünkü İctimaı," *Yeni İkdam*, December 15, 1326/December 28, 1910, p.1; "The Position of the Cabinet," *The Levant Herald and Eastern Express*, December 28, 1910, p.1; and, "Sitzung des Komitees," *Osmanischer Lloyd*, December 28, 1910, p.1.

[162] "Kabinenin Mevkii ve Ekseriyet Fırkasının Dünkü İctimaı," *Yeni İkdam*, December 15, 1326/December 28, 1910, p.1; and, "Turkish Politics: The Committee and the Ministry," *The Times*, December 29, 1910, p.3.

[163] I/III/20, December 18, 1326/December 31, 1910, *Meclis-i Mebusan Zabıt Ceridesi, 1*, pp.716-745. See the preliminary arguments of the Opposition on these issues in, "Kabinenin Mevkii ve Rıza Nur Bey Meselesi," *Yeni İkdam*, December 13, 1326/December 26, 1910, p.2; and, "Kabinenin Mevkii ve İstizahat Meselesi," *Yeni İkdam*, December 16, 1326/December 29, 1910, p.1.

tortures to which he averred members of the Secret Organisation had been subjected.[164]

İsmail Hakkı Bey, monarchist deputy for Gümülcine, declared that the Grand Vezier had threatened to resign if a parliamentary inquiry were voted. This was denied by Hakkı Pasha, who declared that the torture of political suspects did not exist in Turkey. The Chamber was free to discuss the question, and the cabinet would deduce from its vote whether it possessed the confidence of the majority or not. Haydar Bey, a member of the Committee of Union and Progress, advised deputies to pay no attention to attacks on the cabinet. After a further speech by Gümülcineli İsmail Hakkı Bey, Mahmud Şevket Pasha, Minister of War, warned the Chamber not to mix up the names of officers in the question. The debate closed with a speech from Dr. Rıza Nur, deputy for Sinob, who, after thanking deputies on both sides of the Chamber for the interest they had taken in his case, declared that he would be satisfied if his painful experience should hereafter prove the means of obtaining greater liberty for the individual. The motion was then put to vote and defeated by ninety-five votes to sixty-nine, with several Unionist deputies abstaining from recording their votes.[165]

Meanwhile, the issue of Dr. Rıza Nur's arrest in July in connection with the Secret Organisation and allegations of torture were kept alive by the monarchists and continued to be discussed in the opposition news media. In an article in the *Yeni Gazete* of January 3, 1911, Gabriel Nouradunghian, one of the most prominent monarchist politicians and ex-Minister of Commerce and Public Works, protested against the refusal of the Chamber to investigate charges of torture. He pointed out that capricious administrations that interfered with freedom of speech and conscience had sooner or later fallen by means of a just revolt. According to him, indifference on the part of the

[164] I/III/20, December 18, 1326/December 31, 1910, *Meclis-i Mebusan Zabıt Ceridesi*, 1, pp.717-723; and, "The Case of Dr. Riza Nur: Debate in the Turkish Chamber," *The Times*, January 2, 1911, p.7.
[165] I/III/20, December 18, 1326/December 31, 1910, *Meclis-i Mebusan Zabıt Ceridesi*, 1, pp.724-747; "The Case of Dr. Riza Nur: Debate in the Turkish Chamber," *The Times*, January 2, 1911, p.7; and, "The Ottoman Parliament," *The Orient*, 1/38 (January 4, 1911), p.1. See also, Ahmed Bedevi Kuran, *İnkılâp Tarihimiz ve 'Jön Türkler*,' p.300.

deputies to such fundamental rights of humanity gave cause for popular anxiety, criticism, and distrust. It was the duty of the Chamber to find out whether the provisions of the Constitution had, in the case of Dr. Rıza Nur and his co-defendants, been respected or not.[166]

In view of Gabriel Nouradunghian's and other expressions of monarchist dissatisfaction, the government decided to proceed to an investigation, in spite of the refusal of the Chamber to investigate these allegations. On January 5, Mahmud Şevket Pasha ordered the formation of a military court of inquiry to examine the alleged cases of torture of political suspects arrested as members of the Secret Organisation. The press, as a general rule, showed great satisfaction with the decision and expressed the hope that the Minister would vindicate the liberties guaranteed by the Constitution.[167] Convinced of their increasing strength in the Chamber with the closeness of the vote for Lütfi Fikri Bey's motion and the formation of an opposition faction within the Committee of Union and Progress, monarchists were encouraged to begin their campaign against the Unionist leadership in the cabinet.[168]

Their primary targets were Talât Bey, Minister of the Interior, and Cavid Bey, Minister of Finance. In their attempt to oust these prominent Unionists from office, they had also been encouraged by the knowledge that Mahmud Şevket Pasha, too, was highly critical of them, and that in October he

---

[166] "Rıza Nur Bey Meselesi," Yeni İkdam, December 19, 1326/January 1, 1911, p.2; "Gabriel Effendi Nuradungian über den Enquête—Antrag," Osmanischer Lloyd, January 4, 1911, p.1; "Die Verwaltungsenquête über den Fall Risa Nur," Osmanischer Lloyd, January 6, 1911, p.1; and, Gabriel Nouradunghian, "Enquête parlementaire Reddedilmeli mi idi? Edilmemeli mi idi?," Yeni Gazete, December 21, 1326/January 3, 1911, quoted in Tarık Zafer Tunaya, Türkiye'de Siyasi Partiler, 1859-1952, p.289n, and excerpted in The Orient, 1/38 (January 4, 1911), p.4.

[167] "Alleged Torture in Turkey," The Times, January 6, 1911, p.5. The commission of inquiry into the alleged torture of political prisoners was composed of Mahmud Şevket Pasha, Fuad Pasha, Under-Secretary of the Ministry of War, and Ferid Bey, a distinguished artillery officer and formerly President of the İstanbul Court-Martial ("The Alleged Cases of Torture," The Times, January 11, 1911, p.5).

[168] Cemal Kutay, Türkiye İstiklâl ve Hürriyet Mücadeleleri Tarihi, 17, p.9729; Lütfi Simavi, Sultan Mehmed Reşad Han'ın ve Halefinin Sarayında Gördüklerim, 1, pp.138-139; and, Ziya Şakir [Soko], "Hürriyet ve İtilâf Nasıl Doğdu? Nasıl Yaşadı? Nasıl Battı? 9: Heyecan İçinde Bulunan Fırka Âzası Toplanmak İstedi," Tan, November 8, 1937, p.9.

had threatened Hakkı Pasha with resignation if Talât and Cavid Beys remained in the cabinet.[169]

Indeed, in mid-October, there had been serious dissension between Cavid Bey, Minister of Finance, and Mahmud Şevket Pasha, Minister of War, on the issue of the Military Budget. The newly-formed Audit Department had refused to sanction a payment for four hundred thousand liras worth of military stores ordered by the Minister of War on account of the extra-ordinary military Budget for 1909. It gave as the reason for its refusal the fact that this expenditure could only be authorised under the existing Budget Law when the corresponding ex-traordinary receipts for that year's Budget were realised. These extraordinary receipts included the proceeds of the sale of Abdülhamid's jewellery, which was still unsold, and his deposit—a sum of about £2,000,000—in the Deutsche Bank, on which the Turkish Government had not yet been able to lay its hands. Cavid Bey had upheld the decision of the Audit De-partment on grounds of legality.[170]

On the night of October 16 Mahmud Şevket Pasha had visited the Grand Vezier and informed him that he should insist on the financial independence of the Ministries of War and Navy; otherwise either he or Cavid Bey should go. Then, Mahmud Şevket Pasha had suggested that the Grand Vezier should also resign in order to return to power at the head of a new cabinet in which Cavid Bey would be succeeded by Emin Bey, ex-Treasurer of the Salonica province, and Bedros Haladjian by an officer of the General Staff. Hakkı Pasha had suggested that Mahmud Şevket Pasha had better wait until the

---

[169] A.A., Türkei 161, #A17351, Marschall to A. A. #237, October 18, 1910, and, A. La Jonquière, *Histoire de l'empire ottoman depuis les origines jusqu'à nos jours,* Second Edition (Paris: Hachette, 1914), 2, p.271, quoted in Glen Wilfred Swanson, Mahmud Şevket Paşa and the Defense of the Ottoman Empire, p.84; and, Halil Menteşe, "Eski Meclisi Mebusan Reisi Halil Menteşe'nin Hatıraları: 6: Meş-rutiyet Devrinde Bir Buhran Hikayesi," *Cumhuriyet,* October 18, 1946, p.2. See also, Hüseyin Cahid [Yalçın], "Heyet-i Vükelâ'da İhtilâf," *Tanin,* October 5, 1326/October 18, 1910, p.1.

[170] "Heyet-i Vükelâ'da İhtilâf," *Tanin,* October 5, 1326/October 18, 1910, p.1; and, "The Turkish Cabinet: Strained Relations Between Ministers," *The Times,* October 18, 1910, p.5. On the amount of Abdülhamid's bank account in the Deu-tsche Bank and the cash—£275,000—in addition to £120,000 in numerous purses found in the Yıldız Palace in the official search after his dethronement see, Ed-win Pears, *Forty Years in Constantinople: The Recollections of Sir Edwin Pears, 1873-1915,* p.301.

Chamber of Deputies met in November, when a law embodying his views on military finance would be submitted to the representatives of the nation.[171]

Mahmud Şevket Pasha had then visited Talât Bey, but no satisfactory solution had been found. The Committee of Union and Progress was known to be much perturbed at the turn of events.[172] However, the crisis had been averted on October 18; in consequence of the mediation of several of his colleagues, Cavid Bey had accepted certain amendments in the new law of public accounts, which would be discussed by the Grand Vezier and the Under-Secretary of Finance.[173]

The parliamentary party of the Committee of Union and Progress held a meeting on January 5 to discuss the issues concerning Talât and Cavid Beys. *Tanin* of January 6 gave the figures of the voting at the January 5 special meeting of the Committee of Union and Progress at which Talât Bey, Minister of the Interior, and Cavid Bey, Minister of Finance, obtained votes of confidence, the former by eighty-nine votes to fifteen, the latter by ninety-one to four, several members abstaining from voting. The fact that only one hundred and four members of the party out of a nominal total of one hundred and sixty responded to the urgent whip was regarded as a sign of the growing weakness of the party.[174]

---

[171] "The Turkish Cabinet: Strained Relations Between Ministers," *The Times*, October 18, 1910, p.5.

[172] "The Turkish Cabinet: Strained Relations Between Ministers," *The Times*, October 18, 1910, p.5. See also, "Buhran-ı Vükelâ," *Yeni İkdam*, October 5, 1326/ October 18, 1910, p.1.

[173] "Buhran Zail Oldu," *Yeni İkdam*, October 6, 1326/October 19, 1910, p.1; "The Turkish Ministry: Differences Composed," *The Times*, October 19, 1910, p.5; "Buhran-ı Vükelâ," *Yeni İkdam*, October 6, 1326/October 19, 1910, p.2; and, Hüseyin Cahid [Yalçın], "Buhran-ı Vükelâ Şayialarım ve Tefsirat," *Tanin*, October 11, 1326/October 24, 1910, p.1.

[174] *Tanin*, December 24, 1326/January 6, 1911, quoted in "Turkish Politics: The Committee Party," *The Times*, January 7, 1911, p.5; and, "Le parti 'Union et Progrès': Succés de Djavid Bey et de Talaat Bey," *Osmanischer Lloyd*, January 6, 1911, p.4. See also, Kabine ve Ekseriyet Fırkasının Dünkü İctimaı," *Yeni İkdam*, December 24, 1326/January 6, 1911, p.1.

CHAPTER SIX

THE EVENTS OF 1911:
CONTINUING MONARCHIST EFFORTS TO TOPPLE
THE CONSTITUTIONAL REGIME

Monarchist efforts to create an opposition to the Committee of Union and Progress and bring about its downfall through extra-parliamentary means continued despite the exposure of the Secret Organisation. There was a considerable number of officers in the army who were highly critical of the Unionists, and the dispute between Mahmud Şevket Pasha and the Unionist leadership had encouraged them to get organised clandestinely. Colonel Sadık Bey was deeply involved in the organisation.[1]

In late September 1910, Unionist leadership had intercepted a letter by Colonel Sadık Bey, urging the officers at Monastir to join them for a military *putsch*.[2] In December, a number of junior officers in the Second Army Corps at Edirne and the Third Army Corps at Salonica formed an opposition group, criticising the Hakkı Pasha Cabinet for making political appointments in the army.[3] The man behind this movement was again Colonel Sadık Bey, who was arrested in Edirne but was later set free upon pressure.[4]

---

[1] Halil Menteşe, "Eski Meclisi Mebusan Reisi Halil Menteşe'nin Hatıraları: 6: Meşrutiyet Devrinde Bir Buhran Hikâyesi," *Cumhuriyet*, October 18, 1946, p.2.

[2] Halil Menteşe, "Eski Meclisi Mebusan Reisi Halil Menteşe'nin Hatıraları: 6: Meşrutiyet Devrinde Bir Buhran Hikâyesi," *Cumhuriyet*, October 18, 1946, p.2.

[3] F.O. 371/1242/8371, Consul Samson to Marling, Adrianople, December 2, 1910, enclosed in Marling to Sir Edward Grey, Constantinople, January 3, 1911, quoted in Feroz Ahmad, *The Young Turks: The Committee of Union and Progress in Turkish Politics, 1908-1914*, p.85.

[4] F.O. 371/1242/4280, Samson to Sir Gerard Lowther, Adrianople, December 26, 1910, enclosed in Sir Gerard Lowther to Sir Edward Grey, Constantinople, January 3, 1911, quoted in Feroz Ahmad, *The Young Turks: The Committee of Union and Progress in Turkish Politics, 1908-1914*, p.85n; and, F.O. 195/2364, Samson to Sir Gerard Lowther, Adrianople, January 26, 1911, quoted in Glen Wilfred Swanson, *Mahmud Şevket Paşa and the Defense of the Ottoman Empire*, p.87.

216 THE EVENTS OF 1911

Yusuf Ziya Bey, a conservative officer attached to the General Staff and formerly a member of the Committee of Union and Progress, met in January of 1911 with Dr. Nâzım Bey and Ömer Naci Bey. He recommended that Talât Bey and Cavid Bey be induced or compelled to resign their portfolios. He reportedly also suggested that the Ministers in question be offered, as a sort of punishment, the Under-Secretaryships of State for the Interior and Finance respectively.[5] These demands were rejected; but, the monarchist pressure continued. In the last days of January, Rıza Tevfik [Bölükbaşı], the deputy for Edirne and one of the leaders of the monarchist opposition, made a visit to Salonica in order to confer with the leaders of the Committee of Union and Progress.[6]

The threat posed by the machinations of Colonel Sadık Bey and the monarchist opposition in the army along with the general unrest in the Macedonian provinces dictated a change in cabinet policy towards the ethnic minorities whose rebellion against Turkish rule and support for the monarchist cause had made the Unionist leadership sensitive to their demands at a juncture when it had come under attack by the monarchists. In early January, Bulgarian members of the Chamber sent a document to Hakkı Pasha specifying many acts of cruelty and tortures alleged to have been inflicted by the courts martial in Macedonia on Bulgarian Ottomans, and requesting an investigation and the release of innocent men kept in prisons.[7] As a result of pressure, in mid-January, the principle of centralisation in provincial administration which had drawn considerable criticism from the opposition groups in the Chamber, especially among the Albanian, Greek, and Arab deputies, was quietly withdrawn.[8]

The withdrawal of the principle of centralisation, however,

---

[5] "Constantinople Letter," *The Near East*, December 6, 1911, p.127.

[6] "Zur Reise Dr. Risa Tewfiks nach Adrianopel," *Osmanischer Lloyd*, January 29, 1911, p.1; "Empire News: The Provinces," *The Orient*, 1/42 (February 1, 1911), p.6.

[7] "Empire News: The Capital," *The Orient*, 1/42 (February 1, 1911), p.6.

[8] F.O. 371/1244/7134, Sir Gerard Lowther to Sir Edwrad Grey, Pera, January 20, 1911, quoted in Feroz Ahmad, *The Young Turks: The Committee of Union and Progress in Turkish Politics, 1908-1914*, pp.86-87; "Ein Reformplan für die Wilajetsverwaltung," *Osmanischer Lloyd*, January 25, 1911, p.1; and, "Yemen Meselesi ve Kabinenin Siyaseti," *Yeni İkdam*, January 15, 1326/January 28, 1911, p.1.

did not satisfy the monarchist opposition. The opposition wanted more.[9] In mid-February, Lütfi Fikri Bey, deputy for Dersim
and one of the leaders of the monarchist opposition in the
Chamber, submitted a project to the Chamber's Committee on
draft laws, granting a large measure of autonomy to the province of Yemen, where the population had revolted against
Turkish rule in mid-January. He proposed the appointment by
the Sultan of a governor-general who would reside at Sanaa,
and would be assisted by a council of five directors—for the
interior, education, justice, agriculture, and public works—as
well as by a legal counsellor. The legislative power was to be
vested in a diet composed of the tribal chiefs, of representatives
from the cities, of the higher officers of the province, and of a
number of *seyyids*, or men educated in the religious law.
According to Lütfi Fikri Bey's project, the governor-general
was to have absolute veto power, subject only to appeal to the
Grand Vezier.[10]

Although the Unionist leadership ignored the demands of the
discontented officers organised clandestinely in Monastir, Salonica, and Edirne, the issue of ministerial resignations came
up in February in an altogether different context.

One of the issues that created problem between Hakkı Pasha on the one hand and Mahmud Şevket Pasha, the Minister
of War, and the Unionist members of the cabinet on the other
was the prolongation of the state of emergency. On their February 4 meeting, Talât Bey and Mahmud Şevket Pasha had
met and agreed on the necessity of the continuation of the
state of emergency. However, pressed by the monarchist opposition to lift the state of emergency, Hakkı Pasha was reluctant
to its prolongation. At the cabinet meeting on February 6,
when all Unionist ministers insisted on the continuation of
emergency measures, Hakkı Pasha told the cabinet that he
would resign rather than prolong the state of emergency.
After negotiations with Talât Bey on February 7, Hakkı Pasha
agreed to the state of emergency only on the condition of a

[9] "İttihad ve Terakki Fırkası," *Yeni İkdam*, January 24, 1326/February 6,
1911, p.1.
[10] "Proposed Autonomy for Yemen," *The Orient*, 1/46 (March 1, 1911), p.5.

change in the cabinet. He told Talât Bey that, due to fierce monarchist opposition, retention of Bedros Haladjian and Emrullah Efendi in a reconstituted cabinet would be impossible. He also suggested that Halil [Menteşe], instead of Talât Bey, be appointed Minister of the Interior, as Talât Bey, too, was being opposed both by the monarchists and their allies within the military.[11]

The question of ministerial changes constituted the main discussion in the February 9 meeting of Hakkı Pasha and the Unionists members of the cabinet. Hakkı Pasha told the Ministers that his resignation would lead to the formation of a Said Pasha Cabinet, and, as the Unionists did not want this, this solution was out of the question. Therefore the Ministers had to resign individually. After deliberations, it was agreed that the best strategy would be the joint resignations of Bedros Haladjian and Talât Bey during the debates over the Budget in the Chamber. As to Emrullah Efendi, Hakkı Pasha said that he could find no reason for his resignation, as he, along with other cabinet members, had received an overwhelming vote of confidence just two weeks previously. Ürgüplü Hayri Bey, without being able to justify his position, declared his intention of resigning unless Dimitraki Mavrocordato and Rıfat Pasha did not also resign. As a possible solution to the impasse, it was even suggested that, should the Hakkı Pasha Cabinet resign, either Said Pasha or Hüseyin Hilmi Pasha could form the new cabinet with Cavid Bey as the Unionist member along with Mahmud Şevket Pasha as the Minister of War. However, declaring that he had consented to work with Mahmud Şevket Pasha in the cabinet only under extraordinary circumstances and the assurances he got from Hakkı Pasha himself, Cavid Bey objected to this scenario, and said that he would never consider serving in a monarchist dominated cabinet in which Mahmud Şevket Pasha retained his post. The meeting ended without any agreement.[12]

On February 11, Talât Bey handed in his resignation to

---

[11] Mehmed Cavid, "Meşrutiyet Devrine Ait Cavit Bey'in Hatıraları: 14," *Tanin*, September 12, 1943, p.2.

[12] Mehmed Cavid, "Meşrutiyet Devrine Ait Cavit Bey'in Hatıraları: 16," *Tanin*, September 14, 1943, p.2.

Hakkı Pasha.[13] His resignation, given the fact that he was the party leader and the Unionists held a majority in the Chamber and had recently been given a vote of confidence, seemed particularly odd. It provoked considerable comment in the press, which, however, seemed quite unable to give any clear explanation of the event. His resignation, however, was less the result of opposition within either the cabinet or the Chamber as it was of pressure from outside, namely Colonel Sadık Bey's.[14] Indeed, Talât Bey was reported to have informed the members of the parliamentary party of the Committee of Union and Progress, at a meeting held on February 12, that the attacks of opponents within and without the party and the fact that a faction within the Committee of Union and Progress had lately shown signs of want of confidence in certain members of the cabinet had compelled him to withdraw from office. There were rumours that his resignation was only a prelude to further ministerial changes, and it was certain that the position of Cavid Bey and other Unionist ministers was less secure than had been recently the case.[15]

---

[13] Mehmed Cavid, "Meşrutiyet Devrine Ait Cavit Bey'in Hatıraları: 17," *Tanin*, September 15, 1943, p.2; "İstifa Hakkında," and "Talât Bey'in İstifası ve Kabinenin Mevkii," *Yeni İkdam*, January 30, 1326/February 12, 1911, p.1; "Resignation of the Minister of the Interior," *The Levant Herald and Eastern Express*, February 11, 1911, p.1; "Empire News: The Capital," *The Orient*, 1/44 (February 15, 1911), p.6; "Resignation of Talaat Bey," *The Times*, February 11, 1911, p.5; and, "Talât Bey'in İstifası," *Tanin*, January 29, 1326/February 11, 1911, quoted in Feroz Ahmad, *The Young Turks: The Committee of Union and Progress in Turkish Politics, 1908-1914*, p.86.
  At its meeting on February 21, the Committee of Union and Progress elected Talat Bey as President of the parliamentary party of the Committee of Union and Progress, with Seyyid Bey, deputy for İzmir, Ali Münir [Çağıl], deputy for Çorum, Ali Cenani Bey, deputy for Aleppo, Mansur Pasha, deputy for Benghazi, as members of the Executive Council, and Hacı Ali Galib Bey, deputy for Karesi, as Treasurer (*Tanin*, February 9, 1326/February 22, 1911, quoted in Feroz Ahmad, *The Young Turks: The Committee of Union and Progress in Turkish Politics, 1908-1914*, p.87n; and, "İttihad ve Terakki Riyaseti," *Yeni İkdam*, Ferbruary 9, 1326/February 22, 1911, p.2).
[14] Hüseyin Cahid Yalçın, "Meşrutiyet Hatıraları, 1908-1918," *Fikir Hareketleri*, 6 (April 25-October 17, 1936), p.294; Halil Menteşe, "Eski Meclisi Mebusan Reisi Halil Menteşe'nin Hatıraları: 7: Dahiliye Nazırlığım," *Cumhuriyet*, October 19, 1946, p.2; "Resignation of Talaat Bey," *The Times*, February 11, 1911, p.5; "Ministerkrise," *Osmanischer Lloyd*, February 12, 1911, p.1; Hüseyin Cahid [Yalçın], "Dahiliye Nazırı'nın İstifası," *Tanin*, January 30, 1326/February 12, 1911, p.1; and, "Zur Ministerkrise," *Osmanischer Lloyd*, February 14, 1911, p.1. See also, Ahmed İzzet, *Feryadım*, *1*, p.111.
[15] "The Resignation of Talaat Bey," *The Times*, February 13, 1911, p.5; "Dahiliye Nazırının İstifası ve Fırkanın Müzakeratı," *Yeni İkdam*, January 31, 1326/February 13, 1911, pp.1-2; and, "Zur Ministerkrise: Die Sitzung der Partei 'Einheit und Fortschritt'," *Osmanischer Lloyd*, February 14, 1911, p.1. For the advertisement for the meeting see, "İttihad ve Terakki Fırkası," *Tanin*, January 30, 1326/

At a meeting he held with Mahmud Şevket Pasha, Minister of War, and Colonel Mahmud Muhtar Bey, Minister of the Navy, on February 12, Hakkı Pasha informed them of his intention to invite Halil [Menteşe] into his cabinet as Minister of the Interior—to which the Ministers agreed on two conditions: that the cabinet should accept the proposal for a constitutional amendment concerning the dissolution of the Chamber, and that Nâzım Pasha, the Governor of Baghdad who had been exiled there for his role at the monarchist schemes to overthrow the new regime, be recalled from his post to İstanbul immediately.[16] Naturally, the Unionist leadership was against any amendment to the Constitution which might lead to a premature dissolution of the Chamber and call for new elections—especially when the party was not ready for it.[17]

The trial of strength between the military and the Committee of Union and Progress gave rise to serious apprehensions lest Turkey became involved in a grave crisis at a moment when the government needed all its authority and attention for Macedonia, Albania, and Yemen, and for the Baghdad Railway negotiations. The question alleged to have been raised by Mahmud Şevket Pasha as to the future attitude of the Committee of Union and Progress towards the cabinet was regarded as almost an ultimatum. The decisions of the Committee of Union and Progress were consequently awaited with interest, as they were expected to show whether the Unionists were prepared to successfully resist the demands of the military or whether the trend of Turkish politics towards a military dictatorship under Mahmud Şevket Pasha would be accelerated.[18]

The best judges of Turkish affairs were persuaded that the

February 12, 1911, p.1.

[16] Mehmed Cavid, "Meşrutiyet Devrine Ait Cavit Bey'in Hatıraları: 17," *Tanin*, September 15, 1943, p.2.

Nâzım Pasha was recalled to İstanbul on March 17 ("The Baghdad Railway: The Gulf Section," *The Times*, March 18, 1911, p.5; and, "Empire News: The Provinces," *The Orient, 1/49* (March 22, 1911), p.8. See also, "Disorders in Baghdad: Nazim Pasha's Recall," *The Times*, March 27, 1911, p.5; and, "Turkish Policy in Baghdad: Recall of Nazim Pasha," *The Times*, April 10, 1911, p.5).

[17] Mehmed Cavid, "Meşrutiyet Devrine Ait Cavit Bey'in Hatıraları: 18," *Tanin*, September 16, 1943, p.2.

[18] "The Situation in Turkey: Committee and Cabinet," *The Times*, February 15, 1911, p.5.

establishment of military dictatorship was only a question of time, possibly of a very short time, and believed that such an eventuality would clarify the outlook in many respects. The reality was that the Army's position, after the suppression of the *coup* attempt of April 1909, had become supreme, and the only question was whether its supremacy would stand revealed to the world, or continue to be masked. Practically, the issue between Mahmud Şevket Pasha and the Unionist leadership was whether the Army would obey its chiefs alone, or whether it would serve primarily the interests of non-military, *i.e.*, Unionist, politicians.[19]

The Unionists, however, managed to have the Ministers agree to the withdrawal of their conditions; and proceeded with the plan. At the party meeting on February 14, the majority, in conformity with the decisions taken at the meeting between the Unionist leadership and Hakkı Pasha on February 9, decided to withdraw their support from Bedros Haladjian, Minister of Public Works, and Emrullah Efendi, Minister of Education, thus forcing them to resign their posts in the cabinet.[20] At a vote following a heated debate, Bedros Haladjian had obtained only twenty-six votes out of ninety-six.[21] The next day, both handed in their resignations.[22] At a meet-

---

[19] "The Situation in Turkey: Committee and Cabinet," *The Times*, February 15, 1911, p.5. See also, *Le Temps* editorial of February 16, 1911, reproduced in, "Buhran-ı Vükelâ," *Tanin*, February 5, 1326/February 18, 1911, pp.1-2.

[20] Mehmed Cavid, "Meşrutiyet Devrine Ait Cavit Bey'in Hatıraları: 18," *Tanin*, September 16, 1943, p.2; "Zur Ministerkrise: Die heutige Komiteesitzung," *Osmanischer Lloyd*, February 14, 1911, p.1; "İttihad ve Terakki Fırkası'nın Dünkü Müzakeratı," *Tanin*, February 2, 1326/February 15, 1911, p.1; "Ekseriyet Fırkasının Dünkü İctimaı ve Kabinenin Vaziyeti," and "Kabine ve Ekseriyet Fırkası," *Yeni İkdam*, February 2, 1326/February 15, 1911, pp.1-2; and, "The Position of the Cabinet," *The Levant Herald and Eastern Express*, February 15, 1911, p.1.

[21] "The Position of the Cabinet," *The Levant Herald and Eastern Express*, February 15, 1911, p.1; "İttihad ve Terakki Fırkası'nın Dünkü Müzakeratı," *Tanin*, February 2, 1326/February 15, 1911, p.1; and, "Die Ministerkrise: Eine Sitzung des Komitees," *Osmanischer Lloyd*, February 15, 1911, p.1, which gives slightly different figures.

[22] Mehmed Cavid, "Meşrutiyet Devrine Ait Cavit Bey'in Hatıraları: 18," *Tanin*, September 16, 1943, p.2; "Haladjian Efendi'nin İstifası," *Tanin*, February 3, 1236/February 16, 1911, p.1; "Nafia Nazırının İstifası," and, "Maarif Nazırı Emrullah Efendi," *Yeni İkdam*, February 3, 1326/February 16, 1911, p.1; "Turkish Politics: The Committee and the Ministry," *The Times*, February 16, 1911, p.5; "The Ministry of Public Works," *The Levant Herald and Eastern Express*, February 16, 1911, p.1; "The Ministry of Public Instruction," *The Levant Herald and Eastern Express*, February 16, 1911, p.1; "Die Ministerkrise: Die Demission Haladschian Effendis," *Osmanischer Lloyd*, February 16, 1911, p.1; "The Ministry of Public Instruction," *The Levant Herald and Eastern Express*, February 17, 1911, p.1; "The Situation in Turkey: The Cabinet," *The Times*, February 18, 1911, p.5; and, "Empire

ing of the parliamentary party of the Committee of Union and Progress on February 16, sixty-five deputies voted that Halil [Menteşe] should be appointed Minister of the Interior, the remaining forty-eight expressing the opinion that he should remain leader of the party. The vote, although it turned out in favour of the Unionist leadership, clearly showed that the faction within the party was quite strong.[23]

While the government was attempting to make Parliament the political centre of gravity, the monarchist politicians as well as the monarchist press, convinced of their strength, demanded the resignation of the Grand Vezier as the only solution to the crisis. However, strongly supported by the Unionist leadership, Hakkı Pasha, was firmly resolved not to resign, and denied the existence of a crisis, on the ground that the cabinet as a whole was responsible to Parliament as a whole.[24] After negotiations, Halil [Menteşe] accepted the offer, and was appointed Minister of the Interior on February 17.[25] Yet, on February 19, there were vague rumours of further resignations of members of the cabinet, notably of Mahmud Şevket Pasha, Minister of War. Besides, no successors had been appointed to Emrullah Efendi and Bedros Haladjian, whose places had been temporarily filled by Hakkı Pasha and Cavid Bey.[26]

News: The Capital," *The Orient*, 1/45 (February 22, 1911), p.6.

[23] Hüseyin Cahid [Yalçın], "Yeni Dahiliye Nazırı," *Tanin*, February 4, 1326/February 17, 1911, p.1; "Turkish Politics: The Committee and the Ministry," *The Times*, February 17, 1911, p.5; "Die Ministerkrise: Sitzung der Komistees," *Osmanischer Lloyd*, February 17, 1911, p.1; "La situation politique," *The Levant Herald and Eastern Express*, February 17, 1911, p.1; and, "The Ministry of the Interior," *The Levant Herald and Eastern Express*, February 17, 1911, p.1. His name had been circulating in the press as a likely candidate for the Ministry ("Kabinenin Mevkii ve Yeni Dahiliye Nazırı," *Yeni İkdam*, February 1, 1326/February 14, 1911, p.1).

[24] "The Situation in Turkey: The Grand Vizier and the Crisis," *The Times*, February 18, 1911, p.5.

[25] "Kabinenin Mevkii ve Yeni Dahiliye Nazırı," *Yeni İkdam*, February 1, 1326/February 14, 1911, p.1; "Dahiliye Nezareti," *Yeni İkdam*, February 5, 1326/February 18, 1911, p.1; "Der Ministerkrise," *Osmanischer Lloyd*, February 18, 1911, p.1; "The Situation in Turkey: The Cabinet," *The Times*, February 18, 1911, p.5; "Yeni Dahiliye Nazırı," *Yeni İkdam*, February 8, 1326/February 21, 1911, pp.1-2; and, Lütfi Simavi, *Sultan Mehmed Reşad Han'ın ve Halefinin Sarayında Gördüklerim*, 1, p.136. Arar wrongly states that he was appointed Minister on February 19 (İsmail Arar, "Halil Menteşe'nin Hayatı ve Anıları Üzerine Tamamlayıcı Bilgiler," in [Halil Menteşe], *Osmanlı Mebusan Meclisi Reisi Halil Menteşe'nin Anıları*, p.22).

[26] "Die Ministerkrise: Die Arbeitsministerium," *Osmanischer Lloyd*, February 17, 1911, p.1; "The Turkish Cabinet," *The Times*, February 20, 1911, p.5; and, "Münhal Nezaretler," *Tanin*, February 13, 1326/February 26, 1911, p.1.

However, on February 20, no further ministerial changes were reported, but it was generally believed that the life of the cabinet would be brief and troubled.[27] In an attempt to force Hakkı Pasha's resignation, the February 20 issues of *Yeni Gazete* and other monarchist newspapers claimed that his persistent refusal to treat the party vote of non-confidence in one minister as implying want of confidence in the whole cabinet had lowered his prestige.[28] It was anticipated that Cavid Bey, Minister of Finance, would have to face some opposition on the part of the members of both the opposition and the dissident faction within the party on the February 22 sitting of the Chamber of Deputies during which the Budget would be discussed. The position of Rıfat Pasha, Minister for Foreign Affairs, was also said to be insecure, and rumour—which had been officially denied—had even named Reşid Pasha, Ambassador in Vienna, as his successor.[29]

On February 22, Cavid Bey began his Budget statement in a four hours' speech, devoted in part to a reply to the attacks of certain critics, and in part to a review of Turkish financial history since the Revolution, with special reference to the last financial year. he made but a brief reference to the loan negotiations, the failure of which, he said, was not due to any hostility on the part of the French Government. In an attempt to placate both the foreign and the monarchist criticism of Unionist measures to control foreign capital in Turkey, he said that he had never dreamt of attacking any European financial establishment in Turkey—though he had to point out that these establishments had duties to the Turkish Government. As for the friendship of France and Turkey, France had many reasons for desiring to maintain good relations with Turkey—notably her enormous investments in the Turkish Funds and in Turkish commercial and industrial undertakings. Turkey, on the other hand, desired the friendship

---

27 "Buhranın Temadisine Sebep," and, "Kabinenin Mevkii," *Yeni İkdam*, February 7, 1326/February 20, 1911, p.1.
28 "The Turkish Cabinet: Criticism of Hakki Pasha," *The Times*, February 21, 1911, p.5.
29 "Turkish Politics: The Committee of Union and Progress," *The Times*, February 22, 1911, p.5. See also, A. A. Türkei 159, No.2, Copy No.57, "Antisemitische Strömung in der Türkei," Marschall, Pera, March 3, 1911.

of France for sentimental and moral, as well as material, reasons—above all, on account of gratitude for the great French Revolution which, Cavid Bey acknowledged, had first opened their eyes.[30]

Cavid Bey continued his Budget speech on February 23, and characteristically began by protesting against the hypercritical and pessimistic attitude of the Budget Commission. There was no need to fear that the government would demand extraordinary credits for the coming financial year. His estimates showed a revenue of twenty-eight million and six hundred thousand liras, and an expenditure of thirty-four million and five hundred thousand liras. Taking the latter figures first, he pointed out that no great increase was shown in any chapters, except those of the Ministry of Finance, where one hundred and fifty thousand liras had been added for the purchase of coast guard vessels and grants to agriculture, and under the head of debt, of which the increase, close to two million liras, was largely due to increased expenditure for pensions. Military and naval expenditure would amount, in round figures, to thirteen million liras. Though he was not a supporter of the sudden increase in naval expenditure, Cavid Bey stated he recognised that the Budget of the Navy was too small considering the extent of the coastline. The pay and numbers of the gendarmerie and the police would have to be increased. Assuring the Chamber that the War Budget was moderate in proportion to that of other Powers, Cavid Bey admitted that the needs of the Ministry of War were bound to increase annually.[31]

His estimate of revenue, based on the average of the last five years, was found too optimistic by the Budget Commission,

---

[30] I/III/45, February 9, 1326/February 22, 1911, *Meclis-i Mebusan Zabıt Ceridesi*, 3, pp.159-189; "The Ottoman Parliament," *The Orient*, 1/46 (March 1, 1911), p.2; "Die Kammer," *Osmanischer Lloyd*, February 23, 1911, p.1; and, "Turkish Financial Policy: Speech by Djavid Bey," *The Times*, February 23, 1911, p.5. For Yalçın's comments on the speech see, Hüseyin Cahid [Yalçın], "Bütçe Müzakeresi," *Tanin* February 10, 1326/February 23, 1911, p.1. For another editorial see, "Der Finanzminister vor der Kammer," *Osmanischer Lloyd*, February 24, 1911, p.1.

[31] I/III/46, February 10, 1326/February 23, 1911, *Meclis-i Mebusan Zabıt Ceridesi*, 3, pp.193-206; Hüseyin Cahid [Yalçın], "Bütçe," *Tanin*, February 11, 1326/February 24, 1911, p.1; "Die Kammer," *Osmanischer Lloyd*, February 24, 1911, p.1; "The Ottoman Parliament," *The Orient*, 1/46 (March 1, 1911), p.2; and, "The Turkish Budget: Djavid Bey's Optimism," *The Times*, February 25, 1911, p.5.

who had reduced it from twenty-eight million six hundred thousand to twenty-six million and nine hundred thousand liras. Admitting this, Cavid Bey was faced by a deficit of about seven million liras. Unexpended credits and the increase of revenue during the last financial year left him with about three million liras in hand, so that the deficit was reduced to about four million liras, which he proposed to cover by loan. He believed that the government would, in a comparatively near future, arrive at financial equilibrium by the increase of existing revenues. The new house tax, where it was in thorough operation, showed an increase of fifty percent. The government hoped soon to obtain the consent of the Powers to the application of a new income tax, in substitution for the old professional tax, or *temettü vergisi*. The projected four percent increase in the customs duties would bring in a million and a half liras, but the realisation of the increase depended on the Baghdad Railway question, for according to the Convention, the surplus customs revenue had to be affected to the construction of this line. Preliminary discussions were now on foot in regard to the question, and would, he hoped, end favourably for Turkey. The surplus revenues were sufficient for the prolongation of the line to al-Halif; only three hundred thousand liras would be deducted from the proceeds of the proposed four percent customs surtax for this purpose. Cavid Bey also informed the deputies that he was in correspondence with the Public Debt Administration on the subject of the Régie Co-Intéressée des Tabacs de l'Empire Ottoman—or, popularly known as the Régie des Tabacs—which he hoped would be administered as a government monopoly in 1914 instead of a foreign concession. With these possibilities, he hoped in the near future to see the revenue reach thirty-five million liras, and he could confidently promise the Chamber a surplus of five million liras after the coming general elections in 1912. He concluded his Budget speech with a reference to the four railway schemes, which he considered of vital importance—namely, the Baghdad Railway, the İstanbul to Basra Chester scheme, and the Samsun-Sivas and Danube-

Adriatic railways—which he hoped would soon be begun to revolutionise the life of those provinces.[32]

At the March 1 debate on the Budget in the Chamber, İsmail Hakkı Bey, deputy for Gümülcine and leader of the monarchist People's Party, made a long criticism of Cavid Bey's financial policy, at the close of which, after paying lip service to the loyalty of the great majority of the Turkish Jews, he hinted that Cavid Bey had shown undue preference to Jewish capitalists and their agents, some of whom he accused of favouring Zionism. He also drew the attention of the Chamber to the growth of Zionist propaganda in Turkey and to the efforts of the foreign Jewish agents on behalf of that cause. Gümülcineli İsmail Hakkı Bey then treated the Chamber to something of an anti-climax, naming Sir Ernest Cassel and other unlikely persons as presumable Zionists. Hakkı Pasha explained that Sir Ernest Cassel was a member of the Anglican Church, and was an intimate friend of the late King, and therefore a true and loyal friend of Turkey. Answering the statement of Gümülcineli İsmail Hakkı Bey, Talât Bey said that proposals had been made to him and to Cavid Bey by the Jewish General Colonisation Society, which they had been unable to accept. He admitted Zionist activity, but said that the law preventing Jewish immigration into Palestine remained in force.[33]

On March 1, Babanzade İsmail Hakkı Bey, deputy for Baghdad and a prominent Unionist, was appointed Minister of Education in place of Emrullah Efendi.[34] Despite this ap-

[32] I/III/46, February 10, 1326/February 23, 1911, *Meclis-i Mebusan Zabıt Ceridesi*, 3, pp.206-225; Hüseyin Cahid [Yalçın], "Bütçe," *Tanin*, February 11, 1326/February 24, 1911, p.1; "The Ottoman Parliament," *The Orient*, 1/46 (March 1, 1911), p.2; and, "The Turkish Budget: Djavid Bey's Optimism," *The Times*, February 25, 1911, p.5. For the comments on Yalçın's editorial of February 24, 1911, see, "Die osmanische Presse: die türkische Presse," *Osmanischer Lloyd*, February 25, 1911, p.2.

[33] I/III/49, February 16, 1326/March 1, 1911, *Meclis-i Mebusan Zabıt Ceridesi*, 3, pp.311-347; "The Ottoman Parliament," *The Orient*, 1/47 (March 8, 1911), p.1; and, "The Turkish Chamber and Zionism," *The Times*, March 3, 1911, p.5. See also, "Meclis-i Mebusan'ın Hali," *Tanin*, February 18, 1326/March 3, 1911, pp.1-2. For Yalçın's comments on this debate see, Hüseyin Cahid [Yalçın], "Siyonizm," *Tanin*, February 19, 1326/March 4, 1911, p.1.

[34] "Maarif Nezareti," *Tanin*, February 17, 1326/March 2, 1911, p.1; "Sitzung des Komitees," *Osmanischer Lloyd*, March 2, 1911, p.1; Hüseyin Cahid [Yalçın], "Kabine," *Tanin*, February 18, 1326/March 3, 1911, p.1; "The Turkish Chamber and Zionism," *The Times*, March 3, 1911, p.5; "The New Minister of Public Instruction," *The Orient*, 1/47 (March 8, 1911), p.2; and, Edwin Pears, "Develop-

pointment, the Unionist position in the cabinet was somewhat shaky. Reportedly, divergences of opinion had arisen in the cabinet, first as to whether the government could prolong the state of siege without submitting the matter to the Chamber of Deputies, and, secondly, as regards the appointment of a successor to Bedros Haladjian. It was reported that the portfolio of Public Works should be offered to General Sami Pasha, Commander of the Havran Field Force and a kinsman of Mahmud Şevket Pasha, and that Gabriel Nouradunghian should be appointed President of the Council of State with cabinet rank. These proposals had met with strong opposition from the Unionist leadership.[35] In contrast to the weakening position of the Committee of Union and Progress in the cabinet, with the prolongation of the state of siege for an indefinite period of time on March 13, Mahmud Şevket Pasha's position remained as strong as ever.[36]

By mid-April, the Unionist leadership had obtained extensive and reliable information about Colonel Sadık Bey's machinations within the ranks of the party.[37] Even in early March, it was reported from Salonica that violent dissensions prevailed among the Committee of Union and Progress. There was little doubt that the military clubs both at Salonica and at Üsküb and Monastir regarded the proceedings of the Unionist politicians with growing dissatisfaction. Some of the officers, indeed, openly hinted that a great change was in preparation. The officers who had been formerly favourable to the Committee of Union and Progress had changed sides, and the Army was stated to be wholly devoted to Mahmud Şevket Pasha and to be

---

ments in Turkey," p.11. For Babanzade Hakkı Bey's credentials, see, "Der neue Unterrichtsminister," *Osmanischer Lloyd*, March 3, 1911, p.1. His name had been circulating in the press for the Ministry ("İsmail Hakkı Bey," *Yeni İkdam*, February 14, 1326/February 27, 1911, p.2).

[35] "The Turkish Cabinet," *The Times*, March 14, 1911, p.5.

[36] "The State of Siege," *The Times*, March 7, 1911, p.5; F.O. 371/1246/10018, Sir Gerard Lowther to Sir Edward Grey, Pera, March 15, 1911, cited in Feroz Ahmad, *The Young Turks: The Committee of Union and Progress in Turkish Politics, 1908-1914*, p.90; and, "The State of Siege in Constantinople," *The Times*, March 15, 1911, p.5. See also, "The State of Siege in Constantinople," *The Times*, March 17, 1911, p.5.

37 See Ziya Şakir [Soko], "Hürriyet ve İtilâf Nasıl Doğdu? Nasıl Yaşadı? Nasıl Battı? 16: Şehzade'deki Konakta Müzakereler Başlamıştı," *Tan*, November 17, 1937, p.9.

ready to support him should he see fit to proclaim a military dictatorship. Mahmud Şevket Pasha, however, seemed to have little political ambition, and was indisposed to extend the sphere of his activity beyond the Army. Should he resolve to take action, the remnants of constitutionalism would probably disappear, as he was known to have little admiration for parliamentary institutions.[38]

On April 14, Talât Bey, Dr. Nâzım Bey, Hüseyin Cahid [Yalçın], and Cavid Bey met and discussed matters of internal party politics. The matter that needed urgent attention of the Unionist leadership was Colonel Sadık Bey's attempts to form an opposition faction within the party when it had become apparent that trying to establish a strong opposition party by itself had not given the result monarchists desired. The information Unionist leadership received suggested that Colonel Sadık Bey had been trying, with some success, to severe some of the deputies' ties with the Committee of Union and Progress through religious propaganda.[39] Deputies who might be favourably disposed towards religious propaganda were being summoned individually to Colonel Sadık Bey's house where they were being told about the Unionist leadership's involvement with Masonic lodges and the danger it posed to Islam. Reportedly, Colonel Sadık Bey had been trying to win these deputies over by arguments of cleaning the party from those 'Masonic and anti-religious' elements.[40]

Among the deputies who had been contacted by Colonel Sadık Bey were Ali Osman Bey, deputy for Çorum, Hacı Mustafa [Beyman], deputy for Ankara, Abdullah Azmi [Torun],

[38] "Committee and Army," The Times, March 14, 1911, p.5.
[39] Hüseyin Cahid Yalçın, "Meşrutiyet Hatıraları, 1908-1918," Fikir Hareketleri, 6 (April 25-October 17, 1936), p.310; and, Mehmed Cavid, "Meşrutiyet Devrine Ait Cavit Bey'in Hatıraları: 28," Tanin, September 26, 1943, p.2. See also, Şehbenderzade Filibeli Ahmed Hilmi, Muhalefetin İflâsı: İtilâf ve Hürriyet Fırkası, p.34.
[40] Mehmed Cavid, "Meşrutiyet Devrine Ait Cavit Bey'in Hatıraları: 28," Tanin, September 26, 1943, p.2; Halil Menteşe, "Eski Meclisi Mebusan Reisi Halil Menteşe'nin Hatıraları: 7: Dahiliye Nazırlığım," Cumhuriyet, October 19, 1946, p.2; and, Ziya Şakir [Soko], "Hürriyet ve İtilâf Nasıl Doğdu? Nasıl Yaşadı? Nasıl Battı? 22: On Maddelik Program Tereddütlere Yol Açtı," Tan, November 23, 1937, p.9. See also, Şehbenderzade Filibeli Ahmed Hilmi, Muhalefetin İflâsı: İtilâf ve Hürriyet Fırkası, pp.33-34.
There had been an anti-Masonic and anti-Zionist demonstration at Salonica on April 4, 1911, organised by the supporters of Sadık Bey (Orhan Koloğlu, "İttihat ve Terakki'de Komite-Hizb-i Cedid Tartışması Sırasında Yunus Nadi'nin Selânik'te Tokatlanması Olayı," pp.34-35).

deputy for Kütahya, and Mehmed Talât [Sönmez], deputy for Ankara—whose names came as a surprise to the Unionist leadership. There were also familiar names such as İbrahim Vasfi Efendi, deputy for Karesi, Mehmed Hamdi [Yazır], deputy for Antalya, and Hoca Mustafa Sabri Efendi, deputy for Tokad, all of whom had already resigned and joined the People's Party, and Habib Bey, deputy for Bolu, Basri Dukacı, deputy for Dibër, Tokadizade Şekib Bey, deputy for Manisa, Ömer Fevzi Hoca, deputy for Bursa, Ömer Mümtaz Bey, deputy for Kayseri, and İsmail Sıdkı Bey, deputy for Aydın.[41]

Unionist leadership had known for some time the involvement of Naim Bey and Yusuf Ziya Bey, along with a number of army officers, in this monarchist plot to win over some members of the Chamber to their cause. The leadership also learned that Colonel Sadık Bey had sent emissaries to Salonica and Monastir, with instructions to inform the army officers there about the differences of opinion between Mahmud Şevket Pasha and Cavid Bey, in an attempt to discredit the Unionists in the eyes of the military.[42]

Apart from their influence within the military, the monarchist conspiracy had also following in the civilian bureaucracy. Highly critical of many prominent Unionists, such as Cavid Bey, Talât Bey, and Hüseyin Cahid [Yalçın], Avlonyalı Ferid Pasha, Governor of Aydın, was one of those high level bureaucrats who was intimately involved with the monarchist scheme to end Unionist influence in government through unconstitutional methods. He had made several trips to İstanbul within the last month where he had contacted discontented military elements to work out the logistics of a military uprising both in İstanbul and the provinces, to coincide with the formal defections from the Committee of Union and Prog-

---

[41] Mehmed Cavid, "Meşrutiyet Devrine Ait Cavit Bey'in Hatıraları: 29," *Tanin*, September 27, 1943, p.2; and, "Meşrutiyet Devrine Ait Cavit Bey'in Hatıraları: 30," *Tanin*, September 28, 1943, p.2.
    One of the informers was Habib Bey, deputy for Bolu, himself, who first joined the New Faction but then defected back to the Unionist side (Hüseyin Cahid Yalçın, "Meşrutiyet Hatıraları, 1908-1918," *Fikir Hareketleri, 6* (April 25-October 17, 1936), p.310).
[42] Mehmed Cavid, "Meşrutiyet Devrine Ait Cavit Bey'in Hatıraları: 29," *Tanin*, September 27, 1943, p.2.

ress in the Chamber.[43]

His anti-Unionist stand and strong preference for the monarchist cause as well as his involvement in the counter-revolutionary *coup* attempt of April 13, 1909 being public knowledge,
the Unionists also suspected Gerald H. Fitzmaurice, the First
Dragoman of the British Embassy in İstanbul, who had lately
been seen talking with monarchist deputies on certain occasions.[44] Despite the Christian Socialist *Reichspost* of Vienna's
rejection of the insinuation of Unionist newspapers that Fitzmaurice organised the monarchist agitation against the Committee of Union and Progress, the suspicions of the Unionist
leadership were well founded: the conspiracy enjoyed British
support.[45] It was *The Times* correspondent who had reportedly
approached Habib Bey, deputy for Bolu, and informed him
that Cavid Bey had instructed the local branches of the
Committee of Union and Progress to send telegrams denouncing him and Hoca Mecdi Efendi, deputy for Karesi. At the
same time, *The Times* correspondent suggested that Cavid
Bey's expulsion from the Ministry of Finance would result in
increased British investment in Turkey.[46] Upon receiving this
intelligence, Cavid Bey expressed the Unionist concern to
British representatives in two separate interviews—one with
Sir Henry Babington Smith on April 28, and the other with Sir
Adam Block on May 3. Apparently, Sir Adam Block was in
full knowledge of Fitzmaurice's efforts at destabilising the
Unionist-supported cabinet, and expressed his disapproval of
these attempts to Cavid Bey.[47]

[43] Mehmed Cavid, "Meşrutiyet Devrine Ait Cavit Bey'in Hatıraları: 30," *Tanin*, September 28, 1943, p.2.
[44] Mehmed Cavid, "Meşrutiyet Devrine Ait Cavit Bey'in Hatıraları: 29," *Tanin*, September 27, 1943, p.2. See Hüseyin Cahid [Yalçın], "Anarşiye Doğru, 1:
Ecnebi Entrikaları," *Tanin*, April 9, 1327/April 22, 1911, p.1, for the accusations
against Gerald H. Fitzmaurice. For a comment on Yalçın's editorial of April 22,
see, "Stimmen der Presse," *Osmanischer Lloyd*, April 23, 1911, p.1; and, A. A.
Türkei 161/93, Marschall, April 22, 1911. There is ample evidence in a Kedourie
article of the strong anti-Unionist, anti-Masonic and anti-Jewish sentiments Gerald H. Fitzmaurice held (Elie Kedourie, "Young Turks, Freemasons and Jews,"
pp.89-104).
[45] *Reichspost*, April 23, 1911, quoted in "Turkish Politics: Opinion in Vienna," *The Times*, April 25, 1911, p.3.
[46] Hüseyin Cahid Yalçın, "Meşrutiyet Hatıraları, 1908-1918," *Fikir Hareketleri*, 6 (April 25-October 17, 1936), p.310.
[47] Mehmed Cavid, "Meşrutiyet Devrine Ait Cavit Bey'in Hatıraları: 34," *Tanin*, October 4, 1943, p.2; and, "Meşrutiyet Devrine Ait Cavit Bey'in Hatıraları:

By April 18, according to rumours, the number of discontented deputies within the Committee of Union and Progress had risen to about thirty.[48] Other estimates put the number as high as seventy-five, or nearly fifty percent of the party. The dissensions which had long existed in the parliamentary party of the Committee of Union and Progress had come to a head and was likely to lead to important cabinet changes. Organised by Colonel Sadık Bey and other military figures, the dissident faction within the party had mutinied against Talât Bey's leadership.[49] What appeared to have brought the discontent of the deputies to a head was the election of Hüseyin Cahid [Yalçın], editor-in-chief of *Tanin* and a prominent Unionist deputy for İstanbul, as delegate of the Ottoman bondholders on the Council of the Public Debt Administration while he was already a member of the board of the National Bank of Turkey.[50] Some of the provincial Unionist organs in Macedonia, which were controlled by the military officers who had joined Colonel Sadık Bey's attempt to destroy the Committee of Union and Progress from within, were publishing violent attacks on *Tanin* and counselling their readers to boycott the newspaper.[51]

The opposition movement within the party was serious enough to force the leadership to meet with these deputies on

35," *Tanin*, October 5, 1943, p.2.

[48] *Le Jeune Turc* and *La Turquie* of April 19, 1911, both excerpted in "İttihad ve Terakki Fırkası," *Tanin*, April 7, 1327/April 20, 1911, p.2; "Die liberale Partei," *Osmanischer Lloyd*, April 23, 1911, p.1; and, Mehmed Cavid, "Meşrutiyet Devrine Ait Cavit Bey'in Hatıraları: 30," *Tanin*, September 28, 1943, p.2. Şehbenderzade Filibeli Ahmed Hilmi claims that Sadık Bey had personally talked with one hundred and ten deputies belonging to the Committee of Union and Progress (Şehbenderzade Filibeli Ahmed Hilmi, *Muhalefetin İflâsı: İtilâf ve Hürriyet Fırkası*, p.34).

[49] "Turkish Politics: Split in the Committee Party," *The Times*, April 19, 1911, p.5; and, Ziya Şakir [Soko], "Hürriyet ve İtilâf Nasıl Doğdu? Nasıl Yaşadı? Nasıl Battı? 16: Şehzade'deki Konakta Müzakereler Başlamıştı," *Tan*, November 17, 1937, p.9. For Yalçın's rebuttal of the opposition's arguments see, Hüseyin Cahid [Yalçın], "Anarşiye Doğru, 1: Ecnebi Entrikaları," *Tanin*, April 9, 1327/April 22, 1911, p.1.

[50] Hüseyin Cahid Yalçın was elected to this post in place of Hamdi Bey, Director-General of the Imperial Museum, in mid-March by a vote of eight hundred and sixty-four to one against ("Hussein Dschahid Bej türkischer Vertreter bei der Dette Publique," *Osmanischer Lloyd*, March 22, 1911, p.1).

[51] "Turkish Politics: The Split in the Committee Party," *The Times*, April 21, 1911, p.3. See also, "Turkish Politics: The Committee and the Albanian Rising," *The Times*, April 26, 1911, p.5; and, Ziya Şakir [Soko], "Hürriyet ve İtilâf Nasıl Doğdu? Nasıl Yaşadı? Nasıl Battı? 17: İlk Yapılacak İş Umumî Merkezi Dağıtmaktır," *Tan*, November 18, 1937, p.9.

April 19.[52] In an attempt to counter monarchist propaganda, the same day, Talât Bey, President of the parliamentary party of the Committee of Union and Progress, had to issue a statement denouncing that rumours of the dissolution of the party was contrary to facts.[53] On April 20, Talât Bey also met with Colonel Sadık Bey. The latter accused the Unionist leadership of being freemasons and therefore unacceptable to his faction and put forward several demands, including resignations of several ministers from the cabinet and several deputies from the Chamber. The meeting ended without agreement.[54]

Calling itself the New Faction—or, Hizb-i Cedid—the movement represented a conservative insurrection against the supposed radical tendencies of an energetic minority whom the dissidents considered over-represented in the cabinet.[55] The New Faction wanted the resignations of Hakkı Pasha, the Grand Vezier, Musa Kâzım Efendi, the Sheikh-ul-Islam, Cavid Bey, Minister of Finance, and as well as the banishment of Talât Bey, ex-Minister of the Interior, to a remote province after relinquishing his post as President of the Committee of Union and Progress. They also demanded that Hüseyin Cahid [Yalçın], editor of *Tanin*, resign his deputyship.[56]

The New Faction further demanded that the new Ministers be appointed from outside the Chamber, representing, in effect, a return to the practice under the pre-revolutionary absolutist regime—the practice which the Unionists had fought so hard to change, and had finally succeeded in replacing it with a cabinet chosen from among the members of and re-

---

[52] Mehmed Cavid, "Meşrutiyet Devrine Ait Cavit Bey'in Hatıraları: 30," *Tanin*, September 28, 1943, p.2; and, Ziya Şakir [Soko], "Hürriyet ve İtilâf Nasıl Doğdu? Nasıl Yaşadı? Nasıl Battı? 19: Kırmızı Konak Toplantısı Mühim Neticeler Vermişti," *Tan*, November 20, 1937, p.9.

[53] "Beyanname," *Tanin*, April 7, 1327/April 20, 1911, p.2; "Die Komitee-partei," *Osmanischer Lloyd*, April 21, 1911, p.1; and, "Un Communiqué," *The Levant Herald and Eastern Express*, April 21, 1911, p.1. Hacı Âdil [Arda], Secretary-General of the Committee of Union and Progress, issued a similar statement dated April 23, 1911 ("Die politische Lage: Eine Kundgebung der Saloniker Zentralkomitees," *Osmanischer Lloyd*, April 25, 1911, p.1).

[54] Mehmed Cavid, "Meşrutiyet Devrine Ait Cavit Bey'in Hatıraları: 30," *Tanin*, September 28, 1943, p.2.

[55] "Constantinople Letter: The Parliamentary Crisis," *The Near East*, May 10, 1911, p.3. See also, *Stamboul*, April 24, 1911, cited in Korkmaz Alemdar, *Istanbul, 1875-1964: Turkiye'de Yayınlanan Fransızca bir Gazetenin Tarihi*, p.120.

[56] Hüseyin Cahid Yalçın, "Meşrutiyet Hatıraları, 1908-1918," *Fikir Hareketleri*, 6 (April 25-October 17, 1936), p.310.

sponsible to the Parliament. Furthermore, the dissidents also demanded a return to the original Midhatian Constitution—a Constitution which excluded clauses for the establishment of representative government and a liberal democratic regime. The aim of the New Faction was clearly to restore the absolutist monarchical political regime.[57]

At first, it looked as if the dissident deputies within the Committee of Union and Progress led by Colonel Sadık Bey had been completely successful. At the meeting held with dissidents, the Unionist leadership had to accept to consider their demands which might eventually lead to giving certain other concessions. The original regulation stipulating that members should not seek office or concessions had been reaffirmed, while an important modification was introduced granting liberty of action to a minority of the party in the Chamber when in disagreement with a two-thirds majority of the party. Up until then, in these circumstances, the minority had been compelled to vote with the majority. It was quite obvious that this modification would greatly weaken the position of the Unionist leadership in the Chamber and conduce to the instability of ministers.[58]

On April 21, the press and the public, unconvinced by Talât Bey's denial of the existence of serious dissension in the parliamentary party of the Committee of Union and Progress, discussed the rift between what might be described as the governmental and opposition sections of the Committee of Union and Progress. The press, however, was divided along party lines. *Tanin*, along with the Armenian Revolutionary Federation's *Azadamard*, and *La Turquie*, hinted at the dan-

[57] Hüseyin Cahid Yalçın, "Meşrutiyet Hatıraları, 1908-1918," *Fikir Hareketleri*, 6 (April 25-October 17, 1936), p.325; "İttihad ve Terakki Fırkası," *Tanin*, April 9, 1327/April 22, 1911, p.2; "Die politische Krise," *Osmanischer Lloyd*, April 22, 1911, p.1; "Turkish Politics: The Split in the Committee," *The Times*, April 22, 1911, p.5. See also, Ziya Şakir [Soko], "Hürriyet ve İtilâf Nasıl Doğdu? Nasıl Yaşadı? Nasıl Battı? 22: On Maddelik Program Tereddütlere Yol Açtı," *Tan*, November 23, 1937, p.9. See also, Şehbenderzade Filibeli Ahmed Hilmi, *Muhalefetin İflâsı: İtilâf ve Hürriyet Fırkası*, pp.39-40.

[58] "Turkish Politics: The Split in the Committee Party," *The Times*, April 21, 1911, p.3; "Turkish Politics: The Split in the Committee: Opposition Demands," *The Times*, April 22, 1911, p.5; "Fırka Beyannamesi," *Tanin*, April 10, 1327/April 23, 1911, p.2; and, Ziya Şakir [Soko], "Hürriyet ve İtilâf Nasıl Doğdu? Nasıl Yaşadı? Nasıl Battı? 22: On Maddelik Program Tereddütlere Yol Açtı," *Tan*, November 23, 1937, p.9.

gers of internal anarchy and even of a repetition of the events
of April 13, 1909.[59] On the other hand, monarchist papers of
April 21, especially *Yeni İkdam* and *Yeni Gazete,* expressed
their satisfaction with the latest developments in the Committee of Union and Progress. They pointed out that the internal
situation had changed in the last two years, and suggested that
what they misleadingly called "a little more liberalism on
the part of the official majority" would not be harmful to the
interests of the Empire. Congratulating Colonel Sadık Bey and
the discontented deputies in the Chamber for their roles in
recent developments, they expected the existing leadership to
be soon forced to step down and dissidents in the Unionist
ranks to take over the management of the Committee of
Union and Progress.[60] Furthermore, monarchist opposition
hoped that the first result of the alleged agreement between
the dissidents and the Unionist leadership would be the fall of
the Hakkı Pasha Cabinet.[61]

This prompted an immediate response from Hakkı Pasha
and the Unionist leadership. At their meeting on the same
day, they decided to convene the Unionist deputies the following day and either let them know in the strongest of terms
that the country needed stability at this juncture and threaten
them with the government's intention of dissolving the
Chamber and call for new elections should some of the
deputies continue in their efforts to undermine the party, or
invite the dissidents to formally resign from the party, establish their own, and form the government themselves if
they could manage to gather enough votes to support it in the
Chamber.[62]

On April 22, while Hüseyin Cahid [Yalçın] published a
strongly worded editorial in *Tanin,* informing the public of

---

[59] "Turkish Politics: The Split in the Committee," *The Times,* April 22, 1911, p.5.

[60] Mehmed Cavid, "Meşrutiyet Devrine Ait Cavit Bey'in Hatıraları: 31," *Ta-nin,* September 29, 1943, p.2; "İttihad ve Terakki Fırkası'na Edilen Teklifler," *Yeni İkdam,* April 8, 1327/April 21, 1911, p.1; and, "Turkish Politics: The Split in the Committee," *The Times,* April 22, 1911, p.5.

[61] "Turkish Politics: The Split in the Committee Party," *The Times,* April 21, 1911, p.3.

[62] Mehmed Cavid, "Meşrutiyet Devrine Ait Cavit Bey'in Hatıraları: 31," *Ta-nin,* September 29, 1943, p.2.

foreign intervention in the internal politics of Turkey and describing the situation as potentially leading to anarchy and disruption, the monarchist papers prematurely celebrated their success. Cevdet Bey, proprietor of *İkdam*, as well as several followers of Colonel Sadık Bey, had come to the Chamber where they were seen in a particularly joyous mood.[63]

The Unionist leadership, however, managed to turn the table against the dissidents in the party meeting. Before the party meeting, the Unionists could only count on the firm support of fifty to fifty-five deputies.[64] During the debates that lasted for the whole day, the leadership successfully exploited the dissidents' lack of any coherent set of counter-arguments or an alternative programme.[65] The debates ended with the signing of a document by the one hundred and seventy members of the party which stated the recognition of the differences between the leadership and the dissidents on the general principles of the party and the decision that these differences would be fully discussed at the next congress of the party. Thus, the immediate threat to party's potential dissolution was averted.[66]

The Unionists accepted the New Faction's demand that deputies not be allowed to participate in business deals, nor accept government employment. The leadership of the Committee of Union and Progress further agreed that party deputies could only become ministers as long as a two-thirds majority

---

[63] Hüseyin Cahid [Yalçın], "Anarşiye Doğru, 1: Ecnebi Entrikaları," *Tanin*, April 9, 1327/April 22, 1911, p.1. For a comment on Yalçın's editorial of April 22, see, "Stimmen der Presse," *Osmanischer Lloyd*, April 23, 1911, p.1. See also, Mehmed Cavid, "Meşrutiyet Devrine Ait Cavit Bey'in Hatıraları: 31," *Tanin*, September 29, 1943, p.2.

[64] Mehmed Cavid, "Meşrutiyet Devrine Ait Cavit Bey'in Hatıraları: 31," *Tanin*, September 29, 1943, p.2.

[65] Edwin Pears, "Developments in Turkey," pp.14-15; "Eine wichtige Entscheidung: Die Beratung der Komiteepartie," *Osmanischer Lloyd*, April 23, 1911, p.1; and, A. A. Türkei 159, No.2/94, Telegram from Marschall, April 23, 1911.

[66] "Fırka Beyannamesi," *Tanin*, April 10, 1327/April 23, 1911, p.2; Mehmed Cavid, "Meşrutiyet Devrine Ait Cavit Bey'in Hatıraları: 32," *Tanin*, September 30, 1943, p.2; and, "İttihad ve Terakki Fırkası: Dünkü İctima," *Yeni İkdam*, April 10, 1327/April 23, 1911, pp.1-2. See Tunaya for the text of the dissidents' demands which were accepted by the Committee of Union and Progress (Tarık Zafer Tunaya, *Türkiye'de Siyasi Partiler, 1859-1952*, p.186). See also, Feroz Ahmad, *The Young Turks: The Committee of Union and Progress in Turkish Politics, 1908-1914*, pp.87-88. Pears writes that the document was signed by one hundred and fifty-three deputies (Edwin Pears, "Developments in Turkey," p.13).

of the party approved the candidate by secret ballot. Finally, the Unionists also agreed to organise the procedure by which government employees were appointed and dismissed. In return, the New Faction would incorporate elements of the Unionist platform into its formal declaration. These included demands for progress in agriculture, commerce, and industry as well as for increased expenditure on education. Importantly, the New Faction also agreed to support the passage of constitutional amendments restricting the political role of the monarchy.[67]

The monarchist press, including *Yeni İkdam* and *Yeni Gazete*, celebrated the agreement as yet another victory for the opposition. Abdülaziz Mecdi [Tolon], deputy for Karesi and one of the important figures of the New Faction, published an article in *Sabah* in which he defended conservatism, saying that "principles of conservatism would better serve the nation, ninety percent of which were conservatives themselves."[68] Hüseyin Cahid [Yalçın] countered in a lengthy editorial in *Tanin*, accusing Abdülaziz Mecdi [Tolon] of supporting reaction and the restoration of the old regime.[69]

With respect to cabinet changes, the monarchist press was still busy expressing doubt whether the Hakkı Pasha Cabinet would remain in power now that the Unionist leadership yielded to dissident pressure. *Tanin*, however, had no illusions on this score. Its editor, Hüseyin Cahid [Yalçın], declared in an outspoken editorial in the April 24 issue that the leaders of the dissidents, who, he hinted, were actuated by personal jealousies, had decided to overthrow the Sheikh-ul-Islam

---

[67] Hüseyin Cahid Yalçın, "Meşrutiyet Hatıraları, 1908-1918," *Fikir Hareketleri*, 6 (April 25-October 17, 1936), p.326; "İttihad ve Terakki Fırkası, *Yeni İkdam*, April 11, 1327/April 24, 1911, p.2; "Turkish Politics: A New Party Programme," *The Times*, April 24, 1911, p.5; "The Parliamentary Situation," *The Levant Herald and Eastern Express*, April 24, 1911, p.1; and, Edwin Pears, "Developments in Turkey," pp.15-16. See also, Yusuf Hikmet Bayur, *Türk İnkılâbı Tarihi, 2/1*, p.57.

[68] "Konservativ und liberal," *Osmanischer Lloyd*, April 30, 1911, p.1. The same article also appeared in *Yeni İkdam* (Abdülaziz Mecdi [Tolon], "Tenvir-i Hakikat," *Yeni İkdam*, April 16, 1327/April 29, 1911, p.2). For favourable comments on Abdülaziz Mecdi [Tolon]'s views see, "Hizb-i Cedid ve Tenvir-i Hakikat," *Yeni İkdam*, April 16, 1327/April 29, 1911," p.1). See also, "Mecdi Efendi ile bir Mülâkat," *Yeni İkdam*, April 16, 1327/April 29, 1911, p.2.

[69] "Hüseyin Cahid [Yalçın], "Muhafazakârlık, Liberallik," *Tanin*, April 17, 1327/April 30, 1911, p.1. See also, Hüseyin Cahid Yalçın, "Meşrutiyet Hatıraları, 1908-1918," *Fikir Hareketleri*, 6 (April 25-October 17, 1936), p.341.

and the Ministers for Foreign Affairs, of Finance, and of Education. There was little doubt about the truth of the pressure of the dissidents for the resignation of these Ministers, though it was anticipated that the Ministers in question would await the passing of the Budget of the Ministry of Finance before taking any step. Nothing was definitely known as to their possible successors, although there seemed to be consensus of opinion that Reşid Pasha, the Turkish Ambassador in Vienna, was likely to succeed Rıfat Pasha, and that Rasim Pasha would become Minister of the Navy, replacing Mahmud Muhtar Bey.[70]

Despite the joyous mood in the monarchist camp for their relative success at the April 22 meeting of the party, according to information received from trusted Unionist sources within the military, it had become apparent that Colonel Sadık Bey's influence among the officers was negligible. Once this fact was established, Hakkı Pasha and the Unionist members of his cabinet expressed the opinion that Colonel Sadık Bey be dealt with swiftly. There was agreement among the ministers that he should immediately be discharged from the army.[71] Cavid Bey was determined to crush the conspiracy by sending Colonel Sadık Bey before the Court Martial; the headquarters at Salonica was also insistent upon Colonel Sadık Bey's arrest.[72] Among the cabinet members, only Mahmud Şevket Pasha, the Minister of War, was reluctant to take this measure, although he was told by the Grand Vezier that Colonel Sadık Bey's continued presence within the ranks of the army posed a dangerous threat to the stability of the constitutional regime.[73]

---

[70] Hüseyin Cahid [Yalçın], "İtilâf?" *Tanin*, April 11, 1327/April 24, 1911, p.1; and, "Turkish Politics: Comment on the New Programme," *The Times*, April 25, 1911, p.3.

[71] Mehmed Cavid, "Meşrutiyet Devrine Ait Cavit Bey'in Hatıraları: 32," *Tanin*, September 30, 1943, p.2; Ziya Şakir [Soko], "Hürriyet ve İtilâf Nasıl Doğdu? Nasıl Yaşadı? Nasıl Battı? 20: İstanbul'da Yine Epeyce Şayialar Dolaşıyordu," *Tan*, November 21, 1937, p.9; and, Edwin Pears, *Forty Years in Constantinople: The Recollections of Sir Edwin Pears, 1873-1915*, p.307.

[72] Edwin Pears, "Developments in Turkey," p.13; and, Glen Wilfred Swanson, Mahmud Şevket Paşa and the Defense of the Ottoman Empire, p.88.

[73] Mehmed Cavid, "Meşrutiyet Devrine Ait Cavit Bey'in Hatıraları: 32," *Tanin*, September 30, 1943, p.2; Ziya Şakir [Soko], "Hürriyet ve İtilâf Nasıl Doğdu? Nasıl Yaşadı? Nasıl Battı? 21: Mahmut Şevket Paşa ile Talât Bey Karşı Karşıya," *Tan*, November 22, 1937, p.9; and, Edwin Pears, *Forty Years in Constantinople:*

Unsuccessful in their attempts to convince Mahmud Şevket
Pasha of the necessity of Colonel Sadık Bey's discharge from
the army, or, at least, his exile from İstanbul with a commission to either Salonica or İzmir, the Unionist ministers agreed
to jointly resign. Agreeing with most of the points the Unionist ministers made, Hakkı Pasha, nevertheless, told them that
he would try, one more time, to reason with Mahmud Şevket
Pasha.[74] The same day, on April 26, the cabinet received a vote
of confidence by a substantial majority of one hundred and
forty-five to forty-five.[75]

Armed with a strong support behind him in the Chamber,
Hakkı Pasha informed the Sultan that unless Mahmud Şevket
Pasha promptly dealt with Colonel Sadık Bey, he would hand
in the cabinet's resignation. Upon this move, the Sultan sent
an urgent message to Mahmud Şevket Pasha, telling him to
dismiss Colonel Sadık Bey.[76] This produced the desired result,
and on May 1, Mahmud Şevket Pasha finally signed the
papers for Colonel Sadık Bey's exile from İstanbul to Salonica.[77] According to the May 5 issue of the Viennese newspaper
Neue Freie Presse, Colonel Sadık Bey was expected to leave
İstanbul within a week.[78] This was certainly a blow to
Mahmud Şevket Pasha. On his part, Colonel Sadık Bey, on his
arrival at Salonica, was met by a large number of officers, who
greeted him with every sign of enthusiasm, and escorted him

The Recollections of Sir Edwin Pears, 1873-1915, p.307.
    [74] Mehmed Cavid, "Meşrutiyet Devrine Ait Cavit Bey'in Hatıraları: 34," *Ta-nin*, October 4, 1943, p.2; and, Edwin Pears, "Developments in Turkey," p.13.
    [75] I/III/86, April 13, 1326/April 26, 1911, *Meclis-i Mebusan Zabıt Ceridesi*, 5, pp.582-584.
    [76] Edwin Pears, "Developments in Turkey," p.13; Lütfi Simavi, *Sultan Meh-med Reşad Han'ın ve Halefinin Sarayında Gördüklerim*, 1, pp.140-141; and, Meh-med Cavid, "Meşrutiyet Devrine Ait Cavit Bey'in Hatıraları: 34," *Tanin*, October 4, 1943, p.2.
    [77] "Miralay Sadık Bey," *Yeni İkdam*, April 19, 1327/May 2, 1911, p.2; A.A., Türkei 201, #A7812, Marschall to Bethmann Hollweg, Pera, May 13, 1911, quoted in Glen Wilfred Swanson, *Mahmud Şevket Paşa and the Defense of the Ottoman Empire*, p.88; Mehmed Cavid, "Meşrutiyet Devrine Ait Cavit Bey'in Hatıraları: 35," *Tanin*, October 5, 1943, p.2; and, Ziya Şakir [Soko], "Hürriyet ve İtilâf Nasıl Doğdu? Nasıl Yaşadı? Nasıl Battı? 21: Mahmut Şevket Paşa ile Talât Bey Karşı Karşıya," *Tan*, November 22, 1937, p.9. See also, "Die Kabinettskrise: Sadik Bej in Salonik," *Osmanischer Lloyd*, May 7, 1911, p.1; and, Edwin Pears, *Forty Years in Constantinople: The Recollections of Sir Edwin Pears, 1873-1915*, p.307.
    [78] *Neue Freie Presse*, May 5, 1911, quoted in "The Committee Dissensions," *The Times*, May 6, 1911, p.7.

in triumph to his quarters.[79]

The cabinet crisis, however, was not over.[80] The struggle was serious, and for a time looked very dangerous. Monarchist pressure continued unabated. After much private discussion in the Committee of Union and Progress and the cabinet, it was agreed that Cavid Bey and Babanzade İsmail Hakkı Bey, both of whom retained the highest confidence of a large section of the Committee, should resign, but the cabinet should continue in power.[81] Agence Ottomane, the official news agency, which had either denied the existence of a real split in the Committee of Union and Progress or had minimised its importance, confirmed on May 7 the news of Cavid Bey's impending resignation, adding that Babanzade İsmail Hakkı Bey, Minister of Education, had announced his intention of following his colleague's example. The successors to the retiring ministers would, Agence Ottomane said, be chosen *outside* the Committee of Union and Progress by Hakkı Pasha.[82] Thus, only a week after the agreement with the New Faction had been made public, on May 9, *Tanin*, which had been publishing rumours to that effect for some days, announced the resignations of Cavid Bey and Babanzade İsmail Hakkı Bey.[83]

---

[79] "Djavid Bey and the Cabinet: Grand Vizier in Difficulties," *The Times*, May 8, 1911, p.5.

[80] "Turkish Politics: The Committee Party," *The Times*, May 1, 1911, p.5; "Kabinenin İstifası," *Yeni İkdam*, April 19, 1327/May 2, 1911, p.1; and, Edwin Pears, "Developments in Turkey," p.13.

[81] Edwin Pears, "Developments in Turkey," p.13; "Turkish Politics: Position of Djavid Bey," *The Times*, May 5, 1911, p.5; "Rücktritt Dschavid Bejs," *Osmanischer Lloyd*, May 5, 1911, p.1; "Resignation of Djavid Bey," *The Levant Herald and Eastern Express*, May 5, 1911, p.1; "The Turkish Minister of Finance: Position of the Cabinet," *The Times*, May 6, 1911, p.7; and, "The Political Crisis," *The Levant Herald and Eastern Express*, May 6, 1911, p.1. See also, A. A. Türkei 159, No.2/102, Telegram from Marschall, May 4, 1911; A. A. Türkei 159, No.2/104, Telegram from Marschall, May 5, 1911, and A. A. Türkei 159, No.2/105, Telegram from Marschall, May 6, 1911, where Ambassador Marschall relates Cavid Bey's talk with him about his impending resignation.

[82] "Djavid Bey and the Cabinet: Grand Vizier in Difficulties," *The Times*, May 8, 1911, p.5. See also, "Kabinenin Mevkii," *Yeni İkdam*, April 25, 1327/May 8, 1911, p.1.

[83] Hüseyin Cahid [Yalçın], "Cavid ve Hakkı Beylerin İstifası," *Tanin*, April 26, 1327/May 9, 1911, p.1; "Die Krise: Die Demission Dschavid Bejs und Ismail Hakki Bejs," *Osmanischer Lloyd*, May 9, 1911, p.1; Mehmed Cavid, "Meşrutiyet Devrine Ait Cavit Bey'in Hatıraları: 36," *Tanin*, October 6, 1943, p.2; "The Turkish Dissensions: Resignations of Ministers," *The Times*, May 9, 1911, p.7; "The Political Situation," *The Levant Herald and Eastern Express*, May 9, 1911, p.1; Hüseyin Cahid [Yalçın], "İstemezük," *Tanin*, April 27, 1327/May 10, 1911, p.1; "Maarif Na-

It was believed that Sheikh-ul-Islam Musa Kâzım Efendi's resignation was only a matter of weeks. Musa Kâzım Efendi, who was himself a freemason, was under pressure because of Colonel Sadık Bey's agitation against the Masonic Lodges.[84]

A few days before these resignations, on May 3, the Unionist leadership had met with Hakkı Pasha and discussed the situation of the cabinet. They had talked about the possibility of the resignation of the whole cabinet and formation of either a Hüseyin Hilmi Pasha or a Said Pasha Cabinet, with limited Unionist participation. After lengthy deliberations, however, they had decided that Hakkı Pasha remain the Grand Vezier, as they believed that Hüseyin Hilmi Pasha would be too weak a Grand Vezier and thus might strengthen the position of Mahmud Şevket Pasha—which nobody, including the neutral Sultan, wanted—and that Said Pasha might be intimidated to leave office after a very short time. In either scenario, the Unionist ministers as well as Hakkı Pasha was afraid that Mahmud Şevket Pasha would be the single most strong person; on the other hand, leaving him out of office in a reconstituted cabinet would only mean to invite his return to power as a military dictator. In short, there was no choice except for the resignations of the Unionist ministers that the monarchists called for.[85]

Recent events had dealt a serious blow to the prestige of the Committee of Union and Progress.[86] In a May 13 telegram sent from the party headquarters in Salonica to its local party branches, the Unionist leadership tried its best to portray the

zırı," and, "Cavid Bey," *Yeni İkdam*, April 27, 1327/May 10, 1911, p.1; and, "Constantinople Letter: The Party Crisis," *The Near East*, May 17, 1911, p.23. See also, Hüseyin Cahid Yalçın, "Meşrutiyet Hatıraları, 1908-1918," *Fikir Hareketleri*, 6 (April 25-October 17, 1936), p.342; and, Yusuf Hikmet Bayur, *Türk İnkılâbı Tarihi*, 2/1, p.57. For the text of the joint letter of resignation signed by Cavid and Babanzade İsmail Hakkı Beys, see, "İstifaname Sureti," *Tanin*, April 27, 1327/May 10, 1911, p.2, and, "The Turkish Cabinet: New Minister of Finance," *The Times*, May 11, 1911, p.7. For the text of Cavid Bey's farewell letter see, "Cavid Bey'in Vedaı," *Tanin*, April 28, 1327/May 11, 1911, pp.1-2.

[84] "The Political Crisis," *The Levant Herald and Eastern Express*, May 6, 1911, p.1; "Constantinople Letter: The Party Crisis," *The Near East*, May 17, 1911, p.23; "The Committee Dissensions," *The Times*, May 6, 1911, p.7; and, "The Political Situation," *The Levant Herald and Eastern Express*, May 8, 1911, p.1.

[85] Mehmed Cavid, "Meşrutiyet Devrine Ait Cavit Bey'in Hatıraları: 36," *Tanin*, October 6, 1943, p.2.

[86] A. A. Türkei 159, No.2, Mutius to Bethmann Hollweg, Salonica, May 10, 1911. See also, Rifat Uçarol, *Gazi Ahmet Muhtar Paşa: Bir Osmanlı Paşası ve Dönemi*, pp.327-328.

situation in the most favourable of terms, stressing that there was no serious disagreement between the members of the party, that division within was more rumour than reality. The telegram nonetheless ended with a plea for unity.[87]

Many felt that Cavid Bey's forced resignation was both a distinct loss to the country and a serious blow to the Committee of Union and Progress and its ideals.[88] There were public sentiment and regret for Cavid Bey's resignation in İzmir— where *Köylü*, in particular, expressed sorrow for his departure—Beirut, and Salonica.[89] A brilliant and incisive speaker, an energetic parliamentarian, he was the most outstanding personality among the parliamentary leaders of the Committee of Union and Progress. His tenure in office was distinguished by the passage of several much needed reforms, notably the establishment of an Accountant-General's Department and the creation of an Inspectorate—moves which those corrupt provincial officials who had escaped the Ministry of Finance's 'purification' were now beginning to feel.[90]

In the May 13 editorial of *Tanin*, Hüseyin Cahid [Yalçın] wrote that the monarchists had succeeded first to force Talât Bey to resign his post; then Bedros Haladjian was forced to resign. With the forced resignations of Cavid Bey and Babanzade İsmail Hakkı Bey, the Committee of Union and Progress had lost almost all of its most prominent members in the Cabinet.[91] With regard to party affairs, the parliamentary party of

---

[87] *Tanin*, May 1, 1327/May 14, 1911, in Hüseyin Cahid Yalçın, "Meşrutiyet Hatıraları, 1908-1918," *Fikir Hareketleri*, 6 (April 25-October 17, 1936), pp.372-373.

[88] Hüseyin Cahid [Yalçın], "Kabinenin Hal ve Mevkii," *Tanin*, April 24, 1327/May 7, 1911, p.1, and, Hüseyin Cahid [Yalçın], "Cavid ve Hakkı Beylerin İstifası," April 26, 1327/May 9, 1911, p.1; "Die Krise: Dschavid Bej," *Osmanischer Lloyd*, May 10, 1911, p.1 (For a translation of this editorial see, "Cavid Bey," *Tanin*, April 28, 1327/May 11, 1911, p.1); Mehmed Cavid, "Meşrutiyet Devrine Ait Cavit Bey'in Hatıraları: 36," *Tanin*, October 6, 1943, p.2; and, "The New Minister of Finance," *The Orient*, 2/5 (May 17, 1911), p.4. See also, Hüseyin Cahid Yalçın, "Meşrutiyet Hatıraları, 1908-1918," *Fikir Hareketleri*, 6 (April 25-October 17, 1936), pp.357-358; and, A. A. Türkei 159, No.2, Copy No.112, "Parlament, Ministerkrisen und allgemeine Lage in der Türkei," Marschall, May 13, 1911.

[89] "Remaniement du Cabinet," *The Levant Herald and Eastern Express*, May 10, 1911, p.1.

[90] "Constantinople Letter: The Party Crisis," *The Near East*, May 17, 1911, p.23; and, "Turkish Politics: Victory of the Moderates," *The Times*, May 10, 1911, p.10.

[91] Hüseyin Cahid [Yalçın], "İçimizde İhtirasat Uyanıyor!" *Tanin*, April 30, 1327/May 13, 1911, p.1. See also, Hüseyin Cahid Yalçın, "Meşrutiyet Hatıraları, 1908-1918," *Fikir Hareketleri*, 6 (April 25-October 17, 1936), p.358.

the Committee of Union and Progress elected Seyyid Bey, a
moderate Unionist deputy for İzmir, as the new President,
replacing Talât Bey, who had been forced by the New Faction
to withdraw his candidacy for re-election. Seyyid Bey's election was interpreted to be the result of a compromise between
the leaders of the two groups in the party.[92]

Unsatisfied with mere resignations, the monarchists' aim
was to push for the formation of a non-party cabinet. The
Unionists opposed the idea, for if such a cabinet were to take
power, the government would once again be in the hands of
the monarchist pashas of the old regime, signalling the end of
Turkey's new constitutional regime.[93]

The Unionists, however, did succeed in naming moderate
members of their party to the vacant ministerial posts. Abdurrahman Şeref Bey was appointed the Minister of Education,
and Nail Bey, a Committee of Union and Progress senator
who had been Minister of Education in the Hilmi Pasha Cabinet, replaced Cavid Bey as Minister of Finance.[94] The Unionist leadership felt that, though he was not as brilliant as Cavid
Bey, Nail Bey was the best man both for the job as well as
Unionist interests.[95] In the second half of May, however, there
would be two more new appointments to the Cabinet which
would tip the balance against the Committee of Union and
Progress. These were the appointments of Hulusi Bey, Under-
Secretary of the Ministry of Public Works, as Minister of
Public Works on July 4, replacing Bedros Haladjian, and

[92] "Turkish Committee Party: New President Elected," *The Times*, May 15,
1911, p.7. Rumours to that effect had been printed on May 14 ("Fırka İntihabı," *Yeni İkdam*, May 1, 1327/May 14, 1911, p.2).

[93] Hüseyin Cahid Yalçın, "Meşrutiyet Hatıraları, 1908-1918," *Fikir Hareketleri*, 6 (April 25-October 17, 1936), p.358; and, A. A. Türkei 159, No.2, Copy No.112,
"Parlament, Ministerkrisen und allgemeine Lage in der Türkei," Marschall,
May 13, 1911. See also, A. A. Türkei 159, No.2, Copy No.114, Marschall, May 16,
1911, where he relates his talk with Cavid Bey about the political situation.

[94] Edwin Pears, "Developments in Turkey," p.17; "Nail Bej Finanzminister,"
Osmanischer Lloyd, May 10, 1911, p.1; "The Turkish Cabinet: New Minister of Finance," *The Times*, May 11, 1911, p.7; "The Political Situation," *The Levant Herald
and Eastern Express*, May 12, 1911, p.1; "Maliye Nezareti'nde," *Tanin*, April 29,
1327/May 12, 1911, p.2; "Empire News: The Capital," *The Orient*, 2/7 (May 31,
1911), p.6; and, Hüseyin Cahid Yalçın, "Meşrutiyet Hatıraları, 1908-1918," *Fikir
Hareketleri*, 6 (April 25-October 17, 1936), p.357.

[95] Mehmed Cavid, "Meşrutiyet Devrine Ait Cavit Bey'in Hatıraları: 38," *Tanin*, October 8, 1943, p.2; "The New Minister of Finance," *The Orient*, 2/5 (May
17, 1911), p.4; and, "Constantinople Letter: The Party Crisis," *The Near East*, May
17, 1911, p.23.

Istanbulian Efendi, Judicial Inspector, as Minister of Posts and Telegraphs on July 7.[96] What was significant was the fact that neither was a member of either the Senate or the Chamber, indicating a regression to absolutist bureaucratic control of the executive branch.[97]

Meanwhile, anti-Unionist pressure was kept up. *Tanzimat*, an organ of the monarchist opposition, having published a violent attack upon Hüseyin Cahid [Yalçın] in its May 17 issue, and *Tanin* having replied with its usual vigour on May 18, both newspapers were suppressed by order of the Court Martial, which seemingly gave further proof of impartiality by ordering the Greek *Neologos* and the Pan-Islamic *Sırat-ül-Müstakim* to suspend publication.[98] *Tanin* nonetheless continued to appear under such different names as *Cenin*, *Senin* and *Renin* between May 19 and July 27, 1911. Unable to control Mahmud Şevket Pasha and the actions of the Court Martial, it was clear that the Unionist-supported government was essentially powerless against the military.[99]

While *Tanin* was being suppressed, the monarchist press was left free to publish, on May 21, a manifesto of Colonel Sadık Bey criticising Unionist policy and asking the Unionist officers to leave politics by resigning from the party.[100] Only *Osmanischer Lloyd* commented on the true nature of the manifesto by writing that what Colonel Sadık Bey really wanted was the involvement of the military in politics—as

---

[96] "Empire News: The Capital," *The Orient*, 2/12 (July 5, 1911), p.6; "News Items," *The Levant Herald and Eastern Express*, July 5, 1911, p.1; "Policy of Conciliation," *The Times*, July 5, 1911, p.5; "News Items," *The Levant Herald and Eastern Express*, July 7, 1911, p.1; and, Hüseyin Cahid Yalçın, "Meşrutiyet Hatıraları, 1908-1918," *Fikir Hareketleri*, 6 (April 25-October 17, 1936), p.373.

[97] Hüseyin Cahid Yalçın, "Meşrutiyet Hatıraları, 1908-1918," *Fikir Hareketleri*, 6 (April 25-October 17, 1936), p.373.

[98] "Suppression of Turkish Newspaper," *The Times*, May 19, 1911, p.5. For Yalçın's reply to Lütfi Fikri Bey's editorial see, Hüseyin Cahid [Yalçın], "Ahlâksızlık," *Tanin*, May 5, 1327/May 18, 1911, pp.1-2.

[99] "The Suspension of Turkish Newspapers: Two New Journals," *The Times*, May 20, 1911, p.7; and, Hüseyin Cahid Yalçın, "Meşrutiyet Hatıraları, 1908-1918," *Fikir Hareketleri*, 6 (April 25-October 17, 1936), p.373.

[100] Sadık, "İttihad ve Terakki Umumi Kongresi," *Yeni İkdam*, May 8, 1327/May 21, 1911, p.1; "Eine Erklärung des Obersten Sadyk Bej," *Osmanischer Lloyd*, May 21, 1911, p.1; and, "Die Erklärung Sadyk Bejs," *Osmanischer Lloyd*, May 23, 1911, p.1; and, Mehmed Cavid, "Meşrutiyet Devrine Ait Cavit Bey'in Hatıraları: 41," *Tanin*, October 11, 1943, p.2. See also, Feroz Ahmad, *The Young Turks: The Committee of Union and Progress in Turkish Politics, 1908-1914*, pp.90-91.

long as it corresponded to *his* political views.[101] In addition, monarchist *Yeni İkdam* published a letter from Colonel Sadık Bey, in which he demanded his return from Salonica to İstanbul.[102]

Following Colonel Sadık Bey's manifesto, Mahmud Şevket Pasha issued a declaration on May 24, addressing all military officers. Conceding the fact that during the events leading up to the Revolution of 1908 the military was heavily involved in politics, Mahmud Şevket Pasha justified it on grounds of necessity. According to him, as the Revolution had succeeded and the constitutional regime established, there was no justification for the continued involvement of the officers in politics. He ended his declaration with the threat that he would punish all officers who continued to involve themselves in politics.[103]

By May 29, Colonel Sadık Bey was forced to resign and placed on the retired list.[104] He immediately returned from Salonica to İstanbul, where one of Mahmud Şevket Pasha's Aides-de-Camp and many of the principal officers of the Ministry of War came to welcome him on his arrival on May 29.[105] In sharp contrast to ex-Colonel Sadık Bey's reception, the fact that the officers of the local garrison had taken no part in greeting Talât Bey on his visit to Salonica was interpreted as proof that military sympathies in general were on the side of the monarchist dissidents. The belief that this was the case would have encouraged the latter to disregard the menaces of the violent Unionist organs published in Salonica and other

---

[101] *Osmanischer Lloyd*, May 22, 1911, cited in Mehmed Cavid, "Meşrutiyet Devrine Ait Cavit Bey'in Hatıraları: 41," *Tanin*, October 11, 1943, p.2. See also, "Eine Erklärung des Obersten Sadyk Bej," *Osmanischer Lloyd*, May 21, 1911, p.1; and, "Die Erklärung Sadyk Bejs," *Osmanischer Lloyd*, May 23, 1911, p.1.

[102] *Yeni İkdam*, May 11, 1327/May 24, 1911, cited in "Informations," *The Levant Herald and Eastern Express*, May 24, 1911, p.2.

[103] Mahmud Şevket, "Harbiye Nezareti'nden," *Yeni İkdam*, May 11, 1327/May 24, 1911, p.; "The Turkish Army and Politics," *The Times*, May 25, 1911, p.7; Mehmed Cavid, "Meşrutiyet Devrine Ait Cavit Bey'in Hatıraları: 41," *Tanin*, October 11, 1943, p.2; and, Yusuf Hikmet Bayur, *Türk İnkılâbı Tarihi, 2/1*, pp.57-58. See also, Hüseyin Cahid [Yalçın], "Ordu ve Siyasiyat," *Senin*, May 12, 1327/May 25, 1911, p.1.

[104] "News Items," *The Levant Herald and Eastern Express*, May 29, 1911, p.1; "Sadyk Bej," *Osmanischer Lloyd*, June 7, 1911, p.1; and, Glen Wilfred Swanson, Mahmud Şevket Paşa and the Defense of the Ottoman Empire, p.89.

[105] "News Items," *The Levant Herald and Eastern Express*, May 30, 1911, p.1; and, "Turkish Politics: The Army and the Committee," *The Times*, June 2, 1911, p.5.

Macedonian towns, had not one of the bitterest of these newspapers exposed the hollowness of their threats by opening its
columns to a list of names of persons ready to march on
İstanbul and destroy the forces of reaction.[106]

Now a private citizen, ex-Colonel Sadık Bey, however, continued his political activities in İstanbul. Although his subversive activities were geared towards inciting a military unrest with the aim of instituting a monarchist government in
place of a constitutional one, the martial law authorities did
nothing. On its part, the cabinet could not even expel him out
of the capital for fear of opposition from military circles.[107]

The final session of the Chamber of Deputies was particularly sensational. The Senate refused to approve certain articles which the Chamber had appended to the Budget Law for
the year 1911. The articles in question proposed that the
government increase the deductions for pension from the
salaries of the civilian employees from five percent to seven
and a half percent, and slash military pensions by twenty to
twenty-five percent, depending on the beneficiary's seniority.
The Senate maintained that such amendments in pension
law could not singly be 'tacked on' to a money bill. In spite of
the Minister of War's eloquent appeal on his officers' behalf,
the Chamber refused to alter its decision, stating that the
articles in question were an integral part of a larger financial
measure. Finally, the amendments were approved in the
Chamber of Deputies by the Unionist majority. The Senate,
however, proved intransigent, and for eighteen hours both
groups battled it, but to no avail. Daybreak finally ended the
Parliament's third session, the Senate remaining in opposition
to the amendments.[108]

Most felt that the Cabinet would postpone its decision on the
pension issue until Parliament's next session. This ending of
the session in a deadlock created an unsatisfactory impres-

[106] "Turkish Politics: The Army and the Committee," *The Times,* June 2, 1911,
p.5.
[107] Mehmed Cavid, "Meşrutiyet Devrine Ait Cavit Bey'in Hatıraları: 42," *Tanin,* October 12, 1943, p.2.
[108] I/III/75, May 21, 1327/June 3, 1911, *Meclis-i Âyan Zabıt Ceridesi, 3,* pp.472-
499; "Die letzte Kammersitzung," *Osmanischer Lloyd,* June 4, 1911, p.1; "Constantinople Letter," *The Near East,* June 14, 1911, p.119; and, "The Turkish Parliament:
Untoward Close of the Session," *The Times,* June 5, 1911, p.5.

sion, which was heightened by a tardy realisation of the fact that the deficit in the Budget, if exaggerated by opposition deputies, was nevertheless dangerously large. Mahmud Şevket Pasha's failure—his first—to obtain a credit from the Chamber was also much commented upon in parliamentary circles.[109] Public opinion was largely indifferent to the positions taken in the Chamber and in the Senate, save in military circles, where most attacked the Chamber and praised the largely conservative and monarchist Senate.[110] The press was divided on the subject of the conflict between the Senate and the Chamber, monarchist newspapers adopting the contention of the Senate that the Chamber, in voting the addition to the Budget Law of the articles relating to pensions for civilian and military functionaries, was guilty of tacking, while the liberal press followed the majority of the deputies in maintaining that these articles were an integral part of the financial law in question.[111]

Coinciding with the Sultan's state visit to the Albanian provinces in June, civilian members of the Committee of Union and Progress demonstrated throughout Macedonia, hoping to rally enough support to carry the party congress which was to be held in Salonica in late September.[112] Meanwhile, the

---

[109] "The Turkish Parliament: Untoward Close of the Session," *The Times*, June 5, 1911, p.5.

[110] "Constantinople Letter," *The Near East*, June 14, 1911, p.119.

[111] "Mebusan ve Âyan Arasındaki İhtilâf," *Yeni İkdam*, May 23, 1327/June 5, 1911, p.1; "The Parliamentary Conflict in Turkey: An Accusation of 'Tacking'," *The Times*, June 7, 1911, p.5.

[112] "Constantinople Letter," *The Near East*, June 28, 1911, p.167. See also, "Padişahımızın Seyahati," *Yeni İkdam*, May 24, 1327/June 6, 1911, p.1; "The Imperial Visit to Salonika: The Sultan's Departure," *The Times*, June 6, 1911, p.5; "The Sultan's Tour," *The Times*, June 8, 1911, p.5; "Die Reise des Sultans," *Osmanischer Lloyd*, June 8, 1911, p.1; "The Sultan's Tour: Reception at Salonika," *The Times*, June 9, 1911, p.5; "Die Reise des Sultans: Die Beleuchtung von Salonik," *Osmanischer Lloyd*, June 9, 1911, p.1; "Die Reise des Sultans," *Osmanischer Lloyd*, June 10, 1911, p.1; "Die Reise des Sultans," *Osmanischer Lloyd*, June 11, 1911, p.1; "The Sultan's Tour," *The Times*, June 12, 1911, p.5; "The Sultan's Tour: Loyal Welcome at Uskub," *The Times*, June 13, 1911, p.5; "Die Reise des Sultans," *Osmanischer Lloyd*, June 13, 1911, p.1; "The Sultan at Uskub," *The Times*, June 14, 1911, p.7; "Die Reise des Sultans," *Osmanischer Lloyd*, June 14, 1911, p.1; "Die Reise des Sultans," *Osmanischer Lloyd*, June 15, 1911, p.1; "Die Reise des Sultans," *Osmanischer Lloyd*, June 16, 1911, p.1; "Die Reise des Sultans," *Osmanischer Lloyd*, June 17, 1911, p.1; "Die Reise des Sultans," *Osmanischer Lloyd*, June 18, 1911, p.1; "The Sultan at Kossovo: An Amnesty for Rebels," *The Times*, June 19, 1911, p.29; "Die Reise des Sultans," *Osmanischer Lloyd*, June 20, 1911, p.1; "Die Reise des Sultans," *Osmanischer Lloyd*, June 21, 1911, p.1; "Die Reise des Sultans," *Osmanischer*

conservative clique in the party, led by ex-Colonel Sadık Bey, worked hard in Edirne and İstanbul in the hopes of garnering considerable Arab and Albanian support.[113] By August, however, it was certain that the leadership of the Committee of Union and Progress would both disavow and expel ex-Colonel Sadık Bey and his supporters at the upcoming Congress.[114]

By the beginning of July, rumours for a monarchist take-over of government had become rife.[115] Monarchist offensive against the Committee of Union and Progress started with articles in monarchist newspapers calculated to discredit Unionists in the public eye. In its July 4 issue, the monarchist *Şahrah* reproduced the translation of a long article from the well-known Arab divine Sheikh Rashid Rida, of Cairo, which had been recently published by *al-Manar*, an Arabic monthly review devoted to political, religious, and philosophical questions. In the article, which dealt with the causes of the recent split in the Committee of Union and Progress, Sheikh Rashid Rida claimed to have made the acquaintance of the great majority of the senators and deputies of all parties and of many of the leading monarchist statesmen, soldiers, and authors. Ascribing the split in the party to a variety of causes, he claimed that, in the first place, the Unionists had grown unpopular through their interference in all the departments of state. Unionist supporters in the cabinet, the central bureaucracy, and the military were numerous and well organised, and the rules of its party discipline extended even to cabinet ministers who had taken the oath of allegiance to it. In a provocative tone, he alleged that the entire control of the parliamentary party of the Committee of Union and Progress had fallen into the hands of Talât Bey, Cavid Bey, Halil [Menteşe], and Rahmi [Aslan], with Hüseyin Cahid [Yalçın] and Babanzade İsmail Hakkı Bey in the second line. The decisions of a two-

---

Lloyd, June 23, 1911, p.1; "Die Reise des Sultans," *Osmanischer Lloyd*, June 24, 1911, p.1; "Die Sultansreise," *Osmanischer Lloyd*, June 25, 1911, p.1; "The Sultan's Tour: Return from Macedonia," *The Times*, June 26, 1911, p.5; "Die Rückkehr des Sultans," *Osmanischer Lloyd*, June 27, 1911, p.1; and, "Return of the Sultan: An Enthusiastic Reception," *The Times*, June 27, 1911, p.5.

[113] "Constantinople Letter," *The Near East*, June 28, 1911, p.167.

[114] "Constantinople Letter," *The Near East*, August 16, 1911, p.339.

[115] "The Sins of 'Young Turkey'," *The Times*, July 7, 1911, p.5. See also, Yusuf Hikmet Bayur, *Türk İnkılâbı Tarihi*, 2/1, p.56.

thirds majority being binding on the party, the vote of forty members out of a quorum of sixty might carry the day against what he alleged the opposition of the silent majority, and the Unionist leadership was the more certain of success owing to the general belief that it enjoyed the support of Salonica.[116]

Political freemasonry, said Sheikh Rashid Rida, was another cause of the split. He alleged that all the most important members of the Committee of Union and Progress were freemasons, and great efforts were made to induce those members of the cabinet who were not already members to join the lodges. In an attempt to gather political support from the religious conservatives, Ṣahrah article claimed that the object of freemasonry was the separation of the Caliphate from the Sultanate, and the gradual elimination of the shari'a, but its aims were complicated by the presence in the lodges of strong Jewish influences, working in favour of Zionism and also for the exploitation by Jewish capitalists of the Ottoman provinces of Syria and Palestine. Sheikh Rashid Rida wrote that the inner ring of the Committee of Union and Progress also aimed at the turkification of the Empire and the substitution of the Turkish for the Arabic language in certain Asiatic provinces and also as the religious language of the Empire. He concluded his article by ascribing the temporary success of the insurrection within the Committee of Union and Progress to the determined opposition of Colonel Sadık Bey to the Unionist leadership.[117]

Coinciding with the Ṣahrah article, in its July 4 issue, Tanzimat, now appearing under the name of Matbuat, published an interview Lütfi Fikri Bey, its editor, had conducted with Kâmil Pasha. Strongly critical of the Unionists and their domestic policies, Kâmil Pasha answered a question with respect to the situation in Yemen and Albania by saying that he was in favour of decentralisation—which meant giving autonomy, possibly independence, to these nations.[118] Hüseyin Cahid

[116] Ṣahrah, June 21, 1327/July 4, 1911, excerpted in "An Arab on the Internal Situation," The Times, July 12, 1911, p.5.

[117] Ṣahrah, June 21, 1327/July 4, 1911, excerpted in "An Arab on the Internal Situation," The Times, July 12, 1911, p.5.

[118] Matbuat, June 21, 1327/July 4, 1911, quoted in "Déclarations de Kiamil pacha," The Levant Herald and Eastern Express, July 5, 1911, p.1.

[Yalçın] defended Unionist policy in *Tanin*—then appearing under the name of *Renin*; despite this, Kâmil Pasha reiterated his views in a further interview with Lütfi Fikri Bey.[119]

The July 6 issue of *Neue Freie Presse* printed an uncon-firmed report that the aged monarchist Kâmil Pasha was to su-persede Hakkı Pasha as Grand Vezier in order to make peace with the Albanians, who had, once again, revolted in April of 1911 and still continued to resist Turkish military forces.[120] The July 9 issue of the monarchist *Yeni Gazete*—which venti-lated Kâmil Pasha's views on political affairs—urged the gov-ernment to settle the Albanian question once for all by the adoption of a policy of conciliation, and condemned the sys-tem of bargaining with the rebels, to the accompaniment of successive prolongations of the amnesty, as injurious to Turk-ish prestige.[121]

In the first week of July, Nâzım Pasha, who had earlier ap-proached the Unionist leadership with the hopes of gaining political power by the backing of the Committee of Union and Progress, entered into further negotiations for either his Grand Veziership or his Ministry of War. A political opportunist, the monarchist Nâzım Pasha had in mind to exploit the existing differences of opinion between Mahmud Şevket Pasha and the Unionist leadership. Unionists promised nothing, though they told Nâzım Pasha that they had no hard feelings against him.[122]

From Paris, Şerif Pasha and his Parti Radical Ottoman also worked to undermine the Unionist dominated coalition gov-ernment. In a letter sent to *The Near East*, he accused the Committee of Union and Progress in the strongest of terms of being insincere in its belief in liberal democratic principles. Attempting to win the military's support, he attributed the ills of the existing situation to the Committee's hold over the mil-

---

[119] This interview is published in "An Ex-Prime Minister on Turkish Policy," *The Near East*, August 9, 1911, p.316.
[120] *Neue Freie Presse*, July 6, 1911, quoted in "The Sins of 'Young Turkey'," *The Times*, July 7, 1911, p.5, and in "Kâmil Paşa ve Nouradunghian Efendi," *Yeni İkdam*, June 26, 1327/July 9, 1911, p.3.
[121] *Yeni Gazete*, June 26, 1327/July 9, 1911, quoted in "A Mixed Commission to be Sent," *The Times*, July 10, 1911, p.5.
[122] Mehmed Cavid, "Meşrutiyet Devrine Ait Cavit Bey'in Hatıraları: 43," *Tanin*, October 13, 1943, p.2.

itary and its ability to order military operations, stating that
certain commanders took their orders directly from the leadership of the Committee of Union and Progress. Finally, not-
ing that Great Britain had lent its support to the Kâmil Pasha
Cabinet, Şerif Pasha wrote that when the time came to topple
the constitutional regime, he hoped Great Britain would not
deny the monarchists the same help.[123]

On the night of July 10, Zeki Bey, a chief secretary in the Public Debt Administration, was shot dead while returning to his
house in Bakırköy. Zeki Bey, who had been arrested after the
coup attempt of April 13, 1909, but had been acquitted by the
Court Martial, was a clever and hard-hitting monarchist journalist, who had helped at the time of the split in the Committee of Union and Progress to found *Şahrah*, an extremely
monarchist newspaper which, despite sundry changes of
name consequent upon suppressions by the Court Martial, had
not lost an opportunity of attacking the Unionist leadership in
the most vigorous terms. It was suspected that Zeki Bey's murder was committed by extremists, who supposed that he had
entered into negotiations with Colonel Sadık Bey with the object of joining his party. This hypothesis was strengthened by
the arrest of Nâzım Bey, brother of Derviş Bey, Unionist deputy for Serres.[124] A perquisition at the house of a relative of
Nâzım Bey resulted in the discovery of documents which, it
was believed, would throw considerable light on the crime. It
appeared that Zeki Bey had incurred the ire of the Unionists
not only by entering into negotiations with ex-Colonel Sadık
Bey, but by publishing a translation of an article in the Egyptian review *al-Manar* which drew attention to the revolution-

[123] Şerif Pasha, "Turkey and Great Britain," *The Near East*, July 12, 1911, p.221.
[124] "Mystérieux assassinat," *The Levant Herald and Eastern Express*, July 12,
1911, p.1; "Political Murder in Turkey: Two Arrests," *The Times*, July 12, 1911, p.5.
Derviş Bey, who was summoned to appear before the Prosecutor General's Office in
connection with the murder of Zeki Bey, was believed to have fled to Bulgaria
("The Macrikeui Murder," *The Levant Herald and Eastern Express*, July 13, 1911,
p.1; and, "The Difficulties of Turkey: The Murder of Zeki Bey," *The Times*, July 15,
1911, p.5). See also, Ziya Şakir [Soko], "Hürriyet ve İtilâf Nasıl Doğdu? Nasıl Yaşadı? Nasıl Battı? 43: İtilâfçılar Etrafa Cazip Tekliflerde Bulunuyorlar," *Tan*, December 21, 1937, p.9; Yusuf Hikmet Bayur, *Türk İnkılâbı Tarihi*, 2/1, p.58; and, "The
Murder of Zeki Bey: Sentence on the Prisoners," *The Times*, May 27, 1912, p.3.

ary political activity of the Young Turk Masonic Lodges.[125] By July 12, three persons—Nâzım Bey, Ahmed Agha, and Ferid Bey, all of Serres—had been arrested for Zeki Bey's murder. After some unconvincing explanations, they had made admissions of the most damaging character, and were later identified by eyewitnesses of the murder.[126] A preliminary inquiry on August 25 resulted in the committal for trial of Ahmed Agha and Nâzım Bey, the former on a charge of murder, the latter as an accomplice.[127]

The murder appeared to be as stupid as it was criminal. Though the victim was a man of considerable influence and an active supporter of ex-Colonel Sadık Bey, the advantage of eliminating him would hardly have seemed to men in their senses commensurate with the disadvantage of directing foreign attention to the Unionist methods at so critical a moment in Turkish affairs, a moment, moreover, when the Committee of Union and Progress was struggling desperately against the conservative and monarchist forces that had for some months past been getting organised and growing in strength. The fall of Cavid Bey, Minister of Finance, despite the Unionist efforts to maintain him in office, was the first serious sign that things in Turkey were deteriorating. Although the crime appeared to have no direct connection with the insurrection in Albania— save in so far as the victim was a personal friend of the monarchist Albanian deputy İsmail Kemal Bey, who now had been actively working for the success of the Albanian revolt, and that Şahrah had advocated the granting of autonomy to Albania—it was supposed that public disapproval of the murder might strengthen the hands of those monarchist politicians like Kâmil Pasha who desired to give Albanian rebels extensive concessions, which, in effect, amounted to recognising their independence.[128]

---

[125] "The Murder of Zeki Bey: Responsibility for the Crime," *The Times*, July 14, 1911, p.5. See also, Ziya Şakir [Soko], "Hürriyet ve İtilâf Nasıl Doğdu? Nasıl Yaşadı? Nasıl Battı? 43: İtilâfçılar Etrafa Cazip Tekliflerde Bulunuyorlar," *Tan*, December 21, 1937, p.9.

[126] "The Murder of Zeki Bey: A Third Arrest," *The Times*, July 13, 1911, p.5; and, "Mystérieux assassinat," *The Levant Herald and Eastern Express*, July 13, 1911, p.2.

[127] "The Murder of Zeki Bey," *The Times*, August 26, 1911, p.3.

[128] "The Salonika Committee and the Crime," *The Times*, July 13, 1911, p.5.

Lütfi Fikri Bey, deputy for Dersim and editor of *Tanzimat*—
the official organ of the monarchist Moderate Liberals now
appearing under the name of *Merih*—bade farewell to his
readers in the July 13 issue, "until the revolver ceased to be an
instrument of discussion," in a leading article in which he
roundly accused the Unionists of having planned Zeki Bey's
murder.[129]

By mid-July, news of ex-Colonel Sadık Bey's efforts of reorganising the monarchist opposition by accomplishing the
secession of a number of deputies from the Committee of
Union and Progress became rife. The July 18 issue of the
monarchist newspaper *Yeni Gazete* wrote that, at the beginning of the upcoming parliamentary session, several deputies
belonging to the Committee of Union and Progress would
resign to join the Ottoman Union, the party to be formed by
ex-Colonel Sadık Bey.[130] By the end of the month, ex-Colonel
Sadık Bey applied to the authorities to establish a political
journal, *Misak*, as Ottoman Union's official organ.[131] By mid-
September, the preparations for the new party were almost
complete. *Alemdar* of September 14 announced that it would
print the party's programme after the establishment of the
Ottoman Union.[132]

Although rumours, both of an impending cabinet change and
of the convocation of an extraordinary session of Parliament to
which the Albanian policy of the Hakkı Pasha Cabinet was to
be submitted, were current at the end of July, they were
denied by the organs of the Committee of Union and Progress.[133] It was generally believed that there would be no
changes in the cabinet until after the Unionist congress was

[129] "The Murder of Zeki Bey: Responsibility for the Crime," *The Times*, July 14, 1911, p.5; and, "Lütfi Fikri Bey," *Yeni İkdam*, July 2, 1327/July 15, 1911, p.3.
[130] *Yeni Gazete*, July 5, 1327/July 18, 1911, quoted in "News Items," *The Levant Herald and Eastern Express*, July 18, 1911, p.1; and, "Empire News: The Capital," *The Orient*, 2/15 (July 26, 1911), p.6. See also, "Sadık Bey'in Beyanatı," *Yeni İkdam*, July 14, 1327/July 27, 1911, p.3.
[131] "Un nouveau journal," *The Levant Herald and Eastern Express*, July 24, 1911, p.2.
[132] *Alemdar*, September 1, 1327/September 14, 1911, quoted in "Le parti de Sadik bey," *The Levant Herald and Eastern Express*, September 14, 1911, p.2.
133 "Kabinenin Mevkii," *Renin*, July 13, 1327/July 26, 1911, p.1; and, Hüseyin Cahid [Yalçın], "Buhran-ı Vükelâ," *Tanin*, July 16, 1327/July 29, 1911, p.1

held at Salonica in late September. At the congress, the demands of the New Faction would be discussed, and the party would consider the position of ex-Colonel Sadık Bey, who continued to work on behalf of the monarchists and had obtained definite promises of support from between forty and fifty nominally Unionist deputies.[134]

The situation of the cabinet remained a difficult one. It had been fatally handicapped since its reconstruction by a legacy Albanian, Arab, and Macedonian troubles, and the thinly-veiled hostility of the monarchist opposition and the non-Turkish communities. To the discontented elements—Albanian, Arab, Greek, and Bulgarian—must now be added the Armenians of the powerful Armenian Revolutionary Federation, whose organ, *Azadamard*, had started publishing vigorous attacks on the internal policy of the Hakkı Pasha Cabinet, which it compared to that of the Hamidian regime. Annoyance at the shelving of the Chester railway scheme, the revival of attacks on the Armenians of Muş, Bitlis, and Van by Kurdish *beys*, and the loss by the Armenians of the Ministry of Public Works—for which the appointment of Istanbulian Efendi to be Minister of Posts and Telegraphs was regarded as a poor consolation—explained this change of attitude on the part of the best organised political group in Turkey.[135]

The attitude of Muslim İstanbul had also to be taken into account. To the ill-feeling caused by such incidents as the murder of Zeki Bey, and by some misguided attempts which had been made by part of the press to explain away this stupid crime, must be added the discontent engendered by economic causes, notably by the general increase in rents and in the price of food and charcoal which had been a marked feature of the past two years. The latest fires, which had destroyed whole quarters and rendered scores of thousands of people homeless, were not calculated to improve the situation. Rumours of the return of 'elder statesmen,' *i.e.*, Kâmil and Said Pashas, had become rife. However, it was certain that neither

---

[134] "The Internal Situation in Turkey: Widespread Discontent," *The Times*, August 2, 1911, p.3. See also, "Seyyid Bey'in Beyanatı," *Yeni İkdam*, Juky 30, 1327/August 12, 1911, p.2.

[135] "The Internal Situation in Turkey: Widespread Discontent: Armenian Grievances," *The Times*, August 2, 1911, p.3.

Kâmil Pasha nor Hüseyin Hilmi Pasha, nor Ferid Pasha
would accept office without ample guarantees that the Unionists would adopt and enforce a policy of 'hands off' in matters
of internal administration.[136]

On August 9, newspapers announced the appointment of
Rıfat Pasha, Minister for Foreign Affairs, to be Turkish Ambassador to France.[137] The August 12 issue of *Tanin*, commenting on the appointment of Rıfat Pasha as Ambassador in
Paris, hinted that the time of Hakkı Pasha's resignation was
approaching. The cabinet, according to *Tanin*, had outlived its
utility after the resignation of Talât and Cavid Beys, and other
Unionist ministers. Already, a large number of Unionists objected to Hakkı Pasha, whose Cabinet was described by *Tanin*
as a "patchwork cloak retaining few vestiges of its original
Unionist colour."[138] In an interview with *The Near East*, Halil
Halid Bey, a Unionist sympathiser living in England, also
criticised the cabinet, saying that such men as Hakkı Pasha
and Rıfat Pasha, the Minister for Foreign Affairs, men who
had both served the old monarchist regime until the end,
were to be blamed for the diminution, since the early days of
the Revolution, of the new regime's popularity among the European public opinion.[139]

The announcement of Rıfat Pasha's resignation of the Foreign Ministry, the approaching return of Cavid Bey from Kurdistan, and the absence of Halil [Menteşe] from the Sublime
Porte gave rise to rumours of the impending fall of the cabinet,
which was naturally desired by the leadership of the Committee of Union and Progress who wished to see Hakkı Pasha resign before the Unionist congress at Salonica in late September. His resignation would strengthen the demand of the party leadership for an entirely Unionist cabinet, but it was re-

---

[136] "The Internal Situation in Turkey: Widespread Discontent," *The Times*,
August 2, 1911, p.3.
    [137] "Paris Sefareti," *Tanin*, July 27, 1327/ August 9, 1911, p.1; and, "News:
Turkish Ambassador to France," *The Times*, August 10, 1911, p.3.
    [138] "Kabinenin Rengi," *Tanin*, July 30, 1327/August 12, 1911, p.1. For com-
ments on this unsigned editorial see, "Constantinople Letter," *The Near East*, Au-
gust 30, 1911, p.387, and, "Turkish Politics: The Committee and the Cabinet," *The
Times*, August 14, 1911, p.3. See also a further unsigned editorial, "Biraz Daha
İzah," *Tanin*, August 1, 1327/August 14, 1911, p.1.
    [139] Halil Halid Bey's interview is published in "Young Turkey and the En-
glish Press," *The Near East*, August 23, 1911, p.369.

alised that there were difficulties in the way of any scheme that would involve the 'disembarking' of the Grand Vezier during the parliamentary vacation.[140]

Throughout late August, the Turkish press continued to speculate about Hakkı Pasha's resignation and the formation of a Kâmil or Said Pasha Cabinet, all of which would theoretically take place during the first weeks of the Parliament's fourth session in mid-October. Some Unionists hinted that Said Pasha's Cabinet would be transitory, that the Unionists would take advantage of the dispute between the Senate and the Chamber to bring about the dissolution of the Parliament, and that a thoroughly Unionist Cabinet would be placed in power after the Unionist triumph in the general elections.[141]

During late August, Unionist financial policy came once again in direct conflict with the Budget of the Ministry of War. The cabinet was engaged in the discussion of the divergence of opinion which had arisen between Mahmud Şevket Pasha, Minister of War, and Nail Bey, Unionist Minister of Finance, on the subject of the Army Budget for 1912-1913. Nail Bey, who had consistently opposed the tendency prevalent in almost all the Ministries to submit inflated estimates of expenditure at the beginning of each financial year and to ask the Chamber for credits which could not be expended during its course, desired to reduce the Army Estimates from nine million liras to eight million. The Minister of War did not accept the proposal.[142]

Tanin of August 28 asserted that Mahmud Şevket Pasha's refusal to submit the Ministry of War accounts to the direct control of the Accountant General's Department of the Ministry of Finance was the direct the cause of Nail Bey's unwillingness to grant the nine million liras Mahmud Şevket Pasha desired. *Tanin* wrote that however great his confidence in the

---

[140] "The Turkish Ministry," *The Times*, August 25, 1911, p.3.

[141] "Kâmil Paşa'nın Beyanatı," *Yeni İkdam*, July 14, 1327/July 27, 1911, pp.2-3; "Kabinede Tebeddülat," *Yeni İkdam*, July 31, 1327/August 13, 1911, p.2; "Constantinople Letter," *The Near East*, August 16, 1911, p.339; "Kabinenin Mevkii," *Yeni İkdam*, August 9, 1327/August 22, 1911, p.1; and, "Kabinenin Mevkii," *Yeni İkdam*, August 13, 1327/August 26, 1911, p.1.

[142] "Kabinenin Mevkii: Yine Buhran-ı Vükelâ Şayiaları," *Yeni İkdam*, August 15, 1327/August 28, 1911, p.1; and, "Turkish Ministerial Differences: Mahmud Şevket Pasha and Nail Bey," *The Times*, August 29, 1911, p.3.

integrity and patriotism of the Minister of War, no Minister of
Finance would accept an indefinite prolongation of this anom-
alous state of affairs, adding that if Şevket Pasha insisted on its
maintenance, he would find himself unable either to form or
to enter a new cabinet.[143] *Tanin*'s criticisms of Mahmud Şevket Pasha caused considerable comment: they were regarded
as an indication of the hostility of the Unionist leadership.
There was, indeed, no doubt that the Unionist leadership had
taken advantage of the ministerial differences arising on the
Budget question with the object of forcing a cabinet crisis, and,
incidentally, of weakening the position of Mahmud Şevket
Pasha.[144]

The August 29 issue of the conservative daily *Sabah* published an account of a conversation between its editor and
Mahmud Şevket Pasha, who declared that his difference of
opinion with Nail Bey had no reference to the question of the
Army Accounts, but was caused solely by the latter's desire to
reduce the Army Budget.[145] On his part, Nail Bey declared his
determination to resign if the Minister of War insisted on the
increase of the Army Budget. Allegedly, Nail Bey was
supported by Hakkı Pasha.[146] Military feeling, on the whole,
favoured Mahmud Şevket Pasha, who was visited by a deputation of officers. They expressed regret at the criticisms of the
general's policy, and promised him unswerving support.[147]
Although in limited circulation, rumours had been spread by
the monarchists that Mahmud Şevket Pasha had joined ex-
Colonel Sadık Bey's group. In order to avoid further damage,
Hüseyin Cahid [Yalçın], in his editorial in the September 2 issue of *Tanin*, denied the rumours.[148]

---

[143] Hüseyin Cahid [Yalçın], "Bütçe İhtilâfı," *Tanin*, August 15, 1327/August
28, 1911, p.1. For comments on this editorial in the foreign press see, "Turkish
Ministerial Differences: Mahmud Sevket Pasha and Nail Bey," *The Times*, August
29, 1911, p.3.

[144] "Mahmud Shevket and His Colleagues: Activity of the Left," *The Times*,
September 1, 1911, p.3.

[145] *Sabah*, August 16, 1327/August 29, 1911, quoted in "The Turkish Ministerial
Differences," *The Times*, August 30, 1911, p.3.

[146] "The Ministerial Crisis," *The Levant Herald and Eastern Express*, August
29, 1911, p.1; and, "The Crisis in the Turkish Cabinet: The Army Estimates," *The
Times*, August 31, 1911, p.3. See also, "Bütçe İhtilâfı: Maliye Nazırı'nın Beyanatı,"
Yeni İkdam, August 27, 1327/September 9, 1911, p.2.

[147] "The Turkish Ministerial Differences," *The Times*, August 30, 1911, p.3.

[148] Hüseyin Cahid [Yalçın], "Dedikodu," *Tanin*, August 20, 1327/September 2,

By early September, the Unionists approached Mahmud Şevket Pasha and told him about their intention of forming a Hacı Âdil [Arda] Cabinet, in which he was promised to retain his position as Minister of War. Mahmud Şevket Pasha, however, rejected this since he was opposed to the formation of a distinctly Unionist cabinet. Instead, he indicated his willingness of forming a cabinet under his grand veziership, with ministers from the Committee of Union and Progress. He had no objections to Hacı Âdil [Arda] and Cavid Bey as possible ministers in his cabinet. However, as news arrived that the rank and file of the party, which partly remained under the influence of ex-Colonel Sadık Bey, would object to the formation of an outright Unionist cabinet, the Unionist leadership decided to leave the question of a restructured 'Unionist' cabinet until after the end of the party congress to be held in late September.[149]

When it became apparent that the military wing of the monarchist opposition was intransigent and bent on destroying the Committee of Union and Progress rather than negotiate with the Unionists for sharing power, the leadership of the party decided to exclude ex-Colonel Sadık Bey's New Faction and strike a deal with the civilian members of the monarchist opposition. In this attempt to deal with Prince Sabahaddin and others alone, the Unionists also hoped to severe the ties between the two groups, and isolate the military faction, thus eliminating military threat to constitutional rule.

During September, the Unionist leadership entered into negotiations with the monarchist opposition, who had already expressed their desire to share governmental responsibility since July. In addition to tactical reasons calculated to drive a wedge between the two monarchist groups, both domestic troubles—mainly, the unrest in Albania and Yemen—and the international dispute between Italy and Turkey over Tripoli had also made it imperative that Unionists seek support for the formation of a coalition government. Besides, the military

---

1911, p.1. See also, "The Turkish Ministerial Differences," *The Times*, September 4, 1911, p.3.

[149] Mehmed Cavid, "Meşrutiyet Devrine Ait Cavit Bey'in Hatıraları: 44," *Tanin*, October 14, 1943, p.2.

wing of the monarchist opposition led by ex-Colonel Sadık
Bey had been working hard to discredit the Unionists in
public on the issue of the dispute over Tripoli between Turkey
and Italy.[150]

The Unionist leadership first approached Prince Sabahaddin, the leader of the monarchist opposition, and offered him
a post in a Unionist-led coalition government. They also stated
that they were prepared to give concessions on the issue of
centralisation, accepting certain points of Prince Sabahaddin's
decentralisation programme. Though Dr. Nihad Reşad [Bel-
ger], one of Prince Sabahaddin's closest colleagues, expressed
enthusiasm, Prince Sabahaddin rejected the offer, saying that
he was not interested in a cabinet position. Unionist leadership then met with Murad Bey, formerly editor of *Mizan*, in
an effort to enlist his intervention for a rapprochement between the civilian members of the monarchist opposition and
the Committee of Union and Progress.[151]

Additionally, Talât Bey talked with Lütfi Fikri Bey, one of
the opposition leaders in the Chamber, who was busy at that
time trying to establish a monarchist party with the help of ex-
Colonel Sadık Bey to counter Unionist influence in the Chamber. Negotiations started with Lütfi Fikri Bey and other members of the soon-to-be-formally-established Entente Libérale.
Greek deputies would form an important bloc within the new
party. Therefore, Lütfi Fikri Bey demanded that Yorgos Boussios, deputy for Serfidje, and Pantoleon Cosmidis, deputy for
İstanbul and owner of several monarchist newspapers, be included in the proposed coalition government. The Unionists,
however, were categorically opposed to the presence of monarchist Greek deputies in the cabinet and, as a consequence, negotiations broke off.[152]

Then came another dispute between Nail Bey, the Minister
of Finance, and Mahmud Şevket Pasha, the Minister of

---

[150] "Turkey's African Provinces," *The Orient*, 2/23 (September 20, 1911), pp.1 -
2.

[151] Halil Menteşe, "Eski Meclisi Mebusan Reisi Halil Menteşe'nin Hatıraları:
8: Trablusgarp Harbi," *Cumhuriyet*, October 20, 1946, p.2.

[152] Halil Menteşe, "Eski Meclisi Mebusan Reisi Halil Menteşe'nin Hatıraları:
8: Trablusgarp Harbi," *Cumhuriyet*, October 20, 1946, p.2.

War.[153] At the September 12 meeting of the Cabinet, Nail Bey, submitted further reductions of government expenditures for the upcoming financial year. The Ministry of War's budget was to be reduced by one million liras, the Ministry of the Interior's by two hundred and twenty thousand liras, the Ministry of Education's by one hundred and fifty thousand liras, the Ministry of Public Works' by one hundred and fifty thousand liras, and the Ministry of Mines and Forests' by sixty thousand liras. Along with other fiscal measures, these proposed reductions would reduce the budget deficit by two and a half million liras. Expressing their readiness to somewhat reduce their estimates, Nail Bey's colleagues did not, however, think that the deficit could be reduced by more than a million liras. Mahmud Şevket Pasha, in particular, found a reduction of more than one hundred and fifty thousand liras in the military budget completely unacceptable. It was finally agreed that the members of the Cabinet, each accompanied by his chief accountant, would meet at the Ministry of Finance to make a final decision on the matter.[154] Though the question of reductions in the military budget was left unresolved following the meeting, the remainder of the Cabinet yielded to Nail Bey's proposals and made the requisite reductions.[155]

Tanin immediately published an unsigned leading article which criticised the Minister of War, and provoked a certain amount of resentment among the officers of the General Staff.[156] *Nur-u Hakikat*, of Monastir, and *Silâh*, of Salonica— both Unionist newspapers—also published violent attacks on Mahmud Şevket Pasha. The entry of *Silâh* into İstanbul was prohibited.[157] Several Macedonian newspapers, like *Rumeli* and *Silâh*, generally thought to represent the views of the

---

[153] "Bütçe İhtilâfı: Maliye Nazırı'nın Beyanatı," *Yeni İkdam*, August 27, 1327/September 9, 1911, p.2; and, "Constantinople Letter," *The Near East*, September 13, 1911, p.435.

[154] "Turkish Finance and the War Minister," *The Times*, September 13, 1911, p.3; "Bütçe Meselesi," *Tanin*, September 1, 1327/September 14, 1911, p.2; "Bütçe İhtilâfı," *Tanin*, September 2, 1327/September 15, 1911, p.1; and, "Constantinople Letter," *The Near East*, September 20, 1911, p.463.

[155] "Constantinople Letter," *The Near East*, September 27, 1911, p.491.

[156] "Bütçe İhtilâfı," *Tanin*, August 24, 1327/September 6, 1911, p.1; and, "Constantinople Letter," *The Near East*, September 13, 1911, p.435.

[157] "Press Attacks on the Turkish War Minister," *The Times*, September 14, 1911, p.3.

Unionists' military wing, continued publishing bitter attacks
on Mahmud Şevket Pasha's behaviour.[158]

The Congress of the Committee of Union and Progress was
scheduled to open on the last day of September.[159] Cavid and
Talât Beys left İstanbul for Salonica on September 24.[160] Sixty-
one members would take part, fifty-five as ordinary members,
representing the provincial organisations, the Central
Committee of Salonica, the parliamentary party, the Committee inspectors, and the local authorities. Six would be extraordinary members, representing the Senate and the Chamber of
Deputies. Though the Congress would be convened to discuss
vital issues of policy, it was uncertain whether the six representatives of the Senate and the Chamber would have more
than a consultative role.[161]

No previous Unionist congress had been awaited with such
uncertainty as to its outcome; for the movement under ex-Colonel Sadık Bey for the organisation of a secessionist group or
party was so popular in monarchist quarters as to inspire no
little uneasiness in Unionist circles. It was expected that the
congress would make every effort to strengthen the bonds that
united all wings of the party. The recent tour of Cavid Bey and
Ömer Naci Bey in eastern Anatolia, especially in the Van
and Bitlis provinces and along the Black Sea coast, had been
timed to increase the prestige and influence of the Committee
of Union and Progress in that region, and make it possible for
it to win support there during the upcoming 1912 general
elections which would be critical—because two crises were
approaching.[162]

[158] "Constantinople Letter," *The Near East*, September 27, 1911, p.491.
[159] "İttihad ve Terakki Kongresi," *Tanin*, August 29, 1327/September 11, 1911,
p.2; and, "The Salonika Congress," *The Times*, September 15, 1911, p.3.
[160] "Le congrès Union et Progrès," *The Levant Herald and Eastern Express*,
September 25, 1911, p.2.
[161] "Constantinople Letter," *The Near East*, September 20, 1911, p.463.
[162] "The Turkish Elections," *The Times*, September 8, 1911, p.3; and, "Committee of Union and Progress to Meet," *The Orient*, 2/24 (September 27, 1911), p.2.
For the news on Cavid and Ömer Naci Beys' visit to the Eastern provinces see, "Cavid ve Naci Beylerin Seyahati," *Tanin*, July 10, 1327/July 23, 1911, p.3; "Cavid ve
Naci Beylerin Seyahati," *Tanin*, July 20, 1327/August 2, 1911, p.2; "Cavid Bey'in
Konferansı," *Tanin*, July 23, 1327/August 5, 1911, pp.2-3; "Cavid Bey'in Konferansı—Mabad," *Tanin*, July 24, 1327/August 6, 1911, pp.2-3;"Cavid ve Naci Beyler Bitlis'te," *Tanin*, August 4, 1327/August 17, 1911, p.1; "Cavid ve Naci Beylerin Şe-

First, there was the cabinet crisis. Although the divergence of opinion between Mahmud Şevket Pasha and Nail Bey on the subject of the Budget of the Ministry of War would probably be amicably settled, it was a fact that the Hakkı Pasha Cabinet was by no means on a secure footing. A week before the opening of the congress, *Rumeli*, the organ of the Committee of Union and Progress at Salonica, had expressed its dissatisfaction with the way government was run. Failure of the statesmen, *Rumeli* wrote, had made it imperative for the Unionists to take action immediately. Instead of trying to influence the events from outside, the paper recommended taking direct responsibility of governing the country. According to *Rumeli*, only then everybody would see clearly to what extent and for how long a period the statesmen, who had been appointed on the ground of their experience, had been a failure.[163] As the article in *Rumeli* showed, the leadership of the Committee of Union and Progress would prefer running the government directly, rather than controlling the dummy players from behind the screen.[164]

Second, there was the issue of the general elections: the coming session of the Chamber was its fourth and last. Elections would be held for a new Chamber, and it would be in the best interests of the Committee of Union and Progress to patch up the differences between the leadership and the dissidents in the party.[165]

The whole political situation, however, changed on September 28. That day, the Italian Chargé d'Affaires relayed an ultimatum to the Turkish Government, informing it that "in consequence of its failure to meet the demands of the Italian Gov-

refine," *Tanin*, August 4, 1327/August 17, 1911, p.2; "Cavid ve Naci Beyler," *Tanin* August 6, 1327/August 19, 1911, p.1; and, "Cavid Bey'in Avdeti," *Tanin*, August 11, 1327/August 24, 1911, p.1. On Cavid and Ömer Naci Beys' visit to the Eastern provinces see also the consular report from Erzurum, F.O. 424/228, Consul McGregor to Mr. Marling, Erzerum, August 7, 1911, *Further Correspondence Respecting the Affairs of Asiatic Turkey and Arabia*, No.9937, pp.83-84. See also, Fethi Tevetoğlu, *Ömer Naci*, 2nd Edition, pp.127-128. For Cavid Bey's visit to Trabzon see, Kudret Emiroğlu, "Maliye Nazırı Cavit Bey'in Trabzon Gezisi, 1911," pp.328-336.
[163] "Committee and Cabinet," *The Orient*, 2/23 (September 20, 1911), p.3.
[164] "Committee of Union and Progress to Meet," *The Orient*, 2/24 (September 27, 1911), p.2.
[165] "Committee of Union and Progress to Meet," *The Orient*, 2/24 (September 27, 1911), p.2.

ernment, Italian troops would occupy Tripoli and Benghazi."
The Turkish Government was given twenty-four hours to
communicate the news to the garrisons of these towns.[166]

For some weeks past, there had been much diplomatic discussion concerning the Italian demands on Tripoli. Several
cabinet meetings had taken place to discuss the issue.[167] In his
meeting with Cavid Bey on September 20, Hakkı Pasha told
him that war might be unavoidable. Entering into negotiations with the Italian government concerning economic
concessions would be another alternative which neither Hakkı Pasha nor the Unionist leadership wanted.[168] Indeed, the
Turkish Chargé d'Affaires in Paris stated in the September 24
issue of *Le Temps* that he had no knowledge of any negotiations between Turkey and Italy with regard to Tripoli.[169]
Therefore, it was agreed that there was no other way out except for fighting against the Italians should they declare war
on Turkey. Conceding defeat without a fight no matter how
poor the prospects of winning it might be would open up the
way for the eventual dismemberment of the empire.[170]

Turkish Government demanded the intervention of Germany and Austria-Hungary on Turkey's behalf.[171] On September 25, Cavid Bey met with Baron Marschall von Bieber-
stein, the German Ambassador, who, though sympathetic to
the Turkish side, nevertheless suggested that Turkey give
some economic concessions to Italy. He told that there was

---

[166] "Constantinople Letter," *The Near East*, October 11, 1911, p.547; "Italy and
Turkey: Grave Situation," *The Levant Herald and Eastern Express*, September 29,
1911, p.1; Hüseyin Cahid [Yalçın], "İlân-ı Harb," *Tanin*, September 17, 1327/Sep-
tember 30, 1911, p.1; and, Halil Menteşe, "Eski Meclisi Mebusan Reisi Halil Menteşe'nin Hatıraları: 9: Trablusgrap Meselesinin İçyüzüne Dair Vesikalar," *Cumhuriyet*, October 21, 1946, p.2. For the text of the Turkish translation of the Note,
see, "İlân-ı Harb Notası," *Tanin*, September 17, 1327/September 30, 1911, p.1, or,
Yusuf Hikmet Bayur, *Türk İnkılâbı Tarihi, 2/1*, pp.93-95.

[167] "Hüseyin Cahid [Yalçın], "Trablus Garb ve İtalya," *Tanin*, August 23, 1327/
September 5, 1911, p.1; "Italy and Tripoli: Turkish Uneasiness," *The Times*, September 21, 1911, p.3; and, "Hüseyin Cahid [Yalçın], "Trablus Garb," *Tanin*, September 9, 1327/September 22, 1911, p.1.

[168] Mehmed Cavid, "Meşrutiyet Devrine Ait Cavit Bey'in Hatıraları: 45," *Tanin*, October 15, 1943, p.2.

[169] "The Tripoli Question: Benevolent Neutrality of France," *The Times*, September 25, 1911, p.3.

[170] Mehmed Cavid, "Meşrutiyet Devrine Ait Cavit Bey'in Hatıraları: 45," *Tanin*, October 15, 1943, p.2.

[171] "Italy and Turkey," *The Levant Herald and Eastern Express*, September 26,
1911, p.1.

animosity among the European Powers against Turkey for its policy of not letting foreign capital enter into the country. Thus, he insinuated the necessity of giving in to the Italian demands pertaining to economic matters. His behaviour also suggested that Germany would not openly side with Turkey should Italy declare war on Turkey.[172] That same day, Hakkı Pasha talked with the German Ambassador, and acknowledged his readiness to grant certain economic concessions to Italy as long as Tripoli remained Turkish territory.[173]

In the meeting the Unionist leadership held with Hakkı Pasha on the night of September 25, it had also become apparent that Hakkı Pasha had been under fire from the monarchist side on the issue of the Italian conflict. The monarchists had intimidated him so much so that he told the Unionist leadership that the days of the Committee of Union and Progress were numbered and that the formation of a Kâmil Pasha Cabinet was unavoidable.[174]

Under fire both from the Italians and the monarchists, Hakkı Pasha immediately summoned a Council of Ministers to discuss the note the Italian government handed.[175] The Cabinet decided to reply in conciliatory terms, promising to examine Italy's grievances and recognising its privileged economic position in Tripoli—knowing only too well that at best they might postpone the disaster a few days. It was too late. The following afternoon Italy declared war.[176]

---

[172] Mehmed Cavid, "Meşrutiyet Devrine Ait Cavit Bey'in Hatıraları: 45," *Tanin*, October 15, 1943, p.2.

[173] A.A., Türkei 202, #A15215, Marschall to A. A., Therapia, September 25, 1911, cited in Glen Wilfred Swanson, Mahmud Şevket Paşa and the Defense of the Ottoman Empire, p.132.

[174] Mehmed Cavid, "Meşrutiyet Devrine Ait Cavit Bey'in Hatıraları: 45," *Tanin*, October 15, 1943, p.2.

[175] Halil Menteşe, "Eski Meclisi Mebusan Reisi Halil Menteşe'nin Hatıraları: 9: Trablusgrap Meselesinin İçyüzüne Dair Vesikalar," *Cumhuriyet*, October 21, 1946, p.2.

[176] "Italy and Turkey: Declaration of War," *The Levant Herald and Eastern Express*, September 30, 1911, p.1; and, "Constantinople Letter," *The Near East*, October 11, 1911, p.547. For the text of the Italian Note declaring war on Turkey see, Yusuf Hikmet Bayur, *Türk İnkılâbı Tarihi*, 2/1, pp.97-98.

CHAPTER SEVEN

THE SAID PASHA CABINET

Hakkı Pasha resigned immediately following the declaration of war.[1] Said Pasha, despite ill health and advanced age, accepted the grand veziership. As he had better relations with the Unionists than any other statesman of the old regime, the Committee of Union and Progress promised to support the new government.[2] Kâmil Pasha had also been considered for Grand Veziership in monarchist circles, but he refused to serve without guarantees of complete freedom from Unionists intervention, and was duly left out of consideration.[3] The Unionist leaders had feared that were Kâmil Pasha to replace Said Pasha as Grand Vezier their surrender would be universally interpreted as a defeat, and they would lose all the prestige that they had been able to preserve since 1910.[4]

Said Pasha's appointment to grand veziership prompted the monarchist opposition to actively engage in political schemes to prevent the new government's formation under his leader-

---

[1] "Resignation of the Cabinet," *The Levant Herald and Eastern Express*, September 30, 1911, p.1; "Constantinople Letter," *The Near East*, October 11, 1911, p.547; Cemal Kutay, *Türkiye İstiklâl ve Hürriyet Mücadeleleri Tarihi, 17*, p.9789; and, Yusuf Hikmet Bayur, *Türk İnkılâbı Tarihi, 2/1*, p.109.

[2] "Constantinople Letter," *The Near East*, October 11, 1911, p.547; "Said Pasha Grand Vizier," *The Levant Herald and Eastern Express*, September 30, 1911, p.1; and, Hüseyin Cahid [Yalçın], "Said Paşa Kabinesi," *Tanin*, September 18, 1327/ October 1, 1911, p.1. See also, Ziya Şakir [Soko], "Hürriyet ve İtilâf Nasıl Doğdu? Nasıl Yaşadı? Nasıl Battı? 22: On Maddelik Program Tereddütlere Yol Açtı," *Tan*, November 23, 1937, p.9; and, Yusuf Hikmet Bayur, *Türk İnkılâbı Tarihi, 2/1*, p.109.

[3] "Constantinople Letter," *The Near East*, October 11, 1911, p.547. See also, F.O 371/1251/38318, Sir Gerard Lowther to Sir Edward Grey, Constantinople, October 1, 1911, and, Boppe to de Selves, Therapia, October 3, 1911, *Documents Diplomatiques Français, 1871-1914*, Second Series, *14*, no.391 and 580, both quoted in Feroz Ahmad, *The Young Turks: The Committee of Union and Progress in Turkish Politics, 1908-1914*, p.94. According to a rumour, Kâmil Pasha, when requested by the Committee of Union and Progress to accept the position of Grand Vezier, replied that the Sultan alone had the right to offer the post to whomsoever he pleased ("Current Comments," *The Near East*, October 11, 1911, p.559).

[4] "Constantinople Letter," *The Near East*, October 18, 1911, p.575.

ship. Monarchists approached Mahmud Şevket Pasha, offer-
ing to retain him as the Minister of War in a Kâmil Pasha
Cabinet they hoped would replace Hakkı Pasha's. The
emissary for the monarchists was İsmail Hakkı [Mumcu]
Pasha, deputy for Amasya and one of the leaders of the
monarchist opposition in the Chamber. Mahmud Şevket
Pasha, however, declined to accept the monarchist offer and
continued to function in the existing Cabinet.[5]

Said Pasha had great difficulty in forming his Cabinet, and
his success was jeopardised at the last moment by Reşid Pasha's refusal to accept the portfolio for Foreign Affairs.[6] After
much negotiation with the monarchists, the Cabinet was finally formed and announced to the public on October 4.[7] As
the question of the new Minister for Foreign Affairs had not
yet been settled despite strenuous efforts, Said Pasha was also
the Acting Minister for Foreign Affairs in the new cabinet.
Eventually, it was hoped that the Ministry for Foreign Affairs
would go either to Reşid Pasha, Turkish Ambassador in Vienna, or, in the event of his refusal, Asım Bey, Turkish Minister
in Sofia.[8] On October 6, the press prematurely announced that
Reşid Pasha had accepted the portfolio.[9] In fact, he had refused. Whether or not it be true that the refusal of Reşid Pasha
shook confidence in the vitality of the Said Pasha Cabinet as a
whole, it evidently revealed the extreme difficulty of the internal political situation in Turkey.[10] Faced with a monarchist
scheme to thwart his attempts in forming the cabinet, Said Pasha was forced to invite Gabriel Nouradunghian to the Sub-

---

[5] Hüseyin Cahid Yalçın, "Meşrutiyet Hatıraları, 1908-1918," *Fikir Hareketleri*, 7 (October 24, 1936-April 17, 1937), p.4.
[6] "Constantinople Letter," *The Near East*, October 18, 1911, p.575. See also,
Mehmed Cavid, "Meşrutiyet Devrine Ait Cavid Bey'in Hatıraları: 46," *Tanin*, October 16, 1943, p.2; and, Yusuf Hikmet Bayur, *Türk İnkılâbı Tarihi, 2/1*, p.109.
[7] "Yeni Kabine," *Tanin*, September 21, 1327/October 4, 1911, p.1; "Turkish
Ministers and the Committee," *The Times*, October 6, 1911, p.6; and, "The New
Cabinet," *The Levant Herald and Eastern Express*, October 5, 1911, p.1.
[8] "Reşid Paşa," *Yeni İkdam*, September 25, 1327/October 8, 1911, p.1; "Reşid
Paşa," *Yeni İkdam*, September 26, 1327/October 9, 1911, p.1; "Constantinople Letter," *The Near East*, October 11, 1911, p.547; and, "The New Turkish Cabinet," *The
Times*, October 9, 1911, p.6.
[9] "The New Cabinet," *The Levant Herald and Eastern Express*, October 6,
1911, p.1; and, "Italian Action and Its Possible Effects: The Turkish Foreign Minister," *The Times*, October 7, 1911, p.3.
[10] "The Internal Situation in Turkey: Resid Pasha and the Cabinet," *The
Times*, October 9, 1911, p.3.

lime Porte on October 8, and offer him the post.[11] He also refused.[12] Said Pasha, once again, met with Reşid Pasha in the
hopes of convincing him to accept the portfolio. He had a long
interview with Reşid Pasha on the afternoon of October 9, but
the latter definitely rejected the offer.[13] Following this interview, Said Pasha received Asım Bey. Finally, the question
was solved, with the acceptance of the portfolio by Asım Bey,
who had arrived at İstanbul that very same day.[14] Asım Bey
was a genuine Unionist, whose belief in the necessity of reform and progress in Turkey was known to his friends and
acquaintances for many years past.[15]

Mahmud Şevket Pasha remained as Minister of War, as
did Nail Bey as Minister of Finance, Abdurrahman Şeref Bey
as Minister of Education, and Hulusi Bey as Minister of Public
Works. Celal Bey was appointed as the new Minister of the Interior, replacing Halil [Menteşe]. Formerly Governor of Erzurum, Celal Bey was currently Governor of Edirne, and was
popular with the Committee of Union and Progress. Ürgüplü
Hayri Bey was appointed as the new Minister of Justice,
replacing Necmeddin [Kocataş]. He had also provisionally
taken the portfolio of the Ministry of Pious Foundations.
Sheikh-ul-Islam was Musa Kâzım Efendi, a Unionist senator.
Hurşid Pasha, the Chief Aide-de-Camp of the Sultan, filled the
portfolio of the Ministry of the Navy. Krikor Sinapian was appointed as the Minister of Mines and Forests; he was legal advisor in the Ministry of which he now took charge. İbrahim
Soussa, a Syrian Catholic who was Governor of the Archipela-
go, was the new Minister of Posts and Telegraphs.[16]

[11] "The Ministry for Foreign Affairs," The Levant Herald and Eastern Express, October 8, 1911, p.1.
[12] "The New Turkish Cabinet," The Times, October 9, 1911, p.6.
[13] "The Turkish Cabinet," The Times, October 10, 1911, p.3.
[14] "Asım Bey," Yeni İkdam, September 26, 1327/October 9, 1911, p.1; and,
"The Ministry for Foreign Affairs," The Levant Herald and Eastern Express, October 10, 1911, p.1.
[15] "The Turkish Foreign Office: Assim Bey at Constantinople," The Times,
October 10, 1911, p.3.
[16] "Constantinople Letter," The Near East, October 11, 1911, p.547; "Trablus
Garb—İtalya: Yeni Kabine," Tanin, September 22, 1327/October 5, 1911, p.1; "The
New Cabinet," and, "Le nouveau Cabinet," The Levant Herald and Eastern Express,
October 5, 1911, p.1; "The New Cabinet," The Orient, 2/26 (October 11, 1911), p.3;
and, "Turkish Ministers and the Committee," The Times, October 6, 1911, p.6.
In late October, Ürgüplü Hayri Bey, who had been appointed to the post of
Minister of Justice in the Said Pasha Cabinet while provisionally retaining his

Neither Hurşid Pasha, Krikor Sinapian, nor İbrahim Soussa was particularly identified with any party. The absence of any Greek from the cabinet and the retirement of Halil [Menteşe] and Necmeddin [Kocataş] aroused much comment. Halil [Menteşe] had been lately severely criticised by some members of his party for his failure to support Hüseyin Kâzım Bey, the Unionist ex-Governor of İstanbul. Necmeddin [Kocataş] had of late been subjected to attack by *Tanin*, which after two years' silence had unearthed his former association with Necib Melhame in relation to mining and other concessions.[17] On the other hand, the Committee of Union and Progress had pushed for the restoration of Talât and Cavid Beys to their former positions, but failed.[18]

The new cabinet was generally regarded as rather colourless.[19] If it was considered at all Unionist, it was only because it enjoyed a measure of support from the Central Committee of the party at Salonica, and included Ürgüplü Hayri Bey, as its new Minister of Justice, and Celal Bey, as its new Minister of the Interior, both of whom were generally felt to be solid Unionists.[20] Unionists had but little choice in supporting Said Pasha.[21] The leadership was worried that, in the event of their refusal to support the new government, Said Pasha might request the Sultan to dismiss the Chamber of Deputies so that new elections might be organised without consulting the Committee of Union and Progress. This the Unionists were the more anxious to prevent, since their influence had already been diminished by the appointment of Said Pasha.[22] How-

---

place as Minister of Pious Foundations, presented his resignation in the former capacity and retained the Ministry of the Pious Foundations. The portfolio of justice was entrusted to Memduh Bey ("Empire News: The Capital," *The Orient*, 2/29 (November 1, 1911, p.6).

[17] "Turkish Ministers and the Committee," *The Times*, October 6, 1911, p.6.
[18] "The Tragedy of Turkey," *The Near East*, October 11, 1911, p.558.
[19] "Constantinople Letter," *The Near East*, October 18, 1911, p.575; and "Constantinople Letter," *The Near East*, October 11, 1911, p.547. See also, F.O. 371/1252/39063, Sir Gerard Lowther to Sir Edward Grey, Therapia, October 5, 1911, quoted in Feroz Ahmad, *The Young Turks: The Committee of Union and Progress in Turkish Politics, 1908-1914*, p.94.
[20] "Constantinople Letter," *The Near East*, October 11, 1911, p.547; and, "Turkish Ministers and the Committee," *The Times*, October 6, 1911, p.6.
21 Ziya Şakir [Soko], "Hürriyet ve İtilâf Nasıl Doğdu? Nasıl Yaşadı? Nasıl Battı? 23: Gazeteler Fırkanın Kurulduğu Haberini Veriyordu," *Tan*, November 24, 1937, p.9.
[22] "Italian Action and Its Possible Effects: The Salonika Congress," *The*

ever, should the Chamber of Deputies refuse a vote of confidence in Said Pasha's purely provisional cabinet or in a
Unionist cabinet, the leadership of the Committee of Union
and Progress decided to advise the Sultan to dissolve Parliament rather than risk the appointment of either a Kâmil Pasha
or a Hüseyin Hilmi Pasha Cabinet supported by the monarchist opposition and the dissident members of the Committee
of Union and Progress. They dreaded the vengeance of these
older statesmen, neither of whom would accept office without
guarantee that the political activity of the Committee of Union
and Progress, or its branches, to which they attributed much
of the provincial unrest, should immediately cease.[23]

The Said Pasha Cabinet met with the approval of Unionist
newspapers. *Tanin*, while giving qualified support, criticised
the attitude of the opposition. In his editorial column, Hüseyin
Cahid [Yalçın] wrote that he would have been totally satisfied
had there been in the Said Pasha Cabinet a greater number of
experienced statesmen. He expressed the view that what the
country needed was not a party cabinet, not a programme cabinet, but a cabinet for the resistance to the enemy. Declaring
that he would have preferred at such a crisis a union of political leaders, he regretted to observe that some had made no response whatsoever, while others had refused the proffered
posts. The reference was, of course, to Kâmil Pasha and other
monarchist statesmen who had done all in their power to
block the formation of any cabinet which was not dominated
by themselves. Hüseyin Cahid [Yalçın] wrote that the opposition did not appreciate as it should the conciliatory and friendly attitude taken by the Committee of Union and Progress,
which was the majority party in the Chamber. While the
very person, the policy and the independent spirit of Said Pasha ought to be enough to unite under the banner of union
and in face of the duty of national defence both government
and opposition, the monarchist opposition, he added, had
shown their dissatisfaction because their candidates were not
in power. Hüseyin Cahid [Yalçın] took this attitude as proof

Times, October 7, 1911, p.3.
[23] "The Turkish Cabinet: Policy of the Committee Leaders," *The Times*, October 10, 1911, p.3.

that the opposition did not wish an impartial cabinet, but one that should be of their own opinion. Under these circumstances, he predicted that the new cabinet would run into difficulties in the Chamber. Confessing that the new cabinet, taken as a whole, was not a kind to give entire satisfaction to any party, he added that this fact, which in ordinary times might have been seen a sign of weakness, might possibly be a cause of strength at this crisis.[24]

The cabinet was coldly received by the monarchist press. *Yeni Gazete*, a monarchist newspaper reflecting Kâmil Pasha's views, published a severe attack upon the foreign and domestic policy of the Committee of Union and Progress from the pen of Rıza Tevfik [Bölükbaşı], deputy for Edirne and one of the leading members of the monarchist opposition. The publication of this article resulted in the suspension of *Yeni Gazete* and an order to court martial the author.[25] Furthermore, the fact that the Court Martial had warned the press to abstain from all criticism of the government policy was interpreted as a proof that the position of Said Pasha's Cabinet had been but little strengthened by Asım Bey's acceptance of the portfolio of Foreign Affairs. The Court Martial's action seemed to have been caused by the publication in *Tanin* of an editorial in which the government's reluctance to expel Italian subjects had been roundly blamed.[26] A few days later, *Ekklesiastike Aletheia, Proodos, Nea Patris* —all Greek language monarchist newspapers published in İstanbul—and *La Bourse d'Orient*, another monarchist daily, were suspended by order of the Court Martial for publishing articles adjudged by the Court Martial to be dangerous.[27]

La Bourse d'Orient had begun publication in İstanbul in July of 1911 under the editorship of a Spanish Jew by the name of Ximenes. After the massacres of Armenians at Sas-

---

[24] Hüseyin Cahid [Yalçın], "Kabine," *Tanin*, September 23, 1327/October 6, 1911, p.1. See also, "The New Cabinet Criticised," *The Orient*, 2/26 (October 11, 1911), p.3.

[25] "Turkish Ministers and the Committee: Reception by the Press," *The Times*, October 6, 1911, p.6.

[26] "Position of the Turkish Cabinet," *The Times*, October 11, 1911, p.8. For Yalçın's editorial on this issue see, Hüseyin Cahid [Yalçın], "İtalyanların Tardı," *Tanin*, September 27, 1327/October 10, 1911, p.1.

[27] "Empire News: The Capital," *The Orient*, 2/26 (October 11, 1911), p.6.

soun in 1894, he had gone to London representing himself as a Spanish traveller, and had given to Reuter's agency a long dispatch stating that he had travelled through Sassoun and never heard of a massacre there. He alleged as an eye-witness that there had been no such massacre. Such papers as sympathised with Abdülhamid had published this dispatch, adding that, as the man was a Spaniard, he would have no object in lying. For this service to the absolutist regime, he had been given official favour by Abdülhamid.[28]

Military opinion no longer generally supported the Committee of Union and Progress, or even the Minister of War, as had been the case a year ago.[29] Hostility towards Mahmud Şevket Pasha was particularly high, and there were rumours that monarchist pashas such as Nâzım Pasha or Mahmud Muhtar Pasha might replace him at the Ministry. Though the Salonica and Monastir garrisons, *i.e.*, the Third Army Corps, firmly supported the Committee of Union and Progress, it was generally believed that the First Army Corps stationed at İstanbul was equally divided. On the other hand, the Second Army Corps, especially the Kossovo, Edirne and the Rodosto-Dardanelles troops, were openly hostile to the Unionists.[30]

After Hakkı Pasha's fall, various opposition groups began discussing the formation of a coalition party which many estimated could count on the support of as many as one hundred deputies. The coalition would consist of the Moderate Liberals, the People's Party, the Independents, several Albanian deputies, half a dozen Serbian and Bulgarian deputies from Macedonia, a few non-Unionist Armenian deputies, and all the Greek deputies, except for four who had taken the Unionist oath.[31] On October 12, just prior to the opening of the fourth session of the Parliament, they formally announced the formation of this coalition with İsmail Hakkı [Mumcu] Pasha,

---

[28] *Jamanak*, quoted in "Masked Spite and Retaliation," *The Orient*, 2/30 (November 8, 1911), p.3.

[29] "Constantinople Letter," *The Near East*, October 11, 1911, p.547.

[30] "Constantinople Letter," *The Near East*, October 25, 1911, p.603.

[31] "Yeni bir Fırka-i Muhtelife," *Tanin*, October 12, 1327/October 25, 1911, pp.3-4; "Constantinople Letter," *The Near East*, October 25, 1911, p.603. See Tarık Zafer Tunaya, *Türkiye'de Siyasi Partiler, 1859-1952*, p.317, and p.325n for the list of the Albanian deputies.

deputy for Amasya, as its leader.[32] Though still inferior in numbers to the nominal strength of the Committee of Union and Progress, it would be distinctly more powerful than the last session's opposition, which had seldom mustered more than seventy-five votes.[33]

The same day separate meetings were held at the Chamber of Deputies of the monarchist opposition and the adherents of the Unionist majority, the former numbering about sixty-five presided over by Rıza Tevfik [Bölükbaşı], and the latter numbering over eighty. The Unionists first proposed a collective meeting in order to discuss a common programme and to present a united front in this time of national crisis—the continuing war with Italy over Tripoli. The monarchist opposition, however, declined, stating that it was a question of the cabinet, and they had no confidence in the Said Pasha Cabinet. Thereupon, the Unionists proposed to dispatch a joint deputation to obtain from the Grand Vezier a statement of his programme. The monarchists again declined, declaring that such procedure was unconstitutional. The meetings were then continued separately, the opposition deciding to refuse to support the vote of confidence in the Said Pasha Cabinet.[34]

Counting the members of the New Faction, the Unionists could muster about one hundred and thirty votes. The monarchist opposition could count a maximum of about one hundred votes. The balance of about thirty-five deputies, however, included a number of Arabs, whose allegiance was doubtful, and seven or eight members of the Armenian Revolutionary Federation, whose support of the Committee of Union and Progress was not guaranteed. The opposing forces were more or less evenly divided; thus, if the thirty or forty dissidents of the New Faction were to desert the Committee of Union and Progress, it would probably give the monarchist opposition an

---

[32] "The Situation in Constantinople: A Coalition Party," *The Times*, October 13, 1911, p.5; and, Ziya Şakir [Soko], "Hürriyet ve İtilâf Nasıl Doğdu? Nasıl Yaşadı? Nasıl Battı? 23: Gazeteler Fırkanın Kurulduğu Haberini Veriyordu," *Tan*, November 24, 1937, p.9.

[33] "Constantinople Letter," *The Near East*, October 25, 1911, p.603.

[34] "Deputies and the Said Ministry," *The Times*, October 13, 1911, p.5. See also, "Mebusanın Dünkü İctimaı," *Yeni İkdam*, September 30, 1327/October 13, 1911, p.1.

appreciable majority.[35]

Under these circumstances, the Unionist leadership tried to open negotiations with the new coalition's leaders. The monarchist opposition, however, made any discussion conditional on the Unionists' acceptance of the following points: that the Sultan's power to appoint the Grand Vezier be left intact; that the Grand Vezier be allowed to choose his cabinet; that only an adverse vote in the Chamber, as opposed to outside pressure, henceforth be the sole political cause for any member of the cabinet's resignation; that the Parliament should not interfere with the executive branch; and that the government follow a moderate foreign policy.[36]

On October 15, the fourth session of the Parliament opened.[37] Marshal Gazi Ahmed Muhtar Pasha was appointed President of the Senate, and Sharif Ali Haydar Bey, a former Minister of Pious Foundations, Vice-President.[38] At a meeting of the Committee of Union and Progress and opposition groups, the Unionists proposed to re-elect Ahmed Rıza Bey as President of the Chamber, undertaking, however, to vote for the candidate of the opposition for the Vice-Presidency. The opposition was unable to agree to the proposal, as their aim was not to solve the question at hand but still to affect the fall of the Said Pasha Cabinet. So, the question of the cabinet was discussed, the monarchists insisting that Kâmil Pasha should become Grand Vezier. The Unionists were naturally against the proposal, and suggested the selection of a neutral person. The meeting ended with no decision having been arrived at.[39]

The Committee of Union and Progress had first to deal

---

[35] "Constantinople Letter," *The Near East*, October 25, 1911, p.603.

[36] "Constantinople Letter," *The Near East*, October 25, 1911, p.603.

[37] I/IV/1, October 2, 1327/October 15, 1911, *Meclis-i Mebusan Zabıt Ceridesi*, *1*, pp.2-8; "Fourth Parliamentary Session Opens," *The Orient*, 2/27 (October 18, 1911), p.1; Hüseyin Cahid [Yalçın], "Meclis-i Mebusan'ın Küşadı," *Tanin*, October 2, 1327/October 15, 1911, p.1; "Meclis-i Umumi'nin Küşadı," *Tanin*, October 2, 1327/October 15, 1911, p.1; and, Mehmed Cavid, "Meşrutiyet Devrine Ait Cavid Bey'in Hatıraları: 46," *Tanin*, October 16, 1943, p.2.

[38] I/IV/1, October 3, 1327/October 16, 1911, *Meclis-i Mebusan Âyan Ceridesi*, *1*, p.2; "Turkish Parliamentary Situation: Election of President," *The Times*, October 16, 1911, p.5; and, "Empire News: The Capital," *The Orient*, 2/28 (October 25, 1911), p.4.

[39] Mehmed Cavid, "Meşrutiyet Devrine Ait Cavid Bey'in Hatıraları: 46," *Tanin*, October 16, 1943, p.2; "İttihad ve Terakki Fırkası," *Yeni İkdam*, October 1, 1327/October 14, 1911, p.1; and, "Turkish Parliamentary Situation: Election of President," *The Times*, October 16, 1911, p.5.

with its own conservative military wing—the New Faction
led by ex-Colonel Sadık Bey—which was critical of certain
prominent party members. According to accounts of the
Unionist congress published by the Salonica and İstanbul
press, most of the ten demands made by the New Faction had
been either refused or only accepted after their pristine vigour
had been weakened by copious amendments. This was especially the case in regard to the New Faction's demand that the
Committee of Union and Progress should condemn the secret
societies—that is, the Masonic lodges—which occupied themselves with politics.[40] According to the published versions of
the proceedings at Salonica, this was not accepted by the majority on the ground that the existence of a law prohibiting secret political associations made it unnecessary for the Unionists to pass any resolution on this subject. Before the vote for
the Presidency of the Chamber of Deputies, the Unionists sacrificed Emmanuel Carasso in an effort to appease the New Faction and maintain party unity. This news, which appeared at
the October 14 issue of Le Jeune Turc, caused much surprise.[41]
An active Unionist deputy for Salonica, Carasso was
unpopular with the New Faction, mainly because it had demanded the suppression of secret societies in the last of its declaration's ten articles, and Carasso was known to have Masonic ties.[42]

---

[40] Ziya Şakir [Soko], "Hürriyet ve İtilâf Nasıl Doğdu? Nasıl Yaşadı? Nasıl Battı? 22: On Maddelik Program Tereddütlere Yol Açtı," Tan, November 23, 1937,
p.9.

[41] "The Salonika Congress: The Committee and Freemasonry," The Times,
October 16, 1911, p.5; and, "The Committee of Union and Progress," The Times,
October 18, 1911, p.5.

[42] Carasso informed Le Jeune Turc that he had been obliged to obey the dictates of his conscience and leave the parliamentary party of the Committee of
Union and Progress in consequence of the hostile attitude which it had adopted
towards freemasonry and other secret societies. Carasso was Venerable of the well-
known Macedonia Risorta lodge of Salonica at the time of the Revolution, and was
thus enabled to give the revolutionaries great assistance and to obtain their favour.
After the downfall of Abdülhamid, he had shown great activity as a Masonic
propagandist and helped to found many lodges ("Constantinople Letter," The Near
East, October 25, 1911, p.603). For Carasso's Masonic ties see, Angelo Iacovella,
Gönye ve Hilâl: İttihad-Terakki ve Masonluk, pp.39-43.
      Gerald H. Fitzmaurrice, the First Dragoman of the British Embassy, who
was in close touch with the monarchist opposition and leadership of the New
Faction also held strongly anti-Jewish and anti-Masonic views. Partly through his
influential position in the Embassy, Ambassador Sir Gerard Lowther also held
similar prejudices. Thus, he called Carasso, 'a low-class, and dishonest lawyer, an
obsequious, venal and secretive scoundrel, with a mysterious manner.' For Ambas-

The election for the Presidency of the Chamber took place on October 15. In return for Carasso's sacrifice, the New Faction, keeping their side of the bargain, pledged to support Unionist candidates for the Presidency and the Vice-Presidency of the Chamber.[43] Despite all the efforts of the Unionist leadership, altogether only one hundred and fifty deputies participated in the election. Ahmed Rıza Bey was re-elected by eighty-six votes against fifty-five given in favour of the candidate of the opposition, Mahir Said Bey, a nominally independent deputy. Ahmed Rıza Bey had barely succeeded to get the necessary minimum number of votes. Necmeddin [Kocataş] and Halil [Menteşe] received six and three votes respectively.[44]

In order to win the votes of the Arab deputies, the Unionists, at a meeting held on October 15, decided to support the candidacy of Abd al-Hamid az-Zahrawi, a prominent member of the monarchist opposition, for the Vice-Presidency of the Chamber of Deputies. The decision partially confirmed reports that the Committee of Union and Progress desired to diminish the hostility, if it was unable to win the support, of the monarchist opposition by a more conciliatory policy during the existing crisis. At the October 16 sitting of the Chamber, Abd al-Hamid az-Zahrawi was elected as First Vice-President by eighty-six votes.[45] However, the conciliatory overtures of the Committee of Union and Progress did not have much effect on the opposition, who refused the offer of the Vice-Presidency for one of their members—Abd al-Hamid az-Zahrawi

---

sador Sir Gerard Lowther's highly prejudiced views against Carasso and other members of the Committee of Union and Progress see, Sir G. Lowther to Sir C. Hardinge, Constantinople, May 29, 1910, reproduced in full in Elie Kedourie, "Young Turks, Freemasons and Jews," pp.94-103.

[43] "The Salonika Congress: The Committee and Freemasonry," *The Times*, October 16, 1911, p.5; and, "Constantinople Letter," *The Near East*, October 25, 1911, p.603.

[44] I/IV/1, October 2, 1327/October 15, 1911, *Meclis-i Mebusan Zabıt Ceridesi*, *1*, p.8; Mehmed Cavid, "Meşrutiyet Devrine Ait Cavid Bey'in Hatıraları: 46," *Tanin*, October 16, 1943, p.2; "Turkish Parliamentary Situation: Election of President," *The Times*, October 16, 1911, p.5; "The Opening of Parliament," *The Levant Herald and Eastern Express*, October 16, 1911, p.1; and, "Fourth Parliamentary Session Opens," *The Orient*, 2/27 (October 18, 1911), p.1.

[45] I/IV/2, October 3, 1327/October 16, 1911, *Meclis-i Mebusan Zabıt Ceridesi*, *1*, p.13; "Turkish Parliamentary Situation," *The Times*, October 16, 1911, p.5; and, Mehmed Cavid, "Meşrutiyet Devrine Ait Cavid Bey'in Hatıraları: 47," *Tanin*, October 17, 1943, p.2. See also, Ahmed Tarabein, "Abd al-Hamid al-Zahrawi: The Career and Thought of an Arab Nationalist," p.101.

immeditaely tendered his resignation.[46] Consequently, two Unionist deputies, Ruhi al-Khalidi, Arab deputy for Jerusalem, and Emmanuel Emmanuelidis, Greek deputy for İzmir, were elected First and Second Vice-Presidents of the Chamber respectively.[47]

On October 16, Cavid Bey and Hüseyin Cahid [Yalçın] discussed the possibility of the formation of a coalition government. Although they found this idea tempting, they were not sure how the other Unionist leaders would react to such an arrangement. Hüseyin Cahid [Yalçın] had already mentioned this possibility to Said Pasha when he was trying to form his cabinet, but Said Pasha had rejected the idea as being unfeasible.[48] Later during the same day, representatives of the Unionist leadership—Cavid Bey, Talât Bey, Babanzade İsmail Hakkı Bey, and Halil [Menteşe]—met with a group of Armenian deputies consisting of Krikor Zohrab, Karekin Pasturmadjian, and Vartkes Serengülyan.[49]

Pasturmadjian and Serengülyan were sympathetic to the Unionist position. However, representing the monarchist opposition, Zohrab put forward their demands which had been agreed upon at a meeting attended by himself along with Lütfi Fikri Bey, Gümülcineli İsmail Hakkı Bey, Mahir Said Bey, Sıdkı Bey, and Dr. Rıza Nur. Criticising the existing state of affairs, the monarchists claimed that it could not be considered a constitutional regime. Demanding the elimination of the power of the Committee of Union and Progress in governmental affairs, the monarchists complained of what they called the chauvinistic attitude of the Unionists towards the

---

[46] I/IV/2, October 3, 1327/October 16, 1911, *Meclis-i Mebusan Zabıt Ceridesi, 1*, p.15; Mehmed Cavid, "Meşrutiyet Devrine Ait Cavid Bey'in Hatıraları: 47," *Tanin*, October 17, 1943, p.2; "Fourth Parliamentary Session Opens," *The Orient*, 2/27 (October 18, 1911), p.1; "The Turkish Chamber and the Government," *The Times*, October 17, 1911, p.5; and, Ahmed Tarabein, "Abd al-Hamid al-Zahrawi: The Career and Thought of an Arab Nationalist," p.101. See also, Philip S. Khoury, *Urban Notables and Arab Nationalism: The Politics of Damascus, 1860-1920*, p.61.

[47] I/IV/2, October 3, 1327/October 16, 1911, *Meclis-i Mebusan Zabıt Ceridesi, 1*, p.15; "Fourth Parliamentary Session Opens," *The Orient*, 2/27 (October 18, 1911), p.1; and, "The Turkish Chamber and the Government," *The Times*, October 17, 1911, p.5.

[48] Mehmed Cavid, "Meşrutiyet Devrine Ait Cavid Bey'in Hatıraları: 47," *Tanin*, October 17, 1943, p.2.

[49] Mehmed Cavid, "Meşrutiyet Devrine Ait Cavid Bey'in Hatıraları: 48," *Tanin*, October 18, 1943, p.2.

Arabs, Albanians, and other ethnic and religious minorities. Urging the Unionists to change their attitude towards the minorities, the monarchists also asked the lifting of the state of emergency as they claimed that it was not compatible with the notion of constitutional rule. The main point of their demands however was the formation of a Kâmil Pasha Cabinet.[50]

While expressing qualified agreement on most of their demands, the Unionist leadership stood firm on the issue of the appointment of Kâmil Pasha as Grand Vezier. The Unionist leadership argued that not only Kâmil Pasha was not an excellent choice as had been suggested but that his unashamedly pro-British stand on every domestic and foreign issue would compromise Turkey's international position at this juncture. They said that a strongly anglophile vezier such as Kâmil Pasha would totally alienate Germany, while his appointment would not even be well-received by France either. In short, Unionists argued that Kâmil Pasha's appointment to the grand veziership would not be beneficial to Turkey's interests. Furthermore, their total disagreement with Kâmil Pasha would render a coalition government under his grand veziership totally unacceptable to the Committee of Union and Progress. The meeting ended with the Unionists' offer of a formation of a coalition government—presumably under Said Pasha's leadership—which would include three or four opposition deputies as Ministers.[51]

On October 17, the leaders and representatives of the different parliamentary parties held long meetings at which the question of a vote of confidence to the Said Pasha Cabinet was discussed. The Unionists intended to reserve their decision until a further attempt was made to arrive at an agreement with the leaders of the monarchist opposition as to common action. A combined meeting of the opposition groups discussed the possibility of arriving at an understanding during the existing crisis—the war with Italy over Tripoli—with the Committee of Union and Progress, but decided to make the

---

[50] Mehmed Cavid, "Meşrutiyet Devrine Ait Cavid Bey'in Hatıraları: 48," *Tanin*, October 18, 1943, p.2.

[51] Mehmed Cavid, "Meşrutiyet Devrine Ait Cavid Bey'in Hatıraları: 48," *Tanin*, October 18, 1943, p.2.

acceptance by their opponents of certain conditions such as the formation of a non-parliamentary cabinet and the recognition of the grand vezier's right to a form a cabinet in accordance with his own opinions a *sine qua non* of their entering into any combination with the Unionists.[52]

The monarchists had in mind the appointment of Kâmil Pasha as Grand Vezier. In fact, Abdülaziz Mecdi [Tolon] had personally visited the Sultan and requested that Kâmil Pasha be appointed as Grand Vezier in place of Said Pasha. All the members of the royal family were also pressing for Kâmil Pasha's appointment. The Sultan, however, was thoroughly opposed to Kâmil Pasha, and let his views be known to Abdülaziz Mecdi [Tolon]. According to the Sultan, Kâmil Pasha was not a dependable politician, especially in view of the fact that he was a man of the old regime and that several *jurnals* of him written to the ex-Sultan Abdülhamid heavily compromised his integrity.[53] In addition, the mere mention of Kâmil Pasha's name invariably aroused the utmost scorn among the Unionist leadership.[54] Despite this, there were still some hopes among monarchist circles that the Committee of Union and Progress and the opposition would eventually come to a temporary understanding on the basis of a coalition government.[55]

On October 18, Said Pasha read a statement of his government's policy. With respect to domestic affairs, he said that necessary modifications to the Constitution, the definition of the duties of the ministers, laws regarding the administration of the provinces, the elections, military service, and the gendarmerie were contemplated. The financial policy included the increase of revenues by greater customs duties, the uni-

---

[52] "Fırkaların Dünkü İçtimaı," *Yeni İkdam*, October 5, 1327/October 18, 1911, p.1; and, "The Turkish Parliament: Said Pasha's Intentions: Conference of the Opposition Groups," *The Times*, October 19, 1911, p.5.

[53] Mehmed Cavid, "Meşrutiyet Devrine Ait Cavid Bey'in Hatıraları: 52," *Tanin*, October 22, 1943, p.2.

[54] "The Committee of Union and Progress: An Uncompromising Attitude," *The Times*, October 18, 1911, p.5. See also, XXX. 138, Baron von Marschall to the German Foreign Office, Constantinople, October 31, 1911, reproduced in E. T. S. Dugdale (Ed.), *German Diplomatic Documents, 1871-1914, 4: The Descent to the Abyss, 1911-1914*, p.64.

[55] "The Turkish Parliament: Said Pasha's Intentions: Conference of the Opposition Groups," *The Times*, October 19, 1911, p.5.

versal application of the professional tax, or *temettü vergisi*, and new taxes on luxuries. Then, he stated the government's foreign policy. Declaring that the government would defend Ottoman rights at all costs, he added that in order to safeguard the interests of the country, it was proposed to modify the policy hitherto pursued by Turkey and to seek alliances. He promised that the first and foremost task of the government would be to reach a solution of the Tripoli affair such as Turkey considered most favourable to her interests. Expressing desire that Turkey would strengthen her friendly relations with all the Powers, particularly the Balkan states, on a basis of mutual confidence and the recognition of common interests, he assured the Chamber that Turkey had no ambitious designs against any country or any state. Declaring that this constituted the pillar of his cabinet, he promised the pursuance of its execution if the deputies extended to him and his cabinet their confidence.[56]

Delegates of the Committee of Union and Progress and of the opposition met on October 19. The Unionists were represented by Necmeddin [Kocataş], Seyyid Bey, Talât Bey, Ali Cenani Bey, Mehmed Ali Bey, Bedros Haladjian, Emrullah Efendi, and Mecdi Efendi. The opposition was represented by İsmail Hakkı [Mumcu] Pasha, Lütfi Fikri Bey, Gümülcineli İsmail Hakkı Bey, Ahmed Ferid [Tek], Rıza Tevfik [Bölükbaşı], Dr. Rıza Nur, Hamdi Bey, Krikor Zohrab, and Yorgos Boussios. After three hours' discussion, the majority of the delegates decided to inform the Grand Vezier that they would give him a vote of confidence if they received assurances from him that six Ministers—Mahmud Şevket Pasha, Ürgüplü Hayri Bey, Hulusi Bey, Nail Bey, and Abdurrahman Şeref Bey, who belonged to Hakkı Pasha's last Cabinet, and Celal Bey, the new Minister of the Interior—would immediately resign their portfolios. According to *Le Moniteur Oriental* of

---

[56] I/IV/3, October 5, 1327/October 18, 1911, *Meclis-i Mebusan Zabıt Ceridesi, I*, pp.19-21; "Heyet-i Vükelâ Programı," *Tanin*, October 6, 1327/October 19, 1911, pp.2-3; "Heyet-i Cedide-i Vükelânın Hatt-ı Hareketi," *Yeni İkdam*, October 6, 1327/October 19, 1911, p.1; "The Ottoman Parliament," *The Orient, 2/28* (October 25, 1911), p.1; and, "Statement by the Grand Vizier," *The Times*, October 19, 1911, p.5. See also, Cemal Kutay, *Türkiye İstiklâl ve Hürriyet Mücadeleleri Tarihi, 17*, p.9794; and, Mehmed Cavid, "Meşrutiyet Devrine Ait Cavid Bey'in Hatıraları: 50," *Tanin*, October 20, 1943, p.2.

October 20, Said Pasha replied that while he accepted the decision in principle, he would require at least two months to put it into execution. On this point the parties split. The Unionist delegates agreed to temporise. The monarchist opposition, however, refused, and inter-party negotiations ceased then and there.[57]

Later in the day, parliamentary debate on the cabinet programme began. Monarchist deputies Pantoleon Cosmidis, Rıza Tevfik [Bölükbaşı], İsmail Sıdkı Bey, and Lütfi Fikri Bey spoke for the opposition, and Emrullah Efendi replied. Said Pasha then made an impassioned refutation of the charge of inaction, and pleaded for a chance to work for the country.[58] There were moments when the tide seemed turning against the Grand Vezier. However, members of the New Faction with the majority of the Albanian and Armenian deputies rallied to the Committee of Union and Progress, and late at night Said Pasha obtained a vote of confidence by one hundred and twenty-one votes to sixty.[59] The Unionist leadership was so pessimistic in the result of the vote of confidence that they were prepared to regard even a majority of one hundred and ten victorious. A total of one hundred and twenty-one votes, which were above and beyond their expectations, was mainly due to the fact that the bulk of the Armenian deputies had decided, at the last minute, to throw in their support to the Committee of Union and Progress instead of remaining neutral.[60]

The result of the debate was regarded as to a large extent a personal triumph for Said Pasha, who, in spite of his age and

---

[57] "Heyet-i Vükelânın Programı," *Tanin*, October 6, 1327/October 19, 1911, pp.2-3; Mehmed Cavid, "Meşrutiyet Devrine Ait Cavid Bey'in Hatıraları: 50," *Tanin*, October 20, 1943, p.2; "The Turkish Chamber and the Cabinet: A Vote of Confidence," *The Times*, October 20, 1911, p.5; and, "The Ottoman Parliament," *The Orient*, 2/28 (October 25, 1911), p.1.

[58] I/IV/4, October 6, 1327/October 19, 1911, *Meclis-i Mebusan Zabıt Ceridesi*, 1, pp.24-43; "The Ottoman Parliament," *The Orient*, 2/28 (October 25, 1911), p.1; Mehmed Cavid, "Meşrutiyet Devrine Ait Cavid Bey'in Hatıraları: 51," *Tanin*, October 21, 1943, p.2; and, "The Grand Vizier's Speech," *The Times*, October 20, 1911, p.5.

[59] "The Turkish Chamber and the Cabinet: A Vote of Confidence," *The Times*, October 20, 1911, p.5; Mehmed Cavid, "Meşrutiyet Devrine Ait Cavid Bey'in Hatıraları: 51," *Tanin*, October 21, 1943, p.2; "Cabinet Obtains Vote of Confidence," *The Levant Herald and Eastern Express*, October 20, 1911, p.1; and, I/IV/4, October 6, 1327/October 19, 1911, *Meclis-i Mebusan Zabıt Ceridesi*, 1, pp.46-48.

[60] Mehmed Cavid, "Meşrutiyet Devrine Ait Cavid Bey'in Hatıraları: 51," *Tanin*, October 21, 1943, p.2.

infirmity, rose to the occasion in an astonishing manner. He kept the unruly elements thoroughly in hand, and by his speech undoubtedly secured the support of at least twenty waverers or members of the opposition. His position was, of course, far from secure. The demand made by representatives of the monarchist opposition that he should dismiss six of his colleagues was sufficient proof of this. However, his adherents hoped that his success would enable him to obtain support from certain statesmen who had hitherto refused to enter the cabinet, or, at least, to find successors for those six ministers who, according to popular belief, were doomed.[61]

Hopes for a rapprochement between the Unionists and the monarchists were too optimistic. Kâmil Pasha was busy organising a press attack against the new government.[62] In its October 26 issue, the monarchist *Yeni İkdam*, in an effort to force cabinet changes, alleged that Celal Bey, the Unionist Minister of the Interior, had sent in his resignation, and that the Grand Vezier had proposed that office to Avlonyalı Ferid Pasha, formerly Grand Vezier under the old regime.[63] This totally baseless rumour was immediately denied by Said Pasha.[64]

The monarchist opposition nevertheless kept up the campaign to discredit the Committee of Union and Progress in any way imaginable. *Yeni İkdam* published in its October 27 issue the copy of a letter addressed to Seyyid Bey, who had been re-elected to the leadership of the parliamentary party of the Committee of Union and Progress, by Basri Dukacı, deputy for Dibër and a prominent member of the New Faction. Dukacı stated that he had been obliged to sever all connections with the Unionists owing, first, to the refusal of the Central Executive Committee to allow the senators and deputies who were present at the Salonica Congress, to take any effective part in its deliberations; secondly, its continued interference,

---

[61] "The Turkish Chamber and the Cabinet: Said Pasha's Position," *The Times*, October 21, 1911, p.5. See also, Hüseyin Cahid [Yalçın], "Dünkü Celse," *Tanin*, October 7, 1327/October 20, 1911, p.1.

[62] Mehmed Cavid, "Meşrutiyet Devrine Ait Cavid Bey'in Hatıraları: 52," *Tanin*, October 22, 1943, p.2.

[63] *Yeni İkdam*, October 13, 1327/October 26, 1911, quoted in "News Items," *The Levant Herald and Eastern Express*, October 26, 1911, p.1.

[64] "Tekzib-i Resmi," *Yeni İkdam*, October 14, 1327/October 27, 1911, p.4; and, "News Items," *The Levant Herald and Eastern Express*, October 27, 1911, p.1.

despite its promises of amendment, with the cabinet; and thirdly, in consequence of the extent to which personal considerations were still influencing their policy.[65]

Despite monarchist attempts to undermine the liberal democratic order and constant attacks on the Committee of Union and Progress, Unionists had a chance to show their firm commitment to liberal principles—which included the exclusion of the military from involvement in politics—in early November. On November 1, the lately suspended opposition newspaper *Tanzimat,* the editor of which was Lütfi Fikri Bey, reappeared under the name of *Müdafaa-i Hukuk* without permission of the Court Martial. In the October 29 issue of *Tanzimat,* Lütfi Fikri Bey had openly accused the Unionist leadership in Zeki Bey's murder, although there was no strong or concrete evidence in support of this allegation. Besides, the trial of the alleged murderers was still continuing, and no verdict had yet been reached.[66] He continued to attack the Unionists and the judicial system in the November 1 issue of *Müdafaa-i Hukuk.* All the copies exposed for sale were consequently confiscated.[67] Owing to Lütfi Fikri Bey's insistence on the publication of his newspaper, notwithstanding the order for its suppression, on November 4 he was invited to attend before the Court Martial. He refused to comply on the ground of his parliamentary immunity unless he was forced to do so. The police requested him to wait while they telephoned for instructions, but Lütfi Fikri Bey proceeded to the Chamber, where he submitted his case to Ahmed Rıza Bey, the Unionist President of the Chamber. An urgent motion was adopted, unanimously describing Lütfi Fikri Bey's attempted arrest as a clear and insolent violation of the Constitution and inviting the Minister of War to furnish explanations forthwith.[68]

---

[65] "Committee Methods Exposed," *The Times,* October 28, 1911, p.5. See also, "İttihad ve Terakki Fırkası'nda," *Tanin,* October 14, 1327/October 27, 1911, p.3.

[66] Mehmed Cavid, "Meşrutiyet Devrine Ait Cavid Bey'in Hatıraları: 54," *Tanin,* October 24, 1943, p.2.

[67] "The Turkish Press," *The Times,* November 2, 1911, p.5; and, Mehmed Cavid, "Meşrutiyet Devrine Ait Cavid Bey'in Hatıraları: 55," *Tanin,* October 25, 1943, p.2.

[68] "The Turkish Parliament and the Court Martial: The Case of Lutfi Bey," *The Times,* November 6, 1911, p.5; "The Ottoman Parliament," *The Orient,* 2/30 (November 8, 1911), p.1; and, Mehmed Cavid, "Meşrutiyet Devrine Ait Cavid Bey'in Hatıraları: 55," *Tanin,* October 25, 1943, p.2.

At the close of the November 4 debate on the case of Lütfi Fikri Bey, İdris Pasha, the President of the İstanbul Court Martial, arrived at the Chamber and discussed the situation for nearly an hour with the Unionist leadership. He informed them that the Minister of War was ready to take all responsibility for the action of the Court Martial and would furnish the Chamber of Deputies the necessary explanations at a later date. The incident aroused considerable excitement in parliamentary circles, and speculation was rife regarding its possible consequences. While an overwhelming majority of deputies appreciated the firm stand of the Unionist leadership against the Court Martial authorities, some members of the monarchist opposition still expressed scepticism as to the willingness of the Committee of Union and Progress to support the opposition deputy, who identified himself with the anti-Unionist agitation against the Court Martial, on a question of principle.[69]

At the November 6 sitting of the Chamber, a message from the Minister of War was read, promising to be present in person or by delegate on November 8 to answer the interrogation of the previous sitting.[70] The deputies were roused to a high pitch of zeal for the defence of the Constitution against what they deemed an attack by Mahmud Şevket Pasha, whom Rıza Tevfik [Bölükbaşı] did not hesitate to call publicly a "mannequin stuffed with straw." The Chamber decided to insist on the Minister of War attending immediately to offer his explanations.[71] During a prolonged noon recess, Mahmud Şevket Pasha was interviewed, and he stuck to his guns, but sent in his place İdris Pasha, the President of the İstanbul Court Martial, who when the Chamber sat again, explained that Lütfi Fikri Bey had been merely invited to appear before the Court Martial, and that there had been no intention or at-

[69] I/IV/10, October 22, 1327/November 4, 1911, *Meclis-i Mebusan Zabıt Ceridesi, 1,* pp.244-245; "Lütfi Fikri Bey ve Divan-ı Harb ve Meclis-i Mebusan," *Yeni İkdam,* October 23, 1327/November 5, 1911, p.1; and, "The Turkish Parliament and the Court Martial: The Case of Lutfi Bey," *The Times,* November 6, 1911, p.5.

[70] I/IV/11, October 24, 1327/November 6, 1911, *Meclis-i Mebusan Zabıt Ceridesi, 1,* p.261.

[71] I/IV/11, October 24, 1327/November 6, 1911, *Meclis-i Mebusan Zabıt Ceridesi, 1,* pp.261-273; and, "The Ottoman Parliament," *The Orient, 2/30* (November 8, 1911), p.1.

tempt to arrest him; that the Minister of War had been very busy; and that with the ongoing manoeuvres in the vicinity of İstanbul he had been compelled to postpone appearing before the Chamber till November 8. The Chamber chose to consider these explanations insufficient, but agreed to wait two days more for the Minister.[72]

İdris Pasha's statement in the Chamber on November 6 was regarded as an advance version of the explanations which would be given by the Minister of War on November 8.[73] At the November 8 sitting, Mahmud Şevket Pasha appeared before the Chamber and made his reply, which lasted nearly an hour. He gave his reasons for not appearing earlier, and indignantly denied having attempted any violation of the Constitution. He also denied the charge made by some newspapers that he was taking the role of a dictator. He declared his confidence in the Committee of Union and Progress and his unwillingness to take a position in any cabinet to be formed by Kâmil Pasha or anyone else, if not favourable to the Unionists. The Minister then reviewed the career of *Tanzimat* and the subversive articles published therein. He went on to say that the Court Martial had therefore summoned the editor to appear, but that there had been no order to arrest. At the afternoon sitting, Lütfi Fikri Bey answered the speech of Mahmud Şevket Pasha, alleging that it was no mere request to attend that was served on him, but a peremptory order. He also violently criticised the whole attitude of the Minister of War, and the prolongation of martial law in the capital. The Grand Vezier then made a long speech, condemning the violent recriminations of Lütfi Fikri Bey and upholding the Minister of War.[74]

---

[72] I/IV/11, October 24, 1327/November 6, 1911, *Meclis-i Mebusan Zabıt Ceridesi*, 1, pp.274-281; and, "The Ottoman Parliament," *The Orient*, 2/30 (November 8, 1911), p.1.

[73] "The Turkish Political Situation," *The Times*, November 7, 1911, p.7. See also, "Dünkü Ahval," *Yeni İkdam*, October 25, 1327/November 7, 1911, p.1; and, "Lütfi Fikri Bey'in Tevkifi Etrafında," *Yeni İkdam*, October 25, 1327/November 7, 1911, p.2. Seyyid Bey and Bedros Haladjian, both of the Committee of Union and Progress, visited Mahmud Şevket Pasha and urged him to appear before the Chamber ("İttihad ve Terakki Fırkası Reisi," *Yeni İkdam*, October 25, 1327/November 7, 1911, p.2).

[74] I/IV/12, October 26, 1327/November 8, 1911, *Meclis-i Mebusan Zabıt Ceridesi*, 1, pp.287-331; Hüseyin Cahid [Yalçın], "Boşa Gitmemiş bir Celse," *Tanin*, October 27, 1327/November 9, 1911, p.1; and, "The Ottoman Parliament," *The*

The firm stand of the Committee of Union and Progress on this question involving constitutional rights of the deputies produced the desired result: the military accepted its mistake. Minister of War's explanations in the November 8 sitting of the Chamber was an admittance of the military's wrongdoing. Mahmud Şevket Pasha's explanations were interpreted that the Court Martial would in future confine itself to sending written invitations to deputies to furnish it with explanations. The motion proposed by Seyyid Bey, the leader of the parliamentary party of the Committee of Union and Progress, which was accepted by the Chamber on November 9, and the declarations of the Grand Vezier both implied that any attempt on the part of the Court Martial to arrest a deputy during the session would be regarded as an anti-constitutional act.[75]

By mid-November, a rift between Said Pasha and the monarchist-dominated Senate had appeared, and was growing ever wider. This had to do with what the Grand Vezier considered the Senate's independent attitude.[76] Halid Ziya [Uşaklıgil], the Sultan's Secretary and one of the most trusted members of the Committee of Union and Progress, had been nominated for senator.[77] Damad Ferid Pasha, however, opposed his nomination on the ground that the Constitution forbade pluralism, and that officials or officers in active employment could not become senators unless they resigned their posts.[78] Although Halid Ziya [Uşaklıgil]'s resignation in order to accept the office of senator was announced in the November 2

Orient, 2/31 (November 15, 1911), p.2.

[75] I/IV/13, October 27, 1327/November 9, 1911, *Meclis-i Mebusan Zabıt Ceridesi, 1*, pp.336-359; "The Case of Lutfi Bey: Deputies and the Court-Martial," *The Times*, November 10, 1911, p.5; "İstizah Neticelendi," *Yeni İkdam*, October 28, 1327/November 10, 1911, p.1; "The Ottoman Parliament," *The Orient, 2/31* (November 15, 1911), p.2; and, Mehmed Cavid, "Meşrutiyet Devrine Ait Cavid Bey'in Hatıraları: 55," *Tanin*, October 25, 1943, p.2.

[76] Hüseyin Cahid [Yalçın], "Meclis-i Âyan ve Hükûmet," *Tanin*, November 3, 1327/November 16, 1911, p.1; and, "Constantinople Letter," *The Near East*, November 22, 1911, p.63. See also "Constantinople Letter," *The Near East*, November 15, 1911, p.35.

[77] I/IV/1, October 3, 1327/October 16, 1911, *Meclis-i Âyan Zabıt Ceridesi, 1*, p.3; "Nouvelles du Jour," *The Levant Herald and Eastern Express*, October 16, 1911, p.2.

[78] I/IV/1, October 3, 1327/October 16, 1911, *Meclis-i Âyan Zabıt Ceridesi, 1*, pp.4-5; I/IV/2, October 4, 1327/October 17, 1911, *Meclis-i Âyan Zabıt Ceridesi, 1*, pp.13-14; I/IV/6, October 18, 1327/October 31, 1911, *Meclis-i Âyan Zabıt Ceridesi, 1*, pp.38-41; "Constantinople Letter," *The Near East*, November 22, 1911, p.63; and, "Scenes from the Senate," *The Orient, 2/31* (November 15, 1911), p.4.

issues of the newspapers, monarchist opposition was adamant.[79] After a sharp exchange on the Senate floor, opposing
senators led by Hüseyin Hilmi Pasha, were able to carry their
point. They then decided to select a deputation which would
present their case to the Sultan. Vainly, Said Pasha urged
them to reconsider this last decision, pointing out that the Senate would be exceeding its rights if it ignored the government
and communicated directly with the Sultan. Hüseyin Hilmi
Pasha, Gabriel Nouradunghian, and Damad Ferid Pasha,
along with other well known senators maintained that nothing in the Constitution forbade them to do so.[80]

They carried out their protest and communicated to the
Sultan the Senate's protest against the nomination of Halid Ziya [Uşaklıgil] as a senator.[81] The protest note was handed by
the Sultan to Said Pasha, whose reply described the Senate's
action as illegal.[82] However, the Senate, led by Hüseyin Hilmi
Pasha in the struggle with the Said Pasha Cabinet, showed no
signs of readiness to accept the Grand Vezier's ruling.[83]
Though Halid Ziya [Uşaklıgil] resigned his senatorship, Said
Pasha insisted on the question of principle. The matter, however, was left unresolved.[84]

On November 14, rumours were circulated that Nail Bey,
one of the few Ministers of the Said Pasha Cabinet who had
gained both in popularity and prestige of late, contemplated re-

[79] "News Items," *The Levant Herald and Eastern Express*, November 2, 1911, p.1.
[80] I/IV/7, October 22, 1327/November 4, 1911, *Meclis-i Âyan Zabıt Ceridesi, 1*, pp.56-67; "The Turkish Political Situation," *The Times*, November 7, 1911, p.7; "Scenes from the Senate," *The Orient*, 2/31 (November 15, 1911), p.4; and, "Con-stantinople Letter," *The Near East*, November 22, 1911, p.63. See also "Constan-tinople Letter," *The Near East*, November 15, 1911, p.35.
[81] I/IV/9, October 25, 1327/November 7, 1911, *Meclis-i Âyan Zabıt Ceridesi, 1*, pp.81-90; and, I/IV/10, October 29, 1327/November 11, 1911, *Meclis-i Âyan Zabıt Ceridesi, 1*, p.94.
[82] I/IV/11, November 1, 1327/November 14, 1911, *Meclis-i Âyan Zabıt Ceri-desi, 1*, pp.104-108; and, "Scenes from the Senate," *The Orient*, 2/31 (November 15, 1911), p.4.
[83] "Scenes from the Senate," *The Orient*, 2/31 (November 15, 1911), p.4; and, "The Turkish Senate and the Grand Vezier," *The Times*, November 16, 1911, p.5. See also, I/IV/12, November 5, 1327/November 18, 1911, *Meclis-i Âyan Zabıt Ceri-desi, 1*, pp.113-115.
[84] I/IV/13, November 8, 1327/November 21, 1911, *Meclis-i Âyan Zabıt Ceri-desi, 1*, pp.119-137; I/IV/14, November 12, 1327/November 25, 1911, *Meclis-i Âyan Zabıt Ceridesi, 1*, pp.141-143; and, "Political Parties in Turkey," *The Times*, De-cember 5, 1911, p.5.

signing office after the upcoming debate on the Budget. The cause of the decision was ascribed to the hostility of one of his recently appointed colleagues in the cabinet.[85] Of course, the differences of opinion arose on the issue of the military budget. Nail Bey's plea before the Chamber for economy in the control of military expenditure caused much comment in Unionist circles of a general and deservedly favourable character. The obvious incompatibility of his views with the Minister of War naturally aroused some speculation as to the possibility of a further conflict between the Unionist leadership and Mahmud Şevket Pasha. The Unionist stand on the issue of the military budget was extremely courageous, and they had to be congratulated for advocating economy at a moment when all the chauvinist elements in the country were clamouring for the increase of military and naval expenditure.[86]

On November 21, the much talked-about new opposition party, conservative and monarchist in nature, was finally formed under the name of Entente Libérale—or, Hürriyet ve İtilâf Fırkası.[87] Its founders were Damad Ferid Pasha, a well known monarchist senator, ex-Colonel Sadık Bey, the leader of the opposition group New Faction, İsmail Hakkı [Mumcu] Pasha, leader of the Moderate Liberals, Lütfi Fikri Bey, opposition deputy for Dersim, Dr. Rıza Nur, monarchist deputy for Sinob, Rıza Tevfik [Bölükbaşı], monarchist deputy for Edirne, Marshal Fuad Pasha, better known as 'Deli' Fuad Pasha, Süley-

[85] "The Turkish Finance Minister," *The Times*, November 15, 1911, p.5.
[86] I/IV/21, November 14, 1327/November 27, 1911, *Meclis-i Mebusan Zabıt Ceridesi*, 2, pp.71-84; and, "Turkish Finance: A Plea for Economy," *The Times*, November 29, 1911, p.5.
[87] "Kuvvetli bir Lema-ı Ümit," *Yeni İkdam*, November 8, 1327/November 21, 1911, p.1; *Tesisat*, November 8, 1327/November 21, 1911, quoted in Tarık Zafer Tunaya, *Türkiye'de Siyasi Partiler, 1859-1952*, p.316n; "Un nouveau Parti," *The Levant Herald and Eastern Express*, November 21, 1911, p.1; "Yeni bir ·Fırka," *Tanin*, November 9, 1327/November 22, 1911, p.3; "Hürriyet ve İtilâf Fırkası," *Yeni İkdam*, November 9, 1327/November 22, 1911, p.1; "Turkish Politics: Formation of a New Party," *The Times*, November 22, 1911, p.5; and, "Empire News: The Capital," *The Orient*, 2/33 (November 29, 1911), p.6. For the Unionist comments on the formation of the party see, Hüseyin Cahid [Yalçın], "Hürriyet ve İtilâf Fırkası," *Tanin*, November 10, 1327/November 23, 1911, p.1; Hüseyin Cahid [Yalçın], "Hürriyet ve İtilâf Fırkası," *Tanin*, November 11, 1327/November 24, 1911, p.1. See also, Hüseyin Cahid Yalçın, "Meşrutiyet Hatıraları, 1908-1918," *Fikir Hareketleri*, 7 (October 24, 1936-April 17, 1937), p.6; Ahmed Bedevi Kuran, *Osmanlı İmparatorluğunda İnkılâp Hareketleri ve Milli Mücadele*, p.552; and, Yusuf Hikmet Bayur, *Türk İnkılâbı Tarihi*, 2/1, pp.233-234.

man Pasha, retired General of Cavalry, Vefik Pasha, ex-Governor of Konya, 'Abd al-Hamid az-Zahrawi, the well known monarchist Arab deputy for Hama, Mustafa Sabri Efendi, deputy for Tokad, Nazareth Daghavarian, Armenian deputy for Sivas, Volçetrinli Hasan Bey, Albanian deputy for Prishtnë, Basri Dukacı, Albanian deputy for Dibër, and Tahir Hayreddin Bey, son of Tunuslu Hayreddin Pasha and a monarchist journalist.[88]

The administrative council of the party was headed by Damad Ferid Pasha and included ex-Colonel Sadık Bey as its Vice-President, and the following deputies: Dr. Rıza Nur, deputy for Sinob, Lütfi Fikri Bey, deputy for Dersim, Gümülcineli İsmail Hakkı Bey, deputy for Gümülcine, Rıza Tevfik [Bölükbaşı], deputy for Edirne, Mahir Said Bey, deputy for Ankara, İsmail Sıdkı Bey, deputy for Aydın—all of whom were Turks—and, the Albanians Basri Dukacı, deputy for Dibër, and Ahmed Hamdi Efendi, deputy for İpek, and Shukri al-Asali, Arab deputy for Damascus. It also included Siret Bey, a journalist who was known to be a close friend of Prince Sabahaddin, Kemal Midhat Bey, a representative of the Midhat Pasha family, and, Midhat Frashëri, formerly Political Director to the Salonica province.[89]

At its November 23 meeting, the new party elected as its Leader of the parliamentary party İsmail Hakkı [Mumcu] Pa-

[88] Tarık Zafer Tunaya, *Türkiye'de Siyasi Partiler, 1859-1952*, p.315; "Hürriyet ve İtilâf Fırkası," *Yeni İkdam*, November 9, 1327/November 22, 1911, p.2; "News Items," *The Levant Herald and Eastern Express*, November 22, 1911, p.1; "Turkish Politics: Formation of a New Party," *The Times*, November 22, 1911, p.5; "The New Parliamentary Party," *The Orient*, 2/34 (December 6, 1911), p.1; Ahmed Bedevi Kuran, *Osmanlı İmparatorluğunda İnkılâp Hareketleri ve Milli Mücadele*, p.552; and, Ali Birinci, *Hürriyet ve İtilâf Fırkası: II. Meşrutiyet Devrinde İttihat ve Terakki'ye Karşı Çıkanlar*, pp.45-48. See also, Rashid Khalidi, "Ottomanism and Arabism in Syria Before 1914: A Reassessment," p.59; and, Ahmed Tarabein, "Abd al-Hamid al-Zahrawi: The Career and Thought of an Arab Nationalist," p.100.
[89] *Tesisat*, November 11, 1327/November 24, 1911, and *Yeni İkdam*, November 11, 1327/November 24, 1911, both quoted in Tarık Zafer Tunaya, *Türkiye'de Siyasi Partiler, 1859-1952*, p.315; "Le parti de l'Entente Libérale," *The Levant Herald and Eastern Express*, November 25, 1911, p.2; "Constantinople Letter," *The Near East*, November 29, 1911, p.95; and, Hüseyin Cahid Yalçın, "Meşrutiyet Hatıraları, 1908-1918," *Fikir Hareketleri*, 7 (October 24, 1936-April 17, 1937), p.6. See also, Ziya Şakir [Soko], "Hürriyet ve İtilâf Nasıl Doğdu? Nasıl Yaşadı? Nasıl Battı? 25: Günün En Kuvvetli Siması Miralay Sadık Bey'di," *Tan*, November 27, 1937, p.9; and, Ali Birinci, *Hürriyet ve İtilâf Fırkası: II. Meşrutiyet Devrinde İttihat ve Terakki'ye Karşı Çıkanlar*, p.49, and, p.65. For the political career of Shukri al-Asali see, Samir Seikaly, "Shukri al-'Asali: A Case Study of a Political Activist," pp.73-96; and, Philip S. Khoury, *Urban Notables and Arab Nationalism: The Politics of Damascus, 1860-1920*, pp.61-62.

sha and as its Deputy-Leaders Hoca Mustafa Sabri Efendi and Nazareth Daghavarian. The administrative committee consisted of Şeyhzade Zeynelabidin Efendi, deputy for Konya, Said al-Husseini Bey, deputy for Jerusalem, İbrahim Vasfi Efendi, deputy for Karesi, Davud Yusufani Efendi, deputy for Mosul, Ahmed Şükrü Efendi, deputy for Sivas, and Haznedarzade Mahmud Mazhar Bey, deputy for Trabzon.[90]

A majority of the Greek and Albanian deputies supported the new party's programme, but declined to join, stating that such a move would be distasteful to their electors.[91] Nonetheless, there was reason to believe that the Committee of Union and Progress would suffer further defections following publication of the new party's platform. Some monarchists estimated that Entente Libérale might be, in fact, one hundred deputies strong.[92] Indeed, on November 24, it was announced that five Unionists deputies had resigned from the Committee of Union and Progress and joined the Entente Libérale. These deputies were Şükrü Bey, deputy for Maraş, Faradj Sa'id Bey, deputy for 'Asir, Sheikh Bashir al-Ghazzi Efendi, deputy for Aleppo, Muhammad Shawkat ibn Rif'at Pasha, deputy for Divaniye, and Kamil al-As'ad Efendi, deputy for Beirut.[93]

Including the defecting deputies from the Committee of

[90] "Meclis-i Mebusan: Hürriyet ve İtilâf Fırkası," *Yeni İkdam*, November 11, 1327/November 24, 1911, pp.2-3; *Tesisat*, November 11, 1327/November 24, 1911, quoted in Tarık Zafer Tunaya, *Türkiye'de Siyasi Partiler, 1859-1952*, p.315; ; "Hürriyet ve İtilâf Fırkası," *Tanin*, November 11, 1327/November 24, 1911, p.3; "The New Turkish Party," *The Times*, November 24, 1911, p.5; and, "L'Entente Libérale," *The Levant Herald and Eastern Express*, November 24, 1911, p.2.

[91] "Les Grecs et le Nouveau Parti," *The Levant Herald and Eastern Express*, November 29, 1911, p.1; "Constantinople Letter," *The Near East*, November 29, 1911, p.95; and, "Political Parties in Turkey: The New Party," *The Times*, December 5, 1911, p.5. See also, Basil Kondis, *Greece and Albania, 1908-1914*, p.65; Diogenis Xanalatos, "The Greeks and the Turks on the Eve of the Balkan Wars: A Frustrated Plan," p.289; Ziya Şakir [Soko], "Hürriyet ve İtilâf Nasıl Doğdu? Nasıl Yaşadı? Nasıl Battı? 27: Gümülcinelinin İhtirası Arkadaşlarını Bıktırıyordu," *Tan*, November 29, 1937, p.9; Feroz Ahmad, "Unionist Relations with the Greek, Armenian, and Jewish Communities of the Ottoman Empire, 1908-1914," p.415; and, Ali Birinci, *Hürriyet ve İtilâf Fırkası: II. Meşrutiyet Devrinde İttihat ve Terakki'ye Karşı Çıkanlar*, pp.50-51. For the programme of the party see, Mehmet O. Alkan, "Türkiye'de Siyasal Partiler Tarihine Katkı, I: Hürriyet ve İ'tilâf Fırkası'nın İlk Programı ve Nizâmnamesi," pp.50-55.

[92] "Constantinople Letter," *The Near East*, November 29, 1911, p.95; and, "Turkish Politics: Formation of a New Party," *The Times*, November 22, 1911, p.5. See also, Şehbenderzade Filibeli Ahmed Hilmi, *Muhalefetin İflâsı: İtilâf ve Hürriyet Fırkası*, p.41.

[93] "L'Entente Libérale," *The Levant Herald and Eastern Express*, November 24, 1911, p.2.

Union and Progress, the total number of Entente Libérale deputies, however, remained around seventy.[94] This meant that
the new party failed to obtain a majority in the Chamber, and
was thus unable to force the formation of a new government.
In addition, it was not likely that any of the monarchist statesmen, whom rumour described as the real leaders of the new
party, were particularly anxious to accept the responsibility of
office at this particular juncture.[95]

The conservative and monarchist press praised the Entente
Libérale.[96] The conservative *Sabah* of November 23 welcomed
the formation of the new party in the most favourable terms.[97]
The monarchist *Levant Herald and Eastern Express* of
November 27 was also highly jubilant at the establishment of
a distinctly monarchist party.[98] Another monarchist
newspaper, *Yeni İkdam*, wrote that a study of the programme
of the Entente Libérale showed that the party had been
formed, not to domineer and oppress, but to respond to a social
necessity. "Had the country not felt such a need, the nature of
events would not have compelled the formation of this party."
Claiming that the party had accepted the programme prepared
according to convictions, *Yeni İkdam* wrote that in their political consciousness there was nothing save the contents of
that programme. Expressing the wish that the Turkish Chamber should resemble that of England, *Yeni İkdam* went on to
say that they were in favour of having two parties in the
Chamber, as there were in England. In an explicit effort to
merge all the parliamentary groups opposed to the Committee
of Union and Progress within the Entente Libérale, *Yeni İkdam* alleged that there was no group that could not enter the
Entente Libérale as the party's programme was so flexible.
Expressing the view that they did not believe there was in

[94] "L'Entente Libérale," *The Levant Herald and Eastern Express*, November 24, 1911, p.2.
[95] "Constantinople Letter," *The Near East*, November 29, 1911, p.95.
[96] Ziya Şakir [Soko], "Hürriyet ve İtilâf Nasıl Doğdu? Nasıl Yaşadı? Nasıl Battı? 23: Gazeteler Fırkanın Kurulduğu Haberini Veriyordu," *Tan*, November 24, 1937, p.9.
[97] *Sabah*, November 10, 1327/November 23, 1911, quoted in *The Levant Herald and Eastern Express*, November 23, 1911, p.1; and, "The New Parliamentary Party," *The Orient*, 2/34 (December 6, 1911), p.1.
[98] "Le Nouveau parti," *The Levant Herald and Eastern Express*, November 27, 191, p.1.

Turkey a programme more conformed to the country's interests, *Yeni İkdam* did not approve the attitude of the Greek and
Armenian deputies, who held themselves between heaven
and earth. The newspaper urged these deputies to immediately join the Entente Libérale.[99]

The establishment of the new party, as well as its programme, drew sharp criticism from both *Tanin*, and *Rumeli*,
Silâh and other Salonica newspapers. The pro-Unionist press
generally condemned the new party as a public danger.[100]
Writing in the *Tanin* of November 23, and 24, Hüseyin Cahid
[Yalçın] commented that what had brought this group together was not a coherent ideal or point of view, but the wish
to destroy the Committee of Union and Progress along with
the liberal democratic regime it was trying to establish. He
expressed the view that sooner or later dissensions would arise
among the members of this party who held such diverse political opinions.[101] In his newspaper *Isopolitia*, Yorgos Boussios,
Greek deputy for Serfidje, criticised the programme as being
hastily drawn up and wanting the elements needed for a
really useful basis of work, and as being long rather than
stout. *La Liberté* wrote that the new party seemed to be merely
a syndicate of malcontents, whose programme lacked clearness and preciseness on the very points where the various
nationalities were in danger of splitting apart. Reflecting
Unionist viewpoint, *Le Jeune Turc*, said that they still remembered the violent and vehement polemic between Rıza Tevfik
[Bölükbaşı], monarchist deputy for Edirne, and Hoca Basri
Efendi the previous year in the columns of *Yeni Gazete*, each
of them upholding principles and ideas absolutely irreconcilable.[102]

---

[99] 'Program Demek İhtiyac-ı İctimai Demektir," *Yeni İkdam*, November 11,
1327/November 24, 1911, p.1; and, "The New Parliamentary Party," *The Orient*,
2/34 (December 6, 1911), p.1.
[100] Hüseyin Cahid [Yalçın], "Hürriyet ve İtilâf Fırkası," *Tanin*, November 10,
1327/November 23, 1911, p.1; "The New Turkish Party," *The Times*, November 24,
1911, p.5; and, "Constantinople Letter," *The Near East*, December 6, 1911, p.127.
[101] Hüseyin Cahid [Yalçın], "Hürriyet ve İtilâf Fırkası," *Tanin*, November 10,
1327/November 23, 1911, p.1; and, Hüseyin Cahid [Yalçın], "Hürriyet ve İtilâf Fırkası," *Tanin*, November 11, 1327/November 24, 1911, p.1; and, Hüseyin Cahid Yalçın, "Meşrutiyet Hatıraları, 1908-1918," *Fikir Hareketleri*, 7 (October 24, 1936-
April 17, 1937), p.6 and 21. See also Tarık Zafer Tunaya, *Türkiye'de Siyasi Partiler,
1859-1952*, p.318n.
[102] "The New Parliamentary Party," *The Orient*, 2/34 (December 6, 1911), p.1.

On their part, monarchists continued their press attacks against members of the Committee of Union and Progress. Their latest target was Musa Kâzım Efendi, the Sheikh-ul-Islam, who was a freemason. In the eyes of the monarchists, the fact that he was a freemason made his devotion to Islam questionable; he was forced to publicly defend himself as a result of the attacks.[103] In his editorial column in *Tesisat*, Lütfi Fikri Bey called upon the Sheikh-ul-Islam to resign. While writing that it was not just, in an age of liberty of conscience and of religion, to call in question the religious belief of any individual, Lütfi Fikri Bey nevertheless went on to say that when there was the slightest doubt cast on the religious convictions of one occupying one of the highest religious positions, such a person ought at once to resign his position and straightaway defend himself.[104]

Meanwhile, the Entente Libérale decided to enter the İstanbul by-election to be held on December 11, contesting the seat that had been left vacant when Rıfat Pasha, the ex-Minister for Foreign Affairs in the Hakkı Pasha Cabinet, was appointed Turkish Ambassador in Paris.[105] The new party mounted a vigorous propaganda campaign aimed at both the first and second degree electors.[106] Memduh Bey, the new Minister of Justice, had been chosen as the Unionist candidate, but overconfidence marred his campaign. His opponent was Tahir Hayreddin Bey, son of a former Grand Vezier Tunuslu Hay-

---

[103] Musa Kâzım, "Beyanname," *Tanin*, November 15, 1327/November 28, 1911, pp.1-2; and, Musa Kâzım, "Beyanname," *Yeni İkdam*, November 16, 1327/November 29, 1911, p.3. See also, Hüseyin Cahid Yalçın, "Meşrutiyet Hatıraları, 1908-1918," *Fikir Hareketleri*, 7 (October 24, 1936-April 17, 1937), p.21.

[104] "The Sheikh-ul-Islam Under Fire," *The Orient*, 2/34 (December 6, 1911), p.4. See also, "Franmasonluk," *Yeni İkdam*, November 17, 1327/November 30, 1911, p.1.

[105] Hüseyin Cahid [Yalçın], "İstanbul İntihabı Etrafında," *Tanin*, November 16, 1327/November 29, 1911, p.1; "L'Entente Libérale," *The Levant Herald and Eastern Express*, December 5, 1911, p.1; and, "Empire News: The Capital," *The Orient*, 2/34 (December 6, 1911), p.6. See also, "İstanbul Mebusluğu," *Yeni İkdam*, November 16, 1327/November 29, 1911, p.1; and, "Yine İstanbul Mebusluğu," *Yeni İkdam*, November 18, 1327/December 1, 1911, p.1.

[106] For propaganda on behalf of Entente Libérale in the columns of *Yeni İkdam* see, "Hürriyet ve İtilâf Fırkası'nın Beyannamesidir," *Yeni İkdam*, November 19, 1327/December 2, 1911, p.1; and, "İstanbul Müntehib-i Sanileri Hemşehrilerimize," *Yeni İkdam*, November 22, 1327/December 5, 1911, p.1. See also, "Rey Sandıklarına Dikkat," *Yeni İkdam*, November 28, 1327/December 11, 1911, p.1.

reddin Pasha, proprietor of the monarchists' organ *Alemdar*, and one of the Unionists' most outspoken critics.[107]

Two hundred and ninety-four electors participated in the by-elections that were held on December 11. Tahir Hayreddin Bey, the Entente Libérale candidate, received one hundred and ninety-six votes, while Memduh Bey, Minister of Justice and the Unionist candidate, obtained one hundred and ninety-five votes, losing the race by only one vote.[108] Thus, to the surprise of the Committee of Union and Progress as well as his own, Tahir Hayreddin Bey, won by a margin of one vote, thanks largely to Christian support and the recent wave of defections from the Committee of Union and Progress.[109]

Addressing the Entente Libérale supporters, Damad Ferid Pasha claimed that the election of Tahir Hayreddin Bey had shown that the nation had full confidence in the new party, and that Entente Libérale, thus clothed with national confidence, could render noteworthy service to the state. He said that the party had two main objects: one, the establishing of an actual Constitution; the other, the securing of Ottoman unity by full harmony between the various nationalities. While the majority given Tahir Hayreddin Bey was a proof that the former was well appreciated by the Ottoman nation, the latter was already assured, since the Greek and Armenian second degree electors, with few exceptions, had voted almost unanimously for the Entente Libérale candidate.[110]

---

[107] "İstanbul Mebusluğu Namzedleri," *Yeni İkdam*, November 27, 1327/December 10, 1911, p.3; "Constantinople Letter," *The Near East*, December 20, 1911, p.191; Ahmed Bedevi Kuran, *Osmanlı İmparatorluğunda İnkılâp Hareketleri ve Milli Mücadele*, p.553; and, Yusuf Hikmet Bayur, *Türk İnkılâbı Tarihi*, 2/1, p.236. See also, Şehbenderzade Filibeli Ahmed Hilmi, *Muhalefetin İflâsı: İtilâf ve Hürriyet Fırkası*, p.42.

[108] "Legislative Election," and "L'Election d'hier," *The Levant Herald and Eastern Express*, December 12, 1911, p.1; Ahmed Bedevi Kuran, *Osmanlı İmparatorluğunda İnkılâp Hareketleri ve Milli Mücadele*, p.553; and, Hüseyin Cahid Yalçın, "Meşrutiyet Hatıraları, 1908-1918," *Fikir Hareketleri*, 7 (October 24, 1936-April 17, 1937), p.22. Two votes were cast for Şefik Bey and one vote for Şemseddin Bey, a former Minister of Pious Foundations ("L'Election d'hier," *The Levant Herald and Eastern Express*, December 12, 1911, p.1).

[109] "Constantinople Letter," *The Near East*, December 20, 1911, p.191; Mehmed Cavid, "Meşrutiyet Devrine Ait Cavid Bey'in Hatıraları: 60," *Tanin*, October 30, 1943, p.2; Ali Birinci, *Hürriyet ve İtilâf Fırkası: II. Meşrutiyet Devrinde İttihat ve Terakki'ye Karşı Çıkanlar*, pp.103-104; and, Yusuf Hikmet Bayur, *Türk İnkılâbı Tarihi*, 2/1, p.236.

[110] "The Defeat of the Committee of Union and Progress," *The Orient*, 2/36 (December 20, 1911), p.4; and, Ali Birinci, *Hürriyet ve İtilâf Fırkası: II. Meşrutiyet Devrinde İttihat ve Terakki'ye Karşı Çıkanlar*, p.104.

The victory of the Entente Libérale candidate by a single vote caused general surprise. It was ascribed by the monarchist press to the growing unpopularity of the Committee of Union and Progress in the capital and elsewhere.[111] The monarchist *Yeni Gazete* lost no time in claiming that the Committee of Union and Progress had, with the lapse of time, departed from its original basis and was losing ground each day by following a policy of favouritism for its partisans. *Yeni Gazete* went on to say that the nation wished to live under a free and truly constitutional administration, asserting that it would tolerate no oppression from any quarter whatever and it would not forgive those who abused its confidence.[112]

Indeed, there was a decrease in the enthusiastic support accorded to the Committee of Union of Progress in some parts of Anatolia. Despite Cavid Bey's successful visit in the fall of 1911, the Committee's influence in Erzurum, for instance, had become questionable. While dissension plagued the Erzurum branch of the Committee of Union and Progress, two of its local branches in the countryside had ceased to exist, and some of those who remained were said to be leaning towards the newly formed monarchist political party, Entente Libérale. By December, placards denouncing the Committee of Union and Progress and the Constitution were visible throughout the town, and meetings between *mollahs* and other reactionaries were reportedly being held.[113]

There was reason, however, to believe that the Unionists might have held the İstanbul seat had they not presumed too much on the superiority of their organisation and neglected to employ canvassers. In any case, the general elections was still five months ahead, and any deductions from the result of the İstanbul by-election might prove misleading.[114] Writing in

---

[111] "A Constantinople Election: Success of the New Party," *The Times*, December 13, 1911, p.6; Basil Kondis, *Greece and Albania, 1908-1914*, p.66; and, Feroz Ahmad, *The Young Turks: The Committee of Union and Progress in Turkish Politics, 1908-1914*, p.100.

[112] "The Defeat of the Committee of Union and Progress," *The Orient*, 2/36 (December 20, 1911), p.4; and, Mehmed Cavid, "Meşrutiyet Devrine Ait Cavid Bey'in Hatıraları: 60," *Tanin*, October 30, 1943, p.2.

[113] F.O. 424/230, Consul McGregor to Sir Gerard Lowther, Erzerum, December 27, 1911, *Further Correspondence Respecting the Affairs of Asiatic Turkey and Arabia*, No.10075, p.14.

[114] "A Constantinople Election: Success of the New Party," *The Times*, De-

Tanin, Hüseyin Cahid [Yalçın] reminded the fact that at the elections held two years previously one of the opposition candidates had received one hundred and twenty votes, another thirty and a third thirty-five. That is, two years ago, more than one hundred and eighty votes in İstanbul had gone to the opposition. Given these figures, Hüseyin Cahid [Yalçın] wrote that in the course of the two years the opposition had gained only twenty-six votes, claiming that it was no great success. He then draw upon lessons from the Unionist defeat. Admitting that the Committee of Union and Progress could not live on the glorious record of its first success in bringing in the constitutional order, he took it as only natural that the Unionists should be attacked from without, and that treachery should appear from within. Foreseeing possible defections from the party, Hüseyin Cahid [Yalçın] declared that the Committee of Union and Progress, secure on its grand foundations, needed to purify itself. Insisting that the purification be as radical as possible, he declared that those who had joined from personal motives and not from conviction would confer a great benefit on the party by quitting it.[115] There was indeed a defection from the party: *Yeni İkdam* and *The Levant Herald and Eastern Express* of December 14 announced that Mustafa Asım Efendi, deputy for İstanbul, resigned from the Committee of Union and Progress.[116]

On December 13, a rumour which had been circulating for several days crystallised into fact. Said Pasha summoned the Chamber for a special session to propose the modification of Article 35 of the Constitution.[117] Said Pasha's proposal had first

---

cember 13, 1911, p.6; and, Mehmed Cavid, "Meşrutiyet Devrine Ait Cavid Bey'in Hatıraları: 60," *Tanin*, October 30, 1943, p.2.

[115] Hüseyin Cahid [Yalçın], "İstanbul İntihabı," *Tanin*, November 30, 1327/ December 13, 1911, p.1. For excerpts from this editorial see, "The Defeat of the Committee of Union and Progress," *The Orient*, 2/36 (December 20, 1911), p.5. See also, Hüseyin Cahid [Yalçın], "Tavşan ile Kaplumbağanın Hikâyesi," *Tanin*, December 1, 1327/December 14, 1911, p.1.

[116] "Mustafa Asım Efendi'nin İstifanamesi Sureti," *Yeni İkdam*, December 1, 1327/December 14, 1911, p.2; and, "Le parti Union et Progrès," *The Levant Herald and Eastern Express*, December 14, 1911, p.2. See also, Mehmed Cavid, "Meşrutiyet Devrine Ait Cavid Bey'in Hatıraları: 61," *Tanin*, October 31, 1943, p.2.

[117] "Yine Kanunu-u Esasi," *Yeni İkdam*, December 1, 1327/December 14, 1911, p.1; "Constantinople Letter," *The Near East*, December 20, 1911, p.191; "The Turkish Cabinet and the Constitution: The Proposed Amendment," *The Times*,

been discussed in early October during the Unionist Congress in Salonica.[118] Article 35 stated that the Sultan might, in the event of a continued dispute between the Chamber of Deputies and the Cabinet, dissolve the Chamber, should the Senate give its consent.[119] The Committee of Union and Progress decided that it would propose an amendment of the final clause and advocate the abolition of the senatorial veto. The outbreak of war with Italy, however, had prevented any action from being taken at the time. It was generally believed that the Unionists would keep this political card up their sleeve until the next general elections drew near, or, if the electoral outlook was favourable, until a new Chamber had been elected.[120]

Said Pasha's decision to pursue the issue at this moment was the subject of much speculation in political circles. There were three theories: that Said Pasha was intentionally riding for a fall; that he was intentionally risking defeat in the hopes of bringing the cabinet's fall and the opportunity to form a new and stronger cabinet; or, that the Committee of Union and Progress was considering a sort of political *coup*. The supporters of this last view maintained that the Central Committee of the party had been greatly alarmed by its defeat in the İstanbul by-election, and that its leaders, knowing that they could depend on the support of a great majority of the provincial representatives of the Ministry of the Interior, who could do a great deal to control the elections, and fearing that further delay might prove prejudicial to their chances, had decided to play a bold game and strike for the dissolution of the Chamber

---

December 16, 1911, p.5; Hüseyin Cahid [Yalçın], "Kanun-u Esasi'nin Tadili," *Tanin*, December 2, 1327/December 15, 1911, p.1; Hüseyin Cahid Yalçın, "Meşrutiyet Hatıraları, 1908-1918," *Fikir Hareketleri*, 7 (October 24, 1936-April 17, 1937), pp.22-23; and, "Yine Kanun-u Esasi," *Yeni İkdam*, December 1, 1327/December 14, 1911, cited in Feroz Ahmad, *The Young Turks: The Committee of Union and Progress in Turkish Politics, 1908-1914*, p.101n. See also, Ziya Şakir [Soko], "Hürriyet ve İtilâf Nasıl Doğdu? Nasıl Yaşadı? Nasıl Battı? 38: Sait Paşa İttihatçılara Karşı Derin bir Kin Besliyordu," *Tan*, December 15, 1937, p.9; Ahmed Bedevi Kuran, *Osmanlı İmparatorluğunda İnkılâp Hareketleri ve Milli Mücadele*, p.555; and, I/IV/25, December 3, 1327/December 16, 1911, *Meclis-i Mebusan Zabıt Ceridesi*, 2, p.201.

[118] "Constantinople Letter," *The Near East*, December 20, 1911, p.191.

[119] "The Turkish Cabinet and the Constitution: Proposed Modifications," *The Times*, December 14, 1911, p.5; and, "Constantinople Letter," *The Near East*, December 20, 1911, p.191. See also, I/IV/25, December 3, 1327/December 16, 1911, *Meclis-i Mebusan Zabıt Ceridesi*, 2, p.201. For the exact wording of Article 35 see, Tarhan Erdem (Compilor), *Anayasalar ve Seçim Kanunları, 1876-1982*, pp.5-6.

[120] "Constantinople Letter," *The Near East*, December 20, 1911, p.191.

and call for general elections.[121]

This apparently was what the Committee of Union and Progress was aiming at. Having lost the İstanbul by-election, the leadership decided to call for general elections by dissolving the Chamber of Deputies. For this, however, the Committee of Union and Progress needed the unlikely approval of the monarchist-dominated Senate, and the proposed amendment would solve that problem nicely.[122] The December 14 meeting of the parliamentary party of the Committee of Union and Progress, however, was stormy. It was reported that many deputies threatened to leave the party rather than vote for the measure. They were supported by Seyyid Bey, the leader of the parliamentary party, and Emrullah Efendi, ex-Minister of Education. The meeting finally came to an end for want of a quorum, and Seyyid Bey informed the deputies that they were free to vote as they wished. The executive council of the Committee of Union and Progress at Salonica had not yet given its instructions to the party. However, what these instructions might be was foreshadowed in *Tanin* in two leading articles, the work of Babanzade İsmail Hakkı Bey and Hüseyin Cahid [Yalçın], both of whom supported Said Pasha's proposals.[123]

At another meeting the Unionist leadership held on December 16, the question of the modification of Article 35 was discussed. Talât Bey informed the meeting that Salonica insisted on modification. The parliamentary Commission for the Revision of the Constitution, of which Babanzade İsmail Hakkı Bey was Chairman, would accept it, and whatever difficulties might be raised by individual members of the party

---

[121] "Constantinople Letter," *The Near East*, December 20, 1911, p.191; and, William W. Rockhill to Secretary of State P. C. Knox, Constantinople, December 22, 1911, in *Records of the Department of State Relating to Internal Affairs of Turkey, 1910-1929*, Roll 4. See also, Ziya Şakir [Soko], "Hürriyet ve İtilâf Nasıl Doğdu? Nasıl Yaşadı? Nasıl Battı? 38: Sait Paşa İttihatçılara Karşı Derin bir Kin Besliyordu," *Tan*, December 15, 1937, p.9; and, Yusuf Hikmet Bayur, *Türk İnkılâbı Tarihi, 2/1*, p.237.

[122] Hüseyin Cahid Yalçın, "Meşrutiyet Hatıraları, 1908-1918," *Fikir Hareketleri, 7* (October 24, 1936-April 17, 1937), p.22.

[123] Hüseyin Cahid [Yalçın], "Kanunu-u Esasi'nin Tadili," *Tanin*, December 2, 1327/December 15, 1911, p.1; and, Babanzade İsmail Hakkı, "Hürriyet ve Hakimiyet-i Hakikiye Kuvvetlerin Tevazün Etmesine Mütevaffıktır," *Tanin*, December 2, 1327/December 15, 1911, p.1. See also, "The Turkish Cabinet and the Constitution: The Proposed Amendment," *The Times*, December 16, 1911, p.5.

the measure ought to be passed at all costs. Major Hüseyin
Kadri Bey suggested that recalcitrant deputies belonging to the
New Faction could be forced to come into line by the publication or by the threat of publication of *jurnals* relating to
them. Cavid Bey said that it was rather late in the day for such
a measure and advised the party if such a measure was adopted it should confine itself to the publication of the names of
jurnalcis, or the persons who wrote the *jurnals*. The meeting,
which did not seem to have arrived at an absolute agreement
as to the employment of this weapon, then heard a memorandum from Salonica headquarters read and expounded by Talât
Bey and others. After rebuking the İstanbul Committee for
failing to check undue criticism and discussion, the Central
Committee expressed its conviction that safety was to be found
in the strengthening of the Caliphate and Sultanate, and there
was no reason to fear that the throne would abuse its powers.[124]

At the December 16 sitting of the Chamber, Said Pasha explained the modification in a lengthy speech which was re-
peatedly interrupted by the monarchist opposition. Declaring
that the war with Italy had to lead to negotiations for peace,
Said Pasha told the Chamber that a strong and well-balanced
government was needed to bring these negotiations to a successful end. He indignantly denied that he desired to dissolve
the Chamber to reinstate absolutism.[125] Mecdi Efendi said that
however desirable such an amendment to the Constitution
might be, it could not possibly obtain the requisite two-thirds
vote of the deputies, or one hundred and eighty-four out of two
hundred and seventy-six votes, so that it best be referred to the
Parliamentary Commission for the Revision of the Constitution. Lütfi Fikri Bey inveighed against the proposed change,

---

[124] "The Committee and Foreign Affairs," *The Times*, December 26, 1911, p.3.
[125] I/IV/25, December 3, 1327/December 16, 1911, *Meclis-i Mebusan Zabıt Ceridesi*, 2, pp.203-206; Hüseyin Cahid [Yalçın], "Telâşın Hikmeti," *Tanin*, December 4, 1327/December 17, 1911, p.1; "The Ottoman Parliament," *The Orient*, 2/36
(December 20, 1911), p.1; and, "The Cabinet and the Constitution," *The Levant
Herald and Eastern Express*, December 18, 1911, p.1. For the text of Said Pasha's
speech, see also *Takvim-i Vekayi*, December 7, 1327/December 20, 1911. See also,
F.O.371/1263, 51583, Sir Gerard Lowther to Sir Edward Grey, Pera, December 18,
1911, cited in Feroz Ahmad, *The Young Turks: The Committee of Union and
Progress in Turkish Politics, 1908-1914*, p.101n; Mustafa Ragıb Esatlı, "Meşrutiyet
Devrinde: İntihap Mücadelesi Nasıl Yapılıyordu?" *Akşam*, March 11, 1943, p.4;
and, Yusuf Hikmet Bayur, *Türk İnkılâbı Tarihi*, 2/1, p.237.

and especially against making it a matter of urgency. Said Pasha tried to reply, but was so often and so violently interrupted that he finally left the Chamber in disgust. After a recess of half an hour, the Chamber voted to refer the proposed amendment to the Commission, and by a smaller majority agreed to make it a matter of urgency, demanding immediate action and report.[126]

Said Pasha's proposal for the modification of Article 35 was then presented to the Parliamentary Commission for the Revision of the Constitution. As the Commission was chaired by Babanzade İsmail Hakkı Bey, a prominent Unionist deputy for Baghdad, and as nearly two-third of its members were Unionist deputies, there was little doubt that it would support the proposal. The real struggle would come later, as Said Pasha could hardly hope to obtain a two-thirds majority in the Chamber, much less in the Senate.[127]

At the December 18 sitting of the Chamber, Ahmed Ferid [Tek], opposition deputy for Kütahya, presented a written request for an explanation as to what constituted a 'new cabinet' in Article 35 of the Constitution. He also demanded a formal vote on the question of urgency of the previous sitting.[128] In the afternoon sitting, Basri Dukacı, the Albanian opposition deputy for Dibër, presented a written accusation against the Grand Vezier, as being an unchangeable and bitter enemy of the Constitution. President Ahmed Rıza Bey refused to read this motion except in the presence of Said Pasha himself. A tumult arose which soon became a veritable pandemonium, members of the government and opposition parties shouting at

---

[126] I/IV/25, December 3, 1327/December 16, 1911, *Meclis-i Mebusan Zabıt Ceridesi*, 2, pp.206-216; Hüseyin Cahid [Yalçın], "Telâşın Hikmeti," *Tanin*, December 4, 1327/December 17, 1911, p.1; "The Ottoman Parliament," *The Orient*, 2/36 (December 20, 1911), p.1; "The Cabinet and the Constitution," *The Levant Herald and Eastern Express*, December 18, 1911, p.1; and, Cemal Kutay, *Türkiye İstiklâl ve Hürriyet Mücadeleleri Tarihi*, 17, pp.9803-9806. See also, "Dünkü Müzakere," *Yeni İkdam*, December 4, 1327/December 17, 1911, p.1.

[127] "Constantinople Letter," *The Near East*, December 29, 1911, p.223. See also, "The Turkish Cabinet and the Constitution: Proposed Modifications," *The Times*, December 14, 1911, p.5; and, Cemal Kutay, *Türkiye İstiklâl ve Hürriyet Mücadeleleri Tarihi*, 17, p.9806.

[128] I/IV/26, December 5, 1327/December 18, 1911, *Meclis-i Mebusan Zabıt Ceridesi*, 2, pp.224-228; "The Ottoman Parliament," *The Orient*, 2/36 (December 20, 1911), p.2; and, "Scene in the Turkish Chamber," *The Times*, December 19, 1911, p.6.

one another, and barely escaping actual blows. The President, when he could stand it no longer, left the chair and the hall. Seyyid Bey, parliamentary leader of the Committee of Union and Progress, and Haydar Bey, Secretary of the Chamber, tried in vain to quiet down Ömer Fevzi Bey and Şeyhzade Zeynelabidin Efendi, who were known as the two heavy-weights of the Entente Libérale. The deputies, left without a presiding officer, gradually withdrew from the hall, and when Ahmed Rıza Bey returned, he had no deputies to call to order, and no meeting to adjourn.[129]

Tanin of December 19 wrote that neither the Italians—with whom Turkey was at war—nor the revolutionary Bulgarian Internal Organisation which was engaged in acts of violence against Turkish authority in Macedonia were so harmful as the attempted destruction of constitutional order by the monar-chist opposition. *Tanin* wrote that nothing good or useful for the nation could any longer be expected from those whose judgement was so inflamed by ambition or hatred. In addi-tion to the scene in the Chamber, *Tanin* cited an article by Dr. Rıza Nur published in the monarchist newspaper *Tesisat* which, the newspaper claimed, was calculated to provoke the Kurdish population against constituted authority. Indeed, Dr. Rıza Nur had attacked Said Pasha in his *Tesisat* article, saying that the government was on the point of taking from the Kurds the lands they possessed, and giving them to the Armenians. *Tanin* was worried that this distorted version of actual facts would be carried to Kurdistan where the population would be exasperated at seeing themselves about to be dispossessed for the benefit of the Armenians. Under these circumstances, *Tanin* declared, members of the Committee of Union and Progress were of opinion that the greatest patriotic service they could render the country would be to deliver it from this Chamber, or, at least, to resign in a body, so that the Chamber might be dissolved and new elections take place.[130]

---

[129] I/IV/26, December 5, 1327/December 18, 1911, *Meclis-i Mebusan Zabıt Ce-ridesi*, 2, pp.229-230; "The Ottoman Parliament," *The Orient*, 2/36 (December 20, 1911), p.2; and, "Scene in the Turkish Chamber," *The Times*, December 19, 1911, p.6. See also, "Dünkü Niza'," *Yeni Ikdam*, December 6, 1327/December 1911, p.1.

[130] Hüseyin Cahid [Yalçın], "Fesih Değil Tefessüh," *Tanin*, December 6, 1327/December 19, 1911, p.1. For excerpts from this editorial see, "Is the Chamber

It was at precisely this juncture that Unionists raised the question of Palace informers and their *jurnals, i.e.*, secret reports, to Abdülhamid under the absolutist monarchy in order to embarrass and discredit some of the members of the New Faction as well as monarchist members of the opposition party. *Tanin* threatened the opposition with the publication of these *jurnals*.[131] These *jurnals*, in some cases, were prepared by ministers and other officials of the state in accordance with official instructions; others were mere denunciations, inspired by private hostility or the desire for gain and favour. The number of more or less recognised informers under the *ancien régime* was believed to be in excess of eighty thousand.[132]

At the December 20 sitting of the Chamber, Mahmud Şevket Pasha did his best to prevent the publication of these reports, warning the Chamber against the dangers of disunion. Neither Muslim nor Christian would gain from a policy of personal recrimination. He told the Chamber that he was not in favour of the publication of these documents. He also suggested that if the *jurnals* were published, few honest men would remain to carry on the government's business, adding that he himself had refused to dismiss officers guilty of such activity in the past, giving them instead a chance to start afresh and prove their worth under happier conditions.[133] The issue was left unresolved.

Meanwhile the discussion of Article 35 continued without intermission. While the Parliamentary Commission for the Revision of the Constitution examined the problem, delegates, from both the Committee of Union and Progress and the Entente Libérale, met at the invitation of the 'independents,' composed mostly of ex-members of the Committee of Union and Progress and a group of Albanian nationalists, to "dis-

---

of Deputies a Menace?" *The Orient*, 2/37 (December 27, 1911), p.5.
    [131] "Constantinople Letter," *The Near East*, December 29, 1911, p.223.
    [132] "Constantinople Letter," *The Near East*, November 29, 1911, p.95.
    [133] I/IV/27, December 7, 1327/December 20, 1911, *Meclis-i Mebusan Zabıt Ceridesi*, 2, pp.248-257; "The Ottoman Parliament," *The Orient*, 2/37 (December 27, 1911), p.1; and, "Constantinople Letter," *The Near East*, December 29, 1911, p.223. See also, Yusuf Hikmet Bayur, *Türk İnkılâbı Tarihi*, 2/1, p.238; and, William W. Rockhill to Secretary of State P. C. Knox, Constantinople, December 22, 1911, in *Records of the Department of State Relating to Internal Affairs of Turkey, 1910-1929*, Roll 4.

cover a *modus vivendi*".[134]

The demands of the Entente Libérale delegates, however, were more sweeping than their party's strength appeared to justify. They asked for the abolition of martial law in İstanbul, the proclamation of a general amnesty for those banished, exiled, or imprisoned for counter-revolutionary offences, the formation of a neutral cabinet from which prominent Unionists were excluded, and a declaration to be made by the Unionists that officers and officials would be forbidden to enter any political organisation as a member thereof.[135]

The Unionists voted by a large majority in favour of the maintenance of Said Pasha.[136] Though they were at first unwilling to discuss these demands seriously, they would later change their attitude and accept the first two points as well as the last—positions which the Committee of Union and Progress essentially supported.[137] The leadership, for example, had already tried to lift martial law in İstanbul in the hopes of curtailing the military's influence. They had failed, and the Court Martial had then suppressed the pro-Unionist *Tanin*. Some of the Unionist leadership was also not adverse to a political amnesty. In the words of Hüseyin Cahid [Yalçın], it made little sense to exile people like Mizancı Murad Bey while the equally guilty owners, editors and journalists of the monarchist *Yeni İkdam* and *Yeni Gazete* were allowed to remain, publishing anti-Unionist propaganda just as they had done before.[138]

The Unionists, however, absolutely refused to let Said Pasha fall from the Grand Veziership. Although he was not a

---

[134] "Constantinople Letter," *The Near East*, January 5, 1912, p.259; and, Yusuf Hikmet Bayur, *Türk İnkılâbı Tarihi*, 2/1, p.239.

[135] *Tanin*, December 13, 1327/December 26, 1911, in Hüseyin Cahid Yalçın, "Meşrutiyet Hatıraları, 1908-1918," *Fikir Hareketleri*, 7 (October 24, 1936-April 17, 1937), p.23; "News Items," *The Levant Herald and Eastern Express*, December 26, 1911, p.1; "Turkish Party Conflicts: Deputies and Said Pasha," *The Times*, December 26, 1911, p.3; and, "Constantinople Letter," *The Near East*, January 5, 1912, p.259. See also, Yusuf Hikmet Bayur, *Türk İnkılâbı Tarihi*, 2/1, p.239.

[136] "News Items," *The Levant Herald and Eastern Express*, December 26, 1911, p.1.

[137] Hüseyin Cahid Yalçın, "Meşrutiyet Hatıraları, 1908-1918," *Fikir Hareketleri*, 7 (October 24, 1936-April 17, 1937), p.36; and, "Constantinople Letter," *The Near East*, January 5, 1912, p.259.

[138] Hüseyin Cahid Yalçın, "Meşrutiyet Hatıraları, 1908-1918," *Fikir Hareketleri*, 7 (October 24, 1936-April 17, 1937), p.36.

Unionist, the Committee of Union and Progress considered him an able statesman who could withstand outside pressure. The Unionists then would only agree to the formation of a caretaker cabinet of a neutral political complexion as long as Said Pasha was at the helm.[139] After lengthy negotiations between parties on December 26, the Unionists consented to the portfolios of War, Interior, and Foreign Affairs changing hands but on condition that Said Pasha remained Grand Vezier.[140] This was not at all in conformity with the wishes of the Entente Libérale. The Entente Libérale delegates created a scene, swearing that they would never consent to Said Pasha's maintenance. The Unionists stood firm, refused to negotiate on any other basis, and the Entente Libérale, after deliberation, consented. The Entente Libérale delegates then demanded that the Committee of Union and Progress forgo its plan to modify Article 35, pledging not to submit the proposal to the Chamber. The Unionists categorically refused, and the negotiations came to an abrupt end.[141]

Part of the Unionist intransigence on the issue of a new Said Pasha Cabinet had to do with Said Pasha himself. The latter had made it abundantly clear that although he was ready to make concessions to public opinion with respect to martial law and a general amnesty, and although he himself was contemplating replacements within the cabinet, he would not allow the haggling of rival political parties to determine either his position or those of his Ministers. Because Said Pasha's support was necessary for the amendment of Article 35, any idea that the Committee of Union and Progress leadership might have had of giving in on the cabinet issue quickly evaporated. Said Pasha was to be supported at all

---

[139] "İtilâf Olmuyor," *Yeni İkdam*, December 13, 1327/December 26, 1911, p.1; "İtilâf Olacak mı, Olmayacak mı[?]" *Yeni İkdam*, December 14, 1327/December 27, 1911, p.1.; and, Hüseyin Cahid Yalçın, "Meşrutiyet Hatıraları, 1908-1918," *Fikir Hareketleri*, 7 (October 24, 1936-April 17, 1937), p.36.

[140] "The Party Struggle," *The Levant Herald and Eastern Express*, December 27, 1911, p.1.

[141] "Turkish Parties and the Grand Vizier: The Modification of the Constitution," *The Times*, December 27, 1911, p.3; "Turkish Party Politics: End of the Conference," *The Times*, December 28, 1911, p.3; "Constantinople Letter," *The Near East*, January 5, 1912, p.259; and, "Empire News: The Capital," *The Orient*, 2/37 (December 27, 1911), p.6.

costs.[142]

As expected, the Parliamentary Committee for the revision of the Constitution had passed the modified version of Article 35, though there were a few amendments.[143] On the opening of the Chamber on December 27, İbrahim Vasfi Efendi, Entente Libérale deputy for Karesi, on behalf of the opposition, objected to the placing of the proposed constitutional amendment on the order of the day, since this had been done at the close of the previous sitting in the acknowledged default of a quorum. He was seconded by Ahmed Ferid [Tek], deputy for Kütahya, representing the independents, who urged postponing action on Article 35 until January 1, 1912, in order to give the independent group more time to arrange an understanding between the two main parties. On behalf of the Albanian deputies, Hamdi Bey, deputy for Prevesa, urged the necessity of prior settlement of the Albanian crisis. Said Pasha asked for time to consult with his colleagues, and an hour's recess followed, which was devoted to lobbying. When the meeting was again called to order, two motions were presented, one by the Committee of Union and Progress fixing the discussion on December 30, the other by the Entente Libérale, deferring it until January 1, 1912. After considerable sparring, the vote was taken, resulting in the adoption of the Unionist motion by a vote of one hundred and seven to ninety-nine, most of the independents refraining from voting.[144]

---

[142] "Turkish Parties and the Grand Vizier: The Modification of the Constitution," *The Times*, December 27, 1911, p.3; and, "Constantinople Letter," *The Near East*, January 5, 1912, p.259.

[143] "News Items," *The Levant Herald and Eastern Express*, December 22, 1911, p.1; and, Cemal Kutay, *Türkiye İstiklâl ve Hürriyet Mücadeleleri Tarihi*, 17, p.9806. The modified proposal ran as follows:
     Article 35: "In case of a disagreement between the cabinet and the Chamber, if the cabinet insist on its point of view and in case of a formal and repeated refusal on the part of the Chamber, the Sovereign has the right either to change the cabinet or to dissolve the Chamber, on condition that fresh elections be held and the Chamber convoked within three months, and also that the Chamber be not dissolved more than once in the course of a year. The Sovereign also has the right in case of war to decree the temporary suspension of the debates in the Chamber, but on condition that this suspension shall not exceed in duration half the current session of Parliament. In case of the dissolution of the Chamber His Majesty shall be at liberty to have recourse or not to have recourse to the Senate's opinion. If the new Chamber insists on the point of view of its predecessor, its decision must then be accepted" ("Constantinople Letter," *The Near East*, January 5, 1912, p.259).

[144] I/IV/30, December 14, 1327/December 27, 1911, *Meclis-i Mebusan Zabıt Ceridesi*, 2, pp.309-322; "35. Madde," *Yeni İkdam*, December 15, 1327/December

On December 29, all the main parliamentary groups—the Committee of Union and Progress, the Entente Libérale, and the independents—held meetings in the Chamber. It was significant that the meeting of the Committee of Union and Progress was only attended by sixty members of that party. On their part, the independents sent delegates to the Entente Libérale to urge them to agree to the retention of Said Pasha as Grand Vezier. Entente Libérale leadership expressed its willingness to accept the independents' proposal only on the condition that all the other ministers were changed.[145]

As there were one hundred and seven Unionist deputies to the Entente Libérale's ninety-nine, the battle promised to be long and fierce. Twenty-four independents had decided to refrain from voting.[146] The debate, however, did not take place on December 30. The opposition had decided to abstain, and the one hundred and twenty odd Unionist deputies faced only a half-dozen members of the opposition who were present only to insure that the Unionists remained within the bounds of the Constitution.[147] Neither the Entente Libérale deputies, nor the independents, nor the Greeks, nor the Albanians would enter the hall; and the Unionists could not muster a majority without them. At no time were there more than one hundred and thirty-one deputies present, whereas one hundred and forty were necessary for a quorum.[148] During the afternoon sitting, the Grand Vezier addressed President A h-

---

28, 1911, p.1; "The Ottoman Parliament," *The Orient*, 3/1 (January 3, 1912, p.1; and, "Turkish Party Politics: End of the Conference," *The Times*, December 28, 1911, p.3. See also, "Constantinople Letter," *The Near East*, January 5, 1912, p.259.

[145] "News Items," *The Levant Herald and Eastern Express*, December 30, 1911, p.1.

[146] "Constantinople Letter," *The Near East*, January 5, 1912, p.259. The total number of deputies in the Chamber was 278 (Hüseyin Cahid Yalçın, "Meşrutiyet Hatıraları, 1908-1918," *Fikir Hareketleri*, 7 (October 24, 1936-April 17, 1937), p.37).

[147] Hüseyin Cahid [Yalçın], "Meclis-i Mebusan'da Tatil-i Eşgal," *Tanin*, December 18, 1327/December 31, 1911, p.1; "Meclis-i Mebusan'ın Dünkü Manzarası," *Tanin*, December 18, 1327/December 31, 1911, pp.1-3; "Constantinople Letter," *The Near East*, January 12, 1912, p.291. See also, Mehmed Cavid, "Meşrutiyet Devrine Ait Cavid Bey'in Hatıraları: 63," *Tanin*, November 2, 1943, p.2; Mustafa Ragıb Esatlı, "Meşrutiyet Devrinde: İntihap Mücadelesi Nasıl Yapılıyordu?" *Akşam*, March 11, 1943, p.4; and, Ali Birinci, *Hürriyet ve İtilâf Fırkası: II. Meşrutiyet Devrinde İttihat ve Terakki'ye Karşı Çıkanlar*, pp.113-114.

[148] "Meclis-i Mebusan'ın Dünkü Manzarası," *Tanin*, December 18, 1327/December 31, 1911, pp.1-3; Hüseyin Cahid Yalçın, "Meşrutiyet Hatıraları, 1908-1918," *Fikir Hareketleri*, 7 (October 24, 1936-April 17, 1937), p.37; "The Political Situation," *The Levant Herald and Eastern Express*, January 1, 1912, p.1; and, "The Ottoman Parliament," *The Orient*, 3/1 (January 3, 1912), p.1.

med Rıza Bey and said he wished to convey to the nation through the deputies present the views of the cabinet. He said that the prolongation of martial law was a detriment, and should soon be suppressed; that there were some now in prison who should be pardoned; that reforms were needed in Albania; but that the main question was the proposed constitutional amendment, which, he said, was necessary for the establishment of a strong government able to carry out the reforms required by the country. Continuing his speech, he quoted a letter to *Le Temps*, which stated that if Italy was able to prosecute her African venture successfully, it was because of Turkey's internal quarrels. He then retired. After some time, the cabinet returned and Said Pasha announced that the obstructionist tactics of the majority of the deputies compelled him to hand in his resignation, and leave the ground free for those who were greedy for power.[149]

Faced with this monarchist obstruction, Said Pasha resigned that evening.[150] The Unionists, at a meeting held that night, decided to press for Said Pasha's re-appointment to the Grand Vezierate and to render him unswerving obedience and support for the remainder of the Session. Despite the Unionist leadership's determination to support Said Pasha, it was now doubtful whether the Committee of Union and Progress possessed more than a bare majority, if that, in the Chamber. The Entente Libérale, with their Greek allies, mustered nearly one hundred votes. The attitude of the eight or nine members of the Armenian Revolutionary Federation was doubtful. The failure of their group to secure the election of their nominee to

[149] "Meclis-i Mebusan'ın Dünkü Manzarası," *Tanin*, December 18, 1327/December 31, 1911, pp.1-3; "The Ottoman Parliament," *The Orient*, 3/1 (January 3, 1912), p.1; "Parliamentary Crisis in Turkey: Statement by the Grand Vizier," *The Times*, January 1, 1912, p.5; and, "The Political Situation," *The Levant Herald and Eastern Express*, January 1, 1912, p.1. See also, Mehmed Cavid, "Meşrutiyet Devrine Ait Cavid Bey'in Hatıraları: 64," *Tanin*, November 3, 1943, p.2.
[150] "Meclis-i Mebusan Müzakere Salonu'ndaki Dünkü Konferans: Kabinenin İstifası," *Yeni İkdam*, December 18, 1327/December 31, 1911, p.1; "Heyet-i Vükelâya Dair," *Tanin*, December 18, 1327/December 31, 1911, p.1; and, "Parliamentary Crisis in Turkey: Resignation of the Cabinet," *The Times*, January 1, 1912, p.5. See also, Mehmed Cavid, "Meşrutiyet Devrine Ait Cavid Bey'in Hatıraları: 63," *Tanin*, November 2, 1943, p.2; Feroz Ahmad, *The Young Turks: The Committee of Union and Progress in Turkish Politics, 1908-1914*, p.102; and, Yusuf Hikmet Bayur, *Türk İnkılâbı Tarihi*, 2/1, p.239.

the Armenian Patriarchate had shown them that their recent policy was not altogether favourably viewed by the strong conservative element among the Armenians, and the recent abstention of their deputies from voting might signal a prelude to a change of attitude towards the Committee of Union and Progress, which hitherto as a general rule they had supported.[151] Although not deserting the Unionist camp altogether, members of the Armenian Revolutionary Federation declared themselves opposed to the Chamber's dissolution.[152] The situation with the Albanian members of the Committee of Union and Progress, however, was totally different. Seven of the ten Albanian deputies—including Bedri Bey, deputy for İpek and father of Mazhar Bey, Governor of Kossovo during the Albanian insurrection of 1910—who had remained with the Committee of Union and Progress seceded from the party on December 30. Upset with the Unionists' unwillingness to fix a day for the discussion of government policy in Albania, these now realised that the Unionists were committed to a speedy parliamentary dissolution, leaving no time for such discussion. Therefore, they joined the independents.[153]

In an attempt to solve the political deadlock, which, in part, had been caused by the refusal of the independents to participate in the voting, the Sultan sent a message to the independents on December 31, advising them to abandon obstruction. The deputies belonging to the independent group held a meeting on January 1, 1912 to discuss the situation. Although they decided to resume negotiations for an understanding between the Committee of Union and Progress and the Entente Libérale, the success of these efforts was highly improbable. Consequently, the dissolution of the Chamber and fresh elections were regarded as inevitable.[154]

---

[151] "Parliamentary Crisis in Turkey: Resignation of the Cabinet," *The Times,* January 1, 1912, p.5.

[152] "The Turkish Cabinet Crisis," *The Times,* January 3, 1912, p.3; and, "Constantinople Letter," *The Near East,* January 12, 1912, p.291.

[153] "Parliamentary Crisis in Turkey: Resignation of the Cabinet," *The Times,* January 1, 1912, p.5; and, "Constantinople Letter," *The Near East,* January 12, 1912, p.291.

[154] "The Political Deadlock in Turkey: A Government Proclamation," *The Times,* January 2, 1912, p.3. See also, Babanzade İsmail Hakkı, "Obstruction," *Tanin,* December 19, 1327/January 1, 1912, p.1.

The resignation of the cabinet was the logical outcome of the deadlock in the Chamber, and especially the failure of the Unionists to secure even a quorum at the Chamber on December 30. Said Pasha was immediately given the task of forming a new government.[155] This, too, was equally logical, for Said Pasha had not received a rebuff of a vote of non-confidence, nor forfeited his position by any step of which the Sultan did not approve. Moreover, so long as the Committee of Union and Progress was really the party in power, its candidate was the natural choice to head the new cabinet. By their passive resistance, the monarchist opposition had apparently lost rather than gained in the public opinion, especially in view of the fact that in principle they acknowledged themselves in favour of the extension of the powers of the throne. The measure proposed by Said Pasha—that Article 35 of the Constitution be so revised as to give the Sultan power to dissolve the Chamber even without the consent of the Senate—alarmed quite a section of the country, since this had been mistakenly interpreted as the prelude to another *coup d'état* and the assumption of autocratic power. The Entente Libérale had seen here its opportunity to pose as the champion of constitutional liberty, though it knew well that the proposed amendment was not a step towards absolutism.[156]

A power struggle ensued following Said Pasha's resignation. Although the Sultan, pressed by the leadership of the Committee of Union and Progress, immediately re-appointed Said Pasha to form a new government, the monarchists did not give up the fight for political power. *La Liberté* mentioned views expressed in monarchist circles that Damad Ferid Pasha, senator and leader of the Entente Libérale, be appointed Grand Vezier. However, even opponents of the Committee of Union and Progress realised that the monarchists could supply neither the Grand Vezier nor the most important portfolios

---

[155] Hüseyin Cahid [Yalçın], "Said Paşa'nın Dokuzuncu Sadareti," *Tanin*, December 19, 1327/January 1, 1912, p.1; "Buhran-ı Vükelâ," *Tanin*, December 19, 1327/January 1, 1912, p.1; "Parliamentary Crisis in Turkey: Said Pasha Reappointed," *The Times*, January 1, 1912, p.5; and, "The Political Situation," *The Levant Herald and Eastern Express*, January 1, 1912, p.1. See also, Mehmed Cavid, "Meşrutiyet Devrine Ait Cavid Bey'in Hatıraları: 63," *Tanin*, November 2, 1943, p.2; and, Yusuf Hikmet Bayur, *Türk İnkılâbı Tarihi, 2/1*, p.240.

[156] "Said Pasha His Own Successor," *The Orient, 3/1* (January 3, 1912), p.1.

in the cabinet, since the opposition was an aggregation of several groups with but a single feature in common: hatred of the
party in power. Supporters of the Entente Libérale—the Greek,
Albanian, Armenian, and Arab deputies—had all their own
programmes and their separate agendas. These deputies
would naturally be with the opposition—until the Entente Libérale came into power.[157] Despite unfavourable political opinion, an Entente Libérale deputation composed of İsmail Hakkı
[Mumcu] Pasha, leader of the parliamentary party of the Entente Libérale, Hacı Ali al-'Alusi Efendi, deputy for Baghdad,
Yorgos Boussios, deputy for Serfidje, Théodore Pavloff, deputy
for Üsküb, Abd al-Nafi Pasha, deputy for Aleppo, Gümülcineli
İsmail Hakkı Bey, deputy for Gümülcine, Esad Pasha Toptan,
deputy for Durazzo, Volçetrinli Hasan Bey, deputy for Prishtnë, Tahir Hayreddin Bey, deputy for İstanbul, Nazareth Daghavarian, deputy for Sivas, Hoca Mustafa Sabri Efendi, dep-
uty for Tokad, Hacı Bayram Efendi, deputy for İçel, Constantin Constantinidis, deputy for İstanbul, and Shafiq al-
Mu'ayyad al-'Azm, deputy for Damascus, visited the Sultan on
December 31 to ask him to reconsider his decision.[158]

The Damad Ferid Pasha option having failed, the monarchists proposed another combination. The proposed monarchist 'solution' consisted in forming a cabinet whose members would be chosen outside the Chamber, and which would
unite with a conciliatory object the most prominent monarchist or conservative statesmen in the Empire: Hüseyin Hilmi
Pasha, Mahmud Şevket Pasha, Gabriel Nouradunghian, and
the like. The monarchists' choice for the position of the Grand
Vezierate was Kâmil Pasha. Although all of the monarchist
pashas would be willing to serve under him, there was the
absolute impossibility of Said Pasha ever being persuaded to
serve in a cabinet which Kâmil Pasha was the Grand Vezier—

---

[157] *La Liberté*, January 1, 1912, excerpted in "Political Possibilities," *The
Orient*, 3/1 (January 3, 1912), p.2.
[158] "Meclis-i Vükelâ: Muhalefetin Zat-ı Hazret-i Padişahi'ye Müracaatları," *Ta-
nin*, December 19, 1327/January 1, 1912, p.1; "Réunion de l'Entente Libérale," *The
Levant Herald and Eastern Express*, January 1, 1912, p.2; and, Ziya Şakir [Soko],
"Hürriyet ve İtilâf Nasıl Doğdu? Nasıl Yaşadı? Nasıl Battı? 39: İtilâfçılar Fırsat
Gözeterek bir Heyet Gönderdiler," *Tan*, December 16, 1937, p.9. See also, Yusuf
Hikmet Bayur, *Türk İnkılâbı Tarihi*, 2/1, p.240; and, Rifat Uçarol, *Gazi Ahmet
Muhtar Paşa: Bir Osmanlı Paşası ve Dönemi*, p.329.

and there was no question that Said Pasha could be left out of
power. Thus, this combination was also out of the question.[159]

By January 2, official notification of the formation of a new
cabinet had not been published, but there was reason to believe
that Said Pasha had consented to the substitution of Talât Bey
for Celal Bey as Minister of the Interior. Abdurrahman Şeref
Bey had refused to take office again, and his place would probably be taken by Emrullah Efendi.[160] Said Pasha announced
his cabinet on January 3. The cabinet, however, was formed
without Talât Bey.[161] Talât Bey's as well as Cavid Bey's exclusion from the new cabinet was mainly due to Mahmud
Şevket Pasha's objections.[162]

The new Sheikh-ul-Islam was Abdurrahman Nesib Efendi,
former Chief Judge of Egypt. Memduh Bey, Minister of Justice, would act as Minister of the Interior. Emrullah Efendi
took the place of Abdurrahman Şeref Bey as Minister of Education. Aristidi Pasha Yorgandjioglu became Minister of
Mines and Forests. Krikor Sinapian was appointed as the new
Minister of Public Works. There were no other changes.[163]
One of the most significant departures from the previous cabinet was the appointment of Krikor Sinapian, a monarchist, to
the Ministry of Public Works. His predecessor had been
Hulusi Bey whose policy of favouring domestic entrepreneurs
and capitalists at the expense of foreign concessions had provoked anxiety among foreign investors. Krikor Sinapian's ap-

[159] *La Liberté*, January 1, 1912, excerpted in "Political Possibilities," *The
Orient*, 3/1 (January 3, 1912), p.2.
[160] "Yeni Kabine," *Yeni İkdam*, December 21, 1327/January 3, 1912, p.1; "Ye-
ni Heyet-i Vükelâ," *Tanin*, December 21, 1327/January 3, 1912, p.3; "The Turkish
Cabinet Crisis," *The Times*, January 3, 1912, p.3; and, "The New Cabinet," *The
Orient*, 3/1 (January 3, 1912), p.5. See also, William W. Rockhill to Secretary of
State, Constantinople, January 4, 1912, in *Records of the Department of State Relating to Internal Affairs of Turkey, 1910-1929*, Roll 4.
[161] "Yeni Kabine," *Yeni İkdam*, December 22, 1327/January 4, 1912, p.1;
"New Turkish Cabinet," *The Times*, January 4, 1912, p.3; Hüseyin Cahid Yalçın,
"Meşrutiyet Hatıraları, 1908-1918," *Fikir Hareketleri*, 7 (October 24, 1936-April 17,
1937), p.37; and, Mehmed Cavid, "Meşrutiyet Devrine Ait Cavid Bey'in Hatıraları:
64," *Tanin*, November 3, 1943, p.2.
[162] Mehmed Cavid, "Meşrutiyet Devrine Ait Cavid Bey'in Hatıraları: 65," *Tanin*, November 4, 1943, p.2.
[163] "Yeni Heyet-i Vükelâ," *Tanin*, December 21, 1327/January 3, 1912, p.3;
"Yeni Kabine," *Yeni İkdam*, December 22, 1327/January 4, 1912, p.1; "The New
Cabinet," *The Orient*, 3/1 (January 3, 1912), p.5; "New Turkish Cabinet," *The
Times*, January 4, 1912, p.3; and, "The Political Situation," *The Levant Herald and
Eastern Express*, January 4, 1912, p.1.

pointment was clearly calculated to alloy their concern.[164] For
the moment the portfolio of the Interior remained unfilled;
Hacı Âdil [Arda], a moderate member of the Committee of
Union and Progress, would later be named to the post.[165] Despite this, the new Cabinet was devoid of a strong Unionist
presence. In the words of the Unionists, this was a 'Said Pasha
Cabinet,' or a colourless 'Cabinet d'Affaires.'[166]

Immediately following the formation of his new cabinet, Said
Pasha, at the January 3 sitting of the Assembly, presented the
famous amendment to Article 35 of the Constitution, and said
the new cabinet insisted on its being voted.[167] Sıdkı Bey,
opposition deputy for Aydın, claimed that this was really not a
new cabinet, in as much as the previous cabinet had not had
an adverse vote and had no legal right to resign; and that furthermore, the Chamber had no right to discuss this amendment now, since there were other items on the agenda previous to this—referring to the Albanian question. He ended by
presenting a motion that the Senate be consulted as to whether
the present cabinet was or was not to be considered a new cabinet. Hoca Mustafa Sabri Efendi, opposition deputy for Tokad,
gave legal reasons why the claim of the Grand Vezier that the
Chamber had by its obstruction virtually rejected the proposed
amendment could not stand, and said it was evident that the
cabinet was determined to dissolve the Chamber. Hüseyin
Cahid [Yalçın], editor of *Tanin* and Unionist deputy for İs-
tanbul, expressed his disapproval of this speech. The Grand
Vezier vigorously repudiated the charge of wishing to dissolve
the Chamber, and condemned the obstructionist tactics of the
monarchist opposition. Seyyid Bey, leader of the parliamentary party of the Committee of Union and Progress, refuted the

---

[164] "Constantinople Letter," *The Near East*, January 12, 1912, p.291.
[165] Hüseyin Cahid Yalçın, "Meşrutiyet Hatıraları, 1908-1918," *Fikir Hareketleri*, 7 (October 24, 1936-April 17, 1937), p.52.
[166] Hüseyin Cahid Yalçın, "Meşrutiyet Hatıraları, 1908-1918," *Fikir Hareketleri*, 7 (October 24, 1936-April 17, 1937), p.37; and, Mehmed Cavid, "Meşrutiyet
Devrine Ait Cavid Bey'in Hatıraları: 64," *Tanin*, November 3, 1943, p.2.
[167] I/IV/31, December 21, 1327/January 3, 1912, *Meclis-i Mebusan Zabıt Ceridesi*, 2, p.325; Ziya Şakir [Soko], "Hürriyet ve İtilâf Nasıl Doğdu? Nasıl Yaşadı? Nasıl Battı? 40: Sait Paşa Yeni Kabineyi Teşkile Memur Ediliyor," *Tan*, December
17, 1937, p.9. See also, Yusuf Hikmet Bayur, *Türk İnkılâbı Tarihi*, 2/1, p.241.

arguments of Hoca Mustafa Sabri Efendi, and moved that the amendment be immediately discussed. At the demand of Said Pasha, this motion was put before that of Sıdkı Bey, but this led to high words and some very plain but unparliamentary appellatives between Ahmed Ferid [Tek], opposition deputy for Kütahya, and Talât Bey, who were with difficulty separated. Seyyid Bey's motion was carried, the opposition having left the hall, by a vote of one hundred and three to two. The Entente Libérale deputies returned for the vote on referring the legal point to the Senate, which motion was defeated by one hundred votes to ninety.[168]

At the January 4 sitting of the Chamber, Babanzade İsmail Hakkı Bey, Unionist deputy for Baghdad and Chairman of the Parliamentary Commission for the Revision of the Constitution, gave a long explanation of the object of the proposed amendment. Denying that the amending of Article 35 was a blow at the Constitution, he said that it was on the contrary intended to strengthen it. He called attention to the frequency of a dissolution of Parliament in Great Britain, and to the fact that a newly elected set of deputies would represent more accurately the national opinion. France also saw frequent dissolutions. The restriction on the power of the throne to dissolve the Chamber, relating to the consent of the Senate, existed in no other monarchy, and had been introduced from the Constitution of the French Republic, where the Senate was an elective body. If the Chamber had the right to concur for the dissolution of the Senate, it would even up matters, but the existing provision gave the Senate a great advantage over the Chamber.[169]

---

[168] I/IV/31, December 21, 1327/January 3, 1912, Meclis-i Mebusan Zabıt Ceridesi, 2, pp.326-347; [Hüseyin Cahid Yalçın], "Dünkü Celse," Tanin, December 22, 1327/January 4, 1912, p.1; "The Ottoman Parliament," The Orient, 3/2 (January 10, 1912), p.1; and, "The Political Situation," The Levant Herald and Eastern Express, January 4, 1912, p.1. See also, "New Turkish Cabinet," The Times, January 4, 1912, p.3. See also, Cemal Kutay, Türkiye İstiklâl ve Hürriyet Mücadeleleri Tarihi, 17, pp.9807-9809; Ahmed Bedevi Kuran, Osmanlı İmparatorluğunda İnkılâp Hareketleri ve Milli Mücadele, pp.547-548; and, Ahmed Bedevi Kuran, İnkılâp Tarihimiz ve 'Jön Türkler,' pp.301-302.   •
[169] I/IV/32, December 22, 1327/January 4, 1912, Meclis-i Mebusan Zabıt Ceridesi, 2, pp.352-360; "The Ottoman Parliament," The Orient, 3/2 (January 10, 1912), p.1; "Chambre des Députés," The Levant Herald and Eastern Express, January 5, 1912, pp.1-2; and, "The Turkish Chamber and the Cabinet," The Times, January 5, 1912, p.3. See also, "Yine 35. Madde," Yeni İkdam, December 23, 1327/January 5,

Sıdkı Bey replied for the Entente Libérale. He occupied an hour and a half in setting forth the illegality of the procedure of the cabinet, in proposing a constitutional amendment before the cabinet had unfolded their programme or obtained a vote of confidence, and especially without the concurrence of the new Sheikh-ul-Islam, who had not yet arrived from Egypt. He said it was not the Sultan whom the Entente Libérale feared but the Grand Vezier who protested so loudly that he had no desire to dissolve the Chamber while in reality that matter was not in his hands. The debate was afterwards adjourned until January 6.[170]

The continuous obstruction of the Chamber's proceedings by the monarchist deputies led the Unionist leadership to take action. In retaliation, the Unionists again threatened to publish those *jurnals* which members of the opposition had sent to Abdülhamid during the pre-revolutionary period. In an open letter published in the *Tanin* of January 6, Talât Bey accused one of the prominent monarchist members of having written to Abdülhamid, urging him to oppose a constitutional monarchy on the grounds that it would not be beneficial to the country.[171]

The debate on the proposed constitutional amendment was continued on January 6. Babanzade İsmail Hakkı Bey began by answering the arguments of Sıdkı Bey. He said that the refusal to discuss the project was tantamount to a rejection; that in presenting this amendment the new cabinet did present its programme, and that the vote of the Chamber to discuss it immediately was in reality a vote of confidence. He ended his speech by begging the opposition to cease obstructionist tactics and express themselves on the principles of the amendment.[172]

1912, p.1.
    [170] I/IV/32, December 22, 1327/January 4, 1912, *Meclis-i Mebusan Zabıt Ceridesi*, 2, pp.362-371; "The Turkish Chamber and the Cabinet," *The Times*, January 5, 1912, p.3; and, "The Ottoman Parliament," *The Orient*, 3/2 (January 10, 1912), p.1. See also, "Yine 35. Madde," *Yeni Ikdam*, December 23, 1327/January 5, 1912, p.1.
    [171] *Tanin*, December 24, 1327/January 6, 1912, reproduced in its entirety in Hüseyin Cahid Yalçın, "Meşrutiyet Hatıraları, 1908-1918," *Fikir Hareketleri*, 7 (October 24, 1936-April 17, 1937), p.37.
    [172] I/IV/33, December 24, 1327/January 6, 1912, *Meclis-i Mebusan Zabıt Ceridesi*, 2, pp.374-379; and, "The Ottoman Parliament," *The Orient*, 3/2 (January 10,

Daltcheff, deputy for Serres, criticised the government for trying to make itself stronger when the trouble was, it was too strong already. He alleged that the government had used illegal force in Albania, Macedonia, and lately at İştib, where, he claimed, troubles were due to governmental mistakes. In his view, to give such a government more power would be to re-establish absolutism.[173] Boussios, Greek deputy for Serfidje, said that they did not accept the amendment because they did not wish to leave the country in the hands of the Committee of Union and Progress. Pointing out that the Unionists were losing adherents in the Chamber, Boussios declared that a party that mustered only one hundred votes in an assembly composed of two hundred and eighty members could not in any country pretend to have a majority. His advice to the Committee of Union and Progress was to leave the power to others.[174] His speech was well publicised in the monarchist press. *Yeni İkdam* of January 7 praised him for his oratorical gifts and used this opportunity to further attack the Unionists.[175]

At the January 9 sitting of the Chamber, Dr. Rıza Nur, Yorgos Boussios, and Ömer Fevzi Efendi tried obstructionist tactics for a while, but the debate on Article 35 proceeded. 'Abd-al Hamid az-Zahrawi, monarchist deputy for Hama, in a long harangue, aroused harsh feelings by his unfair criticisms. Emmanuel Emmanuelides, Unionist Greek deputy for İzmir, defended the Committee of Union and Progress against the attacks of Boussios.[176] The following day, on January 10, Dr. Rıza Nur and Basri Dukacı, deputy for Dibër, occupied the

---

1912), pp.1-2.

[173] I/IV/33, December 24, 1327/January 6, 1912, *Meclis-i Mebusan Zabıt Ceridesi*, 2, pp.379-380; and, "The Ottoman Parliament," *The Orient, 3/2* (January 10, 1912), p.2.

[174] I/IV/33, December 24, 1327/January 6, 1912, *Meclis-i Mebusan Zabıt Ceridesi*, 2, pp.384-393; "Mr. Boussios's Speech in Parliament," *The Orient, 3/2* (January 10, 1912), pp.3-4.

[175] "Boussios Efendi ve 35. Madde'nin Tadili," *Yeni İkdam*, December 25, 1327/January 7, 1912, p.1. This editorial is also excerpted in "An Able Greek Deputy," *The Orient, 3/2* (January 10, 1912), pp.6-7.

[176] I/IV/34, December 27, 1327/January 9, 1912, *Meclis-i Mebusan Zabıt Ceridesi*, 2, pp.396-417; "The Ottoman Parliament," *The Orient, 3/3* (January 17, 1912), p.1; and, Babanzade İsmail Hakkı, "Müzakere Devam Ediyor," *Tanin*, December 28, 1327/January 10, 1912, p.1. See also, Ahmed Tarabein, "Abd al-Hamid al-Zahrawi: The Career and Thought of an Arab Nationalist," p.101.

whole afternoon sitting in attacking the Unionists and the amendment, being frequently interrupted in most unparliamentary form. Dr. Rıza Nur criticised the government for trying to force the measure while the Grand Vezier was ill, the Sheikh-ul-Islam absent, and the Ministry of the Interior vacant. Alleging that the real object of the cabinet was to strengthen the position not of the Sultan but of their own party, he said he preferred an absolute sovereign who respected the law to a constitutional monarchy which did not. [177] At the January 11 sitting, Rıza Tevfik [Bölükbaşı], one of the leaders of the Entente Libérale, openly cursed the Unionist deputies in an address to the Chamber, denounced the Committee of Union and Progress, and wished calamity on the constitutional regime.[178] By now it was perfectly clear that the opposition's aim did not fall within the bounds of a liberal democra cy; the aim was not merely to criticise the deeds of the Said Pasha Cabinet as one would normally expect in a liberal democratic parliamentary regime but to destroy both the Committee of Union and Progress and the liberal democratic regime.[179]

---

[177] I/IV/35, December 28, 1327/January 10, 1912, *Meclis-i Mebusan Zabıt Ceridesi*, 2, pp.421-456; "Rıza Nur ve Basri Beyler," *Yeni İkdam*, December 29, 1327/January 11, 1912, p.1; [Hüseyin Cahid Yalçın], "Dünkü Celse," *Tanin*, December 29, 1327/January 11, 1912, p.1; and, "The Ottoman Parliament," *The Orient*, 3/3 (January 17, 1912), p.1.

[178] I/IV/36, December 29, 1327/January 11, 1912, *Meclis-i Mebusan Zabıt Ceridesi*, 2, pp.458-485; "Meclis-i Mebusan'da Dünkü Rezalet," *Tanin*, December 30, 1327/January 12, 1912, p.1; [Hüseyin Cahid Yalçın], "Dünkü Müzakerat," *Tanin*, December 30, 1327/January 12, 1912, p.1. See also, Hüseyin Cahid Yalçın, "Meşrutiyet Hatıraları, 1908-1918," *Fikir Hareketleri*, 7 (October 24, 1936-April 17, 1937), p.52. See also, "Tokad Mebusu Mustafa Sabri Efendi," *Yeni İkdam*, December 30, 1327/January 12, 1912, p.1.

[179] *Tanin*, December 27, 1327/January 9, 1912, in Hüseyin Cahid Yalçın, "Meşrutiyet Hatıraları, 1908-1918," *Fikir Hareketleri*, 7 (October 24, 1936-April 17, 1937), p.52.
On the question of the future of liberal democracy and the positions of the Committee of Union and Progress, and the monarchist opposition on this issue, the representative of the American Embassy filed this confidential report: "It may well be believed that the Union and Progress party will not hesitate in its devotion to a representative form of government, to have recourse to even more irregular methods than it recently used in connection with the dissolution of Parliament for maintaining itself in power and 'preserving the Constitution,' as it euphemistically says. Whatever we may think of the success of the present régime and of its maintaining itself in power, its overthrow and the assumption of power by the opposition would be a disaster for the country, for this latter party includes in its ranks all the most bigoted reactionary and inexperienced elements of the political world of Turkey. The sins of commission and omission of the party of Union and Progress are probably great, but it is, so far as I can see, the only one which can bring Turkey through its present troubles" (William W. Rockhill to Secretary of State, Constantinople, January 24, 1912, in *Records of the Department of State Relating to Internal Affairs of Turkey, 1910-1929*, Roll 4).

Backed by the majority of the monarchist-dominated Senate, Hüseyin Hilmi Pasha submitted, on January 9, to the leaders of the two parties a scheme for an understanding. The scheme was based on the main point that the proposed modification of Article 35 be accepted with one amendment—namely, consultation of the Senate to be a necessary preliminary to the dissolution of Parliament. He further proposed that dissolution of the Chamber not to take place in 1912 and that a paragraph providing for this be added to the modified Article. Requesting that party organs abstain from further polemics for the remainder of the session, Hüseyin Hilmi Pasha also asked the Chamber to bind itself to abstain from unnecessary interpellations on penalty of having debates suspended for three months.[180]

However, his attempt to effect a compromise between the warring parties on the question of the amendment of the Constitution ended in failure.[181] In an interview published in the January 12 issue of *La Liberté*, Hüseyin Hilmi Pasha expressed regret that his proposals for a compromise had not been accepted by either side, and added that he did not believe the government would obtain a two-thirds majority, or one hundred and fifty-six votes, for the proposal of the amendment of the Constitution. He told *La Liberté* that the majority of the Senate also opposed to the immediate modification of Article 35. The creation of new senators in order to constitute a majority in favour of the amendment would, in his opinion, have the unfortunate result of lowering the prestige of that body, which, he claimed, should hold the balance of power between the parties. Informing the public that holding of general elections would be inevitable should the Parliament be dissolved, he expressed the opinion that this was not an opportune moment for electoral struggles, which were certain to cause agitation, and might result in disturbances which would only in-

---

[180] "Hüseyin Hilmi Paşa'nın İtilâf Teklifi Ne İmiş!" *Yeni İkdam*, December 27, 1327/January 9, 1912, p.1; "Hüseyin Hilmi Paşa Hazretleri ile Mülâkat," *Yeni İkdam*, December 28, 1327/January 10, 1912, p.1; [Hüseyin Cahid Yalçın], "Son Lâkırdılar," *Tanin*, December 28, 1327/January 10, 1912, p.1; Mehmed Cavid, "Meşrutiyet Devrine Ait Cavid Bey'in Hatıraları: 63," *Tanin*, November 2, 1943, p.2; and, "The Turkish Constitutional Debates: Proposals for a Compromise," *The Times*, January 10, 1912, p.3.
[181] "Notes of the Week," *The Near East*, January 19, 1912, p.321.

crease the malaise from which the whole country had been suffering in consequence of parliamentary rivalries. He added that an understanding between Muslims and Christians and between the Committee of Union and Progress and the Entente Libérale was necessary for the welfare of Turkey. His advice was that the prorogation of the Chamber for three months would be a simple method of putting an end to these polemics, which, he alleged, had been having a bad effect everywhere.[182]

The government decided to put the proposed amendment to a vote in the Chamber at all costs. On January 13, the Chamber narrowly sanctioned the proposal by a vote of one hundred and twenty-four to one hundred and five, which, because this was not a two-thirds majority, effectively meant defeat for the Committee of Union and Progress. The Government then decided to dissolve the Chamber and call for new elections. The new Chamber would meet in three months' time.[183] On January 15, the Sultan transmitted to the Senate an imperial decree informing it of his decision to dissolve the Chamber, and, in conformity with Article 7 of the Constitution, awaiting the Senate's reply.[184] The Senate decided to appoint a commission composed of nine members—Hüseyin Hilmi Pasha, Prince Said Halim Pasha, Mehmed Galib Bey, General Salih Pasha, Bessaraya Efendi, Şerif Cafer Pasha, İsmail Hakkı Bey,

[182] *La Liberté*, January 12, 1912, excerpted in "The Turkish Constitution: Hilmi Pasha on the Outlook," *The Times*, January 15, 1912, p.5. See also, "Hüseyin Hilmi Paşa'nın Beyanatı," *Yeni İkdam*, December 31, 1327/January 13, 1912, p.2.

[183] I/IV/37, December 31, 1327/January 13, 1912, *Meclis-i Mebusan Zabıt Ceridesi*, 2, pp.488-510; "Dünkü Netice," *Yeni İkdam*, January 1, 1327/January 14, 1912, p.1; "Rejection of the Government's Bill: The Dissolution of Parliament," *The Levant Herald and Eastern Express*, January 15, 1912, p.1; "Rejection of the Government Measure," *The Times*, January 15, 1912, p.5; "The Ottoman Parliament," *The Orient*, 3/3 (January 17, 1912), pp.1-2; "Notes of the Week," *The Near East*, January 19, 1912, p.321. See also, Feroz Ahmad, *The Young Turks: The Committee of Union and Progress in Turkish Politics, 1908-1914*, p.102; Ahmed Bedevi Kuran, *Osmanlı İmparatorluğunda İnkılâp Hareketleri ve Milli Mücadele*, p.554; and, Yusuf Hikmet Bayur, *Türk İnkılâbı Tarihi*, 2/1, p.242. See also, William W. Rockhill to Secretary of State, Constantinople, January 24, 1912, in *Records of the Department of State Relating to Internal Affairs of Turkey, 1910-1929*, Roll 4.

[184] I/IV/22, January 2, 1327/January 15, 1912, *Meclis-i Âyan Zabıt Ceridesi*, 1, pp.258-260; "Meclis-i Âyan ve Fesih Meselesi," *Yeni İkdam*, January 2, 1327/January 15, 1912, p.1; "Turkish Chamber to be Dissolved: Imperial Message to the Senate," *The Times*, January 16, 1912, p.8; and, *Tanin*, January 3, 1327/January 16, 1912, cited in Feroz Ahmad, *The Young Turks: The Committee of Union and Progress in Turkish Politics, 1908-1914*, p.102n. See also, Yusuf Hikmet Bayur, *Türk İnkılâbı Tarihi*, 2/1, p.242.

Zareh Efendi Dilber, and General Hüsnü Pasha—to report on
the advisability of a dissolution. As the majority of the members of this commission was sympathetic to the Committee of
Union and Progress, it was expected that the Senate had decided not to raise difficulties.[185] After weighing the pros and
cons, the commission decided that it would be wiser to yield
on this issue of new elections than to enter into a struggle
which would pit the Senate against the Committee of Union
and Progress, the Grand Vezier, and the Sultan.[186] On January
17, the Senate voted thirty-nine to five with one abstention that
the Sultan be advised to dissolve Parliament.[187]

[185] "Âyan'ın Feshi Telakki ve Tezekkürü," Yeni Ikdam, January 3, 1327/Jan-
uary 16, 1912, p.1; "Turkish Chamber to be Dissolved: Imperial Message to the Senate," The Times, January 16, 1912, p.8; and, "The Senate: The Dissolution of Parliament," The Levant Herald and Eastern Express, January 16, 1912, p.1.
[186] "The Dissolution of the Turkish Chamber," The Times, January 17, 1912,
p.5; "The Dissolution of Parliament," The Levant Herald and Eastern Express, January 17, 1912, p.1; "The Chamber Dissolved," The Orient, 3/4 (January 24, 1912),
p.1; and, "Constantinople Letter," The Near East, January 26, 1912, p.359.
[187] "The Turkish Parliament: Expected Dissolution To-Day," The Times, January 18, 1912, p.5; "Meclis-i Âyan'ın Feşhe Muvafakkıyeti," Tanin, January 5,
1327/January 18, 1912, p.1; and, "Meclis-i Âyan Müzakeratı ve Mebusan'ın Feshi,"
Yeni Ikdam, January 5, 1327/January 18, 1912, p.1. See also, Mehmed Cavid, "Meş-
rutiyet Devrine Ait Cavid Bey'in Hatıraları: 66," Tanin, November 5, 1943, p.2;
Ahmed Bedevi Kuran, Osmanlı Imparatorluğunda Inkılâp Hareketleri ve Milli
Mücadele, p.554; Mustafa Ragıb Esatlı, "Meşrutiyet Devrinde: Intihap Mücadelesi
Nasıl Yapılıyordu?" Akşam, March 11, 1943, p.4; and, Yusuf Hikmet Bayur, Türk
Inkılâbı Tarihi, 2/1, p.242. Those who voted against were Avlonyalı Ferid Pasha,
Damad Ferid Pasha, Marshal Fuad Pasha, Georgiades Efendi, and Sheikh Abd-al
Kadir Efendi ("The Dissolution of Parliament," The Levant Herald and Eastern
Express, January 18, 1912, p.1; and, "The Chamber Dissolved," The Orient, 3/4
(January 24, 1912), p.1).

CHAPTER EIGHT

THE GENERAL ELECTIONS OF 1912

The imperial decree dated January 17 for the dissolution of the Chamber of Deputies and calling for the new elections and the constitution of the new Chamber within three months was published in the newspapers of January 18.[1] The elections, it was said, would begin in a month's time. All prophesies concerning the composition and character of the next Parliament were based on mere surmise and had to be accepted with the utmost caution. All that could be said was that while the Committee of Union and Progress had lost ground, there was no proof that the Entente Libérale had gained any access of strength except in Albania and perhaps in the Arab provinces. The general pessimism, accentuated by the ongoing war with Italy over Tripoli, was perhaps the most striking feature of the situation.[2]

Although a definite decision had not been taken with regard to further cabinet changes, there was reason to believe that an influential section of the Committee of Union and Progress wished to strengthen the cabinet by the appointment of Talât Bey as Minister of the Interior, and of Cavid Bey as Minister of Public Works.[3] Immediately after the call for new elections, the Unionist leadership began criticising the Said

---

[1] *Tanin*, January 5, 1327/January 18, 1912, cited in Hüseyin Cahid Yalçın, "Meşrutiyet Hatıraları, 1908-1918," *Fikir Hareketleri*, 7 (October 24, 1936-April 17, 1937), p.52; "The Chamber Dissolved," *The Orient*, 3/4 (January 24, 1912), p.1; "The Dissolution of Parliament," *The Levant Herald and Eastern Express*, January 19, 1912, p.1; and, "The Turkish Chamber: Work of the Past Session," *The Times*, January 19, 1912, p.5. See also, Ziya Şakir [Soko], "Hürriyet ve İtilâf Nasıl Doğdu? Nasıl Yaşadı? Nasıl Battı? 41: İtilâfçılar Son Darbe Altında Afallamışlardı," *Tan*, December 19, 1937, p.9.

[2] "The Turkish Chamber: Work of the Past Session," *The Times*, January 19, 1912, p.5.

[3] "The Turkish Chamber: Work of the Past Session—Rumoured Cabinet Changes," *The Times*, January 19, 1912, p.5.

Pasha Cabinet for being transitory, and for not having accomplished anything new or drastic in the way of institutionalising the Revolution.[4]

The pressures worked. Hacı Âdil [Arda], ex-Governor of Edirne and Secretary-General of the Committee of Union and Progress, was appointed Minister of the Interior on January 22.[5] He was a man of considerable administrative experience, especially in the Customs Administration, and was believed to be of a more moderate and conciliatory disposition than some of his colleagues in the Committee of Union and Progress.[6] In the January 26 issue of *Tanin*, Hüseyin Cahid [Yalçın] welcomed the news of Hacı Âdil Arda's appointment as Minister of the Interior, but expressed worry that there was needed more energetic people in government which had a difficult task to accomplish in the upcoming three months.[7]

Hacı Âdil [Arda] was soon joined by Talât Bey, the new Minister of Posts and Telegraphs, replacing İbrahim Sousa.[8] The official news of his appointment, though, did not appear until February 3.[9] He took up his duties on February 5.[10] Ürgüplü Hayri Bey, another Unionist, was already in the cabinet as Minister of Pious Foundations. However, still unable to have Cavid Bey appointed as Minister of Public Works, *Tanin* kept up the pressure, arguing that because the cabinet had come into power only with the support of the Unionist deputies, it was the Committee of Union and Progress which was largely responsible for the government's actions and policies.

---

[4] [Hüseyin Cahid Yalçın], "Fesihten Sonra," *Tanin*, January 7, 1327/January 20, 1912, p.1; and, Hüseyin Cahid Yalçın, "Meşrutiyet Hatıraları, 1908-1918," *Fikir Hareketleri*, 7 (October 24, 1936-April 17, 1937), p.52.

[5] "Dahiliye Nazırı," *Tanin*, January 9, 1327/January 22, 1912, p.3.

[6] "News Items," *The Levant Herald and Eastern Express*, January 22, 1912, p.1; "The Turkish Cabinet: The Minister of the Interior," *The Times*, January 23, 1912, p.5; and, "Empire News: The Capital, *The Orient*, 3/4 (January 24, 1912), p.7.

[7] [Hüseyin Cahid Yalçın], "Yavaş, Yavaş!" *Tanin*, January 13, 1327/January 26, 1912, p.1. For excerpts of this unsigned editorial see, "Yavash, Yavash!," *The Orient*, 3/5 (January 31, 1912), p.6.

[8] "The Turkish Senate: Appointment of Ahmed Riza Bey," *The Times*, January 25, 1912, p.5; and "Empire News: The Capital," *The Orient*, 3/6 (February 7, 1912), p.7.

[9] "News Items," *The Levant Herald and Eastern Express*, February 3, 1912, p.1; "Posta ve Telgraf Nezareti," *Tanin*, January 23, 1327/February 5, 1912, p.3; and, "Turkish Politics: Talaat Bey's Appointment," *The Times*, February 5, 1912, p.5.

[10] "News Items," *The Levant Herald and Eastern Express*, February 6, 1912, p.1.

Yet, no Minister was a prominent member of the party, and this raised the problem of accountability. Extending this logic, *Tanin* argued that those who were responsible for the policies of the government should also be in the cabinet as well.[11]

After persistent Unionist efforts, the leadership of the Committee of Union and Progress finally managed to have Cavid Bey appointed to a cabinet post. On February 17, Krikor Sinapian having handed in his long-awaited resignation, an Imperial Decree was issued appointing Cavid Bey Minister of Public Works.[12]

By late January, both the Committee of Union and Progress and the Entente Libérale had begun preparations for the upcoming general elections. It was generally expected that the first degree elections would be over by the end of February, the second some time in April. By and large, the Committee of Union and Progress was expected to win.[13]

The Entente Libérale, the main opposition party, consisted of monarchist Turks, Albanians, Arabs of Syria and Iraq, a large majority of Greeks, Bulgarians, and a few of the more conservative Armenian communities.[14] By the end of January, an arrangement had been practically concluded between the Greeks and Bulgarians in Macedonia for common action at the approaching elections. The efforts made by Unionist envoys to sow discord between the Greeks and the Bulgarians appeared to have failed, and the Bulgarians were stated to have rejected the Unionist offer of seven seats in the new Chamber provided that they would not cooperate with the Greeks.[15] An exchange of visits between the Bulgarian Min-

---

[11] Hüseyin Cahid [Yalçın], "İttihad ve Terakki Kabinesi," *Tanin*, January 15, 1327/January 28, 1912, p.1; and, "Said Pasha and the Cabinet: The Rumoured Changes," *The Times*, January 31, 1912, p.5. See also, Hüseyin Cahid Yalçın, "Meşrutiyet Hatıraları, 1908-1918," *Fikir Hareketleri*, 7 (October 24, 1936-April 17, 1937), p.53; and, "Ekseriyete Göre Kabine," *Yeni İkdam*, January 16, 1327/January 29, 1912, p.1.

[12] "New Turkish Minister," *The Times*, February 19, 1912, p.5; "Nafia Nazırı: Cavid Bey," *Yeni İkdam*, February 6, 1327/February 19, 1912, p.1; and, "Nafia Nezareti'nde," *Tanin*, February 8, 1327/February 21, 1912, p.2.

[13] "Constantinople Letter," *The Near East*, February 9, 1912, 427.

[14] "Constantinople Letter," *The Near East*, February 16, 1912, p.459.

[15] "Macedonia and the Young Turks," *The Times*, January 31, 1912, p.5; and, "The Elections in Macedonia," *The Levant Herald and Eastern Express*, February 5, 1912, p.1.

ister in İstanbul and the Greek Ecumenical Patriarch in the last days of January caused considerable comment in political circles. It was quite rightly interpreted as a proof of the friendly relations existing between Greeks and Bulgarians, and their respective Churches.[16] Having joined the Entente Libérale, the Greeks and Bulgarians, together with the help of their clergy, were doing their utmost to undermine the Unionist organisation in Macedonia.[17]

The Unionist concern for the accord reached between the Greeks and the Bulgarians in the Macedonian provinces of the Empire was aggravated by the rapprochement between the Greek and Bulgarian states. Commenting in the *Tanin* of January 31 on the visit of the Crown Prince of Greece to Sofia, Babanzade İsmail Hakkı Bey expressed the Unionist consternation that the 'pompous menacing' Greco-Bulgarian rapprochement was directed against Turkey. As for the possibility that it might lead to interference in the internal affairs of the Empire, Babanzade İsmail Hakkı Bey said that Turkey was strong enough to resist such attempts and could count upon the help of elements oppressed by the foreigners. The article faithfully reflected the apprehensions caused in Unionist circles by the steady improvement in the relations between the Greeks and Bulgarians both within the boundaries of the Empire and outside them.[18]

On the other hand, the Bulgarian leaders and the Albanian chiefs maintained the accord arrived the previous spring. The Albanians, recognising the error they had committed in the Spring of 1911 by beginning the revolt prematurely, were determined to remain quiet for the time being, but to continue their preparations. This decision by the Albanian chiefs had been taken before the announcement of certain reforms on the part of the Committee of Union and Progress, and consequently could not be regarded as the result of the conciliatory

---

[16] "Said Pasha and the Cabinet: The Rumoured Changes," *The Times*, January 31, 1912, p.5.

[17] "The Election Campaign in Turkey," *The Near East*, February 23, 1912, p.510.

[18] Babanzade İsmail Hakkı, "Yunanistan, Bulgaristan," *Tanin*, January 18, 1327/January 31, 1912, p.1. This editorial is also quoted in, "Anxiety of the Young Turks," *The Times*, February 1, 1912, p.5.

attitude of the Unionists towards the Albanians. In any case, the Albanians regarded the promise of reforms as an electoral device and did not take it seriously.[19] On its part, in spite of renewed attempts to draw Albanian support, the Committee of Union and Progress did not expect this constituency to vote in its favour. In fact, the insurrection in the Spring of 1911 and the government's inability to introduce certain promised reforms had made the Albanians the Unionists' most bitter opponents.[20]

By the end of January, the situation in Albania, which was already bad, had considerably worsened. A further complication had arisen in the refusal of the peasants in the Vlorë and Argyrocastro districts—two monarchist constituencies—to pay taxes. Not only had the payment been refused, but the tax collectors had been warned that should they persist in their demands, their lives would be endangered. The inhabitants stated that they were without means and therefore could not pay the amount demanded of them. The opinion of the local officials was that this situation was due to the instigation of certain interested parties—among whom İsmail Kemal Bey, the monarchist Albanian deputy for Berat, figured prominently—who were desirous of creating further difficulties for the government in Albania. The collectors' request for military assistance had been categorically refused by the local military authorities, and the matter had been referred to the Ministry of the Interior.[21]

In consequence of these disturbances, it was officially announced in İstanbul that Hacı Âdil [Arda], Minister of the Interior, would start on a tour of the Macedonian provinces, accompanied by a staff of civilian and military officials. He would be given full powers for the immediate application of remedial measures.[22] Hacı Âdil [Arda] left İstanbul for Sa-

---

[19] "Macedonia and the Young Turks," *The Times*, January 31, 1912, p.5.

[20] "The Election Campaign in Turkey," *The Near East*, February 23, 1912, p.510.

[21] "Trouble in Albania: Peasants' Refusal to Pay Taxes," *The Times*, February 10, 1912, p.5. İsmail Kemal Bey, fearing arrest in consequence of the cessation of parliamentary immunity with the dissolution of the Chamber, had left İstanbul on January 16 ("Flight of a Deputy," *The Times*, January 18, 1912, p.5).

[22] "The Unrest in Turkey: Minister of the Interior's Proposed Tour," *The Times*, February 9, 1912, p.5; and, "Reforms in Asia Minor," *The Times*, February

lonica on February 17 on his tour of inquiry into the condition of the Macedonian and Albanian provinces.[23] The Albanians, however, were determined to resist the Turkish authority. By mid-March it was reported that an Albanian band had ambushed the escort of Hacı Âdil [Arda] on the road between İpek and Gjakovë. Official secrecy was maintained as to the number of victims.[24]

Since the Italian declaration of war, the state of Albania had not improved, while that of Macedonia had gone from bad to worse. The revival of the Bulgarian revolutionary propaganda was one of the worst features of the existing situation. It was generally ascribed to the severities which marked the disarmament of 1910-1911, following the suppression of the revolt by government troops, and which undoubtedly drove some of the Bulgarian peasants to the hills. Given the fact that the average Bulgarian peasant would generally bear the bastinado and worse treatment with dour patience, it was, however, clear that the causes of the discontent lay deeper. The real causes of the revival of the Bulgarian revolutionary propaganda in Macedonia were due to the failure of the new regime to grapple with the agrarian question, the breakdown of the gendarmerie organisation, and the frequent and unpunished massacres of Bulgarian peasants by the hired assassins of Muslim murder clubs.[25]

The situation was not a simple one. It was not only the Muslims who killed the Bulgarian peasantry. Bands of the Bulgarian revolutionary Internal Organisation were busy attacking not only the representatives of the state, but also terrorising the Bulgarian peasantry in an attempt to force them join in their struggle against Turkish rule. On February 17, a bomb explod-

---

14, 1912, p.5. See also, Joseph Swire, *Albania: The Rise of a Kingdom*, pp.112-113; and, Stavro Skendi, *The Albanian National Awakening, 1878-1912*, pp.426-427.
      [23] "New Turkish Minister," *The Times*, February 19, 1912, p.5; and, "Hacı Âdil Beyefendi," *Tanin*, February 8, 1327/February 21, 1912, p.2.
      [24] "Turkish Minister's Tour: Escort Ambushed by Albanians," *The Times*, March 16, 1912, p.5; and, Joseph Swire, *Albania: The Rise of a Kingdom*, p.113. It was no secret that the Governor of Kossovo had informed the government that the news of Hacı Âdil [Arda]'s proposed visit to Albania had failed to produce any tranquilizing effect in the region ("Turkish Home Troubles: The Albanian Unrest," *The Times*, February 2, 1912, p.5).
      [25] "Albanian and Macedonian Grievances: Hadji Adil Bey's Commission," *The Times*, February 24, 1912, p.7.

ed in the police headquarters of the town of Kirchevo, to the north of Monastir, destroying the building and killing one person and injuring five others. The crime was attributed to the Internal Organisation. The day being market day at Kirchevo, it was apparently hoped to provoke further incidents such as occurred at İştib in December, but the authorities took prompt measures to prevent any disturbances, and order was restored.[26]

A few days later, the refusal of the Bulgarian inhabitants of a mill at Petritch in Serres to lend their support to the Internal Organisation was the cause of a particularly revolting crime which was attributed by the authorities to the revolutionary chief Donjo, whose band had attacked the mill and ruthlessly massacred the Bulgarian inhabitants. The peasants being unarmed were unable to defend themselves and inflicted no loss upon the brigands. It had become evident that orders had been issued to the bands that the Bulgarian villages were to be terrorised into extending their hospitality to the revolutionary Internal Organisation.[27]

It was not only Bulgarians that were being assassinated in Macedonia. The situation had considerably deteriorated, and it had almost approached to the level of civil strife in the whole region. By mid-February, the continuation of the series of assassinations of Muslims by Bulgarian bands had given rise to a growing feeling of resentment and anger among the entire Muslim population of Macedonia. It was feared that if the government did not succeed in putting an end to these outrages, it would be very difficult to avoid large scale massacres on both sides.[28]

In an effort to settle the outstanding issues between the Internal Organisation and the Turkish Administration, Şükrü Bey, Under-Secretary of the Ministry of the Interior, and Abdülkerim Bey, Inspector of Public Instruction, went to Sofia to ask the representatives of the Internal Organisation what reforms would satisfy them and under what conditions they

---

[26] "Bomb Outrage in Macedonia," *The Times*, February 19, 1912, p.5.

[27] "Terrorism in Macedonia: Villagers Killed," *The Times*, February 21, 1912, p.5.

[28] "Bulgarian Band Outrages: Moslem Resentment," *The Times*, February 24, 1912, p.7.

would put a stop to the bomb explosions and terrorist activity. The representatives of the Internal Organisation gave the uncompromising reply that the Internal Organisation refused to negotiate with the Turkish Government and would continue its terrorist activity until it attained its object, *i.e.*, autonomy through international European intervention.[29]

Indeed, the aim of the Internal Organisation was to capture the attention of the European Powers. As part of their propaganda effort, Professors Miletich and Georgov, both of Sofia University, had arrived at St. Petersburg in mid-March as delegates of the Internal Organisation to agitate in favour of European intervention against the alleged atrocities perpetrated by the Turkish Government. An international press campaign had already started. In leading articles and interviews, they insisted on the revival of the programme of reforms outlined at the Reval meeting of 1908 between the King of Great Britain and the Czar of Russia. The delegates then proceeded to London and other European capitals.[30] Meanwhile, the Internal Organisation continued its terrorist activities throughout the election campaign. On March 26, it was reported that ten bombs had been found on the Salonica-Monastir railway near Florina.[31]

Another group which was in close touch with the Entente Libérale was the secular as well as the religious leadership of the Greek community. Though sympathetic to the monarchist cause, the Greek community had formally refrained from joining the Entente Libérale up until mid-January despite persistent appeals by the Entente Libérale leadership. With the heated debate on the modification of Article 35 of the Constitution, the consequent dissolution of the Chamber, and the call for general elections, however, conservative Greek deputies decided to formally ally themselves with the Entente Libérale.[32] The conservative *Sabah* and the monarchist *Yeni Gazete*

---

[29] "The Revolutionary Movement in Macedonia: Turkish Overtures Repulsed," *The Times*, March 19, 1912, p.5.
[30] "The Macedonian Agitation: A Mission of Propaganda," *The Times*, March 22, 1912, p.5.
[31] "Bombs on a Turkish Railway," *The Times*, March 27, 1912, p.5.
[32] [Hüseyin Cahid Yalçın], "Rum Meşrutiyet Cemiyeti'yle İtilâf," *Tanin*,

of January 12 informed the public that a protocol had been signed between the two sides and that twenty-two Greek deputies had joined the Entente Libérale.[33] With the protocol, the Entente Libérale guaranteed minorities' rights in the elections, and promised to maintain the rights of the Greek Church.[34] They also pledged that they would support the election of fifty-two Greek deputies to the new Chamber.[35]

The protocol signed between the Greek deputies and the Entente Libérale, formally allying the former to the monarchist opposition, caused consternation in the Unionist camp and indignation among some sections of the Greek population in Anatolia. The Unionists were anxious to obtain the support, or, at least, the neutrality of the Greeks in the upcoming elections.[36] On January 28, Talât Bey and Halil [Menteşe]—two prominent members of the Unionist leadership—visited Joachim Efendi, the Greek Ecumenical Patriarch, and talked about the upcoming elections. In an effort to win the Greek minority to the Unionist side, they proposed cooperation between the Greek community and the Committee of Union and Progress. Reportedly, they promised that all the legitimate demands of the Patriarchate would be granted.[37] On behalf of the Committee of Union and Progress, they also promised that they would allocate thirty-seven seats for the Greek community in the new Chamber. Their offer to Joachim Efendi included a promise of several key governmental positions in the Ministries as well as the offer of the Ministry of Justice to Aristidi Pasha Yorgandjioglu.[38]

As the Unionist offer to Joachim Efendi constituted an effort

---

January 2, 1327/January 15, 1912, p.1. See also, Ziya Şakir [Soko], "Hürriyet ve İtilâf Nasıl Doğdu? Nasıl Yaşadı? Nasıl Battı? 43: İtilâfçılar Etrafa Cazip Tekliflerde Bulunuyorlar," *Tan*, December 21, 1937, p.9

[33] "Les députés grecs," *The Levant Herald and Eastern Express*, January 12, 1912, p.2.

[34] "Les députés grecs et l'Entente Libérale," *The Levant Herald and Eastern Express*, January 13, 1912, p.1.

[35] Caterina Boura, "I vouleftices ecloges stin othomaniki aftocratoria I ellines vouleftes 1908-1918," p.79.

[36] "Said Pasha and the Cabinet: The Rumoured Changes," *The Times*, January 31, 1912, p.5.

[37] "News Items," *The Levant Herald and Eastern Express*, January 29, 1912, p.1; and, Mehmed Cavid, "Meşrutiyet Devrine Ait Cavid Bey'in Hatıraları: 68," *Tanin*, November 7, 1943, p.2.

[38] Caterina Boura, "I vouleftices ecloges stin othomaniki aftocratoria I ellines vouleftes 1908-1918," p.78.

on the part of the Committee of Union and Progress to come to an understanding with the Greek community, this posed a threat to the agreement reached between the Greek deputies and the monarchist Entente Libérale. Therefore, the monarchist press did everything in its power to prevent the conclusion of a definite agreement between the Greek Ecumenical Patriarchate and the Committee of Union and Progress. Press attacks of the Unionist proposals followed. In response to factually distorted monarchist press attacks, Talât Bey and Halil [Menteşe] made a declaration which appeared in the February 3 issues of newspapers, denying that the visit to the Patriarch was to propose the elimination of Greek deputies from the Chamber. They said that the Committee of Union and Progress supported the election of Greek deputies and that the Unionists did not bear any ill-feeling because of an understanding reached between Greek Constitutional League, a conservative political organisation, and the Entente Libérale.[39] On its part, *Amalthia*, a Greek newspaper published in İzmir, criticised Greek alliance with the Entente Libérale, saying that declaring themselves against the Unionists would not be beneficial to the Greek community at large, as the Committee of Union and Progress was expected to have the majority in the next Chamber.[40]

The leadership of the Greek community in İstanbul, however, was decided to oppose the Committee of Union and Progress in the elections. They were also active in trying to recruit other communities in the Entente Libérale camp. On February 10, it was reported that Solon Casanova and Dingas, representatives of the Greek Electoral Club, had entered into negotiations with the Armenian Social Democrat Hnchakian Party, the conservative rival of the Armenian Revolutionary Federation—or, Dashnaktsuthiun—with the object of having a joint action against the Committee of Union and Progress.[41]

---

[39] "News Items," *The Levant Herald and Eastern Express*, February 3, 1912, p.1. See also, "İntihab Propagandaları: Rumlar," *Tanin*, January 22, 1327/February 4, 1912, p.3.

[40] "Elections législatives," *The Levant Herald and Eastern Express*, February 2, 1912, p.2.

[41] "Les élections législatives: Grecs et Arméniens," *The Levant Herald and Eastern Express*, February 10, 1912, p.2.

Convinced of their electoral strength, the Social Democrat Hn-chakian Party, however, also bargained with the Committee of Union and Progress and declared on February 13 that they had decided not to oppose the Unionists in the elections in return for guarantees that their conservative candidates—most importantly, Krikor Zohrab—would not be opposed by the Committee of Union and Progress.[42]

The greatest achievement of the Entente Libérale, however, came in mid-February with the announcement in Salonica that the ulema had decided to leave the Committee of Union and Progress and join the Entente Libérale. As a result of pro-tracted negotiations, the influential ulema, or religious lead-ers, had decided to withdraw their support from the Commit-tee of Union and Progress, and to throw in their lot with the Entente Libérale. In view of the undoubted authority exercised by the ulema over the Muslim population, this was a political change of considerable importance, and one which might well have a most unexpected influence upon the upcoming elections. As some considerable surprise was doubtless mani-fested at the decision of the ulema to aid so substantially the Christian candidates, it was interesting to note that the ulema now claimed that in working in harmony with their Chris-tian brethren they had the sanction of the Koran. The repre-sentatives of the ulema argued that they were convinced not only that in a union of diverse communities of the Empire lay the one way of salvation for Turkey, but that such a union could never now be obtained under the organisation of the Committee of Union and Progress, and could only be effected under the auspices of the Muslim religion and by convincing the Muslims that the Koran not only permitted, but encour-aged, an *entente* with the Christians.[43]

Coinciding with the ulema's statement, the Entente Libér-ale announced the establishment of its Salonica branch. Sheikh Ömer Efendi was chosen as the first president and Se-

---

[42] "Elections Législatives: Les Arméniens," *The Levant Herald and Eastern Express*, February 13, 1912, p.2.
[43] "The Committee of Union and Progress: Hostility of Moslem Priests," *The Times*, February 17, 1912, p.5; and, "The Committee of Union and Progress," *The Levant Herald and Eastern Express*, February 21, 1912, p.1. See also, "The Election Campaign in Turkey," *The Near East*, February 23, 1912, p.510.

lânikli Hamdi Beyzade Âdil Bey as the vice-president of the local branch of the Entente Libérale at Salonica, to which body the local Greek and Bulgarian organisations had already promised their adhesion.[44] The ulema would run their own candidate, Hafız Süleyman Efendi, in Salonica where the organisation and influence of the Entente Libérale would be placed at their disposal. On the other hand, the candidates of the Entente Libérale would receive the hearty support of the ulema throughout the province. The local leaders of the Entente Libérale were very optimistic about their chances at the elections. Counting upon the support of the whole of the Greek and Bulgarian and the religious conservative Muslim population, they hoped to control three quarters of the voting strength of the Salonica province, and thus heavily to defeat the Unionist candidates.[45]

At this time, the Committee of Union and Progress was composed mainly of Turks, with a very respectable number of Arabs from the provinces of Iraq, Yemen, and to a degree, Tripoli.[46] According to press reports, an agreement with Imam Yahya stipulated that there would be twenty-five deputies for Yemen, as opposed to thirteen in the last Chamber.[47] This move was calculated to quiet down the Yemenite rebellion that had been going on for several months, which the government troops had been unable to suppress. The Committee of Union and Progress also enjoyed Jewish support, as well as a small measure of Serbian support. Despite their differences on the issue of Parliament's dissolution, Armenian Revolutionary Federation also remained supporters of the Unionists.[48]

---

[44] Mehmed Cavid, "Meşrutiyet Devrine Ait Cavid Bey'in Hatıraları: 72," *Tanin*, November 11, 1943, p.2. See also, "The Committee of Union and Progress: Hostility of Moslem Priests," *The Times*, February 17, 1912, p.5; and, "The Committee of Union and Progress," *The Levant Herald and Eastern Express*, February 21, 1912, p.1.

[45] "The Committee of Union and Progress: Hostility of Moslem Priests," *The Times*, February 17, 1912, p.5; and, "The Committee of Union and Progress," *The Levant Herald and Eastern Express*, February 21, 1912, p.1.

[46] "Constantinople Letter," *The Near East*, February 16, 1912, p.459.

[47] "Elections législatives," *The Levant Herald and Eastern Express*, February 2, 1912, p.2. See also, "Fazla Mebus İsteriz!" *Tanin*, January 23, 1327/February 5, 1912, p.1.

[48] "Constantinople Letter," *The Near East*, February 16, 1912, p.459.

In an attempt to win the bulk of the Armenian vote in Anatolia, it was announced on February 7 that Ürgüplü Hayri Bey, the Unionist Minister of Pious Foundations, would make a trip to eastern Anatolia. His tour of inspection was connected with the question of the restitution of Armenian properties, seized by the Kurds under the Hamidian regime, to their former legitimate owners.[49] Ever since the establishment of the liberal democratic regime, the issue was on the Unionist agenda; however, Kurdish resistance, supported by monarchist politicians, had effectively blocked the execution of this policy.[50] On February 12, the government announced that it had decided to open a credit of one hundred thousand liras for the settlement of the Armeno-Kurdish land disputes in the eastern provinces. Armenians who had been wrongfully dispossessed and were able to give proof of their title would be reinstated in their old holdings, while compensation would be paid to the Kurdish squatters. Extended powers for the introduction of reforms and the maintenance of order would be conferred on the Governors of Bitlis and Erzurum. These measures were likely to secure the Armenian Revolutionary Federation vote for the Committee of Union and Progress at the upcoming elections.[51]

On February 29, it was formally announced that the Committee of Union and Progress and the Armenian Revolutionary Federation had agreed to join forces. Delegates of both parties signed an agreement for common action at the elections. The protocol also stated that deputies of the two parties would cooperate in the Chamber until the dissolution of the next Parliament.[52] On March 7, it was further announced that the

---

[49] "The Turkish Government and the Armenians," *The Times*, February 8, 1912, p.5. See also, "Hayri Bey'in Namzetliği," *Tanin*, January 22, 1327/February 4, 1912, p.3.

[50] See for example, F.O. 424/226, Sir Gerard Lowther to Sir Edward Grey, Constantinople, February 28, 1911, Enclosure: "Notes on Journey from Van to Erzincan [by Captain L. Molyneux-Seel]," *Further Correspondence Respecting the Affairs of Asiatic Turkey and Arabia, Part I*, pp.109-111; and, F.O. 424/230, Acting Vice-Consul Safrastian to Consul McGregor, Erzerum, December 18, 1911, *Further Correspondence Respecting the Affairs of Asiatic Turkey and Arabia, Part V*, p.5. On this issue see also p.296 of this book.

[51] "Reforms in Asia Minor: Turkey and the Land Question," *The Times*, February 14, 1912, p.5. See also, Dr. [Nazareth] Daghavarian, "Ermenilerin Arazi Meselesi," *Yeni İkdam*, Ferbruary 8, 1327/February 21, 1912, p.1.

[52] "Turkish Committee and the Armenians," *The Times*, March 1, 1912, p.5.

Committee of Union and Progress and the Armenian Revolutionary Federation had been having negotiations on the number of the deputies to represent the Armenian minority. The Armenian Revolutionary Federation had been demanding twenty deputies, as it claimed that this number was justified and represented a figure proportional to the Armenian population in the Empire.[53]

On March 20, Protestant and Catholic Armenians met to discuss to collaborate in the general elections. The majority of the participants were declared to be in favour of cooperating with the Committee of Union and Progress.[54]

The opposition had a large number of newspapers under its control, including such Turkish language dailies as the prominent *Yeni İkdam* and *Yeni Gazete*, as well as most of the minority newspapers.[55]

Writing editorials in *Yeni Gazete*, Yorgos Boussios, the prominent Greek deputy for Serfidje, was one of the Unionists' fiercest opponents. He enjoyed the support of Ahmed Cevdet Bey, the owner of *Yeni İkdam*; and, when Pantoleon Cosmidis, a prominent Greek monarchist deputy for İstanbul, established *Phoni*, a Greek language newspaper, Yorgos Boussios became its editor-in-chief. Apart from its attacks on the Committee of Union and Progress, *Phoni* became known for its highly derogatory and racist propaganda against the Turkish population.[56] In one of its February issues, *Phoni* reproduced an article by E. J. Dillon, of the British newspaper *The Daily Telegraph*, on the internal situation in Turkey.[57] When this article—which was a totally racist and disrespect-

---

[53] "Les élections: L'accord entre l'Union et Progrès et le parti arménien Dachnaktzoutioun," *The Levant Herald and Eastern Express*, March 7, 1912, p.2.

[54] "Les Elections: Les Arméniens," *The Levant Herald and Eastern Express*, March 21, 1912, p.2.

[55] Hüseyin Cahid Yalçın, "Meşrutiyet Hatıraları, 1908-1918," *Fikir Hareketleri*, 7 (October 24, 1936-April 17, 1937), p.53.

[56] "Cosmidis ve Boussios," *Tanin*, February 1, 1327/February 14, 1912, p.3. See also, Hüseyin Cahid Yalçın, "Meşrutiyet Hatıraları, 1908-1918," *Fikir Hareketleri*, 7 (October 24, 1936-April 17, 1937), p.53.

[57] "Cosmidis ve Boussios," *Tanin*, February 1, 1327/February 14, 1912, p.3; "News Items," *The Levant Herald and Eastern Express*, February 16, 1912, p.1; "The Sentence on a Turkish Deputy," *The Times*, February 17, 1912, p.5; and, "Empire News: The Capital," *The Orient*, 3/8 (February 21, 1912), p.7.

ful piece of pseudo-journalism against the Turkish population—came under attack, *Teminat*, another monarchist newspaper owned by İsmail Hakkı [Mumcu] Pasha, deputy for
Amasya and leader of the Entente Libérale, rushed to *Phoni*'s
defence, claiming that the slurs were the result of printing
errors.[58] Nevertheless, *Phoni*'s owner, Pantoleon Cosmidis,
appeared before the Court Martial which sentenced him on
February 15 to four month's imprisonment and a fine of thirty-four liras for publishing articles calculated to excite the public against the government.[59] The Government also ordered
the expulsion of four prominent Greek journalists belonging to
the local press on the ground that they were promoting the
"disunion of races."[60] On February 4, the Court Martial also
sentenced Tahir Hayreddin Bey, monarchist deputy for İstan-
bul, to two months' and ten days' imprisonment for publishing articles in *Bedahat* calculated to bring the government
into disrepute and to cause disorders. The verdict was pronounced *in absentia* as he had already left İstanbul to avoid
arrest.[61] However, Cemal Bey, the owner of *Bedahat* and a
former governor of İzmit, was arrested.[62]

Hoping to publicly discredit the monarchists, *Tanin* published, in its February 16 issue, the text of a letter Kâmil Pasha
had written to the Sultan from Egypt on December 20, 1911
which amounted to nothing less than a wholesale indictment
of the Unionists and their policies. Kâmil Pasha confidently
asserted that owing to the despotic attitude of the Committee of

---

[58] *Tanin*, February 3, 1327/February 16, 1912, quoted in Hüseyin Cahid Yalçın, "Meşrutiyet Hatıraları, 1908-1918," *Fikir Hareketleri*, 7 (October 24, 1936-
April 17, 1937), p.53. *Teminat* was closed down along with *Hedef*, another monarchist newspaper, by the Martial Law authorities on March 30 (*Tanin*, March 18,
1328/March 31, 1912, in Hüseyin Cahid Yalçın, "Meşrutiyet Hatıraları, 1908-
1918," *Fikir Hareketleri*, 7 (October 24, 1936-April 17, 1937), p.164).
[59] Hüseyin Cahid Yalçın, "Meşrutiyet Hatıraları, 1908-1918," *Fikir Hareketleri*, 7 (October 24, 1936-April 17, 1937), p.53; "News Items," *The Levant Herald
and Eastern Express*, February 16, 1912, p.1; "The Turkish Court-Martial: Sentence
on a Deputy," *The Times*, February 16, 1912, p.5; "The Sentence on a Turkish Deputy," *The Times*, February 17, 1912, p.5; and, "Empire News: The Capital," *The
Orient*, 3/8 (February 21, 1912), p.7.
[60] "The Greek Press in Turkey," *The Times*, February 29, 1912, p.5.
[61] Hüseyin Cahid Yalçın, "Meşrutiyet Hatıraları, 1908-1918," *Fikir Hareketleri*, 7 (October 24, 1936-April 17, 1937), p.53; "News Items," *The Levant Herald
Eastern and Eastern Express*, February 5, p.1; and, "Turkish Politics," *The Times*,
February 5, 1912, p.5.
[62] "News Items," *The Levant Herald Eastern and Eastern Express*, February 5,
p.1.

Union and Progress, Turkey was in danger of dismemberment and the Caliphate was threatened. He charged the
Unionists with inability to govern along constitutional lines,
and of resorting therefore to martial law. He claimed that the
Unionists had dismissed competent officials in both the capital and the provinces and had replaced them by
inexperienced and incompetent Unionist followers, whose
unsatisfactory administration was responsible for the troubles
in Albania, Arabia and the Yemen, involving such a waste of
lives as well as money. He threatened that unless the
Unionists relinquished their control, another revolution
would take place, aided by the army, against their despotism.[63]

Kâmil Pasha argued that the Unionists' maladministration
had also caused coldness on the part of European powers towards Turkey. The most interesting feature of the letter was
the reference to the foreign policy of the Unionists. Kâmil
Pasha charged the Committee of Union and Progress with
having alienated old friends, and with having given a pretext
for Italian hostility by its provocative attitude. In his words, a
friendly understanding with Great Britain was hindered by
the Committee of Union and Progress. Kâmil Pasha expressed
the opinion that the Arab world, especially Egypt where the
Khedive was hostile to the Committee of Union and Progress,
would learn from recent events that it could not expect effective protection from Turkey, and Egypt would eventually declare her independence, after coming to an arrangement
whereby she would be assured of the protection of Great Britain. He blamed the Unionists for all the misfortunes which
now afflicted Turkey, demanded the Committee's dissolution
and the lifting of martial law, at the same time, proposing that

---

[63] Hüseyin Cahid [Yalçın], "Kâmil Paşa'nın Arîzası," *Tanin*, February 3,
1327/February 16, 1912, p.1; "Kâmil Paşa'nın Arîzası," *Tanin*, February 3, 1327/
February 16, 1912, p.3—which is excerpted in, "Indictment of Young Turkish Policy," *The Times*, February 17, 1912, p.5, and, "Kiamil Pasha Scores Union and
Progress Committee," *The Orient*, 3/8 (February 21, 1912), p.3. The letter has also
been reproduced in Hilmi Kamil Bayur, *Sadrazam Kâmil Paşa: Siyasi Hayatı*,
pp.308-312. See also, [Kâmil Pasha], "Kâmil Paşa'nın Arîzası," *Yeni İkdam*, February 4, 1327/February 17, 1912, p.1; Ziya Şakir [Soko], "Hürriyet ve İtilâf Nasıl
Doğdu? Nasıl Yaşadı? Nasıl Battı? 47: Kâmil Paşa Mısır'dan Padişah'a Uzun bir
Lâyiha Gönderdi," *Tan*, December 26, 1937, p.9; and, Ziya Şakir [Soko], "Hürriyet
ve İtilâf Nasıl Doğdu? Nasıl Yaşadı? Nasıl Battı? 48: Kral Beşinci George'un Haki-
ki Maksadı Neydi?" *Tan*, December 27, 1937, p.9.

Turkey enter into alliance with Great Britain in order to avoid further international disaster.[64]

By publishing the letter, Hüseyin Cahid [Yalçın] effectively established the complicity of forces both within and outside of the country in the monarchist plan to topple the constitutional regime.[65] Hüseyin Cahid [Yalçın] continued his criticism of Kâmil Pasha in the February 18 issue of *Tanin*. Declaring that the Committee of Union and Progress had a clear conscience and was ready to give an account of its deeds, Hüseyin Cahid [Yalçın] accused Kâmil Pasha of incapacity and wrote that the Committee of Union and Progress had had much better success in international negotiations, as witness the better terms secured by Cavid Bey for a loan than by Kâmil Pasha. In reply to Kâmil Pasha's criticisms of the domestic and foreign policy of the Committee of Union and Progress, Hüseyin Cahid [Yalçın] asked why Kâmil Pasha had not concluded an alliance with Great Britain during his grand vezirship. Reminding him that his government had neither prevented the annexation of Bosnia nor the declaration of Bulgarian independence, Hüseyin Cahid [Yalçın] wrote that if political events were to be regarded as the results of a general scheme of policy, the Italo-Turkish War had to be considered the outcome of an agreement between Italy, France, and Great Britain.[66]

Electoral campaign in the provinces started in late January, almost immediately after the publication of the imperial decree that dissolved the Chamber and called for new elections.

---

[64] "Kâmil Paşa'nın Arîzası," *Tanin*, February 3, 1327/February 16, 1912, p.3 —which is excerpted in "Indictment of Young Turkish Policy," *The Times*, February 17, 1912, p.5, and, "Kiamil Pasha Scores Union and Progress Committee," *The Orient*, 3/8 (February 21, 1912), p.3. The letter has also been reproduced in Hilmi Kamil Bayur, *Sadrazam Kâmil Paşa: Siyasi Hayatı*, pp.308-312.

[65] Bernard Lewis, *The Emergence of Modern Turkey*, 2nd Edition, p.222. See also, Mehmed Cavid, "Meşrutiyet Devrine Ait Cavid Bey'in Hatıraları: 72," *Tanin*, November 11, 1943, p.2; and, Carl von Sax, *Geschichte des Machverfalls der Türkei*, 2nd Edition, pp.589-590. For an interpretation that tries to discredit Unionists on this issue see, Yusuf Hikmet Bayur, *Türk İnkılâbı Tarihi*, 2/1, pp.243-244.

[66] *Tanin*, February 5, 1327/February 18, 1912, quoted in "Kiamil Pasha and the Young Turks," *The Times*, February 20, 1912; and, "Kiamil Pasha Scores Union and Progress Committee," *The Orient*, 3/8 (February 21, 1912), p.3. For *Yeni İkdam*'s rebuttal of *Tanin*'s arguments concerning Kâmil Pasha see, "Kâmil Paşa ve İttihad ve Terakki," *Yeni İkdam*, February 4, 1327/February 17, 1912, p.1.

It was no secret that in the Arab provinces, as well as in parts of Macedonia and Eastern Turkey, disappointed minority nationalists—Greeks, Bulgarians, Albanians, and Armenians— were expected to do their best to overthrow the constitutional regime and the Committee of Union and Progress, resenting as they did its 'Turkification' policy.[67]

Indépendant de Salonique informed in one of its late January issues that the electoral campaign had started in the province of Kossovo, with the local Committee of Union and Progress forming an electoral committee. The Üsküb branch of the Committee of Union and Progress had decided to put forward the candidacies of two Bulgarians and two Turks.[68] Intelligence received by the Committee of Union and Progress had convinced the leadership that Bulgarians had to be given two deputyships; otherwise the Unionists would not have much chance of success at the elections there. On February 8, a deputation on behalf of the Üsküb Serbians visited Talât Bey, protesting that the elimination of the Serbian deputy would constitute an infringement of their rights. In the 1908 Chamber the Serbians had one deputy for the Kossovo province. This time, although the Unionist leadership promised that they would guarantee the election of one Serbian for the province— but not for the Üsküb electoral district—the Serbians were not satisfied, and asked for an additional deputy.[69]

By the beginning of February, the İzmir campaigns were in full swing. By law, the district would elect six deputies: two Turks, two Greeks, one Jew, and one Armenian. Muammer Bey, grandson of Midhat Pasha, was the Entente Libérale candidate. Mustafa Nuri Bey and Seyyid Bey were the Unionist candidates. Muammer Bey, the Entente Libérale candidate, was not expected to win.[70] *Proodos* of February 6 printed the news that a sanguinary conflict took place in early February near the local party headquarters of the Entente Libérale in

---

[67] "The Election Campaign in Turkey," *The Near East*, February 23, 1912, p.510.

[68] "Elections législatives," *The Levant Herald and Eastern Express*, February 2, 1912, p.2.

[69] [Hüseyin Cahid Yalçın], "Fazla Mebus İsteriz!" *Tanin*, January 23, 1327/ February 5, 1912, p.1; and, Mehmed Cavid, "Meşrutiyet Devrine Ait Cavid Bey'in Hatıraları: 72," *Tanin*, November 11, 1943, p.2.

[70] "Notes From Smyrna," *The Near East*, February 23, 1912, p.499.

İzmir between the monarchists and the Unionists. A plain-
clothesman was killed and two gendarmes and three other
persons were wounded.[71] The February 7 issue of *Yeni İkdam*
reported that the events at İzmir had been organised against
Lütfi Fikri Bey, who had begun his electoral campaign for the
Entente Libérale.[72] The official Agence Ottomane denied the
news of the conflict in İzmir between the Unionists and
members of the Entente Libérale in which a policeman was
said to have been killed and two gendarmes wounded.[73]
Yorgos Boussios arrived at İzmir for political campaign on
behalf of the Entente Libérale in the first week of March.[74]
There, he made an important propaganda speech at the
Entente Libérale club.[75] By the second week of March,
Boussios was continuing his propaganda campaign around İz-
mir. On his arrival at Urla, he was met with great enthusiasm.[76]

On his way back from Egypt, Kâmil Pasha stopped in İzmir
as part of the Entente Libérale campaign and met with several
prominent members of the British colony. He consistently opposed the policy of the Committee of Union and Progress. Reportedly, his return to İstanbul was in no small measure due to
his anxiety about the Entente Libérale's political future, and he
expressed dismay at the general situation of the country during the meeting.[77]

By early February, monarchist Arab deputies arrived at
Beirut to campaign for the Entente Libérale, among them Lütfi

---

[71] "News Items," *The Levant Herald and Eastern Express*, February 6, 1912, p.1; and, "Bagarres à Smyrne?," *The Levant Herald and Eastern Express*, February 6, 1912, p.2. See also, Fevzi Demir, İkinci Meşrutiyet Dönemi Meclis-i Mebusan Seçimleri, 1908-1914, p.125.

[72] "Les élections législatives," *The Levant Herald and Eastern Express*, February 7, 1912, p.2; and, "Lütfi Fikri Bey İzmir'de!" *Tanin*, January 26, 1327/February 8, 1912, p.3. See also, Fevzi Demir, İkinci Meşrutiyet Dönemi Meclis-i Mebusan Seçimleri, 1908-1914, p.110.

[73] "News Items," *The Levant Herald and Eastern Express*, February 8, 1912, p.1.

[74] "Les Elections: Boussios effendi à Smyrne," *The Levant Herald and Eastern Express*, March 12, 1912, p.1.

[75] "Les Elections: A Smyrne," *The Levant Herald and Eastern Express*, March 14, 1912, p.2.

[76] "Les Elections: Boussios effendi," *The Levant Herald and Eastern Express*, March 18, 1912, p.2.

[77] "Notes From Smyrna," *The Near East*, March 29, 1912, p.676. See also, "Kiamil Pasha and Conditions in Turkey," *The Times*, March 15, 1912, p.5.

Fikri Bey, the incumbent deputy for Dersim, who had distinguished himself by his fearless attacks on the Committee of Union and Progress.[78] Accompanied by Shukri al-Asali, the Entente Libérale deputy for Damascus, and Abd al-Hamid az-Zahrawi, the Entente Libérale deputy for Hama, Lütfi Fikri Bey held a conference in one of the prominent cafés facing the town square to explain the principles and expose the salient features of his party's policy.[79] The Entente Libérale's position in Beirut—as in several other Arab provinces—was by no means dominant; and the party had enough trouble recruiting committed local leaders, to say nothing of garnering the support of local voters.[80] As the electorate was fairly evenly divided between the two parties, the Entente Libérale hoped to incite more defections. The Committee of Union and Progress, however, rearranged Beirut's electoral districts in order to break up its support for the opposition.[81] As part of the Unionist campaign, Senator Cafer Pasha arrived at Tripoli in Lebanon on March 11 where he was given an enthusiastic reception. It was reported that the Committee of Union and Progress had great chances of success in the area.[82]

After his campaign on behalf of the Entente Libérale candidates at Beirut, Lütfi Fikri Bey proceeded to Damascus, arriving there on February 10, accompanied by Nâzım Pasha.[83] Then, he visited Aleppo. According to reports from Aleppo,

---

[78] Hüseyin Cahid Yalçın, "Meşrutiyet Hatıraları, 1908-1918," *Fikir Hareketleri*, 7 (October 24, 1936-April 17, 1937), p.69; and, Fevzi Demir, İkinci Meşrutiyet Dönemi Meclis-i Mebusan Seçimleri, 1908-1914, p.110. See also, Mustafa Ragıb Esatlı, "Meşrutiyet Devrinde: İntihap Mücadeleleri En Çirkin İhtiraslara Sebep Olmuştu," *Akşam*, March 18, 1943, p.4.

[79] "Notes From Beyrout," *The Near East*, February 23, 1912, p.499. See also, Ahmed Tarabein, "Abd al-Hamid al-Zahrawi: The Career and Thought of an Arab Nationalist," p.101; Samir Seikaly, "Shukri al-'Asali: A Case Study of a Political Activist," p.89; Fevzi Demir, İkinci Meşrutiyet Dönemi Meclis-i Mebusan Seçimleri, 1908-1914, p.110, and p.119; and, Ali Birinci, *Hürriyet ve İtilâf Fırkası: II. Meşrutiyet Devrinde İttihat ve Terakki'ye Karşı Çıkanlar*, p.135.

[80] HHS. PA 32/354, Pinter to Berchtold, Beirut, April 3, 1912, quoted in Hasan Kayalı, Arabs and Young Turks, p.153.

[81] HHS. PA 32/354, Pinter to Berchtold, Beirut, April 3, 1912, quoted in Hasan Kayalı, Arabs and Young Turks, pp.156-157.

[82] "Les Elections: En Syrie," *The Levant Herald and Eastern Express*, March 12, 1912, p.1; and, Fevzi Demir, İkinci Meşrutiyet Dönemi Meclis-i Mebusan Seçimleri, 1908-1914, p.106.

[83] "Nouvelles du Jour," *The Levant Herald and Eastern Express*, February 12, 1912, p.2. See also, Fevzi Demir, İkinci Meşrutiyet Dönemi Meclis-i Mebusan Seçimleri, 1908-1914, p.110.

Lütfi Fikri Bey met with an enthusiastic reception on his arrival there on February 15. Lütfi Fikri Bey was met at the station by the partisans of the Entente Libérale who were very
numerous at Aleppo. The Unionist attempted to organise a
counter-demonstration but they completely failed to do so.[84]
Syria's electorate was evenly divided between the two parties.
Both the Committee of Union and Progress and the Entente
Libérale organised campaign tours throughout the province.[85]
Well aware that some of the Syrian deputies had thrown in
their lot with the monarchist opposition, Unionists also arrived
in the province, and campaigned aggressively. It was important for the Unionists not to lose the Syrian seats wholesale to
the opposition in a place where public opinion was more or
less equally divided.[86] Under the leadership of Senator Cafer
Pasha, the Unionist mission arrived at Aleppo in the first
week of March, where it was enthusiastically received.[87] The
Unionist mission for electoral propaganda, presided by
Senator Cafer Pasha, arrived at Hama by March 15.[88] He arrived at Damascus on March 15. In the name of Cafer Pasha
and the Unionist mission, Sheikh As'ad Tawfiq Efendi Shuqair, incumbent deputy for Acra, made a political speech. The
Syrian press attacked Sheikh As'ad Tawfiq Efendi Shuqair.[89]
According to the monarchist *Teminat*, the Arab newspapers
had printed that Sheikh As'ad Tawfiq Efendi Shuqair represented Zionists.[90] By March 23, Cafer Pasha had arrived at
Jaffa. In a propaganda speech he delivered at Jaffa, he invited

---

[84] "Lütfi Fikri Bey," *Yeni İkdam*, February 3, 1327/February 16, 1912, p.1;
"Lütfi Fikri Bey—Haleb'de," *Yeni İkdam*, February 3, 1327/February 16, 1912, pp.3-
4; and, "News Items," *The Levant Herald and Eastern Express*, February 16, 1912,
p.1. See also, Fevzi Demir, İkinci Meşrutiyet Dönemi Meclis-i Mebusan Seçimleri,
1908-1914, p.110.

[85] Rashid Khalidi, "The 1912 Election Campaign in the Cities of *bilad al-
Sham*," pp.461-471.

[86] HHS. PA 12/205, Pallavicini to Aehrenthal, March 12, 1912, quoted in Hasan Kayalı, Arabs and Young Turks, p.155.

[87] "Les élections: la tournée de Djafer pacha," *The Levant Herald and Eastern
Express*, March 9, 1912, p.2; and, Fevzi Demir, İkinci Meşrutiyet Dönemi Meclis-i
Mebusan Seçimleri, 1908-1914, p.106.

[88] "Les Elections," *The Levant Herald and Eastern Express*, March 15, 1912,
p.2.

[89] "Les Elections: La mission unioniste à Damas," *The Levant Herald and
Eastern Express*, March 16, 1912, p.2.

[90] "Les Elections: A St. Jean d'Acre," *The Levant Herald and Eastern Express*,
March 16, 1912, p.2.

the population to vote for the Unionist candidates.[91]

In the capital, the electoral campaign started in early February. On February 5, Cavid Bey spoke at the Unionist club at Kadıköy. Among the audience there were many Greeks, Armenians, Jews, and even members of the Entente Libérale, in addition to members of the Committee of Union and Progress. His criticism of the Entente Libérale platform made an excellent impression on the audience.[92] Between February 10 and February 14, Cavid Bey gave a series of conferences at the various workers' clubs at İstanbul neighbourhoods, including Beşiktaş, Samatya, Fatih, and Süleymaniye. There was much enthusiasm for his speeches. On account of popular demand, he had to make two speeches at the club at Beşiktaş. At all of the conferences he gave, there were a mixed crowd of Unionist sympathisers as well as devout Muslims and Entente Libérale supporters. Explaining the Unionist policy to his audience, Cavid Bey at the same time strongly criticised not only the Entente Libérale platform but also the socialist viewpoint.[93] Hüseyin Cahid [Yalçın] conducted additional Unionist campaign in İstanbul in mid-February, giving public speeches at the neighbourhoods of Aksaray, Davud Paşa, and Fatih.[94]

The Entente Libérale was also actively campaigning in İstanbul. Rıza Tevfik [Bölükbaşı] and Pantoleon Cosmidis organised an Entente Libérale meeting to be held on the Prince Islands. As İstanbul was still under martial law, organisers of all public meetings had to secure permission from the authorities at least forty-eight hours in advance. In defiance of martial law rules and regulations, the Entente Libérale tried to hold the meeting without the required authorisation. Consequently, Rıza Tevfik [Bölükbaşı] was arrested and given a

---

[91] *Sabah*, March 10, 1328/March 23, 1912, quoted in "Les Elections: A Jaffa," *The Levant Herald and Eastern Express*, March 23, 1912, p.2.

[92] Mehmed Cavid, "Meşrutiyet Devrine Ait Cavid Bey'in Hatıraları: 71," *Tanin*, November 10, 1943, p.2.

[93] Mehmed Cavid, "Meşrutiyet Devrine Ait Cavid Bey'in Hatıraları: 72," *Tanin*, November 11, 1943, p.2; and, "La lutte électorale," *The Levant Herald and Eastern Express*, February 13, 1912, p.1. See also, Tevfik Çavdar, *"Müntehib-i Sani"den Seçmene*, pp.11-12.

[94] Hüseyin Cahid Yalçın, "Meşrutiyet Hatıraları, 1908-1918," *Fikir Hareketleri*, 7 (October 24, 1936-April 17, 1937), p.133; and, "La lutte électorale," *The Levant Herald and Eastern Express*, February 13, 1912, p.1.

twenty-five day prison sentence for not observing the regulations.[95]

The Entente Libérale campaign, however, continued. On February 26, Yorgos Boussios, the incumbent deputy for Serfidje, gave a conference at the Entente Libérale branch at Fındıklı.[96] The February 29 issue of *Ameroliptos* printed the news that Hamid Bey, President of the Koca Mustafa Paşa branch of the Entente Libérale in İstanbul, and Lieutenant-Colonel Ahmed Bey, a retired officer and an influential member of the Entente Libérale, were arrested and imprisoned at the Ministry of War for infractions of martial law rules concerning public meetings.[97] The Entente Libérale leadership immediately addressed a letter to the Grand Vezierate protesting the methods employed in the general elections.[98]

The opposition newspapers of March 5, among which *Yeni İkdam*—now appearing under the name of *İktiham*—was the one that devoted its whole front page to the news, printed the electoral platform of the Entente Libérale. The party platform incorporated many ideas of the Ottoman League for Private Initiative and Decentralisation and reflected the views of Prince Sabahaddin. The party platform promised that laws would be enacted to establish administrative decentralisation, or autonomy; provincial administration would be taken out of the hands of the central government. As the Entente Libérale's main support came from both religious and ethnic minorities, the party paid special attention to the rights and privileges of the minorities in the Empire. Although the electoral system

---

[95] "The Turkish Court-Martial: Sentence on Riza Tewfik Bey," *The Times*, February 21, 1912, p.5; "Another Deputy Imprisoned," *The Levant Herald and Eastern Express*, February 21, 1912, p.1; and, Hüseyin Cahid [Yalçın], "Son Mahkumiyetler," *Tanin*, February 9, 1327/February 22, 1912, p.1. See also, Hüseyin Cahid Yalçın, "Meşrutiyet Hatıraları, 1908-1918," *Fikir Hareketleri*, 7 (October 24, 1936-April 17, 1937), p.69. For the monarchist press' response to Rıza Tevfik [Bölükbaşı]'s imprisonment see, Mustafa Şahin, "Rıza Tevfik'in İkinci Tutuklanışı ve Bazı Tepkiler," pp.6-8.

[96] "Nouvelles du Jour," *The Levant Herald and Eastern Express*, February 27, 1912, p.2.

[97] "News Items," *The Levant Herald and Eastern Express*, March 1, 1912, p.1; and, "Arrestations," *The Levant Herald and Eastern Express*, March 1, 1912, p.2.

[98] *Sabah*, February 18, 1327/March 2, 1912, quoted in "News Items," *The Levant Herald and Eastern Express*, March 2, 1912, p.1.

in existence gave ample protection to the right of minority representation in the Chamber of Deputies, Entente Libérale nevertheless reiterated the point that proportional representation of minorities was one of its main planks, and that it would respect the constituent elements of the Empire.[99]

Entente Libérale's stand on the minority issue went so far as promising the electorate that it would enter into alliances with the other Balkan states in order to guarantee the rights and privileges of the minorities within Turkey.[100] Within the context of international affairs, this promise was as unreal as it was a threat to Turkish territorial integrity, since it was a well-known fact that both Greece and Bulgaria had been having formal talks to enter into a military alliance in an attempt to occupy the Macedonian provinces of Turkey. Promising an alliance with both Greece and Bulgaria, whose ethnic sympathisers within the Turkish borders in touch with these states were already busy working to destabilise the political and social order in Macedonia was an extremely dangerous game to play.

With respect to domestic affairs, the Entente Libérale promised to make changes in both the press law and the penal code, liberalising both. As regards the economic policy, the party stood for lifting all the barriers to private enterprise. Most importantly, the Entente Libérale expressed its determination to eliminate all the existing restrictions to the entrance of foreign capital into Turkey; it promised to facilitate foreign ownership of economic enterprises.[101] As such, the Entente Libérale's economic policy stood diametrically opposite to the one advocated by the Committee of Union and Progress which strived for the elimination of capitulations and raising the customs tariffs so as to help develop the domestic industry owned and operated by Turkish nationals. While the Unionists were attempting to lay the foundations of a liberal economic system with a strong national base under domestic control,

---

[99] "Les élections: Programme électorale de l'Entente Libérale," *The Levant Herald and Eastern Express*, March 5, 1912, p.2.
[100] "Les élections: Programme électorale de l'Entente Libérale," *The Levant Herald and Eastern Express*, March 5, 1912, p.2.
[101] "Les élections: Programme électorale de l'Entente Libérale," *The Levant Herald and Eastern Express*, March 5, 1912, p.2.

the monarchists represented by the Entente Libérale were trying to keep the economic and financial conditions the same as they had existed during the absolutist regime.

By late-February, municipal elections began to take place in almost every town all over Turkey. Needless to say, there was great interest in these elections as they would give a clear indication of what the prospects of the main political parties might be in the upcoming parliamentary elections. As such, municipal elections were observed with great interest by all the interested parties.

One of the earliest and the most important of these municipal elections was the one at Salonica. Salonica was not only one of the most important towns in Turkey but also the birthplace of the Revolution and the stronghold of the Committee of Union and Progress. Therefore, results of the municipal elections there would be, at least psychologically, very important for elections to be held elsewhere, not to speak of its bearing on the parliamentary elections.

By February 18, it was reported from Salonica that the Entente Libérale following was increasing day by day.[102] Although the Unionists had a strong and well-established party organisation there, electoral victory was by no means certain. What was worse, the ulema, whose influence among Muslims was almost equal to that of the priests among the Christians, had held a meeting at Salonica and decided to support the Entente Libérale, or in other words, to work with the Christians against the Unionists.[103] Indeed, the agreement reached between the ulema and the Entente Libérale at Salonica proved to be very effective in capturing the votes of the Muslim population. At the Salonica municipal elections which took place on February 23, the Committee of Union and Progress was defeated. Out of the six seats of the Municipal Coun cil, the Unionists managed to capture only one: İsmail Bey won the elections as the Unionist candidate. The completed returns

---

[102] "Lettre de Salonique," *The Levant Herald and Eastern Express*, February 22, 1912, p.2; and, "Selânik Muhabir-i Mahsusumuzdan," *Yeni İkdam*, February 9, 1327/February 22, 1912, p.4..

[103] "The Election Campaign in Turkey," *The Near East*, February 23, 1912, p.510.

showed that two Greeks, one Jew, and two members of the Entente Libérale had been returned as Councillors. One of the Greek Councillors, M. Hondrodimo, who had headed the poll, was appointed the Mayor of Salonica.[104]

The monarchist press capitalised on the Unionists' failure to capture the majority in the elections for the Municipal Council at Salonica. This was portrayed as a general defeat of the Committee of Union and Progress at the polls. In an attempt to portray the Entente Libérale in the best possible light, the monarchist press also argued that apart from İsmail Bey — who, they claimed, was not a Unionist but and independent — all the other elected councillors belonged to the Entente Libérale. Despite the fact that İsmail Bey sent a protest letter published in the *Tanin* of February 28 pointing out the inaccuracies in the monarchist press' description and interpretation of the election results, the damage to Unionist prestige had already been done.[105]

It was clear that if the Committee of Union and Progress lost Macedonia, its traditional bastion of support, it could barely hope to keep the country together and itself in power.[106] At a meeting Cavid Bey held on March 2 with a Unionist delegation from Salonica, the results of the municipal elections were discussed. It was apparent that intra-party rivalry had played an important part in the Unionist defeat.[107] Nevertheless, as a consequence of this electoral disaster, the leadership of the Committee of Union and Progress took immediate action, and sent invitations to all the local party branches throughout the Empire, asking them to send delegates to an extra-ordinary congress to be held in Salonica in the first week of March.[108]

Despite energetic efforts of the Committee of Union and Progress to win the municipal elections, the results were

---

[104] "Committee Defeat at Salonika," *The Times*, February 27, 1912, p.5; and, Mehmed Cavid, "Meşrutiyet Devrine Ait Cavid Bey'in Hatıraları: 77," *Tanin*, November 16, 1943, p.2.

[105] Mehmed Cavid, "Meşrutiyet Devrine Ait Cavid Bey'in Hatıraları: 77," *Tanin*, November 16, 1943, p.2.

[106] "The Election Campaign in Turkey," *The Near East*, February 23, 1912, p.510.

[107] Mehmed Cavid, "Meşrutiyet Devrine Ait Cavid Bey'in Hatıraları: 78," *Tanin*, November 17, 1943, p.2.

[108] *Sabah*, February 11, 1327/February 24, 1912, quoted in "News Items," *The Levant Herald and Eastern Express*, February 24, 1912, p.1.

mixed and not totally in favour of the Unionists. On March 5, municipal elections took place at Çankırı, a small Anatolian town, where the results were favourable to the Committee of Union and Progress.[109] In the province of Basra, municipal elections that took place at its principal town—Basra—on March 5, the Unionist list won with a large majority.[110] Likewise, at Mardin, a south-eastern Anatolian town, the Unionists won the majority of the seats on the Municipal Council in the elections which were over by March 7.[111]

However, municipal election results at the prominent towns in western Anatolia were not always favourable to the Committee of Union and Progress. For instance, municipal elections held at Eskişehir in early March resulted in the victory of the Entente Libérale candidates who won the majority of the seats on the Municipal Council.[112] By March 20, municipal elections at Eskişehir was over. The final result was favourable to the Entente Libérale. However, on account of electoral irregularities, the elections were declared null and void.[113]

In Balıkesir, where the Municipal Council consisted of five seats, the Committee of Union and Progress won two seats, Entente Libérale one, and independents two.[114] It was considered a victory for the Entente Libérale as the two independents had allied themselves with the Entente Libérale Councillor. At Bandırma, another western Anatolian town, the Entente Libérale won a victory at the municipal elections.[115] However, at Alaşehir, a close-by town, the municipal elections, which were over by March 28, resulted in the victory of the Unionist candidates.[116]

---

[109] "Elections municipales," *The Levant Herald and Eastern Express*, March 7, 1912, p.2.
[110] "Elections municipales," *The Levant Herald and Eastern Express*, March 7, 1912, p.2.
[111] "Les élections," *The Levant Herald and Eastern Express*, March 8, 1912, p.1.
[112] "Les élections," *The Levant Herald and Eastern Express*, March 8, 1912, p.1.
[113] "Les Elections: A Eski Chéhir," *The Levant Herald and Eastern Express*, March 20, 1912, p.2.
[114] "Les élections," *The Levant Herald and Eastern Express*, March 8, 1912, p.1.
[115] "Les Elections: Succès ententiste," *The Levant Herald and Eastern Express*, March 15, 1912, p.2.
[116] "Les Elections: A Smyrne," *The Levant Herald and Eastern Express*, March 28, 1912, p.2.

In central Anatolia, the Unionists won the municipal elections at Ankara which were held on March 14.[117] The results of the municipal elections at Kastamonu also concluded in favour of the Committee of Union and Progress. Hamdi Bey, pharmacist in İstanbul who ran as the Entente Libérale candidate at Kastamonu, received very little support.[118]

By early-March, first degree elections, *i.e.*, the election of the electors, had only taken place in one or two districts. Another two to three weeks had to elapse before any idea of the probable composition of the electors could be formed. It looked, however, that the Unionists would obtain a majority.[119]

By March 14, the first degree elections had been completed at Malkara in Rodosto. Out of a total of twenty-one electors, nineteen belonged to the Entente Libérale and two to the Committee of Union and Progress.[120] By March 22, the first degree elections at Bayramiç, an electoral district of Kale-i Sultaniye, was over. The population unanimously voted for the Unionist candidates. The chosen electors, Lieutenant Atıf [Kamçıl] Bey and Captain Asım Bey, had both played remarkable roles during the Revolution of 1908.[121]

The Entente Libérale would stop at nothing to disturb the peace during the elections. Faced with an apparent loss of support, the monarchist opposition appealed to religious sentiment in an effort to mobilise the voters. As a consequence of reactionary agitation orchestrated by the monarchists, disturbances occurred in Eskişehir, Salonica, and İzmir.[122]

The first degree elections at Eskişehir was scheduled to take

---

[117] "Les Elections," *The Levant Herald and Eastern Express*, March 15, 1912, p.2.

[118] "Les Elections: A Castamouni," *The Levant Herald and Eastern Express*, March 16, 1912, p.2.

[119] "Constantinople Letter," *The Near East*, March 15, 1912, p.603.

[120] "Les Elections: A Malgara," *The Levant Herald and Eastern Express*, March 14, 1912, p.2.

[121] "Les Elections: Aux Dardanelles," *The Levant Herald and Eastern Express*, March 22, 1912, p.2. For Atıf [Kamçıl] Bey's role in the Revolution see, Aykut Kansu, *The Revolution of 1908 in Turkey*, p.91.

[122] For the reactionary agitation at Eskişehir see, Ahmed Şerif, "Eskişehir Vaka-i İrticaiyesi," *Tanin*, March 22, 1328/April 4, 1912, pp.1-2; Ahmed Şerif, "Eskişehir Vaka-i İrticaiyesi," *Tanin*, March 23, 1328/April 5, 1912, pp.1-2; Ahmed Şerif, "Eskişehir Vaka-i İrticaiyesi," *Tanin*, March 24, 1328/April 6, 1912, p.3; and, Ahmed Şerif, "Eskişehir Vaka-i İrticaiyesi," *Tanin*, March 27, 1328/April 9, 1912, p.3.

place on March 24. If public sentiment were to be trusted, Unionist candidates were expected to win.[123] During the elections on March 24, however, there were serious disturbances.[124] Hacı Veli, the local Entente Libérale leader at Eskişehir, provoked the population with religious fanaticism, portraying Unionists as the destroyers of Islam.[125] Excited by monarchist *agents provocateurs*, a group of religious fanatics roamed the town and attacked Unionist sympathisers, accusing them of being atheists.[126] Besides Hacı Veli, the reactionary movement was also organised by Abdurrahman Hoca, who had previously been deeply involved in the counter-revolutionary *coup d'état* of April, 1909.[127] The groups organised under his supervision also called for everybody to vote for the Entente Libérale.[128] Several additional disturbances also took place in the villages surrounding Eskişehir, whereupon two members of the Committee of Union and Progress, Hamdi Bey, Secretary of the Commission for the Verification of Election Procedures, and Haroutioun Ohannessian, went on a tour of inspection accompanied by gendarmes.[129] At Deveköy and Kümbet, reactionaries demonstrated against the electoral commission members and carried on monarchist propaganda.[130] After the success of the Unionists at the elections, the partisans of the Entente Libérale

---

[123] "Les Elections: A Eski Chéhir," *The Levant Herald and Eastern Express*, March 20, 1912, p.2.

[124] "News Items," *The Levant Herald and Eastern Express*, March 25, 1912, p.1. For the full story of the disturbances see, İhsan Güneş, "1912 Seçimleri ve Eskişehir'de Meydana Gelen Olaylar," pp.470-472.

[125] Hüseyin Cahid Yalçın, "Meşrutiyet Hatıraları, 1908-1918," *Fikir Hareketleri*, 7 (October 24, 1936-April 17, 1937), p.150; İhsan Güneş, "1912 Seçimleri ve Eskişehir'de Meydana Gelen Olaylar," p.470; and, Fevzi Demir, "II. Meşrutiyet Dönemi Parlamento Seçimlerinde Din ve Siyaset: Kâbe Örtüsüne Dökülen Şarap ve Kimliği Belirsiz Sakal," p.18.

[126] "Les incidents d'Eski-Chéhir," *The Levant Herald and Eastern Express*, March 26, 1912, p.2.

[127] "Les incidents d'Eski-Chéhir," *The Levant Herald and Eastern Express*, March 29, 1912, p.2.

[128] "Les incidents d'Eski-Chéhir," *The Levant Herald and Eastern Express*, March 26, 1912, p.2; and, İhsan Güneş, "1912 Seçimleri ve Eskişehir'de Meydana Gelen Olaylar," p.471.

[129] *Hakikat*, March 12, 1328/March 25, 1912, quoted in "Les incidents d'Eski-Chéhir," *The Levant Herald and Eastern Express*, March 27, 1912, p.1. See also, İhsan Güneş, "1912 Seçimleri ve Eskişehir'de Meydana Gelen Olaylar," pp.472-474.

[130] "Les incidents d'Eski-Chéhir," *The Levant Herald and Eastern Express*, March 29, 1912, p.2; and, İhsan Güneş, "1912 Seçimleri ve Eskişehir'de Meydana Gelen Olaylar," pp.477-478.

made demonstrations in Eskişehir, shouting, "We want *shari'a!*"[131]

The first degree elections at Eskişehir, which were over by April 4, ended with the victory of the Entente Libérale candidates who captured the majority of the votes.[132] Despite the fact that the Entente Libérale captured the majority of the electorships in Eskişehir, in late April fourteen Entente Libérale candidates were still protesting against what they called electoral irregularities at Eskişehir.[133]

Entente Libérale pursued the policy of monarchist agitation at Salonica as well. On March 27, a serious disturbance occurred at the Langhaza district of Salonica in connection with the first degree elections. A number of armed peasants, incited by monarchist *agents provocateurs*, made a demonstration in the town, shouting slogans that they did not want the liberal regime but that they preferred *shari'a*, and attacked the gendarmes, who were compelled to intervene. In the fight that ensued, ten peasants and one gendarme were killed and twenty gendarmes and peasants were wounded. Many rifles had been seized and order was restored.[134] The ex-mufti of Langhaza, who was involved in the monarchist counter-revolutionary propaganda at Langhaza, was brought to İstanbul for trial.[135]

Although the monarchists conducted a similar religious propaganda campaign in İzmir, their agitation did not adversely affect the elections.[136] On March 27, the first degree

---

[131] "Les troubles d'Eski-Chéhir," *The Levant Herald and Eastern Express*, March 25, 1912, p.1.
[132] "Les Elections: A Eski-Chéhir," *The Levant Herald and Eastern Express*, April 4, 1912, p.2.
[133] "Les Elections: A Eskichéhir," *The Levant Herald and Eastern Express*, April 25, 1912, p.2.
[134] "Troubles à Langhaza: Il y a eu des tués et des blessés," *The Levant Herald and Eastern Express*, March 28, 1912, p.2; "Shooting Affray at Salonika: Eleven Killed," *The Times*, March 28, 1912, p.3; and, "Les incidents de Langhaza," *The Levant Herald and Eastern Express*, March 30, 1912, p.2. See also, Hüseyin Kâzım Kadri, *Meşrutiyet'ten Cumhuriyet'e Hatıralarım*, pp.117-119; Fevzi Demir, İkinci Meşrutiyet Dönemi Meclis-i Mebusan Seçimleri, 1908-1914, p.114; and, Fevzi Demir, "II. Meşrutiyet Dönemi Parlamento Seçimlerinde Din ve Siyaset: Kâbe Örtüsüne Dökülen Şarap ve Kimliği Belirsiz Sakal," pp.15-16.
[135] "Le Chériat et la politique," *The Levant Herald and Eastern Express*, April 3, 1912, p.1.
[136] Hüseyin Cahid Yalçın, "Meşrutiyet Hatıraları, 1908-1918," *Fikir Hareketleri*, 7 (October 24, 1936-April 17, 1937), p.150.

elections took place at İzmir. There was overwhelming support for the Committee of Union and Progress, and Unionists were expected to win by a large majority. The electoral urns were brought to the Municipality amid enthusiastic crowds for the counting of votes. The voters of İzmir's Ninth District comprising the neighbourhoods of Halil Efendi, Tuzcu Hasta Mescidi, Kalafat, Balcı, and Dayı Emir unanimously voted for the two Unionist candidates, Hurşid Bey and Mehmed Niyazi Efendi, both of whom obtained six hundred and fifty votes. The Entente Libérale candidates did not receive any vote. Unionists also won in the first degree elections at Salihli, a town in the Aydın province.[137]

The first degree elections at various Anatolian towns concluded without serious monarchist disturbance. At Kütahya, where the first degree elections were over by April 1, the population voted for the Unionist candidates.[138] Altogether one hundred and twelve electors were chosen for Kütahya, the majority of whom were Unionist sympathisers.[139] In Kayseri, the first degree elections resulted in a Unionist victory; the majority of the electors were Unionist.[140] At Kastamonu, the majority of the electors were Unionist.[141] At Aydıncık, an administrative district of Kastamonu, the Entente Libérale candidate won the first degree elections.[142]

The first degree elections at Trabzon were complete by March 28. Out of the twenty-three electors, twenty-one were Unionists—including the members of the Armenian Revolutionary Federation—as opposed to two Greeks representing the Entente Libérale. Prince Sabahaddin, who had contemplated of putting his candidacy for Trabzon decided not to do so after

---

[137] "Les Elections: A Smyrne," *The Levant Herald and Eastern Express*, March 28, 1912, p.2.
[138] "Les Elections: A Kutahia," *The Levant Herald and Eastern Express*, March 29, 1912, p.2.
[139] "Les Elections: A Kutahia," *The Levant Herald and Eastern Express*, April 1, 1912, p.2.
[140] "Les Elections: A Césarée," *The Levant Herald and Eastern Express*, March 16, 1912, p.2.
[141] "Les Elections: A Castamouni," *The Levant Herald and Eastern Express*, March 25, 1912, p.2.
[142] "Les Elections: Succés ententiste," *The Levant Herald and Eastern Express*, April 3, 1912, p.2.

the results of the first degree elections were made public. [143]

Greek metropolitans of Ephesus, Monastir, Verria, Rhodes, Aenos, Sisaniou, and Çatalca protested in late March against alleged electoral irregularities concerning the number of the electors to represent the Greek minority. [144] At Dedeağaç, Greek and Bulgarian population which totalled forty-five thousand were given seventeen electors, whereas the Turkish population of forty thousand were given twenty-nine electors. Protesting the disproportionate distribution of electors among the different ethnic and religious groups, Greeks and Bulgarians decided not to take part in the elections. [145] On March 21, the Greek Patriarchate in İstanbul registered a complaint with the authorities in regard to alleged election irregularities at İzmir. [146]

First degree elections commenced at various neighbourhoods of İstanbul beginning with the first week of April. First degree elections were scheduled to take place at Kasımpaşa, Hasköy and the Prince Islands between April 3 and 4, at Beşiktaş between April 3 and 7, at Anadolu Hisarı, Beylerbeyi, Arnavutköy, Bebek and Kuruçesme between April 4 and 6, at Fatih between April 4 and 7, at Selimiye between April 6 and 7, and, at Kadıköy, Üsküdar, Yeni Mahalle, Kireçburnu and Tarabya between April 6 and 10. [147]

At Kartal, a suburb of İstanbul, the first degree elections had already been over by March 19. Osman Bey, a Unionist candidate, won the elections with seven hundred and ninety-nine votes to represent Kartal on the second degree elections. [148] Hacı Melcon Efendi, representing the Social Democrat

[143] "Les Elections: A Trébizonde," *The Levant Herald and Eastern Express,* March 29, 1912, p.2. See also, Kudret Emiroğlu, "Trabzon'da Sopalı Seçimler, 1912," pp.42-43.
[144] "Les Elections: Illégalités électorales," *The Levant Herald and Eastern Express,* March 20, 1912, p.2.
[145] "Les Elections: A Dédéagatch," *The Levant Herald and Eastern Express,* March 20, 1912, p.2.
[146] "Les Elections: Nouvelles illégalités," *The Levant Herald and Eastern Express,* March 22, 1912, p.2.
[147] "Les Elections: A Constantinople," *The Levant Herald and Eastern Express,* April 3, 1912, p.2; "Les Elections: A Constantinople," *The Levant Herald and Eastern Express,* April 4, 1912, p.2; and, "Les Elections: A Constantinople," *The Levant Herald and Eastern Express,* April 6, 1912, p.1.
[148] "Les Elections: A Cartal," *The Levant Herald and Eastern Express,* March 19, 1912, p.2; and, "Les Elections: A Cartal," *The Levant Herald and Eastern Express,* March 22, 1912, p.2.

Hnchakian Party, obtained six hundred and seventy-one votes, whereas the Entente Libérale candidate received three hundred and forty-two votes.[149] By March 20, Halil Efendi, a Unionist, was elected with one hundred and ninety-eight votes to represent Gebze, a town close to İstanbul, as its elector in the final elections.[150] Likewise, the first degree elections at Eyüb were already over by April 3 with the overwhelming victory for the Unionist candidates who obtained between four thousand two hundred and sixty-three and four thousand two hundred seventy-five votes as opposed to the monarchist opposition's two hundred twenty and four hundred and eleven votes.[151]

According to the April 6 issue of *İktiham*, the election results at the Prince Islands showed that the Entente Libérale captured the majority of the electorships with nine hundred and seventy-four votes as opposed to one hundred and seventy votes received by the Unionist candidates.[152]

The first degree elections at Büyükdere were over by April 8. The overwhelming majority of the electors were Unionists, who received between two thousand three hundred and sixty-three and two thousand three hundred and fifty-two votes.[153] At Beylerbeyi, Anadolu Hisarı and Bayezid, Unionist candidates obtained the majority of votes.[154] At Fatih, the first degree elections were also over by April 8. About forty-five Unionist candidates, who obtained between thirteen thousand five hundred and ninety and thirteen thousand five hundred and seventy-nine votes, were declared as electors to represent the neighbourhood. The Fatih branch of the Entente Libérale lodged a complaint, accusing the authorities of electoral

---

[149] "Les Elections: A Cartal," *The Levant Herald and Eastern Express*, March 22, 1912, p.2.
[150] "Les Elections: A Guebzé," *The Levant Herald and Eastern Express*, March 20, 1912, p.2.
[151] "Les Elections: Victoire unioniste à Eyoub," *The Levant Herald and Eastern Express*, April 3, 1912, p.2.
[152] "Les Elections: Aux îles des Princes," *The Levant Herald and Eastern Express*, April 6, 1912, p.2.
[153] "Les Elections: A Buyukdéré," *The Levant Herald and Eastern Express*, April 8, 1912, p.2.
[154] "Les Elections: Constantinople," *The Levant Herald and Eastern Express*, April 9, 1912, p.2.

fraud.[155] The Üsküdar section of the Social Democrat Hnchakian Party and the Kızıltoprak branch of the Entente Libérale sent a formal complaint to the office of the Grand Vezierate protesting what they claimed certain election irregularities and declaring that they would therefore abstain from voting in the first degree elections.[156]

The Kadıköy branch of the Entente Libérale also complained about election irregularities and declared that they would abstain from voting.[157] There, the Unionist list obtained six thousand two hundred and forty-three votes as against Entente Libérale's two hundred and nineteen.[158] At Üsküdar, the Unionists obtained between three thousand eight hundred and fifty-two and three thousand eight hundred and forty-four votes as opposed to Entente Libérale's fifty-two votes.[159]

At Beşiktaş, the Unionist candidates received between eleven thousand one hundred and ninety-nine and nine thousand one hundred and ninety-seven votes. The Entente Libérale candidates obtained nine hundred and forty-seven votes. Likewise, at Beykoz and Arnavutköy, candidates of the Committee of Union and Progress won the elections with wide margins.[160] At Tarabya, Unionist candidates were elected with a majority of two hundred and forty-four votes.[161] At Pera, the Entente Libérale list included forty-one Greeks and nine Armenians.[162] Elections there were over by April 16, where ninety-two Unionist candidates won with twenty-six thousand votes.[163]

---

[155] "Les Elections: Constantinople," and "Les Elections: Protestations," *The Levant Herald and Eastern Express*, April 9, 1912, p.2.

[156] "Les Elections: Protestations," *The Levant Herald and Eastern Express*, April 9, 1912, p.2.

[157] "Les Elections: Abstentions," *The Levant Herald and Eastern Express*, April 9, 1912, p.2.

[158] "Les Elections: A Constantinople," *The Levant Herald and Eastern Express*, April 12, 1912, p.2.

[159] "Les Elections: Constantinople," *The Levant Herald and Eastern Express*, April 10, 1912, p.2.

[160] "Les Elections: Constantinople," *The Levant Herald and Eastern Express*, April 10, 1912, p.2.

[161] "Les Elections: A Constantinople," *The Levant Herald and Eastern Express*, April 12, 1912, p.2.

[162] "Les Elections: A Péra," *The Levant Herald and Eastern Express*, April 10, 1912, p.2.

[163] "Les Elections: A Péra," *The Levant Herald and Eastern Express*, April 16, 1912, p.2; and, "The Turkish Elections: Committee Party Success," *The Times*,

Second degree elections did not start until mid-March. Therefore, by the end of March, it was still too early to speak of
election prospects.[164] In late April, elections were still taking
place in such remote areas as Albania, where the population
in general proved more independent than in other parts of the
country.

In the Kossovo province, the sandjak of Üsküb had a total
male population of two hundred and thirty thousand. The
sandjak was entitled to elect five deputies, two of which would
be Muslims, two Bulgarians, and one Serbian.[165]

At Serfidje, Unionist delegation arrived in mid-March for
the election campaign. Hasan Tahsin Bey, from the Audit
Department, did not accept the candidacy for Serfidje. In his
place, Osman Bey, a legal councillor at the Ministry of the Interior, was chosen as candidate. According to *Tanin*, a Unionist electoral success at Serfidje was certain.[166] By April 11, it
was reported that the second degree elections at Serfidje were
turning in favour of the Committee of Union and Progress,
whose candidates were Osman Bey and Gregorius Efendi. By
then, it had become clear that the election of Yorgos Boussios
was highly unlikely. The Greek Constitutional Club, a separatist group which had allied itself with the monarchist opposition in Turkey, declared that it would protest in the Chamber of Deputies against the way the elections were carried out
at Serfidje.[167]

Despite efforts on the part of the government, Albanian constituencies elected several Entente Libérale and independent
candidates.[168] In late January, Avlonyalı Ferid Pasha's brother
Süreyya Vlora approached the Unionist leadership through
intermediaries for his nomination on the Unionist ticket for
the candidacy for Berat. Since it was understood that İsmail

April 18, 1912, p.5.
[164] "Constantinople Letter," *The Near East*, March 15, 1912, p.603.
[165] "Les Elections: A Uskub," *The Levant Herald and Eastern Express*, April 1, 1912, p.2.
[166] "Les Elections: A Serfidjé," *The Levant Herald and Eastern Express*, March 16, 1912, p.2.
[167] "The Elections at Serfidjé," *The Levant Herald and Eastern Express*, April 12, 1912, p.1.
[168] Peter Bartl, *Die albanischen Muslime zur Zeit der nationalen Unabhän-gigkeitsbewegung, 1878-1912*, p.179; Joseph Swire, *Albania: The Rise of a King-dom*, p.113; and, "Constantinople Letter," *The Near East*, May 3, 1912, p.851.

Kemal Bey would not be allowed to run for re-election, he asked to be put on the ballot in place of İsmail Kemal Bey, promising that he would follow the Unionist line in the Chamber in all matters except for those pertaining to Albanian affairs. The Unionist leadership was not enthusiastic about his nomination since it was believed that he was no better than İsmail Kemal Bey.[169] At Berat, İsmail Kemal Bey was not re-elected, the government having prevented him from landing at Vlorë, and having issued orders to the local authorities to arrest him if he landed. Nonetheless, Albanian nationalists were able to elect two of their candidates, Süreyya Vlora and Sami Vrionis.[170] At the elections, Süreyya Vlora obtained sixty-one votes, and Sami Vrionis, sixty votes. The other two unsuccessful candidates, Aziz Pasha Vrione and İsmail Kemal Bey, obtained forty-nine and thirty-seven votes respectively.[171] According to *Hak*, a Unionist organ, Süreyya Vlora, the newly elected deputy for Berat, had accepted the Unionist programme.[172] The Albanians' resistance to official pressure also met with success at İpek, Gjakovë, and Prizren. Necib Draga, Bekir Bey, and Hasan Bey of Prishtnë, the first and last of whom were well known for their nationalist positions and their advocacy of the Latin alphabet, were elected with another Albanian Nationalist deputy for Prishtnë, after a bitter struggle, which at one point seemed likely to end in bloodshed.[173]

---

[169] Mehmed Cavid, "Meşrutiyet Devrine Ait Cavid Bey'in Hatıraları: 69," *Tanin*, November 8, 1943, p.2; and, Ali Birinci, *Hürriyet ve İtilâf Fırkası: II. Meşrutiyet Devrinde İttihat ve Terakki'ye Karşı Çıkanlar*, p.152.

[170] "Constantinople Letter," *The Near East*, May 10, 1912, p.3; and, Feroz Ahmad and Dankwart A. Rustow, "İkinci Meşrutiyet Döneminde Meclisler, 1908-1918," p.266. See also, Stavro Skendi, *The Albanian National Awakening, 1878-1912*, p.426.

[171] "Les Elections: Ismail Kemal bey échoue à Bérat," *The Levant Herald and Eastern Express*, May 4, 1912, p.2. See also, Peter Bartl, *Die albanischen Muslime zur Zeit der nationalen Unabhängigkeitsbewegung, 1878-1912*, p. 179.

[172] *Hak*, April 28, 1328/May 11, 1912, cited in, "Informations: Les Albanais et l'Union," *The Levant Herald and Eastern Express*, May 11, 1912, p.2.

[173] "Constantinople Letter," *The Near East*, May 24, 1912, p.71. Ahmad and Rustow do not give the names of any deputies for Prishtnë for the 1912 Parliament (Feroz Ahmad and Dankwart A. Rustow, "İkinci Meşrutiyet Döneminde Meclisler, 1908-1918," p.266). For the Albanian nationalist campaign Necib Draga waged in Gjakovë see, Stavro Skendi, *The Albanian National Awakening, 1878-1912*, pp.426-428.

Despite its efforts in Monastir, the Committee of Union and Progress won only one out of the five seats, with Ali Fethi [Okyar], the Unionist candidate, obtaining thirty votes. Two seats went to Traianos Nallis, with twenty-nine votes, and the Albanian candidate Mehmed Vasıf Bey, both of whom were on the Entente Libérale ticket; one went to the socialist candidate Pancthé Doreff, and the last seat went to an independent—Dimitrievitch Efendi, who was elected with twenty-eight votes.[174] Except for Ali Fethi [Okyar], all were incumbents. The former replaced Ali Vasfi Bey, an independent Albanian deputy of the 1908 Chamber.[175]

Vildan Efendi, a preacher at İstanbul, was a candidate for Dibër.[176] Basri Bey, ex-deputy for Dibër, declared that he was determined to boycott the elections.[177] Dibër insisted on the election of Basri Bey and no other.[178]

Hacı Ali Efendi, an ulema and President of the Albanian Club at İstanbul, was a candidate for Elbasan.[179] Rasih Bey, ex-President of the Audit Department, was a candidate for Çamlık, in the province of Janina.[180]

In January, the Unionist leadership at İstanbul had gathered intelligence to the effect that there was growing resentment at Salonica against especially Cavid Bey's candidacy. There was even the likelihood that Cavid Bey might not be re-elected due to counter-propaganda waged by Selânikli Hamdi Beyzade Âdil Bey who had organised the ulema against the Committee of Union and Progress. There was also the tactical errors committed by the Unionist Governor of Salonica who had alienated some of the population. Both Selânikli Hamdi

---

[174] "Les Elections: A Monastir," *The Levant Herald and Eastern Express*, April 3, 1912, p.2.
[175] Feroz Ahmad and Dankwart A. Rustow, "İkinci Meşrutiyet Döneminde Meclisler, 1908-1918," p.267.
[176] "Elections législatives: Les candidatures," *The Levant Herald and Eastern Express*, March 4, 1912, p.2.
[177] "Les Elections: Boycottage électoral," *The Levant Herald and Eastern Express*, March 27, 1912, p.2. Despite his statement to the contrary, he was deeply involved in election propaganda on behalf of the Entente Libérale in Monastir (Ali Birinci, *Hürriyet ve İtilâf Fırkası: II. Meşrutiyet Devrinde İttihat ve Terakki'ye Karşı Çıkanlar*, p.135).
[178] "Constantinople Letter," *The Near East*, May 10, 1912, p.3.
[179] "Les élections," *The Levant Herald and Eastern Express*, March 2, 1912, p.2.
[180] "Les élections législatives," *The Levant Herald and Eastern Express*, February 7, 1912, p.2.

Beyzade Âdil Bey and Serezli Hulusi Bey were active in the electoral campaign for their own candidacies. Although they belonged to the opposition, they nevertheless tried to get the nomination of the Committee of Union and Progress, as they judged that they would stand a better chance of winning on the Unionist ticket. Of course, their applications were rejected by the Committee of Union and Progress.[181]

On February 7, Cavid Bey met with Midhat Şükrü [Bleda] and talked about the election prospects at Salonica. Midhat Şükrü [Bleda] assured Cavid Bey that some influential notables of the city backed the Committee of Union and Progress. Midhat Şükrü [Bleda] also related that he had tried convincing Hulusi Bey not to run as a candidate for Salonica but try Serres instead.[182] Despite Midhat Şükrü [Bleda]'s assurances, there was growing concern within the Unionist leadership that all was not going well at Salonica. Local Unionist leadership from Drama visited Cavid Bey on March 7, informing him that his prospects for re-election as deputy for Salonica might be in jeopardy. Local leadership suggested that Cavid Bey put his candidacy from either Kavalla or Drama, where he was extremely popular and therefore was assured of certain victory. When Cavid Bey categorically refused to change his constituency, Midhat Şükrü [Bleda]'s name was put on the list of Unionist candidates for Drama.[183]

By mid-March, news reached to İstanbul that support for Unionist candidates at Salonica were growing day by day, owing, in most part, to the active propaganda campaign conducted by Dr. Nâzım Bey. According to reports, the Unionists had almost regained their former popularity, especially in the town, but in the whole province as well.[184] After meeting with Cavid Bey on March 18, Rahmi [Aslan] departed for Salonica in order to drum up support for the Committee of Union and Progress. He was especially optimistic that there was still a

---

[181] Mehmed Cavid, "Meşrutiyet Devrine Ait Cavid Bey'in Hatıraları: 69," *Tanin*, November 8, 1943, p.2.

[182] Mehmed Cavid, "Meşrutiyet Devrine Ait Cavid Bey'in Hatıraları: 71," *Tanin*, November 10, 1943, p.2.

[183] Mehmed Cavid, "Meşrutiyet Devrine Ait Cavid Bey'in Hatıraları: 80," *Tanin*, November 19, 1943, p.2.

[184] Mehmed Cavid, "Meşrutiyet Devrine Ait Cavid Bey'in Hatıraları: 82," *Tanin*, November 21, 1943, p.2.

likelihood of working with at least some of the Greek electors.[185]

The success of the Unionists at Salonica was not a foregone conclusion, despite the fact that the Committee of Union and Progress had made it its first centre, and that it was, to all intents and purposes, the political capital between 1908 and 1910. There was trouble in Salonica. Owing to discontent among non-Turks, including many of the town's Jewish socialist workers, the loss of confidence in the new regime felt by a section of the merchants, the general effects of the war on trade, and unrest in Macedonia and Albania, the Committee of Union and Progress, which had already thoroughly lost the municipal elections, now stood a good chance of losing a majority of its Chamber seats.[186]

The Unionist electoral campaign in Salonica continued with public appearances of Cavid Bey during the week beginning with April 6. After a dinner party given by the Governor in his honour, Cavid Bey took the opportunity to address the notables of the town gathered for the occasion. He talked about the achievements of the Committee of Union and Progress, attacking those who organised the monarchist opposition in Salonica at the beginning of the electoral campaign and rejecting the baseless allegations with which the monarchists accused the Committee of Union and Progress. His speech especially contained sharply worded condemnation of the attitude of the religious leadership of Salonica which had chosen to ally itself with the monarchist cause. The speech on the whole left a strong impression on the select audience.[187]

Cavid Bey gave a public conference on the night of April 8 at the İttihad ve Terakki Mektebi. Since the Revolution of 1908, Salonica had not seen such a large crowd gathered for a political occasion. The crowd not only totally filled the school building itself but also flowed over to the garden and the street. In his speech which lasted for two hours and extremely well received, Cavid Bey once again talked about the past achieve-

---

[185] Mehmed Cavid, "Meşrutiyet Devrine Ait Cavid Bey'in Hatıraları: 83," *Tanin*, November 22, 1943, p.2.
[186] "Constantinople Letter," *The Near East*, April 12, 1912, p.747.
[187] Mehmed Cavid, "Meşrutiyet Devrine Ait Cavid Bey'in Hatıraları: 90," *Tanin*, November 29, 1943, p.2.

ments as well as the future plans of the Committee of Union and Progress. In particular, he attacked those who claimed during the election campaign that the days of the Committee of Union and Progress had come to an end.[188]

Cavid Bey travelled to Langhaza on April 9. Langhaza was the locality where monarchists had organised a counter-revolutionary demonstration at the early stages of the electoral campaign, demanding the restitution of the absolutist regime as well as the *shari'a*. Denouncing the organisers of the reactionary demonstration and exposing the real intent and purpose of these monarchist *agents provocateurs*, Cavid Bey spoke of the duties of the citizens in protecting the liberal regime and defending the Constitution against monarchist encroachment.[189]

The Entente Libérale candidates for Salonica were Hafız Süleyman Efendi, Osman Âdil Bey, Honeos Efendi, Adamidis Efendi, Vlachoff Efendi, and Asir Salim Efendi.[190] The elections results were close to a landslide victory for the Committee of Union and Progress, which won four of the six seats with Cavid Bey, Major Halil Bey, Emmanuel Carasso, and Rahmi [Aslan].[191] There were eighty-three electors for Salonica. At the elections which were over by April 14, the Unionist list, containing the names of Cavid Bey, Major Halil Bey, Emmanuel Carasso, and Rahmi [Aslan], received seventy-seven votes. The two remaining seats went to independent candidates—Tchikotchanov, a Greek, and, Yurdan Nikolov, a Bulgarian.[192]

According to *Makedonia* of Salonica, the Entente Libérale had strong support in the districts of Kavalla and Drama, two important towns of the Salonica province. The Entente Libér-

[188] Mehmed Cavid, "Meşrutiyet Devrine Ait Cavid Bey'in Hatıraları: 90," *Tanin*, November 29, 1943, p.2; and, "Constantinople Elections: Government and Party Leaders," *The Times*, April 12, 1912, p.5.

[189] Mehmed Cavid, "Meşrutiyet Devrine Ait Cavid Bey'in Hatıraları: 90," *Tanin*, November 29, 1943, p.2.

[190] "Les Elections: A Salonique," *The Levant Herald and Eastern Express*, April 10, 1912, p.2.

[191] Feroz Ahmad and Dankwart A. Rustow, "İkinci Meşrutiyet Döneminde Meclisler, 1908-1918," p.267.

[192] "Les Elections," *The Levant Herald and Eastern Express*, April 15, 1912, p.2; and, "Les Elections: 141 élus," *The Levant Herald and Eastern Express*, April 16, 1912, p.2.

ale candidates were Solon Casanova and Hoca Sabri Efendi.[193] The other candidates for the Entente Libérale were Selânikli Hamdi Beyzade Âdil Bey and Hoca Süleyman Efendi.[194]

Electoral campaign at Serres was not without incidents. Mustafa Nuri Bey, a lawyer at Serres working in the Entente Libérale campaign, was attacked in a public thoroughfare at that town and most brutally handled.[195] Mahir Said Bey, ex-Deputy for Ankara, and Rıza Nur, ex-Deputy for Sinob, protested to the Grand Vezierate and the Ministry of the Interior for Mustafa Nuri Bey's maltreatment at Serres by individuals belonging to the Committee of Union and Progress. The protest letter was also signed by ex-Colonel Sadık Bey, Vice-President of the Entente Libérale.[196] Mustafa Nuri Bey, arrived in İstanbul on February 13. He intended to publish particulars of the incident and calling the attention of the government to the situation in Serres. He would ask the government to take measures for the protection of the partisans of the Entente Libérale.[197]

Public order was once more disturbed in late March at Serres, when officers with divergent political views had a fight among themselves. At the Serres Military Club, a fight broke out between Unionist officers and Ententist officers, leaving several Unionist officers wounded. The matter taken under control, Ententist officers who were found guilty were immediately transferred to another garrison.[198]

At Serres, the five candidates of the Entente Libérale were Hafız Mehmed Rıza Bey, ex-Governor of Siirt, M. Iconomo, a Greek lawyer, Mustafa Bey, Hamid Bey, a judge, and Mustafa Hilmi Bey, Governor of Çorum. At the early stages of the campaign, there was no mention of Derviş Bey, the Unionist

[193] "Les Elections: Candidatures," *The Levant Herald and Eastern Express*, March 18, 1912, p.2.
[194] Mehmed Cavid, "Meşrutiyet Devrine Ait Cavid Bey'in Hatıraları: 78," *Tanin*, November 17, 1943, p.2.
[195] "News Items," *The Levant Herald and Eastern Express*, February 14, 1912, p.1.
[196] "L'Entente Libérale," *The Levant Herald and Eastern Express*, February 9, 1912, p.2. See also, Fevzi Demir, İkinci Meşrutiyet Dönemi Meclis-i Mebusan Seçimleri, 1908-1914, p.126.
[197] "News Items," *The Levant Herald and Eastern Express*, February 14, 1912, p.1.
[198] "Constantinople Letter," *The Near East*, April 5, 1912, p.711.

incumbent deputy for Serres.[199] A graduate of Mekteb-i Mülkiye, Hafız Mehmed Rıza Bey had been appointed Governor
of Siirt on October 20, 1909 and dismissed on November 6,
1910.[200] Mustafa Hilmi Bey was a graduate of Mekteb-i Mülkiye. He was the son of Kocaağazade Hacı Ali Efendi, a notable of Serres.[201]

At Serres, the Unionists could win only one of the five
seats. At Nevrehop, an electoral district of Serres, Unionist candidate Derviş Bey, and opposition candidates Hulusi Bey and
Stoju Hadziev won the elections with thirty-eight votes against
three.[202] Overall, Serres was carried by the independents—
Bulgarian candidates Alexandre Bujnov and Stoju Hadziev,
Greek candidate Dimitris Dingas, and Turkish candidates Hulusi Bey—and Unionist Derviş Bey.[203]

Departing from İstanbul on the night of March 21, Cavid
and Talât Beys arrived at Edirne the following morning,
where they were met with an enthusiastic crowd. Cavid Bey
gave a speech on matters pertaining to public works, emphasising the achievements of the liberal democratic regime in
this field and cautioning the public that although they had
every right to expect the revolutionary regime to achieve even
more, they had to be realistic in their expectations. At another
gathering the same day, Cavid Bey spoke about the proposed
amendment to the Constitution—the famous Article 35—as
well as on the domestic and foreign policy of the Committee
of Union and Progress. Representatives of the Chamber of
Commerce came out into the open and declared themselves
in support of the new regime and the Committee of Union
and Progress. It was also interesting to observe that military
officers stationed at Edirne were supportive of the Unionist
electoral campaign.[204]

[199] "Les Elections: A Serrès," *The Levant Herald and Eastern Express*, March 11, 1912, p.2.
[200] Ali Çankaya, *Yeni Mülkiye Tarihi ve Mülkiyeliler*, 3, p.358.
[201] Ali Çankaya, *Yeni Mülkiye Tarihi ve Mülkiyeliler*, 3, p.435.
[202] "Les Elections: A Sérès," *The Levant Herald and Eastern Express*, April 9, 1912, p.2.
[203] Feroz Ahmad and Dankwart A. Rustow, "İkinci Meşrutiyet Döneminde Meclisler, 1908-1918," p.267.
[204] Mehmed Cavid, "Meşrutiyet Devrine Ait Cavid Bey'in Hatıraları: 84," *Tanin*, November 23, 1943, p.2.

In Gümülcine, there was an active effort to have Gümülcineli İsmail Hakkı Bey, one of the most prominent members
of the monarchist opposition, put on the ballot as the Entente
Libérale candidate.[205] However, the effort to put him on the
ballot was not successful. The electoral campaign of the Entente Libérale also met with physical violence at Gümülcine.
Rıza Tevfik [Bölükbaşı], the prominent Entente Libérale politician who was released from prison on March 16, left İstanbul
on March 21 for an electoral tour in Gümülcine, Kırk Kilise,
Edirne and Salonica.[206] He arrived at Gümülcine on the evening of March 22. The following day, the Greek Archiman-
drite, accompanied by some Greek notables of the town, visited Rıza Tevfik [Bölükbaşı] at his hotel. While he was talking
to his visitors, a party of twenty people arrived at the hotel and
assaulted Rıza Tevfik [Bölükbaşı]. They dragged him to the
railway station, maltreating him on the way. The police intervened and rescued [Bölükbaşı], who was slightly injured.
He was taken to the hospital where his wounds were attended
to. He then went to the residence of Gümülcineli İsmail Hakkı Bey, ex-deputy for Gümülcine, where he stayed.[207] He
continued his campaign in the other towns of Edirne province, arriving at Dedeağaç on March 24. *Tanin* of March 24
reproved the act and invited the authorities to punish the
guilty and take measures to ensure the protection of opposition
deputies in future and prevent such scenes.[208] Other cases of
assault on propagandists of both political parties were reported
from different quarters.[209] At Gümülcine, the electors of Da-

---

[205] "Les Elections: A Gumuldjina," *The Levant Herald and Eastern Express*,
March 26, 1912, p.2.
[206] "News Items," *The Levant Herald and Eastern Express*, March 18, 1912,
p.1.; and, "Les Elections," *The Levant Herald and Eastern Express*, March 23, 1912,
p.2.
[207] "Gümülcine'de Rıza Tevfik Bey," *Tanin*, March 12, 1328/March 25, 1912,
p.4; "Dr. Riza Tewfik Assaulted at Gumuldjina," *The Levant Herald and Eastern
Express*, March 25, 1912, p.1; and, "The Turkish Election Campaign: Assault on Dr.
Riza Tewfik," *The Times*, March 25, 1912, p.5. See also, Fevzi Demir, İkinci Meşrutiyet Dönemi Meclis-i Mebusan Seçimleri, 1908-1914, p.125; Cüneyt Okay, "Kendi Kaleminden 1912 Seçimlerinde Rıza Tevfik'in Dövülmesi: Gümülcine'de Sopalı
Seçimler," pp.18-20; and, Mustafa Ragıb Esatlı, "Meşrutiyet Devrinde: İntihap Mücadeleleri En Çirkin İhtiraslara Sebep Olmuştu," *Akşam*, March 18, 1943, p.4.
[208] "The Turkish Election Campaign: Assault on Dr. Riza Tewfik," *The Times*,
March 25, 1912, p.5. See also, "Rıza Tevfik Bey: Ufak bir Kanun Dersi," *Tanin*,
March 14, 1328/March 27, 1912, pp.3-4.
[209] "Constantinople Letter," *The Near East*, April 5, 1912, p.711.

rıdere voted for Unionist candidates.[210] The successful candidates who got elected were Hacı Âdil [Arda], the Unionist Minister of the Interior, Mehmed Efendi, an ulema, and Mehmed Bey.[211]

The population of Kırk Kilise, where Emrullah Efendi was the Unionist candidate, petitioned that Ali Tevfik Bey, Legal Advisor in the Ministry of Public Works, be also included in the list of candidates.[212]

In neighbouring Rodosto, the Armenian notables of the town sent a petition to the Central Committee of Union and Progress for the inclusion of the candidacy of Simpat Katibian, a graduate of the Paris Law School who was working as a lawyer for the Credit Lyonnais.[213] By the beginning of April, there was grave disagreement between the parties at Rodosto. Armenians refused to support the candidacies of Hagop Boyadjian, the incumbent Armenian deputy for Rodosto, and the two other Unionist candidates—Mazhar Paşazade Veleddin Bey, and Bedri Bey, Governor of Hayrabolu. At the second degree elections that had been held at Malkara in mid-April, the Entente Libérale candidate Emin Efendi, Mufti of Malkara, obtained nineteen out of a total of twenty-two votes.[214]

Unionist candidates for İstanbul were Asım Bey, Minister for Foreign Affairs, Memduh Bey, Minister of Justice, Hulusi Bey, ex-Minister of Public Works, Hüseyin Cahid [Yalçın], incumbent deputy and editor-in-chief of *Tanin*, Bedros Haladjian, incumbent deputy and ex-Minister of Public Works, Vassilakis Orphanidis, a functionary in the Régie des Tabacs, and Faraggi, incumbent deputy. According to an agreement reached between the Committee of Union and Progress and the Armenian community, Krikor Zohrab, one of the most prominent members of the opposition, was also included in

---

[210] "Les Elections: A Gumuldjina," *The Levant Herald and Eastern Express*, March 28, 1912, p.2.

[211] "Les Elections: Résultats à ce jour," *The Levant Herald and Eastern Express*, April 1, 1912, p.2.

[212] "Les Elections: A Kirk-Kilissé," *The Levant Herald and Eastern Express*, March 20, 1912, p.2.

[213] "Les Elections: A Rodosto," *The Levant Herald and Eastern Express*, April 4, 1912, p.2.

[214] "Les Elections: A Rodosto," *The Levant Herald and Eastern Express*, April 11, 1912, p.2.

the Unionist ticket.[215] The final list of Unionist candidates for İstanbul was made public on April 16. The list contained the names of Ahmed Nesimi [Sayman], incumbent deputy, Hüseyin Cahid [Yalçın], Memduh Bey, Yağcı Şefik Bey, a prominent businessman, Hüseyin Haşim [Sanver], a high-level bureaucrat in the Ministry of Finance, Artas Efendi, Greek incumbent deputy for Salonica, Vassilakis Orphanidis, Bedros Haladjian, Albert Vitali Faraggi, and Krikor Zohrab.[216] The Entente Libérale declared that it would not put forward any list in the İstanbul elections, claiming that irregularities in the first degree elections had made the electoral race meaningless.[217]

At first, the Unionist leadership was not absolutely confident that Hüseyin Cahid [Yalçın] could be re-elected from İstanbul. Some were even sure that his re-election was totally impossible. There were suggestions that he should try to put his candidacy from Serres, Drama, or Karesi. Although no decision had been reached as to from where Hüseyin Cahid [Yalçın] would put his candidacy, both Cavid Bey and Hüseyin Cahid [Yalçın] himself thought that it would be strategically unwise for the prestige of the Committee of Union and Progress to change his constituency.[218]

A day before the second degree elections, on April 16, Armenian electors of İstanbul, forty-six in number, declared that they had decided to vote unanimously for the Unionist list, which also incorporated the list of the Armenian Revolutionary Federation.[219] At the İstanbul elections which took place on April 17, the Unionist list obtained the overwhelming majority of the votes. Out of the four hundred and seventy-one electors, four hundred and fifty-seven cast their votes; fourteen electors abstained. All of the candidates on the Unionist ticket

---

[215] "Elections Législatives: Candidatures," *The Levant Herald and Eastern Express*, February 13, 1912, p.2; and, "Les Elections: Les candidats unionistes," *The Levant Herald and Eastern Express*, April 9, 1912, p.2.

[216] "Les Elections: Les candidats de Constantinople," *The Levant Herald and Eastern Express*, April 17, 1912, p.2.

[217] "Les Elections: Les candidats de Constantinople," *The Levant Herald and Eastern Express*, April 17, 1912, p.2.

[218] Mehmed Cavid, "Meşrutiyet Devrine Ait Cavid Bey'in Hatıraları: 69," *Tanin*, November 8, 1943, p.2.

[219] "Les Elections: Les candidats de Constantinople," *The Levant Herald and Eastern Express*, April 17, 1912, p.2.

were elected as deputies, each receiving between four hundred and fifty-seven and four hundred and fifty votes. The other two official candidates that entered the race were independents—Ahmed Saki Bey, representative of the Muslim population of Rethymo, and İzzet Bey, Sub-Governor of Boğazlıyan. Entente Libérale politicians as well as other independents who were not officially running in the İstanbul elections nevertheless got between six and one votes. Among those non-candidates who received one or two votes from the İstanbul electors were Lütfi Fikri Bey, Pantoleon Cosmidis, Nazareth Daghavarian, Tahir Hayreddin Bey, Constantin Constantinidis, Rıza Tevfik [Bölükbaşı], Ahmed Cevdet Bey, editor-in-chief of *İktiham*, and Kâmil Pasha.[220]

In early March, it was announced that Nâzım Bey was an independent candidate for İzmit.[221] Unionist leadership conducted an active electoral campaign at İzmit and the adjoining towns like Adapazarı and Sabanca, for its candidates. Hüseyin Cahid [Yalçın], the incumbent Unionist deputy for İstanbul, accompanied by Ahmed Müfid [Saner], the incumbent Unionist deputy for İzmit, arrived at Adapazarı on March 24 and made a campaign speech on behalf of the Committee of Union and Progress. He also appeared before the public at Sabanca and İzmit, delivering speeches at the local branches of the party.[222]

Papadopoulos, an employee of the Public Debt Administration, was a candidate for Bursa.[223] In late March, Sıdkı Bey, incumbent deputy for Aydın and owner of *Köylü*, arrived at Bursa to make propaganda speeches.[224] At Bursa, a majority of the most prominent ulema had supported the Revolution of 1908, though some did not join the Committee of Union and Progress, but chose, instead, to remain independent. A large

---

[220] "Les Elections: Les députés de Constantinople," *The Levant Herald and Eastern Express*, April 18, 1912, p.2.
[221] "Elections législatives: Les candidatures," *The Levant Herald and Eastern Express*, March 4, 1912, p.2.
[222] Hüseyin Cahid Yalçın, "Meşrutiyet Hatıraları, 1908-1918," *Fikir Hareketleri*, 7 (October 24, 1936-April 17, 1937), p.133; and, "Les Elections: A Ada-Bazar," *The Levant Herald and Eastern Express*, March 25, 1912, p.2.
[223] "Les élections," *The Levant Herald and Eastern Express*, February 5, 1912, p.2.
[224] "Les Elections: A Brousse et à Smyrne," *The Levant Herald and Eastern Express*, March 21, 1912, p.2.

number of lesser ulema, however, did not support the Revolution and these joined the Entente Libérale.[225] As a result of their active campaigning in the villages and towns around Bursa against the Committee of Union and Progress and the principles of the Revolution, the Entente Libérale candidate, Hafız Ahmed Hamdi Efendi, won a seat. The independent, Abdullah Sabri [Karter], also won a seat, as did the Unionist candidates Hasan Rafet [Canıtez] and Rıza Bey.[226]

At Karesi, Abdülaziz Mecdi [Tolon] and İbrahim Vasfi Efendi, both incumbent deputies, lost the elections to Unionist candidates.[227] The Unionist candidates, Hacı Ali Galib Bey and Mehmed Vehbi [Bolak], received twenty-seven and twenty-four votes respectively and were declared the winners. Other successful candidates were Hasan Ferhad Bey, Hüseyin Kadri Bey, and Konstantinos Savapoulos, who obtained twenty-three votes each.[228]

According to *Azadamard*, electoral campaign at Chios started in mid-March. The island's mainly Greek population was divided for about twenty years between the followers of Couvélis and the followers of Canélis. Couvelists formed the majority in the island. Their candidate was Ladopoulos, Chief Translator of the Governor. The Canélist candidate was Achille Arodiago, a graduate of the Galatasaray Lycée in İstanbul. Tchélébidis, the incumbent deputy for Chios, supported the Couvelist candidate.[229]

By mid-March, neither the Committee of Union and Progress nor the Entente Libérale had selected their respective Muslim candidates in İzmir. Only Mehmed Seyyid Bey, one of the leaders of the Committee of Union and Progress, had been put forward by his party, and his election was considered certain. There were still two candidates to be selected

---

[225] Celal Bayar, *Ben de Yazdım*, 2, pp.475-476; and, Fevzi Demir, "II. Meşrutiyet Dönemi Parlamento Seçimlerinde Din ve Siyaset: Kâbe Örtüsüne Dökülen Şarap ve Kimliği Belirsiz Sakal," p.15.
[226] Feroz Ahmad and Dankwart A. Rustow, "İkinci Meşrutiyet Döneminde Meclisler, 1908-1918," p.269.
[227] "Les Elections: A Carassi," *The Levant Herald and Eastern Express*, March 29, 1912, p.2.
[228] "Les Elections: A Karassi," *The Levant Herald and Eastern Express*, April 4, 1912, p.2.
[229] "Les Elections: A Chio," *The Levant Herald and Eastern Express*, March 18, 1912, p.2.

among the Muslim population, and their choice would probably be among staunch supporters of the Committee of Union
and Progress.[230] In mid-March, it was announced that the
Administrative Council of the Aydın Province had designat-
ed the three Greek candidates for İzmir. They were Nicolaki
Tchurukdjioglou, editor of *La Reforme*, and, Tchakiroglou
and Youvanovitch, both medical doctors.[231] However, by late
March it became apparent that the three strongest candidates
for the two Greek seats were D. Dimitriadis, X. Anastassiadis,
and Emmanuel Emmanuelidis. The latter was an incumbent
Unionist deputy for İzmir. Stephen Spartali, who was the Armenian candidate at İzmir, ceded his place to Vahan Bardizbanian, a member of the Armenian Revolutionary Federation.[232] The final list of Armenian candidates for the one Armenian seat were Diran Achnan, Vahan Bardizbanian, and
S. Davidian. As for the Jewish seat, the community was divided: the section of the community siding with the Committee of Union and Progress desired to nominate Nesim Masliah, the incumbent deputy for İzmir, whereas a considerable
majority supported the candidacy of Selim Misrahi.[233]

By mid-March, the impression was gaining ground that
the Committee of Union and Progress candidates would come
in with a large majority.[234] The superior organisation of the
Committee of Union and Progress rendered it almost certain
that its candidates would sweep the polls everywhere.[235] By
April 3, second degree elections were over. The urns were
then carried to the Municipality with great joy by a crowd of
more than fifty thousand people of all classes shouting "Long
Live the Ottomans!" and "Long Live the Committee of Union
and Progress!"[236] One hundred and twenty-five out of a total of

---

[230] "Notes From Smyrna," *The Near East*, March 29, 1912, p.676.

[231] "Les Elections: A Smyrne," *The Levant Herald and Eastern Express*, March 19, 1912, p.2.

[232] "Les Elections: Les résultats dans les provinces," *The Levant Herald and Eastern Express*, March 30, 1912, p.2.

[233] "Notes From Smyrna," *The Near East*, March 29, 1912, p.676.

[234] "Notes From Smyrna," *The Near East*, March 15, 1912, p.606; and, "The Turkish Elections: Sweeping Victory of the Committee," *The Times*, April 9, 1912, p.3.

[235] "Notes From Smyrna," *The Near East*, March 29, 1912, p.676.

[236] "Les Elections: A Smyrne," *The Levant Herald and Eastern Express*, April 3, 1912, p.2.

one hundred and twenty-eight electors had voted in the elections at İzmir. The Unionist candidates obtained one hundred and eight votes. Seventeen Greek electors voted for the Entente Libérale candidates.[237] The Unionists won both Turkish seats with Musa Kâzım Efendi and Mehmed Seyyid Bey, and both Greek seats with Emmanuelidis and Carolidis Efendis. The incumbent Unionist deputy Nesim Masliah also won the Jewish seat.[238] The Greek candidate for the Entente Libérale, M. Conéménos, a medical doctor, obtained only one vote.[239]

In Aydın, the Entente Libérale could not win any of the three seats. The independent, Kâzım Nuri [Çoriş], won one seat, and the Unionists—Yunus Nadi [Abalıoğlu], editor of *Rumeli*, and Ubeydullah [Hatipoğlu]—took the other two.[240]

Sadık Bey, ex-Judge of Edirne, and Besim Bey, ex-Chief Accountant of Tripoli, were candidates for Denizli.[241] Eventually, Sadık Bey and Gani Bey won the elections at Denizli.

At Manisa, Mansurizade Mehmed Said Bey, the incumbent independent deputy, obtained the majority of the votes and was thus re-elected.[242] The other candidates who won the elections were Unionist—Hüseyin Kâzım Kadri Bey, the Governor-General of Salonica, and Mustafa Feyzi Efendi, The President of the Court at Pera.[243] At Soma, the Unionist candidates Hüseyin Kâzım Kadri Bey and Mehmed Sabri [Top-

---

[237] "Les Elections: A Smyrne," *The Levant Herald and Eastern Express*, April 4, 1912, p.2.

[238] "Constantinople Letter," *The Near East*, April 5, 1912, p.711; "Les Elections: Les résultats dans les provinces," *The Levant Herald and Eastern Express*, March 30, 1912, p.2; and, "Les Élections: Résultats à ce jour," *The Levant Herald and Eastern Express*, April 1, 1912, p.2. See also, Feroz Ahmad and Dankwart A. Rustow, "İkinci Meşrutiyet Döneminde Meclisler, 1908-1918," pp.270-271, who mistakenly cite Carolidis as being independent.

[239] "Les Elections: Les résultats dans les provinces," *The Levant Herald and Eastern Express*, March 30, 1912, p.2; and, "Les Elections: Résultats à ce jour," *The Levant Herald and Eastern Express*, April 1, 1912, p.2.

[240] Feroz Ahmad and Dankwart A. Rustow, "İkinci Meşrutiyet Döneminde Meclisler, 1908-1918," p.270.

[241] "Les élections," *The Levant Herald and Eastern Express*, February 5, 1912, p.2.

[242] "Les Elections: Les résultats dans les provinces," *The Levant Herald and Eastern Express*, March 30, 1912, p.2; and, "Les Elections: 38 députés élus," *The Levant Herald and Eastern Express*, April 4, 1912, p.2.

[243] "Les Elections: 38 députés élus," *The Levant Herald and Eastern Express*, April 4, 1912, p.2.

rak] received the majority of the votes.[244]

In mid-March, Halil [Menteşe], the incumbent deputy for Menteşe and former parliamentary leader of the Committee of the Union and Progress, arrived at Muğla where he was met with enthusiastic crowds.[245] He was re-elected on the Unionist ticket for Menteşe.[246] The other seat went to an independent, Ali Haydar [Yuluğ], Governor of Nazilli.[247]

The Unionist candidates for the sandjak of Konya were Mehmed Emin Efendi, the incumbent deputy, Ali Haydar Efendi, Director of Agriculture at Sivas, Tekelizade Rıza Efendi, and Ömer Efendi. The Entente Libérale candidates were Şeyhzade Zeynelabidin Efendi and Mustafa Efendi, both incumbent deputies, Mehmed Efendi, Safvet Efendi, and Ali Rıza Efendi, President of the Civil Court at Konya.[248]

There was an incident at Konya on March 21. At the Alaeddin Mosque, Hoca Mustafa Sabri Efendi, an ulema and the incumbent Entente Libérale deputy for Tokad, made a speech in which he liberally interpreted the Koran, stating that the spirit of Islam preferred a free Christian to an enslaved Muslim. This speech had the intention of both warming the Muslim population to the Entente Libérale which had entered into an electoral alliance with those segments of the Christian population who were actively working for the dissolution of the Empire, and at the same time criticising the Committee of Union and Progress by accusing it of enslaving even the Muslim population.[249] Mustafa Sabri Efendi's provocative speech

---

[244] "Les Elections: Les résultats dans les provinces," *The Levant Herald and Eastern Express*, March 30, 1912, p.2.

[245] "Les Elections: L'ancien leader unioniste," *The Levant Herald and Eastern Express*, March 16, 1912, p.2.

[246] "Les Elections: Les résultats dans les provinces," *The Levant Herald and Eastern Express*, March 30, 1912, p.2; "Les Elections: A Mentéché," *The Levant Herald and Eastern Express*, April 4, 1912, p.2; and, "Constantinople Letter," *The Near East*, April 5, 1912, p.711.

[247] "Les Elections: Les résultats dans les provinces," *The Levant Herald and Eastern Express*, March 30, 1912, p.2; "Les Elections: A Mentéché," *The Levant Herald and Eastern Express*, April 4, 1912, p.2; and, Feroz Ahmad and Dankwart A. Rustow, "İkinci Meşrutiyet Döneminde Meclisler, 1908-1918," p.270. See also, Ali Çankaya, *Yeni Mülkiye Tarihi ve Mülkiyeliler*, 3, pp.939-941.

[248] "Les Elections: A Konia," *The Levant Herald and Eastern Express*, April 3, 1912, p.2.

[249] "Les Elections: Un incident dans une mosquée à Konia," *The Levant Herald and Eastern Express*, March 22, 1912, p.2; and, Ali Birinci, *Hürriyet ve İtilâf Fırkası: II. Meşrutiyet Devrinde İttihat ve Terakki'ye Karşı Çıkanlar*, p.135.

caused a fight to break out. The Governor General of Konya tried to interfere with the intention of keeping the fight within acceptable boundaries. However, it was only after the partisans of the Committee of Union and Progress were kept out of the mosque that the fight subsided.[250]

In early April, a counter-revolutionary agitation erupted at Konya as a consequence of Entente Libérale propaganda in and around the town. According to the *İktiham* of April 11, thirty-eight Entente Libérale agitators had been arrested on charges of making propaganda on behalf of the absolutist regime.[251]

Konya elected an Entente Libérale candidate: the conservative hoca, Şeyhzade Zeynelabidin Efendi.[252] As a matter of fact, Konya was one of the important provinces in Anatolia where none of the Unionist candidates won the elections. The remaining four of a total of five deputyships went to independents Mehmed Emin Efendi, Ali Kemali Efendi, Mehmed Rıza Bey, and Ömer Vehbi [Büyükyalvaç].[253]

Kelekian Efendi was a candidate for Kayseri.[254] The chosen candidate at Kayseri was Soubour Bey, a government official at İstanbul.[255] The population of Kayseri, however, persisted in their demands that Kelekian be also included in the list of candidates.[256] To the Unionists' surprise, the electors of Kayseri insisted on voting for candidates of their own choice. At the second degree elections at Develi in Kayseri, Ömer Mümtaz Bey, the incumbent deputy, obtained seventeen votes, Ahmed Rıfat [Çalık'a], the opposition candidate, thirteen, and Arsen Efendi and Major Ali Galib Bey, the Entente Libérale

---

[250] "Les Elections: Un incident dans une mosquée à Konia," *The Levant Herald and Eastern Express*, March 22, 1912, p.2; and, Ali Birinci, *Hürriyet ve İtilâf Fırkası: II. Meşrutiyet Devrinde İttihat ve Terakki'ye Karşı Çıkanlar*, p.135.

[251] *İktiham*, March 29, 1328/April 11, 1912, cited in, "News Items," *The Levant Herald and Eastern Express*, April 11, 1912, p.1; and, "Les Elections: A Konia," *The Levant Herald and Eastern Express*, April 11, 1912, p.2.

[252] "Constantinople Letter," *The Near East*, May 10, 1912, p.3

[253] Feroz Ahmad and Dankwart A. Rustow, "İkinci Meşrutiyet Döneminde Meclisler, 1908-1918," p.273.

[254] "Elections législatives: Les candidatures," *The Levant Herald and Eastern Express*, March 4, 1912, p.2.

[255] "Les Elections: A Césarée," *The Levant Herald and Eastern Express*, March 16, 1912, p.2.

[256] "Les Elections: A Césarée," *The Levant Herald and Eastern Express*, March 26, 1912, p.2.

candidate, ten each.[257] Kayseri voted for the Entente Libérale candidates and succeeded in electing the opposition candidates, Ali Galib Bey, and Ahmed Rıfat [Çalık'a].[258] Major Ali Galib Bey and Ahmed Rıfat [Çalık'a] were declared winners with seventy-nine and fifty votes respectively. The Unionist candidates, Armenak Efendi, a lawyer, and Ömer Mümtaz Bey, the incumbent deputy for Kayseri, trailed the successful Entente Libérale candidates with forty-five and forty-one votes respectively.[259]

At Kastamonu, Çayhanecioğlu Hüseyin Agha, from the village of Hoca Hacib, organised a demonstration. The group consisting of about one hundred and fifty people marched to the Governor's residence where they demanded the application of the shari'a.[260] At Kastamonu, four deputies were to be elected. Necmeddin [Kocataş], ex-Minister of Justice, Ahmed Mahir Efendi, and Hüsnü Bey were elected on the Unionist ticket.[261]

At Sinob, the second degree elections at Boyabat and Ayancık took place by March 28, where the electors voted for the Unionist candidates. Hasan Fehmi [Tümerkan], ex-deputy for Sinob, and Lieutenant İsmail Hakkı Bey, Aide-de-Camp to the Minister of War, received fifty-five and fifty-one votes respectively, while Dr. Rıza Nur, the incumbent deputy for Sinob and the Entente Libérale candidate, obtained ten votes.[262] Finally, the winners were Hasan Fehmi [Tümerkan] and İsmail Hakkı Bey, the latter replacing Rıza Nur.[263]

By mid-March, Hasan Fehmi [Tümerkan], the incumbent

---

[257] "Les Elections: A Césarée," The Levant Herald and Eastern Express, April 13, 1912, p.2.
[258] Feroz Ahmad and Dankwart A. Rustow, "İkinci Meşrutiyet Döneminde Meclisler, 1908-1918," p.274. See also, Fevzi Demir, İkinci Meşrutiyet Dönemi Meclis-i Mebusan Seçimleri, 1908-1914, p.133.
[259] "Les Elections: Derniers élus," The Levant Herald and Eastern Express, April 15, 1912, p.2.
[260] "Le Chériat et la politique," The Levant Herald and Eastern Express, April 3, 1912, p.1. See also, Fevzi Demir, İkinci Meşrutiyet Dönemi Meclis-i Mebusan Seçimleri, 1908-1914, p.127.
[261] "Les Elections: A Castamouni," The Levant Herald and Eastern Express, March 29, 1912, p.2.
[262] "Les Elections: A Sinope," The Levant Herald and Eastern Express, March 28, 1912, p.2. See also, Fevzi Demir, İkinci Meşrutiyet Dönemi Meclis-i Mebusan Seçimleri, 1908-1914, pp.126-127.
[263] "Les Elections: Résultats à ce jour," The Levant Herald and Eastern Express, April 1, 1912, p.2.

deputy for Sinob, and Hacı Ahmed Hamdi Efendi, incumbent
deputy for Samsun, made speeches in the mosques at Trabzon
on behalf of the Committee of Union and Progress. Commenting on the elections prospects at the Trabzon province, *Tanin*
wrote that the Entente Libérale had support neither at Trabzon
nor at Ordu or Giresun.[264] All reports from Trabzon were optimistic about the electoral success of the Unionist candidates.[265]

However, Trabzon was not immune to monarchist agitation
and provocation. There was a reactionary outburst in Arsin, a
village close to Trabzon, where two *agents provocateurs*, Kü-
çükibrahimoğlu Mehmed Agha and Mehmed Efendi, managed to stir the villagers into shouting slogans that asked for
the application of the *shari'a* and the return to absolutist rule.
However, the *agents provocateurs* were arrested and the demonstration suppressed.[266]

Osman Nuri Efendi, a palace preacher, was a candidate for
Sivas on the Entente Libérale ticket.[267] Nazareth Daghavarian,
the incumbent deputy for Sivas and a founding member of the
Entente Libérale, Hairanian, a member of the Armenian
Revolutionary Federation, and Dikran Zaven, an Armenian
publicist, were Armenian opposition candidates for Sivas.[268]
Dr. Garabet Pashayan, a member of the Armenian
Revolutionary Federation, was the Armenian candidate on
the Unionist ticket.[269] The other candidates who were on the
Unionist ticket were Ömer Şevki Bey, the incumbent deputy,
Mustafa Ziya Bey, and Hoca Emin Efendi.[270] The second de-

---

[264] "Les Elections: A Trébizonde," *The Levant Herald and Eastern Express*,
March 16, 1912, p.2; and, Kudret Emiroğlu, "Trabzon'da Sopalı Seçimler, 1912,"
p.43.
[265] "Les Elections: A Trébizonde," *The Levant Herald and Eastern Express*,
April 13, 1912, p.2.
[266] "Les Elections: A Trébizonde," *The Levant Herald and Eastern Express*,
April 13, 1912, p.2; and, Kudret Emiroğlu, "Trabzon'da Sopalı Seçimler, 1912,"
p.43.
[267] "Les élections," *The Levant Herald and Eastern Express*, February 5, 1912,
p.2.
[268] "Elections législatives: Les candidatures," *The Levant Herald and Eastern
Express*, March 4, 1912, p.2. On Zaven see, "Sivas Mebus Namzedi Dikran Zaven
Efendi," *Tanin*, March 8, 1328/March 21, 1912, pp.3-4.
[269] "Les Elections: Candidats arméniens," *The Levant Herald and Eastern Express*, April 3, 1912, p.2; and, "Les Elections: A Sivas," *The Levant Herald and Eastern Express*, April 4, 1912, p.2.
[270] "Les Elections: A Sivas," *The Levant Herald and Eastern Express*, April 4,

gree elections at Sivas were over by April 4. By and large, the electors voted for the candidates on the Unionist ticket.[271]

Tanin of March 12 announced that Arif Fazıl Efendi, a religious figure and the incumbent deputy for Amasya, was invited to run once again as the Unionist candidate for Amasya.[272] In mid-March, it was confirmed that he would run as the Unionist candidate.[273] At Amasya, the majority of the electors of the towns of Köprü and Mecidözü cast their votes for the Unionist candidate Arif Fazıl Efendi, and independent candidates Hacı Mustafa Efendi and Hasan Rasim Efendi.[274] At Vezirköprü, Mahmud Beyzade Hüseyin Efendi, a Unionist candidate, obtained a majority of the votes, but failing to get the majority of the votes for the whole sandjak of Amasya he lost the elections. At the Amasya elections, İsmail Hakkı [Mumcu] Pasha, the incumbent deputy and the Entente Libérale candidate, managed to obtain only three votes at Vezirköprü.[275] After the final count, Arif Fazıl Efendi, Hacı Mustafa Efendi, and Hasan Rasim Efendi were elected deputies for Amasya, the latter obtaining the great majority of the votes.[276]

At Tokad, the second degree elections were over by April 16. Like in some other Anatolian towns, there were troubles at Zile as a consequence of the counter-revolutionary propaganda by monarchist forces. However, despite the efforts of the monarchist *agents provocateurs*, public order was maintained, and the elections resulted in the victory of three independent candidates—Kemerlizade Şakir Bey of Tokad, Topçuzade Hacı Kâmil Efendi of Zile, and Tahsin Rıza Bey of Niksar.[277]

In Erzurum, where the population had an independent spirit as had been amply shown during the months leading up to the Revolution, the opening of the local branch of the Entente

1912, p.2.
[271] "En Province," *The Levant Herald and Eastern Express*, April 6, 1912, p.2.
[272] "Les Elections: A Amassia," *The Levant Herald and Eastern Express*, March 12, 1912, p.1.
[273] "Les Elections: A Amassia," *The Levant Herald and Eastern Express*, March 16, 1912, p.2.
[274] "En Province," *The Levant Herald and Eastern Express*, April 6, 1912, p.2.
[275] "Les Elections: A Amassia," *The Levant Herald and Eastern Express*, April 6, 1912, p.2.
[276] "En Province," *The Levant Herald and Eastern Express*, April 6, 1912, p.2.
[277] "Notes de Tokat," *The Levant Herald and Eastern Express*, April 29, 1912, p.3.

Libérale in early March created a furore among the citizens
who held demonstrations against the establishment of a monarchist party club at Erzurum. Judging all political activity as
divisive and potentially explosive, especially in a social setting
where ethnic and religious wounds caused by the Hamidian
policy of letting the Kurdish chiefs terrorise the Armenian
peasantry to the point of widespread massacres were still
fresh, the population of Erzurum also expressed its concern for
the existence of the branch of the Committee of Union and
Progress as well as that of the Armenian Revolutionary Federation.[278]

Incumbent Armenian deputies Vartkes Serengülyan and
Karekin Pasturmadjian were candidates for Erzurum.[279]
Vartkes Serengülyan, the incumbent deputy for Erzurum, and
Hüseyin Tosun Bey, Director of Ottoman Telegraph Office
and a Unionist propagandist, arrived at Bayburt on March 4.
Making propaganda speeches in favour of the Committee of
Union and Progress, they explained the conditions of the
agreement reached between the Unionists and the Armenian
Revolutionary Federation.[280] *Haraç*, an Armenian newspaper
published at Erzurum, protested against the candidacy of Hafız
Osman Efendi, a local notable, who had enriched himself by
plundering the properties of the Armenian peasantry.[281]

The elections which ended by April 14 resulted in Unionist victory. Hakim Bey came first with one hundred and seventeen votes. Hüseyin Tosun Bey was elected with one hundred and sixteen votes, Rezak Efendi with ninety-seven, and
Şaban Efendi with seventy-nine votes. The Armenian Revolutionary Federation candidates—Vartkes Serengülyan and Karekin Pasturmadjian—who were supporting the Committee of
Union and Progress also won the elections, receiving one
hundred and six, and one hundred and four votes respec-

---

[278] "Manifestations à Erzeroum," *The Levant Herald and Eastern Express*,
March 5, 1912, p.2.
[279] "Les Elections: Candidats arméniens," *The Levant Herald and Eastern Express*, April 3, 1912, p.2.
[280] "Les Elections: A Baïbourt," *The Levant Herald and Eastern Express*, March
15, 1912, p.2.
[281] "Les Elections: A Erzeroum," *The Levant Herald and Eastern Express*,
March 20, 1912, p.2.

tively.[282]

Zeki Moghamez Bey, a man of letters, was a candidate for Aleppo.[283] At Aleppo, where at Maara the second degree elections were over by April 12, all the electors had voted for the Unionist candidates.[284]

The Unionist-dominated administration at Beirut re-arranged the constituencies. Even with this gerrymandering, Unionist victory was not be complete. Muharrem Misbah won the electoral race as an independent; the other seat went to the incumbent deputy, Kamil al-As'ad, a Shiite Unionist.[285] Acra voted for Sheikh As'ad Tawfiq Efendi Shuqair.[286]

Atıf Bey, a retired officer, was candidate for Damascus.[287] Abd al-Ghani Pasha, and Rafiq Bey were candidates for Damascus.[288] In Damascus, the Unionists were eventually strong enough to eliminate Shukri al-Asali, Rushdi al-Sham'a and Shafiq al-Mu'ayyad al-'Azm, all members of the Entente Libérale and deputies in the Chamber, from the political race; yet they were not dominant enough to have their own candidates elected. The Committee would win only one of four seats in Damascus; the other three were won by independent candidates.[289]

General Hasan Rıza Pasha, Military Commander of Scutari in Albania, was a candidate for Baghdad.[290] On March 12, ex-Colonel Sadık Bey addressed, in the name of the Entente

---

[282] "Les Elections," *The Levant Herald and Eastern Express*, April 15, 1912, p.2; and, "Les Elections: 141 élus," *The Levant Herald and Eastern Express*, April 16, 1912, p.2.

[283] "Elections Législatives: Candidatures," *The Levant Herald and Eastern Express*, February 13, 1912, p.2.

[284] "Les Elections: A Alep," *The Levant Herald and Eastern Express*, April 12, 1912, p.2.

[285] Rashid Khalidi, "Ottomanism and Arabism in Syria Before 1914: A Reassessment," p.59; and, Feroz Ahmad and Dankwart A. Rustow, "İkinci Meşrutiyet Döneminde Meclisler, 1908-1918," p.280.

[286] "Les Elections: En Palestine," *The Levant Herald and Eastern Express*, March 30, 1912, p.2.

[287] "Elections," *The Levant Herald and Eastern Express*, February 17, 1912, p.2.

[288] "Les élections," *The Levant Herald and Eastern Express*, March 6, 1912, p.2.

[289] Samir Seikaly, "Shukri al-'Asali: A Case Study of a Political Activist," p.89; Ahmed Tarabein, "Abd al-Hamid al-Zahrawi: The Career and Thought of an Arab Nationalist," pp.101-102; Philip S. Khoury, *Urban Notables and Arab Nationalism: The Politics of Damascus, 1860-1920*, p.62; and, Feroz Ahmad and Dankwart A. Rustow, "İkinci Meşrutiyet Döneminde Meclisler, 1908-1918," p.280.

[290] "Elections Législatives: Candidatures," *The Levant Herald and Eastern Express*, February 13, 1912, p.2.

Libérale, a letter to the Ministry of the Interior protesting the events at Baghdad.[291]

The elections at Basra was over by April 1. The Unionists lost the elections. Entente Libérale candidates Zuhayrzade Abdullah Bey and Talib won the two seats for Basra.[292] There was concern within the Unionist leadership at İstanbul that other constituencies in the Basra province might also go overboard to the monarchist side.[293]

On March 7, Sharif Ali Haydar Bey, former Minister of Pious Foundations and Vice-President of the Senate, arrived at Medina where he was warmly welcomed by both the civilian and military authorities and the representatives of the Committee of Union and Progress. There was also a large crowd present.[294]

Artillery Captain Abdüllatif Bey was elected deputy for Fizan in late March, replacing Cami [Baykut]. He was one of the early participants in the Revolution of 1908. At Salonica, he was among the revolutionary officers who had fired the first salvo to salute the Revolution.[295]

---

[291] "Les Elections: Une lettre de protestation du chef du l'Entente Libérale," *The Levant Herald and Eastern Express*, March 13, 1912, p.2.

[292] Mehmed Cavid, "Meşrutiyet Devrine Ait Cavid Bey'in Hatıraları: 90," *Tanin*, November 29, 1943, p.2; and, "Les Elections: 4 députés ententistes," *The Levant Herald and Eastern Express*, April 10, 1912, p.2.

[293] Mehmed Cavid, "Meşrutiyet Devrine Ait Cavid Bey'in Hatıraları: 90," *Tanin*, November 29, 1943, p.2.

[294] "Les Elections: A Médine," *The Levant Herald and Eastern Express*, March 22, 1912, p.2.

[295] "Les Elections: Le député du Fezzan," *The Levant Herald and Eastern Express*, March 27, 1912, p.2; and, "Les Elections: Résultats à ce jour," *The Levant Herald and Eastern Express*, April 1, 1912, p.2.

CHAPTER NINE

THE *COUP D'ÉTAT* OF 1912

The Parliament convened on April 18 as scheduled.[1] If somewhat vague on matters of internal policy, the Speech from the Throne was clear enough with regard to the continuation of the war with Italy and the Sublime Porte's absolute refusal to surrender one bit of its sovereignty in Turkish Africa, much less the whole of Tripoli as the Italians had demanded. The news of the attack on the Dardanelles reached Parliament at the outset of the opening ceremony, reportedly causing no alarm.[2]

As expected, the elections had not been totally completed, and without a majority of its deputies in attendance, the Chamber could not begin conducting business.[3] Up until mid-April, about one hundred and sixty-seven deputies had been elected.[4] In mid-May, some one hundred and eighty deputies had arrived at İstanbul, many of whom were members of the Committee of Union and Progress.[5]

With the election nonetheless effectively over, the Committee's leadership returned to the modification of Article 35 of the Constitution. By early May, the cabinet had approved

---

[1] II/I/1, April 5, 1328/April 18, 1912, *Meclis-i Mebusan Zabıt Ceridesi, I,* pp.2-3; "Meclis-i Mebusan'ın Resm-i Küşadı," *İktiham,* April 5, 1328/April 18, 1912, p.1; "Opening of the Turkish Parliament," *The Times,* April 19, 1912, p.8; Hüseyin Cahid [Yalçın], "Meclis-i Mebusan'ın Küşadı," *Tanin,* April 6, 1328/April 19, 1912, p.1; "Yeni Meclis-i Mebusan'ın Küşadı Münasebetiyle," *İktiham,* April 6, 1328/April 19, 1912, p.1; Hüseyin Cahid Yalçın, "Meşrutiyet Hatıraları, 1908-1918," *Fikir Hareketleri,* 7 (October 24, 1936-April 17, 1937), p.165; and, Yusuf Hikmet Bayur, *Türk İnkılâbı Tarihi, 2/1,* p.244.

[2] "Meclis-i Mebusan'ın Resm-i Küşadı: Nutk-u İftitahı," *Tanin* April 6, 1328/April 19, 1912, p.1; "Nutk-u İftitahı," *İktiham,* April 6, 1328/April 19, 1912, p.2; "Opening of the Turkish Parliament," *The Times,* April 19, 1912, p.8; and, "Constantinople Letter," *The Near East,* April 26, 1912, p.815.

[3] Hüseyin Cahid Yalçın, "Meşrutiyet Hatıraları, 1908-1918," *Fikir Hareketleri,* 7 (October 24, 1936-April 17, 1937), p.165.

[4] "Constantinople Letter," *The Near East,* April 26, 1912, p.815.

[5] "Constantinople Letter," *The Near East,* May 17, 1912, p.39.

the proposed modifications which then had to be submitted to the Parliament. The leadership of the Committee of Union and Progress was confident that it would obtain the necessary two-thirds majority in the Chamber of Deputies.[6] With Article 35 passed, the Chamber would then pass the Budget, discuss, and perhaps pass, certain demands for extra-ordinary credits, and then be prorogued.[7] A meeting was held on June 5 at Cavid Bey's house to discuss the proposed amendment ot the Constitution. Said Pasha, and a group of the leaders of the Committee of Union and Progress—Talât Bey, Emrullah Bey, Midhat Şükrü [Bleda], Ahmed Nesimi [Sayman], Ziya Bey, Ürgüplü Mustafa Hayri Bey, and Dr. Nâzım Bey—were all present. Both Said Pasha and Talât Bey had serious reservations concerning the cooperation of the Chamber. Yet, the decision taken by the leaders of the Committe of Union and Progress was to push for the amendment.[8]

The Chamber, as Said Pasha and Talât Bey had feared, refused to cooperate. A majority of the deputies decided that the article in question should be modified so as to give the Sultan, in the case of the Chamber's repeated refusal to accept a proposal supported by the cabinet and acting on the advice of the government, the power to dissolve Parliament and order new elections to be held. The proposal also stipulated that if after the elections, the Chamber persisted in its point of view the government would have to give way. In response, the government attempted to further modify the article, in a proposal which would give the government freedom to disregard the decisions of a newly elected Parliament. This latest proposal encountered so much opposition that it was quickly withdrawn.[9]

On June 22, after some discussion on the floor, the Chamber modified, by a vote of two hundred and five votes to fifteen,

---

[6] "Kanun-u Esasi'nin Tadili," *Tanin*, May 9, 1328/May 22, 1912, pp.1-2; and, "Esbab-ı Mucibe Mazbatası," *Tanin*, May 9, 1328/May 22, 1912, p.2.

[7] "Constantinople Letter," *The Near East*, May 17, 1912, p.39.

[8] Mehmed Cavid, "Meşrutiyet Devrine Ait Cavid Bey'in Hatıraları: 121," *Tanin*, January 2, 1944, p.2.

[9] "Kanun-u Esasi Tadilâtı," *Tanin*, May 30, 1328/June 12, 1912, p.1; "Kanun-u Esasi: Tadilâtın Esbab-ı Mucibesi," *Tanin*, June 5, 1328/June 18, 1912, pp.3-4; "Kanun-u Esasi: Tadilâtın Esbab-ı Mucibesi," *Tanin*, June 6, 1328/June 19, 1912, pp.3-4; and, "Constantinople Letter," *The Near East*, June 21, 1912, p.199.

Article 7.[10] On June 24, the Chamber voted by one hundred and ninety-nine to fifteen Article 35 of the Constitution in accordance with the recommendations of the Committee for the Revision of the Constitution, which had not gone so far as the Government wished.[11]

Meanwhile, the Unionist leadership had also encountered difficulty in selecting an acceptable candidate for the Presidency of the Chamber. Its first choice had been Hacı Âdil [Arda], then on an inspection tour in Macedonia. His nomination, however, had met with strong opposition in the Chamber, and was dropped. Consequently, Halil [Menteşe], a former Minister of the Interior, and leader of the parliamentary group of the Committee, was nominated.[12]

On May 15 Halil [Menteşe] was elected President of the Chamber of Deputies. The First Vice-President was Muhammad Fawzi Pasha al-'Azm, deputy for Damascus, the Second, Bedros Haladjian, deputy for İstanbul and former Minister of Public Works. All three were the nominees of the Committee of Union and Progress.[13]

Rumours of cabinet instability persisted, though it seemed premature to predict any immediate change. Most felt that the Unionists would continue to make use of Said Pasha for just as long as needed, and that when he retired on account of old age, ill health, or under pressure he would probably be succeeded by another 'elder statesman,' meaning, another non-Unionist pasha.[14]

In late May, Nail Bey, Minister of Finance, resigned. He had been appointed to the Ministry in May of 1911, replacing Cavid Bey who had been forced to resign under monarchist attack. A strong advocate of economy, he had followed Cavid

---

[10] II/I/18, June 9, 1328/June 22, 1912, *Meclis-i Mebusan Zabıt Ceridesi, 1,* pp.435-465; and, Yusuf Hikmet Bayur, *Türk İnkılâbı Tarihi, 2/1,* p.244.

[11] II/I/19, June 11, 1328/June 24, 1912, *Meclis-i Mebusan Zabıt Ceridesi, 1,* pp.469-494; "Turkish Constitution: The Chamber and Article 35," *The Times,* June 24, 1912, p.5; and, "Constantinople Letter," *The Near East,* July 5, 1912, p.263.

[12] "Constantinople Letter," *The Near East,* May 17, 1912, p.39.

[13] II/I/5, May 2, 1328/May 15, 1912, *Meclis-i Mebusan Zabıt Ceridesi, 1,* pp.43-45; "Presidency of the Turkish Chamber," *The Times,* May 16, 1912, p.5; and, "Constantinople Letter," *The Near East,* May 24, 1912, p.71. See also, Ahmed Bedevi Kuran, *Osmanlı İmparatorluğunda İnkılâp Hareketleri ve Milli Mücadele,* p.555; and, Yusuf Hikmet Bayur, *Türk İnkılâbı Tarihi, 2/1,* p.244.

[14] "Constantinople Letter," *The Near East,* May 17, 1912, p.39.

Bey's policies and had the pleasure of seeing a distinct improvement in revenues, while his efforts to reduce expenditure, if not entirely successful, had none the less produced an
improvement in the financial situation of the Government.
Cavid Bey was appointed Acting-Minister of Finance, and
would probably succeed him, in which case Bedros Haladjian
would probably replace Cavid Bey as Minister of Public
Works. There were rumours that Asım Bey, Minister for Foreign Affairs, would also resign shortly. As he was not on the
best of terms with Said Pasha and some members of the Committee of Union and Progress, it was certain that such a move
would not be entirely voluntary.[15]

When it realised that it had no hope of capturing political power through constitutional means, the monarchist opposition
decided to resort to a *coup d'état*, one which would center
around the discontented Albanian elements in Macedonia.[16]
Dr. Rıza Nur, one of the leaders of the Entente Libérale, held
talks with Colonel Yakovalı Rıza Bey who was, at the time,
exiled to Sinob for his role in the counter-revolutionary *coup*
attempt of April, 1909. They agreed to work together to provoke
an Albanian rebellion which would ostensibly lead to the
destabilisation and fall of the Unionist government. Just as Dr.
Rıza Nur was arranging for Yakovalı Rıza Bey's escape from
Sinob, the latter was pardoned. He then returned to Albania
where he began organising, as had been planned, the rebellion.[17]

[15] "The Turkish Cabinet: Resignation of the Minister of Finance," *The Times*, May 23, 1912, p.5; and, "Constantinople Letter," *The Near East*, May 31, 1912, p.103. For reasons of his resignation see, "The Turkish Cabinet: Cause of the Finance Minister's Resignation," *The Times*, May 25, 1912, p.5. For speculations on further ministerial changes see, "The Turkish Ministry," *The Times*, May 29, 1912, p.5; and, "The Turkish Cabinet: Reported Differences," *The Times*, May 31, 1912, p.3.
[16] "Discontent in Albania: Hostile Attitude of the Tribes," *The Times*, May 9, 1912, p.5. For Şerif Pasha's letter supporting the Albanians in overthrowing the Committee of Union and Progress regime dated July 5, 1912 see, William W. Rockhill to Secretary of State, in *Records of the Department of State Relating to Internal Affairs of Turkey, 1910-1929*, Roll 4. See also, Stavro Skendi, *The Albanian National Awakening, 1878-1912*, p.430.
[17] Rıza Nur, *Hürriyet ve İtilâf Fırkası Nasıl Doğdu, Nasıl Öldü?* p.63; Peter Bartl, *Die albanischen Muslime zur Zeit der nationalen Unabhängigkeitsbewegung, 1878-1912*, p.180; Joseph Swire, *Albania: The Rise of a Kingdom*, p.120.; and, Ahmet Turan Alkan, *İkinci Meşrutiyet Devrinde Ordu ve Siyaset*, p.125. See also,

Dr. Rıza Nur maintained contact with the Albanian rebels through such intermediaries as Celal Paşazade Emin Bey. This network also included Prince Sabahaddin, who was introduced by Dr. Rıza Nur to Yakovalı Rıza Bey, and helped finance the clandestine operation.[18] Hoca Said Efendi and Necib Draga, both ex-deputies for Üsküb, Volçetrinli Hasan Bey, ex-deputy for Prishtnë, Mehmed Pasha Dralla, Receb Mitrovitza, Bedri Bey of İpek, Salih Yuka, İdris Sefer, and Issa Bolatinatz were among the organisers of the conspiracy.[19]

While leaders of the Entente Libérale were busy coordinating and financially supporting the Albanian rebellion, however, monarchist supporters in the army started a rebellion in the Monastir area on May 6. Some officers left their garrisons and took to the mountains; some were captured and brought to İstanbul.[20] News of this military insurrection would not appear in Turkish newspapers for almost six weeks.

League of Saviour Officers—or, Halâskâr Zabitan Grubu—a secret military organisation, was to become the lynch-pin of the monarchists' plans.[21] One of its leading members, Geli-

---

Ziya Şakir [Soko], "Hürriyet ve İtilâf Nasıl Doğdu? Nasıl Yaşadı? Nasıl Battı? 50: 'İsrar Ediyoruz; Hesaplar Lâyikiyle Tetkik Edilmeli'," *Tan*, December 29, 1937, p.9; and, Yusuf Hikmet Bayur, *Türk İnkılâbı Tarihi, 2/1*, p.262.

[18] Rıza Nur, *Hürriyet ve İtilâf Fırkası Nasıl Doğdu, Nasıl Öldü?* p.63; Stefanaq Pollo and Arben Puto, *The History of Albania from its Origins to the Present Day*, p.144; and, Şehbenderzade Filibeli Ahmed Hilmi, *Muhalefetin İflâsı: İtilâf ve Hürriyet Fırkası*, pp.46-47.

[19] Rıza Nur, *Hürriyet ve İtilâf Fırkası Nasıl Doğdu, Nasıl Öldü?* p.64; Peter Bartl, *Die albanischen Muslime zur Zeit der nationalen Unabhängigkeitsbewegung, 1878-1912*, p.180; J. Swire, *Albania: The Rise of a Kingdom*, p.120; Şehbenderzade Filibeli Ahmed Hilmi, *Muhalefetin İflâsı: İtilâf ve Hürriyet Fırkası*, pp.46-47; and, Celal Bayar, *Ben de Yazdım, 2*, p.500. Hasan Bey, ex-deputy for Prishtnë, and Isa Bolatinatz were identified as two of the most important rebel leaders by the *Times* correspondent ("The Albanian Outbreaks: A Serious Situation," *The Times*, May 13, 1912, p.5; and, "The Albanian Rebels," *The Times*, June 11, 1912, p.5. See also, Aram Andonyan, *Balkan Savaşı*, pp.173-175).

[20] "Plot Against the Turkish Commission," *The Times*, May 9, 1912, p.5; J. Swire, *Albania: The Rise of a Kingdom*, p.119; Aram Andonyan, *Balkan Savaşı*, p.175; Ahmed Bedevi Kuran, *Osmanlı İmparatorluğunda İnkılâp Hareketleri ve Milli Mücadele*, pp.563-565; and, Ahmed Bedevi Kuran, *İnkılâp Tarihimiz ve 'Jön Türkler,'* pp.302-303. One of the rebel officers, Tahsin Bey, was appointed as the Police Commissioner of İstanbul by the monarchist/collaborationist Damad Ferid Pasha Government during the Armistice after World War I. Nafiz Bey, one of the officers who had been captured by the authorities, later became aide-de-camp to Nâzım Pasha who was appointed Minister of War after the *coup d'état* of July 1912 and was killed during the 'Raid on the Sublime Porte' of January 1913 (Celal Bayar, *Ben de Yazdım, 2*, p.499).

[21] Ahmed Bedevi Kuran, *Osmanlı İmparatorluğunda İnkılâp Hareketleri ve Milli Mücadele*, pp.565-566. See also, Bülent Dâver, "Hürriyet ve İtilâf Fırkası," p.97.

bolulu Kemal [Şenkıl] Bey, a staff officer, had contacted
Prince Sabahaddin through Scalieri, a Greek politician.[22]
Prince Sabahaddin had then invited Dr. Rıza Nur and several
other opposition politicians to discuss the prospects of the Albanian rebellion. They agreed that, at this critical juncture, in
order to effect the fall of the Said Pasha Cabinet, the Albanian
rebellion could use the help of a general military upheaval.
Following the meeting, Prince Sabahaddin added his own
views to the League of Saviour Officers' manifesto, and this revised version was secretly printed in large quantities in a print
shop at Pera. Again, Prince Sabahaddin was responsible for fi-
nancing.[23]

Monarchists then set about diligently recruiting army officers.[24] Acting as liaison between the officers on the one hand
and Prince Sabahaddin, Kâmil Pasha, and Nâzım Pasha on
the other, Dr. Rıza Nur also used his residence as the headquarters for the preparation and distribution of counter-revolutionary propaganda.[25] Nâzım Pasha, head of the Council of
War, also served as intermediary between the leadership of
the Entente Libérale and the secret military organisation,
though most communication between the two groups was
highly secret and, in general, the organisation was geared to
disguise its political machinations as a purely military unrest.[26]

In late June, newspapers finally printed news of the revolt
at Monastir, though most downplayed its significance, por-

---

[22] Tarık Zafer Tunaya, *Türkiye'de Siyasi Partiler, 1859-1952*, p.346; and, Fethi
Tevetoğlu, *Ömer Naci*, 2nd Edition, p.138.
[23] Rıza Nur, *Hürriyet ve İtilâf Fırkası Nasıl Doğdu, Nasıl Öldü?* pp.63-65. See
also, Ziya Şakir [Soko], "Hürriyet ve İtilâf Nasıl Doğdu? Nasıl Yaşadı? Nasıl Battı?
51: Prens Sabahattin Bey'in Yalısındaki Toplantılar," *Tan*, December 30, 1937, p.9.
[24] Rıza Nur, *Hürriyet ve İtilâf Fırkası Nasıl Doğdu, Nasıl Öldü?* pp.65-66; and,
Ali Birinci, *Hürriyet ve İtilâf Fırkası: II. Meşrutiyet Devrinde İttihat ve Terakki'ye Karşı Çıkanlar*, pp.166-168. The initial leading members belonging to the
military were Gelibolulu Kemal, Kastamonulu Hilmi, Receb, İbrahim Aşkî, Kudret, 'Rossignol' Hüsnü, Hasan Ali and Tevfik Beys (Fethi Tevetoğlu, *Ömer Naci*,
2nd Edition, pp.137-138).
[25] Rıza Nur, *Hürriyet ve İtilâf Fırkası Nasıl Doğdu, Nasıl Öldü?* pp.65-66. For
the text of this seditious propaganda see, Yusuf Hikmet Bayur, *Türk İnkılâbı Tarihi*, 2/1, pp.252-254.
[26] Süleyman Nazif, *Yıkılan Müessese* (İstanbul: İlhami Fevzi Matbaası, 1927),
pp.9-13, quoted in Celal Bayar, *Ben de Yazdım*, 2, p.532n; and, Rıza Nur, *Hürriyet
ve İtilâf Fırkası Nasıl Doğdu, Nasıl Öldü?* pp.65-66. See also, Ali Birinci, *Hürriyet
ve İtilâf Fırkası: II. Meşrutiyet Devrinde İttihat ve Terakki'ye Karşı Çıkanlar*,
p.169.

traying it as the action of a few disgruntled officers and soldiers who were rebelling against their supervisors.[27] But, the mutiny of troops at Monastir proved to be a more serious problem than was at first indicated.[28] The Government soon realised that it was, in effect, a deliberate revolt against the Cabinet on the part of at least one organisation, ostensibly the League of Saviour Officers, which by itself represented an influential body of military opinion. Although local factors seemed to have caused a premature outbreak at Monastir, there was good reason to believe that the secret military organisation had for some time been contemplating open hostility against the Committee of Union and Progress and that it had only held back on account of the Tripolitan war. With the crisis past, however, the unrest in Albania and monarchist activity combined to strengthened the hands of the malcontents in Monastir.[29]

On the night of June 22 and 23, Captain Tayyar Bey Tetova, an Albanian officer from Dibër and a member of the League of Saviour Officers, left the barracks at Bistritza, three miles from Monastir, with several other officers, some sixty men, several machine guns and 1,000 TLs. He was later joined by more officers and troops, mostly Albanians, though a few were Turks and Christians from Dibër and Perlepe.[30] He then

---

[27] "Beyanname-i Resmi," *Iktiham*, June 15, 1328/June 28, 1912, p.3; "Arnavutluk," *Tanin*, June 15, 1328/June 28, 1912, p.2; "Manastır Firarileri," *Iktiham*, June 15, 1328/June 28, 1912, p.3; "Arnavutluk," *Tanin*, June 16, 1328/June 29, 1912, pp.2-3; "Arnavutluk," *Tanin*, June 18, 1328/July 1, 1912, pp.2-3; Hüseyin Cahid Yalçın, "Meşrutiyet Hatıraları, 1908-1918," *Fikir Hareketleri*, 7 (October 24, 1936-April 17, 1937), p.166. In his statement in the Chamber of Deputies with reference to the situation in Albania, Hacı Âdil [Arda], the Minister of the Interior, was still denying that the Albanians had been contemplating an uprising ("Ministerial Statement," *The Times*, June 6, 1912, p.5).

[28] "Mutiny of Turkish Troops: Albanian Disaffection," *The Times*, June 25, 1912, p.5; "Mutiny of Turkish Troops," *The Times*, June 26, 1912, p.5; "Monastir Mutiny: Political and Military Movement—Fighting with the Insurgents," *The Times*, June 27, 1912, p.8; and, "The Revolt of Troops at Monastir: Spread of the Disaffection," *The Times*, June 28, 1912, p.5.

[29] "Monastir Mutiny: Political and Military Movement—Fighting with the Insurgents," *The Times*, June 27, 1912, p.8; "Notes of the Week," *The Near East*, July 5, 1912, p.261; and, Aram Andonyan, *Balkan Savaşı*, p.176. For the existence of seditious propaganda material—distributed by members of the League of Saviour Officers, and found on the captured mutineers—see, Yusuf Hikmet Bayur, *Türk İnkılâbı Tarihi*, 2/1, pp.255-256.

[30] "Monastir Mutiny: Political and Military Movement—Fighting with the Insurgents," *The Times*, June 27, 1912, p.8; "Bir Mülâzım-ı Saninin Gaybubeti," *Iktiham*, June 15, 1328/June 28, 1912, p.3; "Pirlepe'den Firar Edenler," *Iktiham*, June 15, 1328/June 28, 1912, p. 3; "Firarilerin Mikdarı," *Iktiham*, June 15, 1328/

announced that he and his comrades, organised clandestinely under the name of Protection of the Fatherland—or,
Hıfz-ı Vatan, or Muhafaza-i Vatan—supported the Albanian
insurgents, and sent a telegram to the Government demanding the resignation of the existing Cabinet, the impeachment
of Hakkı Pasha's Cabinet for its lack of military preparations
in Tripoli, as well as the trials of Talât Bey, Cavid Bey, Hüseyin Cahid [Yalçın], Ömer Naci Bey, Dr. Nâzım Bey, Babanzade İsmail Hakkı Bey, and Rahmi [Aslan]—all of whom
were leaders of the Committee of Union and Progress. He also
demanded that the Committee of Union and Progress be prohibited from any further political activity, that army officers'
grievances be addressed, that a General Staff at the Palace be
created, and that new elections be held.[31]

The League of Saviour Officers addressed its demands to
the Council of War, which was conveniently headed by one
of its conspirators, Nâzım Pasha.[32] Acting in his official capacity, Nâzım Pasha urged that the Cabinet give the matter
immediate attention, suggesting that discontent was widespread enough to warrant its resignation.[33] Although the
League of Saviour Officers had demanded that the Sultan preside over the General Staff, apparently to correct certain 'irregularities' in the army's advancement procedures, there could

---

June 28, 1912, p.3; and, "Constantinople Letter," *The Near East*, July 5, 1912, p.263.
See also, Peter Bartl, *Die albanischen Muslime zur Zeit der nationalen Unab-
hängigkeitsbewegung, 1878-1912*, p.181; Süleyman Külçe, *Osmanlı Tarihinde Ar-
navutluk*, p.410; Basil Kondis, *Greece and Albania, 1908-1914*, p.69; Stavro Skendi,
The Albanian National Awakening, 1878-1912, p.430; Ahmet Turan Alkan, *İkinci
Meşrutiyet Devrinde Ordu ve Siyaset*, p.125; Edwin Pears, *Forty Years in Constan-
tinople: The Recollections of Sir Edwin Pears, 1873-1915*, p.325; and, Yusuf Hikmet
Bayur, *Türk İnkılâbı Tarihi, 2/1*, p.257.

[31] "The Revolt of Troops at Monastir: Demand of the Mutineers," *The Times*,
June 28, 1912; "Notes of the Week," *The Near East*, July 5, 1912, p.261; "Constantinople Letter," *The Near East*, July 5, 1912, p.263; Aram Andonyan, *Balkan Savaşı*,
p.176; Peter Bartl, *Die albanischen Muslime zur Zeit der nationalen Unabhängigkeitsbewegung, 1878-1912*, p.181; Stavro Skendi, *The Albanian National Awakening, 1878-1912*, pp.430-431; Ahmet Turan Alkan, *İkinci Meşrutiyet Devrinde Ordu
ve Siyaset*, p.126; and, Süleyman Külçe, *Osmanlı Tarihinde Arnavutluk*, p.406.

[32] Ziya Şakir [Soko], "Hürriyet ve İtilâf Nasıl Doğdu? Nasıl Yaşadı? Nasıl Battı? 52: Sait Paşa Adeta Tehditkâr bir Vaziyet Almıştı," *Tan*, December 31, 1937,
p.9; Ahmet Turan Alkan, *İkinci Meşrutiyet Devrinde Ordu ve Siyaset*, p.134; and,
and Rıza Nur, *Hürriyet ve İtilâf Fırkası Nasıl Doğdu, Nasıl Öldü?* pp.67-67.

[33] "Hurşid Paşa'nın Kabine Hatıraları," *Hayat*, January 23, 1964, p.5, quoted
in Celal Bayar, *Ben de Yazdım, 2*, p.530, and Rıza Nur, *Hürriyet ve İtilâf Fırkası
Nasıl Doğdu, Nasıl Öldü?* p.67.

be no doubt that its demands were primarily political.[34] It had singled out Cavid and Talât Beys, two of the most prominent leaders of the Committee of Union and Progress and ministers in the cabinet, as well as Mahmud Şevket Pasha, the Minister of War; and called for the Committee's dissolution, as well as the new parliament's.[35]

After the news of the outbreak at Monastir, the government summoned the Chamber for the special purpose of passing a bill introduced by Mahmud Şevket Pasha, Minister of War, which would prohibit political activity on the part of officers and troops.[36] In the speech he delivered to the Chamber on July 1, Mahmud Şevket Pasha praised the alliance between officers and Unionists prior to and during the Revolution of 1908. Yet he went on to say that he was generally against the military's involvement in politics and was proposing a bill to that effect.[37] Apart from the Albanian and Entente Libérale deputies, a majority of the Chamber favoured the bill.[38] Nonetheless, Ali Galib Bey, the opposition deputy for Kayseri, criticised the proposal as unconstitutional, adding that if the bill were passed, the fact that the officers and troops of Monastir would automatically be guilty might only provoke them further still.[39] Vartkes Serengülyan, the socialist deputy

---

[34] "Salonika Letter," *The Near East*, July 12, 1912, p.295.

[35] "The Turkish Military Revolt: Divided Government Counsels," *The Times*, June 29, 1912, p.5; "The Turkish Revolt: Pessimism in Vienna," *The Times*, July 4, 1912, p.5; "Salonika Letter," *The Near East*, July 12, 1912, p.295. See also, Ziya Şakir [Soko], "Hürriyet ve İtilâf Nasıl Doğdu? Nasıl Yaşadı? Nasıl Battı? 51: Prens Sabahattin Bey'in Yalısındaki Toplantılar," *Tan*, December 30, 1937, p.9.

[36] II/I/22, June 16, 1328/June 29, 1912, *Meclis-i Mebusan Zabıt Ceridesi*, *1*, pp.537-539; "Mahmud Şevket Paşa'nın Beyanatı," *İktiham*, June 17, 1328/June 30, 1912, p.2; Babanzade İsmail Hakkı, "Asker ve Siyaset," *Tanin*, June 17, 1328/June 30, 1912, p.1; "Asker ve Siyaset," *Tanin*, June 17, 1328/June 30, 1912, p.1; "Notes of the Week," *The Near East*, July 5, 1912, p.261; Hüseyin Cahid Yalçın, "Meşrutiyet Hatıraları, 1908-1918," *Fikir Hareketleri*, 7 (October 24, 1936-April 17, 1937), p.166; and, Ahmet Turan Alkan, *İkinci Meşrutiyet Devrinde Ordu ve Siyaset*, p.133.

[37] II/I/23, June 18, 1328/July 1, 1912, *Meclis-i Mebusan Zabıt Ceridesi*, *1*, pp.543-546; and, Mehmet Saray, "Devlet Yönetiminde Ordunun Yeri ve Rolü Hakkında bir Örnek: İttihat ve Terakki Devrinde Ordunun Millet ve Devlet Yönetimine Tesiri," pp.87-88. See also, Babanzade İsmail Hakkı, "Harbiye Nazırının Nutku," *Tanin*, June 19, 1328/July 2, 1912, p.1; and, Ahmet Turan Alkan, *İkinci Meşrutiyet Devrinde Ordu ve Siyaset*, pp.144-145.

[38] II/I/23, June 18, 1328/July 1, 1912, *Meclis-i Mebusan Zabıt Ceridesi*, *1*, pp.546-549. See also, Mehmet Saray, "Devlet Yönetiminde Ordunun Yeri ve Rolü Hakkında bir Örnek: İttihat ve Terakki Devrinde Ordunun Millet ve Devlet Yönetimine Tesiri," pp.88-89; and, Yusuf Hikmet Bayur, *Türk İnkılâbı Tarihi*, 2/1, p.258.

[39] II/I/23, June 18, 1328/July 1, 1912, *Meclis-i Mebusan Zabıt Ceridesi*, *1*,

for Erzurum, responded to the monarchist rhetoric of Ali Galib Bey by denouncing any political party which leaned on military support.[40] The bill, prohibiting all political meetings and demonstrations by the military, as well as its taking any part in any political struggle, passed that day.[41]

The government's measures to deal with the revolt, however, provoked little more than its own embarrassment. After having announced that loyal troops at Monastir would pursue the deserters rigorously, the Cabinet was informed that the garrison could not be counted upon to take action against its comrades. The government then ordered Abdullah Pasha, its commander in İzmir, to send a detachment of his troops to the afflicted region. However, Abdullah Pasha was also actively working with the monarchists and the Albanian rebels; so he curtly replied that no Turkish officer would take the field against his brother officers. Troops, however, were eventually dispatched to Monastir. Nonetheless, the Government, now aware of the strength and extent of its opposition, was not prepared to risk civil war, and while some pushed for strong military action, others continued to support the ongoing negotiations with Tayyar Bey Tetova conducted through officers of the Monastir and Salonica garrisons who acted as the government's representatives.[42]

Unable to rely on other troops in Macedonia, the Government sent in an entire division from the Dardanelles. Though

---

pp.550-554; and, Mehmet Saray, "Devlet Yönetiminde Ordunun Yeri ve Rolü Hakkında bir Örnek: İttihat ve Terakki Devrinde Ordunun Millet ve Devlet Yönetimine Tesiri," pp.88-89.

[40] II/I/23, June 18, 1328/July 1, 1912, *Meclis-i Mebusan Zabıt Ceridesi, 1,* pp.555-557.

[41] II/I/23, June 18, 1328/July 1, 1912, *Meclis-i Mebusan Zabıt Ceridesi, 1,* pp.570-578; "Troops Sent to Monastir: Officers and Politics," *The Times,* July 2, 1912, p.5; and, "Salonika Letter," *The Near East,* July 12, 1912, p.295. The bill, however, did not become law immediately. Before the other required procedures were carried out, Mahmud Şevket Pasha was forced to resign. After the *coup d'état* of July 1912, Nâzım Pasha, the new monarchist Minister of War, deferring to the wishes of the monarchist deputies, delayed the carrying out of the remaining formalities for three months, and the bill was finally published in October 1912 (*Takvim-i Vekayi,* September 27, 1328/October 10, 1912, cited in Celal Bayar, *Ben de Yazdım, 2,* p.516). See also, Ahmet Turan Alkan, *İkinci Meşrutiyet Devrinde Ordu ve Siyaset,* p.146.

[42] "The Turkish Military Revolt: Official Statements," *The Times,* June 29, 1912, p.5; "The Monastir Mutiny: Situation at Monastir," *The Times,* July 1, 1912, p.5; "The Monastir Mutiny: Hopes of a Compromise," *The Times,* July 3, 1912, p.5; "Notes of the Week," *The Near East,* July 5, 1912, p.261; and, Aram Andonyan, *Balkan Savaşı,* p.176.

it contained elements which were decidedly hostile to the Committee of Union and Progress, the army was by no means unanimously anti-Unionist, and most officers wished to avoid a military conflagration at all costs. These supported a cover-up of the Monastir episode which involved letting the mutineers escape without much punishment. Mahmud Şevket Pasha and the leaders of the Committee of Union and Progress, however, declared that while those deserters who surrendered within a given period would be dealt with as mildly as possible, those who refused would be punished with the utmost severity. Yet, neither the Minister of War nor the Unionists could feel at all secure; they were relying largely on the patriotism of the officer class to prevent any extension of the movement.[43]

There was little doubt that there had been signs of disaffection among the troops at İzmir, Edirne, and to a certain extent Erzurum and Erzincan.[44] At İzmir, the army, six divisions strong and under the command of the anti-Unionist Abdullah Pasha, demonstrated in sympathy with the mutineers.[45] On July 6, the Commander of the Damascus Army Corps detained two officers for their involvement in political demonstrations. The officers of the garrison demanded their release, which was at first refused. The garrison then went on

---

[43] "The Monastir Mutiny: The Committee and the Movement," *The Times*, July 1, 1912, p.5; "Troops Sent to Monastir: Officers and Politics," *The Times*, July 2, 1912, p.5; "The Monastir Mutiny: The Movement of Turkish Troops," *The Times*, July 3, 1912, p.5; "Constantinople Letter," *The Near East*, July 12, 1912, p.295; and, Aram Andonyan, *Balkan Savaşı*, p.176.

[44] "The Monastir Mutiny: The Committee and the Movement," *The Times*, July 1, 1912, p.5; and, "Constantinople Letter," *The Near East*, July 12, 1912, p.295.

[45] "Constantinople Letter," *The Near East*, July 19, 1912, p.323; and, Aram Andonyan, *Balkan Savaşı*, p.176. See also, Ziya Şakir [Soko], "Hürriyet ve İtilâf Nasıl Doğdu? Nasıl Yaşadı? Nasıl Battı? 52: Sait Paşa Adeta Tehditkâr bir Vaziyet Almıştı," *Tan*, December 31, 1937, p.9.
     The American Consul at İzmir filed this report on Abdullah Pasha's complicity in overthrowing the constitutional regime: "I am credibly informed that Abdullah, with various of his officers have been meeting in a house at Seydiköy, near Smyrna, where they have been receiving from forty to fifty cipher telegrams per day from the different military centers of the Empire. ... It is worthy of notice that many of the leading officers of the army are Albanians or Arabs, who have been disaffected by the policy which the Committee has been pursuing with reference to these two provinces. It is more than probable that the recent disturbances in Albania have been approved of if not actually connived at by army officers here and elsewhere" (Consul George Horton to Secretary of State, Smyrna, July 25, 1912, in *Records of the Department of State Relating to Internal Affairs of Turkey, 1910-1929*, Roll 4).

strike, adopting such a hostile attitude that the commander was finally forced to release the officers. Additionally, the commanders of one or two isolated battalions on the Anatolian coastline reported that their officers had made the same demands as the Monastir mutineers.[46]

On the night of July 9, Mahmud Şevket Pasha resigned his portfolio, stating that it would be more fitting for someone else to enforce the new law concerning political activity within the military.[47] As his resignation was the result of an League of Saviour Officers ultimatum, he was the first to be sacrificed to the exigencies of the situation.[48]

Mahmud Şevket Pasha's resignation was followed by that of his cousin and brother-in-law, Hadi Pasha, Chief of the General Staff, who had replaced İzzet Pasha when the latter went to Yemen.[49] Monarchists had been against his appointment to that post.[50] Other high officers were also expected to resign, including İsmail Hakkı Pasha, Chief of Provisions.[51]

[46] "Constantinople Letter," *The Near East*, July 19, 1912, p.323.

[47] "Mahmud Şevket Paşa'nın İstifası," *Tanin*, June 27, 1328/July 10, 1912, p.2; "Harbiye Nazırı'nın İstifası," *İktiham*, June 27, 1328/July 10, 1912, p.1; "The Turkish Cabinet: Committee and War Minister," *The Times*, July 10, 1912, p.5; "The Turkish Mutiny: Resignation of the War Minister, *The Times*, July 11, 1912, p.6; "Constantinople Letter," *The Near East*, July 19, 1912, p.323; Mehmed Cavid, "Meşrutiyet Devrine Ait Cavid Bey'in Hatıraları: 134," *Tanin*, January 15, 1944, p.2; and, Hüseyin Cahid Yalçın, "Meşrutiyet Hatıraları, 1908-1918," *Fikir Hareketleri*, 7 (October 24, 1936-April 17, 1937), p.180. See also, Edwin Pears, *Forty Years in Constantinople: The Recollections of Sir Edwin Pears, 1873-1915*, p..325; Yusuf Hikmet Bayur, *Türk İnkılâbı Tarihi*, 2/1, p.258; Ahmet Turan Alkan, *İkinci Meşrutiyet Devrinde Ordu ve Siyaset*, p.147; and, Aram Andonyan, *Balkan Savaşı*, p.176.

[48] "The Army and the Government," *The Times*, July 11, 1912, p.6; "The Situation in Turkey," *The Near East*, July 19, 1912, p.334; Ziya Şakir [Soko], "Hürriyet ve İtilâf Nasıl Doğdu? Nasıl Yaşadı? Nasıl Battı? 51: Prens Sabahattin Bey'in Yalısındaki Toplantılar," *Tan*, December 30, 1937, p.9; and, Ahmet Turan Alkan, *İkinci Meşrutiyet Devrinde Ordu ve Siyaset*, p.147. See also, Babanzade İsmail Hakkı, "Mahmud Şevket Paşa," *Tanin*, June 28, 1328/July 11, 1912, p.1; and, "Mahmud Shevket's Fall: England and Turkey," *The Times*, July 12, 1912, p.5. Hasan Amca, who belonged to the League of Saviour Officers, has a completely different—and, wrong—view of the event (Hasan Amca, *Doğmayan Hürriyet: Bir Devrin İçyüzü, 1908-1918*, p.101). For Bayur's interpretation of the resignation see, Yusuf Hikmet Bayur, *Türk İnkılâbı Tarihi*, 2/1, pp.259-260.

[49] "The Turkish Mutiny: Resignation of the War Minister, *The Times*, July 11, 1912, p.6; and, "Constantinople Letter," *The Near East*, July 19, 1912, p.323.

[50] "Mahmud Shevket's Fall: Feeling in the Army," *The Times*, July 13, 1912, p.5.

[51] *Tanin*, July 2, 1328/July 15, 1912, cited in Hüseyin Cahid Yalçın, "Meşrutiyet Hatıraları, 1908-1918," *Fikir Hareketleri*, 7 (October 24, 1936-April 17, 1937), p.181; and, Aram Andonyan, *Balkan Savaşı*, pp.176-177. See also, Hasan Amca, *Doğmayan Hürriyet: Bir Devrin İçyüzü, 1908-1918*, p.101; and, Yusuf Hikmet Bayur, *Türk İnkılâbı Tarihi*, 2/1, p.259.

Meanwhile, counter-revolutionaries sent a stream of threatening letters to leaders of the Committee of Union and Progress, expressing their designs to assassinate certain Ministers and leaders of the Committee of Union and Progress, and at the same time, spread rumours designed to destabilise the Government. In İzmir, hand bills printed by the League of Saviour Officers were distributed both among the troops and the civilian population. *Müsavat*, a monarchist paper there, also printed unfounded stories that several Cabinet members, including Mahmud Şevket Pasha, had been assassinated.[52]

Said Pasha asked the Minister of the Navy, Hurşid Pasha, to take over the Ministry of War as Acting Minister. The latter, however, was of the opinion that the whole Cabinet should resign. Under pressure from Said Pasha, he reluctantly accepted and was appointed pending the selection of a successor.[53] Said Pasha then offered the job to Abdullah Pasha, Commander of the Army at İzmir, who declined the offer on the grounds of 'competence.'[54] Nâzım, Turgut Şevket, Abdullah, İbrahim, and Tatar Osman Pashas were all considered possible successors, and although Turgut and Nâzım Pashas had both refused, monarchist press hoped that Nâzım Pasha, who had been holding long talks with the Cabinet, might reconsider.[55] Not wanting to further strain an already delicate situation, the Government clearly hoped to resolve the Ministry question as quickly as possible. There was, however, some hope that the

---

[52] Şerafettin Turan, "İkinci Meşrutiyet Döneminde Ordu-Yönetim İlişkileri," p.74; and, Hüseyin Cahid Yalçın, "Meşrutiyet Hatıraları, 1908-1918," *Fikir Hareketleri*, 7 (October 24, 1936-April 17, 1937), p.181. See also, Mehmet Saray, "Devlet Yönetiminde Ordunun Yeri ve Rolü Hakkında bir Örnek: İttihat ve Terakki Devrinde Ordunun Millet ve Devlet Yönetimine Tesiri," pp.90-91.

[53] "Mahmud Şevket Paşa'nın İstifası," *Tanin*, June 27, 1328/July 10, 1912, p.2; "The Turkish Mutiny: Resignation of the War Minister, *The Times*, July 11, 1912, p.6; Celal Bayar, *Ben de Yazdım*, 2, p.519; Hüseyin Cahid Yalçın, "Meşrutiyet Hatıraları, 1908-1918," *Fikir Hareketleri*, 7 (October 24, 1936-April 17, 1937), p.181; and, Yusuf Hikmet Bayur, *Türk İnkılâbı Tarihi*, 2/1, p.272.

[54] "Mahmud Shevket's Fall: Feeling in the Army," *The Times*, July 13, 1912, p.5; "Harbiye Nazırlığı," *İktiham*, June 29, 1328/July 12, 1912, p.1; and, Hüseyin Cahid Yalçın, "Meşrutiyet Hatıraları, 1908-1918," *Fikir Hareketleri*, 7 (October 24, 1936-April 17, 1937), pp.181-182. See also, Yusuf Hikmet Bayur, *Türk İnkılâbı Tarihi*, 2/4, p.215; and, Rifat Uçarol, *Gazi Ahmet Muhtar Paşa: Bir Osmanlı Paşası ve Dönemi*, pp.332-333.

[55] "The Turkish Mutiny: Resignation of the War Minister, *The Times*, July 11, 1912, p.6; "Harbiye Nezareti," *Tanin*, June 29, 1328/July 12, 1912, p.2; "Harbiye Nazırlığı," "Nâzım Paşa," and, "Osman Paşa," *İktiham*, June 29, 1328/July 12, 1912, p.1; and, "Mahmud Shevket's Fall: The Vacant Ministry of War," *The Times*, July 16, 1912, p.5. See also, Yusuf Hikmet Bayur, *Türk İnkılâbı Tarihi*, 2/1, p.272.

division between those officers who had strictly military grievances, and wanted no more than Mahmud Şevket Pasha's resignation, and those who had a definite political programme, which included the resignation of the Cabinet, the overthrow of the Committee of Union and Progress, and the dissolution of the existing Chamber of Deputies, might bring about a compromise and save the country from a *pronunciamento*.[56]

When Said Pasha asked Nâzım Pasha to take the Ministry of War, the latter had made his acceptance conditional on several points. First, he stated that he would not vigorously pursue the Monastir rebels; second, he demanded that martial law be lifted and a general amnesty declared; third, he wanted the creation of a new office, Supreme Commander, the responsibilities of which would be given to the Minister of War. The Unionist leadership indicated that whereas they were willing to accept the first two conditions, they could not accept the third, pointing out that, as stipulated in the Constitution, only the Sultan himself could be considered Supreme Commander. Nâzım Pasha, however, insisted and was duly passed over as a candidate for the Ministry of War.[57]

Then, Said Pasha offered the position to Mahmud Muhtar Pasha. Made on July 16, this offer would be the Cabinet's last chance to hold its ground.[58] Mahmud Muhtar Pasha predicated his acceptance on conditions similar to the first two Nâzım Pasha had presented, and though the Committee of Union and Progress agreed, he eventually declined the of-

---

[56] "Constantinople Letter," *The Near East*, July 19, 1912, p.323. See also, Şehbenderzade Filibeli Ahmed Hilmi, *Muhalefetin İflâsı: İtilâf ve Hürriyet Fırkası*, pp.47-48.

[57] "Nâzım Paşa," *İktiham*, June 29, 1328/July 12, 1912, p.1; "Mahmud Şevket's Fall: The Difficulties of the Cabinet," *The Times*, July 13, 1912, p.5; "Harbiye Nezareti," *Tanin*, June 30, 1328/July 13, 1912, p.2; "Harbiye Nazırlığı ve Nâzım Paşa," *İktiham*, June 30, 1328/July 13, 1912, p.1; "Nâzım Paşa—Harbiye Nazırlığı," *İktiham*, July 1, 1328/July 14, 1912, p.1; "Turkish Politicians and the War: The Cabinet Crisis," *The Times*, July 15, 1912, p.5; "Nâzım Paşa'nın Şeraiti," *İktiham*, July 4, 1328/July 17, 1912, p.1; Mehmed Cavid, "Meşrutiyet Devrine Ait Cavid Bey'in Hatıraları: 135," *Tanin*, January 16, 1944, p.2; Hüseyin Cahid Yalçın, "Meşrutiyet Hatıraları, 1908-1918," *Fikir Hareketleri*, 7 (October 24, 1936-April 17, 1937), p.181; and, Aram Andonyan, *Balkan Savaşı*, p.177.

[58] "Harbiye Nezareti," *İktiham*, July 4, 1328/July 17, 1912, p.1; "The Situation in Turkey," *The Near East*, July 19, 1912, p.334; and, Mehmed Cavid, "Meşrutiyet Devrine Ait Cavid Bey'in Hatıraları: 136," *Tanin*, January 17, 1944, p.2.

fer.[59] Nonetheless, that day, the press announced that Mahmud Muhtar Pasha had been named to the post. The imperial decree confirming the appointment, however, was never issued.[60]

The pashas had been acting in collusion all along, and their persistent refusals had left the Unionist-backed Said Pasha Cabinet in an extremely difficult position.[61] And it was at this critical juncture that Hurşid Pasha, also involved in the League of Saviour Officers—fearing that if Mahmud Muhtar Pasha were forced to accept the post, the Cabinet might be saved and the *coup* crushed—resigned.[62] His resignation had the intended effect: Despite the advice of Cavid and Talât Beys who had insistently refused to succumb to monarchist intimidation, Said Pasha resigned.[63]

On July 17, the Said Pasha Cabinet resigned—just two days after it had been given an overwhelming one hundred ninety-four to four vote of confidence. That day both Said Pasha and Asım Bey, Minister for Foreign Affairs, had made well-received speeches in the Chamber of Deputies on both the domestic unrest and its effect on international relations.[64]

---

[59] "New Turkish War Minister: Mahmud Mukhtar's Career," *The Times*, July 17, 1912, p.5; "The Sultan and the Crisis: Said Pasha's Resignation," *The Times*, July 19, 1912, p.5; Hüseyin Cahid Yalçın, "Meşrutiyet Hatıraları, 1908-1918," *Fikir Hareketleri*, 7 (October 24, 1936-April 17, 1937), p.182; Mustafa Ragıb Esatlı, *İttihat ve Terakki Tarihinde Esrar Perdesi: Yakup Cemil Niçin ve Nasıl Öldürüldü?* p.100; Mehmed Cavid, "Meşrutiyet Devrine Ait Cavid Bey'in Hatıraları: 136," *Tanin*, January 17, 1944, p.2; Mahmud Muhtar Pasha, *La Turquie*, p.159 (All cited in Feroz Ahmad, *The Young Turks: The Committee of Union and Progress in Turkish Politics, 1908-1914*, p.107). See also, Mahmud Muhtar Paşa, *Maziye Bir Nazar*, p.157. See also, Yusuf Hikmet Bayur, *Türk İnkılâbı Tarihi, 2/4*, pp.215-217; and, Rifat Uçarol, *Gazi Ahmet Muhtar Paşa: Bir Osmanlı Paşası ve Dönemi*, p.333.

[60] "New Turkish War Minister: Mahmud Mukhtar's Career," *The Times*, July 17, 1912, p.5; and, "The Situation in Turkey," *The Near East*, July 19, 1912, p.334.

[61] Ziya Şakir [Soko], "Hürriyet ve İtilâf Nasıl Doğdu? Nasıl Yaşadı? Nasıl Battı? 52: Sait Paşa Adeta Tehditkâr bir Vaziyet Almıştı," *Tan*, December 31, 1937, p.9. See also, Yusuf Hikmet Bayur, *Türk İnkılâbı Tarihi, 2/1*, p.272.

[62] Mahmud Muhtar Paşa, *Maziye Bir Nazar*, p.157; and, Hüseyin Cahid Yalçın, "Meşrutiyet Hatıraları, 1908-1918," *Fikir Hareketleri*, 7 (October 24, 1936-April 17, 1937), p.182.

[63] "Salonika Letter," *The Near East*, July 26, 1912, p.351; Mehmed Cavid, "Meşrutiyet Devrine Ait Cavid Bey'in Hatıraları: 136," *Tanin*, January 17, 1944, p.2; and Hüseyin Cahid Yalçın, "Meşrutiyet Hatıraları, 1908-1918," *Fikir Hareketleri*, 7 (October 24, 1936-April 17, 1937), p.182. See also, Yusuf Hikmet Bayur, *Türk İnkılâbı Tarihi, 2/1*, p.277.

[64] Mehmed Cavid, "Meşrutiyet Devrine Ait Cavid Bey'in Hatıraları: 137," *Tanin*, January 18, 1944, p.2; Babanzade İsmail Hakkı, "Buhrandan Buhrana," *Ta-*

Although Asım Bey had tendered his resignation four
times during the cabinet crisis, Talât Bey had consistently
prevented it. When Hurşid Pasha finally resigned, leaving
both the Ministry of the Navy and of War empty, Said Pasha
had told the leadership of the Committee of Union and Progress that it would be impossible to carry on. In order to gain
time, however, Talât Bey urged Said Pasha to postpone his resignation, and Said Pasha acquiesced, waiting another day before submitting the cabinet's resignation to the Sultan.[65]

The previous Hakkı Pasha Cabinet had been forced to resign, at the beginning of the war with Italy, owing to popular
indignation over its failure to avoid the war or make adequate
preparations for it. Said Pasha had filled the gap with a nominally non-party Cabinet, though before long the Committee of
Union and Progress had seen fit to strengthen its position by
placing some of its leaders in the cabinet. This process of
consolidation was then applied to the Chamber, where the
elections were carefully designed to secure parliamentary
support for the Committee of Union and Progress. From that
moment on, the fate of the cabinet was sealed. Internal dissensions within its ranks became acute; the monarchist opposition now had an invaluable rallying cry, while at the same
time, dissatisfaction among the military could only grow, in-

---

nin, July 5, 1328/July 18, 1912, p.1; "Buhran-ı Vükelâ: Said Paşa'nın İstifası—Esbab-ı İstifa," *Tanin,* July 5, 1328/July 18, 1912, pp.1-2; "İstifa," *Tanin,* July 5, 1328/
July 18, 1912, p.2; "Buhran-ı Vükelâ," "Said Paşa'nın Konağında," and "Kabul-ü
İstifa Tebliği," *İktiham,* July 5, 1328/July 18, 1912, p.1; "Resignation of the Cabinet: Growing Difficulties in Albania," *The Times,* July 18, 1912, p.6; Feroz Ahmad,
*The Young Turks: The Committee of Union and Progress in Turkish Politics,
1908-1914,* p.107; Edwin Pears, *Forty Years in Constantinople: The Recollections of
Sir Edwin Pears, 1873-1915,* p.325; Yusuf Hikmet Bayur, *Türk İnkılâbı Tarihi, 2/I,*
p.275; and, Ahmed Bedevi Kuran, *Osmanlı İmparatorluğunda İnkılâp Hareketleri ve Milli Mücadele,* p.567. See also, Ahmed İzzet, *Feryadım, 1,* p.116. The letter of
resignation was dated July 15, 1912. It was made public with the *Takvim-i Vekayi,*
July 18, 1912. The text of the resignation letter can also be found in Celal Bayar,
Ben de Yazdım, 2, pp.536-537.
    II/I/33, July 2, 1328/July 15, 1912, *Meclis-i Mebusan Zabıt Ceridesi, 2,*
pp.315-336; "The Situation in Turkey," *The Near East,* July 19, 1912, p.334. "Hükûmetin İzahataı: Üç Nutk-u Mühim—Bir Kitle-i İttihad," *Tanin,* July 3, 1328/July
16, 1912, pp.1-4; İbnülemin Mahmud Kemal İnal, *Osmanlı Devrinde Son Sadrıazamlar,* p.1089. Yalçın writes that the Cabinet had received a vote of confidence by
196 votes (Hüseyin Cahid Yalçın, "Meşrutiyet Hatıraları, 1908-1918," *Fikir Hareketleri,* 7 (October 24, 1936-April 17, 1937), p.182).
    [65] Mehmed Cavid, "Meşrutiyet Devrine Ait Cavid Bey'in Hatıraları: 136," *Ta-
nin,* January 17, 1944, p.2; and, Letter of Hakkı Baha [Pars], Unionist deputy for
Bursa, to Celal [Bayar], Unionist local party member, İstanbul, July 12, 1328/July
25, 1912, reproduced in full in Celal Bayar, *Ben de Yazdım, 2,* pp.523-526.

separable as it was from the Unionist policy of consolidating its power.[66]

After Mahmud Şevket Pasha's resignation, the League of Saviour Officers had prepared a proclamation in which they demanded the immediate resignation of the Said Pasha Cabinet, the dissolution of the Chamber, and appointment of Kâmil Pasha to the Grand Vezierate. On July 18, the League of Saviour Officers gave its proclamation to Hurşid Pasha and Nâzım Pasha.[67] Hurşid Pasha brought it to the attention of the Cabinet. The Cabinet members who were present during the ensuing discussion were Said Pasha, Hacı Âdil [Arda], Minister of the Interior, Talât Bey, Minister of Posts, Hayri Bey, Minister of Pious Foundations, and Asım Bey, Minister for Foreign Affairs. Hacı Âdil [Arda] and Talât Bey urged Hurşid Pasha to use force against the rebellious officers. Hurşid Pasha, however, rejected any such plan and recommended that the proclamation be presented to the Sultan.[68] The Cabinet was at an impasse. Said Pasha summoned Nâzım Pasha to the Sublime Porte, but Nâzım Pasha refused, agreeing with Hurşid Pasha that the ultimatum should be immediately referred to the Sultan, something he himself was prepared to do.[69] The Cabinet, however, decided that if the Sultan needed to be informed of the situation, Said Pasha should be the one to do it. Nonetheless, Hurşid Pasha took matters into his own hands and went to the Palace.[70] The Sultan then summoned Said Pasha and requested that the Cabinet draft a conciliatory

---

[66] "The Situation in Turkey," *The Near East*, July 19, 1912, p.334. See also, F.O. 424/232, Major Tyrrell to Mr. Marling, Constantinople, July 29, 1912, *Further Correspondence Respecting the Affairs of Asiatic Turkey and Arabia, Part VII*, No.10164, pp.99-100.

[67] Letter of Hakkı Baha [Pars], Unionist deputy for Bursa, to Celal [Bayar], Unionist local party member, İstanbul, July 12, 1328/July 25, 1912, reproduced in full in Celal Bayar, *Ben de Yazdım*, 2 , pp.523-526. See also, Şehbenderzade Filibeli Ahmed Hilmi, *Muhalefetin İflâsı: İtilâf ve Hürriyet Fırkası*, p.47.

[68] "Hurşid Paşa'nın Kabine Hatıraları," *Hayat*, January 23, 1964, p.5, quoted in Celal Bayar, *Ben de Yazdım*, 2, p.533.

[69] "Hurşid Paşa'nın Kabine Hatıraları," *Hayat*, January 23, 1964, p.5, quoted in Celal Bayar, *Ben de Yazdım*, 2, pp.533-534.

[70] Letter of Hakkı Baha [Pars], Unionist deputy for Bursa, to Celal [Bayar], Unionist local party member, İstanbul, July 12, 1328/July 25, 1912, reproduced in full in Celal Bayar, *Ben de Yazdım*, 2 , pp.523-526. Hursid Pasha claims that he was authorised to see the Sultan and present the military ultimatom ("Hurşid Paşa'nın Kabine Hatıraları," *Hayat*, January 23, 1964, p.5, quoted in Celal Bayar, *Ben de Yazdım*, 2, p.534).

proclamation, addressing the military's grievances. The Cabinet then prepared its proclamation and submitted it for the Sultan's approval. That night, however, Nâzım, Hurşid, and Hadi Pashas revised the proclamation, deleting, among other things, all references to the punishment of rebellious officers. Seeing the altered text in the newspapers the next day, the Cabinet met and declared that this constituted a serious breach of constitutional rules.[71]

On July 17, the Sultan again offered Tevfik Pasha, the monarchist pasha who had been appointed Grand Vezier during the April, 1909 *coup*, the helm of the government.[72] In its response to the League of Saviour Officers, the government reprimanded the rebellious officers for having interfered in politics. The proclamation announced that the Sultan had consulted the Presidents of both the Chamber and the Senate, and with their consent, had invited Tevfik Pasha to take the post of Grand Vezier. The Sultan added that the new cabinet would be composed of those who had wide experience of matters of State, independent views, and that this cabinet would be free from all outside influences.[73] In essence, this meant the establishment of a conservative government composed mostly of old regime pashas—most likely, under the grand veziership of Kâmil Pasha—with the aim of keeping the Unionists out of

[71] Mehmed Cavid, "Meşrutiyet Devrine Ait Cavid Bey'in Hatıraları: 137," *Tanin*, January 18, 1944, p.2; and, Letter of Hakkı Baha [Pars], Unionist deputy for Bursa, to Celal [Bayar], Unionist local party member, İstanbul, July 12, 1328/July 25, 1912, reproduced in full in Celal Bayar, *Ben de Yazdım, 2?*, pp.523-526. For the text of this imperial proclamation see, "Beyanname-i Padişahi," *Tanin*, July 7, 1328/July 20, 1912, p.1.

[72] "Resignation of the Cabinet: Growing Difficulties in Albania," *The Times*, July 18, 1912, p.6; "Meclis Koridorlarında," *İktiham*, July 5, 1328/July 18, 1912, p.2; "Tevfik Paşa'ya Teklif," *Tanin*, July 5, 1328/July 18, 1912, p.2; "The Sultan and the Crisis: Said Pasha's Resignation," *The Times*, July 19, 1912, p.5; Ziya Şakir [Soko], "Hürriyet ve İtilâf Nasıl Doğdu? Nasıl Yaşadı? Nasıl Battı? 52: Sait Paşa Adeta Tehditkâr bir Vaziyet Almıştı," *Tan*, December 31, 1937, p.9; and, Yusuf Hikmet Bayur, *Türk İnkılâbı Tarihi, 2/1*, p.277. Tevfik Pasha was Ambassador at London at this juncture ("The Situation in Turkey," *The Near East*, July 19, 1912, p.334). See also, Hüseyin Cahid Yalçın, "Meşrutiyet Hatıraları, 1908-1918," *Fikir Hareketleri*, 7 (October 24, 1936-April 17, 1937), p.197.

[73] "Notes of the Week," *The Near East*, July 26, 1912, p.349. The whole text of this proclamation, dated July 6, 1328/July 19, 1912, can be found in "Beyanname-i Padişahi," *Tanin*, July 7, 1328/July 20, 1912, p.1, Hüseyin Cahid Yalçın, "Meşrutiyet Hatıraları, 1908-1918," *Fikir Hareketleri*, 7 (October 24, 1936-April 17, 1937), p.197, and İbnülemin Mahmud Kemal İnal, *Osmanlı Devrinde Son Sadrıazamlar*, pp.1713-1714. See also, Yusuf Hikmet Bayur, *Türk İnkılâbı Tarihi, 2/1*, pp.278-279.

power.[74]

Tevfik Pasha's conditions for accepting the Grand Veziership, however, were the lifting of the martial law, the proclamation of general amnesty, the dissolution of the Chamber of Deputies and the abolition of the 'secret' societies and political organisations—meaning, the closing down of the Committee of Union and Progress. Naturally, the Unionists rejected these demands, and Tevfik Pasha was passed over as a nominee for the Grand Veziership.[75]

The situation was clearly deadlocked. As forces operating outside established parliamentary rules had forced the Said Pasha Cabinet to resign, it was clear that the monarchist opposition aspired to a totally anti-Unionist Grand Vezier and cabinet. This could only be thoroughly unacceptable to the Committee of Union and Progress and the predominantly anti-monarchist Chamber.[76] The names of Ferid Pasha and Kâmil Pasha had also been circulated by the monarchists, but the leadership of the Committee of Union and Progress had also successfully resisted their nominations.[77] In the case of Kâmil Pasha, Talât Bey had even urged Halid Ziya [Uşaklıgil], Secretary to the Sultan, to use his influence with the Sultan to block the nomination, indicating that it might well lead to civil war.[78]

---

[74] Yusuf Hikmet Bayur, *Türk İnkılâbı Tarihi*, 2/1, p.279.

[75] Mehmed Cavid, "Meşrutiyet Devrine Ait Cavid Bey'in Hatıraları: 138," *Tanin*, January 19, 1944, p.2; "The Sultan and the Crisis: Tewfik Pasha's Plans," *The Times*, July 19, 1912, p.5; "The Turkish Crisis: Tewfik Pasha to Form a Cabinet," *The Times*, July 20, 1912, p.8; "Buhran-ı Vükelâ: Tevfik Paşa," and "Tevfik Paşa'nın Sadareti Hakkında," *İktiham*, July 7, 1328/July 20, 1912, p.2; "Notes of the Week," *The Near East*, July 26, 1912, p.349; and, Ziya Şakir [Soko], "Hürriyet ve İtilâf Nasıl Doğdu? Nasıl Yaşadı? Nasıl Battı? 52: Sait Paşa Adeta Tehditkâr bir Vaziyet Almıştı," *Tan*, December 31, 1937, p.9. See also, Rifat Uçarol, *Gazi Ahmet Muhtar Paşa: Bir Osmanlı Paşası ve Dönemi*, p.337.

[76] Hüseyin Cahid Yalçın, "Meşrutiyet Hatıraları, 1908-1918," *Fikir Hareketleri*, 7 (October 24, 1936-April 17, 1937), p.197; and, Mehmed Cavid, "Meşrutiyet Devrine Ait Cavid Bey'in Hatıraları: 138," *Tanin*, January 19, 1944, p.2. See also, *Osmanischer Lloyd* of July 19, 1912, excerpted in "Yeni Kabine Hakkında," *İktiham*, July 7, 1328/July 20, 1912, p.2. See also, Şehbenderzade Filibeli Ahmed Hilmi, *Muhalefetin İflâsı: İtilâf ve Hürriyet Fırkası*, pp.52-55.

[77] "Tevfik Paşa Kabinesi," *İktiham*, July 8, 1328/July 21, 1912, p.1; Halid Ziya Uşaklıgil, *Saray ve Ötesi*, 3, p.47; Ali Fuad Türkgeldi, *Görüp İşittiklerim*, p.49; and, Rifat Uçarol, *Gazi Ahmet Muhtar Paşa: Bir Osmanlı Paşası ve Dönemi*, p.338.

[78] "Kiamil Pasha's Position," *The Times*, July 8, 1912, p.5; Halid Ziya Uşaklıgil, *Saray ve Ötesi*, 3, p.47; Ali Fuad Türkgeldi, *Görüp İşittiklerim*, p.49; Mustafa Ragıb Esatlı, *İttihat ve Terakki Tarihinde Esrar Perdesi: Yakup Cemil Niçin ve Nasıl Öldürüldü?* p.106; and, Yusuf Hikmet Bayur, *Türk İnkılâbı Tarihi*, 2/1, pp.279-280.

Described by its adherents as the 'Grand Cabinet,' the new Cabinet was formed on July 21, under the presidency of Gazi Ahmed Muhtar Pasha.[79] It included Gabriel Nouradunghian, the monarchist senator and now Minister for Foreign Affairs, Avlonyalı Mehmed Ferid Pasha, the deposed Grand Vezier of the absolutist regime and now Minister of the Interior, Hüseyin Hilmi Pasha, ex-Grand Vezier and now Minister of Justice, Nâzım Pasha, member of the Council of War and now Minister of War, Mahmud Muhtar Pasha, Minister of the Navy, Said Bey, Under-Secretary of the Ministry of Education and now Minister of Education, Ziya Pasha as Minister of Finance, Damad Şerif Pasha, President of the Civil Bureaucracy Section of the Council of State and now Minister of Public Works, Reşid Pasha, ex-Ambassador to Vienna, now Minister of Commerce and Agriculture, and Muhammad Fawzi Pasha al-'Azm, deputy for Damascus and Vice-President of the Chamber of Deputies, now Minister of Pious Foundations. Kâmil Pasha was named President of the Council of State; Mehmed Cemaleddin Efendi was appointed Sheikh-ul-Islam.[80] With his appointment as Sheikh-ul-Islam Cemaleddin Efendi, who was a member of the Entente Libérale, returned to an office which he had held for many years under the *ancien régime*.[81]

Avlonyalı Mehmed Ferid Pasha, however, had been named to the Ministry of the Interior without either his prior

---

[79] "Muhtar Paşa—Kâmil Paşa Kabinesi, *Iktiham*, July 9, 1328/July 22, 1912, p.1; "New Turkish Cabinet: Mukhtar Pasha Grand Vizier," *The Times*, July 22, 1912, p.5; "Buhranın Nihayeti," *Tanin*, July 9, 1328/July 22, 1912, p.1; and, "Yeni Sadr-ı Âzam," *Tanin*, July 9, 1328/July 22, 1912, p.1. See also, Mehmed Cavid, "Meşrutiyet Devrine Ait Cavid Bey'in Hatıraları: 139," *Tanin*, January 20, 1944, p.2; Hasan Amca, *Doğmayan Hürriyet: Bir Devrin İçyüzü, 1908-1918*, p.105; Ahmed Bedevi Kuran, *Osmanlı İmparatorluğunda İnkılâp Hareketleri ve Milli Mücadele*, p.566; Yusuf Hikmet Bayur, *Türk İnkılâbı Tarihi, 2/1*, pp.279-280; and, Ahmed İzzet, *Feryadım, I*, p.116.

[80] *Takvim-i Vekayi*, July 10, 1328/July 23, 1912, quoted in Celal Bayar, *Ben de Yazdım, 2*, pp.564-565; "The Turkish Cabinet: A Blow to the Extremists," *The Times*, July 23, 1912, p.5; "Constantinople Letter," *The Near East*, August 2, 1912, p.379; and, William W. Rockhill to Secretary of State, Constantinople, July 26, 1912, in *Records of the Department of State Relating to Internal Affairs of Turkey, 1910-1929*, Roll 4. See also, Hüseyin Cahid Yalçın, "Meşrutiyet Hatıraları, 1908-1918," *Fikir Hareketleri, 7* (October 24, 1936-April 17, 1937), p.198. Bayur quite rightly observes that Kâmil Pasha was the 'spiritual leader' of this cabinet (Yusuf Hikmet Bayur, *Türk İnkılâbı Tarihi, 2/1*, p.289).

[81] "The Turkish Cabinet: A Blow to the Extremists," *The Times*, July 23, 1912, p.5. See also, Mehmed Cavid, "Meşrutiyet Devrine Ait Cavid Bey'in Hatıraları: 139," *Tanin*, January 20, 1944, p.2.

knowledge or consent, and he immediately declined the position.[82] Ziya Pasha, the new Minister of Finance, was named as his replacement; in turn, Abdurrahman Bey, a member of the Financial Reform Commission was appointed to the latter's position.[83] However, unable to 'compromise,' Ziya Pasha soon left the Cabinet altogether.[84] Damad Şerif Pasha, the Minister of Public Works, was then appointed in his place, but he too resigned shortly afterwards.[85] The Ministry was then entrusted to Ali Daniş Bey, an Albanian and former governor of Salonica who, after the Revolution, had been dismissed from office for incompetence.[86] Reluctant to appoint such a dubious character, the Sultan had once again offered the post to Avlonyalı Mehmed Ferid Pasha, who had, once again, refused.[87]

But by this time, it was clear that the constant ministerial shuffling was the result of concerted monarchist efforts to force Gazi Ahmed Muhtar Pasha from office, in the hopes of replacing him with Kâmil Pasha. Ferid Pasha had suggested as much in his meetings with Gazi Ahmed Muhtar Pasha.[88]

---

[82] "Ghazi Mukhtar's Cabinet: The Committee and the Government," *The Times*, July 25, 1912, p.5; "Notes of the Week," *The Near East*, July 26, 1912, p.349; "The Turkish Cabinet and the Committee: Withdrawal of Ferid Pasha," *The Times*, July 27, 1912, p.5; "The Turkish Crisis: Cabinet Changes and Appointments," *The Times*, July 29, 1912, p.5; "Constantinople Letter," *The Near East*, August 2, 1912, p.379; Mustafa Ragıb Esatlı, *İttihat ve Terakki Tarihinde Esrar Perdesi: Yakup Cemil Niçin ve Nasıl Öldürüldü?* p.110; and, Mahmud Kemal İnal, *Osmanlı Devrinde Son Sadrıazamlar,* p.1621.

[83] "The Turkish Crisis: Cabinet Changes and Appointments," *The Times*, July 29, 1912, p.5; Mehmed Cavid, "Meşrutiyet Devrine Ait Cavid Bey'in Hatıraları: 140," *Tanin*, January 21, 1944, p.2; Mustafa Ragıb Esatlı, *İttihat ve Terakki Tarihinde Esrar Perdesi: Yakup Cemil Niçin ve Nasıl Öldürüldü?* p.110; and, Celal Bayar, *Ben de Yazdım, 2,* p.565.

[84] Mustafa Ragıb Esatlı, *İttihat ve Terakki Tarihinde Esrar Perdesi: Yakup Cemil Niçin ve Nasıl Öldürüldü?* p.114; Celal Bayar, *Ben de Yazdım, 2,* p.565; and, Yusuf Hikmet Bayur, *Türk İnkılâbı Tarihi, 2/4,* p.225.

[85] "Dahiliye Nezareti," *Tanin*, August 8, 1328/August 21, 1912, p.3; "Şerif Paşa'nın Sebeb-i İstifası," *Tanin*, August 9, 1328/August 22, 1912, p.3; "Boş Nezaretler, " *Tanin*, August 10, 1328/August 23, 1912, p.2; and, Celal Bayar, *Ben de Yazdım, 2,* p.565.

[86] "Dahiliye Nezareti," *Tanin*, August 10, 1328/August 23, 1912, p.2; Mustafa Ragıb Esatlı, *İttihat ve Terakki Tarihinde Esrar Perdesi: Yakup Cemil Niçin ve Nasıl Öldürüldü?* p.115; and, Celal Bayar, *Ben de Yazdım, 2,* p.565.

[87] "Ferid Paşa," *İktiham*, July 13, 1328/July 26, 1912, p.1; "Reşid Bey—Dahiliye Nezareti," *İktiham*, July 14, 1328/July 27, 1912, p.1; and, Celal Bayar, *Ben de Yazdım, 2,* p.566.

[88] Celal Bayar, *Ben de Yazdım, 2,* pp.566-567. See also, Şehbenderzade Filibeli Ahmed Hilmi, *Muhalefetin İflâsı: İtilâf ve Hürriyet Fırkası,* pp.55-56.

The move reportedly began with Hoca Said Efendi, the Entente Libérale's ex-deputy for Üsküb, who, along with several
other Albanian politicians, now openly petitioned to the Palace for these demands.[89]

The blatant instability of the new cabinet worried the Committee of Union and Progress. Whereas monarchists called it
the 'Grand Cabinet,' *Tanin* described it as the 'Cabinet of Revenge,' and along with *Hak*, and, to a lesser degree, *Le Jeune
Turc*, campaigned against it.[90]

On their part, the monarchists realised that the cabinet,
which had come to power without the support either of a parliamentary majority or the Committee of Union and Progress,
left the Entente Libérale vulnerable to retaliation—at least as
long as it failed to dissolve the Parliament.[91]

The League of Saviour Officers—or, Halâskâr Zabitan Grubu—
was a secret military organisation formed sometime in 1911.[92]
Its aim was not only the fall of the Said Pasha Cabinet, but the
complete exclusion of the Committee of Union and Progress
from political life. The organisation hoped to achieve its ends
by threatening the Unionist leadership with nothing short of
violence and death. Accordingly, in a letter dated July 24,
Halid Ziya [Uşaklıgil], the Unionist Secretary to the Sultan,
was told to resign within twenty-four hours and return to
private life or lose his life.[93] On the night of July 29, he, as well
as Lütfi [Simavi], the First Chamberlain, were relieved of their
duties and were replaced by Halid Hurşid Bey, First Secretary
to the Turkish Embassy in Paris, and Rıfat Bey, Assistant
Grand Referandary at the Sublime Porte.[94]

---

[89] Ali Fuad Türkgeldi, *Görüp İşittiklerim*, pp.69-70.

[90] "Meclis ve Hükûmet," *Tanin*, July 19, 1328/August 1, 1912, p.4; "Constantinople Letter," *The Near East*, August 2, 1912, p.379. See also, Rifat Uçarol, *Gazi Ahmet Muhtar Paşa: Bir Osmanlı Paşası ve Dönemi*, p.347.

[91] "Constantinople Letter," *The Near East*, August 2, 1912, p.379; and, Şehbenderzade Filibeli Ahmed Hilmi, *Muhalefetin İflâsı: İtilâf ve Hürriyet Fırkası*, p.52-
54.

[92] Hasan Amca, *Doğmayan Hürriyet: Bir Devrin İçyüzü, 1908-1918*, p.104; Ahmed Bedevi Kuran, *İnkılâp Tarihimiz ve 'Jön Türkler,'* pp.302-303; and, Halid Ziya Uşaklıgil, *Saray ve Ötesi*, 3, pp.40-41. See also, Fethi Tevetoğlu, *Ömer Naci*, 2nd
Edition, pp.137-138.

[93] Halid Ziya Uşaklıgil, *Saray ve Ötesi*, 3, pp.40-41.

[94] "The Turkish Crisis: The Cabinet and the Chamber," *The Times*, July 31,
1912, p.5.

Halil [Menteşe], the Unionist President of the Chamber of Deputies received a similar letter, again, dated July 24.[95] Here, the League of Saviour Officers expressed dissatisfaction with Halil [Menteşe] for having blocked Kâmil Pasha's appointment to the Grand Vezierate, and demanded the dissolution of the Chamber of Deputies. If its demands were not met within forty-eight hours, the League of Saviour Officers promised to assassinate Halil [Menteşe].[96] The latter immediately met with Talât Bey, leader of the Committee of Union and Progress; they decided to take the matter before the Chamber of Deputies.[97]

Halil [Menteşe] presented the letter that following day, and the Chamber reacted energetically.[98] Talât Bey, Seyyid Bey, and Halil [Menteşe] declared that they were prepared to die for the Constitution.[99] Ömer Naci Bey, deputy for Kırk Kilise and a prominent member of the Committee of Union and Progress, made a moving speech in which he denounced the League of Saviour Officers' tactics and aims, and reiterated his and his party's commitment to defend the Revolution and the new constitutional regime against military intervention.[100]

But the most important speech came from Vartkes Seren-

---

[95] Celal Bayar, *Ben de Yazdım*, 2, p.540; and, II/I/40, July 12, 1328/July 25, 1912, *Meclis-i Mebusan Zabıt Ceridesi*, 2, pp.444-449.

[96] The complete text of the letter dated July 11, 1328/July 24, 1912, sent by the Group of Saviour Officers can be found in Celal Bayar, *Ben de Yazdım*, 2, pp.540-541. Hüseyin Cahid Yalçın, "Meşrutiyet Hatıraları, 1908-1918," *Fikir Hareketleri*, 7 (October 24, 1936-April 17, 1937), p.198.

[97] Celal Bayar, *Ben de Yazdım*, 2, p.540.

[98] II/I/40, July 12, 1328/July 25, 1912, *Meclis-i Mebusan Zabıt Ceridesi*, 2, pp.444-449; "The Turkish Chamber: Threatening Letter from the Military League," *The Times*, July 26, 1912, p.5; Mehmed Cavid, "Meşrutiyet Devrine Ait Cavid Bey'in Hatıraları: 140," *Tanin*, January 21, 1944, p.2; and, Mustafa Ragıb Esatlı, *İttihat ve Terakki Tarihinde Esrar Perdesi: Yakup Cemil Niçin ve Nasıl Öldürüldü?* p.109. See also, Yusuf Hikmet Bayur, *Türk İnkılâbı Tarihi*, 2/1, pp.293-294. *İktiham* also published a long proclamation by the League of Saviour Officers on July 25, 1912 ("Halaskâr Zabitan Grubu Beyannamesi," *İktiham*, July 12, 1328/July 25, 1912, p.4). The same proclamation was published in, "Halaskâr Zabitan Grubu'nun Beyannamesi," *Yeni Gazete*, July 12, 1328/July 25, 1912, and, "Halaskâr Zabitan Grubu'nun Programı," *Teminat*, July 12, 1328/July 25, 1912 (Rifat Uçarol, *Gazi Ahmet Muhtar Paşa: Bir Osmanlı Paşası ve Dönemi*, p.358n).

[99] II/I/40, July 12, 1328/July 25, 1912, *Meclis-i Mebusan Zabıt Ceridesi*, 2, pp.444-449; "Constantinople Letter," *The Near East*, August 2, 1912, p.379; Mustafa Ragıb Esatlı, *İttihat ve Terakki Tarihinde Esrar Perdesi: Yakup Cemil Niçin ve Nasıl Öldürüldü?* p.109; and, Hüseyin Cahid Yalçın, "Meşrutiyet Hatıraları, 1908-1918," *Fikir Hareketleri*, 7 (October 24, 1936-April 17, 1937), p.198.

[100] II/I/40, July 12, 1328/July 25, 1912, *Meclis-i Mebusan Zabıt Ceridesi*, 2, pp.445-446. See also Celal Bayar, *Ben de Yazdım*, 2, p.542; and, Fethi Tevetoğlu, *Ömer Naci*, 2nd Edition, pp.139-141.

gülyan, the socialist Armenian deputy for Erzurum, who
joined in the condemnation, adding that they had eliminated
similar charlatans during the pre-revolutionary days and
were prepared to do so again. He went on to say that the
Chamber could not be dissolved through outside pressure, and
he urged his colleagues to turn to the Government for an explanation, at the same time, inviting representatives of the
Government to confess that they had gained power with the
League of Saviour Officers' support. Finally, he ended his
speech by stating that as long as strong adherents to a parliamentary regime remained, the country would never be ruled
by a military dictatorship.[101]

The address was significant in so far as it gave voice to
widespread Unionist dissatisfaction with the way the Said Pasha Cabinet had been forced to resign, and publicly raised the
question of the current military-backed government's legitimacy. Nesim Masliah, a prominent Unionist deputy for İz-
mir, along with the other Jewish and Armenian Unionist
deputies condemned the ultimatum, and demanded that the
Government come to the parliamentary regime's defence.[102]

Meanwhile, monarchist papers were in an unabashedly
festive mood. Not only did they publish the ultimatum in its
entirety, they openly gave the League of Saviour Officers and
its demands their whole-hearted support, urging the Government to obey the rebel officers and dissolve the Chamber.[103]

Eventually, Nâzım Pasha, the monarchist Minister of War,
appeared before the Chamber. He began by saying that the
threatening letter was in all probability a bluff, nonetheless,

[101] II/I/40, July 12, 1328/July 25, 1912, *Meclis-i Mebusan Zabıt Ceridesi*, 2,
pp.446-447. See also, "The Turkish Cabinet and the Committee: Another Military
Threat," *The Times*, July 27, 1912, p.5; and, "The Turkish Crisis: Cabinet Changes
and Appointments," *The Times*, July 29, 1912, p.5.
[102] II/I/40, July 12, 1328/July 25, 1912, *Meclis-i Mebusan Zabıt Ceridesi*, 2,
pp.446-448; "The Turkish Cabinet and the Committee: Another Military Threat,"
The Times, July 27, 1912, p.5; "Constantinople Letter," *The Near East*, August 2,
1912, p.379; Celal Bayar, *Ben de Yazdım*, 2, p.544; and, Hüseyin Cahid Yalçın,
"Meşrutiyet Hatıraları, 1908-1918," *Fikir Hareketleri*, 7 (October 24, 1936-April 17,
1937), p.198.
[103] "Halaskâr Zabitan Grubu Beyannamesi," *İktiham*, July 12, 1328/July 25,
1912, p.4; Hüseyin Cahid Yalçın, "Meşrutiyet Hatıraları, 1908-1918," *Fikir Hareketleri*, 7 (October 24, 1936-April 17, 1937), p.213. Hüseyin Cahid Yalçın, "Hüseyin
Cahid Yalçın'ın 50 Yıllık Siyasi Hatıraları: Meşrutiyet Devri ve Sonrası," No.129,
Halkçı (Yeni Ulus), October 23, 1954, reproduced in Celal Bayar, *Ben de Yazdım*,
2, p.547. See also, Yusuf Hikmet Bayur, *Türk İnkılâbı Tarihi*, 2/1, pp.249-252.

he assured the Chamber that the culprits would be pursued and punished.[104] Seyyid Bey, deputy for İzmir and leader of the parliamentary group of the Committee of Union and Progress, asked Nâzım Pasha what steps he was prepared to take in regard to those newspapers which had publicly endorsed the military organisation's threats. Nâzım Pasha avoided the issue by blaming the press' behaviour on the public and its hunger for sensational news.[105]

Dissatisfied with Nâzım Pasha's answers, the Unionist press attacked the monarchist opposition and took it upon itself to discredit the League of Saviour Officers.[106] Despite threats against Unionist journalists, *Hak* printed an editorial by Süleyman Nazif, entitled "Kılıçlı Siyaset"—*i.e.*, 'Armed Politics,'—which ridiculed the army's motto, "The military is the defender of the Constitutional Regime." The editorial went on to say that the army's sole and proper function was to defend the nation against foreign attack, that it had no place in domestic politics, and that the survival of a constitutional regime depended not on the sword, but on the conscience of the citizenry.[107] The Unionist press also began printing letters which denounced the League of Saviour Officers and supported the constitutional regime, sent by loyal officers in such Macedonian towns as Salonica, İpek, and Senidje.[108]

It became clear that the Committee of Union and Progress would do everything in its power, particularly in the Chamber, to resist the newly formed monarchist Cabinet and its wish to dissolve the Chamber.[109] On their part, the monar-

---

[104] II/I/40, July 12, 1328/July 25, 1912, *Meclis-i Mebusan Zabıt Ceridesi*, 2, p.449; "Meclis-i Mebusan'da," *İktiham*, July 13, 1328/July 26, 1912, p.1; Celal Bayar, *Ben de Yazdım*, 2, pp.544-545; "The Turkish Chamber: Threatening Letter from the Military League," *The Times*, July 26, 1912, p.5; "Constantinople Letter," *The Near East*, August 2, 1912, p.379; Hüseyin Cahid Yalçın, "Meşrutiyet Hatıraları, 1908-1918," *Fikir Hareketleri*, 7 (October 24, 1936-April 17, 1937), p.198; and, Rıza Nur, *Hürriyet ve İtilâf Fırkası Nasıl Doğdu, Nasıl Öldü?* pp.87-88.

[105] II/I/40, July 12, 1328/July 25, 1912, *Meclis-i Mebusan Zabıt Ceridesi*, 2, p.449. See also, Yusuf Hikmet Bayur, *Türk İnkılâbı Tarihi*, 2/1, p.294.

[106] "Constantinople Letter," *The Near East*, August 2, 1912, p.379.

[107] Süleyman Nazif, "Kılıçlı Siyaset," *Hak*, July 12, 1328/July 25, 1912, reprinted in full in Celal Bayar, *Ben de Yazdım*, 2, pp.554-556. For threats against members of the Committee of Union and Progress see, Yusuf Hikmet Bayur, *Türk İnkılâbı Tarihi*, 2/4, p.241.

[108] "Ordunun Beyan-ı Hissiyatı," *Hak*, July 14, 1328/July 27, 1912, reproduced in Celal Bayar, *Ben de Yazdım*, 2, pp.549-551.

[109] Babanzade İsmail Hakkı, "Feshe Doğru İlk Teşebbüs," *Tanin*, July 19, 1328/

chists had already made up their mind and were looking for
a seemingly 'legal' way to dissolve the Chamber.[110] Lütfi Fikri
Bey, an opposition ex-deputy for Dersim, who was known for
his independent views, came up with one solution: "If each
and every deputy were 'persuaded' to resign, then the
Chamber would be automatically dissolved."[111] This was
clearly impossible. On his part, Rıza Nur was publicly engaged in activities in discrediting the general elections and,
therefore, the Chamber of Deputies.[112]

Gazi Ahmed Muhtar Pasha presented the new government's
programme on July 30. Hüseyin Hilmi Pasha, the new Minister of Justice, asked the Chamber for its unconditional support. Under pressure, the deputies approved the government's
programme by a vote of one hundred and twelve to forty-four
that same day.[113]

Armed with an apparent mandate, the Government lost no
time in replacing the Head of Police, as well as the Chief Military Commander in İstanbul, and state of emergency was
promptly lifted. Military and provincial authorities in the

August 1, 1912, p.1; Babanzade İsmail Hakkı, "Fesih Gayr-ı Meşru," *Tanin*, July 21,
1328/August 3, 1912, p.1; "Constantinople Letter," *The Near East*, August 16, 1912,
p.435.

[110] Mehmed Cavid, "Meşrutiyet Devrine Ait Cavid Bey'in Hatıraları: 140,"
Tanin, January 21, 1944, p.2. For Gazi Ahmed Pasha's views for the urgency of the
dissolution see, Rifat Uçarol, *Gazi Ahmet Muhtar Paşa: Bir Osmanlı Paşası ve Dönemi*, pp.361-362.

[111] Hüseyin Cahid Yalçın, "Meşrutiyet Hatıraları, 1908-1918," *Fikir Hareketleri*, 7 (October 24, 1936-April 17, 1937), p.214.

[112] Rıza Nur, "Yeni Kabinenin Heyet-i Muhteremesine: Hükûmetin İntihaba-
ta Müdahalesine ve Binaenaleyh İntihabın Gayr-ı Meşru Olduğuna Dair Vesaik-i
Resmiye," *İktiham*, July 15, 1328/July 28, 1912, pp.1-2.

[113] II/1/43, July 17, 1328/July 30, 1912, *Meclis-i Mebusan Zabıt Ceridesi, 2*,
pp.533-558; "The Turkish Crisis: The Cabinet and the Chamber," *The Times*, July
31, 1912, p.5; "Kabine Meclis-i Mebusan Huzurunda," *İktiham*, July 18, 1328/July
31, 1912, p.1; *Tanin*, July 18, 1328/July 31, 1912, quoted in Hüseyin Cahid Yalçın,
"Meşrutiyet Hatıraları, 1908-1918," *Fikir Hareketleri*, 7 (October 24, 1936-April 17,
1937), p.214; "Yeni Kabine: İtimad Reyi Hakkında," *İktiham*, July 19, 1328/August
1, 1912, p.1; and, William W. Rockhill to Secretary of State, Constantinople, July
31, 1912, in *Records of the Department of State Relating to Internal Affairs of
Turkey, 1910-1929*, Roll 4. See also, Mehmed Cavid, "Meşrutiyet Devrine Ait Cavid
Bey'in Hatıraları: 140," *Tanin*, January 21, 1944, p.2; Rifat Uçarol, *Gazi Ahmet
Muhtar Paşa: Bir Osmanlı Paşası ve Dönemi*, pp.352-354; Mustafa Ragıb Esatlı, *İtti-
hat ve Terakki Tarihinde Esrar Perdesi: Yakup Cemil Niçin ve Nasıl Öldürüldü?*
pp.110-111; and, Yusuf Hikmet Bayur, *Türk İnkılâbı Tarihi, 2/1*, p.293. For an English translation of the cabinet's programme see, William W. Rockhill to Secretary of State, Constantinople, August 2, 1912, in *Records of the Department of State
Relating to Internal Affairs of Turkey, 1910-1929*, Roll 4.

Macedonian provinces were also ordered to exercise leniency with regard to Albanian and other rebels still at large.[114] Finally, those rebels currently in detention were amnestied and immediately set free.[115]

The amnesty drew heavy criticism from the independent daily press in İstanbul, among them *A revelk* and *Jamanak*, two Armenian newspapers. Both attacked the military Government, pointing out that, with few exceptions, it consisted of prominent figures from the old absolutist regime. *Jamanak* went on to say that if the new Government thought it could solve the current crisis by bringing in Hamidian reactionaries, it was dead wrong.[116] *Puzantion*, another Armenian daily, denounced the amnesty, saying that it included not only Hamidian spies, conspirators, and other reactionaries who were involved in the uprising, but also corrupt Hamidian bureaucrats and ministers who had been exiled or imprisoned long before.[117]

Dr. Rıza Nur, one of the conspirators who had brought about the fall of the constitutional regime, remained in close contact with Albanian nationalist/separatist leaders. Towards the end of July, a telegram he had sent to Hoca Said Efendi, the monarchist ex-deputy for Üsküb who was organising the Albanian revolt in Prishtnë, was intercepted. In it, he promised the hodja that the Chamber's dissolution was only a matter of time.

---

[114] "The Turkish Cabinet: Martial Law Suppressed," *The Times*, July 23, 1912, p.5; "The Grand Vizier and Public Order: Police Under Military Officers," *The Times*, July 24, 1912, p.5; Hüseyin Cahid Yalçın, "Meşrutiyet Hatıraları, 1908-1918," *Fikir Hareketleri*, 7 (October 24, 1936-April 17, 1937), p.198; and, Rifat Uçarol, *Gazi Ahmet Muhtar Paşa: Bir Osmanlı Paşası ve Dönemi*, p.356. See also, Basil Kondis, *Greece and Albania, 1908-1914*, p.74.
[115] "Aff-ı Umumi," *İktiham*, July 14, 1328/July 27, 1912, p.1; "Aff-ı Umumi," *İktiham*, July 16, 1328/July 29, 1912, p.2; and, Hüseyin Cahid Yalçın, "Meşrutiyet Hatıraları, 1908-1918," *Fikir Hareketleri*, 7 (October 24, 1936-April 17, 1937), p.214, and p.230. The monarchist politicians forming the new cabinet had gotten in touch with the Albanian rebels as soon as the Said Pasha Cabinet left office (Peter Bartl, *Die albanischen Muslime zur Zeit der nationalen Unabhängigkeitsbewegung, 1878-1912*, p.181).
[116] "Neden Af Olundular?" *Tanin*, July 21, 1328/August 3, 1912, pp.1-2. See also, Hüseyin Cahid Yalçın, "Meşrutiyet Hatıraları, 1908-1918," *Fikir Hareketleri*, 7 (October 24, 1936-April 17, 1937), p.214; and, Aram Andonyan, *Balkan Savaşı*, p.193.
[117] "Af Etrafında," *Tanin*, July 22, 1328/August 4, 1912, p.1; and, Hüseyin Cahid Yalçın, "Meşrutiyet Hatıraları, 1908-1918," *Fikir Hareketleri*, 7 (October 24, 1936-April 17, 1937), p.229. See also, Aram Andonyan, *Balkan Savaşı*, p.193.

The text was printed in *Tanin*.[118]

Local partisans of the Committee of Union and Progress sent telegram after telegram to the Grand Vezier, urging him not to dissolve the Parliament, and threatening to raise a force of ten thousand volunteers if any move were made in this direction.[119] Countless letters and telegrams from concerned citizens of all political convictions throughout the country poured into the Chamber in support of the constitutional regime, denouncing the proclamations and threats of the secret military organisation.[120]

The military Government, however, had found a 'legal' way to dissolve the Chamber by modifying Article 7 of the Constitution which defined the rights of the Sultan. The Cabinet proposed that the article be modified in such a way as to empower the Sultan to dissolve the Chamber under extraordinary circumstances after consultation with the Senate.[121] After a stormy debate, the Chamber sent the Government's proposal to the Commission for the Revision of the Constitution. Realising that the Commission would certainly reject its proposal after delaying its reply for as long as possible, the Government turned to the monarchist-dominated Senate, and a special sitting was scheduled for the morning on Sunday, August 4.[122]

In response, and in order to test the Unionist strength in the Chamber, eight Unionist deputies—Ziya Bey, deputy for Rize, Hasan Fehmi [Tümerkan], deputy for Sinob, Osman Bey,

---

[118] *Tanin*, July 18, 1328/July 31, 1912, in Hüseyin Cahid Yalçın, "Meşrutiyet Hatıraları, 1908-1918," *Fikir Hareketleri*, 7 (October 24, 1936-April 17, 1937), p.230.

[119] F.O. 424/232, Mr. Marling to Sir Edward Grey, Constantinople, August 1, 1912, *Further Correspondence Respecting the Affairs of Asiatic Turkey and Arabia, Part VII*, No.10164, p.86; and, "The Turkish Cabinet and the Committee: Another Military Threat," *The Times*, July 27, 1912, p.5.

[120] "The Turkish Cabinet and the Committee: Another Military Threat," *The Times*, July 27, 1912, p.5; II/1/42, July 16, 1328/July 29, 1912, *Meclis-i Mebusan Zabıt Ceridesi*, 2, pp.487-492; II/1/44, July 18, 1328/July 31, 1912, *Meclis-i Mebusan Zabıt Ceridesi*, 2, pp.561-564; and, Celal Bayar, *Ben de Yazdım*, 2, p.548.

[121] "Meclis'in Feshi," "Fesih Hakkında," and "Tadil Etrafında," *İktiham*, July 22, 1328/August 4, 1912, p.1; Mehmed Cavid, "Meşrutiyet Devrine Ait Cavid Bey'in Hatıraları: 140," *Tanin*, January 21, 1944, p.2; Hüseyin Cahid Yalçın, "Meşrutiyet Hatıraları, 1908-1918," *Fikir Hareketleri*, 7 (October 24, 1936-April 17, 1937), p.230; and, Yusuf Hikmet Bayur, *Türk İnkılâbı Tarihi, 2/1*, p.295.

[122] "Constantinople Letter," *The Near East*, August 16, 1912, p.435. See also, Mehmed Cavid, "Meşrutiyet Devrine Ait Cavid Bey'in Hatıraları: 141," *Tanin*, January 22, 1944, p.2.

deputy for Serfidje, Bedros Haladjian, deputy for İstanbul, Mehmed Münir [Çağıl], deputy for Çorum, Nuri Bey, deputy for Kerbela, İbrahim Fevzi Efendi, deputy for Mosul, and Talât Bey, deputy for Edirne—submitted a petition to the Chamber of Deputies on August 4 which criticised both the actions of the League of Saviour Officers and the laxity on the part of Nâzım Pasha, Minister of War, and the Government towards the rebel officers. The deputies alleged that Nâzım Pasha, far from opening an investigation into counter-revolutionary activity among his officers, had, in fact, invited the League of Saviour Officers members to the Sublime Porte, and congratulated them. The petition also criticised the fact that these officers had complete access to the Chamber without the proper authorities' knowledge or authorisation. The deputies demanded that the Ministry of War be held accountable.[123]

During the closed Senate session that same day, the Government gave its version of the events in Macedonia. Twenty out of sixty garrisons in Albania, it said, had revolted against government authority and joined the uprising, and coupled with the fact that the Committee of Union and Progress on the whole did not enjoy widespread military support, a resolution to the crisis in Albania clearly called for the dissolution of the Chamber of Deputies.[124] Mahmud Şevket Pasha, the ex-Minister of War who had been named senator immediately after his forced resignation, questioned the validity of these allegations as well as the government's logic. He pointed out that a majority of the garrisons in Macedonia had remained loyal and had sent telegrams supporting the constitutional regime— both to the Sublime Porte and to Parliament. These troops, he argued, were perfectly capable of maintaining order; the activities of a few mutinous garrisons were clearly no reason to dissolve the Chamber. The monarchist-dominated Senate, however, paid little attention to his arguments, and proceeded to

---

[123] "Meclis-i Mebusan'da: İstizah Etrafında," *İktiham*, July 22, 1328/August 4, 1912, p.1; and, Hüseyin Cahid Yalçın, "Meşrutiyet Hatıraları, 1908-1918," *Fikir Hareketleri*, 7 (October 24, 1936-April 17, 1937), p.231, and p.245.

[124] "Âyan'da: Celse-i Tarihiye," *Tanin*, July 23, 1328/August 5, 1912, pp.1-2; and, Hüseyin Cahid Yalçın, "Meşrutiyet Hatıraları, 1908-1918," *Fikir Hareketleri*, 7 (October 24, 1936-April 17, 1937), p.245.

make legal arrangements for the Chamber's dissolution.[125]

By a vote of twenty-eight to five, with one undecided, the Senate passed a modified version of Article 35. It then passed an amendment to Article 43 which shortened the parliamentary session to six months, though it could be prolonged for an additional period of time. Because the Senate declared that the present Parliament was a continuation of the Parliament of 1908, making the last elections null and void, and because this Parliament had been sitting for much more than the proscribed term, the Senate authorised the Government to dissolve the Chamber of Deputies.[126]

That night, Halil [Menteşe] rushed to the Palace and implored the Sultan not to issue the decree of dissolution, but to no avail. The Imperial Decree was issued at midnight.[127]

Hoping to mount a counter-attack, the leadership of the Committee of Union and Progress decided to convene the Chamber before the official announcement was made. On the morning of August 5, Halil [Menteşe] did not relay the Imperial Decree to the Chamber. Instead, he simply confirmed that such a decree had been issued, allowing the session to continue as if nothing had happened.[128] After several Albanian deputies had tried unsuccessfully to disrupt the proceedings, Cavid Bey took the floor and made a highly charged

[125] "Âyan'da: Celse-i Tarihiye," *Tanin*, July 23, 1328/August 5, 1912, pp.1-2; and, Hüseyin Cahid Yalçın, "Meşrutiyet Hatıraları, 1908-1918," *Fikir Hareketleri*, 7 (October 24, 1936-April 17, 1937), p.246.

[126] II/I/32, July 22, 1328/August 4, 1912, *Meclis-i Âyan Zabıt Ceridesi*, *1*, p.383; "Âyan'da: Celse-i Tarihiye," *Tanin*, July 23, 1328/August 5, 1912, pp.1-2; "Meclis-i Mebusan'ın Feshi," and "Meclis'in Feshi: İctima-i Fevkalâde," *İktiham*, July 23, 1328/August 5, 1912, pp.1-2; "Fesih Hakkında," *İktiham*, July 25, 1328/August 7, 1912, p.2; "Constantinople Letter," *The Near East*, August 16, 1912, p.435; Mehmed Cavid, "Meşrutiyet Devrine Ait Cavid Bey'in Hatıraları: 141," *Tanin*, January 22, 1944, p.2; Mustafa Ragıb Esatlı, *İttihat ve Terakki Tarihinde Esrar Perdesi: Yakup Cemil Niçin ve Nasıl Öldürüldü?* p.112; and, Yusuf Hikmet Bayur, *Türk İnkılâbı Tarihi*, *2/1*, p.295. Those who voted against were Hüseyin Hüsnü Pasha, Bessaraya Efendi, Musa Kâzım Efendi, Tilkof Efendi, Ahmed Rıza Bey. Mahmud Sevket Pasha was undecided. Some senators had left the Senate in protest during the closed session (Hüseyin Cahid Yalçın, "Meşrutiyet Hatıraları, 1908-1918," *Fikir Hareketleri*, 7 (October 24, 1936-April 17, 1937), p.246; and, Mustafa Ragıb Esatlı, *İttihat ve Terakki Tarihinde Esrar Perdesi: Yakup Cemil Niçin ve Nasıl Öldürüldü?* p.112). See also, Ahmed İzzet, *Feryadım*, *1*, p.117.

[127] "Constantinople Letter," *The Near East*, August 16, 1912, p.435.

[128] Hüseyin Cahid Yalçın, "Meşrutiyet Hatıraları, 1908-1918," *Fikir Hareketleri*, 7 (October 24, 1936-April 17, 1937), p.246; Mehmed Cavid, "Meşrutiyet Devrine Ait Cavid Bey'in Hatıraları: 141," *Tanin*, January 22, 1944, p.2; "Meclis-i Mebusan Riyaseti'nin Telgrafı," *Tanin*, July 24, 1328/August 6, 1912, p.3; and, Yusuf Hikmet Bayur, *Türk İnkılâbı Tarihi*, *2/1*, p.296.

speech, in which he declared that more than the existence of the Chamber was at stake: the rights of the entire nation were under siege.[129] After fierce debate, the Chamber gave the Government a vote of no confidence, and adjourned "till summoned by its President."[130]

Gazi Ahmed Muhtar Pasha arrived at Parliament at 1 p.m. and read the decree of dissolution to a handful of Senators, a dozen monarchist Albanian deputies, as well as Seyyid Talib ibn Receb Bey, deputy for Basra, and Şeyhzade Zeynelabidin Efendi, deputy for Konya. He informed the deputies that the Government would not recognise the morning's proceedings.[131] Halil [Menteşe] went to the Palace, where the Sultan refused to see him. Later, after a scene in the Speaker's room, where Esad Pasha Toptan behaved with such violence that Halil [Menteşe] was forced to summon the police, the Chamber of Deputies was locked up by Ferid Pasha's order and the Cabinet met to discuss the situation.[132]

---

[129] II/I/47, July 23, 1328/August 5, 1912, *Meclis-i Mebusan Zabıt Ceridesi*, 2, pp.647-654; "Bir Celse-i Tarihiye: Şeciyane bir Müdafaa-i Kanun ve Meşrutiyet—Bir Nutk-u Mühim," *Tanin*, July 24, 1328/August 6, 1912, pp.1-2; Mehmed Cavid, "Meşrutiyet Devrine Ait Cavid Bey'in Hatıraları: 141," *Tanin*, January 22, 1944, p.2; Hüseyin Cahid Yalçın, "Meşrutiyet Hatıraları, 1908-1918," *Fikir Hareketleri*, 7 (October 24, 1936-April 17, 1937), p.246; and, Aram Andonyan, *Balkan Savaşı*, p.178.
    See also, Yusuf Hikmet Bayur, *Türk İnkılâbı Tarihi*, 2/1, pp.296-298. Bayur criticises Cavid Bey's speech (Yusuf Hikmet Bayur, *Türk İnkılâbı Tarihi*, 2/1, pp.299-300). Şefik Esad also satirised the speeches of Cavid Bey and Bedros Haladjian in the Chamber (Şefik Esad, "İttihad ve Terakki Komedyası: Gülünçlü Piyes, İki Perde," *İktiham*, July 25, 1328/August 7, 1912, p.1).

[130] II/I/47, July 23, 1328/August 5, 1912, *Meclis-i Mebusan Zabıt Ceridesi*, 2, p.655; "Bir Celse-i Tarihiye: Şeciyane bir Müdafaa-i Kanun ve Meşrutiyet—Bir Nutk-u Mühim," *Tanin*, July 24, 1328/August 6, 1912, pp.1-2; "Meclis-i Mebusan'da Sabık Mebusların Hasbıhali," *İktiham*, July 24, 1328/August 6, 1912, pp.3-4; "Constantinople Letter," *The Near East*, August 16, 1912, p.435; Hüseyin Cahid Yalçın, "Meşrutiyet Hatıraları, 1908-1918," *Fikir Hareketleri*, 7 (October 24, 1936-April 17, 1937), p.247; Aram Andonyan, *Balkan Savaşı*, p.178; and, Yusuf Hikmet Bayur, *Türk İnkılâbı Tarihi*, 2/1, p.298.

[131] "Meclis-i Âyan'da," Tanin, July 24, 1328/August 6, 1912, p.3; "Hatt-ı Hümayun Kıraatı," *Tanin*, July 24, 1328/August 6, 1912, p.3; Mehmed Cavid, "Meşrutiyet Devrine Ait Cavid Bey'in Hatıraları: 141," *Tanin*, January 22, 1944, p.2; Hüseyin Cahid Yalçın, "Meşrutiyet Hatıraları, 1908-1918," *Fikir Hareketleri*, 7 (October 24, 1936-April 17, 1937), p.247; "Constantinople Letter," *The Near East*, August 16, 1912, p.435; Mustafa Ragıb Esatlı, *İttihat ve Terakki Tarihinde Esrar Perdesi: Yakup Cemil Niçin ve Nasıl Öldürüldü?* p.112; Rifat Uçarol, *Gazi Ahmet Muhtar Paşa: Bir Osmanlı Paşası ve Dönemi*, pp.367-368; and, Yusuf Hikmet Bayur, *Türk İnkılâbı Tarihi*, 2/1, p.300.

[132] "Bir Hadise," *Tanin*, July 24, 1328/August 6, 1912, p.3; "Riyaset Odasında bir Hadise," *İktiham*, July 24, 1328/August 6, 1912, p.1; "Constantinople Letter," *The Near East*, August 16, 1912, p.435; and, Yusuf Hikmet Bayur, *Türk İnkılâbı Tarihi*, 2/1, p.301.

Throughout that day, about three hundred loyalist officers demonstrated in Hürriyet-i Ebediye Square. In a proclamation issued that day, they declared their allegiance to the constitutional regime, denounced the rebel officers, and asked for their immediate arrests. They further demanded that those rebel officers be tried and punished.[133]

In a joint declaration, one hundred and sixteen junior officers belonging to the Third Army Corps stationed at Salonica expressed the hope that the Third Army Corps, which had played such a significant role in restoring the constitutional regime after the *coup* attempt of April 1909, would not remain silent in this event too. They especially deplored and denounced those army officers who had both joined the Albanian insurgents' demands for independence and rebelled against the constitutional regime at a time when Turkey was at war with the Italians in Tripoli. They ended their declaration with a firm commitment to liberal democratic principles and the supremacy of parliamentary rule.[134]

---

[133] *Hak*, July 24, 1328/August 6, 1912, p.4, quoted in Mehmet Saray, "Devlet Yönetiminde Ordunun Yeri ve Rolü Hakkında bir Örnek: İttihat ve Terakki Devrinde Ordunun Millet ve Devlet Yönetimine Tesiri," p.91; Hüseyin Cahid Yalçın, "Meşrutiyet Hatıraları, 1908-1918," *Fikir Hareketleri*, 7 (October 24, 1936-April 17, 1937), p.231; and, Celal Bayar, *Ben de Yazdım*, 2, pp.548-549. See also, Rifat Uçarol, *Gazi Ahmet Muhtar Paşa: Bir Osmanlı Paşası ve Dönemi*, p.334; and, Mustafa Ragıb Esatlı, "İntihabatta Parti İhtirası: İntihabatta Muhaliflerin Karşılıklı İhtirasları Felâketler Doğurmuştu," *Akşam*, March 25, 1943, p.3.

[134] *Hak*, July 27, 1328/August 9, 1912, p.1, quoted in Mehmet Saray, "Devlet Yönetiminde Ordunun Yeri ve Rolü Hakkında bir Örnek: İttihat ve Terakki Devrinde Ordunun Millet ve Devlet Yönetimine Tesiri," pp.91-92.

CHAPTER TEN

THE ROAD TO THE FALL OF MONARCHIST RULE

Immediately after the dissolution of the Chamber, the Government re-instituted the state of emergency: organising demonstrations, giving public speeches, making propaganda on behalf of political parties, meeting in political clubs, and publishing editorials or criticisms of a political nature were forbidden.[1] On August 10, Hüseyin Cahid [Yalçın] temporarily closed *Tanin*, the pro-Unionist daily with one of the largest circulation in the capital.[2] After meeting with the Unionist leadership—which itself had moved back to Salonica from İstanbul—Hüseyin Cahid [Yalçın], however, resumed publication on August 21 with an editorial which, though conciliatory in tone, remained firm in its expressed determination to oppose any event considered detrimental to the country.[3]

Several Greek papers, on the other hand, celebrated the Albanian revolt. One of these, *Phoni*, even welcomed the es-

[1] "İdare-i Örfiye," *Tanin*, July 25, 1328/August 7, 1912, Morning Edition, p.3; "Tebliğ," *Tanin*, July 25, 1328/August 7, 1912, Evening Edition, p.4; "Divan-ı Harb-ı Örfî Heyeti," *İktiham*, July 25, 1328/August 7, 1912, p.1; "Fesih ve İdare-i Örfiye," *Tanin*, July 27, 1328/August 9, 1912, p.2; "İdare-i Örfiye," *Tanin*, July 27, 1328/August 9, 1912, p.2; "Selânik'te İdare-i Örfiye," *İktiham*, July 27, 1328/August 9, 1912, p.1; "İdare-i Örfiye Beyannamesinde Tadilât," *İkdam*, July 29, 1328/August 11, 1912, p.2; and, Hüseyin Cahid Yalçın, "Meşrutiyet Hatıraları, 1908-1918," *Fikir Hareketleri*, 7 (October 24, 1936-April 17, 1937), p.247. See also, Rifat Uçarol, *Gazi Ahmet Muhtar Paşa: Bir Osmanlı Paşası ve Dönemi*, p.371.

[2] Hüseyin Cahid [Yalçın], "Zade-i Meşrutiyet olan *Tanin* İhtiyar-ı Tatil Ediyor: Vatanın Mücahede-i Kalemiyeye İhtiyacı Olduğunu Görerek Tatilimi Yarım Bıraktım, Memleketime Koştum. Halbuki İstanbul'a Geldim, Anladım ve *Tanin*'i Muvakkaten Kapamaya Karar Verdim," *Tanin*, July 28, 1328/August 10, 1912, p.1. See also, Hüseyin Cahid Yalçın, "Meşrutiyet Hatıraları, 1908-1918," *Fikir Hareketleri*, 7 (October 24, 1936-April 17, 1937), p.260; and, Mehmed Cavid, "Meşrutiyet Devrine Ait Cavid Bey'in Hatıraları," *Tanin*, January 23, 1944, p.2.

[3] Hüseyin Cahid [Yalçın], "Hal ve Mevki," *Tanin*, August 8, 1328/August 21, 1912, p.1. See also, Hüseyin Cahid Yalçın, "Meşrutiyet Hatıraları, 1908-1918," *Fikir Hareketleri*, 7 (October 24, 1936-April 17, 1937), p.247, 260, and 277; and, Mehmed Cavid, "Meşrutiyet Devrine Ait Cavid Bey'in Hatıraları: 142," *Tanin*, January 23, 1944, p.2.

tablishment of an Albanian state.[4] In telegrams sent to Hasan Bey of Prishtnë, Rıza Nur reiterated monarchist support for the revolt. These were again intercepted and published in *Tanin*.[5]

There were signs, however, that the cabinet was not as unified as it seemed.[6] Ziya Pasha had resigned as Minister of the Interior because, as he put it, he thought himself unfit for the difficult task of restoring internal tranquillity in the face of the Albanian uprising. But it was also due to the underground opposition of the Committee of Union and Progress.[7]

Damad Şerif Pasha, who succeeded Ziya Pasha, was something of a nonentity and was considered Hüseyin Hilmi Pasha's man. Hüseyin Hilmi Pasha, in turn, was thought to be in contact with the Unionist leadership. The *Indépendant de Salonique* confirmed these suspicions by asserting that Hilmi Pasha would be the Unionist nominee for Grand Vezier when the Committee of Union and Progress came back into power.[8]

Following in Ziya Pasha's footsteps, Damad Şerif Pasha demanded a free hand in the appointment and dismissal of governors, sub-governors, and other important provincial officials. Mostly, he wanted the summary dismissal of those governors who had been appointed under the Unionist administration.[9] Hüseyin Hilmi Pasha then gave an interview, not to any of-

---

[4] *Tanin*, July 26, 1328/August 8, 1912, in Hüseyin Cahid Yalçın, "Meşrutiyet Hatıraları, 1908-1918," *Fikir Hareketleri*, 7 (October 24, 1936-April 17, 1937), p.259.

[5] *Tanin*, July 26, 1328/August 8, 1912, in Hüseyin Cahid Yalçın, "Meşrutiyet Hatıraları, 1908-1918," *Fikir Hareketleri*, 7 (October 24, 1936-April 17, 1937), p.259.

[6] "Buhran-ı Vükelâ Şayiaları," *Ikdam*, August 2, 1328/August 15, 1912, p.1; "Heyet-i Vükelâda İhtilâf," *Tanin*, August 8, 1328/August 21, 1912, p.1; "Kabinenin İstifası?" *Tanin*, August 9, 1328/August 22, 1912, p.2; and, "Buhran-ı Vükelâ Etrafında," *Tanin*, August 9, 1328/August 22, 1912, p.2. See also, Mustafa Ragıb Esatlı, *İttihat ve Terakki Tarihinde Esrar Perdesi: Yakup Cemil Niçin ve Nasıl Öldürüldü?* pp.114-115; and, Şehbenderzade Filibeli Ahmed Hilmi, *Muhalefetin İflâsı: İtilâf ve Hürriyet Fırkası*, pp.53-54.

[7] "Dahiliye Nazırının İstifası," *Ikdam*, August 1, 1328/August 14, 1912, p.1; "Ziya Paşa," *Ikdam*, August 2, 1328/August 15, 1912, p.1; Hüseyin Cahid [Yalçın], "Kabine," *Tanin*, August 9, 1328/August 22, 1912, p.1; "Kabinede İtilâf-ı Efkâr Mevcut!: Fakat Nâzırlar bir bir Gidiyor," *Tanin*, August 9, 1328/August 22, 1912, p.2; and, "Constantinople Letter," *The Near East*, August 23, 1912, p.463. See also, Rifat Uçarol, *Gazi Ahmet Muhtar Paşa: Bir Osmanlı Paşası ve Dönemi*, p.384.

[8] "Constantinople Letter," *The Near East*, August 23, 1912, p.463. For the news of his appointment see, "Dahiliye Nezareti," *Ikdam*, August 3, 1328/August 16, 1912, p.1.

[9] Hüseyin Cahid Yalçın, "Meşrutiyet Hatıraları, 1908-1918," *Fikir Hareketleri*, 7 (October 24, 1936-April 17, 1937), p.278. For the rumours of impending dismissals see, "Valilerde Tebeddül," *Ikdam*, July 30, 1328/August 12, 1912, p.2.

ficial organ or monarchist paper, but to *Le Jeune Turc* of August 15, in which he declared that the Cabinet intended to make no widespread changes and had only accepted the resignation of certain governors who had absolutely refused to obey orders. The monarchist press took up the cudgels for Damad Şerif Pasha, saying it was folly to leave the conduct of the next elections in the hands of Unionist officials, whom they accused of gerrymandering the last elections.[10] The Grand Vezier, however, refused to give Damad Şerif Pasha such power, mainly because of Hüseyin Hilmi Pasha's opposition to any such wholesale changes, and Damad Şerif Pasha promptly resigned.[11]

The Cabinet was increasingly divided between such hardliners as Kâmil and Nâzım Pashas and such moderates as Gazi Ahmed Muhtar and Hüseyin Hilmi Pashas, and their differences only worsened. While the Grand Vezier and the Minister of Justice urged a moderate form of repression against the Unionists, the Kâmil Pasha clique was clearly out for revenge.[12] The Entente Libérale's distrust of Hüseyin Hilmi Pasha increased, particularly as preparations for the next elections were still incomplete. For a time, Hilmi Pasha could ignore recriminations of some of the Cabinet members, but on August 21 monarchist pressure forced him to finally resign. He was accused by most of the monarchist Ministers in the Cabinet for his continuing contacts with the Committee of Union and Progress.[13] In an interview with *Tanin* on August

---

[10] "Hüseyin Hilmi Paşa'nın Beyanatı," *Ikdam*, August 3, 1328/August 16, 1912, pp.1-2; "Constantinople Letter," *The Near East*, August 30, 1912, p.491; and, Yusuf Hikmet Bayur, *Türk Inkılâbı Tarihi*, 2/1, p.303. For the news concerning about the reshuffling of governors see, "Valilerde Tebeddül," *Ikdam*, July 30, 1328/August 12, 1912, p.2; "Yeni Valiler Hakkında," *Tanin*, August 13, 1328/August 26, 1912, p.2; "Yeni Tebeddülât," *Tanin*, August 13, 1328/August 26, 1912, p.2). Hüseyin Hilmi Pasha was rumoured to have received a threatening letter from the League of Saviour Officers ("Tehdit Mektupları," *Tanin*, August 12, 1328/August 25, 1912, p.2).

[11] "Dahiliye Nezareti," *Ikdam*, August 7, 1328/August 20, 1912, p.2; and, "Şerif Paşa'nın Sebeb-i İstifası," *Tanin*, August 9, 1328/August 22, 1912, p.1. See also, Rifat Uçarol, *Gazi Ahmet Muhtar Paşa: Bir Osmanlı Paşası ve Dönemi*, p.384.

[12] Mustafa Ragıb Esatlı, *Ittihat ve Terakki Tarihinde Esrar Perdesi: Yakup Cemil Niçin ve Nasıl Öldürüldü?* p.115; and, Hüseyin Cahid Yalçın, "Meşrutiyet Hatıraları, 1908-1918," *Fikir Hareketleri*, 7 (October 24, 1936-April 17, 1937), pp.277-278.

[13] "Kabinede İtilâf-ı Efkâr Mevcut!: Fakat Nazırlar bir bir Gidiyor," *Tanin*, August 9, 1328/August 22, 1912, p.2; "Hüseyin Hilmi Paşa'nın İstifası," *Ikdam*, August 9, 1328/August 22, 1912, p.1; "Osmanlı Buhran-ı Vükelâsı," *Tanin*, August

22, he cited the ongoing monarchist press campaign against him and the worsening domestic situation as the reason for his resignation.[14] Upon the resignation of Hüseyin Hilmi Pasha the *Tanin* printed an editorial in which the Government party, the Entente Libérale, was severely criticised for its lack of concern for the country and for its fighting over the spoils, the distribution of bureaucratic posts among their favourites, at a time of national crisis.[15]

Whatever the cause of Hilmi Pasha's resignation, it marked a change in the character of the government which, once supposedly neutral and 'above mere party politics,' now had a distinctly monarchist bent.[16] A staunch monarchist, Ali Daniş Bey—the controversial Albanian ex-governor of Salonica who had been dismissed for incompetence—was appointed Minister of the Interior. Halim Bey, a moderate monarchist Senator, was appointed Hüseyin Hilmi Pasha's successor at the Ministry of Justice, and Ahmed Reşid [Rey], the ex-governor of Aleppo and ex-editor of the defunct *Şahrah*—one of the fiercest anti-Unionist organs that was ever suppressed by the Court Martial before the monarchist takeover—was named governor of Aydın.[17]

By late August, rumours of further impending resignations had begun to circulate. Supporters of Kâmil Pasha asserted that he, along with Nâzım Pasha and Cemaleddin Efendi, the Sheikh-ul-Islam, were annoyed with Gazi Ahmed Muhtar Pasha's apparent unwillingness to adopt certain measures which

---

13, 1328/August 26, 1912, p.2; and, "Constantinople Letter," *The Near East*, August 30, 1912, p.491. See also, Yusuf Hikmet Bayur, *Türk İnkılâbı Tarihi*, 2/1, p289.

[14] "Kabinede İtilâf-ı Efkâr Mevcut!: Fakat Nazırlar bir bir Gidiyor," *Tanin*, August 9, 1328/August 22, 1912, p.2;. See also, Hüseyin Cahid Yalçın, "Meşrutiyet Hatıraları, 1908-1918," *Fikir Hareketleri*, 7 (October 24, 1936-April 17, 1937), p.278.

[15] Hüseyin Cahid [Yalçın], "Daima Kabine," *Tanin*, August 12, 1328/August 25, 1912, p.1. See also, Hüseyin Cahid Yalçın, "Meşrutiyet Hatıraları, 1908-1918," *Fikir Hareketleri*, 7 (October 24, 1936-April 17, 1937), p.278.

[16] "Hilmi Paşa'nın İstifası," *Tanin*, August 16, 1328/August 29, 1912, pp.3-4.

[17] "Aydın Vilâyeti Valiliği," *İkdam*, August 4, 1328/August 17, 1912, p.2; "Dahiliye Nezareti," *İkdam*, August 10, 1328/August 23, 1912, p.1; "Adliye Nezareti," *İkdam*, August 10, 1328/August 23, 1912, p.1; "Reşid Bey," *İkdam*, August 10, 1328/August 23, 1912, p.1; "Adliye Nezareti," *Tanin*, August 12, 1328/August 25, 1912, p.2; "Dahiliye Nezareti," *Tanin*, August 13, 1328/August 26, 1912, p.2; "Dahiliye Nezareti," *İkdam*, August 13, 1328/August 26, 1912, p.2; and, "Constantinople Letter," *The Near East*, August 30, 1912, p.491. See also, Mustafa Ragıb Esatlı, *İttihat ve Terakki Tarihinde Esrar Perdesi: Yakup Cemil Niçin ve Nasıl Öldürüldü?* pp.115-118; and, Tahsin Uzer, *Makedonya Eşkiyalık Tarihi ve Son Osmanlı Yönetimi*, p.310.

were considered indispensable to the restoration of the monarchist regime. Others declared that Mahmud Muhtar Pasha's presence in the Cabinet was the principal cause of dissension.[18]

Mahmud Muhtar Pasha's position as Minister of the Navy was a difficult one. To begin with, he was an army officer—a fact which only inspired the fleet's hostility. Yet neither did he enjoy the support of his own service: most of his fellow army officers considered him an ambitious but hot-headed officer who had played, none too skilfully, for his own hand in the past, and had at times played the game of the Unionists, who were anathema in most military circles. Monarchists accused him of being in close touch with the Unionist leadership, and drew attention to his recent interview with Talât Bey, lasting for more than an hour, and in which the political situation was discussed with great freedom. Finally, Mahmud Muhtar Pasha had been a member of the Hakkı Pasha Cabinet, which most of the supporters of the Gazi Ahmed Muhtar Pasha Cabinet had laboured to impeach.[19]

That year, the annual congress of the Committee of Union and Progress was to be held not in Salonica, but in İstanbul, or if this was not expedient, Bursa.[20] The leadership needed to maintain the Committee's credibility at all costs, and in this case the price was high: because İstanbul was under martial law, the complete freedom of the proceedings would have to be sacrificed.[21] By late August, though Cavid Bey was still in Salonica, Talât Bey had returned to the capital.[22]

---

[18] "Gazi Paşa İstifa Etmeyecektir," *Tanin*, August 12, 1328/August 25, 1912, p.2; "Kâmil ve Mahmud Muhtar Paşalar," *Tanin*, August 17, 1328/August 30, 1912, p.2; "Ahmed Muhtar Paşa ve Kâmil Paşa," *Tanin*, August 19, 1328/September 1, 1912, p.2; and, "Constantinople Letter," *The Near East*, September 6, 1912, p.519. See also, Rifat Uçarol, *Gazi Ahmet Muhtar Paşa: Bir Osmanlı Paşası ve Dönemi*, p.386.

[19] "Constantinople Letter," *The Near East*, September 6, 1912, p.519.

[20] "İttihad ve Terakki Kongresi," *Tanin*, August 13, 1328/August 26, 1912, p.1; and, Hüseyin Cahid Yalçın, "Meşrutiyet Hatıraları, 1908-1918," *Fikir Hareketleri*, 7 (October 24, 1936-April 17, 1937), p.294. See also, "İttihad ve Terakki Kongresi'nin İctimaı," *İkdam*, August 20, 1328/September 2, 1912, p.2.

[21] Hüseyin Cahid Yalçın, "Meşrutiyet Hatıraları, 1908-1918," *Fikir Hareketleri*, 7 (October 24, 1936-April 17, 1937), p.294.

[22] "İttihad ve Terakki: Bugünkü Vaziyet Hakkında," *Tanin*, August 13, 1328/August 26, 1912, p.3; and, "Salonika Letter," *The Near East*, September 6, 1912, p.520.

Dr. Rıfat Bey's frequent trips between Salonica and the capital were also the subject of speculation. He was a prominent member of the Committee of Union and Progress. Rumour had it that he was negotiating with Hüseyin Hilmi Pasha in an effort to induce the latter to accept the presidency of the Committee. Hilmi Pasha was supposedly not altogether opposed to the idea, provided the Committee of Union and Progress make certain changes in its programme.[23]

Despite this activity, the Committee's position with respect to the upcoming elections was a matter of contention, and the leadership hoped the Congress would settle the question before it was too late. There were two different currents of opinion as to the best course to adopt. Cavid Bey and others advocated complete non-participation as a protest to what they considered the Chamber's illegal dissolution; taking part in them would be a condonation of the dissolution of the Parliament. Others favoured an energetic struggle to maintain the Committee's influence. Among the other topics to be discussed were: the principle of decentralisation, which the Committee leadership had always opposed, the possibility of peace with Italy, as well as certain measures affecting the party's internal organisation and constitution. Some seventy delegates would attend the Congress, and it was expected to last about a week.[24]

The Congress opened in İstanbul on September 2. Hacı Âdil [Arda] was elected President; Talât Bey and Ahmed Nesimi Bey were made Vice-Presidents.[25] Despite protest, two police officers were present throughout the proceedings, appointed by the government in accordance with Article 18 of the Law of Public Meetings—a law which many in the Committee of Union and Progress had helped to pass.[26] The Central Bureau's

[23] "Salonika Letter," *The Near East*, September 6, 1912, p.520.
[24] "İttihad ve Terakki Cemiyeti'nin Kararı," *İkdam*, August 1, 1328/August 14, 1912, p.2, quoting *Osmanischer Lloyd* of August 13, 1912; Mehmed Cavid, "Meşrutiyet Devrine Ait Cavid Bey'in Hatıraları: 142," *Tanin*, January 23, 1944, p.2; and, "Salonika Letter," *The Near East*, September 6, 1912, p.520.
[25] Hüseyin Cahid [Yalçın], "Bir Mukayese," *Tanin*, August 21, 1328/September 3, 1912, p.1; "İttihad ve Terakki Kongresi," *Tanin*, August 21, 1328/September 3, 1912, pp.1-2; and, "Constantinople Letter," *The Near East*, September 13, 1912, p.547.
[26] "İttihad ve Terakki Kongresi'nde Zabıt Memurları," *Senin*, August 23, 1328/September 5, 1912, p.3; Hüseyin Cahid Yalçın, "Meşrutiyet Hatıraları, 1908-1918," *Fikir Hareketleri*, 7 (October 24, 1936-April 17, 1937), p.294; and, "Constan-

report condemned the action of the Senate, whose interpretation of Article 43 was described as "contrary to the spirit
of the Constitution," along with the Government which had
then carried out the illegal dissolution. On September 4, sixty-
three delegates voted in favour of participating in the elections;
fourteen delegates, headed by Dr. Nâzım Bey, voted in opposition, claiming that the Committee's participation in the elections could only legitimise the government's actions.[27]

The Congress ended with the election of Prince Said Halim
Pasha of Egypt as Secretary-General for the following year.[28]
The new Central Committee were also elected, and except for
Rahmi [Aslan], it consisted of the party's leadership—though
men such as Suleiman al-Bostani, Hacı Âdil [Arda], and Hüseyin Kâzım Kadri Bey, ex-governor of Salonica, who were
known for their moderate views now also counted among its
members.[29] The Central Bureau, which was presumably
composed of the Central Committee's leaders, featured Talât
Bey, ex-Minister of the Interior, İsmail Hakkı Bey, ex-governor of Van, Midhat Şükrü [Bleda], ex-deputy for Serres, Abdullah Sabri Efendi, and Ziya Bey.[30]

On the second day of the Congress, September 3, the Government took action and suspended publication of *Tanin*.[31]
The Unionists, however, had already obtained, under differ-

---

tinople Letter," *The Near East*, September 13, 1912, p.547.
  [27] Hüseyin Cahid [Yalçın], "İttihad ve Terakki Kongresi'ne Avdet," *Senin*,
August 24, 1328/September 6, 1912, p.1; "İttihad ve Terakki: Meclis'te ve Kon-
gre'de," *Ikdam*, August 27, 1328/September 9, 1912, p.1; "İttihad ve Terakki: Kon-
grenin Mukarreratı, 1: Meclis-i Mebusan'ın Seddi ve İntihabat-ı Cedide Meselesi—2: İttihad ve Terakki'nin Teşkilâtı, *Tanin*, September 12, 1328/September 25,
1912, p.1; and "Constantinople Letter," *The Near East*, September 13, 1912, p.547.
See also, Mehmed Cavid, "Meşrutiyet Devrine Ait Cavid Bey'in Hatıraları: 143,"
Tanin, January 24, 1944, p.2; and, Mustafa Ragıb Esatlı, *İttihat ve Terakki Tarihinde Esrar Perdesi: Yakup Cemil Niçin ve Nasıl Öldürüldü?* pp.210-216.
  [28] "İttihad ve Terakki Kongresi," *Senin*, August 29, 1328/September 11, 1912,
p.1; and, "İttihad ve Terakki Kongresi," *Senin*, August 30, 1328/September 12,
1912, p.1. "He was a wealthy and well-educated man, who was believed to have
some business ability and was certainly energetic. He knew Europe relatively better than some of the leaders of the Committee of Union and Progress, and was
well-connected with some European politicians. He was believed to be a progressive
by temperament ("Constantinople Letter," *The Near East*, September 20, 1912,
p.575).
  [29] "Constantinople Letter," *The Near East*, September 20, 1912, p.575. See also,
Hüseyin Kâzım Kadri, *Meşrutiyet'ten Cumhuriyet'e Hatıralarım*, p.133.
  [30] "Constantinople Letter," *The Near East*, September 20, 1912, p.575.
  [31] Hüseyin Cahid Yalçın, "Meşrutiyet Hatıraları, 1908-1918," *Fikir Hareketleri*, 7 (October 24, 1936-April 17, 1937), p.309; and, Mehmed Cavid, "Meşrutiyet
Devrine Ait Cavid Bey'in Hatıraları: 143," *Tanin*, January 24, 1944, p.2.

THE ROAD TO THE FALL OF MONARCHIST RULE

ent names, permits to establish several new newspapers, and *Tanin*, in effect, reappeared in the guise of *Cenin*, allegedly under Cavid Bey's direction. When *Cenin* was suppressed a day later, it resurfaced as *Senin* under the direction of Babanzade İsmail Hakkı.[32] On September 5, the Court Martial authorities charged Hüseyin Cahid [Yalçın], Cavid Bey, and Orhan Talât Bey, the paper's manager, for printing subversive material against government orders.[33] On September 11, Hüseyin Cahid [Yalçın] was sentenced to a month in prison; Cavid Bey and Orhan Talât Bey were each given twenty days and were immediately imprisoned.[34] *Senin* published the news the following day, and was immediately closed down. Nonetheless, *Tanin* again resurfaced as *Hak* on September 13 and published a harsh editorial on the trial and the government's treatment of the defendants.[35]

Ardent supporters of the monarchist Cabinet believed that the imprisonment of Cavid Bey and Hüseyin Cahid [Yalçın] would terrify the Unionists, paralyse their efforts in the upcoming elections, and discourage public support. The Committee, they said, would be lucky if it had forty deputies in the next Chamber.[36] But the affair had the opposite effect. Far from silent, the anti-monarchist press made the most of what it considered an unfair, trumped-up trial, and the public outcry was so great, that on September 17, *Tanin* was allowed to resume publication under its own name. As a result of the publicity, large numbers of people visited the imprisoned Union-

---

[32] Hüseyin Cahid Yalçın, "Meşrutiyet Hatıraları, 1908-1918," *Fikir Hareketleri*, 7 (October 24, 1936-April 17, 1937), p.310; and, Mehmed Cavid, "Meşrutiyet Devrine Ait Cavid Bey'in Hatıraları: 143," *Tanin*, January 24, 1944, p.2.

[33] Mehmed Cavid, "Meşrutiyet Devrine Ait Cavid Bey'in Hatıraları: 143," *Tanin*, January 24, 1944, p.2; and, Hüseyin Cahid Yalçın, "Meşrutiyet Hatıraları, 1908-1918," *Fikir Hareketleri*, 7 (October 24, 1936-April 17, 1937), p.310.

[34] "Sermuharrir ve Müdür-ü Mesullerimizin Mahkumiyeti: Divan-ı Harb Kararıyla mı, Nâzım Paşa'nın Emriyle mi?" *Senin*, August 30, 1328/September 12, 1912, p.1; Hüseyin Cahid Yalçın, "Meşrutiyet Hatıraları, 1908-1918," *Fikir Hareketleri*, 7 (October 24, 1936-April 17, 1937), p.326; Mehmed Cavid, "Meşrutiyet Devrine Ait Cavid Bey'in Hatıraları: 144," *Tanin*, January 25, 1944, p.2; and, Aram Andonyan, *Balkan Savaşı*, p.193.

[35] Hüseyin Cahid [Yalçın], "Mukaddime-i İnkısam ve İzmihlâl," *Hak*, August 31, 1328/September 13, 1912, p.1; and, "Biz Ne Diyoruz, Onlar Ne Diyorlar!" *Hak*, August 31, 1328/September 13, 1912, p.1. See also, Hüseyin Cahid Yalçın, "Meşrutiyet Hatıraları, 1908-1918," *Fikir Hareketleri*, 7 (October 24, 1936-April 17, 1937), p.341.

[36] "Constantinople Letter," *The Near East*, September 27, 1912, p.603.

ist leaders which in turn drew the attention of monarchist politicians, among them Lütfi Fikri Bey, who asked that the Martial Law authorities forbid these visits.[37]

A recent cabinet circular which demanded that municipal
council members refrain from any political affiliation also
aroused a measure of opposition. Several local councillors refused to comply with the circular, and in İzmir, the problem
was compounded by the government's dismissal of certain officials who were replaced by well-known adherents of the *ancien régime*.[38] This was the work of Kâmil Pasha.

Kâmil Pasha's influence in the Cabinet rivalled the Grand
Vezier's, and it was because of him that Fuad Bey, a member
of Kâmil Pasha's family, was named Director of Political Affairs for İzmir. He had held the post during the *ancien régime*, had fled the country when the Constitution was proclaimed, and because the Committee considered him reactionary, was excluded from political office during the time
Unionists were in power. In İzmir, the Committee of Union
and Progress was quite strong; but with the formation of the
monarchist Cabinet, the Entente Libérale opened a club and
Dr. Rıza Tevfik [Bölükbaşı], ex-deputy for Edirne and one of
the party's leaders, came from İstanbul for the inauguration.[39]

On September 30, quoting *Osmanischer Lloyd*, the official
German organ in İstanbul, *Tanin* announced that the Great
Powers had arranged to discuss certain reforms which were to
be imposed on the Macedonian provinces. It was also reported
that Great Britain was in complete agreement with the
scheme.[40] Unionists not only considered this a potential
breach of sovereignty, but also a regression to pre-revolutionary days when European Powers had dictated reform mea-

---

[37] Hüseyin Cahid Yalçın, "Meşrutiyet Hatıraları, 1908-1918," *Fikir Hareketleri*, 7 (October 24, 1936-April 17, 1937), p.358. See also, Mehmed Cavid, "Meşrutiyet Devrine Ait Cavid Bey'in Hatıraları: 144," *Tanin*, January 25, 1944, p.2; and,
Mehmed Cavid, "Meşrutiyet Devrine Ait Cavid Bey'in Hatıraları: 145," *Tanin*,
January 26, 1944, p.2.

[38] "İzmir Valisi ... Başladı," *Tanin*, September 10, 1328/September 23, 1912,
p.2; and, "Notes From Smyrna," *The Near East*, September 27, 1912, p.603. See also,
Rifat Uçarol, *Gazi Ahmet Muhtar Paşa: Bir Osmanlı Paşası ve Dönemi*, p.372.

[39] "Notes From Smyrna," *The Near East*, October 11, 1912, p.664.

[40] "Müşterek Nota," *Tanin*, September 17, 1328/September 30, 1912, p.2.

sures and the absolutist regime of Abdülhamid had carried these out without resistance. The association was unnerving, to say the least.[41]

On October 1, the news that the Bulgarian and Serbian armed forces had been put on a state of alert, reached Turkey.[42] Echoing public opinion, the Committee of Union and Progress, declared that it would support a war should the Balkan states decide to attack.[43] The Committee also announced that a demonstration to support Turkish sovereignty and oppose the imposition of any reform scheme of European Powers would be held at Sultan Ahmed Square on October 4.[44] A large crowd attended. Prominent Unionist politicians— Talât Bey, ex-deputy for Edirne and one of the members of the Central Committee, Hasan Fehmi [Tümerkan], ex-deputy for Sinob, Emmanuel Emmanuelidis, ex-deputy for İzmir, Hagop Boyadjian, ex-deputy for Rodosto, Nesim Masliah, ex-deputy for İzmir, Ömer Naci Bey, ex-deputy for Kırk Kilise—as well as Celaleddin Arif Bey, representative for the Bar Association, Bessaraya Efendi, member of the Senate, Ubeydullah [Hatipoğlu] Efendi, and Yusuf [Akçura] made highly charged speeches, defending Turkey's territorial integrity as well as the rights of its citizens.[45]

---

[41] Hüseyin Cahid Yalçın, "Meşrutiyet Hatıraları, 1908-1918," *Fikir Hareketleri,* 7 (October 24, 1936-April 17, 1937), p.373.

[42] "Harb?" *Tanin,* September 19, 1328/October 2, 1912, p.1; Ali Kemal, "Harb İstiyorlarsa Harb Ederiz," *İkdam,* September 19, 1328/October 2, 1912, p.1; "Balkanlarda Seferberlik: Meclis-i Vükelâ Fevkalâde İctimaı," *İkdam,* September 19, 1328/October 2, 1912, p.1; Aram Andonyan, *Balkan Savaşı,* pp.195-198; and, Mustafa Ragıb Esatlı, *İttihat ve Terakki Tarihinde Esrar Perdesi: Yakup Cemil Niçin ve Nasıl Öldürüldü?* p.120.

[43] "İttihad ve Terakki Merkez-i Umumisi'nin Beyannamesi," *Tanin,* September 20, 1328/October 3, 1912, p.1. See also, Hüseyin Cahid Yalçın, "Meşrutiyet Hatıraları, 1908-1918," *Fikir Hareketleri,* 7 (October 24, 1936-April 17, 1937), pp.389-390; and, Mustafa Ragıb Esatlı, *İttihat ve Terakki Tarihinde Esrar Perdesi: Yakup Cemil Niçin ve Nasıl Öldürüldü?* pp.120-121. Şinasi, the editor of *Ahenk*—a pro-Unionist İzmir newspaper—also expressed similar views (Şinasi, "Balkan İttifakı," *Ahenk,* September 18, 1328/October 1, 1912, p.1; Şinasi, "Bir Şayia Münasebetiyle," *Ahenk,* September 20, 1328/October 3, 1912, p.1; and, Şinasi, "Ne Olacak," *Ahenk,* September 21, 1328/October 4, 1912, p.1, all quoted in Zeki Arıkan, "Balkan Savaşı ve Kamuoyu," pp.172-173).

[44] "Harb Mitingi: İttihad ve Terakki Cemiyeti Tarafından Mürettep—Bugün Zevali Saat İkide Sultan Ahmed Meydanı'nda," *Tanin,* September 21, 1328/October 4, 1912, p.1. See also, Hüseyin Cahid Yalçın, "Meşrutiyet Hatıraları, 1908-1918," *Fikir Hareketleri,* 7 (October 24, 1936-April 17, 1937), p.390. See also, Rifat Uçarol, *Gazi Ahmet Muhtar Paşa: Bir Osmanlı Paşası ve Dönemi,* pp.412-413.

[45] "Dünkü Büyük Nümayişler: Harb! Harb!: Sultan Ahmed'te—Harbiye Nezareti'nde—Türbe-i Fatih'te," *Tanin,* September 22, 1328/October 5, 1912, p.3. See

While public opinion and the Committee of Union and Progress vociferously opposed any submission to the European Powers, the monarchist Government showed itself willing to capitulate to outside pressure, and on October 6, it announced its decision to adopt measures based on those prepared by the European Reform Commission for the re-organisation of the Eastern Rumelian Administration which had been created in 1880 according to the stipulations of the Treaty of Berlin. This, however, did nothing to relieve external pressures, and if anything, only worsened the internal situation.[46]

The following day, students organised a meeting at the university, after which a crowd of several hundred, led by Dr. Nâzım Bey, Muhiddin [Birgen] and other Unionists, appeared before the Sublime Porte and called on the Grand Vezier to make an appearance. Gazi Ahmed Muhtar Pasha asked to meet with a delegation, but the crowd refused. Finally, he appeared with his son, Mahmud Muhtar Pasha, and was met with shouts of "Down with the Government!," "We Want no Reforms," "We Want War." Mahmud Muhtar Pasha then spoke. Though based on the agreement of 1880, the reforms, he said, were not identical with those of the Treaty of Berlin— but this was hardly the point, he continued: whatever the case,

---

also, Hüseyin Cahid Yalçın, "Meşrutiyet Hatıraları, 1908-1918," *Fikir Hareketleri*, 7 (October 24, 1936-April 17, 1937), p.405; Aram Andonyan, *Balkan Savaşı*, p.199; and, Mustafa Ragıb Esatlı, *İttihat ve Terakki Tarihinde Esrar Perdesi: Yakup Cemil Niçin ve Nasıl Öldürüldü?* pp.121-123. See also, Mehmed Cavid, "Meşrutiyet Devrine Ait Cavid Bey'in Hatıraları: 146," *Tanin*, January 27, 1944, p.2; and, Yücel Aktar, "1912 Yılı 'Harb Mitingleri' ve Balkan Harbi'ne Etkileri," pp.118-119; and, *idem, İkinci Meşrutiyet Dönemi Öğrenci Olayları, 1908-1918*, pp.87-88.
    Similar demonstrations took place in Kayseri on October 5, in Konya, and in İzmir on October 11. There was another meeting in İzmir organised by the Committee of Union and Progress which took place on October 13 (Zeki Arıkan, "Balkan Savaşı ve Kamuoyu," pp.173-175).
    [46] "Ya Devlet Başa, Ya Kuzgun Leşe," *Tanin*, September 24, 1328/October 7, 1912, p.1; Mehmed Cavid, "Meşrutiyet Devrine Ait Cavid Bey'in Hatıraları: 146," *Tanin*, January 27, 1944, p.2; Hüseyin Cahid Yalçın, "Meşrutiyet Hatıraları, 1908-1918," *Fikir Hareketleri*, 7 (October 24, 1936-April 17, 1937), p.406; "Constantinople Letter," *The Near East*, October 18, 1912, p.692; Aram Andonyan, *Balkan Savaşı*, p.194, and 201-203; Rifat Uçarol, *Gazi Ahmet Muhtar Paşa: Bir Osmanlı Paşası ve Dönemi*, p..414; and, Mustafa Ragıb Esatlı, *İttihat ve Terakki Tarihinde Esrar Perdesi: Yakup Cemil Niçin ve Nasıl Öldürüldü?* pp.123-124. See also, F.O. 424/234, Sir Gerard Lowther to Sir Edward Grey, Constantinople, October 6, 1912, *Correspondence Respecting the Turkish War, Part I*, No.10224, p.179; F.O. 424/234, Sir Edward Grey to Sir Gerard Lowther, Foreign Office, October 11, 1912, *Correspondence Respecting the Turkish War, Part I*, No.10224, p.214; F.O. 424/234, Sir Edward Grey to Sir Gerard Lowther, Foreign Office, October 12, 1912, *Correspondence Respecting the Turkish War, Part I*, No.10224, p.223; and, Yusuf Hikmet Bayur, *Türk İnkılâbı Tarihi, 2/1*, pp.401-406.

the Government would not be bullied either by the Balkan states or the riotous students. Gazi Ahmed Muhtar Pasha spoke along the same lines, shortly before the arrival of troops put an end to the demonstration.[47]

Unsatisfied, the population became increasingly uneasy throughout the evening, and in a move to preempt unrest and silence the opposition, the Government proclaimed martial law, and all newspapers were barred from printing any news of the demonstration.[48] *Tanin* journalists, Aka Gündüz, Hakkı Cemil, Recai Nüzhet, and Ubeydullah [Hatipoğlu] were arrested, and the paper was again closed down on October 12.[49]

The day after the demonstration, on October 8, Montenegro declared war on Turkey.[50] On October 10, Ambassadors of the

---

[47] "Tezahürat-ı Milliye: Darülfünun Milli Alayı," *İkdam*, September 24, 1328/October 7, 1912, p.1; "Osmanlı Darülfünunu ve Dünkü Nümayiş," *Tanin*, September 25, 1328/October 8, 1912, p.3; "Constantinople Letter," *The Near East*, October 18, 1912, p.692; Mehmed Cavid, "Meşrutiyet Devrine Ait Cavid Bey'in Hatıraları: 147," *Tanin*, January 28, 1944, p.2; Hüseyin Cahid Yalçın, "Meşrutiyet Hatıraları, 1908-1918," *Fikir Hareketleri*, 7 (October 24, 1936-April 17, 1937), p.406; Mustafa Ragıb Esatlı, *İttihat ve Terakki Tarihinde Esrar Perdesi: Yakup Cemil Niçin ve Nasıl Öldürüldü?* pp.125-126; Ahmed Bedevi Kuran, *Osmanlı İmparatorluğunda İnkılâp Hareketleri ve Milli Mücadele*, p.570; Aram Andonyan, *Balkan Savaşı*, p.204-207; Yusuf Hikmet Bayur, *Türk İnkılâbı Tarihi, 2/1*, p.406; and, Yusuf Hikmet Bayur, *Türk İnkılâbı Tarihi, 2/4*, p.243. See also, Yücel Aktar, "1912 Yılı 'Harb Mitingleri' ve Balkan Harbi'ne Etkileri," pp.119-123; *idem*, *İkinci Meşrutiyet Dönemi Öğrenci Olayları, 1908-1918*, pp.88-96; and, Rifat Uçarol, *Gazi Ahmet Muhtar Paşa: Bir Osmanlı Paşası ve Dönemi*, pp.415-416.

[48] "Constantinople Letter," *The Near East*, October 18, 1912, p.692; Mehmed Cavid, "Meşrutiyet Devrine Ait Cavid Bey'in Hatıraları: 147," *Tanin*, January 28, 1944, p.2; and, Hüseyin Cahid Yalçın, "Meşrutiyet Hatıraları, 1908-1918," *Fikir Hareketleri*, 7 (October 24, 1936-April 17, 1937), p.406. *Tanin* of September 25, 1328/October 8, 1912, printed the government order barring the press to report the demonstration (Hüseyin Cahid Yalçın, "Meşrutiyet Hatıraları, 1908-1918," *Fikir Hareketleri*, 7 (October 24, 1936-April 17, 1937), p.406).

[49] "Tanin Gazetesine," *Cenin*, September 30, 1328/October 13, 1912, p.1. It reappeared under the name of *Cenin* on October 13 (Hüseyin Cahid Yalçın, "Meşrutiyet Hatıraları, 1908-1918," *Fikir Hareketleri*, 8 (April 24-October 16, 1937), p.5). See also, Mehmed Cavid, "Meşrutiyet Devrine Ait Cavid Bey'in Hatıraları: 147," *Tanin*, January 28, 1944, p.2; Mehmed Cavid, "Meşrutiyet Devrine Ait Cavid Bey'in Hatıraları: 148," *Tanin*, January 29, 1944, p.2; Yücel Aktar, "1912 Yılı 'Harb Mitingleri' ve Balkan Harbi'ne Etkileri," pp.125-126; Ahmed Bedevi Kuran, *Osmanlı İmparatorluğunda İnkılâp Hareketleri ve Milli Mücadele*, p.570; Rifat Uçarol, *Gazi Ahmet Muhtar Paşa: Bir Osmanlı Paşası ve Dönemi*, p.417; and, Aram Andonyan, *Balkan Savaşı*, pp.198-199, and 207.

[50] "Hele Şükür!" *Tanin*, September 26, 1328/October 9, 1912, p.1; "Muharebe Başladı: Evvelâ Karadağ!" *Tanin*, September 26, 1328/October 9, 1912, p.1; "Harb," *İkdam*, September 26, 1328/October 9, 1912, p.1; "Constantinople Letter," *The Near East*, October 18, 1912, p.692; Hüseyin Cahid Yalçın, "Meşrutiyet Hatıraları, 1908-1918," *Fikir Hareketleri*, 8 (April 24-October 16, 1937), p.5; Mehmed Cavid, "Meşrutiyet Devrine Ait Cavid Bey'in Hatıraları: 147," *Tanin*, January 28, 1944, p.2; Mustafa Ragıb Esatlı, *İttihat ve Terakki Tarihinde Esrar Perdesi: Yakup Cemil Niçin ve Nasıl Öldürüldü?* p.127; Aram Andonyan, *Balkan Savaşı*, pp.208-211; *The Other Balkan Wars: A 1913 Carnegie Endowment Inquiry in Retrospect*, p.49;

Great Powers—Austria-Hungary, Great Britain, France,
Russia, and Germany—handed a note urging the Turkish
Government to start immediately discussing the reform proposals. The Turkish Government replied that it had already
accepted the proposal and that it was about to put measures into
effect.[51] On October 13, however, the Bulgarian, Serbian and
Greek governments gave a collective note to Turkey demanding full autonomy for the Macedonian provinces, the appointment of either Belgian or Swiss governors, and the creation of
an independent gendarmerie. They demanded proportional
representation of each nationality in the Chamber of Deputies,
and the creation of a superior council composed of an equal
number of Muslims and Christians and above the authority of
the grand vezier, which would superintend the introduction of
these reforms. The Sublime Porte had to guarantee to inaugu-
rate this new regime, in good faith, within six months and to
recall its order for mobilisation immediately, or the allies
would not answer for the consequences.[52] On October 15,
Turkey severed diplomatic relations with Bulgaria, Serbia,
and Greece; and two days later declared war on both Bulgaria
and Serbia.[53] Greece declared war on Turkey that same day.[54]

---

and, Ahmed Bedevi Kuran, *Osmanlı İmparatorluğunda İnkılâp Hareketleri ve
Milli Mücadele*, p.570. See also, Metin Ayışığı, *Mareşal Ahmet İzzet Paşa: Askerî
ve Siyasî Hayatı*, p.56; and, Edwin Pears, *Forty Years in Constantinople: The Recollections of Sir Edwin Pears, 1873-1915*, p.326.

[51] Babanzade İsmail Hakkı, "Devletlerin Müdahale ve Murakabeye Hakları
Var mı?" *Tanin*, September 28, 1328/October 11, 1912, pp.1-2; "Devletlerin Umur-u
Dahiliyemize Müdahalesi," *Tanin*, September 29, 1328/October 12, 1912, p.1; "No-
tanın Tarihçesi: İş Nasıl Hazırlandı," *Tanin*, September 29, 1328/October 12, 1912,
p.3; "Düvel-i Muazzamanın Notası," *İkdam*, October 2, 1328/October 15, 1912, p.3;
Hüseyin Cahid Yalçın, "Meşrutiyet Hatıraları, 1908-1918," *Fikir Hareketleri, 8*
(April 24-October 16, 1937), p.6; and, Aram Andonyan, *Balkan Savaşı*, p.208. See
also, Yusuf Hikmet Bayur, *Türk İnkılâbı Tarihi, 2/1*, pp.416-419.

[52] Yusuf Hikmet Bayur, *Türk İnkılâbı Tarihi, 2/1*, pp.419-422; N. Dwight Harris, "The Macedonian Question and the Balkan War," p.215; Douglas Dakin, "The
Diplomacy of the Great Powers and the Balkan States, 1908-1914," p.352; and, *The
Other Balkan Wars: A 1913 Carnegie Endowment Inquiry in Retrospect*, p.49. See
also, Mustafa Ragıb Esatlı, *İttihat ve Terakki Tarihinde Esrar Perdesi: Yakup Cemil Niçin ve Nasıl Öldürüldü?* p.128; Metin Ayışığı, *Mareşal Ahmet İzzet Paşa:
Askerî ve Siyasî Hayatı*, p.56; and, Hüseyin Cahid Yalçın, "Meşrutiyet Hatıraları,
1908-1918," *Fikir Hareketleri, 8* (April 24-October 16, 1937), p.22.

[53] "Balkanlarda Harbin Mukaddimesi: İnkıta-ı Münasebat—Meclis-i Vükelâ
Dün Hükûmet-i Osmaniye'nin Bulgaristan, Sırbistan, Yunanistan Hükûmetleriyle
Münasebat-ı Siyasiyesini Kat' Ederek Süferamıza Avdet Emrini Vermiştir," *Cenin*, October 3, 1328/October 16, 1912, p.2; "Harb İlân Edildi mi?" *Cenin*, October
4, 1328/October 17, 1912, p.1; "Yaşasın Harb: Pasaportlar Verildi!: Gece Geç Vakit
Orduya Taarruz Emri—Dün Sabah da Sırb ve Bulgar Sefirlerine Pasaportları Verildi!—Ya Yunanistan?" *Cenin*, October 5, 1328/October 18, 1912, pp.1-2; and,

Though the war overshadowed the domestic political crisis, it also made it easier for the monarchist government to take further action against the Unionists. On October 25 the governor of İstanbul was dismissed and Cemil [Topuzlu] Paşa, son-in-law of Cemaleddin Efendi, was appointed in his place; other important functionaries in the state bureaucracy were also replaced.[55] Rumours that Gazi Ahmed Muhtar Pasha would step down, to be succeeded by Kâmil Pasha, began to circulate, and on October 29, this became a reality.[56] By this time, *Tanin*, as *Senin*, had again been closed down, only to reappear as *Hak* on October 30. In an editorial of that day, Hüseyin Cahid [Yalçın] severely criticised the change of Government at such a critical moment, and as everyone knew that Gazi Ahmed Muhtar Pasha had no intention of resigning, he blamed Kâmil Pasha's ambition for such a change. The government responded by suppressing several more anti-

---

"Harb Başladı: Tebliğ-i Resmi," *Ikdam*, October 5, 1328/October 18, 1912, p.2. See also, Rifat Uçarol, *Gazi Ahmet Muhtar Paşa: Bir Osmanlı Paşası ve Dönemi*, pp.422-423; N. Dwight Harris, "The Macedonian Question and the Balkan War," p.216; *The Other Balkan Wars: A 1913 Carnegie Endowment Inquiry in Retrospect*, p.49; Hüseyin Cahid Yalçın, "Meşrutiyet Hatıraları, 1908-1918," *Fikir Hareketleri*, 8 (April 24-October 16, 1937), p.22; Mustafa Ragıb Eşatlı, *Ittihat ve Terakki Tarihinde Esrar Perdesi: Yakup Cemil Niçin ve Nasıl Öldürüldü?* p.129; Yusuf Hikmet Bayur, *Türk İnkılâbı Tarihi, 2/1*, pp.427-430; Metin Ayışığı, *Mareşal Ahmet İzzet Paşa: Askerî ve Siyasî Hayatı*, p.56; and, "A Year's Retrospect," *The Near East*, January 3, 1913, p.246.

    [54] "Yunanistan ile Ne Oluyor?" *Cenin*, October 6, 1328/October 19, 1912, p.1; "Bütün Hududlarda Muharebe Ediliyor: Bulgaristan—Sırbistan—Karadağ—Yunanistan," *Cenin*, October 6, 1328/October 19, 1912, pp.1-2; "A Year's Retrospect," *The Near East*, January 3, 1913, p.246; and, Hüseyin Cahid Yalçın, "Meşrutiyet Hatıraları, 1908-1918," *Fikir Hareketleri*, 8 (April 24-October 16, 1937), p.22.

    [55] "İstanbul Valiliği," *Ikdam*, October 13, 1328/October 26, 1912, p.4; and, Hüseyin Cahid Yalçın, "Meşrutiyet Hatıraları, 1908-1918," *Fikir Hareketleri*, 8 (April 24-October 16, 1937), p.36. For a different and highly sanitised account of the same appointment see Cemil Topuzlu, *İstibdat, Meşrutiyet, Cumhuriyet Devirlerinde Seksen Yıllık Hatıralarım*, pp.86-87.

    [56] "Buhran-ı Vükelâ Şayiaları," *Senin*, October 15, 1328/October 28, 1912, p.2; Hüseyin Cahid Yalçın, "Meşrutiyet Hatıraları, 1908-1918," *Fikir Hareketleri*, 8 (April 24-October 16, 1937), p.36; [Hüseyin Cahid Yalçın], "Buhran-ı Vükelâ," *Hak*, October 17, 1328/October 30, 1912, p.1; and, "Kâmil Paşa'nın Sadareti," *Ikdam*, October 17, 1328/October 30, 1912, pp.1-2. See also, Hüseyin Cahid Yalçın, "Meşrutiyet Hatıraları, 1908-1918," *Fikir Hareketleri*, 8 (April 24-October 16, 1937), p.38; Rifat Uçarol, *Gazi Ahmet Muhtar Paşa: Bir Osmanlı Paşası ve Dönemi*, pp.434-439; Ahmed Bedevi Kuran, *Osmanlı İmparatorluğunda İnkılâp Hareketleri ve Milli Mücadele*, p.571; and, Hasan Amca, *Doğmayan Hürriyet: Bir Devrin İçyüzü, 1908-1918*, p.118. Serious attempts to install Kâmil Pasha as Grand Vezier had begun on October 4 (Yusuf Hikmet Bayur, *Türk İnkılâbı Tarihi, 2/4*, p.247).

    The British Embassy had foreknowledge about the cabinet change (F.O. 424/234, Sir Gerard Lowther to Sir Edward Grey, Constantinople, October 27, 1912, *Correspondence Respecting the Turkish War, Part I*, No.10224, p.361).

monarchist papers which had joined in *Tanin*'s condemnation.[57] The liberal Egyptian press also criticised Kâmil Pasha's appointment, and *al-Alam* was suppressed for its attacks.[58] The new Grand Vezier immediately announced that the general elections would be postponed indefinitely due to domestic and foreign conditions.[59]

Monarchists celebrated Kâmil Pasha's long-awaited rise to power, feeling that he would restore confidence in a solution to Turkey's problems which would be compatible with the dignity of the Empire. Because he had friendly ties with Great Britain, monarchists felt that in case of need, Great Britain would surely come to Turkey's rescue.[60] In addition, the British were sure to be pleased with the appointment of Ahmed Reşid [Rey] as Minister of the Interior.[61] After the military *coup* of July, 1912, Ahmed Reşid [Rey] had been appointed Governor of Aydın, to the full satisfaction of both the monarchists and the British colony.[62]

---

[57] [Hüseyin Cahid Yalçın], "Buhran-ı Vükelâ," *Hak*, October 17, 1328/October 30, 1912, printed in full in Hüseyin Cahid Yalçın, "Meşrutiyet Hatıraları, 1908-1918," *Fikir Hareketleri*, 8 (April 24-October 16, 1937), pp.53-54; F.O. 424/235, Sir Gerard Lowther to Sir Edward Grey, Constantinople, November 2, 1912, *Correspondence Respecting the Turkish War, Part II*, No.10263, p.96; and, "Constantinople Letter," *The Near East*, November 8, 1912, p.3. *Hak* was suspended—and appeared as *Renin*—for this editorial ("Buhran-ı Vükelâ," *Renin*, October 18, 1328/October 31, 1912—p.1).

[58] "Constantinople Letter," *The Near East*, November 8, 1912, p.2.

[59] "İntihabatın Tehiri," *İkdam*, October 18, 1328/October 31, 1912, p.4; *Renin*, October 18, 1328/October 31, 1912, cited in Hüseyin Cahid Yalçın, "Meşrutiyet Hatıraları, 1908-1918," *Fikir Hareketleri*, 8 (April 24-October 16, 1937), pp.54-55; and, F.O. 424/235, Sir Gerard Lowther to Sir Edward Grey, Constantinople, October 31, 1912, *Correspondence Respecting the Turkish War, Part II*, No.10263, p.96. The rumours to that effect had been printed two days ago as 'information received from reliable sources' ("İntihabatın Tehiri," *Senin*, October 16, 1328/October 29, 1912, p.3).

[60] "Kâmil Paşa," *İkdam*, October 17, 1328/October 30, 1912, p.1; Ali Kemal, "Yine Kâmil Paşa," *İkdam*, October 18, 1328/October 31, 1912, p.1; "Constantinople Letter," *The Near East*, November 8, 1912, p.3; Rifat Uçarol, *Gazi Ahmet Muhtar Paşa: Bir Osmanlı Paşası ve Dönemi*, p.440; Şehbenderzade Filibeli Ahmed Hilmi, *Muhalefetin İflâsı: İtilâf ve Hürriyet Fırkası*, p.50; and, Aram Andonyan, *Balkan Savaşı*, p.189. See also, F.O. 424/234, Sir Gerard Lowther to Sir Edward Grey, Constantinople, October 21, 1912, *Correspondence Respecting the Turkish War, Part I*, No.10224, p.305*.
The news of the appointment of Kâmil Pasha as Grand Vezier was received with pleasure in İzmir by the British colony, many of whose members knew him personally and were on very friendly terms with him ("Notes From Smyrna," *The Near East*, November 22, 1912, p.65).

[61] F.O. 424/235, Sir Gerard Lowther to Sir Edward Grey, Constantinople, November 2, 1912, *Correspondence Respecting the Turkish War, Part II*, No.10263, p.96.

[62] "Notes From Smyrna," *The Near East*, November 22, 1912, p.65; and, F.O.

The battle of Lüleburgaz began on October 28, and ended two days later with a complete Turkish defeat.[63] Though Turkish troops rallied at various points in an effort to delay the Bulgarian advance, by early November, they had been defeated from Çorlu to Istranca. İpek fell to the Montenegrins, and Prizren to the Serbians; the fall of Rodosto to the Bulgarians seemed imminent. The Greeks continued their advance on Salonica, their intention being to isolate the city rather than make a direct attack.[64] And while the Serbian armies were closing in on Monastir, also advancing towards Salonica, King Peter entered Üsküb in triumph, restoring the ancient capital of the Serbs which had been lost some five hundred years before.[65]

Following the Turkish defeat at Kırk Kilise, there were two or three days of official silence during which Nâzım Pasha went to the front and took command. The next official communiqué spoke of fighting on a line between Lüleburgaz and Vize, and the public realised that the Turkish forces had been pushed back half way to the capital.[66]

Another communiqué, issued in İstanbul on November 3, warned that a nation at war could but await its end with patience and courage, and submit with resignation to all its consequences. It went on to announce that while Turkish troops were "successfully holding their own in the Scutari and Janina districts, the Eastern Army in the Lüleburgaz and Vize districts had found itself obliged to retire on the Çatalca lines of defence, in order to enable it to offer a successful resistance."[67]

424/235, Sir Gerard Lowther to Sir Edward Grey, Constantinople, November 2, 1912, Correspondence Respecting the Turkish War, Part II, No.10263, p.96.
[63] Aram Andonyan, Balkan Savaşı, pp.469-482; and, Metin Ayışığı, Mareşal Ahmet İzzet Paşa: Askerî ve Siyasî Hayatı, p.59.
[64] Yusuf Hikmet Bayur, Türk İnkılâbı Tarihi, 2/2, pp.37-45; and, "Notes of the Week," The Near East, November 8, 1912, pp.1-2. Grrek troops entered Salonica on November 8, 1912 (Metin Ayışığı, Mareşal Ahmet İzzet Paşa: Askerî ve Siyasî Hayatı, p.58).
[65] Aram Andonyan, Balkan Savaşı, pp.335-338; Metin Ayışığı, Mareşal Ahmet İzzet Paşa: Askerî ve Siyasî Hayatı, p.58; Edwin Pears, Forty Years in Constantinople: The Recollections of Sir Edwin Pears, 1873-1915, p.326; and, "Notes of the Week," The Near East, November 8, 1912, p.2.
[66] "Constantinople Letter," The Near East, November 8, 1912, p.3. See also, Yusuf Hikmet Bayur, Türk İnkılâbı Tarihi, 2/2, pp.55-56.
[67] "Notes of the Week," The Near East, November 8, 1912, p.1. For the text of the Government communication, which was published in the October 22, 1328/No-

That day, the Turkish government instructed its Ambassadors to request that the Powers intervene towards the immediate cessation of hostilities.[68] The Powers replied that neutrality forbade them to intervene, but that they were ready to offer their mediation should the Turkish Government place itself unreservedly in their hands.[69] The monarchist Government on November 4 at once showed a due appreciation of the position of the Powers, by following up its first application by an appeal "for the collective mediation of the Great Powers, with a view to an immediate cessation of hostilities and the settlement of the conditions of peace."[70] This was tantamount to unconditional surrender. By placing itself unreservedly in the hands of the Great Powers, the monarchist Kâmil Pasha Cabinet effectively conceded defeat, and as surely as if it had surrendered directly, opened itself up to the demands of the Balkan states.[71]

---

vember 4, 1912 issues of newspapers, see Hüseyin Cahid Yalçın, "Meşrutiyet Hatıraları, 1908-1918," *Fikir Hareketleri*, 8 (April 24-October 16, 1937), p.55.

[68] "Notes of the Week," *The Near East*, November 8, 1912, p.1; and, F.O. 424/235, Sir Gerard Lowther to Sir Edward Grey, Constantinople, November 3, 1912, *Correspondence Respecting the Turkish War, Part II*, No.10263, p.51. See also, Yusuf Hikmet Bayur, *Türk İnkılâbı Tarihi*, 2/2, p.60; Mustafa Ragıb Esatlı, *İttihat ve Terakki Tarihinde Esrar Perdesi: Yakup Cemil Niçin ve Nasıl Öldürüldü?* pp.353-354; Metin Ayışığı, *Mareşal Ahmet İzzet Paşa: Askerî ve Siyasî Hayatı*, p.59; Edwin Pears, *Forty Years in Constantinople: The Recollections of Sir Edwin Pears, 1873-1915*, p.328; and, Süleyman Külçe, *Osmanlı Tarihinde Arnavutluk*, p.441.

[69] "Constantinople Letter," *The Near East*, November 15, 1912, p.35; and, F.O. 424/235, Sir G. Buchanan to Sir Edward Grey, St. Petersburg, November 4, 1912, *Correspondence Respecting the Turkish War, Part II*, No.10263, p.68.

[70] "Notes of the Week," *The Near East*, November 8, 1912, p.1; F.O. 424/235, Sir E. Goschen to Sir Edward Grey, Berlin, November 4, 1912, *Correspondence Respecting the Turkish War, Part II*, No.10263, p.69; and, "Hariciye Nazırının Beyantı," *İkdam*, October 23, 1328/November 5, 1912, p.1. See also, Mehmed Cavid, "Meşrutiyet Devrine Ait Cavid Bey'in Hatıraları: 156," *Tanin*, February 6, 1944, p.2; and, Mehmed Cavid, "Meşrutiyet Devrine Ait Cavid Bey'in Hatıraları: 157," *Tanin*, February 7, 1944, p.2. The text of the Note was: "The Imperial Ottoman Government asks the Great Powers for their collective mediation with a view to the immediate cessation of hostilities and the settlement of conditions of peace" (F.O. 424/235, Sir Edward Grey to Sir H. Bax-Ironside, Foreign Office, November 8, 1912, *Correspondence Respecting the Turkish War, Part II*, No.10263, p.114). Bayur wrongly dates this second appeal of the Turkish Goverment as November 5 (Yusuf Hikmet Bayur, *Türk İnkılâbı Tarihi*, 2/2, p.74). For Kâmil Pasha's submissive plea to Sir Edward Grey see, F.O. 800/79, Kiamil Pasha to Sir Edward Grey, November 7, 1912, quoted in Feroz Ahmad, "Great Britain's Relations with the Young Turks, 1908-1914," pp.319-320.

[71] "Notes of the Week," *The Near East*, November 8, 1912, p.1; "Nearing the End," *The Near East*, November 8, 1912, p.16; and, XXXIII. 291, Kühlmann to the German Foreign Office, November 6, 1912, reproduced in E. T. S. Dugdale (Ed.), *German Diplomatic Documents, 1871-1914, 4: The Descent to the Abyss, 1911-1914*, p.119. See also, Hasan Amca, *Doğmayan Hürriyet: Bir Devrin İçyüzü, 1908-1918*, pp.118-119.

At this point, the army declared itself opposed to any cease-fire which might even have vaguely resembled an unconditional surrender. Kâmil Pasha convened a meeting of generals at the Sublime Porte. The generals expressed themselves in favour of resistance, and were supported by Nâzım Pasha and a large number of field officers.[72] The Government suddenly changed its position and declared that it would exhaust all military means before yielding to the mediation of the Powers—news which the Committee of Union and Progress welcomed.[73] The German and Austrian Ambassadors and military advisors at İstanbul had also strongly urged resistance.[74]

This decided, Edirne contrived to hold out for another week. Turkish forces offered fierce resistance, keeping the besieging Bulgarian forces at a respectful distance and inflicting heavy losses. Rodosto did not fall into Bulgarian hands until November 10.[75]

By November 7, the Greek army had advanced within striking distance of Salonica. That evening, the commandant and a representative of the commander of the Turkish army, together with the Consuls-General, discussed proposals for the capitulation of the port and its garrison. The Turkish army was given until the following morning to accept the Greek conditions, and when after further talks no reply was forthcoming, the Greeks advanced. As they drew near the Turkish outposts, however, a letter arrived from the Turkish commander accepting the conditions; the Greeks duly took possession of the city, and on November 9, a Bulgarian division arrived, along with a Serbian regiment. The fate of Salonica would form part of the general settlement after the war, and indications favoured its establishment as an international port.[76]

In the November 9 issue of *Tanin*, Hüseyin Cahid [Yalçın]

---

[72] Yusuf Hikmet Bayur, *Türk İnkılâbı Tarihi*, 2/2, pp.78-82; and, "Constantinople Letter," *The Near East*, November 15, 1912, p.35.

[73] "Constantinople Letter," *The Near East*, November 15, 1912, p.35.

[74] "Constantinople Letter," *The Near East*, November 22, 1912, p.63.

[75] "Notes of the Week," *The Near East*, November 15, 1912, p.34.

[76] "Notes of the Week," *The Near East*, November 15, 1912, p.34. See also, Metin Ayışığı, *Mareşal Ahmet İzzet Paşa: Askerî ve Siyasî Hayatı*, p.58; Basil Kondis, *Greece and Albania, 1908-1914*, p.85; and, Douglas Dakin, "The Diplomacy of the Great Powers and the Balkan States, 1908-1914," p.353.

stated that the Unionists wanted Mahmud Şevket Pasha appointed Commander-General of the Armed Forces.[77] *Tanin* was closed down upon the publication of this editorial, and its appearance under any other name was banned. Hüseyin Cahid [Yalçın] argued that the revocation of newspaper licences was unlawful; the government's reply stated that the law no longer applied.[78]

On November 12, the Kâmil Pasha Cabinet decided to ask its enemies for their terms of peace.[79] The guns ceased to boom along the Çatalca lines, an armistice was proclaimed, and plenipotentiaries were appointed to discuss the terms under which the Balkan states were prepared to ratify peace.[80] The first meeting of the Bulgarian and Turkish plenipotentiaries took place on November 25, and a neutral zone between the two armies along the Çatalca lines was established.[81] Two days later, the delegates met again, and approached the question of the conditions on which an armistice would be granted and accepted. The Turkish Government was extremely reluctant to recognise even the accomplished fact in Thrace, at least in regard to Edirne, which still held out against the Balkan

[77] [Hüseyin Cahid Yalçın], "Muharebeye Devam Edilecekse," *Tanin*, October 27, 1328/November 9, 1912, p.1. See also, Mehmed Cavid, "Meşrutiyet Devrine Ait Cavid Bey'in Hatıraları: 158," *Tanin*, February 8, 1944, p.2; Hüseyin Cahid Yalçın, "Meşrutiyet Hatıraları, 1908-1918," *Fikir Hareketleri, 8* (April 24-October 16, 1937), p.69; and, F.O. 424/235, Sir Gerard Lowther to Sir Edward Grey, Constantinople, November 11, 1912, *Correspondence Respecting the Turkish War, Part II*, No.10263, p.163. See also, Yusuf Hikmet Bayur, *Türk İnkılâbı Tarihi, 2/4*, pp.259-261.

[78] Hüseyin Cahid Yalçın, "Meşrutiyet Hatıraları, 1908-1918," *Fikir Hareketleri, 8* (April 24-October 16, 1937), p.69; and, Mehmed Cavid, "Meşrutiyet Devrine Ait Cavid Bey'in Hatıraları: 160," *Tanin*, February 10, 1944, p.2. The newspaper started publication on January 31, 1913. See also, F.O. 424/235, Sir Gerard Lowther to Sir Edward Grey, Constantinople, November 11, 1912, *Correspondence Respecting the Turkish War, Part II*, No.10263, p.163.

[79] F.O. 424/235, Sir H. Bax-Ironside to Sir Edward Grey, Sophia, November 13, 1912, *Correspondence Respecting the Turkish War, Part II*, No.10263, p.176; F.O. 424/235, Sir Gerard Lowther to Sir Edward Grey, Constantinople, November 17, 1912, *Correspondence Respecting the Turkish War, Part II*, No.10263, p.215; Yusuf Hikmet Bayur, *Türk İnkılâbı Tarihi, 2/2*, p.115; Metin Ayışığı, *Mareşal Ahmet İzzet Paşa: Askerî ve Siyasî Hayatı*, p.61; and, "Why the Young Turks Failed," *The Near East*, November 22, 1912, p.77.

[80] "The Armistice," *The Near East*, November 22, 1912, p.76.

[81] F.O. 424/235, Sir Gerard Lowther to Sir Edward Grey, Constantinople, November 25, 1912, *Correspondence Respecting the Turkish War, Part II*, No.10263, p.344; F.O. 424/235, Sir H. Bax-Ironside to Sir Edward Grey, Sophia, November 26, 1912, *Correspondence Respecting the Turkish War, Part II*, No.10263, p.345; and, "Notes of the Week," *The Near East*, November 29, 1912, p.93. See also, "Mütareke Müzakereleri," *İkdam*, November 13, 1328/November 26, 1912, p.1.

forces.[82]

Apart from Edirne, Scutari too had successfully resisted the Balkan forces, so much so that the Montenegrins had been obliged to enlist the help of Serbian artillery. A decisive attack on Tarabosh was expected any day, though Esad Pasha, the commander of the garrison, was confident his power could hold out indefinitely.[83]

The fall of Monastir which took the life, among others, of Fethi Pasha, the Commander of the Seventh Army Corps, and the successful torpedo attack on the *Hamidiye* by Bulgarian torpedo boats were the chief military events of mid-November. At Çatalca, a meeting was arranged between a Turkish officer and representatives of the allied Balkan armies. The meeting took place, but the Turkish command considered the Balkan terms for armistice too severe, and further negotiations seemed impossible.[84]

The government, however, was once again willing to accept the conditions of the Balkan states on any terms, though the pro-monarchist *İkdam* of November 21 stated that the Government considered the latest Bulgarian demands less than acceptable.[85] A few days later, however, the November 27 issue of *İkdam* announced a cease-fire and the beginning of negotiations, and the monarchist press began advocating peace at all costs.[86] In an *İkdam* editorial of November 28, Mizancı Murad Bey wrote that Turks had to realise that from now on the nation would have to live under the protection of a European power.[87]

It was during this time—between November 16 and 23—

---

[82] "Notes of the Week," *The Near East*, November 29, 1912, p.93.

[83] "Notes of the Week," *The Near East*, November 29, 1912, p.94.

[84] "Constantinople Letter," *The Near East*, November 29, 1912, p.95. See also, Yusuf Hikmet Bayur, *Türk İnkılâbı Tarihi*, 2/2, pp.130-131.

[85] "Sulhe Doğru," *İkdam*, November 8, 1328/November 21, 1912, p.1. See also, Hüseyin Cahid Yalçın, "Meşrutiyet Hatıraları, 1908-1918," *Fikir Hareketleri*, 8 (April 24-October 16, 1937), p.102.

[86] *İkdam*, November 14, 1328/November 27, 1912, cited in Hüseyin Cahid Yalçın, "Meşrutiyet Hatıraları, 1908-1918," *Fikir Hareketleri*, 8 (April 24-October 16, 1937), p.102.

[87] Murad, "Mühlik bir Geçid," *İkdam*, November 15, 1328/November 28, 1912, p.1. Two days later, Mizancı Murad Bey had to 'explain' what he had really meant by the "protection of a European power" (Murad, "İzah," *İkdam*, November 17, 1328/November 30, 1912, p.1). See also, Hüseyin Cahid Yalçın, "Meşrutiyet Hatıraları, 1908-1918," *Fikir Hareketleri*, 8 (April 24-October 16, 1937), p.102.

that the Kâmil Pasha Cabinet ordered the arrests of leading members of the Committee of Union and Progress.[88] On November 16, the Government started arresting prominent members of the Committee of Union and Progress. Further arrests to the number of sixty were to be made in consequence of "evidence of an anti-government plot."[89] Hüseyin Cahid [Yalçın], however, had already left İstanbul for Vienna by sea via Romania on November 12, after the closure of *Tanin* by the Government, and thus escaped arrest. Cavid Bey and Babanzade İsmail Hakkı Bey also escaped arrest—thanks to telephone operators who had intercepted the government's orders.[90] Talât Bey also managed to escape.[91] Arrests by Court Martial of Committee of Union and Progress adherents, including some members of ex-Unionists cabinets, were proceeding with full speed. As some of the most prominent Committee leaders—such as, Cavid Bey, Hüseyin Cahid [Yalçın], Babanzade İsmail Hakkı Bey, and Talât Bey—had been allowed to escape, it was thought that one of the main reasons for these arrests, apart from any anti-government plot, was to strengthen hands of the Kâmil Pasha Cabinet in view of peace negotiations.[92] On November 25, the Court Martial issued a statement, with reference to these arrests, to the effect that it had been proven by admissions and documentary proofs that

---

[88] "Tevkif Edilenler Etrafında," *İkdam*, November 6, 1328/November 19, 1912, p.3; "Constantinople Letter," *The Near East*, November 29, 1912, p.95; and, Hüseyin Cahid Yalçın, "Meşrutiyet Hatıraları, 1908-1918," *Fikir Hareketleri*, 8 (April 24-October 16, 1937), p.70.

[89] Hüseyin Kâzım Kadri, *Meşrutiyet'ten Cumhuriyet'e Hatıralarım*, p.134; and, F.O. 424/235, Sir Gerard Lowther to Sir Edward Grey, Constantinople, November 16, 1912, *Correspondence Respecting the Turkish War, Part II*, No.10263, p.215.

[90] Hüseyin Cahid Yalçın, "Meşrutiyet Hatıraları, 1908-1918," *Fikir Hareketleri*, 8 (April 24-October 16, 1937), p.70; Mehmed Cavid, "Meşrutiyet Devrine Ait Cavid Bey'in Hatıraları: 164," *Tanin*, February 14, 1944, p.2; Mehmed Cavid, "Meşrutiyet Devrine Ait Cavid Bey'in Hatıraları: 165," *Tanin*, February 15, 1944, p.2; and, Mehmed Cavid, "Meşrutiyet Devrine Ait Cavid Bey'in Hatıraları: 166," *Tanin*, February 16, 1944, p.2. See also, Yusuf Hikmet Bayur, *Türk İnkılâbı Tarihi*, 2/4, p.269.

[91] The order for Talât Bey's arrest was published in the *İkdam*, November 1, 1328/November 14, 1912 (Hüseyin Cahid Yalçın, "Meşrutiyet Hatıraları, 1908-1918," *Fikir Hareketleri*, 8 (April 24-October 16, 1937), p.85). See also, Hüseyin Kâzım Kadri, *Meşrutiyet'ten Cumhuriyet'e Hatıralarım*, p.134; and, Mehmed Cavid, "Meşrutiyet Devrine Ait Cavid Bey'in Hatıraları: 168," *Tanin*, February 18, 1944, p.2.

[92] F.O. 424/235, Sir Gerard Lowther to Sir Edward Grey, Constantinople, November 24, 1912, *Correspondence Respecting the Turkish War, Part II*, No.10263, p.301.

Committee adherents and officers in civilian clothes who had organised and participated in pro-war demonstration at the Sublime Porte on October 7 had done so with the object of producing an internal revolution and overthrowing the government, while they had also made a seditious propaganda in the army, urging the men not to fight, "as Kâmil Pasha had sold the European provinces." The Court Martial statement also alleged that a member of the Committee of Union and Progress had enrolled *fedais* to assassinate the Sultan, Minister of War, and other ministers.[93]

İsmail Canbolat, Emmanuel Carasso, Ağaoğlu Ahmed Bey, Necmeddin [Kocataş], Bedros Haladjian, Müştak Bey, Muhiddin [Birgen], manager of *Tanin*, Faik [Kaltakkıran], ex-deputy for Edirne, Rıza Pasha, ex-deputy for Afyon, Süleyman Nazif Bey, ex-governor of Trabzon, Hüseyin Kâzım Bey, one of the editors of *Tercüman-ı Hakikat*, Aka Gündüz, Ubeydullah [Hatipoğlu], Hakkı Cemil Bey, a *Tanin* journalist, Emmanuel Carasso, İsmail Hakkı Pasha and many others had been arrested.[94] Aka Gündüz was sentenced to seven years' detention in a fortress; Ubeydullah [Hatipoğlu] and Hakkı Cemil Bey, were both sentenced to five years' detention in a fortress—all on account of their participation in the student demonstration at the Sublime Porte on October 7.[95] Although the authorities claimed they had discovered a plot against the Government, this move was clearly motivated by the desire to crush the Unionist opposition.[96] The following week saw fur-

---

[93] "Tevkifata Dair: İdare-i Örfiye Beyannamesi," *İkdam*, November 13, 1328/ November 26, 1912, p.1; and, F.O. 424/235, Sir Gerard Lowther to Sir Edward Grey, Constantinople, November 25, 1912, *Correspondence Respecting the Turkish War, Part II*, No.10263, p.344.

[94] "Tevkif Edilenler Etrafında," *İkdam*, November 6, 1328/November 19, 1912, p.3; "Carasso Efendi," *İkdam*, November 7, 1328/November 20, 1912, p.5; "İsmail Hakkı Paşa," *İkdam*, November 16, 1328/November 29, 1912, p.5; "Constantinople Letter," *The Near East*, November 29, 1912, p.95; Mehmed Cavid, "Meşrutiyet Devrine Ait Cavid Bey'in Hatıraları: 168," *Tanin*, February 19, 1944, p.2; and Hüseyin Cahid Yalçın, "Meşrutiyet Hatıraları, 1908-1918," *Fikir Hareketleri*, 8 (April 24-October 16, 1937), p.102. See also, Yusuf Hikmet Bayur, *Türk İnkılâbı Tarihi, 2/4*, p.271.

[95] *İkdam*, November 6, 1328/November 19, 1912, in Hüseyin Cahid Yalçın, "Meşrutiyet Hatıraları, 1908-1918," *Fikir Hareketleri*, 8 (April 24-October 16, 1937), p.87, and "Constantinople Letter," *The Near East*, November 29, 1912, p.95.

[96] "Constantinople Letter," *The Near East*, November 29, 1912, p.95. Even *The Near East* which supported the monarchist cause admitted that the arrests and accusations against Unionist leadership were not "entirely convincing" ("Constantinople Letter," *The Near East*, December 6, 1912, p.123).

ther arrests, and these continued through the first week of December.[97]

Bowing to opposition and resistance, however, Nâzım Pasha and Kâmil Pasha were forced to dismiss the current Court Martial, appointing a new one composed of officers with a reputation for fairness and integrity. All prisoners were subsequently released.[98]

Şerif Pasha, the monarchist who was living in exile in Paris and the owner of the anti-Unionist *Mechroutiette* and other monarchist journals, returned to İstanbul in early December, as well as other members of the monarchist Liberal Union.[99]

On December 5, *İkdam* announced the signing of the armistice.[100] The peace conference was to be held in London on December 16.[101] It was generally believed that the monarchist Kâmil Pasha Government would admit Greece to the negotiations without insisting on an armistice, and would then raise the question of re-supplying the besieged fortresses. Just as it was unlikely that the Bulgarians would consent to the re-supplying of Edirne—which, according to well-informed sources, had to capitulate from lack of provisions in six weeks' time—it was improbable that the Greeks would likewise strengthen Janina, which had proved a hard nut to crack, and had been bolstered by remnants of Zeki Pasha's forces. Edirne, the Albanian frontiers, and the Aegean islands, would all be sources of difficulty and danger during the conference.[102]

Though there were three meetings during the last week of

[97] "Constantinople Letter," *The Near East*, December 13, 1912, p.151.

[98] "Divan-ı Harb Riyaseti," *İkdam*, November 26, 1328/December 9, 1912, p.4; and, "Constantinople Letter," *The Near East*, December 20, 1912, p.179. See also, Ahmed İzzet, *Feryadım, I*, p.141.

[99] "Constantinople Letter," *The Near East*, December 13, 1912, p.151; and, Taner Timur, "Bir İttihatçı Düşmanı: Şerif Paşa ve *Meşrutiyet* Gazetesi," p.19. By early January 1913, however, Şerif Pasha had again left Turkey (Mehmed Cavid, "Meşrutiyet Devrine Ait Cavid Bey'in Hatıraları: 173," *Tanin*, February 23, 1944, p.2).

[100] "Balkanlarda Harb: Mütareke Akdedildi," *İkdam*, November 22, 1328/December 5, 1912, p.1. See also, Hüseyin Cahid Yalçın, "Meşrutiyet Hatıraları, 1908-1918," *Fikir Hareketleri, 8* (April 24-October 16, 1937), p.118.

[101] Yusuf Hikmet Bayur, *Türk İnkılâbı Tarihi, 2/2*, pp.166-176. See also, Ali Kemal, "İlk İctima," *İkdam*, December 4, 1328/December 17, 1912, p.1.

[102] "Constantinople Letter," *The Near East*, December 27, 1912, p.207.

432 THE ROAD TO THE FALL OF MONARCHIST RULE

December, it was not until New Year's Day that negotiations took serious form.[103] On December 28, at their first meeting after the Christmas adjournment, Turkish delegates presented their counter-proposals to the Allied terms. Balkan demands were thoroughly ignored; instead, Turkey proposed that the province of Edirne remain under the full sovereignty and direct administration of the Turkish government, that Macedonia become an autonomous principality under the suzerainty of Turkey, that Albania be constituted an autonomous province under a prince of the Ottoman Imperial House, and that the Aegean islands be retained by Turkey. Crete, it was argued, had been entrusted to the Protecting Powers, and was, therefore, outside the scope of the negotiations. The Allies refused to discuss these proposals, and the Turkish delegates were left to seek further instructions from İstanbul.[104]

When the Conference met again on December 30, the Turkish delegation explained that it had been unable to entirely decipher the telegram it had received from the government, but that it was prepared to continue the negotiations on such points as were clear in the telegraphic instructions. As the Balkan delegates were expecting this, they had decided to authorise Dr. Daneff, a Bulgarian delegate, to attend the conference on their behalf in order to decline to discuss the Turkish side's fragmentary instructions at that time. Reşid Pasha's communication was understood to include a vague allusion to the cession of parts of Macedonia and a proposal to refer certain points at issue to the mediation of the Great Powers. Dr. Daneff requested that Turkey submit the whole of its proposals in writing by January 1.[105]

When the delegates next met, Turkey's proposals were spelled out as follows: first, all occupied territories to the west of the province of Edirne would be ceded, but the determination of the boundaries and status of autonomous Albania would be submitted to the decision of the Great Powers; second, the

---

[103] Yusuf Hikmet Bayur, *Türk İnkılâbı Tarihi*, 2/2, pp.185-208.
[104] Yusuf Hikmet Bayur, *Türk İnkılâbı Tarihi*, 2/2, pp.208-209; and, "Notes of the Week," *The Near East*, January 3, 1913, p.233.
[105] Yusuf Hikmet Bayur, *Türk İnkılâbı Tarihi*, 2/2, pp.209-210; and, "Notes of the Week," *The Near East*, January 3, 1913, p.233. See also, "Sulh Müzakeratı: Dünkü Sulh Müzakeratı," *İkdam*, December 18, 1328/December 31, 1912, pp.1-2.

province of Edirne would remain in direct possession of Turkey, though Turkey and Bulgaria would negotiate any necessary rectification of their frontier; third, though Turkey would not cede any of the Aegean islands, it was prepared to discuss any related questions with the Great Powers; fourth, Turkey was disposed to consent to any resolution put forth by the Great Powers concerning Crete; and, fifth, the points mentioned above would be considered an indivisible whole.[106]

Following some deliberations, Venizelos, the President of the conference for the day, read the Allied response. First, the Allies would accept territories situated to the west of the province of Edirne under the express condition that this cession would apply not only to occupied territory, but also to territory not yet completely occupied. As regards Albania, the Allies maintained their former proposal. Second, the Turkish proposal regarding the province of Edirne itself was unacceptable, as it implied separate agreements, and, moreover, did not grant the territory demanded. The Turkish propositions concerning the Aegean islands and Crete were also unacceptable; the Allies reiterated their former demands as regards the cession of the islands and the abdication of all Turkish rights in Crete.[107]

With the prospects of a settlement somewhat improved, the conference adjourned until January 3. But because the delicate issue of Edirne remained at the centre of further negotiations, the road ahead promised to be difficult. Neither the Bulgarians nor the Turks would not be denied its possession. The issue was also symbolically charged for Turkey, as Edirne had once been the capital of the Empire. The monarchist demand for Great Power mediation, however, indicated that the Kâmil Pasha Government was willing to compromise. Clearly, the government hoped to lessen the blow to Turkey, and European insistence would correspond more adequately with Kâmil Pasha's conception of *force majeure* than would the demands of the Balkan states.

---

[106] Yusuf Hikmet Bayur, *Türk İnkılâbı Tarihi*, 2/2, pp.211-213; Basil Kondis, *Greece and Albania, 1908-1914*, p.101; and, "Notes of the Week," *The Near East*, January 3, 1913, p.233. See also, "Sulh Müzakeratı: Sulh İhtimalâtı Artıyor," *İkdam*, December 19, 1328/January 1, 1913, pp.1-2.

[107] Yusuf Hikmet Bayur, *Türk İnkılâbı Tarihi*, 2/2, pp.212-213; and, "Notes of the Week," *The Near East*, January 3, 1913, p.233.

That the Powers would contemplate a modification of the Allies' demands in regard to Edirne could hardly be expected, but Turkish demands, it was suggested, might be met halfway by arrangements which would leave the mosques of the city under Turkish administration and under extra-territorial guarantees.[108]

By the beginning of January, 1913, rumours of another cabinet change had begun to circulate. Many felt that Kâmil Pasha would soon retire, making way for Hüseyin Hilmi Pasha and a coalition cabinet, and the fact that Nâzım Pasha had recently offered Mahmud Şevket Pasha a post in what he termed a 'reconstructed' cabinet only seemed to confirm this view. Mahmud Şevket Pasha refused, but the fact that the offer had been made was significant; Hüseyin Hilmi Pasha and Mahmud Şevket Pasha had been on extremely friendly terms for years, and many felt that, should the former return to office, he would no doubt extend the offer again. On his part, Hüseyin Hilmi Pasha, however, was not expected to accept office immediately. The ex-Grand Vezier and ex-Inspector-General of Macedonia enjoyed a reputation for shrewdness, and he would hardly want to take office before the settlement of the peace negotiations. Whatever the outcome, the settlement could not but end unfavourably for Turkey, and the public was likely to make any government that signed peace a scapegoat for the sins of its predecessors. It was, therefore, probable that Hüseyin Hilmi Pasha would wait, sounding out the Committee of Union and Progress through Cavid Bey in Vienna, and assessing the feeling of the military through his friend Mahmud Şevket Pasha.[109]

At this juncture, the Unionists tried to exploit differences of

---

[108] "Notes of the Week," *The Near East*, January 3, 1913, p.233. See also, "Müzakerat-ı Sulhiye Hakkında Bab-ı Âli'nin Yeni Kararı," *İkdam*, December 20, 1328/January 2, 1913, p.1; "Sulh Müzakeratı: Dünkü Sulh Müzakeratı," *İkdam*, December 20, 1328/January 2, 1913, p.1; Ali Kemal, "Müşkülâtın En Büyüğü," *İkdam*, December 21, 1328/January 3, 1913, p.1; "Sulh Müzakeratı: Sulhün Esasları," *İkdam*, December 21, 1328/January 3, 1913, pp.1-2; "Osmanlı Teklif-i Mukabili: Evvelsi Günkü İctima," *İkdam*, December 21, 1328/January 3, 1913, p.2

[109] "Constantinople Letter," *The Near East*, January 10, 1913, p.263. See also, XXXIV. 185, Baron von Wangenheim to the German Foreign Office, Constantinople, January 12, 1913, reproduced in E. T. S. Dugdale (Ed.), *German Diplomatic Documents, 1871-1914, 4: The Descent to the Abyss, 1911-1914*, p.156.

opinion among current cabinet members, especially those
between Nâzım Pasha, the Minister of War, who had wanted
to continue the war, and Kâmil Pasha, the Grand Vezier, who
had wanted peace at all costs. Public news of the rift first
appeared in *İkdam* on December 29. The leadership of the
Committee of Union and Progress tried to win Nâzım Pasha
over to its side by showing itself strongly in favour of defending Turkish interests in the Balkans.[110] Shortly after, Talât Bey
reportedly began negotiations with Nâzım Pasha on the issue
for a change in the cabinet and in the policy towards
conducting the peace negotiations.[111] These negotiations did
not long remain confidential; rumours that Nâzım Pasha was
leaning towards the Unionist position began to spread. In a
letter to *İkdam*, however, Nâzım Pasha denied these rumours
and stated that he was not involved with any political party.[112]
With continued reports of dissension within the cabinet, the
government banned all news on such issues, and on January
16, *Tasvir-i Efkâr* was closed down.[113] Yunus Nadi [Abalıoğlu],
its editor-in-chief, and two of his editorial staff members were
put under investigation, along with several other journalists.[114]

As neither side had shown any willingness to compromise,
the peace negotiations remained suspended throughout mid-
January.[115] In the meantime, the Great Powers drew up a

---

[110] "Dahiliye Nazırı ile Mülâkat," *İkdam*, December 16, 1328/December 29,
1912, p.1. See also, Hüseyin Cahid Yalçın, "Meşrutiyet Hatıraları, 1908-1918," *Fikir Hareketleri*, 8 (April 24-October 16, 1937), p.118.

[111] Hüseyin Cahid Yalçın, "Meşrutiyet Hatıraları, 1908-1918," *Fikir Hareketleri*, 8 (April 24-October 16, 1937), p.118; and, Mehmed Cavid, "Meşrutiyet Devrine
Ait Cavid Bey'in Hatıraları: 174," *Tanin*, February 24, 1944, p.2. See also, Sina Akşin, *Jön Türkler ve İttihat ve Terakki*, pp.319-320.

[112] *İkdam*, January 6, 1328/January 19, 1913, cited in Hüseyin Cahid Yalçın,
"Meşrutiyet Hatıraları, 1908-1918," *Fikir Hareketleri*, 8 (April 24-October 16,
1937), p.119. See also, "Kabine Hakkında," *İkdam*, January 1, 1328/January 14,
1912, p.1.

[113] *İkdam*, January 1, 1328/January 14, 1913, and *İkdam*, January 4, 1328/Jan-
uary 17, 1913, cited in Hüseyin Cahid Yalçın, "Meşrutiyet Hatıraları, 1908-1918,"
Fikir Hareketleri, 8 (April 24-October 16, 1937), pp.118-119.

[114] *İkdam*, January 4, 1328/January 17, 1913, cited in Hüseyin Cahid Yalçın,
"Meşrutiyet Hatıraları, 1908-1918," *Fikir Hareketleri*, 8 (April 24-October 16,
1937), p.119.

[115] Yusuf Hikmet Bayur, *Türk İnkılâbı Tarihi*, 2/2, p.214-224. See also, Ali Kemal, "Bab-ı Âli ve Müzakerat-ı Sulhiye," *İkdam*, December 23, 1328/January 5,
1913, p.1; "Sulh Müzakeratı: Harb mi, Sulh mü?" *İkdam*, December 23, 1328/Jan-
uary 5, 1913, pp.1-2; Ali Kemal, "İnkıtâ-ı Müzakerat," *İkdam*, December 24, 1328/
January 6, 1913, p.1; "Sulh Müzakeratı: Son Müzakerat Hakkında," *İkdam*, De-

Collective Note, which was forwarded to their ambassadors in İstanbul for presentation to the Turkish Government. The Note urged Turkey to surrender Edirne and to leave the question of the Aegean islands to the Powers.[116] According to the monarchist Turkish press, which was fairly well informed on the subject, the Powers, after calling attention to Turkey's need for foreign capital in the development of its Asiatic provinces, pointed out that foreign financial support could not be expected until the war was over. Though the Note urged the government to yield Edirne, the Powers promised to take all the necessary steps to obtain concessions from the Bulgarians concerning the mosques, pious foundations, and other religious and historical monuments of the old capital.[117] Kâmil Pasha decided to convene a consultative assembly, ostensibly with a view to divest himself of the responsibility for the decision to surrender Edirne or to renew the war.[118]

The Government did not feel politically strong enough to reply to the Note without consultation. Though Kâmil Pasha and a good number of his ministers supported peace at any price, there was also public opinion to reckon with, not to mention the Committee of Union and Progress, which was against signing of an unjust peace. The consultative assembly consisted of members from the Senate, ulema, Ministry of War,

---

cember 25, 1328/January 7, 1913, p.1; "Sulh Müzakeratı: Dünkü Sulh Müzakeratı," *İkdam*, December 26, 1328/January 8, 1913, p.1; "Sulh Konferansı," *İkdam*, December 27, 1328/January 9, 1913, p.1; "Sulh Müzakeratı ve Düvel-i Muazzamanın Müdahalesi," *İkdam*, December 28, 1328/January 10, 1913, p.1; "Sulh Müzakeratı: Bab-ı Âli Kakarında Sabittir," *İkdam*, December 28, 1328/January 10, 1913, p.1; Ali Kemal, "İnkıtâ Değil Tevakkuf," *İkdam*, December 30, 1328/January 12, 1913, p.1; Ali Kemal, "Avrupa Cidden Sulh İstiyor mu?" *İkdam*, December 31, 1328/January 13, 1913, p.1; and, "Sulh Müzakeratı: Düvel-i Muazzamanın Teşebbüsü," *İkdam*, December 31, 1328/January 13, 1913, p.1.

[116] "Notes of the Week," *The Near East*, January 17, 1913, p.293. See also, "Sulh Müzakeratı: Devletlerin Yeni bir Karar-ı Müştereği," *İkdam*, December 31, 1328/January 13, 1913, p.1; "Sulh Müzakeratı: Düvel-i Muazzamanın Teşebbüsü," *İkdam*, January 2, 1328/January 15, 1913, p.1; and, "Sulh Müzakeratı: Düvel-i Muazzamanın Teşebbüsü," *İkdam*, January 4, 1328/January 17, 1913, p.1.

[117] "Sulh Müzakeratı: Düvel-i Muazzamanın Notası," *İkdam*, January 6, 1328/January 19, 1913, p.1. See also, "Constantinople Letter," *The Near East*, January 24, 1913, p.323; and, Hüseyin Cahid Yalçın, "Meşrutiyet Hatıraları, 1908-1918," *Fikir Hareketleri*, 8 (April 24-October 16, 1937), p.119. For the reaction of the independent press see, "Müdahale Dün Oldu!" *Tercüman-ı Hakikat*, January 5, 1328/January 18, 1913, p.1.

[118] "Notes of the Week," *The Near East*, January 17, 1913, p.293. See also, "Sulh Müzakeratı: Meclis-i Vükelâ," *İkdam*, January 3, 1328/January 16, 1913, p.1; and, "Sulh Müzakeratı: Cevabi Nota Meselesi," *İkdam*, January 7, 1328/January 20, 1913, p.1.

Ministry of Justice, Council of State, Ministry of the Navy, as well as a number of other high ranking administrators. The Sultan approved Kâmil Pasha's decision to convene such an assembly, and it was publicly announced on January 22, the day of its meeting.[119]

The decision to convene a consultative assembly was an indication of the gravity of the situation. Little doubt was entertained of the leanings towards peace at any cost of Kâmil Pasha himself and of the rest of his monarchist Cabinet, but those who were in favour of continuing the war could count on the support of the great bulk of the army officers and the Committee of Union and Progress, which had not ceased to be a factor in the political life of the capital despite constant harassment and the resulting imprisonment of some of its leadership. Many felt that a renewal of hostilities was inevitable.[120] The Committee of Union and Progress and the military were determined to prove that the Turkish army could make a better stand than it had at Lüleburgaz and Kumanovo. Kâmil Pasha, however, desired peace, and, were it left to himself, would have yielded to the demands of the Balkan states.[121]

If the assembly provided Kâmil Pasha with a visible scapegoat should anything go wrong, it certainly had no real power, and the government lost little time in formulating its response to the note. Though the military was prepared to renew hostilities, it recognised that without adequate financial support it would be impossible to wage an effective campaign, and it agreed to support the cabinet's decision to accept the Powers' advice. Then, on January 22, the Grand Council of the Empire, the consultative assembly, met in closed session. Kâmil Pasha presented the facts, and supported by Nâzım Pasha, Minister of War, Gabriel Nouradunghian, Minister for Foreign Affairs, and the Minister of Finance, argued that the war could not be continued with any prospect of success. When

---

[119] "Meclis-i Kebir-i Meşveret," *İkdam*, January 9, 1328/January 22, 1913, p.1; and, "Sulh Müzakeratı: Meclis-i Kebir-i Meşveret," *İkdam*, January 9, 1328/January 22, 1913, p.1—where there is the full list of the invited 'statesmen.' See also, Hüseyin Cahid Yalçın, "Meşrutiyet Hatıraları, 1908-1918," *Fikir Hareketleri, 8* (April 24-October 16, 1937), p.119.

[120] "Notes of the Week," *The Near East*, January 17, 1913, p.293. See also, Ahmed İzzet, *Feryadım, I*, p.144.

[121] "Constantinople Letter," *The Near East*, January 17, 1913, p.295.

the meeting came to an end after four hours of deliberations, the Council was overwhelmingly in favour of accepting the government's point of view. That evening, a statement was issued to the effect that the Council, "trusting in the sentiments of justice of the Great Powers, left to the patriotic hands of a loyal Cabinet the task of working with the effective support which had been promised by the Great Powers for the future prosperity of the country and for the assurance of its vital financial interests."[122] This was tantamount to accepting total defeat and surrendering unconditionally to the demands of the Balkan states.[123]

The unmistakable movement among officers in favour of the continuation of the war was invested with all the importance of a plot, and arrests followed.[124] It was also in mid-January that the monarchists announced their intention of making amendments to the Constitution after the war was over. In a declaration made to the editor of the monarchist *Sabah*, the Sultan pointed out that "the constant changes of Cabinet which had accompanied the introduction of parliamentary government into Turkey had been a grave hindrance to progress and reform." "In the future," he said, "some means must be devised of preventing the frequent changes and reversals of policy which had marked the era of parliamentarism in Turkey." It was clear that these means could only be found in the removal of parliamentary control over the executive branch.[125]

On January 23, the day following the Grand Council's ac-

---

[122] "Notes of the Week," *The Near East*, January 24, 1913, p.321. For the complete text of the Government's statement see "Sulh Müzakeratı: Beyanname-i Resmiye," *İkdam*, January 10, 1328/January 23, 1913, p.1. See also, Hüseyin Cahid Yalçın, "Meşrutiyet Hatıraları, 1908-1918," *Fikir Hareketleri*, 8 (April 24-October 16, 1937), p.135. For the monarchist press' defence of the decision see, "Bab-ı Âli'nin Cevabı Etrafında," *İkdam*, January 10, 1328/January 23, 1913, p.1; and, M., "Musibetten Sonra," *İkdam*, January 10, 1328/January 23, 1913, p.1. For the independent press' reaction see, "Müdahale Etrafında: Bab-ı Âli Düvel-i Muazzamanın Nasihatini Kabul Etti," *Tercüman-ı Hakikat*, January 10, 1328/January 23, 1913, pp.1-2. See also, Ahmed İzzet, *Feryadım, 1*, p.144.
[123] Charles Donald Sullivan, Stamboul Crossings: German Diplomacy in Turkey, 1908 to 1914, p.315. See also, Edwin Pears, *Forty Years in Constantinople: The Recollections of Sir Edwin Pears, 1873-1915*, p.331.
[124] "Notes of the Week," *The Near East*, January 24, 1913, p.321.
[125] "Constantinople Letter," *The Near East*, January 24, 1913, p.323.

quiescence in the Cabinet's proposal to make the Collective Note of the Powers the basis of peace, a small company of mounted Unionist officers rode into the Sublime Porte. Their arrival was the signal for a concerted rush on the part of various groups that had been waiting close by. Enver Bey and Halil [Menteşe] appeared, and, with Cemal Bey, they entered the Porte and asked to see the Grand Vezier. They were followed by Talât Bey, Ömer Naci Bey, and Midhat Şükrü [Bleda], and other leaders of the Committee of Union and Progress. Nâzım Pasha came out of the Council Chamber and was at once shot by a member of the advancing group.[126] His aide-de-camp was also killed, while Nazif Bey, aide-de-camp to the Grand Vezier, after shooting down Nâzım Pasha's assassin, was the third victim.[127] Enver Bey, according to one account, then entered the Council Chamber and informed Kâmil Pasha that he must either resign or swear to continue the war. The Grand Vezier chose the former course, and, armed with his resignation, the Unionists proceeded to the Palace, where they secured the Sultan's assent to the appointment of Mahmud Şevket Pasha as Grand Vezier.[128]

A new Cabinet was formed the same day. It included Prince Said Halim Pasha, President of the Council of State, who also took over the Ministry for Foreign Affairs; Hacı Âdil [Arda], Minister of the Interior; Çürüksulu Mahmud Pasha, Minister of the Navy; İbrahim Bey, Minister of Justice; Ürgüplü Hayri Bey, Minister of Pious Foundations; Celal Bey, Min-

---

[126] Midhat Şükrü Bleda, *İmparatorluğun Çöküşü*, p.75; Mustafa Ragıb Esatlı, *İttihat ve Terakki Tarihinde Esrar Perdesi: Yakup Cemil Niçin ve Nasıl Öldürüldü?* pp.256-273; Hasan Amca, *Doğmayan Hürriyet: Bir Devrin İçyüzü, 1908-1918*, pp.121-122; Ahmed Bedevi Kuran, *Osmanlı İmparatorluğunda İnkılâp Hareketleri ve Milli Mücadele*, p.588; "Notes of the Week," *The Near East*, January 31, 1913, p.349; Charles Donald Sullivan, *Stamboul Crossings: German Diplomacy in Turkey, 1908 to 1914*, p.316; and, Yusuf Hikmet Bayur, *Türk İnkılâbı Tarihi*, 2/2, p.269.

[127] Midhat Şükrü Bleda, *İmparatorluğun Çöküşü*, p.75; Hasan Amca, *Doğmayan Hürriyet: Bir Devrin İçyüzü, 1908-1918*, pp.121-122; Ahmed Bedevi Kuran, *İnkılâp Tarihimiz ve 'Jön Türkler,'* p.319; Ahmed Bedevi Kuran, *Osmanlı İmparatorluğunda İnkılâp Hareketleri ve Milli Mücadele*, p.587; Yusuf Hikmet Bayur, *Türk İnkılâbı Tarihi*, 2/2, p.269; and, "Notes of the Week," *The Near East*, January 31, 1913, p.349.

[128] "Notes of the Week," *The Near East*, January 31, 1913, p.349; and, Mustafa Ragıb Esatlı, *İttihat ve Terakki Tarihinde Esrar Perdesi: Yakup Cemil Niçin ve Nasıl Öldürüldü?* p.274. See also, Yusuf Hikmet Bayur, *Türk İnkılâbı Tarihi*, 2/2, p.270; and, Edwin Pears, *Forty Years in Constantinople: The Recollections of Sir Edwin Pears, 1873-1915*, p.331.

ister of Commerce and Agriculture; Rıfat Bey, Minister of Finance; Bessaraya Efendi, Minister of Public Works; and, Şükrü Bey, Minister of Education.[129] Although not a totally Unionist cabinet, the list of ministers included some moderate members—like Hacı Âdil [Arda], Ürgüplü Hayri Bey and Prince Said Halim Pasha—of the Committee of Union and Progress.[130] Other ministers were all drawn from politicians who could not be accused in any sense of monarchist leanings. Thus, after a lapse of about six months, constitutional regime was once again re-established.

One of the first measures of the new Government was to place the Ministers of Kâmil Pasha's Cabinet under arrest, while numerous other arrests, including those of Ali Kemal Bey, editor of İkdam, Gümülcineli İsmail Bey and Dr. Rıza Nur, were made during the following days.[131] Abdurrahman Bey, Minister of Finance, and Ahmed Reşid [Rey], Minister of the Interior, were confined in prison.[132] The houses of Kâmil Pasha and Cemaleddin Efendi, the Sheikh-ul-Islam in the Kâmil Pasha Cabinet, were surrounded by secret service agents and gendarmes, and all communications addressed to Kâmil Pasha were opened.[133] The monarchist press was suppressed by the new Government and ceased publication for a few days.[134]

The government's next step was to give publicity to the determination not to surrender under any consideration Edirne and the Aegean islands.[135] On January 30 the Sublime Porte

[129] "Notes of the Week," The Near East, January 31, 1913, p.349; Cemal Kutay, Türkiye İstiklâl ve Hürriyet Mücadeleleri Tarihi, 17, p.9968 and 9976; Metin Ayışığı, Mareşal Ahmet İzzet Paşa: Askerî ve Siyasî Hayatı, pp.67-68; and, Yusuf Hikmet Bayur, Türk İnkılâbı Tarihi, 2/2, pp.272-273.
[130] Feroz Ahmad, The Young Turks: The Committee of Union and Progress in Turkish Politics, 1908-1914, pp.122-123; and, Gwynne Dyer, "The Origins of the 'Nationalist' Group of Officers in Turkey, 1908-18," p.128.
[131] Mustafa Ragıb Esatlı, İttihat ve Terakki Tarihinde Esrar Perdesi: Yakup Cemil Niçin ve Nasıl Öldürüldü? p.288; and, "Notes of the Week," The Near East, January 31, 1913, p.349.
[132] Mustafa Ragıb Esatlı, İttihat ve Terakki Tarihinde Esrar Perdesi: Yakup Cemil Niçin ve Nasıl Öldürüldü? pp.284-285; and, "Constantinople Letter," The Near East, January 31, 1913, p.351.
[133] "Constantinople Letter," The Near East, January 31, 1913, p.351. See also, Mutafa Ragıb Esatlı, İttihat ve Terakki Tarihinde Esrar Perdesi: Yakup Cemil Niçin ve Nasıl Öldürüldü? p.287.
[134] "Constantinople Letter," The Near East, January 31, 1913, p.351. İkdam started to re-appear on January 28, 1913.
[135] "Notes of the Week," The Near East, January 31, 1913, p.349; and, Metin

presented to the Austro-Hungarian Ambassador its reply to the Collective Note of the Powers. The document was couched in moderate terms. The Turkish Government stipulated for the retention of the city of Edirne, and proposed to leave to the Powers the disposal of the land on the right bank of the Maritza. The maintenance of Turkish sovereignty over the Aegean islands was insisted upon, but the question of administration was left to the Powers.[136] The note differed from the one prepared by the Kâmil Pasha Cabinet in its demands for economic liberty.[137]

Ayışığı, *Mareşal Ahmet İzzet Paşa: Askerî ve Siyasî Hayatı*, p.67.

[136] Yusuf Hikmet Bayur, *Türk İnkılâbı Tarihi*, 2/2, pp.280-281; Douglas Dakin, "The Diplomacy of the Great Powers and the Balkan States, 1908-1914," pp.359-360; and, "Notes of the Week," *The Near East*, January 31, 1913, p.350.

[137] Yusuf Hikmet Bayur, *Türk İnkılâbı Tarihi*, 2/2, p.281; and, "Constantinople Letter," *The Near East*, February 7, 1913, p.379.

MEMBERS OF THE MECLİS-İ MEBUSAN, 1912

Election results are given starting from the provinces in Macedonia. The total number of deputies from each province is given in parenthesis next to the name of the province in question. The number of deputies from each electoral district is also given in parenthesis. The names of the deputies are—to the degree possible—reflect the original spelling. Their religious convictions or ethnic origins as well as the political parties in which they have been active are given in the two following columns.

The list follows—to a large extent—the method which Feroz Ahmad and Dankwart A. Rustow have used in their article entitled "İkinci Meşrutiyet Döneminde Meclisler, 1908-1918." The inaccuracies in that article have been rectified by consulting several other sources such as *The Levant Herald and Eastern Express.* The list thus rectified has also been checked with the list that appears in İhsan Ezherci's *Türkiye Büyük Millet Meclisi, 1920-1998 ve Osmanlı Meclis-i Mebusan'ı, 1877-1920,* and Fevzi Demir's İkinci Meşrutiyet Dönemi Meclis-i Mebusan Seçimleri, 1908-1914. Sabine Prätor's *Der arabische Faktor in der jungtürkischen Politik* has been used to correct the list of the deputies from the Arabian provinces.

The provinces and sandjaks are listed according to the administrative division of Turkey at the time of the general elections. For this purpose an atlas— *Memalik-i Mahruse-i Şahane'ye Mahsus Mükemmel ve Mufassal Atlas*—and *Salname-i Devlet-i Âliye-i Osmaniye, 1326* are used.

(*) that appears next to the name of a deputy means that the deputy has been re-elected to the Meclis-i Mebusan.

The party affiliations of the deputies are given in the last column. Committee of Union and Progress (İttihad ve Terakki

Cemiyeti) has been abbreviated as 'CUP'; Entente Liberale (Hürriyet ve İtilâf Fırkası) as 'EL'; and, Armenian Revolutionary Federation (Dashnaktsuthiun) as 'ARF.' Independents have been identified as 'I.'

KOSSOVO/ÜSKÜB (11)

Üsküb (4)

Théodore Pavloff*	Bulgarian	LU[1]
Spiro Ristich	Serbian	CUP[2]
Ali Şefik Bey	Albanian	I[3]
Yusuf Bey	Albanian	I[4]

İpek (1)

Hafız İbrahim Efendi*	Albanian	I[5]

Senice/Novi Bazar (1)

Emir Bey	Albanian	I[6]

---

[1] Lawyer (Fevzi Demir, İkinci Meşrutiyet Dönemi Meclis-i Mebusan Seçimleri, 1908-1914, p.167). His name is written as Todor Pavlov in Stojan Makedonski, "Le Regime Jeune-Turc et les Deuxiemes Elections Parlementaires de 1912 en Macedoine et Thrace Orientale," p.66. See also, Feroz Ahmad and Dankwart A. Rustow, "İkinci Meşrutiyet Döneminde Meclisler, 1908-1918," p.266; and, İhsan Ezherli, Türkiye Büyük Millet Meclisi, 1920-1998, ve Osmanlı Meclis-i Mebusanı, 1877-1920, p.219.

[2] Stojan Makedonski, "Le Regime Jeune-Turc et les Deuxiemes Elections Parlementaires de 1912 en Macedoine et Thrace Orientale," p.71; Feroz Ahmad and Dankwart A. Rustow, "İkinci Meşrutiyet Döneminde Meclisler, 1908-1918," p.267; İhsan Ezherli, Türkiye Büyük Millet Meclisi, 1920-1998, ve Osmanlı Meclis-i Mebusanı, 1877-1920, p.210; and, Fevzi Demir, İkinci Meşrutiyet Dönemi Meclis-i Mebusan Seçimleri, 1908-1914, p.167.

[3] Feroz Ahmad and Dankwart A. Rustow, "İkinci Meşrutiyet Döneminde Meclisler, 1908-1918," p.267; İhsan Ezherli, Türkiye Büyük Millet Meclisi, 1920-1998, ve Osmanlı Meclis-i Mebusanı, 1877-1920, p.205; and, Fevzi Demir, İkinci Meşrutiyet Dönemi Meclis-i Mebusan Seçimleri, 1908-1914, p.167.

[4] Feroz Ahmad and Dankwart A. Rustow, "İkinci Meşrutiyet Döneminde Meclisler, 1908-1918," p.267; İhsan Ezherli, Türkiye Büyük Millet Meclisi, 1920-1998, ve Osmanlı Meclis-i Mebusanı, 1877-1920, p.220; and, Fevzi Demir, İkinci Meşrutiyet Dönemi Meclis-i Mebusan Seçimleri, 1908-1914, p.167.

[5] Feroz Ahmad and Dankwart A. Rustow, "İkinci Meşrutiyet Döneminde Meclisler, 1908-1918," p.265; İhsan Ezherli, Türkiye Büyük Millet Meclisi, 1920-1998, ve Osmanlı Meclis-i Mebusanı, 1877-1920, p.210; and, Fevzi Demir, İkinci Meşrutiyet Dönemi Meclis-i Mebusan Seçimleri, 1908-1914, p.166.

[6] "Ouverture du Parlement," The Levant Herald and Eastern Express, April 18, 1912, p.1; Feroz Ahmad and Dankwart A. Rustow, "İkinci Meşrutiyet Döneminde Meclisler, 1908-1918," p.266; İhsan Ezherli, Türkiye Büyük Millet Meclisi, 1920-1998, ve Osmanlı Meclis-i Mebusanı, 1877-1920, p.205; and, Fevzi Demir, İkinci Meşrutiyet Dönemi Meclis-i Mebusan Seçimleri, 1908-1914, p.166.

Prishtnë (1)

Rifat Bey	?	?[7]

Prizren (3)

Abdülaziz Efendi	Albanian	CUP[8]
Hacı Destan Efendi	Albanian	CUP[9]
Tevfik Nazif [Arıcan]	Albanian	CUP[10]

Taşlıca (1)

Mehmed İzzet Pasha	Turk	I[11]

* * *

SCUTARI (3)

Scutari (2)

Murtaza Galib Bey*	Albanian	I[12]

---

[7] "Nouvelles du Jour," *The Levant Herald and Eastern Express*, May 17, 1912, p.2. His deputyship may have been not ratified; because his name is not listed in the official registers.

[8] "Nouvelles du Jour," *The Levant Herald and Eastern Express*, May 2, 1912, p.2; Feroz Ahmad and Dankwart A. Rustow, "İkinci Meşrutiyet Döneminde Meclisler, 1908-1918," p.265; İhsan Ezherli, *Türkiye Büyük Millet Meclisi, 1920-1998, ve Osmanlı Meclis-i Mebusanı, 1877-1920*, p.203; and, Fevzi Demir, İkinci Meşrutiyet Dönemi Meclis-i Mebusan Seçimleri, 1908-1914, p.166.

[9] "Nouvelles du Jour," *The Levant Herald and Eastern Express*, May 2, 1912, p.2; Feroz Ahmad and Dankwart A. Rustow, "İkinci Meşrutiyet Döneminde Meclisler, 1908-1918," p.265; İhsan Ezherli, *Türkiye Büyük Millet Meclisi, 1920-1998, ve Osmanlı Meclis-i Mebusanı, 1877-1920*, p.207; and, Fevzi Demir, İkinci Meşrutiyet Dönemi Meclis-i Mebusan Seçimleri, 1908-1914, p.166.

[10] "Nouvelles du Jour," *The Levant Herald and Eastern Express*, May 2, 1912, p.2; Feroz Ahmad and Dankwart A. Rustow, "İkinci Meşrutiyet Döneminde Meclisler, 1908-1918," p.265; İhsan Ezherli, *Türkiye Büyük Millet Meclisi, 1920-1998, ve Osmanlı Meclis-i Mebusanı, 1877-1920*, p.219; and, Fevzi Demir, İkinci Meşrutiyet Dönemi Meclis-i Mebusan Seçimleri, 1908-1914, p.166.

[11] "Ouverture du Parlement," *The Levant Herald and Eastern Express*, April 18, 1912, p.1; Feroz Ahmad and Dankwart A. Rustow, "İkinci Meşrutiyet Döneminde Meclisler, 1908-1918," p.267; İhsan Ezherli, *Türkiye Büyük Millet Meclisi, 1920-1998, ve Osmanlı Meclis-i Mebusanı, 1877-1920*, p.212; and, Fevzi Demir, İkinci Meşrutiyet Dönemi Meclis-i Mebusan Seçimleri, 1908-1914, p.167.

[12] "Les Elections: A Schkodra," *The Levant Herald and Eastern Express*, May 4, 1912, p.2; Feroz Ahmad and Dankwart A. Rustow, "İkinci Meşrutiyet Döneminde Meclisler, 1908-1918," p.265; İhsan Ezherli, *Türkiye Büyük Millet Meclisi, 1920-1998, ve Osmanlı Meclis-i Mebusanı, 1877-1920*, p.213; and, Fevzi Demir, İkinci

Rıza Bey*   Albanian   I[13]

Drac/Durazzo (1)

Esad Pasha Toptan*   Albanian   I[14]

* * *

JANINA (6)

Janina (2)

Dimitraki Kingos*   Greek   I[15]
Konstantin Sourlas*   Greek   I[16]

Argyrocastro/Ergiri (2)

Despri Vassilaki Efendi   Greek   I[17]
Müfid Bey*   Albanian   EL[18]

Meşrutiyet Dönemi Meclis-i Mebusan Seçimleri, 1908-1914, p.166.

[13] "Les Elections: A Schkodra," *The Levant Herald and Eastern Express*, May 4, 1912, p.2; Feroz Ahmad and Dankwart A. Rustow, "İkinci Meşrutiyet Döneminde Meclisler, 1908-1918," p.265; İhsan Ezherli, *Türkiye Büyük Millet Meclisi, 1920-1998, ve Osmanlı Meclis-i Mebusanı, 1877-1920*, p.216; and, Fevzi Demir, İkinci Meşrutiyet Dönemi Meclis-i Mebusan Seçimleri, 1908-1914, p.166.

[14] "Les Elections: 38 députés élus," *The Levant Herald and Eastern Express*, April 4, 1912, p.2; "Ouverture du Parlement," *The Levant Herald and Eastern Express*, April 18, 1912, p.1; Feroz Ahmad and Dankwart A. Rustow, "İkinci Meşrutiyet Döneminde Meclisler, 1908-1918," p.265; İhsan Ezherli, *Türkiye Büyük Millet Meclisi, 1920-1998, ve Osmanlı Meclis-i Mebusanı, 1877-1920*, p.207; and, Fevzi Demir, İkinci Meşrutiyet Dönemi Meclis-i Mebusan Seçimleri, 1908-1914, p.166.

[15] "Les Elections: A Janina," *The Levant Herald and Eastern Express*, April 25, 1912, p.2; Feroz Ahmad and Dankwart A. Rustow, "İkinci Meşrutiyet Döneminde Meclisler, 1908-1918," p.266; İhsan Ezherli, *Türkiye Büyük Millet Meclisi, 1920-1998, ve Osmanlı Meclis-i Mebusanı, 1877-1920*, p.211; and, Fevzi Demir, İkinci Meşrutiyet Dönemi Meclis-i Mebusan Seçimleri, 1908-1914, p.166.

[16] "Les Elections: A Janina," *The Levant Herald and Eastern Express*, April 25, 1912, p.2; Feroz Ahmad and Dankwart A. Rustow, "İkinci Meşrutiyet Döneminde Meclisler, 1908-1918," p.266; İhsan Ezherli, *Türkiye Büyük Millet Meclisi, 1920-1998, ve Osmanlı Meclis-i Mebusanı, 1877-1920*, p.217; and, Fevzi Demir, İkinci Meşrutiyet Dönemi Meclis-i Mebusan Seçimleri, 1908-1914, p.166.

[17] Feroz Ahmad and Dankwart A. Rustow, "İkinci Meşrutiyet Döneminde Meclisler, 1908-1918," p.266; İhsan Ezherli, *Türkiye Büyük Millet Meclisi, 1920-1998, ve Osmanlı Meclis-i Mebusanı, 1877-1920*, p.220; and, Fevzi Demir, İkinci Meşrutiyet Dönemi Meclis-i Mebusan Seçimleri, 1908-1914, p.166.

[18] Son of the late Noga Pasha ("Turkey: Some Election Results," *The Times*, October 17, 1908, p.7). Feroz Ahmad and Dankwart A. Rustow, "İkinci Meşrutiyet Döneminde Meclisler, 1908-1918," p.266; İhsan Ezherli, *Türkiye Büyük Millet*

Berat (2)

Süreyya Bey Vlora   Albanian   I[19]
Sami Vrionis   Albanian   I[20]

* * *

MONASTIR (10)

Monastir (4)

Janaki Dimitrijevich*   Serbian   I[21]
Traianos Nallis*   Greek   EL[22]
Pantché Doreff*   Bulgarian   Socialist[23]

Meclisi, 1920-1998, ve Osmanlı Meclis-i Mebusanı, 1877-1920, p.214; and, Fevzi Demir, İkinci Meşrutiyet Dönemi Meclis-i Mebusan Seçimleri, 1908-1914, p.166.

[19] He was elected with 61 votes ("Les Elections: Ismail Kemal bey échoue à Bérat," *The Levant Herald and Eastern Express*, May 4, 1912, p.2). Feroz Ahmad and Dankwart A. Rustow, "İkinci Meşrutiyet Döneminde Meclisler, 1908-1918," p.266; İhsan Ezherli, *Türkiye Büyük Millet Meclisi, 1920-1998, ve Osmanlı Meclis-i Mebusanı, 1877-1920*, p.218; and, Fevzi Demir, İkinci Meşrutiyet Dönemi Meclis-i Mebusan Seçimleri, 1908-1914, p.166.

[20] He was elected with 60 votes ("Les Elections: Ismail Kemal bey échoue à Bérat," *The Levant Herald and Eastern Express*, May 4, 1912, p.2). Feroz Ahmad and Dankwart A. Rustow, "İkinci Meşrutiyet Döneminde Meclisler, 1908-1918," p.266; İhsan Ezherli, *Türkiye Büyük Millet Meclisi, 1920-1998, ve Osmanlı Meclis-i Mebusanı, 1877-1920*, p.217; and, Fevzi Demir, İkinci Meşrutiyet Dönemi Meclis-i Mebusan Seçimleri, 1908-1914, p.166.

[21] Medical doctor ("Lettre de Monastir [November 16]," *The Levant Herald and Eastern Express*, November 24, 1908, p.3). He was elected with 28 votes ("Les Elections: A Monastir," *The Levant Herald and Eastern Express*, April 3, 1912, p.2). "Ouverture du Parlement," *The Levant Herald and Eastern Express*, April 18, 1912, p.1; Stojan Makedonski, "Le Regime Jeune-Turc et les Deuxiemes Elections Parlementaires de 1912 en Macedoine et Thrace Orientale," p.71; Feroz Ahmad and Dankwart A. Rustow, "İkinci Meşrutiyet Döneminde Meclisler, 1908-1918," p.267; İhsan Ezherli, *Türkiye Büyük Millet Meclisi, 1920-1998, ve Osmanlı Meclis-i Mebusanı, 1877-1920*, p.206; and, Fevzi Demir, İkinci Meşrutiyet Dönemi Meclis-i Mebusan Seçimleri, 1908-1914, p.167.

[22] He was elected with 29 votes ("Les Elections: A Monastir," *The Levant Herald and Eastern Express*, April 3, 1912, p.2). "Ouverture du Parlement," *The Levant Herald and Eastern Express*, April 18, 1912, p.1; Feroz Ahmad and Dankwart A. Rustow, "İkinci Meşrutiyet Döneminde Meclisler, 1908-1918," p.267; İhsan Ezherli, *Türkiye Büyük Millet Meclisi, 1920-1998, ve Osmanlı Meclis-i Mebusanı, 1877-1920*, p.219; and, Fevzi Demir, İkinci Meşrutiyet Dönemi Meclis-i Mebusan Seçimleri, 1908-1914, p.167.

[23] He was elected with 30 votes ("Les Elections: A Monastir," *The Levant Herald and Eastern Express*, April 3, 1912, p.2). "Ouverture du Parlement," *The Levant Herald and Eastern Express*, April 18, 1912, p.1; Feroz Ahmad and Dankwart A. Rustow, "İkinci Meşrutiyet Döneminde Meclisler, 1908-1918," p.267; İhsan Ezherli, *Türkiye Büyük Millet Meclisi, 1920-1998, ve Osmanlı Meclis-i Mebusanı, 1877-1920*, p.215; and, Fevzi Demir, İkinci Meşrutiyet Dönemi Meclis-i Mebusan Seçim-

Mehmed Vasıf Efendi*	Albanian	EL[24]
Ali Fethi [Okyar]	Turk	CUP[25]

Diber (1)

Şevket [Enön]*	Albanian	EL[26]

Elbasan (1)

Şevket Bey	Albanian	LU[27]

Goritza/Görice (2)

Philip Mishé*	Serbian	I[28]
Süleyman Efendi	Albanian	I[29]

leri, 1908-1914, p.167.

[24] Feroz Ahmad and Dankwart A. Rustow, "İkinci Meşrutiyet Döneminde Meclisler, 1908-1918," p.267; and, İhsan Ezherli, *Türkiye Büyük Millet Meclisi, 1920-1998, ve Osmanlı Meclis-i Mebusanı, 1877-1920*, p.212. His deputyship may have not been ratified; because he is not listed in Fevzi Demir, İkinci Meşrutiyet Dönemi Meclis-i Mebusan Seçimleri, 1908-1914, p.167).

[25] He was elected with 29 votes ("Les Elections: A Monastir," *The Levant Herald and Eastern Express*, April 3, 1912, p.2). "Ouverture du Parlement," *The Levant Herald and Eastern Express*, April 18, 1912, p.1. Feroz Ahmad and Dankwart A. Rustow, "İkinci Meşrutiyet Döneminde Meclisler, 1908-1918," p.267; İhsan Ezherli, *Türkiye Büyük Millet Meclisi, 1920-1998, ve Osmanlı Meclis-i Mebusanı, 1877-1920*, p.204; and, Fevzi Demir, İkinci Meşrutiyet Dönemi Meclis-i Mebusan Seçimleri, 1908-1914, p.167.

[26] Feroz Ahmad and Dankwart A. Rustow, "İkinci Meşrutiyet Döneminde Meclisler, 1908-1918," p.265; İhsan Ezherli, *Türkiye Büyük Millet Meclisi, 1920-1998, ve Osmanlı Meclis-i Mebusanı, 1877-1920*, p.218; and, Fevzi Demir, İkinci Meşrutiyet Dönemi Meclis-i Mebusan Seçimleri, 1908-1914, p.166.

[27] Notable of Elbasan ("Election," *The Levant Herald and Eastern Express*, April 22, 1912, p.2). Feroz Ahmad and Dankwart A. Rustow, "İkinci Meşrutiyet Döneminde Meclisler, 1908-1918," p.265; and, İhsan Ezherli, *Türkiye Büyük Millet Meclisi, 1920-1998, ve Osmanlı Meclis-i Mebusanı, 1877-1920*, p.218; and, Fevzi Demir, İkinci Meşrutiyet Dönemi Meclis-i Mebusan Seçimleri, 1908-1914, p.166.

[28] Medical doctor (Fevzi Demir, İkinci Meşrutiyet Dönemi Meclis-i Mebusan Seçimleri, 1908-1914, p.166). "Les Elections: A Goritza," *The Levant Herald and Eastern Express*, April 10, 1912, p.2; "Les Elections," *The Levant Herald and Eastern Express*, April 13, 1912, p.2; "Ouverture du Parlement," *The Levant Herald and Eastern Express*, April 18, 1912, p.1; Feroz Ahmad and Dankwart A. Rustow, "İkinci Meşrutiyet Döneminde Meclisler, 1908-1918," p.266; İhsan Ezherli, *Türkiye Büyük Millet Meclisi, 1920-1998, ve Osmanlı Meclis-i Mebusanı, 1877-1920*, p.207; and, Fevzi Demir, İkinci Meşrutiyet Dönemi Meclis-i Mebusan Seçimleri, 1908-1914, p.166.

[29] "Les Elections: A Goritza," *The Levant Herald and Eastern Express*, April 10, 1912, p.2; "Les Elections," *The Levant Herald and Eastern Express*, April 13, 1912, p.2; "Ouverture du Parlement," *The Levant Herald and Eastern Express*, April 18, 1912, p.1; Feroz Ahmad and Dankwart A. Rustow, "İkinci Meşrutiyet Döneminde Meclisler, 1908-1918," p.266; İhsan Ezherli, *Türkiye Büyük Millet Meclisi, 1920-1998, ve Osmanlı Meclis-i Mebusanı, 1877-1920*, p.218; and, Fevzi Demir, İkin-

Serfidje (2)

Gregorius Efendi	Greek	I[30]
Osman Bey	Turk	CUP[31]

* * *

SALONICA (12)

Salonica (6)

Mehmed Cavid Bey*	Turk	CUP[32]
Emmanuel Carasso*	Jew	CUP[33]
Mustafa Rahmi [Aslan]*	Turk	CUP[34]
Halil Bey	Turk	CUP[35]

---

ci Meşrutiyet Dönemi Meclis-i Mebusan Seçimleri, 1908-1914, p.166.

[30] "Ouverture du Parlement," *The Levant Herald and Eastern Express*, April 18, 1912, p.1; "The Ottoman Parliament," *The Orient, 3/21* (May 22, 1912); İhsan Ezherli, *Türkiye Büyük Millet Meclisi, 1920-1998, ve Osmanlı Meclis-i Mebusanı, 1877-1920*, p.207; and, Fevzi Demir, İkinci Meşrutiyet Dönemi Meclis-i Mebusan Seçimleri, 1908-1914, p.166.

[31] "Ouverture du Parlement," *The Levant Herald and Eastern Express*, April 18, 1912, p.1; Feroz Ahmad and Dankwart A. Rustow, "İkinci Meşrutiyet Döneminde Meclisler, 1908-1918," p.266; İhsan Ezherli, *Türkiye Büyük Millet Meclisi, 1920-1998, ve Osmanlı Meclis-i Mebusanı, 1877-1920*, p.214; and, Fevzi Demir, İkinci Meşrutiyet Dönemi Meclis-i Mebusan Seçimleri, 1908-1914, p.166.

[32] Graduate of Mekteb-i Mülkiye, Class of 1896 (Ali Çankaya, *Yeni Mülkiye Tarihi ve Mülkiyeliler, 3*, pp.678-717). "Les Elections," *The Levant Herald and Eastern Express*, April 15, 1912, p.2; "Ouverture du Parlement," *The Levant Herald and Eastern Express*, April 18, 1912, p.1; Feroz Ahmad and Dankwart A. Rustow, "İkinci Meşrutiyet Döneminde Meclisler, 1908-1918," p.267; İhsan Ezherli, *Türkiye Büyük Millet Meclisi, 1920-1998, ve Osmanlı Meclis-i Mebusanı, 1877-1920*, p.206; and, Fevzi Demir, İkinci Meşrutiyet Dönemi Meclis-i Mebusan Seçimleri, 1908-1914, p.167.

[33] "Les Elections," *The Levant Herald and Eastern Express*, April 15, 1912, p.2; "Ouverture du Parlement," *The Levant Herald and Eastern Express*, April 18, 1912, p.1; Feroz Ahmad and Dankwart A. Rustow, "İkinci Meşrutiyet Döneminde Meclisler, 1908-1918," p.267; İhsan Ezherli, *Türkiye Büyük Millet Meclisi, 1920-1998, ve Osmanlı Meclis-i Mebusanı, 1877-1920*, p.206; and, Fevzi Demir, İkinci Meşrutiyet Dönemi Meclis-i Mebusan Seçimleri, 1908-1914, p.167.

[34] "Les Elections: 141 élus," *The Levant Herald and Eastern Express*, April 16, 1912, p.2; "Ouverture du Parlement," *The Levant Herald and Eastern Express*, April 18, 1912, p.1; Feroz Ahmad and Dankwart A. Rustow, "İkinci Meşrutiyet Döneminde Meclisler, 1908-1918," p.267; İhsan Ezherli, *Türkiye Büyük Millet Meclisi, 1920-1998, ve Osmanlı Meclis-i Mebusanı, 1877-1920*, p.215; and, Fevzi Demir, İkinci Meşrutiyet Dönemi Meclis-i Mebusan Seçimleri, 1908-1914, p.167.

[35] Major. "Les Elections," *The Levant Herald and Eastern Express*, April 15, 1912, p.2; "Ouverture du Parlement," *The Levant Herald and Eastern Express*, April 18, 1912, p.1; Feroz Ahmad and Dankwart A. Rustow, "İkinci Meşrutiyet Döneminde Meclisler, 1908-1918," p.267; İhsan Ezherli, *Türkiye Büyük Millet Meclisi,*

Kiryaki Kocuno	Greek	I[36]
Jordan Nikolov	Bulgarian	I[37]
Tchikotchanoff	Bulgarian?	I?[38]

Drama (2)

| Rıza Bey* | Turk | CUP[39] |
| Midhat Şükrü [Bleda]* | Turk | CUP[40] |

Serres (4)

| Alexandre Bujnov | Bulgarian | I[41] |
| Hulusi Bey | Turk | I[42] |

1920-1998, ve Osmanlı Meclis-i Mebusanı, 1877-1920, p.208; and, Fevzi Demir, İkinci Meşrutiyet Dönemi Meclis-i Mebusan Seçimleri, 1908-1914, p.167.

[36] Feroz Ahmad and Dankwart A. Rustow, "İkinci Meşrutiyet Döneminde Meclisler, 1908-1918," p.267; İhsan Ezherli, *Türkiye Büyük Millet Meclisi, 1920-1998, ve Osmanlı Meclis-i Mebusanı, 1877-1920*, p.211; and, Fevzi Demir, İkinci Meşrutiyet Dönemi Meclis-i Mebusan Seçimleri, 1908-1914, p.167.

[37] Stojan Makedonski, "Le Regime Jeune-Turc et les Deuxiemes Elections Parlementaires de 1912 en Macedoine et Thrace Orientale," p.68; "Les Elections," *The Levant Herald and Eastern Express*, April 15, 1912, p.2; "Ouverture du Parlement," *The Levant Herald and Eastern Express*, April 18, 1912, p.1; Feroz Ahmad and Dankwart A. Rustow, "İkinci Meşrutiyet Döneminde Meclisler, 1908-1918," p.267; İhsan Ezherli, *Türkiye Büyük Millet Meclisi, 1920-1998, ve Osmanlı Meclis-i Mebusanı, 1877-1920*, p.220; and, Fevzi Demir, İkinci Meşrutiyet Dönemi Meclis-i Mebusan Seçimleri, 1908-1914, p.167.

[38] Medical doctor. "Les Elections: 141 élus," *The Levant Herald and Eastern Express*, April 16, 1912, p.2; and, "Ouverture du Parlement," *The Levant Herald and Eastern Express*, April 18, 1912, p.1. His deputyship may have not been ratified; because his name is not listed in offical records.

[39] "Les Elections," *The Levant Herald and Eastern Express*, April 13, 1912, p.2; "Ouverture du Parlement," *The Levant Herald and Eastern Express*, April 18, 1912, p.1; Feroz Ahmad and Dankwart A. Rustow, "İkinci Meşrutiyet Döneminde Meclisler, 1908-1918," p.267; İhsan Ezherli, *Türkiye Büyük Millet Meclisi, 1920-1998, ve Osmanlı Meclis-i Mebusanı, 1877-1920*, p.216; and, Fevzi Demir, İkinci Meşrutiyet Dönemi Meclis-i Mebusan Seçimleri, 1908-1914, p.167.

[40] "Les Elections," *The Levant Herald and Eastern Express*, April 13, 1912, p.2; "Ouverture du Parlement," *The Levant Herald and Eastern Express*, April 18, 1912, p.1; Feroz Ahmad and Dankwart A. Rustow, "İkinci Meşrutiyet Döneminde Meclisler, 1908-1918," p.267; İhsan Ezherli, *Türkiye Büyük Millet Meclisi, 1920-1998, ve Osmanlı Meclis-i Mebusanı, 1877-1920*, p.213; and, Fevzi Demir, İkinci Meşrutiyet Dönemi Meclis-i Mebusan Seçimleri, 1908-1914, p.167.

[41] Stojan Makedonski, "Le Regime Jeune-Turc et les Deuxiemes Elections Parlementaires de 1912 en Macedoine et Thrace Orientale," p.68; "Les Elections: Les nouveaux députés," *The Levant Herald and Eastern Express*, April 19, 1912, p.2; Feroz Ahmad and Dankwart A. Rustow, "İkinci Meşrutiyet Döneminde Meclisler, 1908-1918," p.267; İhsan Ezherli, *Türkiye Büyük Millet Meclisi, 1920-1998, ve Osmanlı Meclis-i Mebusanı, 1877-1920*, p.206; and, Fevzi Demir, İkinci Meşrutiyet Dönemi Meclis-i Mebusan Seçimleri, 1908-1914, p.167.

[42] "Les Elections: Les nouveaux députés," *The Levant Herald and Eastern Express*, April 19, 1912, p.2; Feroz Ahmad and Dankwart A. Rustow, "İkinci Meşrutiyet Döneminde Meclisler, 1908-1918," p.267; İhsan Ezherli, *Türkiye Büyük Millet*

Stoju Hadziev   Bulgarian   I[43]
Derviş Ragıb Bey   Turk   CUP[44]

* * *

EDİRNE (12)

Edirne (3)

Mehmed Talât Bey*   Turk   CUP[45]
Faik [Kaltakkıran]*   Turk   CUP[46]
Emin Bey   Turk   CUP[47]

Meclisi, 1920-1998, ve Osmanlı Meclis-i Mebusanı, 1877-1920, p.209; and, Fevzi Demir, İkinci Meşrutiyet Dönemi Meclis-i Mebusan Seçimleri, 1908-1914, p.167.

[43] Stojan Makedonski, "Le Regime Jeune-Turc et les Deuxiemes Elections Parlementaires de 1912 en Macedoine et Thrace Orientale," p.68; "Les Elections: Les nouveaux députés," *The Levant Herald and Eastern Express*, April 19, 1912, p.2; Feroz Ahmad and Dankwart A. Rustow, "İkinci Meşrutiyet Döneminde Meclisler, 1908-1918," p.267; İhsan Ezherli, *Türkiye Büyük Millet Meclisi, 1920-1998, ve Osmanlı Meclis-i Mebusanı, 1877-1920*, p.210; and, Fevzi Demir, İkinci Meşrutiyet Dönemi Meclis-i Mebusan Seçimleri, 1908-1914, p.

[44] "Les Elections: Les nouveaux députés," *The Levant Herald and Eastern Express*, April 19, 1912, p.2; İhsan Ezherli, *Türkiye Büyük Millet Meclisi, 1920-1998, ve Osmanlı Meclis-i Mebusanı, 1877-1920*, p.206; and, Fevzi Demir, İkinci Meşrutiyet Dönemi Meclis-i Mebusan Seçimleri, 1908-1914, p.167.

[45] "Les Elections: Nouveaux députés unionistes," *The Levant Herald and Eastern Express*, April 12, 1912, p.2; "Les Elections," *The Levant Herald and Eastern Express*, April 13, 1912, p.2; "Ouverture du Parlement," *The Levant Herald and Eastern Express*, April 18, 1912, p.1; Feroz Ahmad and Dankwart A. Rustow, "İkinci Meşrutiyet Döneminde Meclisler, 1908-1918," p.268; İhsan Ezherli, *Türkiye Büyük Millet Meclisi, 1920-1998, ve Osmanlı Meclis-i Mebusanı, 1877-1920*, p.219; and, Fevzi Demir, İkinci Meşrutiyet Dönemi Meclis-i Mebusan Seçimleri, 1908-1914, p.168.

[46] "Les Elections: Nouveaux députés unionistes," *The Levant Herald and Eastern Express*, April 12, 1912, p.2; "Les Elections," *The Levant Herald and Eastern Express*, April 13, 1912, p.2; "Ouverture du Parlement," *The Levant Herald and Eastern Express*, April 18, 1912, p.1; Feroz Ahmad and Dankwart A. Rustow, "İkinci Meşrutiyet Döneminde Meclisler, 1908-1918," p.268; İhsan Ezherli, *Türkiye Büyük Millet Meclisi, 1920-1998, ve Osmanlı Meclis-i Mebusanı, 1877-1920*, p.207; and, Fevzi Demir, İkinci Meşrutiyet Dönemi Meclis-i Mebusan Seçimleri, 1908-1914, p.168.

[47] "Les Elections: Nouveaux députés unionistes," *The Levant Herald and Eastern Express*, April 12, 1912, p.2; "Les Elections," *The Levant Herald and Eastern Express*, April 13, 1912, p.2; "Ouverture du Parlement," *The Levant Herald and Eastern Express*, April 18, 1912, p.1; Feroz Ahmad and Dankwart A. Rustow, "İkinci Meşrutiyet Döneminde Meclisler, 1908-1918," p.268; İhsan Ezherli, *Türkiye Büyük Millet Meclisi, 1920-1998, ve Osmanlı Meclis-i Mebusanı, 1877-1920*, p.206; and, Fevzi Demir, İkinci Meşrutiyet Dönemi Meclis-i Mebusan Seçimleri, 1908-1914, p.168.

Dedeağaç (1)

Manavoğlu Süleyman Bey*	Turk	CUP[48]

Gelibolu (1)

Hafız Hüseyin Ulvi Bey	Turk	I[49]

Gümülcine (3)

Hacı Mehmed Âdil [Arda]*	Turk	CUP[50]
Mehmed Hilmi Bey*	Turk	CUP[51]
Müderris Mehmed Bey	Turk	CUP[52]

Kırk Kilise (2)

Emrullah Efendi*	Turk	CUP[53]

---

[48] Captain. "Les Elections: Résultats à ce jour," *The Levant Herald and Eastern Express*, April 1, 1912, p.2; "Ouverture du Parlement," *The Levant Herald and Eastern Express*, April 18, 1912, p.1; Feroz Ahmad and Dankwart A. Rustow, "İkinci Meşrutiyet Döneminde Meclisler, 1908-1918," p.268; İhsan Ezherli, *Türkiye Büyük Millet Meclisi, 1920-1998, ve Osmanlı Meclis-i Mebusanı, 1877-1920*, p.218; and, Fevzi Demir, İkinci Meşrutiyet Dönemi Meclis-i Mebusan Seçimleri, 1908-1914, p.167.

[49] "Les Elections: Pas un député d'opposition!" *The Levant Herald and Eastern Express*, April 9, 1912, p.2; Feroz Ahmad and Dankwart A. Rustow, "İkinci Meşrutiyet Döneminde Meclisler, 1908-1918," p.268; İhsan Ezherli, *Türkiye Büyük Millet Meclisi, 1920-1998, ve Osmanlı Meclis-i Mebusanı, 1877-1920*, p.209; and, Fevzi Demir, İkinci Meşrutiyet Dönemi Meclis-i Mebusan Seçimleri, 1908-1914, p.167.

[50] "Les Elections: Résultats à ce jour," *The Levant Herald and Eastern Express*, April 1, 1912, p.2; "Ouverture du Parlement," *The Levant Herald and Eastern Express*, April 18, 1912, p.1; Feroz Ahmad and Dankwart A. Rustow, "İkinci Meşrutiyet Döneminde Meclisler, 1908-1918," p.267; İhsan Ezherli, *Türkiye Büyük Millet Meclisi, 1920-1998, ve Osmanlı Meclis-i Mebusanı, 1877-1920*, p.207; and, Fevzi Demir, İkinci Meşrutiyet Dönemi Meclis-i Mebusan Seçimleri, 1908-1914, p.167.

[51] "Les Elections: Résultats à ce jour," *The Levant Herald and Eastern Express*, April 1, 1912, p.2; "Ouverture du Parlement," *The Levant Herald and Eastern Express*, April 18, 1912, p.1; Feroz Ahmad and Dankwart A. Rustow, "İkinci Meşrutiyet Döneminde Meclisler, 1908-1918," p.267; İhsan Ezherli, *Türkiye Büyük Millet Meclisi, 1920-1998, ve Osmanlı Meclis-i Mebusanı, 1877-1920*, p.212; and, Fevzi Demir, İkinci Meşrutiyet Dönemi Meclis-i Mebusan Seçimleri, 1908-1914, p.167.

[52] "Les Elections: Résultats à ce jour," *The Levant Herald and Eastern Express*, April 1, 1912, p.2; "Ouverture du Parlement," *The Levant Herald and Eastern Express*, April 18, 1912, p.1; Feroz Ahmad and Dankwart A. Rustow, "İkinci Meşrutiyet Döneminde Meclisler, 1908-1918," p.268; İhsan Ezherli, *Türkiye Büyük Millet Meclisi, 1920-1998, ve Osmanlı Meclis-i Mebusanı, 1877-1920*, p.211; and, Fevzi Demir, İkinci Meşrutiyet Dönemi Meclis-i Mebusan Seçimleri, 1908-1914, p.167.

[53] Graduate of Mekteb-i Mülkiye, Class of 1882 (Ali Çankaya, *Yeni Mülkiye Tarihi ve Mülkiyeliler*, 3, pp.96-102). "Les Elections," *The Levant Herald and Eastern Express*, April 13, 1912, p.2; "Ouverture du Parlement," *The Levant Herald and*

Ömer Naci Bey   Turk   CUP[54]

Tekfurdağı [Tekirdağ]/Rodosto (2)

Agop Boyadjian*   Armenian   I[55]
Bedreddin Bey   Turk   CUP?[56]

* * *

İSTANBUL (10)

İstanbul (10)

Hüseyin Cahid [Yalçın]*   Turk   CUP[57]
Albert Vitali Faraggi*   Jew   I[58]
Bedros Haladjian*   Armenian   CUP[59]

Eastern Express, April 18, 1912, p.1; Feroz Ahmad and Dankwart A. Rustow, "İkinci Meşrutiyet Döneminde Meclisler, 1908-1918," p.268; İhsan Ezherli, *Türkiye Büyük Millet Meclisi, 1920-1998, ve Osmanlı Meclis-i Mebusanı, 1877-1920*, p.207; and, Fevzi Demir, İkinci Meşrutiyet Dönemi Meclis-i Mebusan Seçimleri, 1908-1914, p.168.

[54] "Les Elections," *The Levant Herald and Eastern Express*, April 13, 1912, p.2; "Ouverture du Parlement," *The Levant Herald and Eastern Express*, April 18, 1912, p.1; Feroz Ahmad and Dankwart A. Rustow, "İkinci Meşrutiyet Döneminde Meclisler, 1908-1918," p.268; İhsan Ezherli, *Türkiye Büyük Millet Meclisi, 1920-1998, ve Osmanlı Meclis-i Mebusanı, 1877-1920*, p.215; and, Fevzi Demir, İkinci Meşrutiyet Dönemi Meclis-i Mebusan Seçimleri, 1908-1914, p.168.

[55] Feroz Ahmad and Dankwart A. Rustow, "İkinci Meşrutiyet Döneminde Meclisler, 1908-1918," p.268; and, Fevzi Demir, İkinci Meşrutiyet Dönemi Meclis-i Mebusan Seçimleri, 1908-1914, p.168.

[56] Feroz Ahmad and Dankwart A. Rustow, "İkinci Meşrutiyet Döneminde Meclisler, 1908-1918," p.268; İhsan Ezherli, *Türkiye Büyük Millet Meclisi, 1920-1998, ve Osmanlı Meclis-i Mebusanı, 1877-1920*, p.206; and, Fevzi Demir, İkinci Meşrutiyet Dönemi Meclis-i Mebusan Seçimleri, 1908-1914, p.168.

[57] Graduate of Mekteb-i Mülkiye, Class of 1896 (Ali Çankaya, *Yeni Mülkiye Tarihi ve Mülkiyeliler*, 3, pp.648-678). "Ouverture du Parlement," *The Levant Herald and Eastern Express*, April 18, 1912, p.1; Feroz Ahmad and Dankwart A. Rustow, "İkinci Meşrutiyet Döneminde Meclisler, 1908-1918," p.268; İhsan Ezherli, *Türkiye Büyük Millet Meclisi, 1920-1998, ve Osmanlı Meclis-i Mebusanı, 1877-1920*, p.209; and, Fevzi Demir, İkinci Meşrutiyet Dönemi Meclis-i Mebusan Seçimleri, 1908-1914, p.168.

[58] "Ouverture du Parlement," *The Levant Herald and Eastern Express*, April 18, 1912, p.1; Feroz Ahmad and Dankwart A. Rustow, "İkinci Meşrutiyet Döneminde Meclisler, 1908-1918," p.268; İhsan Ezherli, *Türkiye Büyük Millet Meclisi, 1920-1998, ve Osmanlı Meclis-i Mebusanı, 1877-1920*, p.207; and, Fevzi Demir, İkinci Meşrutiyet Dönemi Meclis-i Mebusan Seçimleri, 1908-1914, p.168.

[59] Lawyer (Feroz Ahmad and Dankwart A. Rustow, "İkinci Meşrutiyet Döneminde Meclisler, 1908-1918," p.268). "Ouverture du Parlement," *The Levant Herald and Eastern Express*, April 18, 1912, p.1; İhsan Ezherli, *Türkiye Büyük Millet*

Ahmed Nesimi [Sayman]*	Turk	CUP[60]
Krikor Zohrab*	Armenian	EL[61]
Yorgaki Artas	Greek	I[62]
Hüseyin Haşim [Sanver]	Turk	CUP[63]
Memduh Bey	Turk	CUP[64]
Orphanidis Efendi	Greek	I[65]
Yağcı Şefik Bey	Turk	CUP[66]

* * *

Meclisi, 1920-1998, ve Osmanlı Meclis-i Mebusanı, 1877-1920, p.208; and, Fevzi Demir, İkinci Meşrutiyet Dönemi Meclis-i Mebusan Seçimleri, 1908-1914, p.168.

[60] "Ouverture du Parlement," The Levant Herald and Eastern Express, April 18, 1912, p.1; Feroz Ahmad and Dankwart A. Rustow, "İkinci Meşrutiyet Döneminde Meclisler, 1908-1918," p.269; İhsan Ezherli, Türkiye Büyük Millet Meclisi, 1920-1998, ve Osmanlı Meclis-i Mebusanı, 1877-1920, p.204; and, Fevzi Demir, İkinci Meşrutiyet Dönemi Meclis-i Mebusan Seçimleri, 1908-1914, p.168.

[61] "Ouverture du Parlement," The Levant Herald and Eastern Express, April 18, 1912, p.1; Feroz Ahmad and Dankwart A. Rustow, "İkinci Meşrutiyet Döneminde Meclisler, 1908-1918," p.269; İhsan Ezherli, Türkiye Büyük Millet Meclisi, 1920-1998, ve Osmanlı Meclis-i Mebusanı, 1877-1920, p.220; and, Fevzi Demir, İkinci Meşrutiyet Dönemi Meclis-i Mebusan Seçimleri, 1908-1914, p.168.

[62] "Ouverture du Parlement," The Levant Herald and Eastern Express, April 18, 1912, p.1; Feroz Ahmad and Dankwart A. Rustow, "İkinci Meşrutiyet Döneminde Meclisler, 1908-1918," p.269; İhsan Ezherli, Türkiye Büyük Millet Meclisi, 1920-1998, ve Osmanlı Meclis-i Mebusanı, 1877-1920, p.220; and, Fevzi Demir, İkinci Meşrutiyet Dönemi Meclis-i Mebusan Seçimleri, 1908-1914, p.168.

[63] Graduate of Mekteb-i Mülkiye, Class of 1891 (Ali Çankaya, Yeni Mülkiye Tarihi ve Mülkiyeliler, 3, p.476). "Ouverture du Parlement," The Levant Herald and Eastern Express, April 18, 1912, p.1; Feroz Ahmad and Dankwart A. Rustow, "İkinci Meşrutiyet Döneminde Meclisler, 1908-1918," p.269; İhsan Ezherli, Türkiye Büyük Millet Meclisi, 1920-1998, ve Osmanlı Meclis-i Mebusanı, 1877-1920, p.209; and, Fevzi Demir, İkinci Meşrutiyet Dönemi Meclis-i Mebusan Seçimleri, 1908-1914, p.168.

[64] "Ouverture du Parlement," The Levant Herald and Eastern Express, April 18, 1912, p.1; Feroz Ahmad and Dankwart A. Rustow, "İkinci Meşrutiyet Döneminde Meclisler, 1908-1918," p.269; İhsan Ezherli, Türkiye Büyük Millet Meclisi, 1920-1998, ve Osmanlı Meclis-i Mebusanı, 1877-1920, p.212; and, Fevzi Demir, İkinci Meşrutiyet Dönemi Meclis-i Mebusan Seçimleri, 1908-1914, p.168.

[65] "Ouverture du Parlement," The Levant Herald and Eastern Express, April 18, 1912, p.1; Feroz Ahmad and Dankwart A. Rustow, "İkinci Meşrutiyet Döneminde Meclisler, 1908-1918," p.269; İhsan Ezherli, Türkiye Büyük Millet Meclisi, 1920-1998, ve Osmanlı Meclis-i Mebusanı, 1877-1920, p.219; and, Fevzi Demir, İkinci Meşrutiyet Dönemi Meclis-i Mebusan Seçimleri, 1908-1914, p.169.

[66] Menemenlioğlu Rıfat Pasha's brother (Feroz Ahmad and Dankwart A. Rustow, "İkinci Meşrutiyet Döneminde Meclisler, 1908-1918," p.269). "Ouverture du Parlement," The Levant Herald and Eastern Express, April 18, 1912, p.1; İhsan Ezherli, Türkiye Büyük Millet Meclisi, 1920-1998, ve Osmanlı Meclis-i Mebusanı, 1877-1920, p.208; and, Fevzi Demir, İkinci Meşrutiyet Dönemi Meclis-i Mebusan Seçimleri, 1908-1914, p.169.

Sandjak of ÇATALCA (1)

Hafız Süleyman Efendi   Turk   CUP[67]

Sandjak of İZMİT (3)

Anastas Mihailidis*   Greek   I[68]
Ahmed Müfid [Saner]*   Turk   I[69]
İsmail Canbulat   Turk   CUP[70]

* * *

HÜDAVENDİGÂR (13)

Bursa (4)

Abdullah Sabri [Karter]*   Turk   I[71]

---

[67] Ulema ("Les Elections: Nouveaux députés unionistes," *The Levant Herald and Eastern Express*, April 12, 1912, p.2). "Les Elections," *The Levant Herald and Eastern Express*, April 13, 1912, p.2; "Ouverture du Parlement," *The Levant Herald and Eastern Express*, April 18, 1912, p.1; Feroz Ahmad and Dankwart A. Rustow, "İkinci Meşrutiyet Döneminde Meclisler, 1908-1918," p.268; İhsan Ezherli, *Türkiye Büyük Millet Meclisi, 1920-1998, ve Osmanlı Meclis-i Mebusanı, 1877-1920*, p.218; and, Fevzi Demir, İkinci Meşrutiyet Dönemi Meclis-i Mebusan Seçimleri, 1908-1914, p.168.

[68] "Les Elections: A Ismid," *The Levant Herald and Eastern Express*, April 23, 1912, p.2; Feroz Ahmad and Dankwart A. Rustow, "İkinci Meşrutiyet Döneminde Meclisler, 1908-1918," p.269; İhsan Ezherli, *Türkiye Büyük Millet Meclisi, 1920-1998, ve Osmanlı Meclis-i Mebusanı, 1877-1920*, p.205; and, Fevzi Demir, İkinci Meşrutiyet Dönemi Meclis-i Mebusan Seçimleri, 1908-1914, p.169.

[69] Graduate of Mekteb-i Mülkiye, Class of 1890 (Ali Çankaya, *Yeni Mülkiye Tarihi ve Mülkiyeliler*, 3, pp.417-418). "Les Elections: A Ismid," *The Levant Herald and Eastern Express*, April 23, 1912, p.2; Feroz Ahmad and Dankwart A. Rustow, "İkinci Meşrutiyet Döneminde Meclisler, 1908-1918," p.269; İhsan Ezherli, *Türkiye Büyük Millet Meclisi, 1920-1998, ve Osmanlı Meclis-i Mebusanı, 1877-1920*, p.204; and, Fevzi Demir, İkinci Meşrutiyet Dönemi Meclis-i Mebusan Seçimleri, 1908-1914, p.169.

[70] "Les Elections: A Ismid," *The Levant Herald and Eastern Express*, April 23, 1912, p.2; Feroz Ahmad and Dankwart A. Rustow, "İkinci Meşrutiyet Döneminde Meclisler, 1908-1918," p.269; İhsan Ezherli, *Türkiye Büyük Millet Meclisi, 1920-1998, ve Osmanlı Meclis-i Mebusanı, 1877-1920*, p.210; and, Fevzi Demir, İkinci Meşrutiyet Dönemi Meclis-i Mebusan Seçimleri, 1908-1914, p.169.

[71] Graduate of Mekteb-i Mülkiye, Class of 1889 (Ali Çankaya, *Yeni Mülkiye Tarihi ve Mülkiyeliler*, 3, pp.394-397). "Ouverture du Parlement," *The Levant Herald and Eastern Express*, April 18, 1912, p.1; Feroz Ahmad and Dankwart A. Rustow, "İkinci Meşrutiyet Döneminde Meclisler, 1908-1918," p.269; İhsan Ezherli, *Türkiye Büyük Millet Meclisi, 1920-1998, ve Osmanlı Meclis-i Mebusanı, 1877-1920*, p.203; and, Fevzi Demir, İkinci Meşrutiyet Dönemi Meclis-i Mebusan Seçimleri, 1908-1914, p.169.

Hasan Rafet [Canıtez]	Turk	CUP[72]
Hafız Ahmed Hamdi Efendi	Turk	EL[73]
Rıza Bey	Turk	CUP[74]

Karahisar-ı Sahib [Afyon] (3)

Hoca Mehmed Kâmil [Mitas]*	Turk	I[75]
Kethüdazade Salim Bey*	Turk	I[76]
Hacı Ahmed Bedri Efendi	Turk	I[77]

Ertuğrul [Bilecik] (2)

| Mehmed Sadık Bey* | Turk | I[78] |
| Hakkı Baha [Pars] | Turk | CUP[79] |

---

[72] "Les Elections: Résultats à ce jour," *The Levant Herald and Eastern Express,* April 1, 1912, p.2; "Ouverture du Parlement," *The Levant Herald and Eastern Express,* April 18, 1912, p.1; Feroz Ahmad and Dankwart A. Rustow, "İkinci Meşrutiyet Döneminde Meclisler, 1908-1918," p.269; İhsan Ezherli, *Türkiye Büyük Millet Meclisi, 1920-1998, ve Osmanlı Meclis-i Mebusanı, 1877-1920,* p.215; and, Fevzi Demir, İkinci Meşrutiyet Dönemi Meclis-i Mebusan Seçimleri, 1908-1914, p.169.

[73] Feroz Ahmad and Dankwart A. Rustow, "İkinci Meşrutiyet Döneminde Meclisler, 1908-1918," p.269; İhsan Ezherli, *Türkiye Büyük Millet Meclisi, 1920-1998, ve Osmanlı Meclis-i Mebusanı, 1877-1920,* p.203; and, Fevzi Demir, İkinci Dönemi Meclis-i Mebusan Seçimleri, 1908-1914, p.169.

[74] Military Doctor (Feroz Ahmad and Dankwart A. Rustow, "İkinci Meşrutiyet Döneminde Meclisler, 1908-1918," p.269; "Les Elections: Résultats à ce jour," *The Levant Herald and Eastern Express,* April 1, 1912, p.2). "Ouverture du Parlement," *The Levant Herald and Eastern Express,* April 18, 1912, p.1; İhsan Ezherli, *Türkiye Büyük Millet Meclisi, 1920-1998, ve Osmanlı Meclis-i Mebusanı, 1877-1920,* p.216; and, Fevzi Demir, İkinci Meşrutiyet Dönemi Meclis-i Mebusan Seçimleri, 1908-1914, p.169.

[75] "Ouverture du Parlement," *The Levant Herald and Eastern Express,* April 18, 1912, p.1; Feroz Ahmad and Dankwart A. Rustow, "İkinci Meşrutiyet Döneminde Meclisler, 1908-1918," p.272; İhsan Ezherli, *Türkiye Büyük Millet Meclisi, 1920-1998, ve Osmanlı Meclis-i Mebusanı, 1877-1920,* p.210; and, Fevzi Demir, İkinci Meşrutiyet Dönemi Meclis-i Mebusan Seçimleri, 1908-1914, p.172.

[76] "Ouverture du Parlement," *The Levant Herald and Eastern Express,* April 18, 1912, p.1; Feroz Ahmad and Dankwart A. Rustow, "İkinci Meşrutiyet Döneminde Meclisler, 1908-1918," p.272; İhsan Ezherli, *Türkiye Büyük Millet Meclisi, 1920-1998, ve Osmanlı Meclis-i Mebusanı, 1877-1920,* p.216; and, Fevzi Demir, İkinci Meşrutiyet Dönemi Meclis-i Mebusan Seçimleri, 1908-1914, p.172.

[77] "Ouverture du Parlement," *The Levant Herald and Eastern Express,* April 18, 1912, p.1; Feroz Ahmad and Dankwart A. Rustow, "İkinci Meşrutiyet Döneminde Meclisler, 1908-1918," p.272; İhsan Ezherli, *Türkiye Büyük Millet Meclisi, 1920-1998, ve Osmanlı Meclis-i Mebusanı, 1877-1920,* p.204; and, Fevzi Demir, İkinci Meşrutiyet Dönemi Meclis-i Mebusan Seçimleri, 1908-1914, p.172.

[78] Feroz Ahmad and Dankwart A. Rustow, "İkinci Meşrutiyet Döneminde Meclisler, 1908-1918," p.269; İhsan Ezherli, *Türkiye Büyük Millet Meclisi, 1920-1998, ve Osmanlı Meclis-i Mebusanı, 1877-1920,* p.212; and, Fevzi Demir, İkinci Meşrutiyet Dönemi Meclis-i Mebusan Seçimleri, 1908-1914, p.169.

[79] Feroz Ahmad and Dankwart A. Rustow, "İkinci Meşrutiyet Döneminde Meclisler, 1908-1918," p.269; İhsan Ezherli, *Türkiye Büyük Millet Meclisi, 1920-*

Kütahya (4)

Abdullah Azmi [Torun]*	Turk	CUP[80]
Hatibzade Ahmed Cemal Bey*	Turk	I[81]
Yenibahçeli Nail Bey	Turk	CUP[82]
Küpelizade Sadık Bey	Turk	I[83]

* * *

Sandjak of KARESİ [Balıkesir] (5)

Hacı Ali Galib Bey*	Turk	I[84]
Konstantin Savapoulos*	Greek	I[85]

1998, ve *Osmanlı Meclis-i Mebusanı, 1877-1920*, p.208; and, Fevzi Demir, İkinci Meşrutiyet Dönemi Meclis-i Mebusan Seçimleri, 1908-1914, p.169.

[80] Lawyer (Feroz Ahmad and Dankwart A. Rustow, "İkinci Meşrutiyet Döneminde Meclisler, 1908-1918," p.271). "Les Elections," *The Levant Herald and Eastern Express*, April 13, 1912, p.2; "Ouverture du Parlement," *The Levant Herald and Eastern Express*, April 18, 1912, p.1; İhsan Ezherli, *Türkiye Büyük Millet Meclisi, 1920-1998, ve Osmanlı Meclis-i Mebusanı, 1877-1920*, p.203; and, Fevzi Demir, İkinci Meşrutiyet Dönemi Meclis-i Mebusan Seçimleri, 1908-1914, p.172.

[81] "Les Elections," *The Levant Herald and Eastern Express*, April 13, 1912, p.2; "Ouverture du Parlement," *The Levant Herald and Eastern Express*, April 18, 1912, p.1; Feroz Ahmad and Dankwart A. Rustow, "İkinci Meşrutiyet Döneminde Meclisler, 1908-1918," p.271; İhsan Ezherli, *Türkiye Büyük Millet Meclisi, 1920-1998, ve Osmanlı Meclis-i Mebusanı, 1877-1920*, p.206; and, Fevzi Demir, İkinci Meşrutiyet Dönemi Meclis-i Mebusan Seçimleri, 1908-1914, p.172.

[82] "Les Elections," *The Levant Herald and Eastern Express*, April 13, 1912, p.2; "Ouverture du Parlement," *The Levant Herald and Eastern Express*, April 18, 1912, p.1; Feroz Ahmad and Dankwart A. Rustow, "İkinci Meşrutiyet Döneminde Meclisler, 1908-1918," p.271; İhsan Ezherli, *Türkiye Büyük Millet Meclisi, 1920-1998, ve Osmanlı Meclis-i Mebusanı, 1877-1920*, p.214; and, Fevzi Demir, İkinci Meşrutiyet Dönemi Meclis-i Mebusan Seçimleri, 1908-1914, p.172.

[83] "Les Elections," *The Levant Herald and Eastern Express*, April 13, 1912, p.2; "Ouverture du Parlement," *The Levant Herald and Eastern Express*, April 18, 1912, p.1; Feroz Ahmad and Dankwart A. Rustow, "İkinci Meşrutiyet Döneminde Meclisler, 1908-1918," p.271; İhsan Ezherli, *Türkiye Büyük Millet Meclisi, 1920-1998, ve Osmanlı Meclis-i Mebusanı, 1877-1920*, p.216; and, Fevzi Demir, İkinci Meşrutiyet Dönemi Meclis-i Mebusan Seçimleri, 1908-1914, p.172.

[84] "Les Elections: Pas un député d'opposition!" *The Levant Herald and Eastern Express*, April 9, 1912, p.2; "Ouverture du Parlement," *The Levant Herald and Eastern Express*, April 18, 1912, p.1; Feroz Ahmad and Dankwart A. Rustow, "İkinci Meşrutiyet Döneminde Meclisler, 1908-1918," p.271; İhsan Ezherli, *Türkiye Büyük Millet Meclisi, 1920-1998, ve Osmanlı Meclis-i Mebusanı, 1877-1920*, p.204; and, Fevzi Demir, İkinci Meşrutiyet Dönemi Meclis-i Mebusan Seçimleri, 1908-1914, p.171.

[85] "Les Elections: Pas un député d'opposition!" *The Levant Herald and Eastern Express*, April 9, 1912, p.2; "Ouverture du Parlement," *The Levant Herald and Eastern Express*, April 18, 1912, p.1; Feroz Ahmad and Dankwart A. Rustow, "İkinci Meşrutiyet Döneminde Meclisler, 1908-1918," p.271; İhsan Ezherli, *Türkiye Büyük*

Hasan Ferhad Bey	Turk	CUP[86]
Mehmed Vehbi [Bolak]	Turk	CUP[87]
Hüseyin Kadri Bey	Turk	CUP[88]

* * *

Sandjak of KALE-İ SULTANİYE (2)

Çanakkale [Biga] (2)

| Atıf [Kamçıl]* | Turk | CUP[89] |
| Kâzım Bey | Turk | CUP[90] |

* * *

Millet Meclisi, 1920-1998, ve Osmanlı Meclis-i Mebusanı, 1877-1920, p.217; and, Fevzi Demir, İkinci Meşrutiyet Dönemi Meclis-i Mebusan Seçimleri, 1908-1914, p.171.

[86] "Les Elections: Pas un député d'opposition!" *The Levant Herald and Eastern Express,* April 9, 1912, p.2; "Ouverture du Parlement," *The Levant Herald and Eastern Express,* April 18, 1912, p.1; Feroz Ahmad and Dankwart A. Rustow, "İkinci Meşrutiyet Döneminde Meclisler, 1908-1918," p.271; İhsan Ezherli, *Türkiye Büyük Millet Meclisi, 1920-1998, ve Osmanlı Meclis-i Mebusanı, 1877-1920,* p.207; and, Fevzi Demir, İkinci Meşrutiyet Dönemi Meclis-i Mebusan Seçimleri, 1908-1914, p.171.

[87] "Les Elections: Pas un député d'opposition!" *The Levant Herald and Eastern Express,* April 9, 1912, p.2; "Ouverture du Parlement," *The Levant Herald and Eastern Express,* April 18, 1912, p.1; Feroz Ahmad and Dankwart A. Rustow, "İkinci Meşrutiyet Döneminde Meclisler, 1908-1918," p.271; İhsan Ezherli, *Türkiye Büyük Millet Meclisi, 1920-1998, ve Osmanlı Meclis-i Mebusanı, 1877-1920,* p.212; and, Fevzi Demir, İkinci Meşrutiyet Dönemi Meclis-i Mebusan Seçimleri, 1908-1914, p.172.

[88] "Les Elections: Pas un député d'opposition!" *The Levant Herald and Eastern Express,* April 9, 1912, p.2; "Ouverture du Parlement," *The Levant Herald and Eastern Express,* April 18, 1912, p.1; Feroz Ahmad and Dankwart A. Rustow, "İkinci Meşrutiyet Döneminde Meclisler, 1908-1918," p.271; İhsan Ezherli, *Türkiye Büyük Millet Meclisi, 1920-1998, ve Osmanlı Meclis-i Mebusanı, 1877-1920,* p.209; and, Fevzi Demir, İkinci Meşrutiyet Dönemi Meclis-i Mebusan Seçimleri, 1908-1914, p.172.

[89] "Les Elections: Pas un député d'opposition!" *The Levant Herald and Eastern Express,* April 9, 1912, p.2; "Ouverture du Parlement," *The Levant Herald and Eastern Express,* April 18, 1912, p.1; İhsan Ezherli, *Türkiye Büyük Millet Meclisi, 1920-1998, ve Osmanlı Meclis-i Mebusanı, 1877-1920,* p.205; and, Fevzi Demir, İkinci Meşrutiyet Dönemi Meclis-i Mebusan Seçimleri, 1908-1914, p.170.

[90] "Les Elections: Pas un député d'opposition!" *The Levant Herald and Eastern Express,* April 9, 1912, p.2; "Ouverture du Parlement," *The Levant Herald and Eastern Express,* April 18, 1912, p.1; İhsan Ezherli, *Türkiye Büyük Millet Meclisi, 1920-1998, ve Osmanlı Meclis-i Mebusanı, 1877-1920,* p.211; and, Fevzi Demir, İkinci Meşrutiyet Dönemi Meclis-i Mebusan Seçimleri, 1908-1914, p.170.

CEZAYİR BAHR-I SEFİD (2)

Mytilene (1)

Dimitraki Sava Efendi	Greek	I[91]

Chio/Sakız (1)

Ehlefes Abodyako Efendi	Greek	I[92]

* * *

AYDIN (17)

İzmir (6)

Emmanuel Emmanuelidis*	Greek	CUP[93]
Vahan Bardizbanian	Armenian	ARF[94]
Pavlis Carolidis*	Greek	I[95]

---

[91] Feroz Ahmad and Dankwart A. Rustow, "İkinci Meşrutiyet Döneminde Meclisler, 1908-1918," p.270; İhsan Ezherli, *Türkiye Büyük Millet Meclisi, 1920-1998, ve Osmanlı Meclis-i Mebusanı, 1877-1920*, p.206; and, Fevzi Demir, İkinci Meşrutiyet Dönemi Meclis-i Mebusan Seçimleri, 1908-1914, p.170.

[92] Achille Bodiano? ("Nouvelles du Jour," *The Levant Herald and Eastern Express*, April 27, 1912, p.2). Feroz Ahmad and Dankwart A. Rustow, "İkinci Meşrutiyet Döneminde Meclisler, 1908-1918," p.270; İhsan Ezherli, *Türkiye Büyük Millet Meclisi, 1920-1998, ve Osmanlı Meclis-i Mebusanı, 1877-1920*, p.206; and, Fevzi Demir, İkinci Meşrutiyet Dönemi Meclis-i Mebusan Seçimleri, 1908-1914, p.170.

[93] "Les Elections: Résultats à ce jour," *The Levant Herald and Eastern Express*, April 1, 1912, p.2; "Ouverture du Parlement," *The Levant Herald and Eastern Express*, April 18, 1912, p.1; Feroz Ahmad and Dankwart A. Rustow, "İkinci Meşrutiyet Döneminde Meclisler, 1908-1918," p.270; İhsan Ezherli, *Türkiye Büyük Millet Meclisi, 1920-1998, ve Osmanlı Meclis-i Mebusanı, 1877-1920*, p.206; and, Fevzi Demir, İkinci Meşrutiyet Dönemi Meclis-i Mebusan Seçimleri, 1908-1914, p.170.

[94] "Les Elections: Résultats à ce jour," *The Levant Herald and Eastern Express*, April 1, 1912, p.2; "Ouverture du Parlement," *The Levant Herald and Eastern Express*, April 18, 1912, p.1; Feroz Ahmad and Dankwart A. Rustow, "İkinci Meşrutiyet Döneminde Meclisler, 1908-1918," p.270; İhsan Ezherli, *Türkiye Büyük Millet Meclisi, 1920-1998, ve Osmanlı Meclis-i Mebusanı, 1877-1920*, p.219; and, Fevzi Demir, İkinci Meşrutiyet Dönemi Meclis-i Mebusan Seçimleri, 1908-1914, p.171.

[95] Professor of history in Athens University (Feroz Ahmad and Dankwart A. Rustow, "İkinci Meşrutiyet Döneminde Meclisler, 1908-1918," p.271). "Les Elections: Résultats à ce jour," *The Levant Herald and Eastern Express*, April 1, 1912, p.2; "Ouverture du Parlement," *The Levant Herald and Eastern Express*, April 18, 1912, p.1; İhsan Ezherli, *Türkiye Büyük Millet Meclisi, 1920-1998, ve Osmanlı Meclis-i Mebusanı, 1877-1920*, p.215; and, Fevzi Demir, İkinci Meşrutiyet Dönemi Meclis-i Mebusan Seçimleri, 1908-1914, p.171.

Nesim Masliah*	Jew	CUP[96]
Mehmed Seyyid Bey*	Turk	CUP[97]
Musa Kâzım Bey	Turk	CUP[98]

Aydın (3)

Kâzım Nuri [Çoriş]	Turk	I[99]
Yunus Nadi [Abalıoğlu]	Turk	CUP[100]
Ubeydullah [Hatiboğlu]*	Turk	CUP[101]

[96] "Les Elections: Résultats à ce jour," *The Levant Herald and Eastern Express*, April 1, 1912, p.2; "Ouverture du Parlement," *The Levant Herald and Eastern Express*, April 18, 1912, p.1; Feroz Ahmad and Dankwart A. Rustow, "İkinci Meşrutiyet Döneminde Meclisler, 1908-1918," p.271; İhsan Ezherli, *Türkiye Büyük Millet Meclisi, 1920-1998, ve Osmanlı Meclis-i Mebusanı, 1877-1920*, p.214; and, Fevzi Demir, İkinci Meşrutiyet Dönemi Meclis-i Mebusan Seçimleri, 1908-1914, p.171.

[97] Lawyer ("Les députés," *The Levant Herald and Eastern Express*, November 11, 1908, p.2). "Les Elections: Résultats à ce jour," *The Levant Herald and Eastern Express*, April 1, 1912, p.2; "Ouverture du Parlement," *The Levant Herald and Eastern Express*, April 18, 1912, p.1; Feroz Ahmad and Dankwart A. Rustow, "İkinci Meşrutiyet Döneminde Meclisler, 1908-1918," p.271; İhsan Ezherli, *Türkiye Büyük Millet Meclisi, 1920-1998, ve Osmanlı Meclis-i Mebusanı, 1877-1920*, p.217; and, Fevzi Demir, İkinci Meşrutiyet Dönemi Meclis-i Mebusan Seçimleri, 1908-1914, p.170.

[98] "Les Elections: Résultats à ce jour," *The Levant Herald and Eastern Express*, April 1, 1912, p.2; "Ouverture du Parlement," *The Levant Herald and Eastern Express*, April 18, 1912, p.1; Feroz Ahmad and Dankwart A. Rustow, "İkinci Meşrutiyet Döneminde Meclisler, 1908-1918," p.271; İhsan Ezherli, *Türkiye Büyük Millet Meclisi, 1920-1998, ve Osmanlı Meclis-i Mebusanı, 1877-1920*, p.213; and, Fevzi Demir, İkinci Meşrutiyet Dönemi Meclis-i Mebusan Seçimleri, 1908-1914, p.171.

[99] "Les Elections: 141 élus," *The Levant Herald and Eastern Express*, April 16, 1912, p.2; "Ouverture du Parlement," *The Levant Herald and Eastern Express*, April 18, 1912, p.1; Feroz Ahmad and Dankwart A. Rustow, "İkinci Meşrutiyet Döneminde Meclisler, 1908-1918," p.270; İhsan Ezherli, *Türkiye Büyük Millet Meclisi, 1920-1998, ve Osmanlı Meclis-i Mebusanı, 1877-1920*, p.211; and, Fevzi Demir, İkinci Meşrutiyet Dönemi Meclis-i Mebusan Seçimleri, 1908-1914, p.170.

[100] "Les Elections: 141 élus," *The Levant Herald and Eastern Express*, April 16, 1912, p.2; "Ouverture du Parlement," *The Levant Herald and Eastern Express*, April 18, 1912, p.1; Feroz Ahmad and Dankwart A. Rustow, "İkinci Meşrutiyet Döneminde Meclisler, 1908-1918," p.270; İhsan Ezherli, *Türkiye Büyük Millet Meclisi, 1920-1998, ve Osmanlı Meclis-i Mebusanı, 1877-1920*, p.220; and, Fevzi Demir, İkinci Meşrutiyet Dönemi Meclis-i Mebusan Seçimleri, 1908-1914, p.170.

[101] "Les Elections: 141 élus," *The Levant Herald and Eastern Express*, April 16, 1912, p.2; "Ouverture du Parlement," *The Levant Herald and Eastern Express*, April 18, 1912, p.1; Feroz Ahmad and Dankwart A. Rustow, "İkinci Meşrutiyet Döneminde Meclisler, 1908-1918," p.270; İhsan Ezherli, *Türkiye Büyük Millet Meclisi, 1920-1998, ve Osmanlı Meclis-i Mebusanı, 1877-1920*, p.219; and, Fevzi Demir, İkinci Meşrutiyet Dönemi Meclis-i Mebusan Seçimleri, 1908-1914, p.170.

Denizli (2)

Fraşerli Gani Bey*	Albanian	CUP[102]
Sadık Bey	Turk	"CUP"[103]

Menteşe [Muğla] (2)

Halil [Menteşe]*	Turk	CUP[104]
Ali Haydar [Yuluğ]*	Turk	I[105]

Saruhan [Manisa] (4)

Ali Haydar Bey*	Turk	CUP[106]
Mansurizade Mehmed	Turk	I[107]

---

[102] "Les Elections: A Dénizli," *The Levant Herald and Eastern Express*, April 10, 1912, p.2; "Les Elections," *The Levant Herald and Eastern Express*, April 13, 1912, p.2; "Ouverture du Parlement," *The Levant Herald and Eastern Express*, April 18, 1912, p.1; Feroz Ahmad and Dankwart A. Rustow, "İkinci Meşrutiyet Döneminde Meclisler, 1908-1918," p.270; İhsan Ezherli, *Türkiye Büyük Millet Meclisi, 1920-1998, ve Osmanlı Meclis-i Mebusanı, 1877-1920*, p.207; and, Fevzi Demir, İkinci Meşrutiyet Dönemi Meclis-i Mebusan Seçimleri, 1908-1914, p.170.

[103] According to Ahmed Reşid [Rey], he was a Unionist sympathiser (Ahmed Reşid Rey, *Gördüklerim, Yaptıklarım, 1890-1922*, p.133). "Les Elections: A Dénizli," *The Levant Herald and Eastern Express*, April 10, 1912, p.2; "Les Elections," *The Levant Herald and Eastern Express*, April 13, 1912, p.2; "Ouverture du Parlement," *The Levant Herald and Eastern Express*, April 18, 1912, p.1; Feroz Ahmad and Dankwart A. Rustow, "İkinci Meşrutiyet Döneminde Meclisler, 1908-1918," p.270; İhsan Ezherli, *Türkiye Büyük Millet Meclisi, 1920-1998, ve Osmanlı Meclis-i Mebusanı, 1877-1920*, p.216; and, Fevzi Demir, İkinci Meşrutiyet Dönemi Meclis-i Mebusan Seçimleri, 1908-1914, p.170.

[104] "Les Elections: 38 députés élus," *The Levant Herald and Eastern Express*, April 4, 1912, p.2; "Ouverture du Parlement," *The Levant Herald and Eastern Express*, April 18, 1912, p.1; Feroz Ahmad and Dankwart A. Rustow, "İkinci Meşrutiyet Döneminde Meclisler, 1908-1918," p.270; İhsan Ezherli, *Türkiye Büyük Millet Meclisi, 1920-1998, ve Osmanlı Meclis-i Mebusanı, 1877-1920*, p.208; and, Fevzi Demir, İkinci Meşrutiyet Dönemi Meclis-i Mebusan Seçimleri, 1908-1914, p.170.

[105] Sub-Governor of Nazilli ("Les Elections: 38 députés élus," *The Levant Herald and Eastern Express*, April 4, 1912, p.2). "Ouverture du Parlement," *The Levant Herald and Eastern Express*, April 18, 1912, p.1; Feroz Ahmad and Dankwart A. Rustow, "İkinci Meşrutiyet Döneminde Meclisler, 1908-1918," p.270; İhsan Ezherli, *Türkiye Büyük Millet Meclisi, 1920-1998, ve Osmanlı Meclis-i Mebusanı, 1877-1920*, p.204; and, Fevzi Demir, İkinci Meşrutiyet Dönemi Meclis-i Mebusan Seçimleri, 1908-1914, p.170.

[106] Feroz Ahmad and Dankwart A. Rustow, "İkinci Meşrutiyet Döneminde Meclisler, 1908-1918," p.271; İhsan Ezherli, *Türkiye Büyük Millet Meclisi, 1920-1998, ve Osmanlı Meclis-i Mebusanı, 1877-1920*, p.209; and, Fevzi Demir, İkinci Meşrutiyet Dönemi Meclis-i Mebusan Seçimleri, 1908-1914, p.171.

[107] "Les Elections: 38 députés élus," *The Levant Herald and Eastern Express*, April 4, 1912, p.2; "Ouverture du Parlement," *The Levant Herald and Eastern Express*, April 18, 1912, p.1; Feroz Ahmad and Dankwart A. Rustow, "İkinci Meşrutiyet Döneminde Meclisler, 1908-1918," p.271; İhsan Ezherli, *Türkiye Büyük Millet Meclisi, 1920-1998, ve Osmanlı Meclis-i Mebusanı, 1877-1920*, p.216; and, Fevzi De-

Said Bey*

Mustafa Feyzi Efendi	Turk	CUP[108]
Hüseyin Kâzım Kadri Bey	Turk	CUP[109]
Mehmed Sabri [Toprak]	Turk	CUP[110]

* * *

KONYA (13)

Konya (5)

Mehmed Emin Efendi*	Turk	I[111]
Seyhzade Zeynelabidin Efendi*	Turk	EL[112]
Ali Kemali Efendi	Turk	I[113]

---

mir, İkinci Meşrutiyet Dönemi Meclis-i Mebusan Seçimleri, 1908-1914, p.171.

[108] President of the Court at Pera ("Les Elections: 38 députés élus," *The Levant Herald and Eastern Express*, April 4, 1912, p.2). "Ouverture du Parlement," *The Levant Herald and Eastern Express*, April 18, 1912, p.1; Feroz Ahmad and Dankwart A. Rustow, "İkinci Meşrutiyet Döneminde Meclisler, 1908-1918," p.271; İhsan Ezherli, *Türkiye Büyük Millet Meclisi, 1920-1998, ve Osmanlı Meclis-i Mebusanı, 1877-1920*, p.213; and, Fevzi Demir, İkinci Meşrutiyet Dönemi Meclis-i Mebusan Seçimleri, 1908-1914, p.171.

[109] Governor-General of Salonica ("Les Elections: 38 députés élus," *The Levant Herald and Eastern Express*, April 4, 1912, p.2). "Ouverture du Parlement," *The Levant Herald and Eastern Express*, April 18, 1912, p.1. He resigned his deputy-ship, and left for his post at Salonica ("Nouvelles du Jour," *The Levant Herald and Eastern Express*, May 10, 1912, p.2). See also, Feroz Ahmad and Dankwart A. Rustow, "İkinci Meşrutiyet Döneminde Meclisler, 1908-1918," p.271; İhsan Ezherli, *Türkiye Büyük Millet Meclisi, 1920-1998, ve Osmanlı Meclis-i Mebusanı, 1877-1920*, p.209; and, Fevzi Demir, İkinci Meşrutiyet Dönemi Meclis-i Mebusan Seçimleri, 1908-1914, p.171.

[110] Elected in place of Hüseyin Kâzım Kadri Bey? Feroz Ahmad and Dankwart A. Rustow, "İkinci Meşrutiyet Döneminde Meclisler, 1908-1918," p.271; İhsan Ezherli, *Türkiye Büyük Millet Meclisi, 1920-1998, ve Osmanlı Meclis-i Mebusanı, 1877-1920*, p.212; and, Fevzi Demir, İkinci Meşrutiyet Dönemi Meclis-i Mebusan Seçimleri, 1908-1914, p.171.

[111] Feroz Ahmad and Dankwart A. Rustow, "İkinci Meşrutiyet Döneminde Meclisler, 1908-1918," p.273; İhsan Ezherli, *Türkiye Büyük Millet Meclisi, 1920-1998, ve Osmanlı Meclis-i Mebusanı, 1877-1920*; and, Fevzi Demir, İkinci Meşrutiyet Dönemi Meclis-i Mebusan Seçimleri, 1908-1914, p.174.

[112] Feroz Ahmad and Dankwart A. Rustow, "İkinci Meşrutiyet Döneminde Meclisler, 1908-1918," p.273; İhsan Ezherli, *Türkiye Büyük Millet Meclisi, 1920-1998, ve Osmanlı Meclis-i Mebusanı, 1877-1920*, p.220; and, Fevzi Demir, İkinci Meşrutiyet Dönemi Meclis-i Mebusan Seçimleri, 1908-1914, p.174.

[113] Feroz Ahmad and Dankwart A. Rustow, "İkinci Meşrutiyet Döneminde Meclisler, 1908-1918," p.273; İhsan Ezherli, *Türkiye Büyük Millet Meclisi, 1920-1998, ve Osmanlı Meclis-i Mebusanı, 1877-1920*, p.205; and, Fevzi Demir, İkinci Meşrutiyet Dönemi Meclis-i Mebusan Seçimleri, 1908-1914, p.174.

Mehmed Rıza Bey   Turk   I[114]
Ömer Vehbi [Büyükyalvaç]   Turk   I[115]

Burdur (1)

Ali Galib Bey   Turk   I[116]

[Hamid-i Abad] Isparta (2)

Burhanzade Hacı Eşref   Turk   I[117]
  Efendi*
Ağlarcazade Mustafa Hakkı   Turk   CUP[118]
  Bey

Niğde (3)

Ürgüplü Mustafa Hayri Bey*   Turk   CUP[119]
Muhiddin Bey*   Turk   CUP[120]

---

[114] Feroz Ahmad and Dankwart A. Rustow, "İkinci Meşrutiyet Döneminde Meclisler, 1908-1918," p.273; İhsan Ezherli, *Türkiye Büyük Millet Meclisi, 1920-1998, ve Osmanlı Meclis-i Mebusanı, 1877-1920*, p.212; and, Fevzi Demir, İkinci Meşrutiyet Dönemi Meclis-i Mebusan Seçimleri, 1908-1914, p.174.

[115] Feroz Ahmad and Dankwart A. Rustow, "İkinci Meşrutiyet Döneminde Meclisler, 1908-1918," p.273; İhsan Ezherli, *Türkiye Büyük Millet Meclisi, 1920-1998, ve Osmanlı Meclis-i Mebusanı, 1877-1920*, p.215; and, Fevzi Demir, İkinci Meşrutiyet Dönemi Meclis-i Mebusan Seçimleri, 1908-1914, p.174.

[116] Feroz Ahmad and Dankwart A. Rustow, "İkinci Meşrutiyet Döneminde Meclisler, 1908-1918," p.272; İhsan Ezherli, *Türkiye Büyük Millet Meclisi, 1920-1998, ve Osmanlı Meclis-i Mebusanı, 1877-1920*, p.204; and, Fevzi Demir, İkinci Meşrutiyet Dönemi Meclis-i Mebusan Seçimleri, 1908-1914, p.173.

[117] "Ouverture du Parlement," *The Levant Herald and Eastern Express*, April 18, 1912, p.1; Feroz Ahmad and Dankwart A. Rustow, "İkinci Meşrutiyet Döneminde Meclisler, 1908-1918," p.272; İhsan Ezherli, *Türkiye Büyük Millet Meclisi, 1920-1998, ve Osmanlı Meclis-i Mebusanı, 1877-1920*, p.207; and, Fevzi Demir, İkinci Meşrutiyet Dönemi Meclis-i Mebusan Seçimleri, 1908-1914, p.172.

[118] "Ouverture du Parlement," *The Levant Herald and Eastern Express*, April 18, 1912, p.1; Feroz Ahmad and Dankwart A. Rustow, "İkinci Meşrutiyet Döneminde Meclisler, 1908-1918," p.272; İhsan Ezherli, *Türkiye Büyük Millet Meclisi, 1920-1998, ve Osmanlı Meclis-i Mebusanı, 1877-1920*, p.213; and, Fevzi Demir, İkinci Meşrutiyet Dönemi Meclis-i Mebusan Seçimleri, 1908-1914, p.172.

[119] Lawyer (Feroz Ahmad and Dankwart A. Rustow, "İkinci Meşrutiyet Döneminde Meclisler, 1908-1918," p.274). "Les Elections: Pas un député d'opposition!" *The Levant Herald and Eastern Express*, April 9, 1912, p.2; "Ouverture du Parlement," *The Levant Herald and Eastern Express*, April 18, 1912, p.1; İhsan Ezherli, *Türkiye Büyük Millet Meclisi, 1920-1998, ve Osmanlı Meclis-i Mebusanı, 1877-1920*, p.209; and, Fevzi Demir, İkinci Meşrutiyet Dönemi Meclis-i Mebusan Seçimleri, 1908-1914, p.175.

[120] "Les Elections: Pas un député d'opposition!" *The Levant Herald and Eastern Express*, April 9, 1912, p.2; "Ouverture du Parlement," *The Levant Herald and Eastern Express*, April 18, 1912, p.1; Feroz Ahmad and Dankwart A. Rustow, "İkinci

Ananias Efendi   Greek   I[121]

Teke [Antalya] (2)

İdris Bey   Turk   I[122]
Münir Bey   Turk   I[123]

* * *

ANKARA (12)

Ankara (4)

Halil Halid Bey   Turk   CUP[124]
Hacı Mustafa [Beyman]*   Turk   CUP[125]

Meşrutiyet Döneminde Meclisler, 1908-1918," p.274; İhsan Ezherli, *Türkiye Büyük Millet Meclisi, 1920-1998, ve Osmanlı Meclis-i Mebusanı, 1877-1920*, p.213; and, Fevzi Demir, İkinci Meşrutiyet Dönemi Meclis-i Mebusan Seçimleri, 1908-1914, p.175.

[121] "Les Elections: Pas un député d'opposition!" *The Levant Herald and Eastern Express*, April 9, 1912, p.2; "Ouverture du Parlement," *The Levant Herald and Eastern Express*, April 18, 1912, p.1; Feroz Ahmad and Dankwart A. Rustow, "İkinci Meşrutiyet Döneminde Meclisler, 1908-1918," p.274; İhsan Ezherli, *Türkiye Büyük Millet Meclisi, 1920-1998, ve Osmanlı Meclis-i Mebusanı, 1877-1920*, p.205; and, Fevzi Demir, İkinci Meşrutiyet Dönemi Meclis-i Mebusan Seçimleri, 1908-1914, p.175.

[122] "Ouverture du Parlement," *The Levant Herald and Eastern Express*, April 18, 1912, p.1; Feroz Ahmad and Dankwart A. Rustow, "İkinci Meşrutiyet Döneminde Meclisler, 1908-1918," p.272; İhsan Ezherli, *Türkiye Büyük Millet Meclisi, 1920-1998, ve Osmanlı Meclis-i Mebusanı, 1877-1920*, p.210; and, Fevzi Demir, İkinci Meşrutiyet Dönemi Meclis-i Mebusan Seçimleri, 1908-1914, p.173.

[123] "Ouverture du Parlement," *The Levant Herald and Eastern Express*, April 18, 1912, p.1; Feroz Ahmad and Dankwart A. Rustow, "İkinci Meşrutiyet Döneminde Meclisler, 1908-1918," p.272; İhsan Ezherli, *Türkiye Büyük Millet Meclisi, 1920-1998, ve Osmanlı Meclis-i Mebusanı, 1877-1920*, p.214; and, Fevzi Demir, İkinci Meşrutiyet Dönemi Meclis-i Mebusan Seçimleri, 1908-1914, p.173.

[124] "Les Elections: Derniers élus," *The Levant Herald and Eastern Express*, April 15, 1912, p.2; "Ouverture du Parlement," *The Levant Herald and Eastern Express*, April 18, 1912, p.1; Feroz Ahmad and Dankwart A. Rustow, "İkinci Meşrutiyet Döneminde Meclisler, 1908-1918," p.273; İhsan Ezherli, *Türkiye Büyük Millet Meclisi, 1920-1998, ve Osmanlı Meclis-i Mebusanı, 1877-1920*, p.208; and, Fevzi Demir, İkinci Meşrutiyet Dönemi Meclis-i Mebusan Seçimleri, 1908-1914, p.174.

[125] "Les Elections: Derniers élus," *The Levant Herald and Eastern Express*, April 15, 1912, p.2; "Ouverture du Parlement," *The Levant Herald and Eastern Express*, April 18, 1912, p.1; Feroz Ahmad and Dankwart A. Rustow, "İkinci Meşrutiyet Döneminde Meclisler, 1908-1918," p.273; İhsan Ezherli, *Türkiye Büyük Millet Meclisi, 1920-1998, ve Osmanlı Meclis-i Mebusanı, 1877-1920*, p.213; and, Fevzi Demir, İkinci Meşrutiyet Dönemi Meclis-i Mebusan Seçimleri, 1908-1914, p.174.

Nusret Sadullah [Ayaşlıoğlu]   Turk   CUP[126]
Mehmed Talât [Sönmez]*   Turk   CUP[127]

Çorum (2)

Ali Mehmed Münir [Çağıl]*   Turk   CUP[128]
Ali Osman Bey*   Turk   CUP[129]

Kayseri (2)

Ali Galib Bey   Turk   EL[130]
Ahmed Rıfat [Çalık'a]   Turk   I[131]

---

[126] "Les Elections: Derniers élus," *The Levant Herald and Eastern Express*, April 15, 1912, p.2; "Ouverture du Parlement," *The Levant Herald and Eastern Express*, April 18, 1912, p.1; Feroz Ahmad and Dankwart A. Rustow, "İkinci Meşrutiyet Döneminde Meclisler, 1908-1918," p.273; İhsan Ezherli, *Türkiye Büyük Millet Meclisi, 1920-1998, ve Osmanlı Meclis-i Mebusanı, 1877-1920*, p.214; and, Fevzi Demir, İkinci Meşrutiyet Dönemi Meclis-i Mebusan Seçimleri, 1908-1914, p.174

[127] "Les Elections: Derniers élus," *The Levant Herald and Eastern Express*, April 15, 1912, p.2; "Ouverture du Parlement," *The Levant Herald and Eastern Express*, April 18, 1912, p.1; Feroz Ahmad and Dankwart A. Rustow, "İkinci Meşrutiyet Döneminde Meclisler, 1908-1918," p.273; İhsan Ezherli, *Türkiye Büyük Millet Meclisi, 1920-1998, ve Osmanlı Meclis-i Mebusanı, 1877-1920*, p.219; and, Fevzi Demir, İkinci Meşrutiyet Dönemi Meclis-i Mebusan Seçimleri, 1908-1914, p.174.

[128] "Les Elections: Derniers élus," *The Levant Herald and Eastern Express*, April 15, 1912, p.2; "Ouverture du Parlement," *The Levant Herald and Eastern Express*, April 18, 1912, p.1; Feroz Ahmad and Dankwart A. Rustow, "İkinci Meşrutiyet Döneminde Meclisler, 1908-1918," p.274; İhsan Ezherli, *Türkiye Büyük Millet Meclisi, 1920-1998, ve Osmanlı Meclis-i Mebusanı, 1877-1920*, p.212; and, Fevzi Demir, İkinci Meşrutiyet Dönemi Meclis-i Mebusan Seçimleri, 1908-1914, p.175.

[129] "Les Elections: Derniers élus," *The Levant Herald and Eastern Express*, April 15, 1912, p.2; "Ouverture du Parlement," *The Levant Herald and Eastern Express*, April 18, 1912, p.1; Feroz Ahmad and Dankwart A. Rustow, "İkinci Meşrutiyet Döneminde Meclisler, 1908-1918," p.274; İhsan Ezherli, *Türkiye Büyük Millet Meclisi, 1920-1998, ve Osmanlı Meclis-i Mebusanı, 1877-1920*, p.205; and, Fevzi Demir, İkinci Meşrutiyet Dönemi Meclis-i Mebusan Seçimleri, 1908-1914, p.175.

[130] Major. Elected with 79 votes ("Les Elections: Derniers élus," *The Levant Herald and Eastern Express*, April 15, 1912, p.2). "Ouverture du Parlement," *The Levant Herald and Eastern Express*, April 18, 1912, p.1; Feroz Ahmad and Dankwart A. Rustow, "İkinci Meşrutiyet Döneminde Meclisler, 1908-1918," p.274; İhsan Ezherli, *Türkiye Büyük Millet Meclisi, 1920-1998, ve Osmanlı Meclis-i Mebusanı, 1877-1920*, p.204; and, Fevzi Demir, İkinci Meşrutiyet Dönemi Meclis-i Mebusan Seçimleri, 1908-1914, p.175.

[131] Elected with 50 votes ("Les Elections: Derniers élus," *The Levant Herald and Eastern Express*, April 15, 1912, p.2). "Ouverture du Parlement," *The Levant Herald and Eastern Express*, April 18, 1912, p.1. The invalidation of his deputyship came up for discussion in the Chamber of Deputies on May 13, 1912 ("Le Parlement," *The Levant Herald and Eastern Express*, May 14, 1912, p.2). Feroz Ahmad and Dankwart A. Rustow, "İkinci Meşrutiyet Döneminde Meclisler, 1908-1918," p.274; İhsan Ezherli, *Türkiye Büyük Millet Meclisi, 1920-1998, ve Osmanlı Meclis-i Mebusanı, 1877-1920*, p.204; and, Fevzi Demir, İkinci Meşrutiyet Dönemi Meclis-i Mebusan Seçimleri, 1908-1914, p.175.

Kırşehir (2)

Benliağazade Ali Rıza Bey*	Turk	I[132]
Mahmud Mahir Efendi*	Turk	I[133]

Yozgat (2)

Ahmed Münir Bey	Turk	CUP[134]
Kınacızade Şakir Bey	Turk	CUP[135]

* * *

KASTAMONU (12)

Kastamonu (4)

Hacı Ahmed Mahir Efendi*	Turk	CUP[136]
Necmeddin [Kocataş]*	Turk	CUP[137]

---

[132] "Les Elections: 141 élus," *The Levant Herald and Eastern Express*, April 16, 1912, p.2; "Ouverture du Parlement," *The Levant Herald and Eastern Express*, April 18, 1912, p.1; Feroz Ahmad and Dankwart A. Rustow, "İkinci Meşrutiyet Döneminde Meclisler, 1908-1918," p.274; İhsan Ezherli, *Türkiye Büyük Millet Meclisi, 1920-1998, ve Osmanlı Meclis-i Mebusanı, 1877-1920*, p.205; and, Fevzi Demir, İkinci Meşrutiyet Dönemi Meclis-i Mebusan Seçimleri, 1908-1914, p.175.

[133] Lawyer at İstanbul ("Les députés," *The Levant Herald and Eastern Express*, November 11, 1908, p.2). "Les Elections: 141 élus," *The Levant Herald and Eastern Express*, April 16, 1912, p.2; "Ouverture du Parlement," *The Levant Herald and Eastern Express*, April 18, 1912, p.1; Feroz Ahmad and Dankwart A. Rustow, "İkinci Meşrutiyet Döneminde Meclisler, 1908-1918," p.274; İhsan Ezherli, *Türkiye Büyük Millet Meclisi, 1920-1998, ve Osmanlı Meclis-i Mebusanı, 1877-1920*, p.211; and, Fevzi Demir, İkinci Meşrutiyet Dönemi Meclis-i Mebusan Seçimleri, 1908-1914, p.175.

[134] Feroz Ahmad and Dankwart A. Rustow, "İkinci Meşrutiyet Döneminde Meclisler, 1908-1918," p.274; İhsan Ezherli, *Türkiye Büyük Millet Meclisi, 1920-1998, ve Osmanlı Meclis-i Mebusanı, 1877-1920*, p.214; and, Fevzi Demir, İkinci Meşrutiyet Dönemi Meclis-i Mebusan Seçimleri, 1908-1914, p.175.

[135] "Nouvelles du Jour," *The Levant Herald and Eastern Express*, May 14, 1912, p.2; Feroz Ahmad and Dankwart A. Rustow, "İkinci Meşrutiyet Döneminde Meclisler, 1908-1918," p.274; İhsan Ezherli, *Türkiye Büyük Millet Meclisi, 1920-1998, ve Osmanlı Meclis-i Mebusanı, 1877-1920*, p.218; and, Fevzi Demir, İkinci Meşrutiyet Dönemi Meclis-i Mebusan Seçimleri, 1908-1914, p.175.

[136] Lawyer (Feroz Ahmad and Dankwart A. Rustow, "İkinci Meşrutiyet Döneminde Meclisler, 1908-1918," p.272). "Les Elections," *The Levant Herald and Eastern Express*, April 13, 1912, p.2; "Ouverture du Parlement," *The Levant Herald and Eastern Express*, April 18, 1912, p.1; İhsan Ezherli, *Türkiye Büyük Millet Meclisi, 1920-1998, ve Osmanlı Meclis-i Mebusanı, 1877-1920*, p.204; and, Fevzi Demir, İkinci Meşrutiyet Dönemi Meclis-i Mebusan Seçimleri, 1908-1914, p.173.

[137] Lawyer (Feroz Ahmad and Dankwart A. Rustow, "İkinci Meşrutiyet Döne-

İsmail Mahir Efendi	Turk	CUP[138]
Hüsnü Bey	Turk	I[139]

Bolu (4)

Mehmed Habib Bey*	Turk	EL[140]
Rıfat Kâmil [Madenci]	Turk	CUP[141]
Taşhancızade Mustafa Zeki Efendi*	Turk	I[142]
Yusuf Ziya [Özenci]	Turk	CUP[143]

---

minde Meclisler, 1908-1918," p.272). "Les Elections," *The Levant Herald and Eastern Express*, April 13, 1912, p.2; "Ouverture du Parlement," *The Levant Herald and Eastern Express*, April 18, 1912, p.1; İhsan Ezherli, *Türkiye Büyük Millet Meclisi, 1920-1998, ve Osmanlı Meclis-i Mebusanı, 1877-1920*, p.214; and, Fevzi Demir, İkinci Meşrutiyet Dönemi Meclis-i Mebusan Seçimleri, 1908-1914, p.173.

[138] "Les Elections," *The Levant Herald and Eastern Express*, April 13, 1912, p.2; "Ouverture du Parlement," *The Levant Herald and Eastern Express*, April 18, 1912, p.1; Feroz Ahmad and Dankwart A. Rustow, "İkinci Meşrutiyet Döneminde Meclisler, 1908-1918," p.272; İhsan Ezherli, *Türkiye Büyük Millet Meclisi, 1920-1998, ve Osmanlı Meclis-i Mebusanı, 1877-1920*, p.210; and, Fevzi Demir, İkinci Meşrutiyet Dönemi Meclis-i Mebusan Seçimleri, 1908-1914, p.173.

[139] "Les Elections," *The Levant Herald and Eastern Express*, April 13, 1912, p.2; "Ouverture du Parlement," *The Levant Herald and Eastern Express*, April 18, 1912, p.1; Feroz Ahmad and Dankwart A. Rustow, "İkinci Meşrutiyet Döneminde Meclisler, 1908-1918," p.272; İhsan Ezherli, *Türkiye Büyük Millet Meclisi, 1920-1998, ve Osmanlı Meclis-i Mebusanı, 1877-1920*, p.209; and, Fevzi Demir, İkinci Meşrutiyet Dönemi Meclis-i Mebusan Seçimleri, 1908-1914, p.173.

[140] Major. "Les Elections: A Bolou," *The Levant Herald and Eastern Express*, April 15, 1912, p.2; Feroz Ahmad and Dankwart A. Rustow, "İkinci Meşrutiyet Döneminde Meclisler, 1908-1918," p.272; İhsan Ezherli, *Türkiye Büyük Millet Meclisi, 1920-1998, ve Osmanlı Meclis-i Mebusanı, 1877-1920*, p.207; and, Fevzi Demir, İkinci Meşrutiyet Dönemi Meclis-i Mebusan Seçimleri, 1908-1914, p.173.

[141] "Les Elections: A Bolou," *The Levant Herald and Eastern Express*, April 15, 1912, p.2; Feroz Ahmad and Dankwart A. Rustow, "İkinci Meşrutiyet Döneminde Meclisler, 1908-1918," p.272; İhsan Ezherli, *Türkiye Büyük Millet Meclisi, 1920-1998, ve Osmanlı Meclis-i Mebusanı, 1877-1920*, p.216; and, Fevzi Demir, İkinci Meşrutiyet Dönemi Meclis-i Mebusan Seçimleri, 1908-1914, p.173.

[142] Feroz Ahmad and Dankwart A. Rustow, "İkinci Meşrutiyet Döneminde Meclisler, 1908-1918," p.272; İhsan Ezherli, *Türkiye Büyük Millet Meclisi, 1920-1998, ve Osmanlı Meclis-i Mebusanı, 1877-1920*, p.214; and, Fevzi Demir, İkinci Meşrutiyet Dönemi Meclis-i Mebusan Seçimleri, 1908-1914, p.173.

[143] "Les Elections: A Bolou," *The Levant Herald and Eastern Express*, April 15, 1912, p.2; Feroz Ahmad and Dankwart A. Rustow, "İkinci Meşrutiyet Döneminde Meclisler, 1908-1918," p.272; İhsan Ezherli, *Türkiye Büyük Millet Meclisi, 1920-1998, ve Osmanlı Meclis-i Mebusanı, 1877-1920*, p.220; and, Fevzi Demir, İkinci Meşrutiyet Dönemi Meclis-i Mebusan Seçimleri, 1908-1914, p.173.

Kengiri [Çankırı] (2)

| Hacı Mehmed Tevfik [Durlanık]* | Turk | I[144] |
| Hazırlıklızade Mehmed Sabri Efendi | Turk | CUP[145] |

Sinob (2)

| Hasan Fehmi [Tümerkan]* | Turk | CUP[146] |
| İsmail Hakkı Bey | Turk | CUP[147] |

* * *

TRABZON (15)

Trabzon (7)

| Eyübzade İzzet Bey* | Turk | I[148] |

---

[144] Ulema. "Les Elections: A Tchangiri," *The Levant Herald and Eastern Express*, April 11, 1912, p.2; "Les Elections," *The Levant Herald and Eastern Express*, April 13, 1912, p.2; "Ouverture du Parlement," *The Levant Herald and Eastern Express*, April 18, 1912, p.1; Feroz Ahmad and Dankwart A. Rustow, "İkinci Meşrutiyet Döneminde Meclisler, 1908-1918," p.273; İhsan Ezherli, *Türkiye Büyük Millet Meclisi, 1920-1998, ve Osmanlı Meclis-i Mebusanı, 1877-1920*, p.219; and, Fevzi Demir, İkinci Meşrutiyet Dönemi Meclis-i Mebusan Seçimleri, 1908-1914, p.174.

[145] "Les Elections: A Tchangiri," *The Levant Herald and Eastern Express*, April 11, 1912, p.2; "Les Elections," *The Levant Herald and Eastern Express*, April 13, 1912, p.2; "Ouverture du Parlement," *The Levant Herald and Eastern Express*, April 18, 1912, p.1; Feroz Ahmad and Dankwart A. Rustow, "İkinci Meşrutiyet Döneminde Meclisler, 1908-1918," p.273; İhsan Ezherli, *Türkiye Büyük Millet Meclisi, 1920-1998, ve Osmanlı Meclis-i Mebusanı, 1877-1920*, p.212; and, Fevzi Demir, İkinci Meşrutiyet Dönemi Meclis-i Mebusan Seçimleri, 1908-1914, p.174.

[146] "Les Elections: Résultats à ce jour," *The Levant Herald and Eastern Express*, April 1, 1912, p.2; "Ouverture du Parlement," *The Levant Herald and Eastern Express*, April 18, 1912, p.1; Feroz Ahmad and Dankwart A. Rustow, "İkinci Meşrutiyet Döneminde Meclisler, 1908-1918," p.274; İhsan Ezherli, *Türkiye Büyük Millet Meclisi, 1920-1998, ve Osmanlı Meclis-i Mebusanı, 1877-1920*, p.209; and, Fevzi Demir, İkinci Meşrutiyet Dönemi Meclis-i Mebusan Seçimleri, 1908-1914, p.175.

[147] He replaced Rıza Nur ("Les Elections: Résultats à ce jour," *The Levant Herald and Eastern Express*, April 1, 1912, p.2). "Ouverture du Parlement," *The Levant Herald and Eastern Express*, April 18, 1912, p.1; Feroz Ahmad and Dankwart A. Rustow, "İkinci Meşrutiyet Döneminde Meclisler, 1908-1918," p.274; İhsan Ezherli, *Türkiye Büyük Millet Meclisi, 1920-1998, ve Osmanlı Meclis-i Mebusanı, 1877-1920*, p.210; and, Fevzi Demir, İkinci Meşrutiyet Dönemi Meclis-i Mebusan Seçimleri, 1908-1914, p.175.

[148] Lawyer (Feroz Ahmad and Dankwart A. Rustow, "İkinci Meşrutiyet Döneminde Meclisler, 1908-1918," p.277). "Les Elections: A Trébizonde [April 11],"

Matheos Cofidis*	Greek	I[149]
Nemlizade Ali Osman [Güley]	Turk	CUP[150]
Nemlizade Hacı Osman Bey*	Turk	I[151]
Hafız Mehmed [Engin]	Turk	CUP[152]
Falcızade Mahmud Memduh Efendi	Turk	I[153]
Servet Bey	Turk	CUP[154]

The Levant Herald and Eastern Express, April 13, 1912, p.2; "Les Elections: A Trébizonde," *The Levant Herald and Eastern Express*, April 24, 1912, p.2; İhsan Ezherli, *Türkiye Büyük Millet Meclisi, 1920-1998, ve Osmanlı Meclis-i Mebusanı, 1877-1920*, p.210; and, Fevzi Demir, İkinci Meşrutiyet Dönemi Meclis-i Mebusan Seçimleri, 1908-1914, p.179.

[149] "Les Elections: A Trébizonde [April 11]," *The Levant Herald and Eastern Express*, April 13, 1912, p.2; "Les Elections: A Trébizonde," *The Levant Herald and Eastern Express*, April 24, 1912, p.2; Feroz Ahmad and Dankwart A. Rustow, "İkinci Meşrutiyet Döneminde Meclisler, 1908-1918," p.277; İhsan Ezherli, *Türkiye Büyük Millet Meclisi, 1920-1998, ve Osmanlı Meclis-i Mebusanı, 1877-1920*, p.211; and, Fevzi Demir, İkinci Meşrutiyet Dönemi Meclis-i Mebusan Seçimleri, 1908-1914, p.179.

[150] He was Sub-Governor of Dibër ("Les Elections: A Trébizonde [April 11]," *The Levant Herald and Eastern Express*, April 13, 1912, p.2). "Les Elections: A Trébizonde," *The Levant Herald and Eastern Express*, April 24, 1912, p.2. See also, Ali Çankaya, *Yeni Mülkiye Tarihi ve Mülkiyeliler*, 3, p.591; Feroz Ahmad and Dankwart A. Rustow, "İkinci Meşrutiyet Döneminde Meclisler, 1908-1918," p.277; İhsan Ezherli, *Türkiye Büyük Millet Meclisi, 1920-1998, ve Osmanlı Meclis-i Mebusanı, 1877-1920*, p.205; and, Fevzi Demir, İkinci Meşrutiyet Dönemi Meclis-i Mebusan Seçimleri, 1908-1914, p.179.

[151] "Les Elections: A Trébizonde [April 11]," *The Levant Herald and Eastern Express*, April 13, 1912, p.2; "Les Elections: A Trébizonde," *The Levant Herald and Eastern Express*, April 24, 1912, p.2; Feroz Ahmad and Dankwart A. Rustow, "İkinci Meşrutiyet Döneminde Meclisler, 1908-1918," p.277; İhsan Ezherli, *Türkiye Büyük Millet Meclisi, 1920-1998, ve Osmanlı Meclis-i Mebusanı, 1877-1920*, p.214; and, Fevzi Demir, İkinci Meşrutiyet Dönemi Meclis-i Mebusan Seçimleri, 1908-1914, p.179.

[152] President of the Penal Court at Samsun ("Les Elections: A Trébizonde [April 11]," *The Levant Herald and Eastern Express*, April 13, 1912, p.2). Feroz Ahmad and Dankwart A. Rustow, "İkinci Meşrutiyet Döneminde Meclisler, 1908-1918," p.277; İhsan Ezherli, *Türkiye Büyük Millet Meclisi, 1920-1998, ve Osmanlı Meclis-i Mebusanı, 1877-1920*, p.208; and, Fevzi Demir, İkinci Meşrutiyet Dönemi Meclis-i Mebusan Seçimleri, 1908-1914, p.179.

[153] "Les Elections: A Trébizonde [April 11]," *The Levant Herald and Eastern Express*, April 13, 1912, p.2; "Les Elections: A Trébizonde," *The Levant Herald and Eastern Express*, April 24, 1912, p.2; Feroz Ahmad and Dankwart A. Rustow, "İkinci Meşrutiyet Döneminde Meclisler, 1908-1918," p.277; İhsan Ezherli, *Türkiye Büyük Millet Meclisi, 1920-1998, ve Osmanlı Meclis-i Mebusanı, 1877-1920*, p.211; and, Fevzi Demir, İkinci Meşrutiyet Dönemi Meclis-i Mebusan Seçimleri, 1908-1914, p.179.

[154] Inspector of public instruction ("Les Elections: A Trébizonde [April 11]," *The Levant Herald and Eastern Express*, April 13, 1912, p.2). Feroz Ahmad and Dankwart A. Rustow, "İkinci Meşrutiyet Döneminde Meclisler, 1908-1918," p.277; İhsan Ezherli, *Türkiye Büyük Millet Meclisi, 1920-1998, ve Osmanlı Meclis-i Mebusanı, 1877-1920*, p.217; and, Fevzi Demir, İkinci Meşrutiyet Dönemi Meclis-i Mebusan Seçimleri, 1908-1914, p.179.

Canik [Samsun] (4)

Süleyman Necmi [Selmen]*	Turk	CUP[155]
Hoca Ahmed Hamdi Efendi*	Turk	I[156]
Ahmed Hakkı Bey	Turk	I[157]
Aynizade Talât Avni Bey	Turk	CUP[158]

Gümüşhane (2)

Mısırlızade Hayri Bey*	Turk	I[159]
Hasan Fehmi [Ataç]	Turk	CUP[160]

---

[155] Son of a Bafra landowner, and a graduate of Mekteb-i Mülkiye, Class of 1893 (Ali Çankaya, *Yeni Mülkiye Tarihi ve Mülkiyeliler, 3*, pp.532-533). "Les Elections: Au Djanik," *The Levant Herald and Eastern Express*, April 13, 1912, p.2; "Les Elections: 141 élus," *The Levant Herald and Eastern Express*, April 16, 1912, p.2; "Ouverture du Parlement," *The Levant Herald and Eastern Express*, April 18, 1912, p.1; Feroz Ahmad and Dankwart A. Rustow, "İkinci Meşrutiyet Döneminde Meclisler, 1908-1918," p.274; İhsan Ezherli, *Türkiye Büyük Millet Meclisi, 1920-1998, ve Osmanlı Meclis-i Mebusanı*, p.218; and, Fevzi Demir, İkinci Meşrutiyet Dönemi Meclis-i Mebusan Seçimleri, 1908-1914, p.175.

[156] Ulema ("Lettre de Samsoun" [November 27], *The Levant Herald and Eastern Express*, December 8, 1908, p.3). "Les Elections: Au Djanik," *The Levant Herald and Eastern Express*, April 13, 1912, p.2; "Les Elections: 141 élus," *The Levant Herald and Eastern Express*, April 16, 1912, p.2; "Ouverture du Parlement," *The Levant Herald and Eastern Express*, April 18, 1912, p.1; Feroz Ahmad and Dankwart A. Rustow, "İkinci Meşrutiyet Döneminde Meclisler, 1908-1918," p.274; İhsan Ezherli, *Türkiye Büyük Millet Meclisi, 1920-1998, ve Osmanlı Meclis-i Mebusanı, 1877-1920*, p.204; and, Fevzi Demir, İkinci Meşrutiyet Dönemi Meclis-i Mebusan Seçimleri, 1908-1914, p.175.

[157] "Les Elections: Au Djanik," *The Levant Herald and Eastern Express*, April 13, 1912, p.2; "Les Elections: 141 élus," *The Levant Herald and Eastern Express*, April 16, 1912, p.2; "Ouverture du Parlement," *The Levant Herald and Eastern Express*, April 18, 1912, p.1; Feroz Ahmad and Dankwart A. Rustow, "İkinci Meşrutiyet Döneminde Meclisler, 1908-1918," p.274; İhsan Ezherli, *Türkiye Büyük Millet Meclisi, 1920-1998, ve Osmanlı Meclis-i Mebusanı, 1877-1920*, p.204; and, Fevzi Demir, İkinci Meşrutiyet Dönemi Meclis-i Mebusan Seçimleri, 1908-1914, p.175.

[158] "Les Elections: Au Djanik," *The Levant Herald and Eastern Express*, April 13, 1912, p.2; "Les Elections: 141 élus," *The Levant Herald and Eastern Express*, April 16, 1912, p.2; "Ouverture du Parlement," *The Levant Herald and Eastern Express*, April 18, 1912, p.1; Feroz Ahmad and Dankwart A. Rustow, "İkinci Meşrutiyet Döneminde Meclisler, 1908-1918," p.275; İhsan Ezherli, *Türkiye Büyük Millet Meclisi, 1920-1998, ve Osmanlı Meclis-i Mebusanı, 1877-1920*, p.219; and, Fevzi Demir, İkinci Meşrutiyet Dönemi Meclis-i Mebusan Seçimleri, 1908-1914, p.175.

[159] "Les Elections," *The Levant Herald and Eastern Express*, April 15, 1912, p.2; "Ouverture du Parlement," *The Levant Herald and Eastern Express*, April 18, 1912, p.1; Feroz Ahmad and Dankwart A. Rustow, "İkinci Meşrutiyet Döneminde Meclisler, 1908-1918," p.277; İhsan Ezherli, *Türkiye Büyük Millet Meclisi, 1920-1998, ve Osmanlı Meclis-i Mebusanı, 1877-1920*, p.209; and, Fevzi Demir, İkinci Meşrutiyet Dönemi Meclis-i Mebusan Seçimleri, 1908-1914, p.178.

[160] "Les Elections," *The Levant Herald and Eastern Express*, April 15, 1912, p.2); "Ouverture du Parlement," *The Levant Herald and Eastern Express*, April 18, 1912, p.1; Feroz Ahmad and Dankwart A. Rustow, "İkinci Meşrutiyet Döneminde Meclisler, 1908-1918," p.277; İhsan Ezherli, *Türkiye Büyük Millet Meclisi, 1920-1998, ve Osmanlı Meclis-i Mebusanı, 1877-1920*, p.208; and, Fevzi Demir, İkinci

Lazistan [Rize] (2)

Çürüksulu Ahmed Bey [Pasha]*	Turk	CUP[161]
Ziya Molla Bey	Turk	CUP[162]

* * *

SİVAS (13)

Sivas (5)

Emin Edib Bey	Turk	I[163]
Şemseddinzade Mustafa Ziya Bey*	Turk	I[164]
Hüsnü Bey*	Turk	I[165]

Meşrutiyet Dönemi Meclis-i Mebusan Seçimleri, 1908-1914, p.178.

[161] "Les Elections: A Trébizonde," *The Levant Herald and Eastern Express*, April 11, 1912, p.2; "Les Elections: 141 élus," *The Levant Herald and Eastern Express*, April 16, 1912, p.2; "Ouverture du Parlement," *The Levant Herald and Eastern Express*, April 18, 1912, p.1; Feroz Ahmad and Dankwart A. Rustow, "İkinci Meşrutiyet Döneminde Meclisler, 1908-1918," p.278; İhsan Ezherli, *Türkiye Büyük Millet Meclisi, 1920-1998, ve Osmanlı Meclis-i Mebusanı, 1877-1920*, p.204; and, Fevzi Demir, İkinci Meşrutiyet Dönemi Meclis-i Mebusan Seçimleri, 1908-1914, p.179.

[162] "Les Elections: A Trébizonde," *The Levant Herald and Eastern Express*, April 11, 1912, p.2; "Les Elections: 141 élus," *The Levant Herald and Eastern Express*, April 16, 1912, p.2; "Ouverture du Parlement," *The Levant Herald and Eastern Express*, April 18, 1912, p.1; Feroz Ahmad and Dankwart A. Rustow, "İkinci Meşrutiyet Döneminde Meclisler, 1908-1918," p.278; İhsan Ezherli, *Türkiye Büyük Millet Meclisi, 1920-1998, ve Osmanlı Meclis-i Mebusanı, 1877-1920*, p.220; and, Fevzi Demir, İkinci Meşrutiyet Dönemi Meclis-i Mebusan Seçimleri, 1908-1914, p.179.

[163] Feroz Ahmad and Dankwart A. Rustow, "İkinci Meşrutiyet Döneminde Meclisler, 1908-1918," p.275; İhsan Ezherli, *Türkiye Büyük Millet Meclisi, 1920-1998, ve Osmanlı Meclis-i Mebusanı, 1877-1920*, p.206; and, Fevzi Demir, İkinci Meşrutiyet Dönemi Meclis-i Mebusan Seçimleri, 1908-1914, p.176.

[164] "Les Elections: A Sivas," *The Levant Herald and Eastern Express*, April 11, 1912, p.2; "Les Elections," *The Levant Herald and Eastern Express*, April 13, 1912, p.2; "Ouverture du Parlement," *The Levant Herald and Eastern Express*, April 18, 1912, p.1; Feroz Ahmad and Dankwart A. Rustow, "İkinci Meşrutiyet Döneminde Meclisler, 1908-1918," p.275; İhsan Ezherli, *Türkiye Büyük Millet Meclisi, 1920-1998, ve Osmanlı Meclis-i Mebusanı, 1877-1920*, p.214; and, Fevzi Demir, İkinci Meşrutiyet Dönemi Meclis-i Mebusan Seçimleri, 1908-1914, p.176.

[165] Medical doctor (Feroz Ahmad and Dankwart A. Rustow, "İkinci Meşrutiyet Döneminde Meclisler, 1908-1918," p.275). "Les Elections: A Sivas," *The Levant Herald and Eastern Express*, April 11, 1912, p.2; "Les Elections," *The Levant Herald and Eastern Express*, April 13, 1912, p.2; "Ouverture du Parlement," *The Levant Herald and Eastern Express*, April 18, 1912, p.1; İhsan Ezherli, *Türkiye Büyük Millet Meclisi, 1920-1998, ve Osmanlı Meclis-i Mebusanı, 1877-1920*, p.209; and, Fevzi

Karabet Paşayan   Armenian   I[166]
Ömer Şevki Bey*   Turk   I[167]

Amasya (3)

Fazıl Arif Efendi*   Turk   CUP[168]
Hacı Mustafa Tevfik Efendi   Turk   I[169]
Hasan Rasim Bey   Turk   I[170]

Karahisar-i Şarki (2)

Hafızzade Mehmed Vasfi   Turk   CUP[171]
[Seçer]
Kürdzade Zihni Efendi   Kurd?   "CUP"[172]

Demir, İkinci Meşrutiyet Dönemi Meclis-i Mebusan Seçimleri, 1908-1914, p.176.

[166] Medical doctor (Feroz Ahmad and Dankwart A. Rustow, "İkinci Meşrutiyet Döneminde Meclisler, 1908-1918," p.275). "Les Elections: A Sivas," *The Levant Herald and Eastern Express*, April 11, 1912, p.2; "Les Elections," *The Levant Herald and Eastern Express*, April 13, 1912, p.2; "Ouverture du Parlement," *The Levant Herald and Eastern Express*, April 18, 1912, p.1; İhsan Ezherli, *Türkiye Büyük Millet Meclisi, 1920-1998, ve Osmanlı Meclis-i Mebusanı, 1877-1920*, p.215; and, Fevzi Demir, İkinci Meşrutiyet Dönemi Meclis-i Mebusan Seçimleri, 1908-1914, p.176.

[167] Medical doctor (Feroz Ahmad and Dankwart A. Rustow, "İkinci Meşrutiyet Döneminde Meclisler, 1908-1918," p.275). "Les Elections: A Sivas," *The Levant Herald and Eastern Express*, April 11, 1912, p.2; "Les Elections," *The Levant Herald and Eastern Express*, April 13, 1912, p.2; "Ouverture du Parlement," *The Levant Herald and Eastern Express*, April 18, 1912, p.1; İhsan Ezherli, *Türkiye Büyük Millet Meclisi, 1920-1998, ve Osmanlı Meclis-i Mebusanı, 1877-1920*, p.215; and, Fevzi Demir, İkinci Meşrutiyet Dönemi Meclis-i Mebusan Seçimleri, 1908-1914, p.176.

[168] "Les Elections," *The Levant Herald and Eastern Express*, April 13, 1912, p.2; "Ouverture du Parlement," *The Levant Herald and Eastern Express*, April 18, 1912, p.1; Feroz Ahmad and Dankwart A. Rustow, "İkinci Meşrutiyet Döneminde Meclisler, 1908-1918," p.275; İhsan Ezherli, *Türkiye Büyük Millet Meclisi, 1920-1998, ve Osmanlı Meclis-i Mebusanı, 1877-1920*, p.205; and, Fevzi Demir, İkinci Meşrutiyet Dönemi Meclis-i Mebusan Seçimleri, 1908-1914, p.176.

[169] Mufti (Fevzi Demir, İkinci Meşrutiyet Dönemi Meclis-i Mebusan Seçimleri, 1908-1914, p.176). "Les Elections," *The Levant Herald and Eastern Express*, April 13, 1912, p.2; "Ouverture du Parlement," *The Levant Herald and Eastern Express*, April 18, 1912, p.1; Feroz Ahmad and Dankwart A. Rustow, "İkinci Meşrutiyet Döneminde Meclisler, 1908-1918," p.275; and, İhsan Ezherli, *Türkiye Büyük Millet Meclisi, 1920-1998, ve Osmanlı Meclis-i Mebusanı, 1877-1920*, p.208.

[170] "Les Elections," *The Levant Herald and Eastern Express*, April 13, 1912, p.2; "Ouverture du Parlement," *The Levant Herald and Eastern Express*, April 18, 1912, p.1; Feroz Ahmad and Dankwart A. Rustow, "İkinci Meşrutiyet Döneminde Meclisler, 1908-1918," p.275; İhsan Ezherli, *Türkiye Büyük Millet Meclisi, 1920-1998, ve Osmanlı Meclis-i Mebusanı, 1877-1920*, p.209; and, Fevzi Demir, İkinci Meşrutiyet Dönemi Meclis-i Mebusan Seçimleri, 1908-1914, p.176.

[171] "Les Elections: Les nouveaux députés," *The Levant Herald and Eastern Express*, April 19, 1912, p.2; İhsan Ezherli, *Türkiye Büyük Millet Meclisi, 1920-1998, ve Osmanlı Meclis-i Mebusanı, 1877-1920*, p.212; and, Fevzi Demir, İkinci Meşrutiyet Dönemi Meclis-i Mebusan Seçimleri, 1908-1914, p.178.

[172] "Les Elections: Les nouveaux députés," *The Levant Herald and Eastern Ex-

Tokad (3)

Topçuzade Hacı Kâmil Efendi	Turk	I[173]
Kemerlizade Şakir Bey	Turk	I[174]
Tahsin Rıza Bey	Turk	CUP[175]

* * *

ERZURUM (8)

Erzurum (6)

Karekin Pasturmadjian*	Armenian	ARF[176]
Vartkes Serengülyan*	Armenian	ARF[177]

---

press, April 19, 1912, p.2; Feroz Ahmad and Dankwart A. Rustow, "İkinci Meşrutiyet Döneminde Meclisler, 1908-1918," p.277; İhsan Ezherli, *Türkiye Büyük Millet Meclisi, 1920-1998, ve Osmanlı Meclis-i Mebusanı, 1877-1920,* p.220; and, Fevzi Demir, İkinci Meşrutiyet Dönemi Meclis-i Mebusan Seçimleri, 1908-1914, p.178.

[173] Notable of Zile ("Notes de Tokat," *The Levant Herald and Eastern Express,* April 29, 1912, p.3). "Ouverture du Parlement," *The Levant Herald and Eastern Express,* April 18, 1912, p.1; "Notes de Tokat," *The Levant Herald and Eastern Express,* April 29, 1912, p.3; Feroz Ahmad and Dankwart A. Rustow, "İkinci Meşrutiyet Döneminde Meclisler, 1908-1918," p.275; İhsan Ezherli, *Türkiye Büyük Millet Meclisi, 1920-1998, ve Osmanlı Meclis-i Mebusanı, 1877-1920,* p.207; and, Fevzi Demir, İkinci Meşrutiyet Dönemi Meclis-i Mebusan Seçimleri, 1908-1914, p.176.

[174] Notable of Tokad ("Notes de Tokat," *The Levant Herald and Eastern Express,* April 29, 1912, p.3). "Ouverture du Parlement," *The Levant Herald and Eastern Express,* April 18, 1912, p.1; "Notes de Tokat," *The Levant Herald and Eastern Express,* April 29, 1912, p.3; Feroz Ahmad and Dankwart A. Rustow, "İkinci Meşrutiyet Döneminde Meclisler, 1908-1918," p.275; İhsan Ezherli, *Türkiye Büyük Millet Meclisi, 1920-1998, ve Osmanlı Meclis-i Mebusanı, 1877-1920,* p.218; and, Fevzi Demir, İkinci Meşrutiyet Dönemi Meclis-i Mebusan Seçimleri, 1908-1914, p.176.

[175] Notable of Niksar ("Notes de Tokat," *The Levant Herald and Eastern Express,* April 29, 1912, p.3). "Ouverture du Parlement," *The Levant Herald and Eastern Express,* April 18, 1912, p.1; "Notes de Tokat," *The Levant Herald and Eastern Express,* April 29, 1912, p.3; Feroz Ahmad and Dankwart A. Rustow, "İkinci Meşrutiyet Döneminde Meclisler, 1908-1918," p.275; İhsan Ezherli, *Türkiye Büyük Millet Meclisi, 1920-1998, ve Osmanlı Meclis-i Mebusanı, 1877-1920,* p.219; and, Fevzi Demir, İkinci Meşrutiyet Dönemi Meclis-i Mebusan Seçimleri, 1908-1914, p.176.

[176] "Les Elections: 141 élus," *The Levant Herald and Eastern Express,* April 16, 1912, p.2; "Ouverture du Parlement," *The Levant Herald and Eastern Express,* April 18, 1912, p.1; Feroz Ahmad and Dankwart A. Rustow, "İkinci Meşrutiyet Döneminde Meclisler, 1908-1918," p.278; İhsan Ezherli, *Türkiye Büyük Millet Meclisi, 1920-1998, ve Osmanlı Meclis-i Mebusanı, 1877-1920,* p.211; and, Fevzi Demir, İkinci Meşrutiyet Dönemi Meclis-i Mebusan Seçimleri, 1908-1914, p.179.

[177] "Les Elections: 141 élus," *The Levant Herald and Eastern Express,* April 16, 1912, p.2; "Ouverture du Parlement," *The Levant Herald and Eastern Express,* April 18, 1912, p.1; Feroz Ahmad and Dankwart A. Rustow, "İkinci Meşrutiyet Döneminde Meclisler, 1908-1918," p.278; İhsan Ezherli, *Türkiye Büyük Millet Meclisi, 1920-1998, ve Osmanlı Meclis-i Mebusanı, 1877-1920,* p.219; and, Fevzi Demir, İkin-

Hacı Lütfullah Vehbi Efendi	Turk	I[178]
Raif [Dinç]	Turk	CUP[179]
Şaban Efendi	Turk	I[180]
Hüseyin Tosun Bey	Turk	I[181]

Bayezid (1)

| Süleyman Sudi [Acarbay]* | Turk | CUP[182] |

Erzincan (1)

| Halet [Sağıroğlu] | Turk | CUP[183] |

* * *

ci Meşrutiyet Dönemi Meclis-i Mebusan Seçimleri, 1908-1914, p.179.

[178] Feroz Ahmad and Dankwart A. Rustow, "İkinci Meşrutiyet Döneminde Meclisler, 1908-1918," p.278; İhsan Ezherli, *Türkiye Büyük Millet Meclisi, 1920-1998, ve Osmanlı Meclis-i Mebusanı, 1877-1920*, p.211; and, Fevzi Demir, İkinci Meşrutiyet Dönemi Meclis-i Mebusan Seçimleri, 1908-1914, p.179.

[179] Feroz Ahmad and Dankwart A. Rustow, "İkinci Meşrutiyet Döneminde Meclisler, 1908-1918," p.278; İhsan Ezherli, *Türkiye Büyük Millet Meclisi, 1920-1998, ve Osmanlı Meclis-i Mebusanı, 1877-1920*, p.215; and, Fevzi Demir, İkinci Meşrutiyet Dönemi Meclis-i Mebusan Seçimleri, 1908-1914, p.179.

[180] "Les Elections: 141 élus," *The Levant Herald and Eastern Express*, April 16, 1912, p.2; "Ouverture du Parlement," *The Levant Herald and Eastern Express*, April 18, 1912, p.1; Feroz Ahmad and Dankwart A. Rustow, "İkinci Meşrutiyet Döneminde Meclisler, 1908-1918," p.278; İhsan Ezherli, *Türkiye Büyük Millet Meclisi, 1920-1998, ve Osmanlı Meclis-i Mebusanı, 1877-1920*, p.218; and, Fevzi Demir, İkinci Meşrutiyet Dönemi Meclis-i Mebusan Seçimleri, 1908-1914, p.179.

[181] "Les Elections: 141 élus," *The Levant Herald and Eastern Express*, April 16, 1912, p.2; "Ouverture du Parlement," *The Levant Herald and Eastern Express*, April 18, 1912, p.1; Feroz Ahmad and Dankwart A. Rustow, "İkinci Meşrutiyet Döneminde Meclisler, 1908-1918," p.278; İhsan Ezherli, *Türkiye Büyük Millet Meclisi, 1920-1998, ve Osmanlı Meclis-i Mebusanı, 1877-1920*, p.209; and, Fevzi Demir, İkinci Meşrutiyet Dönemi Meclis-i Mebusan Seçimleri, 1908-1914, p.179.

[182] Feroz Ahmad and Dankwart A. Rustow, "İkinci Meşrutiyet Döneminde Meclisler, 1908-1918," p.278; İhsan Ezherli, *Türkiye Büyük Millet Meclisi, 1920-1998, ve Osmanlı Meclis-i Mebusanı, 1877-1920*, p.218; and, Fevzi Demir, İkinci Meşrutiyet Dönemi Meclis-i Mebusan Seçimleri, 1908-1914, p.180.

[183] "Les Elections: Pas un député d'opposition!" *The Levant Herald and Eastern Express*, April 9, 1912, p.2; "Ouverture du Parlement," *The Levant Herald and Eastern Express*, April 18, 1912, p.1; Feroz Ahmad and Dankwart A. Rustow, "İkinci Meşrutiyet Döneminde Meclisler, 1908-1918," p.277; İhsan Ezherli, *Türkiye Büyük Millet Meclisi, 1920-1998, ve Osmanlı Meclis-i Mebusanı, 1877-1920*, p.208; and, Fevzi Demir, İkinci Meşrutiyet Dönemi Meclis-i Mebusan Seçimleri, 1908-1914, p.178.

VAN (2)

Van (2)

Midhat [Altıok]	Turk	I[184]
Onnik Terezekyan Virmiyan	Armenian	I[185]

* * *

BİTLİS (5)

Bitlis (1)

Nusret Sadullah Feyzi [Eren]	Turk	I[186]

Genc [Bingöl] (1)

Mehmed Emin Efendi*	Turk	CUP[187]

Muş (2)

Kegham Der Garabetian*	Armenian	I[188]

---

[184] Medical doctor (Feroz Ahmad and Dankwart A. Rustow, "İkinci Meşrutiyet Döneminde Meclisler, 1908-1918," p.278). İhsan Ezherli, *Türkiye Büyük Millet Meclisi, 1920-1998, ve Osmanlı Meclis-i Mebusanı, 1877-1920*, p.213; and, Fevzi Demir, İkinci Meşrutiyet Dönemi Meclis-i Mebusan Seçimleri, 1908-1914, p.180.

[185] Feroz Ahmad and Dankwart A. Rustow, "İkinci Meşrutiyet Döneminde Meclisler, 1908-1918," p.278; İhsan Ezherli, *Türkiye Büyük Millet Meclisi, 1920-1998, ve Osmanlı Meclis-i Mebusanı, 1877-1920*, p.214; and, Fevzi Demir, İkinci Meşrutiyet Dönemi Meclis-i Mebusan Seçimleri, 1908-1914, p.180.

[186] Feroz Ahmad and Dankwart A. Rustow, "İkinci Meşrutiyet Döneminde Meclisler, 1908-1918," p.278; İhsan Ezherli, *Türkiye Büyük Millet Meclisi, 1920-1998, ve Osmanlı Meclis-i Mebusanı, 1877-1920*, p.216; and, Fevzi Demir, İkinci Meşrutiyet Dönemi Meclis-i Mebusan Seçimleri, 1908-1914, p.180.

[187] "Ouverture du Parlement," *The Levant Herald and Eastern Express*, April 18, 1912, p.1; Feroz Ahmad and Dankwart A. Rustow, "İkinci Meşrutiyet Döneminde Meclisler, 1908-1918," p.278; İhsan Ezherli, *Türkiye Büyük Millet Meclisi, 1920-1998, ve Osmanlı Meclis-i Mebusanı, 1877-1920*, p.212; and, Fevzi Demir, İkinci Meşrutiyet Dönemi Meclis-i Mebusan Seçimleri, 1908-1914, p.180.

[188] Feroz Ahmad and Dankwart A. Rustow, "İkinci Meşrutiyet Döneminde Meclisler, 1908-1918," p.278; İhsan Ezherli, *Türkiye Büyük Millet Meclisi, 1920-1998, ve Osmanlı Meclis-i Mebusanı, 1877-1920*, p.211; and, Fevzi Demir, İkinci Meşrutiyet Dönemi Meclis-i Mebusan Seçimleri, 1908-1914, p.180.

Hacı İlyas Sami [Muş]*   Turk   CUP[189]

Siird (1)

Nâzım [Mağgönül]   Turk   I[190]

* * *

MAMURET ÜL-AZİZ (6)

Mamuret-ül-Aziz [Harput] (3)

Hacı Mehmed Nuri Efendi*   Turk   I[191]
Hacı Osman Bey   Turk   I[192]
Esperzade Mustafa Safvet   Turk   I[193]
  Efendi

---

[189] Feroz Ahmad and Dankwart A. Rustow, "İkinci Meşrutiyet Döneminde Meclisler, 1908-1918," p.278; İhsan Ezherli, *Türkiye Büyük Millet Meclisi, 1920-1998, ve Osmanlı Meclis-i Mebusanı, 1877-1920*, p.207; and, Fevzi Demir, İkinci Meşrutiyet Dönemi Meclis-i Mebusan Seçimleri, 1908-1914, p.180.

[190] Feroz Ahmad and Dankwart A. Rustow, "İkinci Meşrutiyet Döneminde Meclisler, 1908-1918," p.278; İhsan Ezherli, *Türkiye Büyük Millet Meclisi, 1920-1998, ve Osmanlı Meclis-i Mebusanı, 1877-1920*, p.214; and, Fevzi Demir, İkinci Meşrutiyet Dönemi Meclis-i Mebusan Seçimleri, 1908-1914, p.180.

[191] "Les Elections: Les nouveaux députés," *The Levant Herald and Eastern Express*, April 20, 1912, p.2; "Les Elections: A Maamouret-ul-Aziz," *The Levant Herald and Eastern Express*, April 24, 1912, p.2; Feroz Ahmad and Dankwart A. Rustow, "İkinci Meşrutiyet Döneminde Meclisler, 1908-1918," p.277; İhsan Ezherli, *Türkiye Büyük Millet Meclisi, 1920-1998, ve Osmanlı Meclis-i Mebusanı, 1877-1920*, p.212; and, Fevzi Demir, İkinci Meşrutiyet Dönemi Meclis-i Mebusan Seçimleri, 1908-1914, p.178.

[192] Veterinary inspector ("Election," *The Levant Herald and Eastern Express*, April 22, 1912, p.2). "Les Elections: Les nouveaux députés," *The Levant Herald and Eastern Express*, April 20, 1912, p.2; "Les Elections: A Maamouret-ul-Aziz," *The Levant Herald and Eastern Express*, April 24, 1912, p.2; Feroz Ahmad and Dankwart A. Rustow, "İkinci Meşrutiyet Döneminde Meclisler, 1908-1918," p.277; İhsan Ezherli, *Türkiye Büyük Millet Meclisi, 1920-1998, ve Osmanlı Meclis-i Mebusanı, 1877-1920*, p.208; and, Fevzi Demir, İkinci Meşrutiyet Dönemi Meclis-i Mebusan Seçimleri, 1908-1914, p.178.

[193] "Les Elections: Les nouveaux députés," *The Levant Herald and Eastern Express*, April 20, 1912, p.2; "Les Elections: A Maamouret-ul-Aziz," *The Levant Herald and Eastern Express*, April 24, 1912, p.2; Feroz Ahmad and Dankwart A. Rustow, "İkinci Meşrutiyet Döneminde Meclisler, 1908-1918," p.277; İhsan Ezherli, *Türkiye Büyük Millet Meclisi, 1920-1998, ve Osmanlı Meclis-i Mebusanı, 1877-1920*, p.214; and, Fevzi Demir, İkinci Meşrutiyet Dönemi Meclis-i Mebusan Seçimleri, 1908-1914, p.178.

Dersim [Tunceli] (1)

Salim Bey   Turk   I[194]

Malatya (2)

Osman Avni Efendi   Turk   I[195]
Hoca Mehmed Tevfik Efendi*   Turk   I[196]

* * *

DİYAR-I BEKİR (6)

Diyar-ı Bekir [Diyarbakır] (2)

Pirinççizade Fevzi Bey*   Kurd   I[197]
Mehmed Zülfi [Tigrel]   Turk   CUP[198]

---

[194] He replaced Lütfi Fikri Bey ("Les Elections: Résultats à ce jour," *The Levant Herald and Eastern Express*, April 1, 1912, p.2). "Ouverture du Parlement," *The Levant Herald and Eastern Express*, April 18, 1912, p.1; Feroz Ahmad and Dankwart A. Rustow, "İkinci Meşrutiyet Döneminde Meclisler, 1908-1918," p.277; İhsan Ezherli, *Türkiye Büyük Millet Meclisi, 1920-1998, ve Osmanlı Meclis-i Mebusanı, 1877-1920*, p.216; and, Fevzi Demir, İkinci Meşrutiyet Dönemi Meclis-i Mebusan Seçimleri, 1908-1914, p.178.

[195] Mufti ("Les Elections: Derniers élus," *The Levant Herald and Eastern Express*, April 15, 1912, p.2). "Ouverture du Parlement," *The Levant Herald and Eastern Express*, April 18, 1912, p.1; Feroz Ahmad and Dankwart A. Rustow, "İkinci Meşrutiyet Döneminde Meclisler, 1908-1918," p.276; İhsan Ezherli, *Türkiye Büyük Millet Meclisi, 1920-1998, ve Osmanlı Meclis-i Mebusanı, 1877-1920*, p.214; and, Fevzi Demir, İkinci Meşrutiyet Dönemi Meclis-i Mebusan Seçimleri, 1908-1914, p.177.

[196] Ulema. "Les Elections: Derniers élus," *The Levant Herald and Eastern Express*, April 15, 1912, p.2; "Ouverture du Parlement," *The Levant Herald and Eastern Express*, April 18, 1912, p.1; Feroz Ahmad and Dankwart A. Rustow, "İkinci Meşrutiyet Döneminde Meclisler, 1908-1918," p.276; İhsan Ezherli, *Türkiye Büyük Millet Meclisi, 1920-1998, ve Osmanlı Meclis-i Mebusanı, 1877-1920*, p.212; and, Fevzi Demir, İkinci Meşrutiyet Dönemi Meclis-i Mebusan Seçimleri, 1908-1914, p.177.

[197] "En province," *The Levant Herald and Eastern Express*, April 6, 1912, p.2; "Ouverture du Parlement," *The Levant Herald and Eastern Express*, April 18, 1912, p.1; Feroz Ahmad and Dankwart A. Rustow, "İkinci Meşrutiyet Döneminde Meclisler, 1908-1918," p.276; İhsan Ezherli, *Türkiye Büyük Millet Meclisi, 1920-1998, ve Osmanlı Meclis-i Mebusanı, 1877-1920*, p.207; and, Fevzi Demir, İkinci Meşrutiyet Dönemi Meclis-i Mebusan Seçimleri, 1908-1914, p.177.

[198] "En province," *The Levant Herald and Eastern Express*, April 6, 1912, p.2; "Ouverture du Parlement," *The Levant Herald and Eastern Express*, April 18, 1912, p.1; Feroz Ahmad and Dankwart A. Rustow, "İkinci Meşrutiyet Döneminde Meclisler, 1908-1918," p.276; İhsan Ezherli, *Türkiye Büyük Millet Meclisi, 1920-1998, ve Osmanlı Meclis-i Mebusanı, 1877-1920*, p.220; and, Fevzi Demir, İkinci Meşrutiyet

Argani-Maden (1)

Ziya Bey   Turk   I[199]

Mardin (2)

Hasan Lâmi Efendi   Turk   I[200]
Said Bey*   Turk   I[201]

Siverek (1)

Müftüzade İsmail Hakkı Bey*   Turk   CUP[202]

* * *

ALEPPO (10)

Aleppo (6)

Sadık Bey ar-Rifa'i   Arab   I[203]

Dönemi Meclis-i Mebusan Seçimleri, 1908-1914, p.177.

[199] "Ouverture du Parlement," *The Levant Herald and Eastern Express*, April 18, 1912, p.1; Feroz Ahmad and Dankwart A. Rustow, "İkinci Meşrutiyet Döneminde Meclisler, 1908-1918," p.276; İhsan Ezherli, *Türkiye Büyük Millet Meclisi, 1920-1998, ve Osmanlı Meclis-i Mebusanı, 1877-1920*, p.220; and, Fevzi Demir, İkinci Meşrutiyet Dönemi Meclis-i Mebusan Seçimleri, 1908-1914, p.177.

[200] Feroz Ahmad and Dankwart A. Rustow, "İkinci Meşrutiyet Döneminde Meclisler, 1908-1918," p.276; İhsan Ezherli, *Türkiye Büyük Millet Meclisi, 1920-1998, ve Osmanlı Meclis-i Mebusanı, 1877-1920*, p.209; and, Fevzi Demir, İkinci Meşrutiyet Dönemi Meclis-i Mebusan Seçimleri, 1908-1914, p.177.

[201] Feroz Ahmad and Dankwart A. Rustow, "İkinci Meşrutiyet Döneminde Meclisler, 1908-1918," p.276; İhsan Ezherli, *Türkiye Büyük Millet Meclisi, 1920-1998, ve Osmanlı Meclis-i Mebusanı, 1877-1920*, p.216; and, Fevzi Demir, İkinci Meşrutiyet Dönemi Meclis-i Mebusan Seçimleri, 1908-1914, p.177.

[202] Son of Müftüzade Ahmed Sabri Efendi, one of the notables of Diyarbakır; and, graduate of Mekteb-i Mülkiye, Class of 1893 (Ali Çankaya, *Yeni Mülkiye Tarihi ve Mülkiyeliler*, 3, p.511). "Les Elections: Nouveaux députés unionistes," *The Levant Herald and Eastern Express*, April 12, 1912, p.2; "Les Elections," *The Levant Herald and Eastern Express*, April 13, 1912, p.2; "Ouverture du Parlement," *The Levant Herald and Eastern Express*, April 18, 1912, p.1; Feroz Ahmad and Dankwart A. Rustow, "İkinci Meşrutiyet Döneminde Meclisler, 1908-1918," p.276; İhsan Ezherli, *Türkiye Büyük Millet Meclisi, 1920-1998, ve Osmanlı Meclis-i Mebusanı, 1877-1920*, p.210; and, Fevzi Demir, İkinci Meşrutiyet Dönemi Meclis-i Mebusan Seçimleri, 1908-1914, p.177.

[203] F.O. 195/2429/2309, Fontana to Sir Gerard Lowther, Aleppo, May 2, 1912, quoted in Rashid Khalidi, *British Policy Towards Syria and Palestine, 1906-1914*, p.258; Sabine Prätor, *Der arabische Faktor in der jungtürkischen Politik: Eine*

Muhammad Baha ad-Din al-Amiri	Arab	I[204]
Artin Boşgezenian*	Armenian	CUP[205]
Ali Cenani Bey*	Turk	I[206]
Hamid 'Abd al-Ghafur Bey	Arab	I[207]
Sheikh Hacı Mustafa Efendi	Turk	CUP[208]

Maraş (2)

Kadızade Hacı Hasan Fehmi Efendi*	Turk	I[209]

Studie zum osmanischen Parlament der II. Konstitution, 1908-1918, p.238; Feroz Ahmad and Dankwart A. Rustow, "İkinci Meşrutiyet Döneminde Meclisler, 1908-1918," p.279; İhsan Ezherli, *Türkiye Büyük Millet Meclisi, 1920-1998, ve Osmanlı Meclis-i Mebusanı, 1877-1920*, p.216; and, Fevzi Demir, İkinci Meşrutiyet Dönemi Meclis-i Mebusan Seçimleri, 1908-1914, p.180.

[204] Sabine Prätor, *Der arabische Faktor in der jungtürkischen Politik: Eine Studie zum osmanischen Parlament der II. Konstitution, 1908-1918*, p.238; Feroz Ahmad and Dankwart A. Rustow, "İkinci Meşrutiyet Döneminde Meclisler, 1908-1918," p.279; İhsan Ezherli, *Türkiye Büyük Millet Meclisi, 1920-1998, ve Osmanlı Meclis-i Mebusanı, 1877-1920*, p.212; and, Fevzi Demir, İkinci Meşrutiyet Dönemi Meclis-i Mebusan Seçimleri, 1908-1914, p.180.

[205] Sabine Prätor, *Der arabische Faktor in der jungtürkischen Politik: Eine Studie zum osmanischen Parlament der II. Konstitution, 1908-1918*, p.238; Feroz Ahmad and Dankwart A. Rustow, "İkinci Meşrutiyet Döneminde Meclisler, 1908-1918," p.279; İhsan Ezherli, *Türkiye Büyük Millet Meclisi, 1920-1998, ve Osmanlı Meclis-i Mebusanı, 1877-1920*, p.205; and, Fevzi Demir, İkinci Meşrutiyet Dönemi Meclis-i Mebusan Seçimleri, 1908-1914, p.180.

[206] F.O. 195/2429/2309, Fontana to Sir Gerard Lowther, Aleppo, May 2, 1912, quoted in Rashid Khalidi, *British Policy Towards Syria and Palestine, 1906-1914*, p.258; "Election," *The Levant Herald and Eastern Express*, April 22, 1912, p.2; Sabine Prätor, *Der arabische Faktor in der jungtürkischen Politik: Eine Studie zum osmanischen Parlament der II. Konstitution, 1908-1918*, p.238; Feroz Ahmad and Dankwart A. Rustow, "İkinci Meşrutiyet Döneminde Meclisler, 1908-1918," p.279; İhsan Ezherli, *Türkiye Büyük Millet Meclisi, 1920-1998, ve Osmanlı Meclis-i Mebusanı, 1877-1920*, p.204; and, Fevzi Demir, İkinci Meşrutiyet Dönemi Meclis-i Mebusan Seçimleri, 1908-1914, p.180.

[207] F.O. 195/2429/2309, Fontana to Sir Gerard Lowther, Aleppo, May 2, 1912, quoted in Rashid Khalidi, *British Policy Towards Syria and Palestine, 1906-1914*, p.258; Sabine Prätor, *Der arabische Faktor in der jungtürkischen Politik: Eine Studie zum osmanischen Parlament der II. Konstitution, 1908-1918*, p.238; Feroz Ahmad and Dankwart A. Rustow, "İkinci Meşrutiyet Döneminde Meclisler, 1908-1918," p.279; İhsan Ezherli, *Türkiye Büyük Millet Meclisi, 1920-1998, ve Osmanlı Meclis-i Mebusanı, 1877-1920*, p.208; and, Fevzi Demir, İkinci Meşrutiyet Dönemi Meclis-i Mebusan Seçimleri, 1908-1914, p.180.

[208] Sabine Prätor, *Der arabische Faktor in der jungtürkischen Politik: Eine Studie zum osmanischen Parlament der II. Konstitution, 1908-1918*, p.238; and, Fevzi Demir, İkinci Meşrutiyet Dönemi Meclis-i Mebusan Seçimleri, 1908-1914, p.180.

[209] Feroz Ahmad and Dankwart A. Rustow, "İkinci Meşrutiyet Döneminde Meclisler, 1908-1918," p.275; İhsan Ezherli, *Türkiye Büyük Millet Meclisi, 1920-1998, ve Osmanlı Meclis-i Mebusanı, 1877-1920*, p.208; and, Fevzi Demir, İkinci Meşrutiyet Dönemi Meclis-i Mebusan Seçimleri, 1908-1914, p.176.

Hacı Evliya Efendi   Turk   I[210]

Urfa (2)

Sheikh Safvet [Yetkin]*   Turk   CUP[211]
Ömer Edib Bey   Turk   I[212]

* * *

ADANA (5)

Adana (1)

Abdullah Faik [Çopuroğlu]*   Turk   EL[213]

Cebel-i Bereket [Dörtyol] (1)

Hasan Sezai Bey   Turk   CUP[214]

---

[210] Feroz Ahmad and Dankwart A. Rustow, "İkinci Meşrutiyet Döneminde Meclisler, 1908-1918," p.275; İhsan Ezherli, *Türkiye Büyük Millet Meclisi, 1920-1998, ve Osmanlı Meclis-i Mebusanı, 1877-1920*, p.207; and, Fevzi Demir, İkinci Meşrutiyet Dönemi Meclis-i Mebusan Seçimleri, 1908-1914, p.176.

[211] "Les Elections," *The Levant Herald and Eastern Express*, April 13, 1912, p.2; "Ouverture du Parlement," *The Levant Herald and Eastern Express*, April 18, 1912, p.1; Feroz Ahmad and Dankwart A. Rustow, "İkinci Meşrutiyet Döneminde Meclisler, 1908-1918," p.276; İhsan Ezherli, *Türkiye Büyük Millet Meclisi, 1920-1998, ve Osmanlı Meclis-i Mebusanı, 1877-1920*, p.218; and, Fevzi Demir, İkinci Meşrutiyet Dönemi Meclis-i Mebusan Seçimleri, 1908-1914, p.177.

[212] "Les Elections," *The Levant Herald and Eastern Express*, April 13, 1912, p.2; "Ouverture du Parlement," *The Levant Herald and Eastern Express*, April 18, 1912, p.1; Feroz Ahmad and Dankwart A. Rustow, "İkinci Meşrutiyet Döneminde Meclisler, 1908-1918," p.276; İhsan Ezherli, *Türkiye Büyük Millet Meclisi, 1920-1998, ve Osmanlı Meclis-i Mebusanı, 1877-1920*, p.215; and, Fevzi Demir, İkinci Meşrutiyet Dönemi Meclis-i Mebusan Seçimleri, 1908-1914, p.177.

[213] His deputyship was confirmed with some objections in the Chamber ("The Ottoman Parliament," *The Orient*, 3/25 (June 19, 1912). Feroz Ahmad and Dankwart A. Rustow, "İkinci Meşrutiyet Döneminde Meclisler, 1908-1918," p.275; İhsan Ezherli, *Türkiye Büyük Millet Meclisi, 1920-1998, ve Osmanlı Meclis-i Mebusanı, 1877-1920*, p.203; and, Fevzi Demir, İkinci Meşrutiyet Dönemi Meclis-i Mebusan Seçimleri, 1908-1914, p.177.

[214] Feroz Ahmad and Dankwart A. Rustow, "İkinci Meşrutiyet Döneminde Meclisler, 1908-1918," p.276; İhsan Ezherli, *Türkiye Büyük Millet Meclisi, 1920-1998, ve Osmanlı Meclis-i Mebusanı, 1877-1920*, p.209; and, Fevzi Demir, İkinci Meşrutiyet Dönemi Meclis-i Mebusan Seçimleri, 1908-1914, p.177.

İç İli [Silifke] (1)

Hafız Emin [İnankor]	Turk	CUP[215]

Kozan (1)

Ali İlmî Fani [Bilgili]	Turk	EL[216]

Mersin (1)

Süleyman Sadık Pasha	Turk	I[217]

* * *

BEIRUT (7)

Beirut (2)

Kamil al-As'ad*	Arab	CUP[218]
Muharram Efendi Misbah	Arab	I[219]

---

[215] "Les Elections: A Itch il," *The Levant Herald and Eastern Express*, April 8, 1912, p.2; "Ouverture du Parlement," *The Levant Herald and Eastern Express*, April 18, 1912, p.1; Feroz Ahmad and Dankwart A. Rustow, "İkinci Meşrutiyet Döneminde Meclisler, 1908-1918," p.273; İhsan Ezherli, *Türkiye Büyük Millet Meclisi, 1920-1998, ve Osmanlı Meclis-i Mebusanı, 1877-1920*, p.208; and, Fevzi Demir, İkinci Meşrutiyet Dönemi Meclis-i Mebusan Seçimleri, 1908-1914, p.174.

[216] Feroz Ahmad and Dankwart A. Rustow, "İkinci Meşrutiyet Döneminde Meclisler, 1908-1918," p.273; İhsan Ezherli, *Türkiye Büyük Millet Meclisi, 1920-1998, ve Osmanlı Meclis-i Mebusanı, 1877-1920*, p.204; and, Fevzi Demir, İkinci Meşrutiyet Dönemi Meclis-i Mebusan Seçimleri, 1908-1914, p.174.

[217] "Les Elections: 141 élus," *The Levant Herald and Eastern Express*, April 16, 1912, p.2; "Ouverture du Parlement," *The Levant Herald and Eastern Express*, April 18, 1912, p.1; Feroz Ahmad and Dankwart A. Rustow, "İkinci Meşrutiyet Döneminde Meclisler, 1908-1918," p.273; İhsan Ezherli, *Türkiye Büyük Millet Meclisi, 1920-1998, ve Osmanlı Meclis-i Mebusanı, 1877-1920*, p.216; and, Fevzi Demir, İkinci Meşrutiyet Dönemi Meclis-i Mebusan Seçimleri, 1908-1914, p.174.

[218] "Les Elections: Résultats à ce jour," *The Levant Herald and Eastern Express*, April 1, 1912, p.2; "Ouverture du Parlement," *The Levant Herald and Eastern Express*, April 18, 1912, p.1; Sabine Prätor, *Der arabische Faktor in der jungtürkischen Politik: Eine Studie zum osmanischen Parlament der II. Konstitution, 1908-1918*, p.241; Feroz Ahmad and Dankwart A. Rustow, "İkinci Meşrutiyet Döneminde Meclisler, 1908-1918," p.280; İhsan Ezherli, *Türkiye Büyük Millet Meclisi, 1920-1998, ve Osmanlı Meclis-i Mebusanı, 1877-1920*, p.211; and, Fevzi Demir, İkinci Meşrutiyet Dönemi Meclis-i Mebusan Seçimleri, 1908-1914, p.181.

[219] F.O. 195/2389/24/1989, Cumberbatch to Sir Gerard Lowther, Beirut, April 19, 1912, quoted in Rashid Khalidi, *British Policy Towards Syria and Palestine, 1906-1914*, p.258; "Ouverture du Parlement," *The Levant Herald and Eastern Ex-*

Acra (1)

Sheikh As'ad Tawfiq Efendi   Arab   EL?[220]
Shuqair*

Latakia (1)

'Abd al-Wahid Efendi Harun   Arab   I[221]

Nablus (1)

Haydar Bey Tufan   Arab   I[222]

---

press, April 18, 1912, p.1; Sabine Prätor, *Der arabische Faktor in der jungtürkischen Politik: Eine Studie zum osmanischen Parlament der II. Konstitution, 1908-1918*, p.241; Feroz Ahmad and Dankwart A. Rustow, "İkinci Meşrutiyet Döneminde Meclisler, 1908-1918," p.280; İhsan Ezherli, *Türkiye Büyük Millet Meclisi, 1920-1998, ve Osmanlı Meclis-i Mebusanı, 1877-1920*, p.213; and, Fevzi Demir, İkinci Meşrutiyet Dönemi Meclis-i Mebusan Seçimleri, 1908-1914, p.181.

[220] Khalidi writes that he was a loyal Unionist (Rashid Khalidi, "The 1912 Election Campaign in the Cities of *bilad' al-Sham*," p.470). F.O. 195/2389/24/1989, Cumberbatch to Sir Gerard Lowther, Beirut, April 19, 1912, quoted in Rashid Khalidi, *British Policy Towards Syria and Palestine, 1906-1914*, p.258; "Les Elections: Nouveaux députés unionistes," *The Levant Herald and Eastern Express*, April 12, 1912, p.2; "Les Élections," *The Levant Herald and Eastern Express*, April 13, 1912, p.2; "Ouverture du Parlement," *The Levant Herald and Eastern Express*, April 18, 1912, p.1; Sabine Prätor, *Der arabische Faktor in der jungtürkischen Politik: Eine Studie zum osmanischen Parlament der II. Konstitution, 1908-1918*, p.241; Feroz Ahmad and Dankwart A. Rustow, "İkinci Meşrutiyet Döneminde Meclisler, 1908-1918," p.280; İhsan Ezherli, *Türkiye Büyük Millet Meclisi, 1920-1998, ve Osmanlı Meclis-i Mebusanı, 1877-1920*, p.207; and, Fevzi Demir, İkinci Meşrutiyet Dönemi Meclis-i Mebusan Seçimleri, 1908-1914, p.181.

[221] F.O. 195/2389/24/1989, Cumberbatch to Sir Gerard Lowther, Beirut, April 19, 1912, quoted in Rashid Khalidi, *British Policy Towards Syria and Palestine, 1906-1914*, p.258; "Les Elections: Derniers élus," *The Levant Herald and Eastern Express*, April 15, 1912, p.2; "Ouverture du Parlement," *The Levant Herald and Eastern Express*, April 18, 1912, p.1; Sabine Prätor, *Der arabische Faktor in der jungtürkischen Politik: Eine Studie zum osmanischen Parlament der II. Konstitution, 1908-1918*, p.239; Feroz Ahmad and Dankwart A. Rustow, "İkinci Meşrutiyet Döneminde Meclisler, 1908-1918," p.279; İhsan Ezherli, *Türkiye Büyük Millet Meclisi, 1920-1998, ve Osmanlı Meclis-i Mebusanı, 1877-1920*, p.203; and, Fevzi Demir, İkinci Meşrutiyet Dönemi Meclis-i Mebusan Seçimleri, 1908-1914, p.181.

[222] F.O. 195/2389/24/1989, Cumberbatch to Sir Gerard Lowther, Beirut, April 19, 1912, quoted in Rashid Khalidi, *British Policy Towards Syria and Palestine, 1906-1914*, p.258; "Les Elections: Nouveaux députés unionistes," *The Levant Herald and Eastern Express*, April 12, 1912, p.2; "Les Elections," *The Levant Herald and Eastern Express*, April 13, 1912, p.2; "Ouverture du Parlement," *The Levant Herald and Eastern Express*, April 18, 1912, p.1; Sabine Prätor, *Der arabische Faktor in der jungtürkischen Politik: Eine Studie zum osmanischen Parlament der II. Konstitution, 1908-1918*, p.241; Feroz Ahmad and Dankwart A. Rustow, "İkinci Meşrutiyet Döneminde Meclisler, 1908-1918," p.280; İhsan Ezherli, *Türkiye Büyük Millet Meclisi, 1920-1998, ve Osmanlı Meclis-i Mebusanı, 1877-1920*, p.209; and, Fevzi Demir, İkinci Meşrutiyet Dönemi Meclis-i Mebusan Seçimleri, 1908-1914, p.182.

Tripoli (2)

Sheikh Muhammed Efendi   Arab   I²²³
al-Djisr
Sa'adallah Efendi Molla   Arab   I²²⁴

* * *

Sandjak of JERUSALEM [Kudüs-ü Şerif] (3)

Jerusalem (3)

Ahmad 'Arif Efendi   Arab   I²²⁵
al-Husayni
Ruhi al-Khalidi Bey*   Arab   I²²⁶

F.O. 195/2389/24/1989, Cumberbatch to Sir Gerard Lowther, Beirut, April 19, 1912, quoted in Rashid Khalidi, *British Policy Towards Syria and Palestine, 1906-1914*, p.258; "Les Elections: 141 élus," *The Levant Herald and Eastern Express*, April 16, 1912, p.2; "Ouverture du Parlement," *The Levant Herald and Eastern Express*, April 18, 1912, p.1; Sabine Prätor, *Der arabische Faktor in der jungtürkischen Politik: Eine Studie zum osmanischen Parlament der II. Konstitution, 1908-1918*, p.239; Feroz Ahmad and Dankwart A. Rustow, "İkinci Meşrutiyet Döneminde Meclisler, 1908-1918," p.280; İhsan Ezherli, *Türkiye Büyük Millet Meclisi, 1920-1998, ve Osmanlı Meclis-i Mebusanı, 1877-1920*, p.212; and, Fevzi Demir, İkinci Meşrutiyet Dönemi Meclis-i Mebusan Seçimleri, 1908-1914, p.181.

F.O. 195/2389/24/1989, Cumberbatch to Sir Gerard Lowther, Beirut, April 19, 1912, quoted in Rashid Khalidi, *British Policy Towards Syria and Palestine, 1906-1914*, p.258; "Les Elections: 141 élus," *The Levant Herald and Eastern Express*, April 16, 1912, p.2; "Ouverture du Parlement," *The Levant Herald and Eastern Express*, April 18, 1912, p.1; Sabine Prätor, *Der arabische Faktor in der jungtürkischen Politik: Eine Studie zum osmanischen Parlament der II. Konstitution, 1908-1918*, p.239; Feroz Ahmad and Dankwart A. Rustow, "İkinci Meşrutiyet Döneminde Meclisler, 1908-1918," p.280; İhsan Ezherli, *Türkiye Büyük Millet Meclisi, 1920-1998, ve Osmanlı Meclis-i Mebusanı, 1877-1920*, p.216; and, Fevzi Demir, İkinci Meşrutiyet Dönemi Meclis-i Mebusan Seçimleri, 1908-1914, p.181.

F.O. 195/2389/24/2342, Satow to Sir Gerard Lowther, Jerusalem, May 7, 1912, quoted in Rashid Khalidi, *British Policy Towards Syria and Palestine, 1906-1914*, p.258; "Les Elections: A Jérusalem," *The Levant Herald and Eastern Express*, May 4, 1912, p.2; Sabine Prätor, *Der arabische Faktor in der jungtürkischen Politik: Eine Studie zum osmanischen Parlament der II. Konstitution, 1908-1918*, p.242; Feroz Ahmad and Dankwart A. Rustow, "İkinci Meşrutiyet Döneminde Meclisler, 1908-1918," p.280; İhsan Ezherli, *Türkiye Büyük Millet Meclisi, 1920-1998, ve Osmanlı Meclis-i Mebusanı, 1877-1920*, p.204; and, Fevzi Demir, İkinci Meşrutiyet Dönemi Meclis-i Mebusan Seçimleri, 1908-1914, p.182.

Khalidi writes that he was a loyal Unionist (Rashid Khalidi, "The 1912 Election Campaign in the Cities of *bilad al-Sham*," p.470). F.O. 195/2389/24/2342, Satow to Sir Gerard Lowther, Jerusalem, May 7, 1912, quoted in Rashid Khalidi, *British Policy Towards Syria and Palestine, 1906-1914*, p.258; "Les Elections: A Jérusalem," *The Levant Herald and Eastern Express*, May 4, 1912, p.2; Sabine Prätor, *Der arabische Faktor in der jungtürkischen Politik: Eine Studie zum osmanischen*

Uthman Efendi an-Nashashibi	Arab	I[227]

* * *

SYRIA/DAMASCUS (10)

Damascus (4)

Muhammad Fawzi Pasha al-'Azm	Arab	I[228]
'Abd ar-Rahman Pasha Yusuf*	Arab	CUP[229]

Parlament der II. Konstitution, 1908-1918, p.242; Feroz Ahmad and Dankwart A. Rustow, "İkinci Meşrutiyet Döneminde Meclisler, 1908-1918," p.280; İhsan Ezherli, *Türkiye Büyük Millet Meclisi, 1920-1998, ve Osmanlı Meclis-i Mebusanı, 1877-1920*, p.216; and, Fevzi Demir, İkinci Meşrutiyet Dönemi Meclis-i Mebusan Seçimleri, 1908-1914, p.182.

[227] F.O. 195/2389/24/2342, Satow to Sir Gerard Lowther, Jerusalem, May 7, 1912, quoted in Rashid Khalidi, *British Policy Towards Syria and Palestine, 1906-1914*, p.258; "Les Elections: A Jérusalem," *The Levant Herald and Eastern Express*, May 4, 1912, p.2; Sabine Prätor, *Der arabische Faktor in der jungtürkischen Politik: Eine Studie zum osmanischen Parlament der II. Konstitution, 1908-1918*, p.242; Feroz Ahmad and Dankwart A. Rustow, "İkinci Meşrutiyet Döneminde Meclisler, 1908-1918," p.281; İhsan Ezherli, *Türkiye Büyük Millet Meclisi, 1920-1998, ve Osmanlı Meclis-i Mebusanı, 1877-1920*, p.214; and, Fevzi Demir, İkinci Meşrutiyet Dönemi Meclis-i Mebusan Seçimleri, 1908-1914, p.182.

[228] F.O. 195/2389/24/1989, Devey to Sir Gerard Lowther, Damascus, April 16, 1912, quoted in Rashid Khalidi, *British Policy Towards Syria and Palestine, 1906-1914*, p.258; "Les Elections: Pas un député d'opposition!" *The Levant Herald and Eastern Express*, April 9, 1912, p.2; "Ouverture du Parlement," *The Levant Herald and Eastern Express*, April 18, 1912, p.1. He was elected Vice-President of the parliamentary party of the Committee of Union and Progress ("Le parti unioniste à la Chambre," *The Levant Herald and Eastern Express*, May 13, 1912, p.2). He was elected Vice-President of the Chamber of Deputies with 256 of 165 votes ("Le Parlement," *The Levant Herald and Eastern Express*, May 16, 1912, p.2). Sabine Prätor, *Der arabische Faktor in der jungtürkischen Politik: Eine Studie zum osmanischen Parlament der II. Konstitution, 1908-1918*, p.240; Feroz Ahmad and Dankwart A. Rustow, "İkinci Meşrutiyet Döneminde Meclisler, 1908-1918," p.280; İhsan Ezherli, *Türkiye Büyük Millet Meclisi, 1920-1998, ve Osmanlı Meclis-i Mebusanı, 1877-1920*, p.212; and, Fevzi Demir, İkinci Meşrutiyet Dönemi Meclis-i Mebusan Seçimleri, 1908-1914, p.181.

[229] Khalidi writes that he was a loyal Unionist (Rashid Khalidi, "The 1912 Election Campaign in the Cities of *bilad al-Sham*," p.470). F.O. 195/2389/24/1989, Devey to Sir Gerard Lowther, Damascus, April 16, 1912, quoted in Rashid Khalidi, *British Policy Towards Syria and Palestine, 1906-1914*, p.258; "Les Elections: Pas un député d'opposition!" *The Levant Herald and Eastern Express*, April 9, 1912, p.2; "Ouverture du Parlement," *The Levant Herald and Eastern Express*, April 18, 1912, p.1; Sabine Prätor, *Der arabische Faktor in der jungtürkischen Politik: Eine Studie zum osmanischen Parlament der II. Konstitution, 1908-1918*, p.240; Feroz Ahmad and Dankwart A. Rustow, "İkinci Meşrutiyet Döneminde Meclisler, 1908-1918," p.280; İhsan Ezherli, *Türkiye Büyük Millet Meclisi, 1920-1998, ve Osmanlı Meclis-i Mebusanı, 1877-1920*, p.203; and, Fevzi Demir, İkinci Meşrutiyet Dönemi

Amin Efendi Tarazi	Arab	I[230]
'Abd al-Muhsin Efendi Ustuwani	Arab	I[231]

Hama (2)

Khalid al-Barazi Efendi*	Arab	EL[232]
Seyyid Haşim Edib Bey	Turk	CUP[233]

Homs (1)

Mehmed Şefik Bey	Turk	CUP[234]

Meclis-i Mebusan Seçimleri, 1908-1914, p.181.

[230] F.O. 195/2389/24/1989, Devey to Sir Gerard Lowther, Damascus, April 16, 1912, quoted in Rashid Khalidi, *British Policy Towards Syria and Palestine, 1906-1914*, p.258; "Les Elections: Pas un député d'opposition!" *The Levant Herald and Eastern Express*, April 9, 1912, p.2; "Ouverture du Parlement," *The Levant Herald and Eastern Express*, April 18, 1912, p.1; Sabine Prätor, *Der arabische Faktor in der jungtürkischen Politik: Eine Studie zum osmanischen Parlament der II. Konstitution, 1908-1918*, p.240; Feroz Ahmad and Dankwart A. Rustow, "İkinci Meşrutiyet Döneminde Meclisler, 1908-1918," p.280; İhsan Ezherli, *Türkiye Büyük Millet Meclisi, 1920-1998, ve Osmanlı Meclis-i Mebusanı, 1877-1920*, p.206; and, Fevzi Demir, İkinci Meşrutiyet Dönemi Meclis-i Mebusan Seçimleri, 1908-1914, p.181.

[231] F.O. 195/2389/24/1989, Devey to Sir Gerard Lowther, Damascus, April 16, 1912, quoted in Rashid Khalidi, *British Policy Towards Syria and Palestine, 1906-1914*, p.258; "Les Elections: Pas un député d'opposition!" *The Levant Herald and Eastern Express*, April 9, 1912, p.2; "Ouverture du Parlement," *The Levant Herald and Eastern Express*, April 18, 1912, p.1; Sabine Prätor, *Der arabische Faktor in der jungtürkischen Politik: Eine Studie zum osmanischen Parlament der II. Konstitution, 1908-1918*, p.240; Feroz Ahmad and Dankwart A. Rustow, "İkinci Meşrutiyet Döneminde Meclisler, 1908-1918," p.280; İhsan Ezherli, *Türkiye Büyük Millet Meclisi, 1920-1998, ve Osmanlı Meclis-i Mebusanı, 1877-1920*, p.203; and, Fevzi Demir, İkinci Meşrutiyet Dönemi Meclis-i Mebusan Seçimleri, 1908-1914, p.181.

[232] "Les Elections: 4 députés ententistes," *The Levant Herald and Eastern Express*, April 10, 1912, p.2; "Les Elections," *The Levant Herald and Eastern Express*, April 13, 1912, p.2; "Ouverture du Parlement," *The Levant Herald and Eastern Express*, April 18, 1912, p.1; Sabine Prätor, *Der arabische Faktor in der jungtürkischen Politik: Eine Studie zum osmanischen Parlament der II. Konstitution, 1908-1918*, p.239; Feroz Ahmad and Dankwart A. Rustow, "İkinci Meşrutiyet Döneminde Meclisler, 1908-1918," p.279; İhsan Ezherli, *Türkiye Büyük Millet Meclisi, 1920-1998, ve Osmanlı Meclis-i Mebusanı, 1877-1920*, p.208; and, Fevzi Demir, İkinci Meşrutiyet Dönemi Meclis-i Mebusan Seçimleri, 1908-1914, p.181. He is not listed in F.O. 195/2389/24/1989, Devey to Sir Gerard Lowther, Damascus, April 16, 1912, quoted in Rashid Khalidi, *British Policy Towards Syria and Palestine, 1906-1914*, p.258.

[233] Sabine Prätor, *Der arabische Faktor in der jungtürkischen Politik: Eine Studie zum osmanischen Parlament der II. Konstitution, 1908-1918*, p.239; Feroz Ahmad and Dankwart A. Rustow, "İkinci Meşrutiyet Döneminde Meclisler, 1908-1918," p.279; İhsan Ezherli, *Türkiye Büyük Millet Meclisi, 1920-1998, ve Osmanlı Meclis-i Mebusanı, 1877-1920*, p.217; and, Fevzi Demir, İkinci Meşrutiyet Dönemi Meclis-i Mebusan Seçimleri, 1908-1914, p.181. He is not listed in F.O. 195/2389/24/1989, Devey to Sir Gerard Lowther, Damascus, April 16, 1912, quoted in Rashid Khalidi, *British Policy Towards Syria and Palestine, 1906-1914*, p.258.

[234] Feroz Ahmad and Dankwart A. Rustow, "İkinci Meşrutiyet Döneminde

Havran (2)

İsma'il Hariri Efendi   Arab   I[235]
Rashid Bey Tali'   Arab   CUP[236]

Kerak (1)

Muhammad 'Ataullah   Arab   I[237]
Efendi al-Ayyubi

* * *

Meclisler, 1908-1918," p.279; İhsan Ezherli, *Türkiye Büyük Millet Meclisi, 1920-1998, ve Osmanlı Meclis-i Mebusanı, 1877-1920*, p.218; and, Fevzi Demir, İkinci Meşrutiyet Dönemi Meclis-i Mebusan Seçimleri, 1908-1914, p.181.

[235] F.O. 195/2389/24/1989, Devey to Sir Gerard Lowther, Damascus, April 16, 1912, quoted in Rashid Khalidi, *British Policy Towards Syria and Palestine, 1906-1914*, p.258. His name is given as İsmail Harari Bey in "Les Elections: Pas un député d'opposition!" *The Levant Herald and Eastern Express*, April 9, 1912, p.2; and, "Ouverture du Parlement," *The Levant Herald and Eastern Express*, April 18, 1912, p.1. Sabine Prätor, *Der arabische Faktor in der jungtürkischen Politik: Eine Studie zum osmanischen Parlament der II. Konstitution, 1908-1918*, p.241; Feroz Ahmad and Dankwart A. Rustow, "İkinci Meşrutiyet Döneminde Meclisler, 1908-1918," p.279; İhsan Ezherli, *Türkiye Büyük Millet Meclisi, 1920-1998, ve Osmanlı Meclis-i Mebusanı, 1877-1920*, p.210; and, Fevzi Demir, İkinci Meşrutiyet Dönemi Meclis-i Mebusan Seçimleri, 1908-1914, p.181.

[236] F.O. 195/2389/24/1989, Devey to Sir Gerard Lowther, Damascus, April 16, 1912, quoted in Rashid Khalidi, *British Policy Towards Syria and Palestine, 1906-1914*, p.258; "Les Elections: Pas un député d'opposition!" *The Levant Herald and Eastern Express*, April 9, 1912, p.2; "Ouverture du Parlement," *The Levant Herald and Eastern Express*, April 18, 1912, p.1; Sabine Prätor, *Der arabische Faktor in der jungtürkischen Politik: Eine Studie zum osmanischen Parlament der II. Konstitution, 1908-1918*, p.241; Feroz Ahmad and Dankwart A. Rustow, "İkinci Meşrutiyet Döneminde Meclisler, 1908-1918," p.279; İhsan Ezherli, *Türkiye Büyük Millet Meclisi, 1920-1998, ve Osmanlı Meclis-i Mebusanı, 1877-1920*, p.216; and, Fevzi Demir, İkinci Meşrutiyet Dönemi Meclis-i Mebusan Seçimleri, 1908-1914, p.181.

[237] Sub-Governor of Homs ("Les Elections: A Kérak," *The Levant Herald and Eastern Express*, April 10, 1912, p.2). He was a graduate of Mekteb-i Mülkiye, Class of 1897 (Ali Çankaya, *Yeni Mülkiye Tarihi ve Mülkiyeliler*, 3, p.730). "Les Elections," *The Levant Herald and Eastern Express*, April 13, 1912, p.2; F.O. 195/2389/24/1989, Devey to Sir Gerard Lowther, Damascus, April 16, 1912, quoted in Rashid Khalidi, *British Policy Towards Syria and Palestine, 1906-1914*, p.258; "Ouverture du Parlement," *The Levant Herald and Eastern Express*, April 18, 1912, p.1; Sabine Prätor, *Der arabische Faktor in der jungtürkischen Politik: Eine Studie zum osmanischen Parlament der II. Konstitution, 1908-1918*, p.242; Feroz Ahmad and Dankwart A. Rustow, "İkinci Meşrutiyet Döneminde Meclisler, 1908-1918," p.281; İhsan Ezherli, *Türkiye Büyük Millet Meclisi, 1920-1998, ve Osmanlı Meclis-i Mebusanı, 1877-1920*, p.212; and, Fevzi Demir, İkinci Meşrutiyet Dönemi Meclis-i Mebusan Seçimleri, 1908-1914, p.182.

Sandjak of DAYR az-ZOR (1)

Zor (1)

Mehmed Nuri Efendi   Turk   I[238]

* * *

MOSUL (8)

Mosul (4)

Hacı Salih Sa'di Efendi   Arab   I[239]
Hasan Fa'iq Bey   Arab   I[240]
İbrahim Fawzi Efendi   Arab   I[241]
Hacı Muhammad Pasha   Arab   EL[242]

---

[238] Sabine Prätor, *Der arabische Faktor in der jungtürkischen Politik: Eine Studie zum osmanischen Parlament der II. Konstitution, 1908-1918*, p.238; Feroz Ahmad and Dankwart A. Rustow, "İkinci Meşrutiyet Döneminde Meclisler, 1908-1918," p.279; İhsan Ezherli, *Türkiye Büyük Millet Meclisi, 1920-1998, ve Osmanlı Meclis-i Mebusanı, 1877-1920*, p.212; and, Fevzi Demir, İkinci Meşrutiyet Dönemi Meclis-i Mebusan Seçimleri, 1908-1914, p.180.

[239] Sabine Prätor, *Der arabische Faktor in der jungtürkischen Politik: Eine Studie zum osmanischen Parlament der II. Konstitution, 1908-1918*, p.235; Feroz Ahmad and Dankwart A. Rustow, "İkinci Meşrutiyet Döneminde Meclisler, 1908-1918," p.284; İhsan Ezherli, *Türkiye Büyük Millet Meclisi, 1920-1998, ve Osmanlı Meclis-i Mebusanı, 1877-1920*, p.216; and, Fevzi Demir, İkinci Meşrutiyet Dönemi Meclis-i Mebusan Seçimleri, 1908-1914, p.184.

[240] Sabine Prätor, *Der arabische Faktor in der jungtürkischen Politik: Eine Studie zum osmanischen Parlament der II. Konstitution, 1908-1918*, p.235; Feroz Ahmad and Dankwart A. Rustow, "İkinci Meşrutiyet Döneminde Meclisler, 1908-1918," p.284; İhsan Ezherli, *Türkiye Büyük Millet Meclisi, 1920-1998, ve Osmanlı Meclis-i Mebusanı, 1877-1920*, p.208; and, Fevzi Demir, İkinci Meşrutiyet Dönemi Meclis-i Mebusan Seçimleri, 1908-1914, p.184.

[241] Sabine Prätor, *Der arabische Faktor in der jungtürkischen Politik: Eine Studie zum osmanischen Parlament der II. Konstitution, 1908-1918*, p.235; Feroz Ahmad and Dankwart A. Rustow, "İkinci Meşrutiyet Döneminde Meclisler, 1908-1918," p.284; İhsan Ezherli, *Türkiye Büyük Millet Meclisi, 1920-1998, ve Osmanlı Meclis-i Mebusanı, 1877-1920*, p.210; and, Fevzi Demir, İkinci Meşrutiyet Dönemi Meclis-i Mebusan Seçimleri, 1908-1914, p.184.

[242] Sabine Prätor, *Der arabische Faktor in der jungtürkischen Politik: Eine Studie zum osmanischen Parlament der II. Konstitution, 1908-1918*, p.235; İhsan Ezherli, *Türkiye Büyük Millet Meclisi, 1920-1998, ve Osmanlı Meclis-i Mebusanı, 1877-1920*, p.207; and, Fevzi Demir, İkinci Meşrutiyet Dönemi Meclis-i Mebusan Seçimleri, 1908-1914, p.184.

Kerkük (3)

Hacı Mehmed Ali Bey*	Turk?	I[243]
Bahaeddin Bey	Turk?	I[244]
Abdullah Safi al-Ya'qubi	Arab	I[245]
Efendi		

Süleymaniye (1)

Babanzade Hikmet Bey	Kurd	CUP[246]

* * *

BAGHDAD (7)

Baghdad (4)

Sasun Ezechiel [Hasgayl]*	Jew	CUP[247]

---

[243] Sabine Prätor, *Der arabische Faktor in der jungtürkischen Politik: Eine Studie zum osmanischen Parlament der II. Konstitution, 1908-1918*, p.235; Feroz Ahmad and Dankwart A. Rustow, "İkinci Meşrutiyet Döneminde Meclisler, 1908-1918," p.283; İhsan Ezherli, *Türkiye Büyük Millet Meclisi, 1920-1998, ve Osmanlı Meclis-i Mebusanı, 1877-1920*, p.211; and, Fevzi Demir, İkinci Meşrutiyet Dönemi Meclis-i Mebusan Seçimleri, 1908-1914, p.184.

[244] Sabine Prätor, *Der arabische Faktor in der jungtürkischen Politik: Eine Studie zum osmanischen Parlament der II. Konstitution, 1908-1918*, p.235; Feroz Ahmad and Dankwart A. Rustow, "İkinci Meşrutiyet Döneminde Meclisler, 1908-1918," p.283; İhsan Ezherli, *Türkiye Büyük Millet Meclisi, 1920-1998, ve Osmanlı Meclis-i Mebusanı, 1877-1920*, p.205; and, Fevzi Demir, İkinci Meşrutiyet Dönemi Meclis-i Mebusan Seçimleri, 1908-1914, p.184.

[245] Sabine Prätor, *Der arabische Faktor in der jungtürkischen Politik: Eine Studie zum osmanischen Parlament der II. Konstitution, 1908-1918*, p.235; Feroz Ahmad and Dankwart A. Rustow, "İkinci Meşrutiyet Döneminde Meclisler, 1908-1918," p.283; İhsan Ezherli, *Türkiye Büyük Millet Meclisi, 1920-1998, ve Osmanlı Meclis-i Mebusanı, 1877-1920*, p.203; and, Fevzi Demir, İkinci Meşrutiyet Dönemi Meclis-i Mebusan Seçimleri, 1908-1914, p.184.

[246] Sabine Prätor, *Der arabische Faktor in der jungtürkischen Politik: Eine Studie zum osmanischen Parlament der II. Konstitution, 1908-1918*, p.235; Feroz Ahmad and Dankwart A. Rustow, "İkinci Meşrutiyet Döneminde Meclisler, 1908-1918," p.284; İhsan Ezherli, *Türkiye Büyük Millet Meclisi, 1920-1998, ve Osmanlı Meclis-i Mebusanı, 1877-1920*, p.209; and, Fevzi Demir, İkinci Meşrutiyet Dönemi Meclis-i Mebusan Seçimleri, 1908-1914, p.184.

[247] "Les Elections: A Bagdad," *The Levant Herald and Eastern Express*, April 24, 1912, p.2; Sabine Prätor, *Der arabische Faktor in der jungtürkischen Politik: Eine Studie zum osmanischen Parlament der II. Konstitution, 1908-1918*, p.235; Feroz Ahmad and Dankwart A. Rustow, "İkinci Meşrutiyet Döneminde Meclisler, 1908-1918," p.283; İhsan Ezherli, *Türkiye Büyük Millet Meclisi, 1920-1998, ve Osmanlı Meclis-i Mebusanı, 1877-1920*, p.217; and, Fevzi Demir, İkinci Meşrutiyet

Fu'ad Bey ad-Daftari   Arab?   I[248]
Nakibzade Sayyid   Arab   I[249]
Muhyi ad-Din al-Kaylani Efendi
Süleymanzade Murad Bey   Arab   I[250]

Divaniye (1)

Babanzade İsmail Hakkı*   Kurd   CUP[251]

Kerbela (2)

Defterizade Fu'ad Saniya   Arab   I[252]

Dönemi Meclis-i Mebusan Seçimleri, 1908-1914, p.183.

[248] "Les Elections: A Bagdad," *The Levant Herald and Eastern Express*, April 24, 1912, p.2; Sabine Prätor, *Der arabische Faktor in der jungtürkischen Politik: Eine Studie zum osmanischen Parlament der II. Konstitution, 1908-1918*, p.235; Feroz Ahmad and Dankwart A. Rustow, "İkinci Meşrutiyet Döneminde Meclisler, 1908-1918," p.283; İhsan Ezherli, *Türkiye Büyük Millet Meclisi, 1920-1998, ve Osmanlı Meclis-i Mebusanı, 1877-1920*, p.207; and, Fevzi Demir, İkinci Meşrutiyet Dönemi Meclis-i Mebusan Seçimleri, 1908-1914, p.183.

[249] "Les Elections: A Bagdad," *The Levant Herald and Eastern Express*, April 24, 1912, p.2; Sabine Prätor, *Der arabische Faktor in der jungtürkischen Politik: Eine Studie zum osmanischen Parlament der II. Konstitution, 1908-1918*, p.235; Feroz Ahmad and Dankwart A. Rustow, "İkinci Meşrutiyet Döneminde Meclisler, 1908-1918," p.283; İhsan Ezherli, *Türkiye Büyük Millet Meclisi, 1920-1998, ve Osmanlı Meclis-i Mebusanı, 1877-1920*, p.217; and, Fevzi Demir, İkinci Meşrutiyet Dönemi Meclis-i Mebusan Seçimleri, 1908-1914, p.183.

[250] "Les Elections: A Bagdad," *The Levant Herald and Eastern Express*, April 24, 1912, p.2; Sabine Prätor, *Der arabische Faktor in der jungtürkischen Politik: Eine Studie zum osmanischen Parlament der II. Konstitution, 1908-1918*, p.235; Feroz Ahmad and Dankwart A. Rustow, "İkinci Meşrutiyet Döneminde Meclisler, 1908-1918," p.283; İhsan Ezherli, *Türkiye Büyük Millet Meclisi, 1920-1998, ve Osmanlı Meclis-i Mebusanı, 1877-1920*, p.213; and, Fevzi Demir, İkinci Meşrutiyet Dönemi Meclis-i Mebusan Seçimleri, 1908-1914, p.183.

[251] "Les Elections: 38 députés élus," *The Levant Herald and Eastern Express*, April 4, 1912, p.2; "Ouverture du Parlement," *The Levant Herald and Eastern Express*, April 18, 1912, p.1; Sabine Prätor, *Der arabische Faktor in der jungtürkischen Politik: Eine Studie zum osmanischen Parlament der II. Konstitution, 1908-1918*, p.236; İhsan Ezherli, *Türkiye Büyük Millet Meclisi, 1920-1998, ve Osmanlı Meclis-i Mebusanı, 1877-1920*, p.210; and, Fevzi Demir, İkinci Meşrutiyet Dönemi Meclis-i Mebusan Seçimleri, 1908-1914, p.183. Ahmad and Rustow mistakenly list him as Deputy for Baghdad (Feroz Ahmad and Dankwart A. Rustow, "İkinci Meşrutiyet Döneminde Meclisler, 1908-1918," p.283).

[252] "Les Elections: Résultats à ce jour," *The Levant Herald and Eastern Express*, April 1, 1912, p.2; "Ouverture du Parlement," *The Levant Herald and Eastern Express*, April 18, 1912, p.1; Sabine Prätor, *Der arabische Faktor in der jungtürkischen Politik: Eine Studie zum osmanischen Parlament der II. Konstitution, 1908-1918*, p.236; Feroz Ahmad and Dankwart A. Rustow, "İkinci Meşrutiyet Döneminde Meclisler, 1908-1918," p.283; İhsan Ezherli, *Türkiye Büyük Millet Meclisi, 1920-1998, ve Osmanlı Meclis-i Mebusanı, 1877-1920*, p.207; and, Fevzi Demir, İkinci Meşrutiyet Dönemi Meclis-i Mebusan Seçimleri, 1908-1914, p.183.

Efendi
Nuri Efendi   Turk   I[253]

* * *

BASRA (9)

Basra (4)

Zuhayrzade Abdullah	Arab	EL[254]
Seyyid Talib ibn Receb*	Arab	EL[255]
'Abd al-Wahhab al-Qirtas	Arab	I[256]
Pasha*		
Babanzade Ahmed Naim Bey	Kurd	CUP[257]

---

[253] "Les Elections: Résultats à ce jour," *The Levant Herald and Eastern Express*, April 1, 1912, p.2; "Ouverture du Parlement," *The Levant Herald and Eastern Express*, April 18, 1912, p.1; Sabine Prätor, *Der arabische Faktor in der jungtürkischen Politik: Eine Studie zum osmanischen Parlament der II. Konstitution, 1908-1918*, p.236; Feroz Ahmad and Dankwart A. Rustow, "İkinci Meşrutiyet Döneminde Meclisler, 1908-1918," p.283; İhsan Ezherli, *Türkiye Büyük Millet Meclisi, 1920-1998, ve Osmanlı Meclis-i Mebusanı*, and, Fevzi Demir, İkinci Meşrutiyet Dönemi Meclis-i Mebusan Seçimleri, 1908-1914, p.183.

[254] "Les Elections: 4 députés ententistes," *The Levant Herald and Eastern Express*, April 13, 1912, p.2; "Ouverture du Parlement," *The Levant Herald and Eastern Express*, April 18, 1912, p.1; Sabine Prätor, *Der arabische Faktor in der jungtürkischen Politik: Eine Studie zum osmanischen Parlament der II. Konstitution, 1908-1918*, p.236; Feroz Ahmad and Dankwart A. Rustow, "İkinci Meşrutiyet Döneminde Meclisler, 1908-1918," p.282; İhsan Ezherli, *Türkiye Büyük Millet Meclisi, 1920-1998, ve Osmanlı Meclis-i Mebusanı, 1877-1920*, p.203; and, Fevzi Demir, İkinci Meşrutiyet Dönemi Meclis-i Mebusan Seçimleri, 1908-1914, p.183.

[255] Chamber. "Les Elections; 4 députés ententistes," *The Levant Herald and Eastern Express*, April 13, 1912, p.2; "Ouverture du Parlement," *The Levant Herald and Eastern Express*, April 18, 1912, p.1; Sabine Prätor, *Der arabische Faktor in der jungtürkischen Politik: Eine Studie zum osmanischen Parlament der II. Konstitution, 1908-1918*, p.236; Feroz Ahmad and Dankwart A. Rustow, "İkinci Meşrutiyet Döneminde Meclisler, 1908-1918," p.282; İhsan Ezherli, *Türkiye Büyük Millet Meclisi, 1920-1998, ve Osmanlı Meclis-i Mebusanı, 1877-1920*, p.219; and, Fevzi Demir, İkinci Meşrutiyet Dönemi Meclis-i Mebusan Seçimleri, 1908-1914, p.183.

[256] Sabine Prätor, *Der arabische Faktor in der jungtürkischen Politik: Eine Studie zum osmanischen Parlament der II. Konstitution, 1908-1918*, p.236; Feroz Ahmad and Dankwart A. Rustow, "İkinci Meşrutiyet Döneminde Meclisler, 1908-1918," p.282; İhsan Ezherli, *Türkiye Büyük Millet Meclisi, 1920-1998, ve Osmanlı Meclis-i Mebusanı, 1877-1920*, p.203; and, Fevzi Demir, İkinci Meşrutiyet Dönemi Meclis-i Mebusan Seçimleri, 1908-1914, p.183.

[257] Sabine Prätor, *Der arabische Faktor in der jungtürkischen Politik: Eine Studie zum osmanischen Parlament der II. Konstitution, 1908-1918*, p.236; Feroz Ahmad and Dankwart A. Rustow, "İkinci Meşrutiyet Döneminde Meclisler, 1908-1918," p.282; İhsan Ezherli, *Türkiye Büyük Millet Meclisi, 1920-1998, ve Osmanlı Meclis-i Mebusanı, 1877-1920*, p.204; and, Fevzi Demir, İkinci Meşrutiyet Dönemi Meclis-i Mebusan Seçimleri, 1908-1914, p.183.

Ammare (2)

'Abd al-Madjid ash-Shawi	Arab	CUP? [258]
'Abd ar-Razzaq Munir	Arab	CUP? [259]

Müntefik (3)

Ferid Paşazade 'Abd al-Muhsin Bey*	Arab	CUP [260]
Djamil Sidqi az-Zahawi Efendi	Arab	I [261]
Muhammad Hamza Bey	Kurd	I [262]

* * *

JIDDAH (1)

Sharif Faisal Efendi	Arab	EL [263]

---

[258] He did not attend the Chamber of Deputies (Sabine Prätor, *Der arabische Faktor in der jungtürkischen Politik: Eine Studie zum osmanischen Parlament der II. Konstitution, 1908-1918*, p.237).

[259] He did not attend the Chamber of Deputies (Sabine Prätor, *Der arabische Faktor in der jungtürkischen Politik: Eine Studie zum osmanischen Parlament der II. Konstitution, 1908-1918*, p.237).

[260] Sabine Prätor, *Der arabische Faktor in der jungtürkischen Politik: Eine Studie zum osmanischen Parlament der II. Konstitution, 1908-1918*, p.237; Feroz Ahmad and Dankwart A. Rustow, "İkinci Meşrutiyet Döneminde Meclisler, 1908-1918," p.282; İhsan Ezherli, *Türkiye Büyük Millet Meclisi, 1920-1998, ve Osmanlı Meclis-i Mebusanı, 1877-1920*, p.203; and, Fevzi Demir, İkinci Meşrutiyet Dönemi Meclis-i Mebusan Seçimleri, 1908-1914, p.183.

[261] Sabine Prätor, *Der arabische Faktor in der jungtürkischen Politik: Eine Studie zum osmanischen Parlament der II. Konstitution, 1908-1918*, p.237; Feroz Ahmad and Dankwart A. Rustow, "İkinci Meşrutiyet Döneminde Meclisler, 1908-1918," p.282; İhsan Ezherli, *Türkiye Büyük Millet Meclisi, 1920-1998, ve Osmanlı Meclis-i Mebusanı, 1877-1920*, p.206; and, Fevzi Demir, İkinci Meşrutiyet Dönemi Meclis-i Mebusan Seçimleri, 1908-1914, p.183.

[262] Sabine Prätor, *Der arabische Faktor in der jungtürkischen Politik: Eine Studie zum osmanischen Parlament der II. Konstitution, 1908-1918*, p.237; Feroz Ahmad and Dankwart A. Rustow, "İkinci Meşrutiyet Döneminde Meclisler, 1908-1918," p.283; İhsan Ezherli, *Türkiye Büyük Millet Meclisi, 1920-1998, ve Osmanlı Meclis-i Mebusanı, 1877-1920*, p.208; and, Fevzi Demir, İkinci Meşrutiyet Dönemi Meclis-i Mebusan Seçimleri, 1908-1914, p.183.

[263] Sabine Prätor, *Der arabische Faktor in der jungtürkischen Politik: Eine Studie zum osmanischen Parlament der II. Konstitution, 1908-1918*, p.243; Feroz Ahmad and Dankwart A. Rustow, "İkinci Meşrutiyet Döneminde Meclisler, 1908-1918," p.281; İhsan Ezherli, *Türkiye Büyük Millet Meclisi, 1920-1998, ve Osmanlı Meclis-i Mebusanı, 1877-1920*, p.218; and, Fevzi Demir, İkinci Meşrutiyet Dönemi Meclis-i Mebusan Seçimleri, 1908-1914, p.182.

HEDJAZ (2)

Mecca (2)

Sharif Abdallah Efendi*	Arab	EL [264]
Sheikh Hasan Shaibi Efendi*	Arab	EL [265]

* * *

YEMEN (12)

Sanaa (5)

Seyyid Ahmad Khabbani Bey	Arab	I [266]
Nuri Bey	Turk	I [267]
Seyyid Hussein ibn 'Ali	Arab	I [268]

---

[264] "Les Elections: Nouveaux députés unionistes," *The Levant Herald and Eastern Express*, April 12, 1912, p.2; "Les Elections," *The Levant Herald and Eastern Express*, April 13, 1912, p.2; "Ouverture du Parlement," *The Levant Herald and Eastern Express*, April 18, 1912, p.1; Sabine Prätor, *Der arabische Faktor in der jungtürkischen Politik: Eine Studie zum osmanischen Parlament der II. Konstitution, 1908-1918*, p.243; Feroz Ahmad and Dankwart A. Rustow, "İkinci Meşrutiyet Döneminde Meclisler, 1908-1918," p.282; İhsan Ezherli, *Türkiye Büyük Millet Meclisi, 1920-1998, ve Osmanlı Meclis-i Mebusanı, 1877-1920*, p.218; and, Fevzi Demir, İkinci Meşrutiyet Dönemi Meclis-i Mebusan Seçimleri, 1908-1914, p.183.

[265] "Les Elections: Nouveaux députés unionistes," *The Levant Herald and Eastern Express*, April 12, 1912, p.2; "Les Elections," *The Levant Herald and Eastern Express*, April 13, 1912, p.2; "Ouverture du Parlement," *The Levant Herald and Eastern Express*, April 18, 1912, p.1; Sabine Prätor, *Der arabische Faktor in der jungtürkischen Politik: Eine Studie zum osmanischen Parlament der II. Konstitution, 1908-1918*, p.243; Feroz Ahmad and Dankwart A. Rustow, "İkinci Meşrutiyet Döneminde Meclisler, 1908-1918," p.282; İhsan Ezherli, *Türkiye Büyük Millet Meclisi, 1920-1998, ve Osmanlı Meclis-i Mebusanı, 1877-1920*, p.209; and, Fevzi Demir, İkinci Meşrutiyet Dönemi Meclis-i Mebusan Seçimleri, 1908-1914, p.183.

[266] Colonel ("The Ottoman Parliament," *The Orient*, 3/27 (July 3, 1912), p.1). Sabine Prätor, *Der arabische Faktor in der jungtürkischen Politik: Eine Studie zum osmanischen Parlament der II. Konstitution, 1908-1918*, p.245; Feroz Ahmad and Dankwart A. Rustow, "İkinci Meşrutiyet Döneminde Meclisler, 1908-1918," p.281; İhsan Ezherli, *Türkiye Büyük Millet Meclisi, 1920-1998, ve Osmanlı Meclis-i Mebusanı, 1877-1920*, p.217; and, Fevzi Demir, İkinci Meşrutiyet Dönemi Meclis-i Mebusan Seçimleri, 1908-1914, p.182.

[267] Sabine Prätor, *Der arabische Faktor in der jungtürkischen Politik: Eine Studie zum osmanischen Parlament der II. Konstitution, 1908-1918*, p.245; Feroz Ahmad and Dankwart A. Rustow, "İkinci Meşrutiyet Döneminde Meclisler, 1908-1918," p.281; İhsan Ezherli, *Türkiye Büyük Millet Meclisi, 1920-1998, ve Osmanlı Meclis-i Mebusanı, 1877-1920*, p.214; and, Fevzi Demir, İkinci Meşrutiyet Dönemi Meclis-i Mebusan Seçimleri, 1908-1914, p.182.

[268] Sabine Prätor, *Der arabische Faktor in der jungtürkischen Politik: Eine*

'Abd al-Qadir Efendi
Seyyid Ali İbrahim Efendi   Arab   I²⁶⁹
Seyyid Ahmad Yahya   Arab   I²⁷⁰
al-Kabsi Efendi*

Hodeidah (5)

Mustafa Fehmi Bey   Turk   I²⁷¹
Muharrem Hıfzı Bey   Turk   I²⁷²
Hakkı İlhami Bey   Turk   I²⁷³
Mustafa Zühdü Efendi*   Turk   I²⁷⁴

Studie zum osmanischen Parlament der II. Konstitution, 1908-1918, p.245; Feroz Ahmad and Dankwart A. Rustow, "İkinci Meşrutiyet Döneminde Meclisler, 1908-1918," p.282; İhsan Ezherli, *Türkiye Büyük Millet Meclisi, 1920-1998, ve Osmanlı Meclis-i Mebusanı, 1877-1920*, p.217; and, Fevzi Demir, İkinci Meşrutiyet Dönemi Meclis-i Mebusan Seçimleri, 1908-1914, p.182.

[269] Sabine Prätor, *Der arabische Faktor in der jungtürkischen Politik: Eine Studie zum osmanischen Parlament der II. Konstitution, 1908-1918*, p.245; Feroz Ahmad and Dankwart A. Rustow, "İkinci Meşrutiyet Döneminde Meclisler, 1908-1918," p.282; İhsan Ezherli, *Türkiye Büyük Millet Meclisi, 1920-1998, ve Osmanlı Meclis-i Mebusanı, 1877-1920*, p.217; and, Fevzi Demir, İkinci Meşrutiyet Dönemi Meclis-i Mebusan Seçimleri, 1908-1914, p.182.

[270] Sabine Prätor, *Der arabische Faktor in der jungtürkischen Politik: Eine Studie zum osmanischen Parlament der II. Konstitution, 1908-1918*, p.245; Feroz Ahmad and Dankwart A. Rustow, "İkinci Meşrutiyet Döneminde Meclisler, 1908-1918," p.282; İhsan Ezherli, *Türkiye Büyük Millet Meclisi, 1920-1998, ve Osmanlı Meclis-i Mebusanı, 1877-1920*, p.217; and, Fevzi Demir, İkinci Meşrutiyet Dönemi Meclis-i Mebusan Seçimleri, 1908-1914, p.182.

[271] Sabine Prätor, *Der arabische Faktor in der jungtürkischen Politik: Eine Studie zum osmanischen Parlament der II. Konstitution, 1908-1918*, p.244; Feroz Ahmad and Dankwart A. Rustow, "İkinci Meşrutiyet Döneminde Meclisler, 1908-1918," p.282; İhsan Ezherli, *Türkiye Büyük Millet Meclisi, 1920-1998, ve Osmanlı Meclis-i Mebusanı, 1877-1920*, p.213; and, Fevzi Demir, İkinci Meşrutiyet Dönemi Meclis-i Mebusan Seçimleri, 1908-1914, p.182.

[272] Sabine Prätor, *Der arabische Faktor in der jungtürkischen Politik: Eine Studie zum osmanischen Parlament der II. Konstitution, 1908-1918*, p.244; Feroz Ahmad and Dankwart A. Rustow, "İkinci Meşrutiyet Döneminde Meclisler, 1908-1918," p.282; İhsan Ezherli, *Türkiye Büyük Millet Meclisi, 1920-1998, ve Osmanlı Meclis-i Mebusanı, 1877-1920*, p.209; and, Fevzi Demir, İkinci Meşrutiyet Dönemi Meclis-i Mebusan Seçimleri, 1908-1914, p.182.

[273] Sabine Prätor, *Der arabische Faktor in der jungtürkischen Politik: Eine Studie zum osmanischen Parlament der II. Konstitution, 1908-1918*, p.244; Feroz Ahmad and Dankwart A. Rustow, "İkinci Meşrutiyet Döneminde Meclisler, 1908-1918," p.282; İhsan Ezherli, *Türkiye Büyük Millet Meclisi, 1920-1998, ve Osmanlı Meclis-i Mebusanı, 1877-1920*, p.208; and, Fevzi Demir, İkinci Meşrutiyet Dönemi Meclis-i Mebusan Seçimleri, 1908-1914, p.182.

[274] Sabine Prätor, *Der arabische Faktor in der jungtürkischen Politik: Eine Studie zum osmanischen Parlament der II. Konstitution, 1908-1918*, p.244; Feroz Ahmad and Dankwart A. Rustow, "İkinci Meşrutiyet Döneminde Meclisler, 1908-1918," p.282; İhsan Ezherli, *Türkiye Büyük Millet Meclisi, 1920-1998, ve Osmanlı Meclis-i Mebusanı, 1877-1920*, p.220; and, Fevzi Demir, İkinci Meşrutiyet Dönemi Meclis-i Mebusan Seçimleri, 1908-1914, p.182.

Seyyid Yahya Pasha   Arab   I[275]

'Asir (2)

Seyyid Yusuf Fazıl Bey   Arab   I[276]
Hüseyin Hüsameddin Efendi Turk   I[277]

* * *

TRIPOLI (9)

Tripoli (3)

Farhad Efendi*   Arab   EL[278]
Mahmud Naci Bey*   Turk   I[279]
Muhammad Muhtar Ka'bar   Arab   I[280]

---

[275] Sabine Prätor, *Der arabische Faktor in der jungtürkischen Politik: Eine Studie zum osmanischen Parlament der II. Konstitution, 1908-1918*, p.244; Feroz Ahmad and Dankwart A. Rustow, "İkinci Meşrutiyet Döneminde Meclisler, 1908-1918," p.282; İhsan Ezherli, *Türkiye Büyük Millet Meclisi, 1920-1998, ve Osmanlı Meclis-i Mebusanı, 1877-1920*, p.217; and, Fevzi Demir, İkinci Meşrutiyet Dönemi Meclis-i Mebusan Seçimleri, 1908-1914, p.182.

[276] Sabine Prätor, *Der arabische Faktor in der jungtürkischen Politik: Eine Studie zum osmanischen Parlament der II. Konstitution, 1908-1918*, p.244; Feroz Ahmad and Dankwart A. Rustow, "İkinci Meşrutiyet Döneminde Meclisler, 1908-1918," p.281; İhsan Ezherli, *Türkiye Büyük Millet Meclisi, 1920-1998, ve Osmanlı Meclis-i Mebusanı, 1877-1920*, p.217; and, Fevzi Demir, İkinci Meşrutiyet Dönemi Meclis-i Mebusan Seçimleri, 1908-1914, p.182.

[277] Sabine Prätor, *Der arabische Faktor in der jungtürkischen Politik: Eine Studie zum osmanischen Parlament der II. Konstitution, 1908-1918*, p.244; Feroz Ahmad and Dankwart A. Rustow, "İkinci Meşrutiyet Döneminde Meclisler, 1908-1918," p.281; İhsan Ezherli, *Türkiye Büyük Millet Meclisi, 1920-1998, ve Osmanlı Meclis-i Mebusanı, 1877-1920*, p.209; and, Fevzi Demir, İkinci Meşrutiyet Dönemi Meclis-i Mebusan Seçimleri, 1908-1914, p.182.

[278] "Les Elections: Résultats à ce jour," *The Levant Herald and Eastern Express*, April 1, 1912, p.2; "Ouverture du Parlement," *The Levant Herald and Eastern Express*, April 18, 1912, p.1; Sabine Prätor, *Der arabische Faktor in der jungtürkischen Politik: Eine Studie zum osmanischen Parlament der II. Konstitution, 1908-1918*, p.246; Feroz Ahmad and Dankwart A. Rustow, "İkinci Meşrutiyet Döneminde Meclisler, 1908-1918," p.284; İhsan Ezherli, *Türkiye Büyük Millet Meclisi, 1920-1998, ve Osmanlı Meclis-i Mebusanı, 1877-1920*, p.207; and, Fevzi Demir, İkinci Meşrutiyet Dönemi Meclis-i Mebusan Seçimleri, 1908-1914, p.184.

[279] "Les Elections: Résultats à ce jour," *The Levant Herald and Eastern Express*, April 1, 1912, p.2; "Ouverture du Parlement," *The Levant Herald and Eastern Express*, April 18, 1912, p.1; Sabine Prätor, *Der arabische Faktor in der jungtürkischen Politik: Eine Studie zum osmanischen Parlament der II. Konstitution, 1908-1918*, p.246; Feroz Ahmad and Dankwart A. Rustow, "İkinci Meşrutiyet Döneminde Meclisler, 1908-1918," p.284; İhsan Ezherli, *Türkiye Büyük Millet Meclisi, 1920-1998, ve Osmanlı Meclis-i Mebusanı, 1877-1920*, p.211; and, Fevzi Demir, İkinci Meşrutiyet Dönemi Meclis-i Mebusan Seçimleri, 1908-1914, p.184.

[280] Sabine Prätor, *Der arabische Faktor in der jungtürkischen Politik: Eine*

| Sadık Bey* | Turk | I[281] |
| Hadi Kenan Bey | Turk? | ?[282] |

Benghazi (3)

Ömer Mansur Pasha*	Turk	I[283]
Yusuf Shatwan*	Arab	EL[284]
'Abd al-Qadir 'Anani Pasha	Arab	I[285]

Cebel-i Garbi (2)

| Suleiman al-Baruni Efendi* | Arab | I[286] |
| Feyzullah Efendi az-Zubayr | Arab | I[287] |

Studie zum osmanischen Parlament der II. Konstitution, 1908-1918, p.246; Feroz Ahmad and Dankwart A. Rustow, "İkinci Meşrutiyet Döneminde Meclisler, 1908-1918," p.284; İhsan Ezherli, *Türkiye Büyük Millet Meclisi, 1920-1998, ve Osmanlı Meclis-i Mebusanı, 1877-1920*, p.212; Fevzi Demir, İkinci Meşrutiyet Dönemi Meclis-i Mebusan Seçimleri, 1908-1914, p.184.

[281] "Les Elections: Résultats à ce jour," *The Levant Herald and Eastern Express*, April 1, 1912, p.2; and, "Ouverture du Parlement," *The Levant Herald and Eastern Express*, April 18, 1912, p.1. His deputyship may have not been ratified; because he is not listed in official registers.

[282] "Les Elections: Les nouveaux députés," *The Levant Herald and Eastern Express*, April 19, 1912, p.2. His deputyship may have not been ratified; because he is not listed in official registers.

[283] Sabine Prätor, *Der arabische Faktor in der jungtürkischen Politik: Eine Studie zum osmanischen Parlament der II. Konstitution, 1908-1918*, p.246; Feroz Ahmad and Dankwart A. Rustow, "İkinci Meşrutiyet Döneminde Meclisler, 1908-1918," p.284; İhsan Ezherli, *Türkiye Büyük Millet Meclisi, 1920-1998, ve Osmanlı Meclis-i Mebusanı, 1877-1920*, p.215; and, Fevzi Demir, İkinci Meşrutiyet Dönemi Meclis-i Mebusan Seçimleri, 1908-1914, p.184.

[284] Sabine Prätor, *Der arabische Faktor in der jungtürkischen Politik: Eine Studie zum osmanischen Parlament der II. Konstitution, 1908-1918*, p.246; Feroz Ahmad and Dankwart A. Rustow, "İkinci Meşrutiyet Döneminde Meclisler, 1908-1918," p.284; İhsan Ezherli, *Türkiye Büyük Millet Meclisi, 1920-1998, ve Osmanlı Meclis-i Mebusanı, 1877-1920*, p.220; and, Fevzi Demir, İkinci Meşrutiyet Dönemi Meclis-i Mebusan Seçimleri, 1908-1914, p.184.

[285] Sabine Prätor, *Der arabische Faktor in der jungtürkischen Politik: Eine Studie zum osmanischen Parlament der II. Konstitution, 1908-1918*, p.246; Feroz Ahmad and Dankwart A. Rustow, "İkinci Meşrutiyet Döneminde Meclisler, 1908-1918," p.284; İhsan Ezherli, *Türkiye Büyük Millet Meclisi, 1920-1998, ve Osmanlı Meclis-i Mebusanı, 1877-1920*, p.203; and, Fevzi Demir, İkinci Meşrutiyet Dönemi Meclis-i Mebusan Seçimleri, 1908-1914, p.184.

[286] "Les Elections: Résultats à ce jour," *The Levant Herald and Eastern Express*, April 1, 1912, p.2; Sabine Prätor, *Der arabische Faktor in der jungtürkischen Politik: Eine Studie zum osmanischen Parlament der II. Konstitution, 1908-1918*, p.246; Feroz Ahmad and Dankwart A. Rustow, "İkinci Meşrutiyet Döneminde Meclisler, 1908-1918," p.284; İhsan Ezherli, *Türkiye Büyük Millet Meclisi, 1920-1998, ve Osmanlı Meclis-i Mebusanı, 1877-1920*, p.218; and, Fevzi Demir, İkinci Meşrutiyet Dönemi Meclis-i Mebusan Seçimleri, 1908-1914, p.184.

[287] Sabine Prätor, *Der arabische Faktor in der jungtürkischen Politik: Eine Studie zum osmanischen Parlament der II. Konstitution, 1908-1918*, p.246; Feroz Ahmad and Dankwart A. Rustow, "İkinci Meşrutiyet Döneminde Meclisler, 1908-

Fizan (1)

Cami [Baykut]*	Turk	I[288]
Abdüllâtif Bey	Turk?	?[289]

* * *

1918," p.284; İhsan Ezherli, *Türkiye Büyük Millet Meclisi, 1920-1998, ve Osmanlı Meclis-i Mebusanı, 1877-1920*, p.207; and, Fevzi Demir, İkinci Meşrutiyet Dönemi Meclis-i Mebusan Seçimleri, 1908-1914, p.184.

[288] "Les Elections: Au Fezzan," *The Levant Herald and Eastern Express*, April 25, 1912, p.2; Sabine Prätor, *Der arabische Faktor in der jungtürkischen Politik: Eine Studie zum osmanischen Parlament der II. Konstitution, 1908-1918*, p.246; Feroz Ahmad and Dankwart A. Rustow, "İkinci Meşrutiyet Döneminde Meclisler, 1908-1918," p.284; İhsan Ezherli, *Türkiye Büyük Millet Meclisi, 1920-1998, ve Osmanlı Meclis-i Mebusanı, 1877-1920*, p.206; and, Fevzi Demir, İkinci Meşrutiyet Dönemi Meclis-i Mebusan Seçimleri, 1908-1914, p.184.

[289] Replacing Cami Bey? ("Les Elections: Résultats à ce jour," *The Levant Herald and Eastern Express*, April 1, 1912, p.2). "Ouverture du Parlement," *The Levant Herald and Eastern Express*, April 18, 1912, p.1. His deputyship may have not been ratified; because he is not listed in official registers.

BIBLIOGRAPHY

Official Documents

Germany, Türkei 159, No.2, R 13795, Türkische Staatsmänner, Volume 10
(August 7, 1908-May 5, 1909)
——, Türkei 159, No.2, R 13796, Türkische Staatsmänner, Volume 11 (May
6, 1909-September 30, 1910)
——, Türkei 159, No.2, R 13797, Türkische Staatsmänner, Volume 12
(October 1, 1910-June 30, 1913)
——, Türkei 161, R 13817, Türkische Ministerium, Volume 2 (September
15, 1891-February 18, 1909)
——, Türkei 161, R 13818, Türkische Ministerium, Volume 3 (February 19,
1909-December 31, 1911)
——, Türkei 167, R 13898, Die Türkische Presse, Volume 4 (December 1,
1908-June 30, 1909)
——, Türkei 167, R 13899, Die Türkische Press, Volume 5 (July 1, 1909-June
30, 1910)
——, Türkei 167, R 13910, Die Türkische Presse, Volume 1 (August 1, 1908-
December 31, 1912)
——, Türkei 181, R 14045, Allgemeine türkische Politik, Volume 1 (February
1889-September 30, 1911)
——, Türkei 198, R 14161, Die Jungtürken, Volume 7 (June 1, 1911-February
2, 1916)
——, Türkei 201, R 14171, Verfassung und Parlament der Türkei, Volume 5
(December 13, 1908-April 30, 1909)
Great Britain, "The Counter-Revolution and the Fall of Abdul-Hamid," in G.
P. Gooch and H. Temperley (Eds.), *British Documents on the
Origins of the War, 1898-1914*, Volume 5: *The Near East* (London:
HMSO, 1928)
——, "The Young Turkish Revolution," in G. P. Gooch and H. Temperley
(Eds.), *British Documents on the Origins of the War, 1898-1914*,
Volume 5: *The Near East* (London: HMSO, 1928), pp.247-307.
——, *Further Correspondence Respecting the Affairs of Asiatic Turkey and
Arabia*, No.9618 (London: HMSO, February 1910) [F.O.424/221]
——, *Further Correspondence Respecting the Affairs of Asiatic Turkey and
Arabia*, No.9707 (London: HMSO, July 1910) [F.O.424/222]
——, *Further Correspondence Respecting the Affairs of Asiatic Turkey and
Arabia, Part I*, No.9923 (London: HMSO, October 1911) [F.O.424/
226]
——, *Further Correspondence Respecting the Affairs of Asiatic Turkey and
Arabia, Part III*, No.9937 (London: HMSO, December 1911)
[F.O.424/228]

——, *Further Correspondence Respecting the Affairs of Asiatic Turkey and Arabia, Part V,* No.10075 (London: HMSO, June 1912) [F.O.424/230]

——, *Further Correspondence Respecting the Affairs of Asiatic Turkey and Arabia, Part VII,* No.10164 (London: HMSO, March 1913) [F.O.424/232]

——, *Correspondence Respecting the Turkish War, Part I,* No.10224 (London: HMSO, May 1913) [F.O.424/234]

——, *Correspondence Respecting the Turkish War, Part II,* No.10263 (London: HMSO, July 1913) [F.O.424/235]

United States of America, *Records of the Department of State Relating to Internal Affairs of Turkey, 1910-1929,* Microfilm Roll 4 (Washington, D.C.: The National Archives, 1961)

Newspapers and Periodicals

Berliner Tageblatt und Handels Zeitung (Berlin)
İkdam (İstanbul) When the newspaper was closed down by the censors, *İkdam* appeared under the names of *Yeni İkdam* and *İktiham.*
The Levant Herald and Eastern Express (İstanbul)
The Near East (London)
The Nineteenth Century and After (London)
The Orient (İstanbul)
Osmanischer Lloyd (İstanbul)
Resimli Kitab (İstanbul)
La Revue (Paris)
Tanin (İstanbul) *Tanin* also appeared under the names of *Yeni Tanin, Cenin, Senin, Renin* and *Hak* when it was closed down by the censors. *Hak,* as *Tanin,* should not be confused by *Hak,* another pro-Unionist newspaper that was published in İstanbul as well.
Tercüman-ı Hakikat (İstanbul)
The Times (London)
Vossische Zeitung (Berlin)

Other Sources

Ahmad, Feroz, "Great Britain's Relations with the Young Turks, 1908-1914," *Middle Eastern Studies,* 2 (October 1965-July 1966), pp.302-329.
——, *The Making of Modern Turkey* (London and New York: Routledge, 1993)
——, "Unionist Relations with the Greek, Armenian, and Jewish Communities of the Ottoman Empire, 1908-1914," in Benjamin Braude and Bernard Lewis (Eds.), *Christians and Jews in the Ottoman Empire: The Functioning of a Plural Society,* Volume 1: *The Central Lands* (New York and London: Holmes and Meier Publishers, Inc., 1982), pp.401-434.
——, *The Young Turks: The Committee of Union and Progress in Turkish Politics, 1908-1914* (Oxford: Oxford University Press, 1969)

Ahmad, Feroz and Dankwart A. Rustow, "İkinci Meşrutiyet Döneminde Meclisler, 1908-1918," *Güney-Doğu Avrupa Araştırmaları Dergisi*, Nos.4-5 (1976), pp.245-284.

Akşin, Sina, *31 Mart Olayı* (Ankara: A. Ü. Siyasal Bilgiler Fakültesi Yayını, 1970)

——, "31 Mart Olayına Değin Sabahattin Bey ve Ahrar Fırkası," *A. Ü. Siyasal Bilgiler Fakültesi Dergisi, 27/3* (1973), pp. 541-560.

——, "Fedâkâran-ı Millet Cemiyeti," *A. Ü. Siyasal Bilgiler Fakültesi Dergisi, 29/1-2* (March-June 1974), pp.125-136.

——, *Jön Türkler ve İttihat ve Terakki*, 2nd Printing (Ankara: İmge Kitabevi, 1998)

Aktar, Yücel, "1912 Yılı 'Harb Mitingleri' ve Balkan Harbi'ne Etkileri," in Ramiz Ertem (Ed.), *İkinci Askeri Tarih Semineri: Bildiriler* (Ankara: Genelkurmay Askeri Tarih ve Stratejik Etüt Başkanlığı Yayınları, 1985), pp.114-139.

——, *İkinci Meşrutiyet Dönemi Öğrenci Olayları, 1908-1918* (İstanbul: İletişim Yayınları, 1990)

Alkan, Ahmet Turan, *İkinci Meşrutiyet Devrinde Ordu ve Siyaset* (Ankara: Cedit Matbuat ve Neşriyat A. Ş., 1992)

Alkan, Mehmet Ö., "Türkiye'de Siyasal Partiler Tarihine Katkı, I: Hürriyet ve İ'tilâf Fırkası'nın İlk Programı ve Nizâmnamesi," *Toplumsal Tarih*, No.2 (February 1994), pp.49-55.

Amca, Hasan, *Doğmayan Hürriyet: Bir Devrin İçyüzü, 1909-1918*, 2nd Printing (İstanbul: Arba Yayınları, 1989)

Arıkan, Zeki, "Balkan Savaşı ve Kamuoyu," in Hikmet Köksal (Ed.), *Dördüncü Askeri Tarih Semineri: Bildiriler* (Ankara: Genelkurmay Askeri Tarih ve Stratejik Etüt Başkanlığı Yayınları, 1989), pp.168-190.

Ayışığı, Metin, *Mareşal Ahmet İzzet Paşa: Askerî ve Siyasî Hayatı* (Ankara: Türk Tarih Kurumu Yayını, 1997)

Bartl, Peter, *Die albanischen Muslime zur Zeit der nationalen Unabhängigkeitsbewegung, 1878-1912* (Wiesbaden: Otto Harrassowitz, 1968)

Bayar, Celal, *Ben de Yazdım: Milli Mücadeleye Giriş*, 8 Volumes (İstanbul: Baha Matbaası, 1965-1972)

Bayur, Hilmi Kamil, *Sadrazam Kâmil Paşa: Siyasi Hayatı* (Ankara: Sanat Basımevi, 1954)

Bayur, Yusuf Hikmet, *Türk İnkılâbı Tarihi*, 3 Volumes in 9 Parts (Ankara: Türk Tarih Kurumu Yayını, 1940-1967)

Birinci, Ali, *Hürriyet ve İtilâf Fırkası: II. Meşrutiyet Devrinde İttihat ve Terakki'ye Karşı Çıkanlar* (İstanbul: Dergâh Yayınları, 1990)

Bleda, Midhat Şükrü, *İmparatorluğun Çöküşü* (İstanbul: Remzi Kitabevi, 1979)

Boura, Caterina, "I vouleftices ecloges stin othomaniki aftocratoria I ellines vouleftes 1908-1918," *Deltio Kentrou Mikrasiatikon Spoudon, 4* (1983), pp.69-85.

Bozkurt, Gülnihâl, *Alman-İngiliz Belgelerinin ve Siyasî Gelişmelerin Işığında Gayrimüslim Osmanlı Vatandaşlarının Hukukî Durumu, 1839-1914* (Ankara: Türk Tarih Kurumu Yayını, 1989)

Buxton, Noel, "The Young Turks," *The Nineteenth Century and After, 65* (January-June 1909), pp.16-24.

Cavid, Mehmed, "Meşrutiyet Devrine Dair Cavit Bey'in Hatıraları," *Tanin*, August 3, 1943-December 22, 1946.

Cemaleddin, Mehmed, *Siyasi Hatıralar, 1908-1913* [Edited by Ziyaeddin Engin] (İstanbul: Tercüman Yayınları, 1978)

Cevad, Ali, *İkinci Meşrutiyetin İlânı ve Otuzbir Mart Hadisesi* [Prepared for publication by Faik Reşit Unat] (Ankara: Türk Tarih Kurumu Yayını, 1960)

Çankaya, Ali, *Yeni Mülkiye Tarihi ve Mülkiyeliler*, 8 Volumes (Ankara: Mars Matbaası, 1968-1971)

Çavdar, Tevfik, *"Müntehib-i Sani"den Seçmene* (Ankara: V Yayınları, 1987)

——, *Talat Paşa: Bir Örgüt Ustasının Yaşam Öyküsü* (Ankara: Dost Kitabevi Yayınları, 1984)

Çoker, Fahri, "II. Meşrutiyet Meclisi'nde Sadrazamın Çekilmesine Neden Olan Bahriyeliler," *Tarih ve Toplum*, No.67 (July 1989), pp.9-12.

Dakin, Douglas, "The Diplomacy of the Great Powers and the Balkan States, 1908-1914," *Balkan Studies, 3* (1962), pp.327-374.

Danişmend, İsmail Hami, *Sadr-ı-a'zam Tevfik Paşa'nın Dosyasındaki Resmi ve Hususi Vesikalara Göre: 31 Mart Vak'ası* (İstanbul: İstanbul Kitabevi, 1961)

Dâver, Bülent, "Hürriyet ve İtilâf Fırkası," in Hikmet Köksal (Ed.), *Dördüncü Askeri Tarih Semineri: Bildiriler* (Ankara: Genelkurmay Askeri Tarih ve Stratejik Etüt Başkanlığı Yayınları, 1989), pp.95-107.

Demir, Fevzi, "II. Meşrutiyet Dönemi Parlamento Seçimlerinde Din ve Siyaset: Kâbe Örtüsüne Dökülen Şarap ve Kimliği Belirsiz Sakal," *Toplumsal Tarih*, No.64 (April 1999), pp.13-17.

——, İkinci Meşrutiyet Dönemi Meclis-i Mebusan Seçimleri, 1908-1914 (Ph. D. Dissertation, Dokuz Eylül Üniversitesi, İzmir, 1995)

Dillon, E. J., "A Clue to the Turkish Tangle," *The Contemporary Review, 95* (January-June 1909) pp.743-756.

——, "Fate's Little Ironies in Turkey," *The Contemporary Review, 98* (July-December, 1910), pp.375-379.

Dugdale, Edgar Trevelyan Stratford (Ed.), *German Diplomatic Documents, 1871-1914*, 4 Volumes [Selected and translated by E. T. S. Dugdale; with a preface by Rt. Hon. Sir Rennell Rodd and an introduction by J. W. Headlam-Morley] (London: Methuen and Co., Ltd., 1928-1931)

Dwight, Harry Griswold, *Constantinople: Old and New* (New York: Charles Scribner's Sons, 1915)

Dyer, Gwynne, "The Origins of the 'Nationalist' Group of Officers in Turkey, 1908-18," *Journal of Contemporary History, 8/4* (October 1973), pp.121-164.

Ege, Nezahet Nurettin (Ed.), *Prens Sabahaddin: Hayatı ve İlmî Müdafaaları* (İstanbul: Güneş Neşriyatı, 1977)

Emil, Birol, *Mizancı Murad Bey: Hayatı ve Eserleri* (İstanbul: İ. Ü. Edebiyat Fakültesi Yayını, 1979)

Emiroğlu, Kudret, *Anadolu'da Devrim Günleri: İkinci Meşrutiyet'in İlânı, Temmuz-Ağustos 1908* (Ankara: İmge Kitabevi, 1999)

——, "Maliye Nazırı Cavit Bey'in Trabzon Gezisi, 1911," in İ. Gündağ Kayaoğlu, Öner Ciravoğlu and Cüneyt Akalın (Eds.), *Bir Tutkudur Trabzon* (İstanbul: Yapı Kredi Kültür Sanat Yayıncılık Ticaret ve Sanayi A. Ş., 1997), pp.328-336.

Emiroğlu, Kudret, "Trabzon'da Sopalı Seçimler, 1912," *Tarih ve Toplum*, No.97 (January 1992), pp.41-46.

Erdem, Tarhan (Compilor), *Anayasalar ve Seçim Kanunları, 1876-1982* (İstanbul: Milliyet Yayınları, 1982)

Erdinç, Erol Şadi and Faruk Ilıkan, "Osmanlı İttihad ve Terakki Cem'iyyeti Merkez-i Umûmî'si Yazışmalarından Örnekler," *Toplumsal Tarih*, No.9 (September 1994), pp.40-41.

Esatlı, Mustafa Ragıb, "İntihabatta Parti İhtirası: İntihabatta Muhaliflerin Karşılıklı İhtirasları Felâketler Doğurmuştu," *Akşam*, March 25, 1943, p.3.

——, *İttihat ve Terakki Tarihinde Esrar Perdesi: Yakup Cemil Niçin ve Nasıl Öldürüldü?* (İstanbul: Akşam Kitaphanesi, 1933)

——, "Meşrutiyet Devrinde: İntihap Mücadeleleri En Çirkin İhtiraslara Sebep Olmuştu," *Akşam*, March 18, 1943, p.4.

——, "Meşrutiyet Devrinde: İntihap Mücadelesi Nasıl Yapılıyordu?" *Akşam*, March 11, 1943, p.4.

Ezherli, İhsan, *Türkiye Büyük Millet Meclisi, 1920-1998, ve Osmanlı Meclis-i Mebusanı, 1877-1920*, 2nd Edition (Ankara: T.B.M.M. Kültür, Sanat ve Yayın Kurulu Yayınları, 1998)

Farhi, David, "The *Şeriat* as a Political Slogan—or the 'Incident of the 31st Mart'," *Middle Eastern Studies*, 7 (1971), pp.275-299.

Farkas, Paul, *Staatsstreich und Gegenrevolution in der Türkei* (Berlin: Verlag von Puttkammer und Mühlbrecht, 1909)

Güneş, İhsan, "1912 Seçimleri ve Eskişehir'de Meydana Gelen Olaylar," *Belleten*, 56 (1992), pp.459-482.

Güresin, Ecvet, *31 Mart İsyanı* (İstanbul: Habora Kitabevi Yayınları, 1969)

Hale, William, *Turkish Politics and the Military* (London and New York: Routledge, 1994)

Halid, Halil, "The Origin of the Revolt in Turkey," *The Nineteenth Century and After*, 65 (January-June 1909), pp.755-760.

Harris, N. Dwight, "The Macedonian Question and the Balkan War," *The American Political Science Review*, 7 (1913), pp.197-216.

Iacovella, Angelo, *Gönye ve Hilâl: İttihad-Terakki ve Masonluk* [Translated by Tülin Altınova] (İstanbul: Tarih Vakfı Yurt Yayınları, 1998)

International Commission to Inquire into the Causes and Conduct of the Balkan Wars, *The Other Balkan Wars: A 1913 Carnegie Endowment Inquiry in Retrospect* [With a New Introduction and Reflections on the Present Conflict by George F. Kennan] (Washington, D. C.: Carnegie Endowment for International Peace, 1993)

Işık, Hüseyin, "İkinci Meşrutiyet'in İlânında ve Korunmasında Silahlı Kuvvetlerimizin Rolü," in Ramiz Ertem (Ed.), *İkinci Askeri Tarih Semineri: Bildiriler* (Ankara: Genelkurmay Askeri Tarih ve Stratejik Etüt Başkanlığı Yayınları, 1985), pp.42-65.

İnal, İbnülemin Mahmud Kemal, *Osmanlı Devrinde Son Sadrıazamlar* (Ankara: T. C. Milli Eğitim Bakanlığı Yayını, 1940-1953)

İzzet, Ahmed, *Feryadım*, Volume 1 (İstanbul: Nehir Yayınları, 1992)

Kadri, Hüseyin Kâzım, *Meşrutiyet'ten Cumhuriyet'e Hatıralarım* [Prepared for publication by İsmail Kara] (İstanbul: İletişim Yayınları, 1991)

Kâmil Paşa, "Explanatory Memorandum by the Late Grand Vizier, Kiamil Pasha," Appendix to Demetrius Georgiades, *Is the Regeneration of*

Turkey Possible? (London: Kegan Paul, Trench, Trübner and Co., Ltd., 1910)

Kansu, Aykut, *1908 Devrimi* [Translated by Ayda Erbal] (İstanbul: İletişim Yayınevi, 1995)

———, "Dünden Bugüne 1908 Devrimi," *Toplumsal Tarih*, No.55 (July 1998), pp.4-11.

———, *The Revolution of 1908 in Turkey* (Leiden, New York and Cologne: E. J. Brill, 1997)

Kars, H. Zafer, *1908 Devrimi'nin Halk Dinamiği* (İstanbul: Kaynak Yayınları, 1997)

Kayalı, Hasan, *Arabs and Young Turks: Ottomanism, Arabism, and Islamism in the Ottoman Empire, 1908-1918* (Berkeley, Los Angeles and London: University of California Press, 1997)

———, Arabs and Young Turks: Turkish-Arab Relations in the Second Constitutional Period of the Ottoman Empire, 1908-1918 (Ph. D. Dissertation, Harvard University, 1988)

Kedourie, Elie, "Young Turks, Freemasons and Jews," *Middle Eastern Studies*, 7 (1971), pp.89-104.

Kemal, Ali, *Ömrüm* [Prepared for publication by Zeki Kuneralp] (İstanbul: İSİS Yayımcılık Ltd., 1985)

Kemal, Ismail, *The Memoirs of Ismail Kemal Bey* [Edited by Sommerville Story; with a preface by William Morton Fullerton] (London: Constable, 1920)

Khalidi, Rashid, "The 1912 Election Campaign in the Cities of *bilad al-Sham*," *International Journal of Middle East Studies*, 16 (1984), pp.461-474.

———, *British Policy Towards Syria and Palestine, 1906-1914: A Study of the Antecedents of the Hussein-McMahon Correspondence, the Sykes-Picot Agreement and the Balfour Declaration* (London: Published for the Middle East Centre, St. Antony's College, Oxford, by Ithaca Press, 1980)

———, "Ottomanism and Arabism in Syria Before 1914: A Reassessment," Rashid Khalidi, Lisa Anderson, Muhammad Muslih and Reeva S. Simon (Eds.), *The Origins of Arab Nationalism* (New York: Columbia University Press, 1991), pp.50-69.

Khoury, Philip S., *Urban Notables and Arab Nationalism: The Politics of Damascus, 1860-1920* (Cambridge: Cambridge University Press, 1983)

Kleinert, Claudia, *Die Revision der Historiographie des Osmanischen Reiches am Beispiel von Abdülhamid II: Das späte Osmanische Reich im Urteil türkischer Autoren der Gegenwart, 1930-1990* (Berlin: Klaus Schwarz Verlag, 1995)

Koloğlu, Orhan, "İttihat ve Terakki'de Komite-Hizb-i Cedid Tartışması Sırasında Yunus Nadi'nin Selânik'te Tokatlanması Olayı," *Tarih ve Toplum*, No.116 (August 1993), pp.34-35.

Kondis, Basil, *Greece and Albania, 1908-1914* (Thessaloniki: Institute for Balkan Studies, 1976)

Kuran, Ahmed Bedevi, *İnkılâp Tarihimiz ve İttihad ve Terakki* (İstanbul: Tan Matbaası, 1948)

———, *İnkılâp Tarihimiz ve 'Jön Türkler'* (İstanbul: Tan Matbaası, 1945)

Kuran, Ahmed Bedevi, *Osmanlı İmparatorluğunda İnkılâp Hareketleri ve Milli Mücadele*, 2nd Edition (İstanbul: Çeltüt Matbaası, 1959)

Kutay, Cemal, *Bir 'Geri Dönüş'ün Mirası: 31 Mart'ın 90. Yılında Laik Cumhuriyet Karşısında Derviş Vahdetiler Cephesi*, 2nd Edition (İstanbul: Aksoy Yayıncılık Sanayi ve Ticaret A. Ş., 1999)

———, *Türkiye İstiklâl ve Hürriyet Mücadeleleri Tarihi*, 20 Volumes (İstanbul: İstanbul Matbaası, 1957-1962)

———, *Üç Paşalar Kavgası* (İstanbul: Tarih Yayınları, 1964)

Külçe, Süleyman, *Osmanlı Tarihinde Arnavutluk* (İzmir: n.p., 1944)

Leipnik, Ferdinand L., "The Future of the Ottoman Empire," *The Contemporary Review*, 97 (January-June, 1910), pp.291-301.

Lepsius, Johannes, Albrecht Mendelssohn-Bartholdy and Friedrich Thimme (Eds.), *Die Grosse Politik der Europäischen Kabinette, 1871-1914*, 40 Volumes (Berlin: Deutsche Verlagsgesellschaft für Politik und Geschichte, 1922-1927)

Lewis, Bernard, *The Emergence of Modern Turkey*, 2nd Edition (London, Oxford, New York: Oxford University Press, 1968)

Macfie, A. L., *The End of the Ottoman Empire, 1908-1923* (London and New York: Addison Wesley Longman Ltd., 1998)

Makedonski, Stojan, "Le Regime Jeune-Turc et les Deuxiemes Elections Parlamentaires de 1912 en Macedoine et Thrace Orientale," *Etudes Balkaniques*, 14/2 (1978), pp.58-71.

McCullagh, Francis, *The Fall of Abd-ul-Hamid* [With a Preface by His Excellency Mahmud Shefket Pasha] (London: Methuen and Co., Ltd., 1910)

Mehmetefendioğlu, Ahmet, "Hüseyin Hilmi Paşa Hükûmetinin İstifası ve Lynch Şirketi," *Tarih ve Toplum*, No.164 (August 1997), pp.13-19.

———, "İttihat ve Terakki ve Siyasi Müsteşarlıklar," *Toplumsal Tarih*, No.43 (July 1997), pp.32-37.

———, "İttihat ve Terakki'nin 1909 Kongresi," *Toplumsal Tarih*, No.55 (July 1998), pp.20-29.

Menteşe, Halil, "Eski Meclis-i Mebusan Reisi Halil Menteşe'nin Hatıraları," *Cumhuriyet*, October 13-December 11, 1946.

———, *Osmanlı Mebusan Meclisi Reisi Halil Menteşe'nin Anıları* [Prepared for publication with an Introduction by İsmail Arar] (İstanbul: Hürriyet Vakfı Yayınları, 1986)

Mevlânzade Rıfat, *31 Mart: Bir İhtilâlin Hikâyesi*, 2nd printing [Prepared for publication by Berîre Ülgenci] (İstanbul: Pınar Yayınları, 1996)

Midhat, Ali Haydar, *Hatıralarım, 1872-1946* (İstanbul: Mithat Akşit Yayını, 1946)

Muhtar, Mahmud, *Maziye Bir Nazar* (İstanbul: Matbaa-ı Ahmed İhsan ve Şürekası, 1341 [1925])

Nasrullah, Mehmed, Mehmed Rüşdü and Mehmed Eşref (Eds.), *Memalik-i Mahruse-i Şahane'ye Mahsus Mükemmel ve Mufassal Atlas* (İstanbul: Şirket-i Hayriye Matbaası, 1325 [1909])

Nur, Rıza, *Cemiyet-i Hafiye* [Prepared for publication by Ahmed Nezih Galitekin] (İstanbul: İşaret Yayınları, 1995)

———, *Hayat ve Hatıratım*, 4 Volumes (İstanbul: Altındağ Yayınları, 1967-1968)

Nur, Rıza, *Hürriyet ve İtilâf Fırkası Nasıl Doğdu, Nasıl Öldü?* [Prepared for publication by İlhami Yalınkılıç] (İstanbul: Kitabevi, 1996)

Okay, Cüneyt, "Kendi Kaleminden 1912 Seçimlerinde Rıza Tevfik'in Dövülmesi: Gümülcine'de Sopalı Seçimler," *Toplumsal Tarih*, No.64 (April 1999), pp.18-20.

Orhon, Alpaslan, "Erzurum ve Erzincan'da '31 Mart Olayı' ile İlgili Ayaklanmalar ve Bastırılışları," in Ramiz Ertem (Ed.), *İkinci Askeri Tarih Semineri: Bildiriler* (Ankara: Genelkurmay Askeri Tarih ve Stratejik Etüt Başkanlığı Yayınları, 1985), pp.93-113.

Pears, Edwin, "The Crisis in Turkey," *The Contemporary Review*, 95 (January-June, 1909), pp.511-526.

——, "Developments in Turkey," *The Contemporary Review*, 97 (January-June, 1910), pp.692-716.

——, *Forty Years in Constantinople: The Recollections of Sir Edwin Pears, 1873-1915* (New York: D. Appleton and Company, 1916)

——, *Life of Abdul Hamid* (New York: Henry Holt and Company, 1917)

——, "Turkey: Developments and Forecasts," *The Contemporary Review*, 95 (January-June, 1909), pp.707-725.

Pollo, Stefanaq and Arben Puto, *The History of Albania from its Origins to the Present Day* [Translated by Carol Wiseman and Ginnie Hole] (London, Boston and Henley: Routledge and Kegan Paul, 1981)

Poynter, Mary A., *When Turkey Was Turkey: In and Around Constantinople* (London: George Routledge and Sons, Ltd., 1921)

Prätor, Sabine, *Der arabische Faktor in der jungtürkischen Politik: Eine Studie zum osmanischen Parlament der II. Konstitution, 1908-1918* (Berlin: Klaus Schwarz Verlag, 1993)

Ramsay, William M., *The Revolution in Constantinople and Turkey: A Diary* (London: Hodder and Stoughton, 1909)

Rey, Ahmed Reşid, *Gördüklerim, Yaptıklarım, 1890-1922* (İstanbul: Türkiye Yayınevi, 1945)

Rıza, Ahmed, *Meclis-i Mebusan ve Ayan Reisi Ahmed Rıza Bey'in Anıları* [Prepared for publication by Bülent Demirbaş] (İstanbul: Arba Yayınları, 1988)

Salaheddin, Mehmed, *Mağdur ve Mazlum Osmanlı Milleti'nin Nazar-ı Mutalaa ve İntibahına: Bildiklerim—İttihad ve Terakki Cemiyeti'nin Maksad-ı Tesis ve Suret-i Teşkili ve Devlet-i Âliye-i Osmaniye'nin Sebeb-i Felâket ve İnkısamı* (Kahire: Emin Hindiye Matbaası, 1334 [1918])

Saray, Mehmet, "Devlet Yönetiminde Ordunun Yeri ve Rolü Hakkında bir Örnek: İttihat ve Terakki Devrinde Ordunun Millet ve Devlet Yönetimine Tesiri," in Ramiz Ertem (Ed.), *İkinci Askeri Tarih Semineri: Bildiriler* (Ankara: Genelkurmay Askeri Tarih ve Stratejik Etüt Başkanlığı Yayınları, 1985), pp.85-92.

Sax, Carl von, *Geschichte des Machverfalls der Türkei bis Ende des 19 Jahrhunderts und die Phasen der 'Orientalischen Frage' bis auf die Gegenwart*, 2nd Edition (Vienna: Manzsche k. u. k. Hof-Verlags und Universitäts Buchhandlung, 1913)

Seikaly, Samir, "Shukri al-'Asali: A Case Study of a Political Activist," Rashid Khalidi, Lisa Anderson, Muhammad Muslih and Reeva S. Simon

(Eds.), *The Origins of Arab Nationalism* (New York: Columbia University Press, 1991), pp.73-96.

Simavi, Lütfi, *Sultan Mehmed Reşad Han'ın ve Halefinin Sarayında Gördüklerim*, 2 Volumes (İstanbul: Kanaat Kitabhanesi, 1340 [1924])

Skendi, Stavro, *The Albanian National Awakening, 1878-1912* (Princeton: Princeton University Press, 1967)

Soko, Ziya Şakir, "Hürriyet ve İtilâf Nasıl Doğu? Nasıl Yaşadı? Nasıl Battı?" *Tan*, October 29, 1937-March 14, 1938

——, *Sultan Hamid'in Son Günleri* (İstanbul: Muallim Fuat Gücüyener Anadolu Türk Kitap Deposu, 1943)

Sonyel, Salâhi R., "The Turco-Armenian 'Adana Incidents' in the Light of Secret British Documents, July, 1908-December, 1909," *Belleten, 51* (1987), pp.1291-1338.

Sullivan, Charles Donald, Stamboul Crossings: German Diplomacy in Turkey, 1908 to 1914 (Ph. D. Dissertation, Vanderbilt University, 1977)

Swanson, Glen Wilfred, Mahmud Şevket Paşa and the Defense of the Ottoman Empire: A Study of War and Revolution during the Young Turk Period (Ph. D. Dissertation, Indiana University, 1970)

Swenson, Victor R., "The Military Rising in Istanbul, 1909," *Journal of Contemporary History, 5/4* (October 1970), pp.171-184.

Swire, Joseph, *Albania: The Rise of a Kingdom* (London: Williams and Norgate, Ltd., 1929)

Şahin, Mustafa, "Cemiyet mi, Eşkıya Çetesi mi?" *Tarih ve Toplum*, No.107 (November, 1992), pp.57-59.

——, "Rıza Tevfik'in İkinci Tutuklanışı ve Bazı Tepkiler," *Tarih ve Toplum*, No.107 (November 1992), pp.6-8.

Şehbenderzade Filibeli Ahmed Hilmi, *Muhalefetin İflâsı: İtilâf ve Hürriyet Fırkası* [Prepared for publication by Ahmet Eryüksel] (İstanbul: Nehir Yayınları, 1991)

Şeref, Abdurrahman, *Son Vak'anüvis Abdurrahman Şeref Efendi Tarihi: II. Meşrutiyet Olayları, 1908-1909* [Prepared for publication by Bayram Kodaman and Mehmet Ali Ünal] (Ankara: Türk Tarih Kurumu Yayını, 1996)

Şerif, *Bir Muhalifin Hatıraları: İttihat ve Terakki'ye Muhalefet* [prepared for publication by A. Özalp] (İstanbul: Nehir Yayınları, 1990)

——, "Les Continuateurs d'Abdul-Hamid, I," *La Revue, 84* (January 1-February 15, 1910), pp.305-315.

——, "Les Continuateurs d'Abdul-Hamid, II: Leurs Finance—Leur Administration," *La Revue, 88* (October 1-December 15, 1910), pp.13-30.

——, "Les Continuateurs d'Abdul-Hamid, III: Le Comité 'Union et Progrès' et notre Politique Extérieure," *La Revue, 88* (October 1-December 15, 1910), pp.569-580

——, "La Faillite des Continuateurs d'Abdul-Hamid," *La Revue, 93* (November 1-December 15, 1911), pp.35-48.

——, "Turkey and Great Britain," *The Near East*, July 12, 1911, p.221.

Tansel, Fevziye Abdullah, "Mizancı Mehmed Murad Bey," *İ. Ü. Edebiyat Fakültesi Tarih Dergisi, 2* (1950-1951), pp.67-88.

Tarabein, Ahmed, "Abd al-Hamid al-Zahrawi: The Career and Thought of an Arab Nationalist," in Rashid Khalidi, Lisa Anderson, Muhammad

Muslih and Reeva S. Simon (Eds.), *The Origins of Arab Nationalism* (New York: Columbia University Press, 1991), pp.97-119.

Tekeli, İlhan and Selim İlkin, *Osmanlı İmparatorluğu'nda Eğitim ve Bilgi Üretim Sisteminin Oluşumu ve Dönüşümü* (Ankara: Türk Tarih Kurumu Yayını, 1993)

Tevetoğlu, Fethi, *Ömer Naci*, 2nd Edition (Ankara: T. C. Kültür ve Turizm Bakanlığı Yayınları, 1987)

Timur, Taner, "Bir İttihatçı Düşmanı: Şerif Paşa ve *Meşrutiyet* Gazetesi," *Tarih ve Toplum*, No.72 (December 1989), pp.17-20.

Topuzlu, Cemil, *İstibdat, Meşrutiyet, Cumhuriyet Devirlerinde 80 Yıllık Hatıralarım*, 2nd Edition [Prepared for publication by Hüsrev Hatemi and Aykut Kazancıgil] (İstanbul: İ. Ü. Cerrahpaşa Tıp Fakültesi Yayını, 1982)

Tunaya, Tarık Zafer, *Türkiye'de Siyasi Partiler, 1859-1952* (İstanbul: Doğan Kardeş Yayınları A. Ş., 1952)

Turan, Şerafettin, "İkinci Meşrutiyet Döneminde Ordu-Yönetim İlişkileri," in Ramiz Ertem (Ed.), *İkinci Askeri Tarih Semineri: Bildiriler* (Ankara: Genelkurmay Askeri Tarih ve Stratejik Etüt Başkanlığı Yayınları, 1985), pp.66-84.

Türkgeldi, Ali Fuad, *Görüp İşittiklerim* (Ankara: Türk Tarih Kurumu Yayını, 1949)

Türkmen, Zekeriya, *Osmanlı Meşrutiyetinde Ordu-Siyaset Çatışması* (İstanbul: İrfan Yayımcılık, 1993)

Uçarol, Rifat, *Gazi Ahmet Muhtar Paşa: Bir Osmanlı Paşası ve Dönemi* (İstanbul: Milliyet Yayınları, 1976)

Uşaklıgil, Halid Ziya, *Saray ve Ötesi*, 3 Volumes (İstanbul: Hilmi Kitabevi, 1940-1941)

Uzer, Tahsin, *Makedonya Eşkiyalık Tarihi ve Son Osmanlı Yönetimi*, 2nd Printing (Ankara: Türk Tarih Kurumu Yayını, 1987)

Xanalatos, Diogenis, "The Greeks and the Turks on the Eve of the Balkan Wars: A Frustrated Plan," *Balkan Studies*, *3* (1962), pp.277-296.

Yalçın, Hüseyin Cahid, "Meşrutiyet Hatıraları, 1908-1918," *Fikir Hareketleri*, No.71 (February 28, 1935)-No.224 (February 5, 1938)

——, *Talât Paşa* (İstanbul: Yedigün Neşriyatı, 1943)

Yöntem, Ali Canip, "Hizb-i Cedid," *Yakın Tarihimiz*, 2 (May 31- August 23, 1962), pp.353-355.

Zürcher, Erik J., *Turkey: A Modern History*, Revised Edition (London and New York: I. B. Tauris and Co., Ltd., 1997)

INDEX